INTERNATIONAL ECON[...]
General Editor: John

HUMAN RIGHTS IN INTERNATIONAL INVESTMENT LAW AND ARBITRATION

Human Rights in International Investment Law and Arbitration

Edited by
PM DUPUY
F FRANCIONI
and
EU PETERSMANN

OXFORD
UNIVERSITY PRESS

OXFORD
UNIVERSITY PRESS

Great Clarendon Street, Oxford OX2 6DP

Oxford University Press is a department of the University of Oxford.
It furthers the University's objective of excellence in research, scholarship,
and education by publishing worldwide in

Oxford New York

Auckland Cape Town Dar es Salaam Hong Kong Karachi
Kuala Lumpur Madrid Melbourne Mexico City Nairobi
New Delhi Shanghai Taipei Toronto
With offices in
Argentina Austria Brazil Chile Czech Republic France Greece
Guatemala Hungary Italy Japan South Korea Poland Portugal
Singapore Switzerland Thailand Turkey Ukraine Vietnam

Oxford is a registered trade mark of Oxford University Press
in the UK and in certain other countries

Published in the United States
by Oxford University Press Inc., New York

ISBN 978-0-19-957819-1

Printed and bound in Great Britain by
CPI Antony Rowe, Chippenham and Eastbourne

General Editor's Preface

The editors and authors of this book have produced a remarkable and enormously significant work which explores not only a cutting-edge combination of attention to a fast-growing segment of the legal profession, but also the relationship of that segment to the profoundly important subjects of human rights and constitutional developments. A reader is well advised first to read the outstanding introductory chapter by Professor Petersmann, one of the three editors, in which he introduces the book and each part of the book. These 30 pages or so are so profound in themselves as to evoke awe, as well as the appreciation of the talent and diligence which went into planning the conferences involved and the follow-up literature in this book which relates to those conferences.

The relationship of human rights law to international economic law is a very complex subject itself, and one which has a growing number of contributors, but nevertheless poses extraordinary puzzles stimulating deep examination and troublesome concepts which need to be disentangled. This book thrusts itself into the middle of these concepts by examining the essential role of human rights in international economic adjudication and arbitration, moving to examination of the troublesome ideas of 'balancing' as it occurs in four different juridical institutions, and then exploring what the authors term to be 'case studies' which explore in depth specific jurisprudential subjects such as 'fair and equitable' treatment, 'proportionality', corporate environment, health policy, and non-discriminatory norms. This is a truly ambitious task, remarkably well executed.

In some ways this book complements a previous book in this IEL series of the Oxford University Press. In 2005, the Press was pleased to publish in the IEL series a book entitled 'Human Rights and International Trade', edited by Professor Thomas Cottier, Professor Joost Pauwelyn, and Elisabeth Burgi Bonanomi. The editor's Foreword to that book emphasized the complexity and conceptual difficulty of the topic with many sentences which could be applied to this 2009 book. It also referred to different viewpoints emphasized by the human rights advocates compared to the economic law professionals, and how important it was to achieve some melding of these different viewpoints. Then, as now, it was noted that the issue of human rights implications for international economic law subjects was recognized by cutting-edge scholars to be inevitably involved in the policy and litigation of these two broad fields of law. This current 2009 book clearly advances the thinking which has motivated both books. Hopefully there will be more books as outstanding as this one to come in the future.

JOHN H JACKSON

Contents

III. JUDICIAL 'BALANCING' OF ECONOMIC LAW AND HUMAN RIGHTS IN REGIONAL COURTS

IV. CASE STUDIES ON PROTECTION STANDARDS AND SPECIFIC HUMAN RIGHTS IN INVESTOR-STATE ARBITRATION

Detailed Contents

III. JUDICIAL 'BALANCING' OF ECONOMIC LAW AND HUMAN RIGHTS IN REGIONAL COURTS

Table of Cases

List of Abbreviations

AB	Appellate Body
ACHPR	African Charter on Human and Peoples' Rights
ACHR	American Convention on Human Rights
ACIJ	Asociación Civil por la Igualdad y la Justicia
ACP	African, Caribbean, and Pacific
ADR	alternative dispute resolution
AF	Additional Facility
AJIL	American Journal of International Law
ASEAN	Association of Southeast Asian Nations
BIT	Bilateral Investment Treaty
BLM	Bureau of Land Management
BRA	Boston Redevelopment Authority
BSE	Bovine Spongiform Encephalopathy
BVerfGE	Bundesverfassungsgericht Entscheidungen
BYIL	British Yearbook of International Law
CAFTA	Central American Free Trade Agreement
CAO	Compliance Advisor/Ombudsman
CARICOM	Caribbean Community
CARIFORUM	Caribbean Forum of ACP States
CDCA	California Desert Conservation Area
CDPA	California Desert Protection Act 1994
CELS	Centro de Estudios Legales y Sociales
CESCR	Committee on Economic, Social, and Cultural Rights
CIEL	Centre for International Environmental Law
CIL	customary international law
COMESA	Common Market of Eastern and Southern Africa
CRC	Convention on the Rights of the Child
CSICH	Convention for the Safeguarding of Intangible Cultural Heritage
CSO	civil society organisation
CUPW	Canadian Union of Postal Workers
CVD	countervailing duty
DCF	discounted cash flow
DOI	Department of the Interior
DSB	Dispute Settlement Body
DSU	Dispute Settlement Understanding
EC	European Community
EU	European Union
ECHR	European Convention of Human Hights

ECommHR	European Commission of Human Rights
ECtHR	European Court of Human Rights
ECJ	European Court of Justice
ECT	Energy Charter Treaty
ECSC	European Coal and Steel Community
ECT	Energy Charter Treaty
EEA	European Economic Area
EEAA	European Economic Area Agreement
EFTA	European Free Trade Area
EFTAn	European Free Trade Association
EHRR	European Human Rights Reports
EJIL	European Journal of International Law
EPA	Economic and Partnership Agreement
ESCR	Economic, Social, and Cultural Rights
EUI	European University Institute
EURATOM	European Atomic Energy Community
FAO	Food and Agriculture Organization
FCN	Friendship, Commerce, and Navigation
FCTC	Framework Convention on Tobacco Control
FET	fair and equitable treatment
FETS	fair and equitable treatment standard
FIDH	International Federation for Human Rights
FIPPA	Foreign Investment Promotion and Protection Agreement
FLPMA	Federal Law Policy and Management Act 1976
FTA	Free Trade Agreement
FTC	Free Trade Commission
GA	General Assembly
GAL	global administrative law
GATS	General Agreement on Trade in Services
GATT	General Agreement on Tariffs and Trade
GCC	Gulf Council Cooperation
GDR	German Democratic Republic
HR	human rights
HRLJ	Human Rights Law Journal
IACHR	Inter-American Court of Human Rights
IACommHR	Inter-American Commission of Human Rights
IASHR	Inter-American system of human rights
ICC	International Chamber of Commerce
ICCPR	International Covenant on Civil and Political Rights
ICESCR	International Covenant on Economic, Social and Cultural Rights
ICJ	International Court of Justice
ICLQ	International & Comparative Law Quarterly
ICSID	International Centre for Settlement of Investment Disputes
ICSID Convention	Convention on the Settlement of Investment Disputes between States and National of Other States

ICSID Review FILJ	ICSID Review Foreign Investment Law Journal
IEL	international economic law
IFC	International Finance Corporation
IIA	international investment agreement
IISD	International Institute for Sustainable Development
ILC	International Law Commission
ILM	International Law Materials
ILO	International Labour Organization
ILR	International Law Review
IMF	International Monetary Fund
IMS	International Minimum Standard
Int.	International
IP	intellectual property
Iran-USCTR	Iran-US Claims Tribunal
ITLOS	International Tribunal for the Law of the Sea
ITWF	International Transport Workers Federation
J Int Arb	Journal of International Arbitration
JWIT	Journal of World Investment and Trade
LEAT	Lawyers' Environmental Action Team
LHRC	Legal and Human Rights Centre
MAI	Multilateral Agreement on Investment
MEA	multilateral environmental agreement
MERCOSUR	Mercado Comun del Sur
MFN	Most Favoured Nation
MFNT	Most-Favoured-Nation treatment
MIGA	Multilateral Investment Guarantee Agency
MNE	multinational enterprise
MSA	Master Settlement Agreement
MSCP	multi-storey car park
MST	minimum standard of treatment
MTBE	methyl tertiary butyl ether
NAAEC	North American Agreement on Environmental Cooperation
NAFTA	North American Free Trade Agreement
NGO	Non-Governmental Organisation
NT	National Treatment
NYU	New York University
OAS Charter	Charter of the Organization of the American States
OECD	Organization for Economic Cooperation and Development
OSPAR	Convention for the Protection of the Marine Environment of the North-East Atlantic
P–A	principle-agent framework
PCA	Partnership and Cooperation Agreement
PCB	polychlorinated biphenyl
PCIJ	Permanent Court of International Justice
RIAA	Reports of International Arbitral Awards
SAA	Stabilization and Association Agreement
SD	sustainable development

SMRA	Surface Mining Reclamation Act
SSA	Sacred Sites Act
TBR	Trade Barriers Regulation
TGNP	Tanzania Gender Networking Programme
TRIMS	Trade Related Investment Measures
TRIPS	Trade Related Intellectual Property Rights
TTM	Thai Tobacco Monopoly
UC	University of California
UDHR	Universal Declaration on Human Rights
UN	United Nations
UNCHR	UN Commission on Human Rights
UNCITRAL	UN Commission on International Trade Law
UNCLOS	UN Convention on the Law of the Sea
UNCTAD	UN Conference on Trade and Development
UNCTC	UN Commission on Transnational Corporations
UNDP	UN Development Programme
UNESCO	UN Educational, Scientific, and Cultural Organization
US	United States
USSC	US Supreme Court
VAT	Value Added Tax
VCLT	Vienna Convention on the Law of Treaties
WHC	World Heritage Convention
WHL	World Heritage List
WHO	World Health Organization
WIPO	World Intellectual Property Organization
WIR	World Investment Report
WSSD	World Summit on Sustainable Development
WTO	World Trade Organization

List of Contributors

Julien Cantegreil, formerly a member of the Cabinet of the Minister of Economics, Finance, and Industry (France), is now enseignant-chercheur in Comparative Law and International Law at the Ecole normale supérieure and member of the Chair of International Law at the Collège de France. His last paper on arbitration appeared in G Aguilar Alvarez and WM Reisman (eds), *The Reasons Requirement in International Investment Arbitration* (2008). He is also currently teaching Jurisprudence at the Sorbonne and Redactor-in-Chief of the *Archives de Philosophie du Droit* (Dalloz). A graduate in Economics from the Ecole normale supérieure (Paris), and in Law from the Sorbonne and the Yale Law School, he holds a BA, an MPhil, and the Agrégation in Philosophy.

Pasquale De Sena is Professor of International Law and International Human Rights Law at the University of Naples 'Federico II' (since 2004). He was Visiting Professor at the International Institute of Human Rights 'René Cassin' (Strasbourg, 2008, 2007); at the University of Valencia (2008); and at the University of Strasbourg 'Robert Schuman' (2007). He was Visiting Scholar at the Hague Academy of International Law (1988, 1989); at the Max Planck Institute for Public International Law and Comparative Public Law (1995); and at the European Court of Human Rights (1998, 2001, 2002, 2007). He has published two books and has written extensively in the field of public international law, with specific regard to international human rights law. He is a Member of the Board of Editors and General Editor of the journal *Diritti umani e diritto internazionale* (*Human Rights and International Law*, 2007 to present).

Bruno De Witte is Professor of European Union Law at the European University Institute, Florence (joint chair of the Law Department and the Robert Schuman Centre) and Co-director of the Academy of European Law at the EUI. He holds a law degree from the University of Leuven and a PhD from the European University Institute. He was Professor of European Law at the Universiteit Maastricht (the Netherlands) from 1989 to 2000. His main fields of interest include EU law, including amongst other things the relations between EU law and national law, and between international law and EU law; the protection of fundamental rights; the horizontal division of powers (between the institutions) and the vertical division of powers (with the Member States); and constitutional reform. Other fields of interest include the European, international, and comparative legal regulation of culture, media, education, and language use, and the protection of minorities.

Angelos Dimopoulos is currently a PhD Candidate at the European University Institute. His research explores topics in EU external relations law and international investment law and he has published articles dealing with EU external economic relations. Mr Dimopoulos holds an LLM from the University of Cambridge, a Magister Legum (MLE) from the University of Hannover, and a law degree from the University of Thessaloniki. He has worked as a practising lawyer, a trainee for the European Commission, DG Trade and as a research assistant, and he is a member of the Thessaloniki Bar Association.

Pierre-Marie Dupuy is Professor of Public International Law at the Graduate Institute of International and Development Studies in Geneva. He is on leave from the Université de Paris II (Panthéon-Assas) and was Professor at the European University Institute in Florence from 2000 to September 2008. Professor Dupuy has an extensive experience in the field of international dispute settlement and international arbitration, including in the framework of ICSID and UNCITRAL. He gave the general course of public international law at the Hague Academy of International Law in 2000 (Rec 2003, Vol 297).

Francesco Francioni (Jur Dr, Florence, LLM Harvard) is Professor of International Law and Human Rights at the European University Institute, Florence, and at the Law Faculty of the University of Siena. He is also General Editor of the *Italian Yearbook of International Law*, member of the Board of Editors of the *European Journal of International Law*, member of the American Law Institute and of the Executive Board of the European Society of International Law, and member of the Italian delegation at many diplomatic conferences and international negotiations, especially in the field of environmental law and cultural heritage. He has taught courses at the Hague Academy of International Law (1995), Cornell Law School (1983 to 1986), Texas Law School (1988 to 2007), and Oxford University (1999 to 2003).

Florian Grisel is a graduate of the Institut d'Etudes Politiques de Paris and Columbia University, working at Lévy Kaufmann-Kohler, a law firm specializing in the field of international arbitration, after working as legal counsel at the World Bank and teaching law at Université Paris I (Panthéon-Sorbonne). He is completing a doctorate in law at the Université Paris I (Panthéon-Sorbonne) and is a candidate for a LLM degree at the Yale Law School, 2010.

James Harrison is an Assistant Professor at the University of Warwick. James's core research interests focus upon analysing the broader social impact of economic laws and regulations. In much of his work he has utilized a human rights methodology for analysis. He has recently published a book entitled *The Human Rights Impact of the World Trade Organisation*. He has worked as a consultant for a number of international organizations, including the Council of Europe, the Office of the High Commissioner of Human Rights, Amnesty International, Article 19, and the Canadian Council for International Cooperation. He was previously a practising human rights lawyer.

Moshe Hirsch is the Maria Von Hofmamsthal Professor of International Law at the Hebrew University of Jerusalem (Law Faculty and Department of International Relations), Director of the International Law Forum, Hebrew University, and a member of the Global Faculty at the Centre for Energy and Petroleum Law and Policy at the University of Dundee. Professor Hirsch specializes in international economic law (trade, investment, and economic development) and public international law. His recent publications include a chapter on 'Interactions between Investment and Non-Investment Obligations in International Investment Law' (published in the *Oxford Handbook of International Law on Foreign Investment* (2008)) as well as an article on 'The Sociology of International Economic Law' (published in the *European Journal of International Law* (2008)).

Ioana Knoll-Tudor holds a PhD in international law from the European University Institute (Florence) and a Master of Arts in European Law from the College of Europe (Natolin). She is the author of a book on the fair and equitable treatment standard in the international law of foreign investment published by Oxford University Press in March 2008 and of a number of articles about various issues of investment and trade law. Ioana is a qualified Spanish lawyer (member of the Madrid bar) and is currently practising at Gide Loyrette Nouel in Warsaw.

Ursula Kriebaum is Professor of Public International Law at the University of Vienna, Department of European, International, and Comparative Law. She received her legal education at the University of Vienna (Austria) and the University of Bourgogne (Dijon, France). She received the Diploma of the International Human Rights Institute – Strasbourg in 1995, her Dr jur (JD) with distinction in 1999 (torture prevention in Europe – doctoral thesis, Verlag Österreich, 2000, 785 pp), and her Dr jur habil in 2008 (property protection in international law, a comparative study of international investment law and human rights law – 'habilitation' thesis – Duncker & Humblot, 2008, 623 pp) (both University of Vienna). She is the author of several publications in the fields of human rights law and international investment law. Her primary research interests lie in the areas of international and European human rights law and international investment protection law and arbitration. She teaches International Law at the University of Vienna and is professorial lecturer at Diplomatische Akademie Wien (Vienna School of International Studies, Austria). She also acts as a consultant for law firms. She has worked in the office of the legal adviser of the Austrian Ministry of Foreign Affairs and was legal expert in the team of the Austrian Special Envoy for Holocaust Restitution Issues. She was delegate to the UN Preparatory Committee for an International Criminal Court. She was appointed as a candidate for the 2007 election as judge at the European Court of Human Rights by the Austrian Government.

Jasper Krommendijk holds an LLM degree in International Law and Law of International Organizations from the University of Groningen, Faculty of Law (the Netherlands). His LLM thesis dealt with balancing international investment law and human rights. He previously completed bachelor degrees in International Relations and International and European Law at the same university. He was formerly an intern at the Dutch Ministry of Economic Affairs, working on issues relating to the EC Services Directive.

Dr Lahra Liberti is Advisor on International Investment Law, Investment Division, Directorate for Financial and Enterprise Affairs, OECD, Paris. Prior to her appointment at the OECD, she worked as a Research Fellow in Public International Law at the British Institute of International and Comparative Law in London and at the University of Rome (La Sapienza). Lahra holds a law degree from the University of Rome (La Sapienza) (*magna cum laude*) and a doctorate in International Law and European Law from both the University of Rome (La Sapienza) and the University of Paris I (Panthéon-Sorbonne). She is a qualified attorney in Italy.

She has worked as a legal consultant for law firms in Rome and she has been visiting researcher at the United Nations, Geneva, and at the Max Planck Institute for Comparative Public Law and International Law, Heidelberg. She has also participated at the Centre for Studies and Research of the Hague Academy of International Law in 'New Aspects of International Investment Law'. She is the author of various articles on international investment law issues and specifically on investments and human rights (L Liberti, 'Investissements et droits de l'homme' in P Kahn and T Wälde (eds), *New*

Aspects of International Investment Law (2007) 791–852). She has acted as editor-in-chief for a special issue of the International Law Forum (ILA Review) on the responsibility of multinational corporations under international law. She has lectured students at the University of Rome (La Sapienza).

Elisa Morgera (PhD, European University Institute; LLM, University College London) is a Legal Officer in the Development Law Service of the Food and Agriculture Organization of the United Nations. Her PhD thesis (to be published by Oxford University Press in 2009) focuses on emerging standards of corporate accountability in international environmental law.

John Morijn is a researcher in the Law Department of the European University Institute and a lecturer in Human Rights Law at the University of Groningen, Faculty of Law (the Netherlands). His PhD research concerns issues relating to balancing human rights and EU and WTO law. He is a member of the European Social Charter Academic Network and served on the board of academic advisors of the Trade and Human Rights Partnership Project.

Pedro Nikken is emeritus Professor and has been Dean of the Faculty of Juridical and Political Sciences of the Universidad Central de Venezuela. He was Founder Member and former President of the Inter-American Institute of Human Rights, and Judge and former President of the Inter-American Court of Human Rights. Currently he serves as a member of many ICSID tribunals and is Vice President of the International Commission of Jurists. He has written many books and articles on international human rights.

Dr Federico Ortino is Reader in International Economic Law at King's College, London. He is Member of the ILA Committee on International Trade Law and co-rapporteur to the ILA Committee on the Law of Foreign Investment; Founding Committee Member, Society of International Economic Law; and Editorial Board Member, *Journal of International Economic Law*. He was previously, Director, Investment Treaty Forum, the British Institute of International and Comparative Law, London; Adjunct Professor at the Universities of Florence and Trento; Emile Noël Fellow and Fulbright Scholar at the NYU Jean Monnet Centre, New York; and Legal Officer at the United Nations Conference on Trade and Development, Geneva. He holds an LLB from the University of Florence; an LLM from Georgetown University Law Centre; and a PhD from the European University Institute.

Riccardo Pavoni is Associate Professor of International Law at the Faculty of Law of the University of Siena (Italy). He holds an M Jur degree from the University of Oxford. He is a member of the Editorial Board of the Oxford Reports on International Law in Domestic Courts, and Associate Editor of the *Italian Yearbook of International Law*. Currently, his main research areas are the relationship between domestic and international law, international environmental law, and the law of immunity.

Ernst-Ulrich Petersmann is Professor of International and European Law and Head of the Law Department at the European University Institute, Florence. Previously, he was professor at Geneva University and its Graduate Institute of International Studies (1993 to 2001) as well as at the Universities of St Gallen and Fribourg (1990 to 1996). Professor Petersmann practised international economic law during more than 30 years as legal adviser/consultant in GATT, the WTO, and the German Ministry of Economic

Affairs, as German representative in numerous international organizations, and as chairman, member, or legal adviser on numerous GATT and WTO dispute settlement panels. Since 2000, he continues to be chairman of the International Trade Law Committee of the International Law Association.

Clara Reiner graduated from the University of Vienna in 2007 and is currently working as a research assistant for Professor Schreuer at the Institute of International Law of the University of Vienna. In the course of her studies, she spent a year in Paris where she studied at Sciences Po (Institut d'Etudes Politiques de Paris) and worked at the International Court of Arbitration of the ICC as an intern. Upon returning to Vienna and before graduating, she also worked as an assistant in the European Centre of Tort and Insurance Law.

Christoph Schreuer is Professor of International Law at the University of Vienna, Austria. He holds degrees from the Universities of Vienna, Cambridge, and Yale. He has spent most of his academic career at the Department of International Law of the University of Salzburg, Austria. From 1992 to 2000 he was the Edward B Burling Professor of International Law and Organization at the Paul H Nitze School of Advanced International Studies (SAIS) of the Johns Hopkins University in Washington, DC. Over an academic career spanning more than 40 years, he has published numerous articles and several books in the field of international law. He has covered such diverse areas as human rights, adjudication by national and international courts and tribunals, sovereign immunity, the law of international organizations, the sources of international law, and the future of sovereignty. Since 1992 he has concentrated on international investment law and has written many articles and several books on the subject. The main product of this activity is *The ICSID Convention: A Commentary* (2009). He has worked on numerous investment arbitration cases in the capacity of legal expert, counsel, and arbitrator.

Alec Stone Sweet works in the fields of comparative and international politics, comparative and international law, and European integration. His most recent book is *A Europe of Rights: The Impact of the ECHR on National Legal Systems* (2008). Other books include *The Birth of Judicial Politics in France* (1992), *European Integration and Supranational Governance* (1998), *Governing with Judge* (2000), *The Institutionalization of Europe* (2001), *The Politics of Delegation* (2002), *On Law, Politics, and Judicialization* (2003), and *The Judicial Construction of Europe* (2004). Prior to coming to Yale, he was Official Fellow, Nuffield College, Oxford, and has held visiting professorships in universities in Aix-en-Provence, Florence, Madrid, Paris, Stockholm, and Vienna. He is presently engaged in a long-term project on the development of (private, a-national) systems of governance for transnational business.

Pierre Thielbörger is a doctoral candidate in law at the European University Institute in Florence. He holds degrees in law and journalism from the University of Hamburg, and has previously studied at the Humboldt University Berlin and at McGill University. His PhD project concerns the development and evolution of the human right to water in international and domestic legal systems. He currently undertakes research on law and public policy at Harvard Kennedy School and Harvard Law School.

Valentina Sara Vadi is a qualified lawyer and researcher/PhD candidate at the European University Institute, Florence. She holds degrees in international law and political science from the University of Siena and a Magister Juris (LLM) from the University of Oxford in European and Comparative Law. She has published several articles concerning investment law, cultural heritage, and intellectual property and is member of the Board of Editors of the *European Journal of Legal Studies*. She has worked as research assistant at the Academy of European Law, the European University Institute, and the University of Oxford.

Jeff Waincymer is Professor of International Trade Law at the Faculty of Law, Monash University in Melbourne, Australia. Jeff's research is primarily in the fields of international trade law, arbitration, and taxation. He is the author of *WTO Litigation: Procedural Aspects of Formal Dispute Settlement* (2002) and *Australian Income Tax: Principles and Policy* (2nd edn, 1993) and is a joint author of *A Practical Guide to International Commercial Arbitration* and also *International Trade Law: Commentary and Materials* (2nd edn, 2004). Jeff is also a qualified practitioner. He is an Australian Government Nominee as a non-governmental panellist for the WTO and has acted as a panellist. He is also a nominated ICSID panellist and has been an ICC-appointed arbitrator. Jeff is Co-convenor of the International Trade and Business Interest Group of the Law Council of Australia.

Jacques Werner is mainly acting as an international arbitrator in commercial and investment cases. He is the Chairman of the Geneva Global Arbitration Forum, Visiting Professor at Hunan Normal University Law School, Changsha, China and City University of Hong Kong. He may be contacted at wernerp@iprolink.ch

PART I

INTRODUCTION AND SUMMARY OF THE BOOK

1

Introduction and Summary: 'Administration of Justice' in International Investment Law and Adjudication?

Ernst-Ulrich Petersmann

Over the past two decades, foreign direct investment flows have rapidly grown to US$1.8 trillion (2007). The number of publicly known treaty-based investment disputes in the context of the more than 2,500 bilateral investment treaties (BITs) and some 250 free trade areas now exceeds 300, more than half of which have been adjudicated over the past five years. In the absence of a single multilateral investment treaty and worldwide investment institution, judicial interpretation and application of the applicable treaty and customary law rules often lack coherence and transparency; their input-legitimacy (for example, in terms of respect for human rights, citizen rights, and democratic governance), output-legitimacy (for example, in terms of serving the general interests of all stakeholders rather than one-sidedly favouring investor interests), and effectiveness (for example, in terms of just and legally coherent dispute settlements) remain controversial among governments, lawyers, and civil society, for example, in case of mutually inconsistent judgments, one-sided 'balancing' among public and private interests being involved, lack of appellate review procedures, high social costs of confidential arbitration awards of millions of US dollars' damages for foreign investors, and perceived lack of a 'level playing field' for all interests involved (for example, regarding less-developed defendant states with inadequate financial, legal, and technical resources).

This book includes the revised contributions to two international conferences organized by Professors Pierre-Marie Dupuy, Francesco Francioni, and Ernst-Ulrich Petersmann at the European University Institute (EUI) in Florence in 2007. The editors gratefully acknowledge the financial support from the EUI Research Council and the editorial assistance from our EUI doctoral candidates Angelos Dimopoulos, Pierre Thielbörger, and Valentina Vadi. The research questions analysed in this book have been neglected in international law and dispute settlement practice and merit additional academic research in view of the ever-increasing number of international economic disputes, investor-state arbitral awards, and related decisions by other national and international courts:

- Why do national and international courts, investor-state arbitral tribunals, and alternative jurisdictions for the settlement of transnational investment disputes and other economic disputes, in their judicial review of treaty claims and related contract claims (for example, regarding alleged government interferences into property rights), refer so rarely to the customary law requirement of settling 'disputes concerning treaties, like other international disputes ... in conformity with the principles of justice and international law', including 'universal respect for, and observance of, human rights and fundamental freedoms for all', as codified in the Vienna Convention on the Law of Treaties (VCLT, Preamble)?

- Could the variety of alternative dispute settlement fora for international investment disputes – such as private commercial arbitration, national courts, investor-state arbitration based on BITs or regional agreements (like Chapter 11 of NAFTA), regional economic or human rights courts, worldwide courts (like the International Court of Justice), and alternative dispute settlement bodies (for example, in the World Trade Organization) – administer justice in more coherent ways, and reduce the risks of legal and jurisdictional fragmentation in international law, by reviewing their textual, contextual, and teleological interpretations of international treaties from the constitutional perspective of the judicial task of settling disputes 'in conformity with principles of justice' and the universal human rights obligations of governments?

- Is the ever-larger number of international courts, investor-state tribunals, and judicial dispute settlements contributing to the emergence of an international customary procedural law – for instance, by clarifying principles of evidence, inherent judicial powers to adopt preliminary decisions, granting provisional measures, suspending proceedings, enjoining parties from pursuing other proceedings, interpreting or revising judgments, exercising 'judicial comity' in case of competing or overlapping jurisdictions, and admitting *amicus curiae* submissions?

- What are the relationships between judicial clarification of principles of 'procedural justice' (like 'hear the other side', precedent following, judicial justification of relevant differences in the concrete dispute, and similarities justifying different treatment or analogies) and substantive 'principles of justice' underlying national and international law applicable in the respective jurisdiction? Are judicial clarification and protection of relevant constitutional rights and 'principles of justice' less democratic than legislative protection of constitutional principles, rights, and obligations?

- Are 'principles of justice' relevant context also for the judicial clarification of the often indeterminate, substantive treaty standards in international investment law (like 'fair and equitable treatment', protection of legitimate expectations, 'national treatment', 'full protection and security', and access to justice) in the settlement of transnational economic disputes with due regard to obligations of governments to protect human rights *erga omnes*, for example, also vis-à-vis third parties adversely affected by investment disputes (for example, if investors and host state authorities colluded in circumventing human rights or other *jus cogens* obligations)?

- Are there lessons to be learnt for adjudication in investment law from judicial dispute settlement in European economic law among the 30 Member States of the European Economic Area (EEA) – for instance, from the judicial interpretation of individual economic rights under EC and EEA law in conformity with the human rights obligations under the European Convention of Human Rights (ECHR)? Does the trend from unilateral and bilateral towards multilateral investment regulation – with due regard for national sovereignty (for example, to regulate investments in conformity with 'constitutional requirements' of transparency, non-discrimination, due process of law, and proportionality of restrictions of individual rights) – facilitate judicial interpretations of investment law in conformity with the multilateral human rights obligations of all states? Is anything gained from describing investment law and adjudication as part of 'global administrative law' and of 'multilevel constitutionalism' limiting governmental restrictions of individual freedom (like freedom of profession), labour rights, and property rights?

The legal, comparative, and empirical case studies in this book offer answers to these complex questions in four parts:

- The Introduction summarizes the main conclusions of Parts II to IV and, together with Chapters 7 to 12, places them into the broader context of 'principles of justice', 'global administrative law', and 'multilevel constitutionalism' that may be relevant for judicial 'administration of justice' in international economic law (IEL) and investor-state arbitration.

- Part II includes contributions by leading academics and arbitrators clarifying the 'constitutional dimensions' of transnational investment disputes and investor-state arbitration, as reflected in the increasing number of arbitral awards and *amicus curiae* submissions addressing human rights concerns and related arguments of human rights bodies. As the multilevel regulation of human rights, investments, and adjudication differs among countries and regional systems, the seven contributions to Part II offer diverse perspectives by private and public lawyers from different countries and different legal systems illustrating the need for legal and 'constitutional pluralism'.

- This need for 'principle-oriented ordering' and 'normative congruence' of diverse national, regional, and worldwide legal regimes is further demonstrated in the four contributions in Part III, written by leading academics and judges, on the pertinent dispute settlement practices and legal interpretation methods of regional economic courts and human rights courts, which increasingly interpret IEL with due regard to the human rights obligations of the governments concerned. The references in arbitration awards to the methods of 'judicial balancing' in regional courts illustrate the potential relevance of such comparative analyses and 'dialogues' among courts.

- Part IV includes 12 case studies on potential human rights dimensions of specific 'protection standards' (for example, for defining the legitimate scope of property rights, 'fair and equitable treatment', and non-discrimination), applicable law (for example, national and international human rights law and rules on 'corporate social accountability'), procedural law issues (for example, in case of *amicus curiae* submissions), and specific fundamental rights (for example, to protection of human health, access to water, protection of the environment, own property without arbitrary government interference, procedural rights of access to justice, indigenous peoples' rights), as they are increasingly being discussed in investor-state arbitration and related *amicus curiae* briefs. Rather than seeking to 'extract water from stones', the case studies do not only discuss the still limited examples of human rights discourse in investor-state arbitral awards. They also probe the *potential* legal relevance of investor-state arbitration (as a 'secondary rule' in terms of Professor Hart's concept of law as a union of 'primary' and 'secondary' rules) for the judicial recognition, interpretation, and 'balancing' of 'primary rules' (for example, of investment law and human rights law) in the light of 'principles of justice', as defined by national and international law. Even though the open-textured investment treaty obligations offer a wide margin of interpretation that enables judges to avoid conflicts between human rights and investment law requirements (for example, of 'fair and equitable treatment'), the case studies illustrate the often diverse conceptions in national and international legal systems of how courts and arbitral tribunals should reconcile economic law, human rights, judicial procedures, and investor-state arbitration, with due regard to the customary law requirement of settling disputes 'in conformity with principles of justice' and human rights. If 'principles of justice' and human rights are perceived also as part of the 'rules of recognition' calling for judicial review of state-centred conceptions of international law, then judicial administration of justice in investor-state arbitration may justify citizen-oriented interpretations also of arbitration *procedures* (for example, admission of *amicus curiae* briefs by citizens adversely affected by the foreign investments concerned) and of the legitimate role of judges and arbitrators in the settlement of investor-state disputes with adverse effects on third parties and democratic decision-making.[1]

I. Judicial Administration of Justice in IEL?

The unpredicted, sudden breakdown of parts of the international financial and banking system in 2008, and its welfare-reducing effects on millions of citizens all over the world (for example, in terms of unemployment and loss of savings and pensions), illustrate the urgent need for reassessing the prevailing conceptions of international market regulation, IEL, and their underlying constitutional assumptions (for example, regarding 'rational choices' by individuals, markets, and governments in the current global financial crisis with unpredictable, systemic repercussions on society, the economy, and polities). The two predominant perspectives on the relation of justice to international law have focused on 'rule-following' (for example, in the sense of H Kelsen's unified conception of national and international law as deriving from the same basic 'Grundnorm'[2]) and on international agreement (for example, on 'international law among states', 'international law among peoples', and 'contractual justice' among citizens as legal subjects of human rights and constitutional rights).[3] Yet, following the universal recognition of inalienable human rights by all 192 UN Member States, both legal paradigms are confronted with 'constitutional problems':

- Rule-following (for example, in the Rawlsian sense of 'justice as regularity' or 'formal justice') and procedural justifications of substantive principles of

---

[1] On criticism of international investment law as one-sidedly privileging foreign investor rights over democratic market regulation, see D Schneidermann, *Constitutionalizing Economic Globalization. Investment Rules and Democracy's Promise* (2008). On Hart's distinction between 'primary rules of obligation' (requiring human beings to do or abstain from certain actions) and 'secondary rules' for changing law, adjudicating disputes, and identifying valid rules ('rules of recognition'), and his distinction between 'justice or injustice of the *law*' and 'justice or injustice of the administration of the law', see HLA Hart, *The Concept of Law* (2nd edn, 1994) 81–94, 160–161. If, as it is suggested in this Introduction, the customary law requirement of 'settling disputes in conformity with the principles of justice' is part also of national and international 'rules of recognition', then national and international courts may have sufficient jurisdiction and 'margin of appreciation' for interpreting and reconciling international investment rules in conformity with the respective domestic constitutional requirements of 'public order' and respect for principles of democracy, protection of human rights, and dispute settlement in conformity with 'principles of justice'.

[2] Cf H Kelsen, *The General Theory of Law and State* (1945) 325 ff; and *Principles of International Law* (1952), where Kelsen formulated the basic customary norm of the national and international legal order as follows: 'The states ought to behave as they have customarily behaved' (at 417–418), allowing revolution and the principle of effectiveness to be law-creating facts.

[3] On the modern relevance of the Kantian legal theory of justice, notably of its emphasis on the mutual complementarities of national, international, and cosmopolitan constitutional guarantees of human dignity, liberty, and equality to be protected by judicial guarantees of rule of law across state borders, cf EU Petersmann, 'How to Constitutionalize International Law and Foreign Policy for the Benefit of Civil Society?' [1998] Michigan Journal of International Law 20, 1–30.

justice by means of 'fair procedures' and 'social contracts' are often based
on assumptions of 'strict compliance' in a law-abiding, ideal society without conflicts (as in Rawls' theory of justice). Yet, such ideal theories of
'formal' and 'procedural justice' may be irrelevant for 'the problems of
partial compliance theory (which) are the pressing and urgent matters',[4]
notably in international relations beyond constitutional democracies.
While community-oriented areas of law (like constitutional law, social law,
and family law) focus on the cooperative and social nature of human
beings, economic law and competition remain characterized by antagonistic rivalry and conflicting self-interests (for example, among bank
managers and shareholders, profit-maximizing investors, and consumers
interested in low prices). Disputes over non-compliance by governments
with their self-imposed international economic obligations remain ubiquitous, notwithstanding the increasing acceptance of compulsory jurisdiction for third-party adjudication in private and public IEL (which
corroborates what philosophers like I Kant have described as the 'civilizing
force' of mutually beneficial economic cooperation among citizens
across frontiers and of their privately agreed 'law merchant').[5] As long as
neither citizens nor most parliaments effectively control intergovernmental
economic regulation and adjudication, justice in dispute resolution – as
explicitly required by the customary rules of treaty interpretation as well as
by Article 1 of the UN Charter – may offer a more acceptable paradigm for
judicial and constitutional protection of rule of law in international economic relations than comprehensive theories of justice (for example, for
restructuring the international economic order) on which the 192 UN
Member States and their citizens are unlikely to ever agree.[6]

[4] The quotation is from J Rawls, *A Theory of Justice* (revised edn, 1999) 8, who justifies his
focus on 'ideal theory' for a strictly law-abiding society in the following terms: 'The reason for
beginning with ideal theory is that it provides, I believe, the only basis for the systematic grasp of
these more pressing problems ... At least, I shall assume that a deeper understanding can be gained
in no other way, and that the nature and aims of a perfectly just society is the fundamental part of
the theory of justice'.
[5] Cf EU Petersmann, 'The Contribution of Free and Fair Trade to Constitutional Liberty and
Justice' in F Trentmann (ed), *Is Free Trade Fair?* (2008) 60–71.
[6] On the need for respecting 'reasonable disagreement' and the 'morality of conflicts', see
S Besson, *The Morality of Conflict. Reasonable Disagreement and the Law* (2005). On the distinction
between ideal and non-ideal theories of justice, see Rawls, n 4 above, 216: 'The intuitive idea is to
split the theory of justice into two parts. The first or ideal part assumes strict compliance and works
out the principles that characterize a well-ordered society under favourable circumstances. It
develops the conception of a perfectly just basic structure and the corresponding duties and obligations of persons under the fixed constraints of human life. My main concern is with this part of
the theory. Non-ideal theory, the second part, is worked out after an ideal conception of justice has
been chosen; only then do the parties ask which principles to adopt under less happy conditions.
This division of the theory has, as I have indicated, two rather different subparts. One consists of
the principles for governing adjustments to natural limitations and historical contingencies, and the
other of principles for meeting injustices.' The term 'constitutional law' is used in my publications
in the Kantian sense of national, international, and cosmopolitan constitutional safeguards of equal

- As explained already in Kantian legal theory and acknowledged in UN human rights law, the universal recognition of inalienable human rights deriving from respect for human dignity (for example, in terms of reasonable autonomy and responsibility of citizens) requires interpreting the 'sovereign equality of states', and the transnational and intergovernmental regulation of international economic cooperation among citizens, in conformity with the universal obligations to protect human rights and rule of law *erga omnes*.[7] IEL and international organizations, like states, derive their legitimacy from respecting, promoting, and protecting equal human rights and voluntary cooperation of free and equal citizens under the rule of law. Just as modern human rights law and democratic constitutionalism are consistent with Kant's 'categorical imperative' of protecting equal human rights by cosmopolitan constitutional law, so can the legalization and judicialization of IEL be seen as confirming the Kantian prediction that legal and judicial protection of mutually beneficial trade and investments can promote rule of law also in transnational relations among antagonistic citizens and foreign governments as long as IEL and courts respect human rights and the legitimate diversity of citizens and constitutional democracies.

For the above-mentioned reasons, this book focuses less on international 'conventional justice' and 'justice as reciprocity' among states than on the emergence of citizen-oriented 'constitutional justice', and on the impact of human rights and 'transformative justice' on 'contractual justice' among citizens, in the sense of an increasing 'judicialization', 'constitutionalization', and judicial clarification of rights-based 'principles of justice' in IEL, as reflected in the increasing recourse by private investors and non-governmental organizations to third-party adjudication and arbitration in international trade and investment law enabling judges to settle disputes, 'declare the law', and 'administer justice' in conformity with human rights obligations of governments. Independent and impartial third-party adjudication may not only be the oldest paradigm of administration of justice on the basis of 'rule of law' (for example, in the formal sense of

---

liberties under the rule of law inside and across states, cf I Kant, 'Perpetual Peace' in H Reiss (ed), *I.Kant – Political Writings* (1971) 98 ff. Kant rightly emphasizes that it is only through constitutional rules that a multitude of rational, antagonistic egoists can be transformed into a 'people', 'state', cosmopolitan 'civil society', and rule-of-law system protecting equal liberties and human rights. In view of the interdependence between national, international, and transnational rule of law, the normative legitimacy of state sovereignty depends on such multilevel, constitutional safeguards of human rights limiting the 'savage freedom' (Kant) of individuals and of states in the state of nature at all levels of human interactions.

[7] On the need for a cosmopolitan re-interpretation of IEL law with due regard to the human rights obligations of all UN Member States (as common normative justification of national and international law), see EU Petersmann, 'State Sovereignty, Popular Sovereignty and Individual Sovereignty: From Constitutional Nationalism to Multilevel Constitutionalism in International Economic Law?' in W Shan, P Simons and D Singh (eds), *Redefining Sovereignty in International Economic Law* (2008) 27–60.

identifying valid rules of law and rule-following), hearing both sides (*audia alteram partem*), judicial protection of equal rights and procedures, and judicial reasoning justifying the peaceful, legally binding settlement of disputes (for example, by judicial reference to legal precedents and judicial justification of relevant similarities and differences in the concrete dispute). From the popular juries judging the complaints against Socrates (399 BC) and Jesus Christ up to today's international criminal court proceedings, judicial proceedings also raise systemic, constitutional dimensions of conflict resolution and rule of law, notably in situations where the parties disagree on the applicable principles of justice and on principle-oriented interpretation of rules.[8] The judicial administration and clarification of 'principles of justice' – such as formal justice (for example, in the sense of treating like cases alike and following precedents), distributive justice (for example, in the sense of judicial and constitutional attention to particular circumstances justifying differential treatment), and 'corrective justice' (for example, in the sense of just punishment or compensation) – has often been instrumental in triggering broader legal reforms by challenging citizens and governments (even if the judicial reasoning remained limited to the context of a specific dispute) to reconsider the systemic, legal implications of judicial determination of legal 'principles of justice'. Arguably, the ever-more comprehensive, individual rights of 'access to justice' in human rights law and IEL, and the resulting 'judicialization' and 'constitutionalization' of international trade and investment law, reflect a systemic strengthening of 'principles of justice' as part of the constitutional foundations of modern IEL.

It remains controversial, especially in international law, to what extent the concept of 'judicial administration of justice' should be based on notions of rule-following (rule of law), procedural justice (for example, impartiality, 'hear the other side'), substantive equality (for example, 'treat like cases alike and different cases differently'), distributive justice (for example, 'reasonable' and 'equitable' administration of justice, proportionality), and 'corrective justice' (for example, by means of just compensation) whenever these diverse dimensions of justice may seem to collide (for example, if governments request domestic courts to refrain from protecting citizens against governmental violations of international law). The universal recognition of human rights and the increasing recognition of compulsory jurisdiction for judicial settlement of transnational economic disputes are of constitutional significance not only for administering procedural and substantive justice in concrete disputes, but also for clarifying the systemic dimensions of IEL

---

[8] On the distinction between rules (whose limited scope of application and categorical 'if-then structure' apply in an 'all-or-nothing fashion' determining the outcome of a dispute irrespective of any other legal arguments made) and principles (as 'optimization requirements' requiring 'weighing and balancing' among competing principles to be realized in the whole legal order) as mutually exclusive sub-categories of legal norms, see R Alexy, *A Theory of Fundamental Rights* (2002). On the increasing recourse – eg in international human rights law, labour law, trade and investment law and adjudication – to 'principle-oriented' interpretations and adjudication, see Chapter 8.

and its 'rules of recognition' (for example, as defined in Article 38 of the ICJ Statute).[9] As human rights norms and international economic treaties tend to include both 'rules' and principles to be realized in the whole legal order (for example, the *human dignity* core of human rights acknowledged in human rights conventions, the 'principles' explicitly referred to in WTO agreements and in BITs), principle-oriented judicial interpretations and 'balancing' in individual disputes may progressively clarify general rules by 'optimizing' legal principles in particular conflicts, thereby promoting progressive development of the interpretation of general treaty provisions in response to what is considered to be factually and normatively possible by the judges and by the parties in particular disputes.[10]

II. Is There a Role for Human Rights in Investor-State Arbitration and International Economic Adjudication?

International law at the beginning of the 21st century is characterized by the legal obligations of all 192 UN Member States to respect and protect human rights as well as by the ever-more comprehensive, multilevel legal regulation and judicial protection of transnational economic cooperation among citizens. International investment law remains unique by granting private foreign investors direct access to international arbitral tribunals, often without prior exhaustion of local remedies, in order to challenge governmental restrictions of investor rights and claim damages for governmental breaches of investment law. Yet, as explained in Chapters 4 and 5, investors and host states only rarely invoke human rights in investment disputes (for example, in case of torture and imprisonment of the investor, public emergency measures of the host state); and investor-state arbitral tribunals remain reluctant to examine human rights

---

[9] Cf Hart, n 1 above, 111–112: 'The case for calling the rule of recognition "law" is that the rule providing for the identification of other rules of the system may well be thought a defining feature of a legal system ... the ultimate rule of recognition may be regarded from two points of view: one is expressed in the external statement of fact that the rule exists in the actual practice of the system; the other is expressed in the internal statements of validity made by those who use it in identifying the law.' See also Hart's Postscript (n 1), edited by PA Bulloch and J Raz, where Hart acknowledges (at 247, 250, 258) that a rule of recognition may include also substantive criteria of justice and morality, such as censure by judges determining the correct recognition of legal sources.

[10] On the warning by J Habermas that Alexy's optimization thesis ('law of balancing') and judicial application of constitutional rules as including also principles risk destroying the 'firewall' between rules and principles in case of 'irrational balancing' (eg if constitutional rights are outweighed by goal-oriented collective goods), and on Alexy's defence emphasizing the possibility of rational judicial 'balancing' and adjudicating individual rights without undermining constitutional rules and the proper role of democratic legislatures, see Alexy, n 8 above, 388–390. Neither Alexy nor Habermas address the different context of international courts and arbitral bodies, whose case law is not effectively controlled by parliamentary legislatures and whose jurisprudence on permissible limitations of individual freedoms may be less constrained by constitutional requirements of proportionality and of individual access to justice.

arguments raised in *amicus curiae* submissions or on their own initiative (for example, as part of 'contextual interpretation' *proprio motu* following the principle of *jura novit curia*) if human rights have not been argued by the parties. The dynamic yet 'fragmented' development of investment law, human rights law, and international economic adjudication may lead to more coherent interpretations of these ever-more important areas of international law only to the extent that judges and courts cooperate (for example, by means of 'judicial comity') and respect that human rights and 'sovereign equality' among states must protect legitimate diversity among citizens and democratic polities.

Most international investment disputes and investor-state arbitrations relate to legal claims based on investment contracts and international investment treaties that include choice of law clauses and jurisdiction clauses referring, directly or indirectly (for example, by means of references to international law in the applicable law of the host state), to the domestic law of the host state and to 'such rules of international law as may be applicable' (ICSID Convention, Article 42). The 'sovereign equality' of states, the diversity of national legal and democratic traditions, and the legal protection of the private autonomy and property rights of investors inevitably entail a 'fragmentation' of international investment law (for example, as reflected in ad hoc arbitration based on the more than 2,500 BITs concluded among states) as well as of national and international dispute settlement jurisdictions. Yet, this inevitable diversity of national and international legal regimes and jurisdictions tends to be progressively reduced by the ever-larger number of investment-related, national and international court judgments, arbitral awards, and other dispute settlement reports clarifying not only common principles of the procedural law of international dispute settlement bodies,[11] but also promoting mutually coherent interpretations of internationally agreed standards of legal protection, regulation, expropriation, and dispute settlement.[12] This 'judicial harmonization', notwithstanding the lack of formal legal obligations (such as *stare decisis*) among ad hoc arbitral tribunals or competing arbitral institutions (such as the International Chamber of Commerce, the London Court of International Arbitration, and the WIPO Arbitration Center), is facilitated by 'contextual', 'systematic', 'dynamic', and 'effective interpretations' of investment law, often with due regard to applicable non-investment law (for example, pursuant to VCLT, Article 31) in view of the fact that international investment agreements explicitly state (unlike the narrower 'applicable law clauses' in Articles 7 and 17 of the Dispute Settlement Understanding of the World Trade Organization) that tribunals should consider 'international law as

---

[11] Cf C Brown, *A Common Law of International Adjudication* (2007).

[12] Cf P Muchlinski, F Ortino, and C Schreuer (eds), *Oxford Handbook of International Investment Law* (2008); and R Dolzer and C Schreuer, *Principles of International Investment Law* (2008). It is characteristic that also the Index of the latter book does not refer to 'justice' as a concern of investment law and adjudication.

applicable'.[13] For example, an increasing number of investor-state arbitral awards examine claims whether investment rules (for example, on national treatment and 'fair and equitable treatment') should be construed in conformity with pertinent WTO obligations of the state concerned.[14]

As illustrated by the seven contributions to Part II, the dynamically evolving case law of private commercial arbitration, national and international courts, investor-state arbitration based on international investment treaties, and alternative dispute settlement proceedings (for example, in the WTO) suggests that – in spite of the lack of a centralized structure of international law and of an integrated judicial system coordinating competing and often overlapping jurisdictions – courts increasingly use the customary methods of 'systematic' treaty interpretation and 'general principles of law' (in terms of Article 38(3)(c) of the ICJ Statute) as well as 'constitutional interpretation' (for example, in the judicial review of the lawfulness and 'proportionality' of government interferences into investor rights) for resolving investment disputes, and for avoiding conflicting court judgments, by interpreting investment contracts and investment treaties in their broader context of national and international law. The judicial settlement of investment disputes and the 'judicial dialogues' (for example, about principles of *res judicata*, *lis alibi pendens*, abuse of process, public order, and *forum non conveniens*) and 'comity' among courts confirm the increasingly systemic and 'constitutional' features of IEL and of judicial protection of individual rights and rule of law in the international division of labour.[15] Occasional inconsistencies among investor-state arbitral awards (for example, regarding judicial interpretations of a 'state of necessity' as legal justification of host state restrictions of investor rights) illustrate that the increasing number of national and international tribunals, without appellate review or other

---

[13] On the contested question of whether international law has only a 'complementary role' vis-à-vis domestic investment law (eg in order to fill a '*lacuna*' in domestic law) or also a 'corrective role' vis-à-vis domestic rules that are inconsistent with international law, see E Gaillard and Y Banifatemi, 'The Meaning of "and" in Article 42(1), Second Sentence, of the Washington Convention: The Role of International Law in the ICSID Choice of Law Process' (2003) 18 *ICSID Review* 375–411, 399. See also *Eastern Sugar v Czech Republic*, Partial Award, 27 March 2007 (UNCITRAL Arbitration, Stockholm Chamber of Commerce) (Netherlands/Czech Republic BIT), at para 196: 'This does not mean that international law applies only when it is in conflict with national law. On the contrary, it means that international law generally applies. It is not just a gap-filling law. It is only where international law is silent that the Arbitral Tribunal should consider before reaching any decision how non conflicting provisions of Czech law might be relevant, and if so, could be taken into account.'

[14] Cf *Pope and Talbot v Canada*, Award on the Merits, 10 April 2001, 7 ICSID Reports 102 at para 45. In July 2001, the NAFTA Free Trade Commission issued legally binding 'Notes of Interpretation of Certain NAFTA Chapter 11 Provisions' stating, inter alia, that – contrary to previous interpretations by NAFTA tribunals – the 'fair and equitable treatment standard' must be understood only as a reference to the customary international 'minimum standard of treatment'. The new Art 6(5) in the US Model BIT of 2004 on expropriation and compensation clarifies explicitly that: 'This Article does not apply to the issuance of compulsory licenses granted in relation to intellectual property rights in accordance with the TRIPS Agreement.'

[15] Cf AM Slaughter, 'A Global Community of Courts' [2003] Harvard International Law Journal 44, 191.

effective hierarchical rules, render uniformity of judicial decisions not only impossible; the inevitable legal and judicial fragmentation of BITs and related investment disputes may also promote 'collective learning processes' that may gradually prompt governments and courts to overcome conflicting regulatory and judicial approaches to investment rules and related disputes.

In Chapter 2 on 'Unification Rather than fragmentation of International Law? The Case of International Investment Law and Human Rights Law', Professor PM Dupuy compares the normative origins of these two distinct branches of international law, assessing the historical anteriority of the obligations of states with regard to the rights of aliens – including their property rights – which appeared well before a new body of law developed with regard to human rights protection in general. This explains for one part some substantial similarities existing between these two sets of rules, as illustrated in particular by the way in which the principle of fair and equitable treatment of foreign investments is applied by arbitral tribunals. He illustrates how judges and arbitrators – in their judicial interpretation and clarification of indeterminate investment rules and incomplete treaty regulations (for example, on procedural powers of courts and judicial remedies) – can resort to principles of treaty interpretation, customary rules, 'general principles of law', judicial precedents, and human rights obligations of governments in order to avoid conflicts among fragmented jurisdictions, treaty regimes, diverse judicial interpretations, and domestic implementing rules. For instance, recourse to general principles of law as applied in the practice of other courts (for example, 'proportionality balancing' in regional economic and human rights courts), or 'contextual interpretation' of BITs in conformity with the human rights obligations of the host state and home state involved in order to clarify the duties of the host state towards the foreign investor and the 'corporate accountability' of investors, may enable arbitral tribunals to reconcile the judicial interpretations of human rights courts (for example, of the lawful limits of government interferences into property rights) with diverse interpretative approaches of investment courts (for example, using 'police power doctrines' or 'sole effects doctrines' for delimiting legitimate private and public interests).

In Chapter 3 on 'Access to Justice, Denial of Justice and International Investment Law', Professor F Francioni analyses the concept of access to justice in international investment law. Although customary international law does not provide for an individual right of access to justice before international tribunals, treaty law has been gradually recognizing and consolidating an indisputable right of access to international justice by private investors in the field of foreign investment law. Following the recent growth of bilateral and regional investment treaties and of investment arbitration, the right of access to justice for the investor has shifted from access to national courts and inter-state claims to the investor-state arbitration where private actors have direct access to an international arbitral tribunal without the traditional need for the interposition of their national state in diplomatic protection. This paradigm shift undermines the traditional dogma of international law under which only states have rights, and tends to blur the traditional dichotomy between alien rights and human rights. The focus on the individual as the right holder is the hallmark of the international law of human rights. Professor Francioni examines the implications of this opening of the international remedial process to individuals and private entities and focuses on three distinct but inter-related aspects of the emergence of access to justice as a human right in the field of foreign investment:

- the extent to which human rights considerations may influence the assessment of the international legality of the host state's interference with foreign property;
- the emerging claim of access to justice for the host state population when the operation of the foreign investment is deemed adversely to affect societal goods – thus, third-party participation to the arbitral process is scrutinized; and
- the way in which access to justice may be reconciled with the traditional rule of sovereign immunity with regard to claims of extra-territorial investors, as is the case in the placement of financial instruments, such as bonds, in the global market.

In Chapter 4 on 'Human Rights and Investment Arbitration', Professor C Schreuer and C Reiner discuss the role of human rights in international investment arbitration, focusing on issues such as jurisdiction, applicable law, and invocation of human rights during proceedings. The authors highlight certain similarities among human rights law and investment law, for example, regarding substantive norms such as prohibition of discrimination and protection of property that are common to both investment and human rights law. Both human rights and investment law are fundamental to the process of the emancipation of the individual from the state – for instance, by providing for legal and judicial remedies of the individual vis-à-vis governmental restrictions. The authors also notice that, in other respects, human rights and investment law differ dramatically.

- First, at the procedural level, investment law grants more rights to the individual. Many human rights treaties either do not provide for the possibility of individual complaints by private persons or, where they do, require prior exhaustion of local remedies as a condition for the exercise of jurisdiction by the international body.
- Second, the paradox of nationality in investment law is alien to human rights law, which guarantees rights irrespective of any specific nationality.
- Third, with regard to the substantive issue of expropriation, the all-or-nothing approach adopted by arbitral tribunals is less nuanced than the proportionality test applied in the jurisprudence of the European Court of

Human Rights (ECtHR) on the protection of property rights against governmental interferences.

The authors point out that the role of human rights in investment arbitration is likely to increase; yet, it remains controversial whether the arbitral system is the best suited for dealing with breaches of human rights – for example, in view of the lack of transparency and legitimacy of confidential arbitration proceedings without adequate legal safeguards for third parties (for example, of workers) and general citizen interests (for example, of consumers) that may be adversely affected by investment disputes.

In Chapter 5 on 'Investment Tribunals and Human Rights: Divergent Paths', Professor M Hirsch likewise identifies common traits as well as basically different characteristics of international human rights and investment laws. Developments in both spheres reflect fundamental structural changes in international law since World War II enhancing the legal protection of individuals (including foreign investors) as well as of various associations and legal persons that are active in these spheres (such as non-governmental organizations and transnational corporations). One of the most fundamental commonalities to both international human rights and investment law is the asymmetric legal relationship between sovereign states and individuals, including foreign investors, namely the legally superior position of states vis-à-vis individuals and foreign investors. Consequently, legal rules and institutions developed in these spheres strive to compensate the inferior position of individuals and investors under the domestic law by enhancing legal protection at the international level. While these two branches of international law address a structurally similar challenge, they have evolved differently along the private/public divide. Hirsch discusses the case law of international investment tribunals that have encountered arguments regarding the applicability and relevance of international human rights law to investment disputes, and analyses the respective judicial approaches in investment awards and certain factors leading investment tribunals to adopt a reserved approach towards international human rights law. Hirsch highlights the divergences of these two legal fields along the private/ public divide, as well as the 'de-politicization strategy' of some arbitral tribunals aimed at evading divisive human rights issues.

In Chapter 6 on 'Limits of Commercial Investor-State Arbitration: Need for Appellate Review', J Werner – a leading practitioner and arbitrator in international investment law – explains why investor-state arbitration is often wrongfully likened to international commercial arbitration among private parties. Investor-state arbitrations involve not only private business interests, but also public policies of the host state and citizen rights. Arbitral awards on investor-state disputes risk lacking credibility and democratic acceptability if they overrule, in non-transparent proceedings, democratically legitimate government decisions on grounds of investor-state contracts. Similar to the introduction of appellate review in the GATT/WTO dispute settlement system, the transparency, legitimacy, and legal coherence of investor-state arbitration could be enhanced by introduction of an appellate instance.

In Chapter 7 on 'Transnational Investment Arbitration: From Delegation to Constitutionalization?', Professor A Stone Sweet and F Grisel compare different 'Principal-Agent' (P-A) models of arbitration and adjudication, and then apply them as a means of focusing empirical attention on how investor-state arbitration is, in fact, evolving. Readers will be familiar with the traditional distinction between, on the one hand, state-centred conceptions of international judges as agents of states with mandates limited by public international law; and, on the other hand, private law conceptions of commercial arbitrators settling private disputes on the basis of private contracts. Stone Sweet and Grisel argue that the arbitral world is being gradually transformed through a process of 'judicialization', which blurs the traditional distinctions and raises important constitutional issues. They illustrate their argument with reference to the increasing recourse to judicial precedents, balancing, the review of the 'proportionality' of state restrictions on investors' rights, and the increasing calls for appellate review of the decisions of investor-state arbitral tribunals.

In Chapter 8 on 'Constitutional Theories of International Economic Adjudication and Investor-State Arbitration', Professor EU Petersmann gives an overview of the diverse 'constitutional approaches' of the European Court of Justice (ECJ), the European Free Trade Area (EFTA) Court, the ECtHR, and national courts throughout Europe – for example, in their judicial review of governmental interferences into economic freedoms and other fundamental rights on the basis of judicial interpretation and application of 'constitutional principles' (such as due process of law, legality, non-discrimination, necessity, proportionality, and limited delegation of powers), with due regard to the human rights obligations of the governments concerned. One reason for the disregard of investor-state arbitral tribunals and intergovernmental dispute settlement bodies (such as the ICJ and WTO dispute settlement bodies) for the customary law requirement of settling international disputes 'in conformity with principles of justice' and human rights is due to inadequate 'constitutional checks and balances' – for example, on the self-interests of governments in limiting their legal and judicial accountability for discriminatory restrictions of transnational trade and investments. The principles of 'commutative justice', 'contractual justice', and 'conventional justice' underlying private commercial arbitration (like party autonomy, *pacta sunt servanda, volenti non fit injuria*) differ fundamentally from the principles of 'constitutional justice' limiting governments and public national and international courts. The judicial task of settling disputes with due regard to the constitutional rights of citizens and constitutional restraints of governance powers is essential for maintaining an 'overlapping consensus' on 'principles of justice' among states and citizens with competing self-interests and conflicting conceptions for a good life, social justice and an efficient regulation of the economy. Even though human rights arguments have hardly ever been raised in GATT and WTO dispute settlement proceedings and were examined also by the ECJ in only very few cases among the thousands of ECJ judgments, they may be important parts of the 'relevant context' and democratic legitimacy of judicial settlements of investment disputes with due regard to all parties concerned, including adversely affected interests of third parties (such as workers, consumers, and tax payers affected by investment decisions).

III. Judicial 'Balancing' of Economic Law and Human Rights in Regional Courts

The four case studies in Part III are limited to the EC Court, the ECtHR, and the Inter-American Court of Human Rights; they focus on the respective judicial approaches to the protection of economic and other fundamental rights of complainants vis-à-vis alleged abuses of governmental or private powers, including the controversial question of whether international courts should limit their standards of review by respecting national 'margins of appreciation'.[16] While the EC Court and EFTA Court interpret and review national and European economic law with due regard to the human rights guarantees in the ECHR as well as in European constitutional law (such as the 'common constitutional principles' protected by the ECJ), the international economic dispute settlement bodies based on the North American Free Trade Agreement (for example, NAFTA chapter 20 panels), the Caribbean Court of Justice, the Mercosur ad hoc tribunals and the recently established Permanent Review Court of Mercosur have hardly ever interpreted economic law in the light of the Inter-American Convention on Human Rights, for instance because the parties to the disputes (such as Canada and the United States) never ratified the Inter-American Convention on Human Rights. The references in arbitral awards to the diverse regional approaches to 'balancing' economic rights, human rights, and public interest legislation illustrate the potential relevance of comparative legal and judicial studies for the future evolution of investor-state arbitration.

In Chapter 9 on 'Balancing of Economic Law and Human Rights in the European Court of Justice', Professor B de Witte explains the approach of the

---

[16] Cf E Benvenisti, 'Margin of Appreciation, Consensus and Universal Standards' [1999] Journal of International Law and Politics 31, 843–854, who argues that 'where national procedures are notoriously prone to failure, most evident when minority rights and interests are involved, no margin and no consensus should be tolerated. Anything less than the assumption of full responsibility would amount to breach of a duty by international human rights organs' (at 853–854). Yet, Benvenisti's more general claim – that 'margin of appreciation, with its principled recognition of moral relativism, is at odds with the concept of the universality of human rights' (at 844) – overlooks that UN human rights law often provides only for minimum standards that protect individual and democratic diversity (at least as long as legitimate democratic regulation of human rights remains non-discriminatory and proportionate). F Ni Aolain, 'The Emergence of Diversity: Differences in Human Rights Jurisprudence' [1995] Fordham Int'l Law Journal 19, 114 ff, argues (at 119) that constitutional democracies should be granted wider margins than non-democratic states.

ECJ to the use of human rights principles in the application and interpretation of economic Community law. This question arises in three different constellations:

- when the Court is called to examine economic regulation by the European Union legislator in the light of fundamental rights;
- when the Court is called to examine economic regulation by the Member States in the light of fundamental rights; and
- when the Court examines private interference with economic activities in the light of fundamental rights.

The chapter examines these three constellations in turn, giving each time one or more examples of how the ECJ operates. The latter two situations are those that are most directly related to the core theme of the volume, namely human rights issues arising in investment disputes. Professor de Witte emphasizes the special features of the European Union legal order, both in substantive and institutional terms, which explain why human rights questions relating to economic investment decisions are dealt with in a very different way here, compared to other arenas of international law.

In Chapter 10 on 'Economic and Non-Economic Values in the Case Law of the European Court of Human Rights', Professor P de Sena argues that the relationship between ECtHR case law relating to protection of property rights (Protocol 1, Article 1) and the traditional principles of international law on foreign investments swings between a tendency to apply these principles, adapting them to the frame of reference of the Convention, and a tendency to overcome them. The first trend displays itself when the rights of property come to the fore viewed in their specific and traditional dimension, as purely economic rights. It concerns the notion of property itself, the 'corporate veil' principle, and the determination of the amount of compensation to be awarded in cases of expropriation. The different tendency to overcome the traditional legal regime of foreign investments can be found when violations of other protected rights of considerable social (non-economic) interest come to the fore, together with interferences with the right of property. In such cases, the Court has tended both to extend the concept of property and to judge disproportionate these interferences in the light of the social relevance of the individual interests at stake.

In Chapter 11 on 'Is the European Court of Human Rights an Alternative to Investor-State Arbitration?', Professor U Kriebaum discusses – in the light of some recent decisions in which the ECtHR decided on typical investment issues – to what extent the ECtHR can replace or complement international arbitration bodies, and under what conditions investors can and should file their claim at the ECtHR rather than at the traditional bodies for the settlement of investment disputes. The analysis focuses on a variety of indicators concerning jurisdiction and merits. By means of its judicial protection of property rights and 'possessions', the ECtHR already operates as one among many other European bodies responsible for the settlement of investment disputes. Resorting to the ECtHR can also entail significant disadvantages for investors, such as the lack of protection of indirect damages, the procedural requirement to first exhaust local remedies, and the risk of an only partial compensation. Nevertheless, wherever jurisdiction through arbitral tribunals is incomplete, the ECtHR could bridge the gap for the investor – for example, in cases in which the investor does not hold a nationality that would grant him access to an arbitral investment tribunal under one of the BITs concluded with the host state; or in cases in which these BITs focus on certain violations (such as expropriation) without providing for other standards of protection such as fair and equitable treatment. A further advantage is the proportionality approach developed by the ECtHR, which allows for a balancing of interests between the host state and the investor and does not necessitate 'all or nothing decisions' with regard to compensation. Professor Kriebaum concludes that the ECtHR is no real alternative, but rather a remedy of second and last resort complementary to traditional arbitral investment tribunals for investors.

In Chapter 12 on 'Balancing of Human Rights and Investment Law in the Inter-American System of Human Rights', Professor P Nikken recalls that the inter-American system of human rights protects property as an individual right. However, the system is not the forum to protect business activity against arbitrary acts of the state. The practice of the Commission and the Court resists mixing wholly economic interests with human rights protection, even if property is involved in the conflict. The inter-American case law contains some solutions for conflicts of law. In cases of conflict between indigenous property and private property, the Court's jurisprudence suggests that human rights prevail over economic rights. Indigenous property is fully protected because it has a function that goes beyond pure economics. In contrast, the protection of other forms of private property is limited to compensation for expropriation. The implicit rule seems to be that in case of conflict between property realizing significant human rights and property satisfying mere economic interests, the former should prevail. The inter-American jurisprudence also suggests that the 'high purposes' of human rights treaties and non-applicability of reciprocity in them could become new tools for the resolution of conflicts with 'economic' conventions, especially BITs. The state's obligations under investment law could hardly be invoked as lawful justification for not fulfilling its human rights obligations. In principle, human rights must always prevail over rights related to international business. The payment of adequate compensation is the solution to meet investment commitments incompatible with human rights obligations. Although broadly based on speculations from the Inter-American Court's case law, this conclusion is rooted in the purpose of human rights treaties and the fundamental principles that sustain contemporary international law.

IV. Investor-State Arbitration and Human Rights – Case Studies on 'Protection Standards' and Human Rights

Part IV includes 12 case studies on diverse human rights dimensions of recent investor-state arbitration.

Chapter 13 by Professor J Waincymer on 'Balancing Property Rights and Human Rights in Expropriation' concentrates on one aspect of international legal rules and their adjudication, namely the protection of property rights through expropriation norms and the way in which the articulation and adjudication of these may impact upon human rights goals. The purpose of this chapter is two-fold: first, to consider whether anti-expropriation norms are a barrier to human rights promotion through their content, application, or even the regulatory chill effects that might flow from expansive indirect takings norms; and, second, to consider to what extent the development of comprehensive and balanced tests at the interface of potentially conflicting international governance regimes places great responsibility on adjudicators to expand upon the more open-ended norms that typically arise from treaty negotiations. A subsidiary question is whether the traditionally private field of international arbitration is as well suited to perform this function as a more permanent body such as the Appellate Body of the WTO or a body with broad public international law expertise such as the International Court of Justice. After examining the trends in the jurisprudence, the author suggests that, on the one hand, a fair balance is generally being achieved; but, on the other hand, the need to determine politically sensitive questions such as when governmental policies are reasonable and proportionate poses particular challenges for private adjudicators in the arbitral field.

Chapter 14 by Dr I Tudor-Knoll on 'Fair and Equitable Treatment in Investment Disputes under ICSID' scrutinizes the possible interactions between human rights and investor-state arbitration, focusing on the role that the fair and equitable treatment (FET) standard might play in such interaction. The FET standard is found in most of the 2,500 BITs signed between more than 170 countries in the world as well as in some multilateral and regional conventions; it is therefore important first to establish the sources and content of this standard. Thus, the first part of her contribution inquires into the conventional and customary sources of the FET and discusses the concrete situations in which the FET standard has already been applied. The second part of her contribution focuses on the relationship between FET and human rights norms. She first enquires into the rationale of applying human rights norms in international investment law cases since most BITs do not contain a specific reference to human rights. The contribution then specifically focuses on the scenarios in which FET may interact with human rights norms, discussing both situations that have already been encountered in the existent case law, and situations that may arise in the future. Indeed, the final part of this contribution examines and expands upon the possible scenarios where FET and human rights are likely to overlap, and on the options that arbitrators have when required to rule on them.

Chapter 15 by Dr F Ortino on 'Non-Discriminatory Treatment in Investment Disputes under ICSID' analyses the principle of non-discrimination on the basis of the nationality of the investor (such as the national treatment standard) as one of the key legal guarantees provided to foreign investors by international investment agreements. As these guarantees may directly restrain states' legislative, administrative, or judicial measures taken to implement a host of public policies (industrial, fiscal, environmental, labour, health, etc), their potential impact (whether positive or negative) on human rights is not difficult to perceive. Given the general and undefined nature of the non-discrimination principle, its meaning and import can only be elucidated by arbitration, the chosen mechanism for the settlement of investment disputes. Based on an examination of the growing body of arbitral jurisprudence, the chapter argues that there still exists a wide margin of inconsistency in the way in which arbitral tribunals interpret the national treatment standard (even when contained in the same international instrument). Although it is still early to determine the full extent of the impact of the national treatment standard on human rights, there is ample scope for treaty makers and arbitral tribunals to ensure that international investment law is drafted and interpreted in accordance with human rights law. The chapter emphasizes that the diversity of treaty language and the diversity of the interpretation of this language may represent a very useful learning ground for policy makers in the field. International law on foreign investment is still in its formative years; rules, institutions, and stakeholders are still being identified and formed.

Chapter 16 by J Cantegreil on 'Implementing Human Rights in the NAFTA Regime: The Potential of the Pending Case *Glamis Corp v USA*' takes a critical view of NAFTA's Chapter 11 impact on human rights, focusing on the pending *Glamis v United States* case. Looking at the facts and the claims raised, the author identifies the environmental and cultural human rights at stake, and assesses where to locate the legal issues concerning human rights upon which the tribunal will have to decide. He argues that if the tribunal adopts the current arbitral jurisprudence on the questions of expropriation and fair and equitable treatment, it will be another award prioritizing investors' rights over human rights concerns in the NAFTA regime. In fact, the *Glamis* litigation presents a striking example of the dangers posed by investor arbitration on the recognition and effective protection of human rights; it highlights how much can be lost in the arbitral process. As a result, the author takes a proactive look, proposing a framework for litigation promoting human rights within the NAFTA regime. Arguing in favour of an internalization of human rights norms in the NAFTA regime and of a multilevel interaction of the different actors, the author devises strategies for the parties and the tribunal to achieve this goal using the available legal tools.

Chapter 17 by Dr J Harrison on 'Human Rights Arguments in *Amicus Curiae* Submissions: Promoting Social Justice?' analyses the impact of human rights interventions of civil society organisations (CSOs) in international investment arbitration proceedings. The chapter provides a history of the *amicus* submissions so far made by CSOs, and highlights the prevalence of human rights arguments in these submissions. It argues that there is a clear rationale for engaging with a range of issues raised in investment arbitration cases (for example, provision of water services, indigenous land and culture, etc) utilizing a human rights framework. The language and legal obligations of human rights appear to have an important impact in terms of ensuring that *amicus* submissions of civil society groups are accepted by tribunals. However, there are fundamental problems in the way in which this mechanism has been utilized by tribunal panels, including: the problems of viewing *amici* as both experts and advocates; lack of expertise among the tribunal with regard to human rights; the inherently complex task of understanding the legal obligations to which human rights give rise in an investment law context; and the mistaken view that the *amicus* procedure can legitimize the tribunal process without effective participation. There are concerns that *amicus* submissions raising human rights concerns are likely to be marginalized by tribunals in the future. Continued failure in meaningful engagement would demonstrate the procedural and substantive barriers to real interaction between the two legal regimes (international human rights law and international investment law). The author concludes by arguing that continued superficial engagement with human rights by investment panels might weaken the edifice of international law in the eyes of those outsiders to the international legal system who seek to engage with it.

Chapter 18 by J Krommendijk and J Morijn on '"Proportional" by What Measure? Balancing Investor Interests and Human Rights by Way of Applying the Proportionality Principle in Investor-State Arbitration' explores the possibility of applying the proportionality principle, which is currently used by the ECtHR in its jurisprudence, in investor-state arbitration and, particularly, in expropriation-related claims. The authors argue that when states' obligations flowing from international investment treaties and human rights law come into tension, the application of the 'proportionality test' in the course of investor-state arbitration concerning expropriation may represent one of the routes through which a balancing of human rights protection imperatives and investor interests can take place. The complexity of this interplay relates to the fact that interests on both sides of the balance have human rights aspects. The authors then trace the arbitral practice with regard to expropriation claims to examine how state and investor interests are being balanced. There appears to be a recently emerging, but as yet still ambiguous, practice of proportionality testing in this context. The appropriateness of expropriatory measures alleged to be justified by human rights considerations is first measured from the investment law perspective. Second, arbitrators seem equally to have added a human rights proportionality measurement to their balancing exercise, particularly by reference to the case law of the ECtHR. By virtue of 'double proportionality' testing, investor-state arbitration practice may be merging investment and human rights law proportionality standards – a development that is to be encouraged.

Chapter 19 by V Vadi on 'Reconciling the Human Rights to Health with Investor Rights: The Case of Tobacco' explores the linkage between investment law and international instruments protecting public health, focusing on the specific issue of tobacco control. Since the recent inception of the WHO Framework Convention on Tobacco Control, which has established cognitive and normative consensus for promoting global public health through tobacco control, states have gradually adopted a series of measures to comply with this convention. However, international investment governance risks undermining the goal of tobacco control – for example, by facilitating access to tobacco products, increasing competition, and lowering tobacco prices. In addition, some regulatory measures adopted by the host state with a view to tobacco control might be deemed to be a form of indirect expropriation, as they have an economic impact on foreign property, including trademarks. After analysing the relevant legal framework, this contribution explores the potential conflict areas between investment governance and tobacco regulation and proposes some legal tools that might help to reconcile the interests at stake. In particular, the author proposes recourse to customary rules of treaty interpretation. As investment law is part of international law, it has to be consistent with its norms. The jurisprudence of both the ECtHR and the ECJ concerning tobacco control and the property rights of tobacco companies illustrates that the right to property is not an absolute right; it may be restricted on grounds of the general interest, such as the protection of public health. As public health and investment protection are not irreconcilable objectives, interpreters and policy makers need to reconcile them carefully through interpretation and treaty making.

Chapter 20 by P Thielbörger on 'The Human Right to Water v Investor Rights' recalls that the human right to water is still not clearly accepted as a binding human right in international law. This absence of a clear legal status makes the settlement of important legal investment disputes in the field of water privatization even more difficult. In detailed case studies, Thielbörger holds that the notion of the right to water shows only little advantage for the states in the arbitral settlement of these disputes, and these advantages occur only in indirect and subtle ways. States must therefore take care of the protection and promotion of the right to water themselves, namely *before* water disputes even arise. They must try to include references to the right to water in the concession contracts with the investors – and thereby *make* the right part of the applicable law – in order to ensure stable water prices and high water quality. States should also pay tribute to the right as a right of the people, by making public input and participation possible at all stages of the privatization. Thielbörger concludes that exactly because of this unsettled status of the right in international law, it will also be a special responsibility of arbitrators to consider this 'neglected' right and protect it as part of the minimum human right standard that can under no circumstances be neglected.

Chapter 21 by Dr E Morgera on 'Human Rights Dimensions of Corporate Environmental Accountability' focuses on the impact of environmental human rights on foreign investors' operations and the role of intergovernmental organisations in ensuring that such operations respect internationally agreed minimum standards. In the context of international practice related to *corporate environmental accountability*, she scrutinizes the preventive role of intergovernmental organisations vis-à-vis foreign investors' actual or potential negative impacts on environmental human rights in the country in which they are operating. The author explores the growing international practice spearheaded by international organisations of 'translating' inter-state obligations into normative benchmarks adapted to the reality of private operators, mainly foreign investors, based upon the interpretation and implementation of a combination of international soft and hard law instruments. The contribution therefore assesses the relevance for foreign investment of corporate environmental accountability.

Chapter 22 by Professor R Pavoni on 'Environmental Rights, Sustainable Development, and Investor Rights' examines the increasing number of international investment disputes where issues relating to environmental rights, sustainable development, and foreign investment protection were inextricably intertwined, in order to determine whether arbitrators have approached such interrelationships by taking environmental and sustainable development principles into consideration. He identifies the status and relevance accorded to environmental principles and obligations, of either a customary or treaty nature, in investor-state disputes. His purpose is to shed some light on the extent to which arbitrators are prepared to take into account the obligation of host states to protect the environment and their citizens' right to a healthy environment. The author shows how environmental principles and rights may effectively find their way into the arbitral process also by way of rules and concepts that are internal to investment law, such as the 'like circumstances of investors test' for the purposes of non-discrimination obligations. The final part of the chapter focuses on the relationship between investment law and the exercise of environmental participatory rights (information, public participation, and access to justice in environmental matters) at the national level. While various investor-state tribunals have indeed touched upon issues of environmental democracy and subsidiarity, they have not developed a consistent and sound approach in that respect. This risks undermining a basic tenet of the contemporary law of human rights and sustainable development.

Chapter 23 by Dr L Liberti on 'The Relevance of Non-Investment Treaty Obligations in the Assessment of Compensation' explores whether and to what extent a measure adopted by the state *in the furtherance* of international obligations other than those provided for in the investment treaty bears any consequences not only in the appreciation of state liability, but also in the determination of the quantum of compensation and in the choice of the method of valuation. The review of ICSID jurisprudence shows considerable shifts in the appreciation of this issue. The relevance of non-investment treaty obligations in the assessment of compensation was excluded by the arbitral tribunal in *Compañia del Desarollo de Santa Elena SA v Republic of Costa Rica*. By strictly relying on the 'sole effect doctrine', the arbitral tribunal left no room for an argument that the existence of international obligations to protect the environment has a bearing on the nature and measure of compensation. In the case *Siemens v Argentina*, the tribunal, while not excluding the relevance *in abstracto*, refused to endorse it *in concreto*, since the human-rights-based defence put forward by the respondent was not sufficiently substantiated. In *SPP v Egypt*, the arbitral tribunal expressly acknowledged the relevance of the international obligations deriving from the UNESCO Convention for the Protection of the World Cultural and Natural Heritage in terms of determining the methodology of valuation of the tourist project, affected by the reclassification of the Pyramids Plateau as a protected area. In particular, the discounted cash flow method was not deemed appropriate to award compensation since it would have resulted in the calculation of profits for activities on the Pyramids Plateau after the date of registration of the area with the World Heritage Committee. From that date forward, the claimants' activities on the Pyramids Plateau would have been in conflict with the Convention and therefore in violation of international law. As a consequence, any profits that might have resulted from such activities were deemed to be non-compensable. The *SPP v Egypt* case sets a useful precedent in that it clearly shows how international obligations arising under different areas of international law can be specifically relevant not only in the appreciation of the legal nature of the taking, but also in the choice of the method of valuation affecting the *quantum* of compensation.

Chapter 24 by A Dimopoulos on 'EU Free Trade Agreements: An Alternative Model for Addressing Human Rights in Foreign Investment Regulation and Dispute Settlement?' explores whether EC Free Trade and Investment Agreements (FTAs) present a new, alternative model for addressing human rights in foreign investment regulation and dispute settlement. The author provides an overview of the scope of foreign investment regulation in EC FTAs, highlighting their limited, but innovative, approach to foreign investment. The contribution then describes the dispute settlement mechanisms in the EC's FTAs and doubts their suitability for investment disputes in view of their failure to address fully the demands of investors and home and host countries. The author considers the effectiveness and suitability of EC FTAs for addressing the human rights implications of foreign investment regulation and emphasizes the importance given to human rights as an objective of EC FTAs and as an 'essential element' of the agreements; the human rights clauses reflect linkages between foreign investment and human rights, yet without addressing the practical concerns arising from the interaction between foreign investment and human rights. The innovative provisions on investors' behaviour and minimum standards found in the EC's Economic Partnership Agreement with the Caribbean Forum of ACP States (CARIFORUM) give a direct, more elaborate role to human rights considerations, safeguarding minimum standards and respecting national choices serving specific public policy goals. Taking into account the dynamic character of the EC's FTAs, the author concludes with the future challenges and perspectives for FTAs, notably in view of the EC's willingness to deal with the challenges posed by the interaction between foreign investment and human rights.

V. Conclusions: The Need for a Constitutional Theory of International Economic Adjudication

In his *Nicomachean Ethics*, Aristotle discussed a variety of conceptions of conventional justice (for example, in terms of rule-following), distributional justice (for example, in terms of equal treatment and fairness in distribution), corrective justice (for example, in civil and criminal courts), reciprocal justice (for example, in terms of the reciprocal return to one's contribution to a mutually beneficial society), and political justice (for example, in terms of 'the rule of reason' rather than 'the rule of a man' as 'guardian of equality and fairness' among 'men who are free and equal' and 'whose mutual relationship is regulated by law'), emphasizing that 'the judge restores equality' and is of particular importance for 'equitable justice' (for example, in terms of a 'rectification of law where law falls short by reason of its universality').[17] The worldwide recognition by all 192 UN Member States of 'inalienable' human rights deriving from respect for human dignity reflects the modern, increasingly universal recognition that – in the words of the American philosopher J Rawls – 'each person possesses an inviolability founded on justice that even the welfare of society as a whole cannot override'; 'justice is the first virtue of social institutions, as truth is of systems of thought'.[18] Yet, even though modern constitutional theories (including Rawls' theory of 'justice as fairness') and human rights offer important criteria for the moral assessment of rules and other social institutions that structure social relations among free and equal citizens,[19] modern

---

[17] Aristotle, *Nicomachean Ethics* (M Ostwald (ed), 1999), book V (the quotations are at 122, 129 ff, 142). [18] Rawls, n 4 above, 3.

[19] The moral assessment of individual and collective actions within the basic structure of rules is the domain of ethics and justice as a virtue of personal conduct. Principles of social justice for designing and improving a just national and international order remain dependent on moral analysis of such social conduct (eg the individual responsibility of citizens to participate in designing and maintaining their society's institutional order) and of the 'circumstances of justice' (eg the rational egoism and limited altruism of individuals constrained by scarcity of resources in their pursuit of a good life) that make just rules and institutions necessary for a stable social order protecting peaceful cooperation among free and equal citizens with diverse conceptions for a good life and for social justice. Whether morality evolved from conventional practices (eg within caring communities) and justice is a rational solution to the natural condition of fear and conflicts of short-term interests remains as controversial as it was in the times of Aristotle, cf J O'Manique, *The Origins of Justice. The Evolution of Morality, Human Rights and the Law* (2002).

international law and dispute settlement practices continue to be characterized by fundamental disagreement on the role of international courts and on how judges should interpret and apply international law rules with due regard to the diversity of their underlying conventional, egalitarian, redistributive, corrective, or commutative 'principles of justice'.[20] Hence, it is understandable that most international courts pragmatically avoid references to 'principles of justice' that are likely to remain deeply contested among reasonable people.

A. The Need for Clarifying 'Constitutional Justice' and 'Transformative Justice' in Transnational Economic Adjudication

John Rawls' *Theory of Justice* emphasizes that – in view of the 'fact of reasonable pluralism' and the 'fact that in a democratic regime political power is regarded as the power of free and equal citizens as a collective body' – the democratic exercise of coercive power over one another is democratically legitimate only when 'political power ... is exercised in accordance with a constitution (written or unwritten) the essentials of which all citizens, as reasonable and rational, can endorse in the light of their common human reason'.[21] Empirical evidence and social theory confirm this constitutional premise that a society's legal and institutional order may be improved, and politically supported over time, by constitutional agreement on political 'principles of justice' of a higher legal rank, provided the constitutional principles respect and protect the legitimate diversity of moral, religious, and political conceptions of citizens and can be freely supported by all reasonable citizens.[22] Such an 'overlapping consensus' on a limited 'political conception of justice' can help to justify, maintain, and adapt a stable social order, endorsed by citizens with competing world views, provided the principles respect and protect basic human needs and remain compatible with the enduring reality of diverse, and partially conflicting, moral, religious, and other world views of citizens. As illustrated by the role of courts in European integration law, coherent 'principles of political justice' are also of decisive importance for judicial conflict resolution and 'transformative justice' limiting abuses of power at national and international levels of public and private governance.

In conformity with the tripartite objective of Rawls' *Theory of Justice* to promote an 'overlapping consensus' among citizens on (1) a common moral justification of (2) principles of political justice for (3) the design, and adjustment over time, of the 'basic structure' of a stable social order, Rawls conceived his *Theory of Justice* as having three tiers: (1) the 'original position' on the top level is

---

[20] For an overview of the diverse state-centred and citizen-centred theories of adjudication, see chapter 8.   [21] J Rawls, *Justice as Fairness: A Restatement* (E Kelly (ed), 2001) 41.
[22] On this 'idea of a well-ordered society' respecting the 'fact of reasonable pluralism' and pursuing only a limited conception of 'political justice', see J Rawls, *Political Liberalism* (1993) 35 ff.

a contractualist, meta-constitutional thought experiment necessary for ensuring 'justice as fairness' in (2) the social agreement, on the middle level, on two principles of justice[23] (with two priority rules) that constitutionally guide and restrain, on the bottom tier, the (3) 'basic structure' of rules concretizing and institutionalizing the 'principles of justice' through their constitutional, legislative, and judicial application so as to sustain a stable order for social cooperation among citizens with fundamental interests in a good life, in a shared public conception of justice, and in successfully pursuing their chosen life plans.[24] The Rawlsian four-stage sequence prioritizes substantive principles of distributive justice over the judicial determination of 'corrective justice' (for example, awarding 'just compensation' for the injustice done by one party to another) and 'transformative justice' through judicial procedures.

As citizens are not only shaped and bound by, but also collectively responsible for, their social order, the Rawlsian constitutional theory justifies constitutional rules as resulting from 'justice as fairness', and as being in the rational self-interest of all reasonable citizens affected by the rules. In order to protect the 'constitutional contract' from being distorted by differential bargaining power and potential threats favouring certain contracting parties, the reasoning of citizens and balancing of their diverse interests must take place behind a 'veil of ignorance' (Rawls) ensuring equal consideration for all citizens. In such an 'original position', all individual interests are represented fairly, and the constitutional principles of justice protect equal access of citizens to the 'social primary goods' essential for their individual wellbeing (for example, equal basic liberties, rights, and opportunities).[25] Hence, 'justice as fairness' (Rawls) suggests that also the principles of justice and basic rules, democratic institutions, and 'courts of justice' justified by such a 'constitutional contract' are to be accepted as fair and *just* by all individuals living under this social order.

As discussed in Chapter 8, Rawls' individualist theory of justice for constitutional democracies differs from his communitarian theory of justice for an 'international law among peoples' and does not elaborate on the judicial functions of 'courts of justice' in international relations. Yet, Rawls' theory of justice explains why a constitutional theory of adjudication must inevitably be derived from a meta-constitutional theory of 'principles of justice' and from the positive, legal concretization of 'principles of justice' in constitutional law, legislation,

---

[23] Rawls' first statement of the two principles reads as follows: 'First: each person is to have an equal right to the most extensive scheme of equal basic liberties compatible with a similar scheme of liberties for others. Second: social and economic inequalities are to be arranged so that they are both (a) reasonably expected to be to everyone's advantage, and (b) attached to positions and offices open to all' (Rawls, n 4 above, 53).

[24] According to Rawls, n 4 above, his 'idea of a four-stage sequence' of choice of principles followed by their constitutional, legislative, and judicial application 'is suggested by the United States Constitution and its history' (172, n 1).

[25] Cf Rawls, n 4 above, 52 ff, 78 ff; on the lexical priority of basic liberties (which may be reduced only for the sake of basic liberties, but not for the sake of any other social primary goods), see 36 ff.

democratic institutions, and judicial protection of rule of law. As constitutions, legislation and international agreements can regulate dynamically changing social relations only in incomplete ways: judicial interpretation, application, and protection of incomplete and often indeterminate rules inevitably entails 'filling gaps' and clarifying the contested meaning of general rules. Notably, judicial conceptions of 'rule of law' – not only in terms of legal restraints on power, but also in terms of a stable legal order for society enabling its constitutionally limited self-governance – are inevitably influenced by judicial conceptions of 'principles of justice'. Rawls infers from his theory of justice that, 'in a constitutional regime with judicial review, public reason is the reason of its supreme court'; and it is of constitutional importance for the 'overlapping, constitutional consensus' necessary for a stable and just society among free, equal, and rational citizens who are likely to remain deeply divided by conflicting moral, religious, and philosophical doctrines.[26]

Yet, just as all constitutional theories of justice and adjudication remain contextual and democratically contested, so the Rawlsian theory of justice as constitutional impartiality and judicial protection of individual rights and 'rule of law' remains controversial, notably Rawls' inadequate proposals for an international 'Law of Peoples'.[27] For example, as an alternative to Rawls' 'original position' as the basis for 'justice as fairness', the ethical theory of T Scanlon[28] and the theory of justice by B Barry[29] posit participants who are aware of their identities and motivated to seek agreement under conditions of impartiality and terms that nobody could reasonably reject. The constitutional protection of human rights of access to justice (for example, in the sense of individual access to legal and judicial remedies – compare ECHR, Articles 6 and 13) and of independent courts administering justice impartially, subject to 'due process of law', are examples of constitutional justice as multilevel judicial protection of fundamental rights and 'rule of law' as constitutional restraints on 'rule by men' and their 'rule by law'.[30]

B. The Need for Clarifying the 'Constitutional Dimensions' of Judicial Interpretation Methods

The 1969 Vienna Convention on the Law of Treaties was drafted at a time when human rights remained deeply contested and suppressed in many states; hence, the diplomats negotiating the VCLT focused on international treaties among

---

[26] J Rawls, n 22 above, 231 ff.

[27] Cf EU Petersmann, 'Human Rights, International Economic Law and Constitutional Justice' (2008) 19 European Journal of International Law 769–798, and the Comment by E Howse as well as the Rejoinder by Petersmann in (2008) 19 European Journal of International Law 995–960.

[28] T Scanlon, *What We Owe to Each Other* (1998).

[29] BM Barry, *Justice as Impartiality* (Vol II of *A Treatise on Social Justice* (1995)).

[30] On the dialectic developments of constitutional rights and principles of justice restraining the instrumental 'governance by law', see Chapter 8.

states and their synallagmatic interrelationships of rights and duties among states. Although drafted as a general treaty applicable to all international treaty relationships among states, the VCLT 'contains many hidden assumptions that are not justified in respect of human rights treaties'[31] and neither adequately reflect the constitutional functions of human rights treaties nor the 'internationalization of national constitutions' and the 'constitutionalization of international law' (for example, resulting from the recognition of *jus cogens* and from the hierarchical legal structures of the law of many international organisations).[32] The VCLT's codification (in its Preamble) of the customary law requirement of settling 'disputes concerning treaties, like other international disputes ... in conformity with the principles of justice and international law', including 'universal respect for, and observance of, human rights and fundamental freedoms for all', recalls the constitutional functions of courts to interpret and apply international law in conformity with principles of justice and *erga omnes* human rights obligations. For example, according to the ECtHR:

the Court's obligation is to have regard to the special character of the Convention as a constitutional instrument of European public order for the protection of individual human beings and its role, as set out in Article 19 of the Convention, is to ensure the observance of the engagements undertaken by the Contracting Parties.[33]

Similarly, the ECJ, the EFTA Court, and investor-state tribunals emphasize their judicial function of protecting rule of international law with due regard to the rights of producers, investors, traders, consumers, and other citizens against arbitrary interferences by governments and other abuses of public and private power. Just as the idea of law has always been related to justice,[34] and human rights law consistently emphasizes 'that human rights should be protected by the rule of law',[35] so is the focus on rule of international law, legal security, legal remedies, and judicial protection of individual rights a defining element of modern international economic law.

The functional interrelationships between law, judges, and justice are reflected in legal language from antiquity (for example, in the common core of the Latin terms *jus*, *judex*, and *justitia*) up to modern times (compare the Anglo-American legal traditions of speaking of courts of justice, and giving judges the title of Mr Justice, Lord Justice, or Chief Justice). The three dimensions of

---

[31] Cf M Scheinin, 'Impact on the Law of Treaties' in MT Kamminga and M Scheinin (eds), *The Impact of Human Rights on General International Law* (2008) 23 ff.

[32] Cf EU Petersmann, 'Human Rights, Markets and Economic Welfare: Constitutional Functions of the Emerging UN Human Rights Constitution' in F Abbott, C Breining, and T Cottier (eds), *International Trade and Human Rights* (2006) 29–67.

[33] ECtHR, Grand Chamber, *Bankovic and ors against Belgium and ors*, inadmissibility decision of 12 December 2001 (123 ILR 94).

[34] On the ancient Greek concept of 'law as participation in the idea of justice', and the need to relate justice not only to the value of equality, see CJ Friedrich, *The Philosophy of Law in Historical Perspective* (1963) chs II and XX.

[35] Universal Declaration of Human Rights, 1948, Preamble.

'constitutional justice' (discussed above) explain why the constitutional functions of courts of justice must likewise depend on their respective judicial conceptions of:

- the constitutive instruments, inherent powers, and statutory functions of
  courts within national and international legal systems;

- the 'constitutional principles' agreed upon in the respective international
  agreements and diverse national constitutions of the contracting parties; and

- the judicial conceptions of the meta-constitutional 'principles of justice'
  underlying human rights, democratic constitutionalism, and modern
  international law (notably UN human rights law).

The need for legal and judicial clarification of the legitimate functions and principles in the 'administration of justice' by international economic courts must also
take into account the prevailing dispute settlement practices and their judicial
contribution to 'transformative justice' (such as the 'judicial constitutionalization'
of European economic law by the EC Court of Justice, the EFTA Court, the
ECtHR, and national courts cooperating with these European courts in their
judicial protection of individual rights). Parts II and III of this book confirm the
far-reaching contribution of courts to the transformation of national and international economic law and human rights law: just as national and European
constitutional, civil, economic, and human rights courts increasingly cooperate in
their protection of rule of European law across the 47 Member States of the
Council of Europe on the basis of an 'overlapping consensus' on common principles of European 'constitutional justice', so have the more than 380 WTO
dispute settlement proceedings and the ever-increasing number of already more
than 300 investor-state arbitral awards contributed to legal security and rule of
international law for the benefit of a welfare-enhancing international division of
labour. Both European courts and WTO dispute settlement bodies increasingly
complement their textual, contextual, and teleological methods of interpreting
international treaties by 'constitutional review' of whether principles of fairness
and 'justice' (such as limited delegation of powers, rule of law, good faith, non-
discrimination, transparency, necessity and 'proportionality' of governmental
restrictions of freedom, and legal security) are being respected. Yet, the case studies
in Part IV of this book also illustrate that 'judicial comity' and conditional *'solange*
cooperation' among courts (namely, 'as long as' the essential constitutional principles of national and international jurisdictions are mutually respected) are far
less developed in international investment law and investor-state arbitration based
on BITs and multilateral investment treaties (such as NAFTA Chapter 11 and the
ICSID Convention) that do not include explicit commitments to respect for
constitutional human rights guarantees. The case studies in Part IV contribute to
the clarification of the potential relevance of 'principles of justice' in transnational
investment disputes by challenging certain judicial practices and identifying
important research questions that need further analysis.

C. Is 'Constitutional Justice' Also an Appropriate Paradigm for Commercial Arbitration in Investor-State Disputes?

The procedural similarities between international commercial arbitration regarding 'contract claims' and investor-state arbitration regarding 'treaty claims' hide important legal differences:

- commercial arbitration is based on private consent to arbitrate (for example, in a contractual 'clause compromissoire') rather than on public law 'arbitration without privity';

- investment treaties insist more often on an amicable negotiation period as a procedural requirement prior to recourse to arbitration;

- commercial arbitration focuses on alleged breaches of an international commercial contract or a related non-contractual dispute rather than on governmental breaches of international law obligations vis-à-vis foreign investors;

- while a commercial arbitral tribunal shall usually 'apply the rules of law which it determines to be appropriate' (International Chamber of Commerce (ICC), Article 17), public law investment arbitration tends to provide that the 'Tribunal shall decide a dispute in accordance with such rules of law as may be agreed by the parties. In the absence of such agreement, the Tribunal shall apply the law of the Contracting State party to the dispute and such rules of international law as may be applicable' (ICSID, Article 42);

- investment treaties often include 'umbrella clauses' which elevate breaches of investor-state contracts to breaches also of BITs;

- compared with concession contracts concluded by a state *jure gestionis* (yet without prejudice to state immunity from execution), investment treaties are *acta jure imperii* with more evident public law and public interest dimensions;

- in contrast to the increasing publicity of investment arbitration (for example, in terms of admissibility of *amicus curiae* briefs and, according to some recent agreements, public access to pleading and public hearings), confidentiality and privacy of hearings continue to be respected in commercial arbitration;

- while commercial arbitration awards remain confidential absent express consent or challenges in national courts, public investment arbitration procedures and awards (for example, pursuant to ICSID procedures) are increasingly published and contribute to the creation of 'legal precedents' (for example, in the judicial interpretation of the standards of protection in BITs);

- while the *lex arbitri* may be important in commercial arbitration (for example, for obtaining evidence, support, or annulment by national courts), investment arbitration (for example, pursuant to ICSID procedures) provides for a self-contained regime without reference to local courts;

- the international legal obligation to enforce commercial awards (for example, pursuant to Article III of the New York Convention) is subject to limited judicial review by domestic courts (compare New York Convention, Article V); awards rendered pursuant to ICSID procedures must be executed without further analysis by the domestic judiciary (compare ICSID, Article 53f) and are only subject to ICSID annulment proceedings.[36]

The commercial law principles of party autonomy, contractual freedom, agreed mediation, and confidential arbitration reflect principles of 'contractual justice' (for example, *pacta sunt servanda* and *volenti non fit injuria*) that focus on the intent of private contracting parties rather than on the will of the home and host states of investors. Private arbitrators have self-interests in interpreting their mandate as being limited to dispute settlement among the parties, as well as in avoiding human rights arguments that were not raised by the parties (*non ultra petita*). Yet, also privately agreed arbitration entails duties to act 'judicially' (for example, by protecting a fair trial and due process of law, respect for 'public order', and *jus cogens*) – although, in some jurisdictions, there is no opportunity for concurrent court control, and the aggrieved party must wait for the end of the proceedings before he or she may challenge the award.[37] The state consent to investor-state disputes tends to be part of public law instruments (for example, BITs and national investment laws) which recognize that investor-state disputes – even if they involve 'contract claims' rather than 'treaty claims'[38] – often affect public interests (for example, of workers and consumers, and general citizen interests affected by foreign investments). The public law dimensions of investor-state disputes are also reflected in many other features of investor-state arbitration – for example, their function to replace litigation in domestic courts and diplomatic protection, to offer remedies also against violations of international law (as explicitly stated in NAFTA, Article 1131, the Energy Charter Treaty, Article 26, and in many BITs), the increasing admission of *amici curiae* submissions to arbitral tribunals, or the subsequent albeit limited judicial review of arbitral awards in the process of their recognition and enforcement in foreign countries.

The famous *Lüth case* judgment by the German Constitutional Court (concerning a private boycott against a film produced by a former Nazi film director) of 1958 – in which the Court inferred from Article 1(3) of the German Basic Law that fundamental constitutional rights (such as the general personality right and freedom of expression protected by Articles 2 and 5 of the Basic Law), apart from

[36] On these differences between commercial arbitration and public law arbitration, see N Blackaby, 'Investment Arbitration and Commercial Arbitration' in LA Mistelis and DM Lew (eds), *Pervasive Problems in International Arbitration* (2006) 217–234.

[37] Cf A Redfern and M Hunter, *Law and Practice of International Commercial Arbitration* (3rd edn, 1999) 5–20 ff.

[38] On this important distinction, see BM Cremades and DJ Cairns, 'Contract and Treaty Claims and Choice of Forum in Foreign Investment Disputes' in N Horn (ed), *Arbitrating Foreign Investment Disputes. Procedural and Substantive Legal Aspects* (2004) 325 ff.

granting individual rights, also prescribe objective constitutional values that apply to the whole legal order and must be taken into account in judicial interpretation of general private law clauses[39] – illustrates the potential relevance of constitutional law for the interpretation and judicial protection of private law. As discussed in Chapters 8 to 10 of this book, the EC Court of Justice likewise reviews respect for fundamental economic freedoms and labour rights also in relations among private actors, just as the ECtHR emphasizes the 'objective constitutional order' established by the ECHR. The mere fact that commercial investor-state arbitration is based on mutual agreement does not change the fact that concession contracts remain subject to constitutional law, regulatory state powers, and human rights.[40] The case law of the European courts, and the explicit recognition (for example, in the Preamble to the EU Charter of Fundamental Rights) that European fundamental rights 'entail responsibilities and duties with regard to other persons, to the human community and to future generations', illustrate that 'principles of justice' and other constitutional restraints in international law may also affect and constitutionally limit private and commercial law practices, including investor-state arbitration based on BITs concluded by EU Member States that must be decided with due regard for EC law and its guarantees of fundamental rights.[41]

D. Protection of Individual Rights by International Investment Law and Adjudication

The equal procedural status of private and state parties in investor-state arbitration, and the development of the customary international law prohibition of 'denial of justice'[42] into human rights of access to justice[43] and to judicial protection of human rights, reflect the increasing recognition of citizens as legal subjects and 'democratic owners' of international law. Can the human rights

---

[39] BVerfGE 7, 198 (15 January 1958); cf H Rösler, 'Harmonizing the German Civil Code of the 19th Century with a Modern Constitution – The Lüth Revolution 50 Years Ago in Comparative Perspective' [2008] Tulane European and Civil Law Forum 23, 1 ff.

[40] Cf A Jacsic, *Arbitration and Human Rights* (2002), who emphasizes that 'States Parties to the human rights treaties undertake to create an objective legal order' (85); 'the violation of the European public order gives rise to a duty to deny the recognition of any legal act which is performed in contravention of such an order' (87); 'human rights norms are applicable to voluntary arbitration procedure and to any proceedings which are capable of affecting the rights and freedoms guaranteed by the human rights instruments' (215); and the 'parties cannot and are not supposed to waive the irreducible core of procedural guarantees, such as the right to an independent and impartial court, the right to a fair trial and the due process of law which are *sine qua non* for liberty, dignity, justice and ... the rule of law principle' (218). See also G Van Harten, *Investment Treaty Arbitration and Public Law* (2007) ch 6.

[41] Cf C Söderlund, 'Intra-EU BIT Investment Protection and the EC Treaty' (2007) 24 Journal of International Arbitration 455–468.

[42] On the customary law requirement of providing decent justice to foreigners and 'to create and maintain a system of justice which ensures that unfairness to foreigners either does not happen, or is corrected', see ch 3 and J Paulsson, *Denial of Justice in International Law* (2006) 7, 36.

[43] Cf ch 3 below and F Francioni (ed), *Access to Justice as a Human Right* (2007).

obligations of governments justify judicial clarification of the often indeterminate BIT standards of protection in conformity with intergovernmental obligations to protect individual rights (for example, investor rights protected in bilateral investment treaties, human rights protected in UN conventions, intellectual property rights protected in WIPO conventions, labour and social rights protected in ILO conventions, individual freedoms of trade protected in WTO rules and regional trade agreements) and *individual* judicial remedies, subject to legitimate 'public interest' regulation? To what extent does the exponential growth of investor-state arbitration and related human rights jurisprudence offer evidence for the emergence of new customary international law?

International investments have become of existential importance for job opportunities and human welfare of many people in many countries. Yet, their private, local, national, regional, and worldwide regulation remains incomplete, notably regarding potential conflicts among investor interests (for example, in low taxes, low competition, low labour, and banking and environmental standards enabling higher profits), worker interests (for example, in high labour and social standards), general citizen interests (for example, in maximizing consumer welfare rather than investor welfare), and bureaucratic self-interests (for example, in discretionary powers, protection rents generated by collaboration with foreign investors, and additional income flowing from nationalizations of foreign investments). Democratic governance requires not only transparent discussion and fair balancing of these diverse interests of investors, workers, consumers, citizens, and national, transnational, and intergovernmental actors. Constitutional democracy also calls for legal and judicial protection of the constitutional rights of investors (for example, property rights, freedom of profession and establishment, access to justice, and freedom of contract), workers (for example, core labour rights and human rights), citizens (for example, rights to democratic governance, freedom of opinion, protection of general consumer welfare, and human rights), and of local, national, regional, and worldwide governance institutions. The multilevel regulation of international trade, investments, and dispute settlement illustrates the need for multilevel constitutional safeguards of individual rights against abuses of public and private power at national, transnational, and international levels.[44]

As recalled in Chapters 8 to 11, the ECJ, the ECtHR, and the EFTA Court successfully transformed the intergovernmental EC treaties and the ECHR into constitutional orders founded on respect for human rights.[45] Their 'judicial

[44] Cf EU Petersmann, 'Multilevel Trade Governance Requires Multilevel Constitutionalism' in C Joerges and EU Petersmann (eds), *Constitutionalism, Multilevel Trade Governance and Social Regulation* (2006) ch 1.
[45] On the judicial 'balancing' of economic and non-economic fundamental rights, and the diverse 'constitutional interpretations' of economic rules, by the ECJ, the EFTA Court, and the ECtHR, see chs 8–11. On Professor Howse's misleading rejection of this European 'judicial balancing' with due regard to comprehensive guarantees of human rights as '*Lochner* jurisprudence' (as practised by the US Supreme Court during the 1930s), see Petersmann, n 27 above.

constitutionalization' of intergovernmental treaty regimes was accepted by citizens, national courts, parliaments, and governments because the judicial 'European public reason' protected individual rights and European 'public goods' (like the EC's common market) more effectively than state-centered interpretations focusing on discretionary government powers. The *'solange* method' of cooperation among European courts 'as long as' (which means 'solange' in German language) constitutional rights are adequately protected, reflects an 'overlapping constitutional consensus' on the need for 'constitutional justice' in European law. Yet, such 'constitutional interpretations' of intergovernmental agreements for the benefit of rights of citizens remain deeply controversial outside Europe,[46] just as the conception of investment treaty arbitration as commercial arbitration, or the 'internationalization' of investor-state contracts by means of international arbitration and 'umbrella clauses' (transforming contract claims into treaty claims), remain legally and politically contested.

Whereas some investor-state tribunals see the primary objective of BITs in international legal and judicial protection of investor rights in order to compensate for the weaker legal status of aliens in host states,[47] others reject one-sided interpretations in favour of foreign investors by emphasizing that the treaty objectives of promoting economic development 'utilize investor protection as a means to an end'[48]; the increasing number of explicit BIT exceptions reserving state rights to protect non-economic public interests confirm the need for 'a balanced interpretation ... taking into account both State sovereignty and the State's responsibility to create an adapted and evolutionary framework for the development of economic activities, as well as the necessity to protect foreign investment and its continuing flow'.[49] The successful cooperation among national and international courts in European integration suggests that judicial recourse to 'general principles of law' (such as respect for human rights, limited delegation of powers, non-discrimination, necessity, and proportionality of government restrictions of individual rights) offers legal criteria for judicial 'balancing' of public and private interests, and for coordinating competing jurisdictions and judicial review standards in international investment disputes,

---

[46] Cf the criticism by G Van Harten, n 40 above, 136 ff, of likening the 'investor rights approach' to legal and judicial remedies under human rights law.

[47] See, eg *Siemens AG v Argentina*, ICSID Case No ARB/02/08, Decision on Jurisdiction, 3 August 2004, at para 81: 'The Tribunal shall be guided by the purpose of the Treaty as expressed in its title and preamble. It is a treaty "to protect" and "to promote" investments ... The intention of the parties is clear. It is to create favorable conditions for investments and to stimulate private initiative'; *SGS Société Générale de Surveillance S.A. v the Philippines*, ICSID Case No ARB/02/6 of 29 January 2004, at para 116: 'It is legitimate to resolve uncertainties in its interpretation so as to favour the protection of covered investments.'

[48] Van Harten, n 40 above, 140 ('the preambular language of investment treaties does not provide a basis for adopting a presumption in favour of safeguarding the claimant against the state').

[49] Cf *El Paso Energy International Co v Argentina*, ICSID Case No ARB/03/15, Decision on Jurisdiction, 27 April 2006, at paras 66–70.

which must complement judicial recourse to private law and 'conflict of law' principles (such as judicial comity, *res judicata*, and *litis pendens*). The successive agreements among NAFTA Member States to limit the NAFTA jurisprudence regarding the NAFTA minimum standard of treatment and expropriation standard[50] illustrate that, in constitutional democracies as well as in European integration law, state liability for public interest regulation of the economy must remain limited; the legal clarification of the general investment protection standards by the judiciary remains subject to democratic legislation.

E. Further Strengthening of Cooperation among National and International Courts and Investor-State Tribunals in Their Judicial Protection of Rule of Law and Individual Rights?

International courts established by multilateral treaty systems (like the ICJ, the International Tribunal for the Law of the Sea, the ECJ, the EFTA Court, and the ECtHR) often emphasize that – in addition to their dispute settlement functions to administer justice between the parties to the dispute and to render legally binding judgments with due regard to all relevant facts, legal claims, and applicable rules – their jurisprudence also serves 'public functions' beyond the concrete dispute: for example, in terms of clarifying and progressively developing incomplete or indeterminate treaty rules, 'providing security and predictability' of their respective treaty systems (compare Dispute Settlement Understanding, Article 3), and taking into account also systemic third-party interests beyond those of the parties to the dispute.[51] Even if private commercial arbitration, state courts, investor-state arbitration, and inter-state adjudication operate in different legal and institutional contexts, they are all established by legal instruments, with limited judicial mandates to settle disputes through impartial and independent, legally binding decisions whose legitimacy derives from respect for 'rule of law', predetermined rules of procedure, and 'principles of justice'. The 'public functions' of these alternative jurisdictions for the settlement of transnational investment disputes (such as proper administration of international justice, clarification of investment law's legal limitations of private autonomy, and protection of legitimate public interests), the inherent powers of courts for realizing their judicial functions, and the appropriate methods of judicial reasoning (for example, 'proportionality balancing' of governmental restrictions of property rights in order to promote other fundamental rights of

---

[50] Cf n 14 above and Van Harten, n 40 above, 145–146.

[51] Cf Brown, n 11 above, 72 ff. On the diverse 'judicial functions', see S Wittich, 'The Judicial Functions of the International Court of Justice' in I Buffard, J Crawford, A Pellet, and S Wittich (eds), *International Law between Universalism and Fragmentation* (2008) 981–999. On perceiving adjudication not only as a means of settling disputes, but also as a form of social ordering, see already LL Fuller, 'The Forms and Limits of Adjudication' [1978] Harvard Law Review 92, 353–409.

citizens) need to be further clarified through 'judicial dialogues', 'deliberative democracy', and academic research.

Depending on their respective 'constitutional context', applicable laws, and procedures, different jurisdictions may settle investment disputes in diverse ways. The limited legal grounds (for example, under the 1958 New York Convention on Recognition and Enforcement of Foreign Arbitral Awards) for refusal of recognition and enforcement of arbitral awards in state courts, or for annulment of ICSID awards in ICSID annulment proceedings, reflect the need for 'international comity' in the judicial protection of rule of law in the world-wide division of labour among some 200 sovereign states with diverse legal systems. If international treaties establish a legal and 'dispute settlement *system*' (compare DSU, Article 3 and EC Treaty, Articles 220 ff) with legal and pro-cedural hierarchies at national and international levels, multilevel judicial cooperation may justify judicial interpretations of the judicial system as entailing 'systemic obligations' (for example, of 'consistent interpretation' in conformity with legal 'precedents'), providing for higher degrees of legal 'security and pre-dictability to the multilateral trading system' (DSU, Article 3). Yet, in the absence of explicit provisions for cooperation among different jurisdictions (for example, by means of international preliminary rulings at the request of state courts), the legal obligations of courts to avoid or solve jurisdictional conflicts leave broad judicial discretion (for example, in terms of 'judicial comity', judicial self-restraint, and 'consistent interpretation' aimed at preventing conflicting judgments), as illustrated by the EC Court's refusal to review whether EC acts are in conformity with the EC's international legal obligations under WTO law, the Law of the Sea Convention, or with legally binding dispute settlement rul-ings of WTO dispute settlement bodies.[52] Mutual respect and conditional 'solange'-cooperation among courts with overlapping or conflicting jurisdic-tions, and judicial regard to legally binding precedents by other courts are more consistent with the common task of courts to protect rule of law and administer justice than judicial disregard for the systemic functions of international law and of multilevel judicial protection of constitutionally limited self-government of citizens across frontiers. As long as governments refrain from regulating coop-eration among international courts more precisely, it remains an important task of judges to develop criteria for more coherent cooperation among competing or overlapping jurisdictions (for example, based on the Anglo-American doctrine of *forum non conveniens*) so as to protect rule of law and legal coherence among courts more effectively, especially inside multilevel legal and judicial systems like international trade and investment law.

[52] Cf H Sauer, *Jurisdiktionskonflikte in Mehrebenensystemen* (2008), according to whom a 'legal obligation of the ECJ to invalidate Community law provisions which have been declared inter-nationally unlawful by a WTO dispute settlement decision directly follows from Article 300 para.7 of the EC Treaty if the time-limit for implementation has exceeded' (at 538).

VI. Complementary Functions of 'Constitutional' and 'Global Administrative Law' Approaches to Investment Law

The need for adapting national and international legal systems to the increasing 'globalization' of international relations and to their inadequate intergovernmental regulation continues to prompt citizens, governments, and courts to insist on respect for constitutional and administrative law principles limiting intergovernmental regulation so as to protect democratic legitimacy, rule of law, and judicial protection of fundamental rights also in transnational relations beyond states. 'Multilevel constitutionalism', 'global administrative law' (GAL), and 'legal pluralism' offer complementary approaches for constituting and constraining multilevel governance for the ever-more important supply of international public goods:

- 'Multilevel constitutionalism' suggests that – just as virtually all UN Member States have found it necessary to adopt national constitutions for the collective supply of *national public goods* – multilevel governance for the supply of *international public goods* likewise requires constitutional methods for overcoming the 'collective action problems', for example, by means of international treaties constituting institutions with limited rule-making, administrative, and judicial powers that provide for citizen participation and remain democratically accountable and subject to judicial review.[53]

- 'GAL' focuses more narrowly on the legal limitation of intergovernmental regulation and administration by use of administrative law principles (such as transparency, participation, reasoned decisions, and judicial review) that inevitably differ depending on the context of international organizations (e.g. UN, ILO, WTO, and EC administrative regulations) and on the diverse administrative law traditions at national levels.[54]

- Legal and constitutional pluralism emphasizes the legitimate diversity of constitutional and administrative law principles at national and international levels and the need for 'pluralist ordering devices' (such as respect for fundamental rights protecting individual and democratic diversity, subsidiarity, 'proportionality balancing', and respect for 'margins of

[53] Cf Petersmann, n 44 above, inferring from the various 'market failures' and 'governance failures' in the intergovernmental supply of international public goods that the 'collective action problems' (like the 'jurisdiction gap', 'participation gap', 'incentive gap', and 'constitutional gap') cannot be overcome without recourse to 'constitutional methods' (such as limited delegation of powers, and multilevel legal and judicial protection of rule of law).
[54] Cf N Krisch and B Kingsburgy (eds), 'Symposium: Global Governance and Global Administrative Law in the International Legal Order' [2006] European Journal of International Law 17, 1–278; and S Cassese et al (eds), *Global Administrative Law* (2nd edn, 2008).

appreciation') promoting mutual respect and normative congruence among specialized and often 'fragmented' legal regimes.[55]

As all three approaches focus on diverse regulatory problems, their constitutional, administrative and coordination strategies tend to be complementary. Hence, proposals for conceptualizing 'investment treaty arbitration as a species of global administrative law'[56] do not obviate the need for acknowledging the legitimate diversity of constitutional principles underlying national and international administrative law and adjudication; for example, as discussed in Chapter 8, international tribunals may find that international rules prescribing a US administrative law doctrine (such as the US 'Chevron doctrine' of judicial deference incorporated into Article 17.6(i) of the WTO Agreement on Antidumping Law) may be inapplicable in the different constitutional context of a worldwide legal system without parliamentary oversight. The multilevel constitutional and administrative law principles reflect different dimensions of multilevel governance problems that must be legally conceptualized and judicially construed in mutually coherent ways. Just as GATT/WTO law protects national sovereignty to use transparent, non-discriminatory, and efficient policy instruments for whatever national policy objectives a WTO member decides to pursue, so have investor-state tribunals rightly emphasized that the 'general body of precedent usually does not treat regulatory action as amounting to expropriation'[57]:

> As a matter of general international law, a non-discriminatory regulation for a public purpose, which is enacted in accordance with due process and which affects, *inter alios*, a foreign investor or investment is not deemed expropriatory and compensable unless specific commitments had been given by the regulating government to the then putative foreign investor contemplating investment that the government would refrain from such regulation.[58]

Investor-state arbitral tribunals must clarify – by means of independent judicial review of whether regulatory measures 'are reasonable with respect to their goals, the deprivation of economic rights and the legitimate expectations of who suffered such deprivation'[59] – the international legal limits of legitimate government regulation; the 'determination of a breach of the obligation of "fair and equitable treatment" by the host State must be made in the light of the high measure of deference that international law generally extends to the right of domestic authorities to regulate matters within their own border.'[60]

---

[55] Cf Petersmann, n 27 above; and M Rosenfeld, 'Rethinking Constitutional Ordering in an Era of Legal and Ideological Pluralism' [2008] International Journal of Constitutional Law 6, 415–455.

[56] Cf G Van Harten and M Loughlin, 'Investment Treaty Arbitration as a Species of Global Administrative Law' [2006] European Journal of International Law 17, 121–150.

[57] *Myers Inc v Canada*, 13 November 2000, (2000) 40 ILM 1408 ff, para 281.

[58] *Methanex v USA*, 3 August 2005, (2005) 44 ILM 1343, 1456, para 7.

[59] *Tecmed SA v Mexico*, 29 May 2003, (2004) 43 ILM 133 ff, para 122.

[60] *Saluka Investments BV v Czech Republic*, 17 March 2006, ICSID, paras 204 ff.

The case studies in Part IV of this book confirm that the legal 'protection standards' of international investment law (such as non-discrimination, 'fair and equitable treatment', and protection of private property), the compulsory jurisdiction of international tribunals for the judicial protection of investor rights and rule of law, and the worldwide enforceability of such arbitral awards in domestic legal systems reveal 'a remarkable trend towards constitutionalization' also in international investment law.[61] Multilevel judicial review on the basis of international constitutional and administrative law principles may correct deficiencies in national decision-making procedures without preventing legitimate regulation necessary for protection of public interests. Rather than undermining constitutional democracy, IEL and multilevel judicial protection of rule of law are preconditions for individual and democratic self-governance in the globally interdependent, worldwide division of labour among states and citizens with diverse self-interests and preferences. As illustrated by the EC Treaty's guarantee (in Article 18 EC) of a general freedom of all EU citizens to reside and move freely in the territory of all 27 EC Member States, IEL may be instrumental for promoting human welfare and 'rule of law' far beyond economic cooperation among citizens. For example, the independent WTO memberships of China, Hong Kong, Macau, and Taiwan, like China's acceptance of investor-state arbitration, have promoted legal and judicial reforms inside China that have enhanced rule of law also among these separate Chinese customs territories. The multilevel legal and judicial protection of international investments contributes to 'domesticating' international power politics by transnational rule of law systems. The more IEL and its judicial protection respect and protect human rights, the better are the chances for transforming international rule of law among states into a cosmopolitan legal system protecting also rule of law among free citizens across frontiers.

---

[61] Cf P Behrens, 'Towards the Constitutionalization of International Investment Protection' [2007] *Archiv des Völkerrechts* 45, 153–179.

PART II

IS THERE A ROLE FOR HUMAN RIGHTS IN INVESTOR-STATE ARBITRATION AND INTERNATIONAL ECONOMIC ADJUDICATION?

2

Unification Rather than Fragmentation of International Law? The Case of International Investment Law and Human Rights Law

Pierre-Marie Dupuy

I. Introduction

International investments law and human rights law are still perceived – albeit most likely not for long – by a number of scholars or practitioners as two separate branches of international law, with no substantial overlap. Human rights are *per essence* focused on individual human beings. While investors can be individuals, international investments law deals mostly with investors envisaged as legal persons, not individuals, the investor being in most cases a private corporation. This explains in part why human rights are still rarely invoked in international arbitrations dealing with international investments, be it by the investor or by the state hosting the investment.

Nevertheless, concerning investors, the legal concept and the economic reality of *property* is at the core of any international investment, and this concept was recognized as a fundamental right as far back as the 1789 French Declaration of human rights. Governments, for their part, often turn to foreign corporations to achieve the privatization of formerly public services.[1] Foreign investors, as a consequence, are led to supply public services, such as drinkable water or electricity, or attend to the management of hazardous waste or that of public transport. Even if the state retains some legal responsibility as to the organization and management of these privatized services of general interest, the foreign investor may in turn be confronted by claims raised by private consumers, sometimes involving human rights issues. In general terms, due in large part to the activism of components of the civil society, be it at the national or international level, the idea of a necessity of developing several types of *corporate*

---

[1] See U Kriebaum, 'Privatizing Human Rights, The Interface between Investment Protection and Human Rights' in Reinisch and Kriebaum (eds), *The Law of International Relations, Liber amicorum Hanspeter Neuhold* (2007) 165–189.

liability is gaining increasing currency. The very fact that, from a technical viewpoint, private corporations are not subjects of public international law is generally not perceived, at least by non-governmental organisations (NGOs), as an obstacle for the furthering of such claims in favour of a responsibility incumbent on the private suppliers of public services.

Clearly, as already demonstrated by a number of cases,[2] national judges or international arbitrators may read and interpret the implications of a seizure of property by a host state or the management of a public service by a private investor in human rights terms. In other terms, one can arguably fathom that the current multiplication of situations in which issues both of international investments law and of human rights may be raised is a contemporary trend, albeit still nascent, but which could very well be a central feature in the development of these seemingly two distinct branches of international law.

Now, as regards their *origin*, their *content*, and the *procedural* means of adjudication of their respective implementation, the international law of investments and the law of human rights are usually considered, be it by scholars or by arbitrators, as wholly distinct, autonomous, or even antagonistic legal domains – this perception partaking to and seemingly reinforcing the very fashionable and catch-all concept of 'fragmentation'. The present chapter will assess the relevance of such a claim by briefly and successively exploring these three aspects: *origins*, *content*, and *means of adjudication*.

II. Origins

The law of international investments is currently undergoing swift and significant developments. This is due in large part to the proliferation of a patchwork of bilateral and multilateral treaties, including of a regional reach. Indeed, at present, there are over 2,300 bilateral investment treaties (BITs) and several multilateral ones, which set forth norms aimed at the protection of foreign investment, including 1,700 already in force in 2005.[3] Parallel to this trend, investment arbitration has demonstrated over more than 15 years to be an effective and increasingly successful means for the settlement of disputes between states and foreign private investors, and has brought with it an array of new normative developments. These recent trends could tend to give the wrong impression that, from a historical viewpoint, international investments law is more recent than human rights law, which can be dated back to the adoption of

---

[2] See in particular the UNCITRAL case of *Biloune v Ghana*, in which the Syrian investor had been arrested and held in custody without charge and finally deported from Ghana to Togo; *Biloune and Marine Drive Complex Ltd v Ghana Investments Centre and the Government of Ghana* (UNCITRAL), Award on Jurisdiction and Liability, 27 October 1989, ILR 184. See also ch 4 below.

[3] UNCTAD, Research Note, Recent Developments in International Investment Agreements, 30 August 2005, UNCTAD/WEB/ITE/IIT/2005.

the UN Charter, together with the 1948 Universal Declaration. However, one may contend that, in terms of historical origins if not precise date of birth, the international protection of foreign investments clearly *preceded* the recognition at the international level of fundamental human rights. This is merely due to the fact that customary international law relating to the protection of citizens abroad or the parallel establishment of international customary obligations incumbent on the territorial state to protect alien property had already crystallized at the turn of the 20th century, if not even a little earlier. This was somewhat ironically illustrated by the fact that, when approaching the codification of the law of state responsibility in the middle of the 1950s, the very first Special Rapporteur to the International Law Commission, Professor Garcia Amador, erroneously started by considering the necessity of codifying the primary norms of state responsibility for damages caused to aliens – a demonstration of the close historical connection between the development of the primary rules governing state obligations towards aliens, including in terms of breach of acquired rights and secondary rules governing state responsibility in general.[4]

Indeed, as early as the second half of the 19th century, with the progression of the industrial revolution, private investments were made by foreign persons, often individuals, originating from already industrialized countries and coming into less or not yet developed ones. It is also in this very context that some of the procedural rules governing access to the exercise of diplomatic protection (like the prior exhaustion of local remedies) were consolidated. Moreover, a number of substantial state obligations concerning aliens were established then, including a series of minimum standards of protection which gained in substance and authority between the end of the 19th and beginning of the 20th century, relating in particular to the concept of *acquired rights.*[5]

In other terms, the history of modern international law shows that the *alien* preceded chronologically the *individual*, understood as the human being, a fact which can be easily explained by the structure of the classical Westphalian international legal framework. The legal status of aliens is still directly linked to the state from which they have received their nationality; by contrast, in the modern human rights legal framework, individuals do not derive their international legal identity from any link with a sovereign state, activated through the legal means of nationality. The inherent rights borne by individuals derive from their inherent nature as a human being. As a consequence, there is, from a conceptual point of view, a significant difference between the sets of rules governing respectively the protection of aliens and human rights.[6] The de-nationalization of individuals deemed to be endowed with specific rights is at the core of the international recognition of human rights, and this characteristic

---

[4] See *Yearbook of the International Law Commission* (1957) vol 1, 154–172.
[5] See in particular R Lillich (ed), *International Law of State Responsibility for Injuries to Aliens* (1983) 412.   [6] See PM Dupuy, *Droit international public* (2008) 217 ff.

can be considered as a major progress, at least if one takes as a criterion its acceptance by states themselves. This development is of such a fundamental nature and entails such legal consequences that it accounts for the persistent resistance, if not the negation, of human rights by so many states, including, at times, some of those which have played a major role in their historical development.

There is another differentiation between the alien and the human considered as the bearer of inherent international rights that is well known, but should be recalled here: while the protection of aliens is still conditioned by the reciprocity of inter-state relations, the protection of individual human rights has an *objective* character, as it does not depend on the reciprocity of rights and obligations between sovereign states. By contrast, the progressive transformation of the private foreign investor as an individual into a private legal corporation endowed with a private legal personality has not fundamentally changed the *problématique*, as the possession of a given *nationality* still governs the identification of the investor as a *foreign* one.[7]

However, an apparent paradox may be underlined: in most cases, and not only in the framework of the Washington Convention of 1965 which created the ICSID, prior exhaustion of local remedies together with the invocation of diplomatic protection is no longer a precondition. In particular, according to Article 26.1 of the ICSID Convention and depending on a number of other conditions, the investor can have *direct* access to international arbitration.[8] At the same time, regional conventions dealing with the protection of human rights still maintain the rule of exhaustion of local remedies as a prerequisite for the injured individual to have access to the competent regional human rights court.

The paradox is nevertheless superficial in nature: in most cases, there is a direct link between respondent states and individuals wishing to have access to a human rights international tribunal as the latter are nationals of the state against which the claim is lodged. As regards private foreign investors, on the other hand, it is precisely to overcome the uncertainties of diplomatic protection that foreign investors have been granted a direct access to international arbitration – particularly in the aftermath of the famous ICSID arbitration in the *AAPL v Sri Lanka* case.[9] This possibility was introduced in an effort to counterweight their uneasy position as foreigners, as within the general international legal framework they would otherwise have to rely on the goodwill of their state of nationality to have their investment protected.

Nevertheless, the nationality test continues to play a key role in the law of investments whereas, as recalled above, it is no longer a decisive feature of human rights law, at least in terms of substance. Most international investment

---

[7] See PM Dupuy, 'Théorie des droits de l'homme et fondements du droit international' in *Archives de philosophie du droit* (1987).

[8] See R Dolzer and C Schreuer, *Principles of International Investment Law* (2008).

[9] *AAPL v Sri Lanka*, ICSID Case No ARB/87/3, Award, 27 June 1990.

treaties, typically bilateral ones, are contracted in favour of the respective nationals of the states parties to the agreement. The investor's nationality remains decisive for the jurisdiction of an arbitral tribunal, and it is also key to the application of substantial protection standards. The consent to arbitration clause included in most BITs limits the jurisdiction of arbitral tribunals to the nationals of the two contracting states, while the ICSID Convention, under Article 25, restricts the access to international arbitration to the persons (be they 'natural' or 'juridical') who do not hold the nationality of the state party against which they wish to complain.

In all cases, the claim according to which the legal status of the alien chronologically preceded that of the individual as a human being is further demonstrated by the significant similarities if not even the correspondence between a number of principles pertaining to the treatment of foreign investors by host states and some human rights rules and principles. While the basis of their respective legal status remains distinct, from a historical viewpoint, it is the alien who was the first recipient of what are now fundamental human rights. Indeed, general principles originally pertaining to the protection of foreigners have later on been transferred and generalized to the protection of human beings in general, be they nationals or not.[10] All in all, this makes a comparison between the content of both sets of rights all the more relevant.

III. Content

The respective content of fundamental human rights as principles partaking beyond doubt in international customary law and some of the principles of international investments law are to be considered from two different viewpoints: one is the viewpoint of the investor; the other is that of the host state.

A. Human Rights and Investors' Rights

As the rights of aliens, including their economic rights linked to property, can to a large extent be perceived as the precursors of human rights, notwithstanding, as already noted, their much narrower basis – that of nationality as opposed to the inherent character of the rights born by individuals – it is no surprise to find not only apparent but also clearly substantial similarities between the two sets of rights, for instance between a number of principles aimed at safeguarding the investor's interests and human rights principles pertaining to international civil

---

[10] See, for instance, LE Peterson and KR Gray, *International Human Rights in Bilateral Investment Treaties and in Investment Treaty Arbitration* (2003), available at <http://www.iisd.org/pdf/2003/investment_int_human_rights_bits.pdf>. See also Report of the High Commissioner for Human Rights, 'Human Rights, Trade and Investment', 2 July 2003, E/CN.4/Sub.2/2003/9.

and economic rights. However, such a comparison must be drawn cautiously, bearing in mind the fact that a number of states are still reluctant to recognize the customary nature of a number of principles relating to the treatment and protection of investments, as was still evident when the Guiding Principles adopted by the World Bank in 1992 were listed.[11]

Be it for the treatment of investments or within the human rights legal framework, the concept of non-discrimination plays a key role, even though in some cases the host state still retains some margin of appreciation as to the choice of foreign investors and their access on its territory. As a consequence, judges or arbitrators often draw a comparison between the rights granted to national and foreign investors placed in an identical situation.

By contrast, in general the definition of the content of another general principle, such as the fair and equitable treatment of foreign investments, is established on a case-by-case basis in view of all relevant circumstances, thus affording the judge and/or the arbitrator with a degree of flexibility in the exercise of their jurisdiction.

Although the principle of fair and equitable treatment is not systematically ascribed the same definition in all international investment treaties, there is still a common ground to all of its different legal perceptions.[12] In this context, even more than that of human rights law, the adjudicating process makes it necessary to refer to international standards; these standards have evolved over time and, contrary to what has been held at some point regarding the NAFTA framework, they are not necessarily to be understood as 'minimum standards'. As rightly pointed out by Judge Asante in his opinion in *AAPL Sri Lanka*:

the requirement as to the fair and equitable treatment, full protection and security and not discrimination treatment all underscore the general obligation of the host State to exercise due diligence in protecting foreign investment in its territories, an obligation that derives from customary international law.[13]

This position has been reiterated several times, for instance in the *Lauder* case.[14] We are here indeed very close to the diligence that, under contemporary international law, a 'well-governed state' must display to ensure the respect of basic human rights on its territory, including, under some conditions, private property rights.

As regards, again, the implications of the fair and equitable treatment principle, the denial of justice caused by the breach of the state's obligation to provide the

---

[11] See in particular I Shihata, *Legal Treatment of Foreign Investment. The World Bank Guidelines* (1993); and P Juillard, 'L'évolution des sources du droit des investissements' RCADI 1994-VI, Vol 250, 13-214.

[12] See I Tudor, *The Fair and Equitable Treatment Standard in the International Law of Foreign Investment* (2008) 315. Foreword by PM Dupuy; see also ch 14 below.

[13] *Asian Agricultural Products Ltd v Sri Lanka*, ICSID Case No ARB/87/3, Award, 27 June 1990, at para 639.

[14] *Ronald Lauder v Czech Republic*, UNCITRAL, Award, 3 September 2001, at para 292.

investor with a non-discriminatory access to justice is also to be considered.[15] As stated by Professor Greenwood concerning the *Loewen* case,[16] a denial of justice may be defined in general terms as consisting in the breach of the obligation 'to maintain and make available to aliens a fair and effective system of justice', understood as belonging to deeply entrenched customary international law.[17] In the same case, the tribunal noted that the positive obligation bearing on the host state under international law is 'to provide a fair trial of a case to which a foreigner is a party'.[18] Interestingly enough, this 'positive obligation' does indeed correspond, within the human rights legal framework, to that of the states parties to the International Covenant on Civil and Political Rights under Article 14. Furthermore, foreigners are not to be considered only as such. They may and must at the same time be considered as human beings endowed with the same right to a fair trial.

Unlike other tribunals, which retain a much stricter perception of their own jurisdiction, the ICSID tribunal in *Mondev v United States* made express reference to general international law as a basis to define the scope of a 'denial of justice'. The tribunal referred in particular not only to the case law of the International Court of Justice in the *ELSI* case, but also to human rights standards as defined by the European Court of Human Rights, particularly concerning Article 6(1) of the European Convention on Human Rights.[19]

In the same vein, reference to the general principle of good faith plays a central role, be it in the human rights legal framework or that of international investments law, as illustrated among others in the *Metalclad* case.[20]

More generally, good faith as a general principle is of interest to both human rights and the international treatment of the investor. In the *Tecmed* case,[21] in particular, reference was made to the legitimate expectations of the investor, as defined according to a certain number of criteria of reasonableness. It was rightly pointed out by the tribunal in *Mondev* that 'a State may treat foreign investment unfairly and inequitably without necessarily acting in bad faith',[22] but this does

---

[15] See ch 3 below.
[16] *Loewen Group Inc and Raymond Loewen v United States of America*, ICSID Case No ARB (AF) 98/3, Final Award, 26 June 2003, at para 129, Professor Ch Greenwood, second opinion, at para 79.   [17] See among others J Paulson, *Denial of Justice in International Law* (2005).
[18] *Loewen*, n 16 above, at para 132.
[19] For further comments on this case, see ch 3 below.
[20] In *Metalclad*, the tribunal was led to analyse the way in which the denial of the construction permit to the investor demonstrated bad faith from part of the concerned local public authority. See *Metalclad Corp v United States of Mexico*, ICSID Case No ARB (AF)/97/1, Final Award, 30 August 2000, at para 91. For further comments on the denial of justice in relation to the breach of the principle of fair and equitable treatment, see ch 14 below.
[21] See in particular F Dupuy, 'La protection de l'attente légitime des parties au contrat, étude de droit international des investissements à la lumière du droit comparé', Thèse co-tutelle Humboldt Universität./Université Paris 2, November 2007.
[22] *Mondev International Ltd v United States of America*, ICSID Case No ARB(AF)/99/2, Final Award, 11 October 2002, at para 116.

not lessen the importance of the principle, be it as regards the application of a fair and equitable treatment to investors or that of human rights.

Furthermore, the same could be said when the arbitrary and discriminatory character of an action or omission of the host state is at issue. Arbitrariness has thus been defined in particular in *Tecmed* as an action which 'shocks or at least surprises a sense of juridical propriety'.[23]

At this point, but this would go far beyond the scope of this chapter, it would be necessary to explore the underlying and deep entrenched relationship between the principle of fair and equitable treatment and a series of basic human rights, including the right to propriety, the right to a fair trial, and many others. This can be established through the common reference to 'equity' understood as the search for the elementary respect of justice, inherent to the application of the rule of law (*equity infra legem*), as set out in the categorization drawn by the International Court of Justice in the *North Sea Continental Shelf* case in 1969.[24]

The protection of foreign investment against expropriation by the host state, be it direct or 'creeping' or indirect, is also an important field of confrontation between human rights and investments law. Treaties related to the protection of investments provide for the protection against direct and indirect expropriation without fair compensation. Although a number of authors, in particular Philippe Juillard, draw a clear distinction between standards of treatment and standards of protection of international investments,[25] the legality of the conditions in which an expropriation has been carried out in a given case is generally examined by arbitral tribunals in clear connection with the applicable principles of treatment as listed and defined in the applicable BIT when such a dispute arises, as is increasingly the case, in the context of a 'treaty claim'.

A difficulty is raised by the fuzzy borderline between regulatory takings and police power.[26] As is well known, one of the most classical standards covered by BITs consists in the prohibition of uncompensated expropriations. Nevertheless, if the expropriation is justified by a public purpose, non-discriminatory, carried out under due process of law, and compensated by a prompt, adequate, and effective compensation, it will remain lawful. To a large extent, the human rights legal framework can in turn be helpful in reducing the uncertainty of the law in the definition of what constitutes effectively a public purpose. Non-discrimination is also a criterion common to human rights and to the international law of investments; and the same could be said as regards the definition of what constitutes an *equitable* compensation. In this context, interesting comparisons can be drawn between the case law of the European Court of Justice concerning

---

[23] *Técnicas Medioambientales, Tecmed SA v Mexico*, ICSID Case No ARB/00/2, Final Award, 29 May 2003, at para 154.
[24] *North Sea Continental Shelf* case, *Germany v Denmark and the Netherlands*, Judgment, 20 February 1969, ICJ Reports (1969), at para 88.   [25] See Juillard, n 11 above.
[26] See SR Ratner, 'Regulatory Takings in Institutional Context: Beyond the Fear of Fragmented International Law' (2008) 102 AJIL 3 475–528.

the balancing of economic law and human rights,[27] and that of regional human rights courts.[28] In general terms, in international investments law, measures that affect an investment without amounting to a true taking of property, but only lower its value, are not considered as expropriatory. On the contrary, if the economic use of the investment has been rendered impossible due to an initiative undertaken by the state, expropriation will be considered to have taken place. Here, in particular, the property protection clause included in the European Convention of Human Rights covers a larger spectrum of situations, the term 'other interference' in the case law of the ECHR being given an extensive understanding on the basis of Article 1, First Protocol additional to the European Convention.[29]

B. Human Rights Invoked by the Host State against the Investor

States are under an obligation to respect the human rights of all individuals living on their territory. At times, there may be situations in which these obligations, in particular when interpreted as *positive* ones,[30] may be in contradiction with other obligations, which the same state, acting as a host of foreign investments, has been led to accept.[31] In any event, when entering into privatization agreements, the host state has a duty to ascertain that there is no such contradiction, even potentially. Referring to the European Convention of Human Rights, the European Commission of Human Rights already recalled in 1958 a general rule of inter-temporal international law according to which 'it is clear that, if a State contracts treaty obligations and subsequently concludes another international agreement which disables it from performing its obligations under the first treaty, it will be answerable for any resulting breach of its obligations under the earlier treaty'.[32] As a consequence, when concluding a BIT, the state involved must take into consideration its human rights obligations. This is true, as stated explicitly by the European Commission, in the case of ratified international human rights conventions. However, the same inter-temporal rule is also applicable as regards international human rights customary rules.

More generally, a number of difficulties may arise out of a number of economic, social, and cultural rights which – especially when they have not yet been

---

[27] See ch 9 below.

[28] See chs 10 and 11 below, both on the European Court of Human Rights, and ch 12.

[29] See G Cohen-Jonathan, 'L'article 1 du Protocole n° 1 et le droit international des contrats et de l'arbitrage' in IDHAE, *La protection du droit de propriété par la Cour européenne des droits de l'homme* (2005) 53–60.

[30] ie obligations to take positive and concrete steps aimed at achieving progressively the full realization of the rights of the people living on their spatial area of jurisdiction.

[31] For an illustration, see the *Aguas del Tunari, SA v Bolivia* case, ICSID Case No ARB/02/3, which was eventually settled by negotiation among the parties. It dealt with a water supply contract of which the city of Cochabamba was dependent. See Kriebaum, n 1 above, 169.

[32] ECommHR, Decision no 235/56 of 10 June 1958, Yearbook 2, 256, at 300.

commented upon by the UN CESCR as regards the Covenant on Economic, Social, and Cultural Rights – may be the object of different interpretations, as their exact meaning and bearing are not necessarily always stripped of all ambiguity.[33] This relative indeterminacy may in some cases be considerably reduced by referring to specific standards, particularly those established by international organisations. One may refer in this respect to the human right to water, analysed in further depth in the present book by Pierre Thielbörger.[34]

According to this right, as defined by the CESCR in its General Comment No 15 of 26 November 2002,[35] in direct conjunction with the right to an adequate living standard protected by Article 11.1 of the Covenant, everyone is entitled to sufficient, safe, acceptable, physically accessible, and affordable water for personal and domestic use.[36] In particular, the Committee pointed out among other considerations that the concerned state must prevent private companies based on its territory from interfering in any way with the enjoyment of the right to water or from compromising equal, affordable, and physical access to sufficient, safe, and accessible water.[37] This comment was made against the background of a number of disputes concerning water supply services, which had arisen earlier between private foreign investors and public authorities.

In cases where the state has failed to act in accordance with its obligations when concluding the contract with a foreign investor and is subsequently challenged with protests and complaints emanating from the population, it may then be led to try to remedy the situation by introducing new regulations. Those, in turn, might be perceived by the concerned investors as affecting the fair and equitable treatment they were expecting. One may argue, however, that in such situations, for their expectations to be considered as 'legitimate', investors must also have taken due notice of the state's obligations deriving from its human rights obligations. It seems clear that the attitude as well as the practices of partners in an investment potentially affecting the fundamental rights of the population are bound to evolve in the near future.

As a matter of fact, not only the attitude, but also the legal culture of the parties to a dispute – be it the claimants or the respondents – are of relevance for the arbitrator when taking into account any human rights dimensions in the settlement of a dispute between a host state and a foreign private investor. On the side of the state, whose position is usually that of respondent, the arbitrators may be able to grant due consideration to an argument based on the state's obligations pertaining to the economic and social rights of the population living on its territory. However, this will only be possible if the state successfully

---

[33] See Kriebaum, n 1 above, 172 ff.   [34] See ch 20 below.

[35] General Comment No 15 of the CESCR, E/C.12/2002/11 of 20 January 2003.

[36] See P-M Dupuy, 'Le droit à l'eau, droit de l'homme ou droit des Etats?' in M Kohen (ed), *Liber amicorum Lucius Caflish* (2007) 701–717.

[37] General Comment No 15, n 36 above, para 24.

demonstrates and documents the extent to which such obligations made it necessary to hinder the legal situation of the concerned investor in a concrete case.

In this context, one can point again to the unclear border line between regulatory takings and police powers.[38] In two recent cases in particular, respectively *Azurix v Argentina* and *Siemens v Argentina*, it was deemed that the argument put forth by the respondent according to which the strict protection of the investor's property rights could potentially violate protected human rights had not sufficiently been grounded to be considered in relation to the merits of these two cases.[39] Such a stance is explained by the fact that in both cases, the human rights argument was raised by the host state to justify an exception to the fulfilment of its international obligations towards the foreign private investor deriving from the concerned BIT.

Indeed, central here is the question of the effective extent of the jurisdiction of a given arbitral tribunal. Such a tribunal is primarily endowed by the parties with the power of settling an international investment's dispute: does this specific scope of jurisdiction entitle the arbitral tribunal to consider also arguments based on human rights? In this respect, the issue of whether public international law is or is not 'fragmented' takes on eventually not only a theoretical dimension, but an actually practical and concrete one for the arbitrators as well as for the parties.

As will be seen in the next and final part of this chapter, as well as in the rest of this book, while one may show that, indeed, the arbitral tribunal has the possibility to take into account human rights arguments, this can only be done after a careful balancing of a number of elements.

IV. Means of Adjudication

The adjudication of international investment disputes between a foreign private investor and a state shares at least one element with human rights disputes submitted to an international judge: in both situations, the entity in charge of adjudicating the dispute is usually a specialized body, be it a regional human rights tribunal, a human rights Committee, or an international investments arbitral tribunal.[40] In each case, the judge or the arbitrator will adjudicate the case on the basis of a specific instrument from which it derives a special jurisdiction.

---

[38] See Ratner, n 26 above, 475–528.

[39] *Azurix v Argentina*, ICSID Case No ARB/01/12, Award, 14 July 2006, at para 254; and *Siemens v Argentina*, ICSID Case No ARB/02/08, Award, 6 February 2007, at para 75.

[40] This remains the main trend even if, as in the *Barcelona Traction* case (*Barcelona Traction, Light and Power Co, Ltd, Belgium v Spain*, ICJ Reports (1970)) or the *ELSI* case (*Elettronica Sicula S.p.A. (ELSI), US v Italy*), ICJ Reports 15 (1989), the ICJ has known of disputes dealing directly with international private investment.

Thus, in particular, the clause governing the scope of the jurisdiction of the adjudicating body is the primary element in determining whether and the extent to which public international law may be applicable. An international arbitrator may nevertheless also take into account human rights law, either on the basis of municipal law or of applicable rules of public international law.

A. The Compromissory Clause and Public International Law

From a legal point of view, the jurisdiction of all adjudicative bodies is precisely defined and refers to the settlement of special categories of disputes: human rights on the one hand and international investments on the other. Concerning the second set of disputes, the arbitral tribunal must start by considering and analysing the wording of the compromissory clause laid down in the BIT and/or in the contract, jointly with Article 25 of the 1965 Washington Convention if the dispute is to be settled by an ICSID tribunal, so as to determine the scope of its jurisdiction.

In this respect, a key element will be to assess whether the relevant disposition contains any reference to public international law. This is in particular the case for Article 42 of the ICSID Convention, which sets out that in the absence of an agreement of the parties on the applicable law, 'the Tribunal shall apply the law of the Contracting State party to the dispute (including its rules on the conflict of laws) *and* such rules of international law as may be applicable'. Article 1131 of the NAFTA indicates that the tribunal 'shall decide the issues in dispute in accordance with this Agreement and applicable rules of international law', a wording which can be found again in substance under Article 26(6) of the Energy Charter Treaty. In such cases, it is quite evident that the applicability of public international law raises no difficulty, including that part of *general* international law (namely, customary international law) which entails a set of obligations to protect fundamental human rights, ranging from the right to life to the principle of non-discrimination based on race or sex, including rights that have a peremptory character as they belong to *jus cogens* – which, contrary to what has been alleged for too long, is rather easily identifiable in its content.

As convincingly demonstrated by Professor Emmanuel Gaillard and Dr Banifatemi on the basis of a careful analysis of the *travaux préparatoires* as well as of international arbitral case law, the meaning of 'and' in Article 42(1), second sentence, of the ICSID Convention does make it possible for arbitrators, in the absence of any explicit choice of law by the parties, to resort to international law 'not only as a functional element of the choice of law process but also as a body of substantive rules'.[41] In this situation, and according to the ICSID Executive

---

[41] E Gaillard and Y Banifatemi, 'The Meaning of "and" in Article 42(1), Second Sentence, of the Washington Convention: The Role of International Law in the ICSID Choice of Law Process' (2003) 18 ICSID Review Foreign Investment Law Journal 397.

Director, 'the term "international law" as used in this context should be understood in the sense given to it by Article 38(1) of the Statute of the International Court of Justice', which covers as is well known international treaties, customary international law, and general principles. This possibility to rely on public international law is all the more reinforced by the increasingly growing number of 'treaty claims', whereby investors make a claim on the basis of an alleged violation of international law rules. What is true in the case of ICSD, Article 25 is quite evidently equally true in the case of claims based on the NAFTA or on the Energy Charter Treaty, which, as already recalled above, explicitly mention international law as an applicable legal framework by the concerned tribunals.

The arbitrator has therefore the possibility to apply human rights customary international law, and may even have to refer, should the case arise, to the way in which the principles at issue have been interpreted and applied by human rights courts. This is what the arbitrators in the *Mondev* and particularly in the *Tecmed* cases did. Concerning the second case, in particular, which was arbitrated in 2003 under the BIT between Spain and Mexico and related to Mexico's closure of a landfill, the tribunal had to establish whether Mexico's regulation pertaining to the protection of the environment was expropriatory. To do so, the arbitrators relied on the test of proportionality between the harm to the investor caused by the measures taken and the public interest at stake. They explicitly found inspiration in the European Court of Human Rights' case law, in that they assessed the evidence, or lack thereof, of an environmental harm and of a major opposition by the population against the landfill so as to determine whether the complete termination of the investment was or was not disproportionate.[42]

As rightly pointed out in the conclusions of the Study Group of the ILC on the fragmentation of international law in 2006[43] – an argument which had already been put forth earlier, in particular by the WTO Appellate Body in its very first report – international treaty provisions cannot be interpreted *in a vacuum* as they all belong to the same legal order, namely the international one. This provides the *ratio legis* for the classical rule of treaty interpretation as laid down under Article 31.3.c of the Vienna Convention on the Law of Treaties, according to which 'there should be taken into account, together with the context any relevant rules of international law applicable in the relation between the parties'.[44]

---

[42] *Técnicas Medioambientales, Tecmed*, n 23 above, at paras 165–172.

[43] 'Conclusions of the work of the Study Group on the Fragmentation of International Law: Difficulties arising from the Diversification and Expansion of International Law' (2006), adopted by the ILC at its 56th session. *Yearbook of the International Law Commission* (2006), Vol II, Pt Two.

[44] The identification of the parties involved does not raise any difficulty in the case of a BIT or a multilateral treaty limited to a restricted number of parties, as is the case in particular for the NAFTA.

Arbitrators should not be disconcerted by a rule whose general wording may appear extremely broad at first glance. Guidance for application was provided by the International Court of Justice in the *Oil Platform* case of 2003. Having to interpret Article I of the 1955 Treaty of Friendship and Commerce between the United States and Iran, a type of treaty which presents some similarities with the modern BITs, the Court recalled that:

> under the general rules of treaty interpretation, as reflected in the 1989 Vienna Convention on the Law of Treaties, interpretation must take into account 'any relevant rules of international law applicable in the relations between the parties' (Art. 31, para. 3 (c). The Court cannot accept that Article XX, paragraph 1 (d) of the 1955 Treaty was intended to operate wholly independently of the relevant rules of international law on the use of force, so as to be capable of being successfully invoked, even in the limited context of a claim for breach of the Treaty, in relation to an unlawful use of force. The application of the relevant rules of international law relating to this question thus forms an integral part of the task of interpretation entrusted to the Court by Article XXI, paragraph 2, of the 1955 Treaty.[45]

As a consequence, it befalls the judge or the arbitrator, in consideration of the overall context of the case, to justify their understanding of the provision(s) of a treaty[46] in order to determine the effective legal relationship prevailing between this (or these) provision(s) and another obligation binding on the same state and which could interfere in some way with the legal conditions under which the rule laid down by the treaty clause at issue was to be applied.

However, the customary principle of interpretation codified under Article 31.2.c of the Vienna Convention does *not*, as such, authorize the adjudicating body competent for interpreting a treaty clause to put it in relation with any kind of other international law rule. First, the bearing and scope of what could be termed the 'external' obligation (namely, the obligation external to the international law of investment) should be carefully assessed in order to determine the extent to which it should be taken into account when interpreting rules established by an investment treaty; secondly, this 'external rule' must be evidenced as bearing a substantial legal relationship with the provision under interpretation. In this respect, the international arbitrator, and in particular if he or she is not familiar with general public international law, should definitely rely on the substance and rationale of the argument made by the party invoking the 'external rule' – which in this case would be a human rights one – so as to determine whether such a rule effectively interferes with the implementation of the international investment provision under consideration.[47]

---

[45] *Case concerning Oil Platforms (Iran v United States of America)*, Judgment, 6 November 2003, ICJ Reports 2003, at para 41.

[46] In particular in consideration of the arguments invoked by one party.

[47] May it concern the treatment or protection of that investment or the way in which it must be realized in the host state.

As demonstrated by cases quoted above,[48] the arbitrator, whose competence for the adjudication of international investment disputes relies primarily on the basis of international investments law, can indeed technically take into account human rights arguments. Because of the specialized character of his or her jurisdiction, this is only possible, however, if the party invoking a human rights obligation demonstrates that there is effectively a potentiality of its having interfered with the origin and/or development of the investments dispute. The arbitrator is bound by his or her legal dialogue with the parties, as he or she has the obligation to answer their respective arguments. As a consequence, it is primarily for them to learn how to deal with human rights law in the framework of an international law dispute.[49] In that respect, as in many others, the arbitrator is thus dependent on the parties to the case.

B. International Human Rights Law as Applied with Reference to Municipal Law or to Private International Law

Even in cases when the compromissory clause does not make any reference as to the applicability of public international law, there are other ways for an international arbitrator to refer, if necessary, to the obligation incumbent on the host state to respect its human rights obligations.

A first possibility is provided in situations in which the municipal law applicable to a state contract, namely, in most cases, that of the host state, establishes a constitutional link between public international law and the municipal legal order. When, in particular, the national Constitution of the host state contains an option in favour of monism granting primacy to public international law, the latter partakes in the law applicable to the dispute. This does not mean that the concerned state will be able without constraint to avail itself of the relevant provisions of its Constitution so as to shun its obligations towards the foreign investor; but when negotiating a contract with a host state, the potential investor should take due notice of the constitutional law that could affect the implementation or interpretation of its contract with that state. As regards the latter, it should be noted that, when negotiating the treaty, it has the obligation – based in any event on good faith – to indicate to the potential investor the constitutional requirements which could have an impact on the contract, particularly when the object of this contract is of general and public interest, as is often the case. Moreover, in a number of cases, not only the

---

[48] *Azurix v Argentina* and *Siemens v Argentina*, n 39 above.
[49] In this sense, the claim according to which international arbitrators are driven by 'ideological' reasons is deemed to account for their reluctance so far to refer to this branch of public international law, is inconsistent – at least in a number of cases. Indeed, there are few cases where a human rights argument can be effectively raised. Moreover, in this context, the legal training of the parties to the dispute themselves, and their ability (or inability) to identify and draw a substantive rationale on a human rights claim should the case arise, play a central role.

constitutional legal framework of a given state must be taken into account, but also the case law of its national courts and tribunals as to what is deemed to be prohibited by the *national public policy* ('ordre public national'). Such prohibitions indeed often refer to the protection of fundamental human rights.

Parallel to the applicability of national law to a given case of international commercial arbitration is that of a *transnational* public policy ('ordre public transnational') – the existence of which having been long demonstrated, and particularly brilliantly by Professor Pierre Lalive in a seminal article dating back to 1985.[50] This author based his argumentation on two cases in particular, both related to actual practices of slavery, the first dealt with by the London Mixed Commission as early as 1855, in the case of the ship 'Créole', and the second, in 1875, in a case concerning the ship 'Marie Luz'.[51] This claim was later further strengthened in a case of corruption or bribery, in which Mr Lagergren acting as sole arbitrator in the framework of a 1963 ICC arbitration forcefully asserted that 'contracts which seriously violate *bonos mores* or international public policy are invalid', adding that 'such corruption is an international evil; it is contrary to good morals and to an international public policy common to the community of nations'.[52]

Interestingly enough, although he was applying French law to the contract, the arbitrator formulated his conviction of corruption not only on the basis of a national legislation, but also on a general principle of law understood as enunciating a rule of international public policy. This case, which arose in the context of a commercial arbitration, can be compared with a recent transnational one, involving a state and a private investor: in the ICSID case *Work Ltd v Republic of Kenya*, of 4 October 2006, the tribunal stated that:

in light of domestic laws and international conventions relating to corruption, and in light of the decisions taken in the matter by courts and international tribunals, this Tribunal is convinced that bribery is contrary to the international public policy of most, if not all States, or to use another formula, to transnational public policy. Thus, claims based on contracts of corruption or on contracts obtained by corruption cannot be upheld by this Arbitral Tribunal.[53]

As already evidenced by the two early cases of 1855 and 1875 dealing with instances of slavery – an issue which is per se at the core of the human rights upheld by the contemporary international community – it is thus quite clear that arbitrators can, on their own initiative, invoke an issue of blatant violation of fundamental human rights deemed to be incompatible with the 'transnational public policy' referred to in the recent case mentioned above. One can note,

---

[50] See P Lalive, 'Ordre public transnational (ou réellement international) et arbitrage international' [1986] Revue de l'arbitrage 329–373.   [51] n 50 above, 336–337.
[52] ICC Award No 1110, quoted by Lalive, n 50 above, 336.
[53] *Work Ltd v Kenya*, ICSID Case No ARB/00/7 of 4 October 2006, at para 157.

furthermore, that, unsurprisingly, the prohibitions that are thus identified coincide generally if not all with that part of fundamental human rights which is currently acknowledged, this time on the basis of *public* international law, as belonging to *jus cogens*, namely customary peremptory international law.[54]

V. General Conclusion

The development, in parallel, of human rights law and international investments law should not be deemed as substantiating the thesis of the 'fragmentation of international law' – a claim which has been much too easily received among scholars, regardless of the analysis put forth in the conclusions of the International Law Commission,[55] as well as by a number of authors.[56]

These two sets of legal regimes belong to the same legal order, namely the international one. If one considers their respective origins and content, there are indeed substantive points of contact between the two. One can furthermore argue that given the growing importance of human rights within the international legal order, arbitrators with jurisdiction over international investment disputes will undoubtedly be increasingly confronted with such rights – be they invoked by the investor or by the host state. An important socio-legal element in this respect is to be considered, namely the growing attention paid by a number of international NGOs to the inter-relations between these two legal domains. As mentioned in the introduction to this chapter, the very fact that, from a classical viewpoint, international corporations are as yet not considered as fully fledged subjects of international law should not be regarded as raising a major obstacle to claim that there should or even must be an international *corporate liability* compelling these non-state actors to respect fundamental human rights: this liability should be read as a condition of reciprocity to the responsibility incumbent on states to protect the human rights of the population based on their territory. This very important issue is further explored in the present book.[57]

However, as regards the adjudication of investments disputes in general, this interaction between international investments law and human rights law cannot be claimed lightly, be it by host states or by foreign private investors. Indeed, the party to a dispute invoking a human rights argument – be it the state or the

---

[54] See PM Dupuy, 'Jus Cogens' in Andriantsimbazovina, Gaudin, Marguénaud, Rials and Sudre (eds), *Dictionnaire des droits de l'homme* (2008) 566–570; see also T Meron, 'On a Hierarchy of International Human Rights' (1986) 80 AJIL 1–23.

[55] See 'Conclusions of the Work of the Study Group on the Fragmentation of International Law', n 43 above, Pt Two, http://untreaty.un.org/ilc/texts/instruments/english/draft%20articles/ 1_9_2006.pdf.

[56] See in particular PM Dupuy, 'L'unité de l'ordre juridique international, cours général de droit international public' RCADI, Vol 297 (2003).   [57] See ch 21 below.

investor – must demonstrate substantively that the human rights at issue effectively impact on the implementation of the investment at stake. This constraint is explained by the fact that the arbitrator's jurisdiction is specifically limited to the settlement of disputes arising out of a given international investment.

This being said, depending on the terms of the compromissory clause (whether or not it expressly mentions public international law as an applicable legal framework to the dispute), the arbitrator may have the possibility to rely, in particular, on the international rules of interpretation of treaties, to find technical means to take into account the potential relevance of a specific human rights element to the substance of the investments dispute. In this regard, the customary rule codified under Article 31.3.c of the Vienna Convention on the Law of Treaties plays a key role. This can also be done through other means, may they derive from the application of the municipal law chosen by the parties to the state contract or that of principles of *transnational public policy* which, including the protection of a number of fundamental human rights, can be directly invoked by the arbitrator him- or herself. The following contributions to this book will of course be of great value to elaborate further and moderate these provisional conclusions.

3

Access to Justice, Denial of Justice, and International Investment Law

Francesco Francioni

I. A Brief Historical Introduction

Denial of justice lies at the heart of the development of international law on the treatment of aliens and of foreign investment. At the same time this notion is inextricably linked to the broader concept of access to justice, understood as the individual's right to obtain the protection of the law and the availability of legal remedies before a court or other equivalent mechanism of judicial or quasi-judicial protection. Intuitively, this type of protection is a *sine qua non* condition for any type of constitutional democracy, where the rule of law and the independence of the courts, rather than the benevolence of the ruler, provide the fundamental guarantees of individual rights and freedoms.

Yet, historically, access to justice has remained problematic for aliens. Even before the formation of the modern nation state, the need for a minimum degree of protection of the life, security, and property of aliens established in, or visiting, a foreign land had emerged in the late Middle Ages, especially in the context of the flourishing trade between the Italian maritime Republics – such as Venice and Genoa – and the Mediterranean areas under Muslim dominion. In these areas, foreign merchants coming from the Christian world could not expect the protection of the universal system of Roman law that had guaranteed the political and legal unity of the ancient Mediterranean world. On the contrary, they encountered diffidence and marginalization by local authorities and, more fundamentally, they had to deal with the difficulty of reconciling their need for personal and economic security with the rigid system of the personality of the law in the Islamic world. This system, informed by the close interpenetration of Islamic law and religion, was a powerful obstacle to the application of legal guarantees of contractual and property rights of non Muslims under the *lex loci*.[1]

---

[1] On the evolution of international law in the context of the mutual contamination and cultural exchange between the Christian World and Islam, see the magisterial analysis by R Ago, 'Pluralism and the Origin of the International Community' (1977) 3 Italian Yearbook of International Law 3.

The pragmatic response to this normative and jurisdictional mismatch was the development of special extraterritorial legal regimes for commercial establishments, trade centres, and warehouses maintained in Muslim land (*fondaci*) by foreign merchants and the gradual recognition of a system of *in situ* protection of foreign merchants by agents of the foreign power of which they were nationals.[2] This practice constitutes a precedent of the modern idea of 'free zones' and, more importantly, formed the basis of the early development of consular relations and of the later emergence of that special branch of customary international law that goes under the name of 'minimum standard of treatment of aliens'.

History tells us also that this early model of international protection of foreign economic interests later degenerated into forms of sheer economic dominance and of colonial imposition by the European powers. The extreme manifestation of this development was the system of 'capitulations', a radical form of extraterritorial imposition of foreign law and jurisdiction in the receiving state, which served to exempt their citizens from the sovereignty of the host state. Capitulations were gradually eliminated in the first part of the 20th century and became incompatible with the principle of de-colonization later implemented within the framework of the UN Charter.

However, the institution of consular protection remains. Therefore, the principle of the 'minimum standard of justice' to be reserved to aliens and their economic interests under customary international law also remains. An integral part of this standard is the principle of 'access to justice'. This principle presupposes that the individual who has suffered an injury in a foreign country at the hands of public authorities or of private entities must be afforded the opportunity to obtain redress before a court of law or appropriate administrative agency. Only when 'justice' is not delivered, either because judicial remedies are not available or the administration of justice is so inadequate, deficient, or deceptively manipulated so as to deprive the injured alien of effective remedial process, can the alien invoke 'denial of justice': a wrongful act for which international responsibility may arise and in relation to which an interstate claim and diplomatic protection may be presented by the national state of the victim.

Therefore, in its historical evolution, access to justice is inseparable from the 'minimum standard of treatment of aliens'. This is confirmed by the customary rule requiring prior exhaustion of local remedies as a precondition of diplomatic protection. This rule presupposes the international obligation of every state to ensure access to courts to aliens and to administer justice in accordance with minimum standards of fairness and due process.

However, the principle of access to justice, as an integral part of customary international law on the treatment of aliens, guarantees only access to remedial

---

[2] L Ferrari Bravo, *Lezioni di diritto internazionale* (1993) 25.

process within the territory and under the law of the host state. Customary international law does not provide for an individual right of access to justice before international tribunals. Nor, by the same token, does it provide a right of access to the courts of a third state, for which, in principle, the alleged mistreatment of an alien in another state remains *res inter alios acta*.

The major leap forward in the field of foreign investment law is represented by the recognition and consolidation of an indisputable right of access to international justice by private investors and by the extension of this right to the courts of third states to the extent that their cooperation is necessary in order to enforce international investment awards.[3] (A third state is a state different from the host state and the national state of the alien.) Following the phenomenal development in the past 25 years of bilateral investment treaties, regional trade agreements, such as NAFTA,[4] and, more importantly, of investment arbitration, the right of access to justice for the investor has shifted from inter-state claims to the private-to-state arbitration where private actors have direct access to 'international' remedial process without the traditional need for the interposition of their national state in diplomatic protection. This shift of focus has important consequences. First, it undermines the traditional dogma of international law[5] under which only states have international rights and the state intervening to protect its nationals injured abroad asserts its own right rather than the right of the injured person, with the consequence that the claimant state may dispose at its own discretion of such right and of the eventual compensation it has been able to obtain. Secondly, and what is more relevant for the general theme of this book, the 'internationalization' of the right of access to justice of private actors tends to blur the traditional boundary between aliens' rights and human rights. This is so because the private actors to which this right is recognized free themselves from the traditional tutelage of their national state and become empowered with the capacity to assert their individual rights and interests before an international dispute settlement body. This focus on the individual as the title holder of rights is the hallmark of the international law of human rights.[6]

---

[3] See Art 54 of the 1965 Convention on the Settlement of Investment Disputes between States and Nationals of Other States, 575 UNTS 159. Paragraph 1 of this Article provides that: 'Each Contracting State shall recognize an award rendered pursuant to this Convention as binding and enforce the pecuniary obligations imposed by that award within its territories as if it were a final judgment of a court in that State'.

[4] North American Free Trade Agreement between Canada, the United States, and Mexico, entered into force on 1 January 1994, (1993) 32 ILM 289.

[5] *Mavrommatis Palestine Concessions*, PCIJ Rep Series A No 2, 30 August 1924, at 12.

[6] It is significant that also in the ILC Articles on Diplomatic Protection this tendency to take into account the rights of the injured person, beside the traditional right of the state which exercises diplomatic protection, has found an echo in the 'recommended practices' annexed to the Articles. See ILC *Draft Articles on Diplomatic Protection* (2006), Official Records of the General Assembly, Sixty first Session, Supplement No 10 (A/61/10).

This potential convergence of traditional aliens' rights with human rights in the field of access to justice is the conceptual point of departure for the following analysis, which will focus on three distinct but inter-linked aspects of the operation of the right of access to justice in the field of foreign investment law. The first aspect concerns the extent to which human rights considerations may influence the assessment of the international legality of the host state's interference with the investor's rights and on his or her ability to obtain judicial or arbitral protection for his or her investment. The second aspect relates to the emerging claim of access to justice for the host state population when the operation of the foreign investment is deemed adversely to affect their environment or other societal goods. The third aspect concerns the way in which access to justice may be reconciled with the traditional rule of sovereign immunity when the state of the investment adopts a measure with extraterritorial effect that adversely impacts the property right of foreign investors especially in the field of financial instruments with worldwide circulation. I will examine these three aspects in light of recent arbitral practice.

II. Access to Justice as an Investor's Right

Several recent investment disputes have highlighted that access to justice may continue to be problematic even in the presence of investment guarantees under bilateral or multilateral treaties.

The most well known, dare say notorious, case is *Loewen Group v the United States*,[7] concerning a claim by a Canadian company against the United States under NAFTA Chapter 11[8] and alleging discriminatory treatment, expropriation, and breach of fair and equitable standard as a consequence of litigation before the courts of Mississippi. Loewen had been sued by a local business competitor in the funeral industry who complained of predatory behaviour and restrictive business practices by the much larger Canadian company. During the jury trial, the strategy of the plaintiff was to emphasize the merits of the local business, its commitment to serving the local community, and its struggle against allegedly predatory practices of foreign corporate competitors. According to Loewen's complaint, the whole trial was pervaded by continuous references to nationality and patriotism – with counsel for the plaintiff likening the struggle of his client with his wartime heroic effort against the Japanese.[9] The jury verdict

---

[7] *Loewen Group Inc and Raymond Loewen v United States of America*, ICSID Case No ARB (AF)/98/3, 26, 26 June 2003, 42 ILM 811.

[8] Since 1978, the Administrative Council of the Centre for the Settlement of Investment Disputes has authorized the Secretariat to administer arbitral proceedings concerning investment disputes between parties to the 1966 ICSID Convention and nationals of states which are not parties to the Convention.   [9] *Loewen*, n 8 above, at para 61.

awarded US$500 million to the plaintiff, of which US$400 million constituted punitive damages. Appeal of the decision was possible under Mississippi law; but state law required the posting of a financial bond in the amount of 125 per cent of the award in order to suspend the execution of the award pending the appeal. Faced with this prohibitive amount of the required bond and the prospect of immediate execution of the exorbitant verdict, Loewen settled the case.

In the ICSID arbitral proceeding against the United States, Loewen alleged violation of the NAFTA anti-discrimination provision under Article 1102, of the principles of minimum standard of treatment of aliens under Article 1105, and of the expropriation provision of Article 1110. The US defence was that basically no governmental measure could be attributed to the United States and that the loss of Loewen was solely attributable to the outcome of a civil suit between two private companies for which the United States could not be held accountable.

What makes this case so interesting for the purpose of our discussion on access to justice is the rather schizophrenic attitude of the arbitral panel which, on the one hand, expressly recognized the flaws in the administration of justice by the Mississippi court, but, on the other hand, declined to enter into the merit of the case because of the alleged failure by the plaintiff to exhaust local remedies in the United States and of his inability to satisfy the rule of continuity of claims (in the meantime, Loewen becoming incorporated in the United States). In the words of the panel:

... the conduct of the trial judge was so flawed that it constituted a miscarriage of justice amounting to a manifest injustice as that expression is understood in international law[10] ... the trial involving O'Keefe and Loewen was a disgrace. By any standard of evaluation, the trial judge failed to afford Loewen the process that was due ... the methods employed by the jury and countenanced by the judge were the antithesis of due process.[11]

In a surprising ending of the saga, the arbitral tribunal went at length to explain why, even in the face of manifest injustice, a remedy could not be granted:

A reader following our account of the injustices which were suffered by Loewen ... in the courts of Mississippi could well be troubled to find that they emerge from the present long and costly proceedings with no remedy at all ... There was unfairness here towards the foreign investor. Why not use the weapons at hand to put it right? ... This human reaction has been present in our minds throughout but we must be on guard against allowing it to control our decision ... the interest of the international investing community demand that we must observe the principles which we have been appointed to apply and stay our hands.

This is an extraordinary statement. What are the principles the panel was appointed to apply? It seems clear that such principles are those clearly expressed in NAFTA Chapter 11: namely, non-discrimination, prohibition of

---

[10] *Loewen* Ibid. at para 54.   [11] *Loewen* Ibid. at paras 119 and 122.

uncompensated expropriation, and minimum standard of justice under international law. This standard certainly includes access to effective remedial process. However, rather than focusing on these principles and standards, the panel preferred to apply a purely formalistic notion of 'denial of justice' coinciding with the absolute finality of abstractly available legal remedies, no matter how uncertain and remote they might have been. What was at stake in this case was the possibility of a petition for certiorari before the US Supreme Court to seek the annulment of the Mississippi verdict. However, this remedy was purely speculative. To consider its abstract availability a legal obstacle to the admissibility of the investor's claim is not consistent with international judicial practice on the matter.

In the *ELSI* case – cited by the tribunal to support the view that the local remedies rule is part of customary international law – the International Court of Justice (ICJ) applied this rule subject to the test of reasonableness and effectiveness. In that case, involving a claim by the United States against Italy, the ICJ correctly rejected Italy's claim that the US investor had failed to exhaust in Italy a theoretically possible action in tort by the parent company, once all civil and administrative actions had been already exhausted by the Italian subsidiary against local and national authorities. The Court applied the rule of exhaustion of local remedies together with the rule of reason, which required that Italy should prove the effectiveness of the further remedy in order to foreclose the admissibility of the international claim:

> Italy contends that Raytheon and Matchlett could have based such an action before the Italian courts on Article 2043 of the Italian Civil Code, which provides that 'Any act . . . which causes wrongful damages to another person implies that the wrongdoer is under and obligation to pay compensation for those damages'. . . . In the present case, however it was for Italy to show, as a matter of fact, the existence of a remedy which was open to the United States stockholders and which they failed to employ. The Chamber does not consider that Italy has discharged that burden.[12]

Had the arbitral tribunal applied the above rule of reason, it would have put on the defendant state the burden of proving that petition to the Supreme Court would have, *as a matter of fact*, provided a remedy for the aggrieved investor. This did not happen. Instead, this arbitral decision has shown that, paradoxically, the rule of prior exhaustion of local remedies has received a more reasonable and flexible application in the context of an inter-state claim before the ICJ – where the primary focus on state rights would justify a more rigorous application of the rule and more deference to state sovereignty – than in private-to-state arbitration, where the primary objective is the protection of the private rights of the investor.

---

[12] ICJ, *Case Concerning Elettronica Sicula Spa (ELSI)*, Judgment, 20 July 1989, ICJ Reports 1989, at paras 61 and 62.

To conclude, this is a bad precedent for access to justice. It is also a bad precedent for the investment community which can hardly benefit from an extreme and unrealistic application of the rule of prior exhaustion of local remedies when the risk of grave loss is imminent and miscarriage of justice has been acknowledged. All the more so in a case such as this when the alien is facing the threat of the execution of an exorbitant verdict of punitive damages – which remain highly contested in international law – and when further judicial protection is barred by excessive bail.[13]

Unlike *Loewen*, the ICSID tribunal in *Mondev v United States*[14] made express reference to international law and to international judicial precedents[15] in order to define the boundaries of the right of access to justice and the corresponding scope of the notion of 'denial of justice'. The case concerned again a NAFTA Chapter 11 claim filed by a Canadian company against the United States for the alleged discriminatory expropriation without compensation of the claimant's rights arising from a commercial real estate development contract entered into with the City of Boston and the Boston Redevelopment Authority. When a dispute arose out of the execution of the contract, the investor successfully sought damages before the courts of Massachusetts, only to see the favourable jury verdict reversed by the State Supreme Court on grounds of domestic sovereign immunity of local regulatory authorities. Was the application of the doctrine of statutory immunity of local authority a denial of the right of access to justice? The ICSID tribunal provided a negative answer to this question. First, it reiterated the principles that under investment treaties parties have the option to seek local remedies and if, in doing so, they lose on the merits, 'it is not the function of NAFTA tribunals to act as courts of appeals'. Second, and most important for our discussion, the tribunal adopted a rather restrictive notion of 'denial of justice'. Building on previous arbitral precedents, such as *Azinian v Mexico*,[16] the tribunal concluded that the exercise of regulatory powers by local government authorities and the application of statutory immunity in respect of the exercise of their official functions could not give rise to a claim of unlawful expropriation under NAFTA.

In spite of this negative outcome, the *Mondev* decision displays a rare consideration of international judicial practice in the determination of the scope of access to justice. Not only does it make express reference to the case law of the ICJ, in particular to the *ELSI* judgment, but it also takes into consideration the human rights standard guaranteed by Article 6(1) of the European Convention

---

[13] For a critical analysis of this case, see the forum discussion in JWIT, February 2005, Vol 6, with contributions by J Werner and M Meldelson, 80–97.

[14] *Mondev International Ltd v United States of America*, ICSID (Additional Facility) Case No ARB(AF)/99/2, Award, 11 October 2002, 42 ILM 85.

[15] See in particular the reference to the *ELSI* case at para 127.

[16] *Robert Azinian, Kenneth Davitian and Ellen Baca v Mexico*, ICSID (Additional Facility) Case No ARB(AF)/97/2, Award, 1 November 1999, 39 ILM 537, at 552.

on Human Rights.[17] This provision, as is well known, requires that in order to right a wrong a court must be open to recourse and that 'fair and public hearings within a reasonable time by an independent and impartial tribunal established by law' are guaranteed by the state. Ultimately, the award in *Mondev* concludes that Article 6(1) is too advanced to provide a criterion for decision in investment arbitration. However, it is noteworthy that an arbitral award has considered even *in abstracto* that a provision contained in a human right instrument to which neither the respondent nor the national state of the claimant were parties could have provided a criterion to determine the scope of the right of access to justice.

In the view of this writer, a better solution would have been to arrive at the identification of an international standard on access to justice taking into account the law and practice of international human rights bodies – including the European Court of Human Rights – and then ask whether functional immunity of the respondent's regulatory bodies could serve a legitimate objective so as to justify an exception of that right in the particular circumstances of the case. This would have helped the consolidation of an international standard on access to justice as a right of aliens and a human right alike, and without compromising the possibility of subjecting this right to restrictions necessary and proportionate to safeguard a legitimate objective, such as the interest of regulatory bodies to pursue democratically deliberated public policies, without fear of being held liable for their decisions.[18]

In this brief overview of the arbitral practice on investors' right of access to justice it is useful to mention also a recent ICSID award that sheds light on the procedural dimension of the right of access to justice. In *Saipem v Bangladesh*, the claimant, an Italian company operating in the oil and gas industry, complained of a violation of the Italy-Bangladesh bilateral investment treaty as a consequence of an allegedly unlawful interference with the investment contract by the combined action of Petrobangla, a Bangadeshi public instrumentality, and Bangladeshi courts. The contract concerned the construction of a natural gas pipeline. As the project was significantly delayed because of strong opposition by the local population, a dispute arose over contract performance. Saipem initiated arbitration proceedings under the rules of the International Chamber of Commerce (ICC) and Petrobangla responded by filing an application before the court of Dacha seeking revocation of the ICC's authority to deal with the case.

---

[17] European Convention for the Protection of Human Rights and Fundamental Freedoms, 4 November 1950, 213 UNTS 222.
[18] If this approach had been followed in *Mondev*, it would have been easy for the panel to realize that also in relation to Article 6(1) of the European Convention on Human Rights, the European Court has accepted a wide range of procedural and substantive restrictions, including immunities of public institutions. For a review of the relevant practice, see F Francioni, 'The Right of Access to Justice under Customary International Law' in F Francioni (ed), *Access to Justice as a Human Right* (2007) 33 ff. In the same volume, see also the specific contribution by M Scheinin, 'Access to Justice before Human Rights Bodies: Reflections on the Practice of the UN Human Rights Committee and the European Court of Human Rights' 135–152.

At the same time, Petrobangla seized the courts with an application seeking an injunction to stay all further arbitration proceedings. The Supreme Court of Bangladesh granted a restraining order enjoining Saipem from pursuing further ICC arbitration. The ICC tribunal proceeded with the arbitration and awarded damages to Saipem, notwithstanding the Bangladeshi injunction to stay all proceedings. At this point Petrobangla filed a suit before the High Court division of the Supreme Court of Bangladesh seeking the annulment of the award: the Court held that there was no award to annul; the ICC arbitration had proceeded illegally, in violation of the Bangladeshi restraining order, and thus the award had to be considered null and void. Saipem filed an ICSID claim invoking the bilateral investment treaty between Italy and Bangladesh and claiming that Bangladesh had violated its obligations toward the foreign investor under Article 5 of the BIT. The ICSID tribunal has affirmed its jurisdiction rejecting Bangladesh's preliminary objection to admissibility based on the alleged 'abuse of process' – namely, seeking to enforce an allegedly invalid ICC award under the guise of an ICSID claim – on the basis of the correct recognition that Saipem's claims simply deal with an allegedly wrongful interference by Bangladeshi courts with the arbitration process and with the investor's ability to obtain judicial protection of his rights.[19] On 30 June 2009 the arbitral tribunal delivered its award in the merits (ICSID Case ARB/05/07). It confirmed that the right to arbitrate under a contract can form the object of expropriation, and, more important for the theme of this chapter, that a local judicial intervention in an arbitral process can amount to a violation of international law when it constitutes a manifest abuse of supervisory powers. The award has not been published yet.

III. Access to Justice by Individuals and Groups Affected by the Investment

The increasing impact of foreign investment on the sphere of social life of the host state has raised the question of whether the principle of access to justice, as successfully developed to the benefit of investors through the provision of binding arbitration, ought to be matched by a corresponding right to remedial process for individuals and groups adversely affected by the investment in the host state. This question arises especially in circumstances in which the foreign investment has an actual or potential impact on the health, the environment, or socio-cultural values of the host state population. Under normal circumstances,

---

[19] *Saipem Spa v Bangladesh*, ICSID Case No ARB/05/07, Decision on Jurisdiction and Recommendation on Provisional Measures, 21 March 2007. It is interesting to note that in this decision at paras 130 and 132 the Tribunal made a reference to the case law of the ECtHR to support the finding that rights under judicial decisions are protected property and that court decisions nullifying them may amount to expropriation.

the right of access to court for local population should be guaranteed by the law and the justice system of the host state. However, the peculiar feature of modern investment law is that the host state ultimately delegates to an international mechanism of dispute settlement – ICSID, NAFTA, etc – the resolution of disputes arising from the investment within its territory. This delegation undercuts the authority of national courts to deal with investment disputes and makes the judicial protection that they may provide against harm caused by the investor subject to extensive review by compulsory international arbitration. Court decisions in the host state upholding complaints brought by private parties against a foreign investor may be attacked by the investor before an arbitral tribunal on the ground that they constitute wrongful interference with the investment. Thus, how can we safeguard in these conditions access to justice for citizens and social groups who are or have the well-found fear of being injured by the investment or by the modalities of its conduct in the host state?

At the substantive level, an answer to this question can be found in the role that the defendant state may play in introducing health, environmental, or social concerns on behalf of its citizens or social groups in the arbitration process. This would permit opening the arbitration to private claims that the host state would endorse in a sort of reverse model of diplomatic protection: the territorial state would espouse the claim of its own citizens against the investor rather than vice versa. This approach has its limits. First, it presupposes that the state is willing to take up the claim of individuals and social groups against the investor. This reproduces the paternalistic model of governmental espousal of private claims which does little to advance the individual right of access to justice. Second, the host state may not be interested in bringing the health, environmental, or social concerns to bear on the arbitration process, especially when the state has authorized the investment against the wishes of special segments of the population. Third, the terms of reference of the arbitral tribunal may leave little room for the consideration of counter-claims brought on behalf and in the interest of the local population.

This notwithstanding, a certain role can be carved out for the host state as a guarantor of the right of its own population to have access to justice within the mechanism of investment arbitration. First, the host state may demand that the applicable law in the arbitration of the investment dispute include provisions of its own domestic law which bind the foreign investors to the respect of health, environmental, or social standards that the local population deems to be endangered by the investment. This is consistent with Article 42(1) of the ICSID Convention, which provides that, absent contrary stipulation by the parties, the tribunal 'shall apply the law of the Contracting State party to the dispute'. In addition, one could argue that a progressive interpretation of the 'fair and equitable standard', which has been systematically adopted in the BITs practice and in regional agreements such as NAFTA, entails that the investor who seeks equity for the protection of his investment must also be accountable, under principles of equity and fairness, toward the host state population affected by the investment. It is difficult to conceive equity as a one-sided concept: equity always requires fair and equitable balancing of competing interests, in this case the interests of the investor and of individuals and social groups who seek judicial protection against possible adverse impacts of the investment on their life or their environment.[20]

The second approach to safeguarding the right of access to justice of the local population is the recourse to international mechanisms for the protection of human rights, whenever they are available and are open to individual recourses. One of the most important precedents in this context is the decision of the Inter-American Court of Human Rights in the case of *Awas Tingni v Nicaragua*.[21] This case arose out of a dispute between the indigenous community of Awas Tingni and the government of Nicaragua as a consequence of this government decision to grant a foreign company a concession for logging in an area claimed by Awas Tingni as ancestral land subject to traditional tenure. After a complex series of litigations before Nicaraguan courts, the matter was brought before the Inter-American Commission of Human Rights and subsequently before the Inter-American Court. The result of these proceedings was the cancellation of the logging concession by the government of Nicaragua and the recognition by the Inter-American Court that under the American Convention on Human Rights the customary right of the Awas Tingni community over the disputed land had to be respected together with their right to the preservation of their cultural integrity. Nicaragua was found responsible for the violation of Article 25 of the Convention, which guarantees the right to judicial protection of everyone 'to simple and prompt recourse, or any other effective recourse ... for protection against acts that violate his fundamental rights'.[22]

Another important precedent of local communities' action to counteract the harmful impact of foreign investments is the 2001 case of *Social and Economic Rights Action (SERAC) v Nigeria*, where the African Commission on Human and Peoples' Rights affirmed its jurisdiction to hear a complaint that foreign oil and gas investments were causing serious health and environmental harm to the Ogoni people in the Niger delta. The Commission found that no effective remedies had been made available to the complainants by the Nigerian authorities and held that the oil exploration and production activities by foreign investors had caused an intolerable level of pollution, severe environmental degradation, and serious health damage so as to threaten the very existence of the Ogoni people.[23] These

---

[20] On the concept of 'fair and equitable treatment' in foreign investment practice, see the detailed study by I Tudor, 'Great Expectations. The "Fair and Equitable Treatment" Standard in the International Law of Foreign Investment', PhD Thesis, European University Institute, 2006. Generally on the role of equity in international economic law, see 'Equity' in *Max Planck Encyclopaedia of Public International Law* (forthcoming).

[21] *Mayana (Sumo) Awas Tingni Community v Nicaragua*, I/A Court HR (ser C) No 124 (15 June 2005).

[22] American Convention on Human Rights, Signed in San José, Costa Rica, 22 November 1969, entered into force 18 July 1978, (1969) 9 ILM 101.

[23] For a discussion of this case, see C Nwobike, 'The African Commission on Human and Peoples' Rights and the Demystification of Second and Third Generation Rights under the African Charter' (2005) 1 African Journal of Legal Studies 129, 131.

precedents attest that when remedies are available under human rights treaties, investors' rights do not stand in the way of the recognition of individuals' and groups' right of access to justice. However, since access by individuals and groups to international mechanisms of human rights protection remains dependent on specific treaty regimes, this option is of limited use, and is mostly available at regional level, for the purpose of providing a forum to remedy abuses or wrongful damage caused by the investor to the local population.

A third approach to improve the opportunities of access to justice by the host state population is through the indirect means of *amici curiae*'s participation in investment arbitration. As is known, the institution of *amici curiae* is a product of common law culture and more particularly of the US practice where the adjudicatory function is open to the participation of individuals or entities who, without being parties to the litigation, are capable nevertheless of providing useful factual information and legal insights in addition to those provided by the disputing parties. *Amici curiae* are not interveners in a technical sense, since they do not vindicate their own rights. Their function as instruments of access to justice is only indirect. However, to the extent that *amici curiae* briefs bring into the arbitral proceedings factual and legal considerations concerning the safeguarding of public goods, such as human and environmental health or the preservation of local cultural heritage, they can become a powerful tool to widen the scope of investment arbitration so as to encompass consideration of public policy concerns with regard to the adverse effects of an investment. This is an important rationale for *amici curiae*, in view of the extensive limitation that investment arbitration produces on the host state's sovereignty with regard to a wide range of matters traditionally reserved to domestic jurisdiction. Such limitations become apparent when we observe that regulatory measures in the field of public health, environmental quality, security, or socio-cultural affairs have become subject to penetrating review by investment arbitration under standards of discrimination, transparency, good faith, and fairness, with a profound impact on the ability of the state to pursue primary public goods and general interest of the society. This is why *amici curiae* participation has become and will remain in the foreseeable future an important feature of the administration of justice in the field of foreign investments.

Although this type of participation is still not contemplated in proceedings before the International Court of Justice, petitions for *amici curiae* intervention have been accepted in the practice of international dispute settlement bodies and, more recently, have been formally codified in the rules of procedure of relevant treaty bodies. First, WTO practice, notwithstanding the absence of specific provisions in the Dispute Settlement Understanding (DSU),[24] has

---

[24] Understanding on Rules and Procedures Governing the Settlement of Disputes, Annex 2 of the Marrakesh Agreement Establishing the World Trade Organization, (1994) 33 ILM 1197 ff, in force since 1 January 1995.

allowed the presentation of briefs by *amici curiae* in a large number of cases on the basis of an expansive interpretation of the rules of procedure. This development, although initially opposed by certain developing countries in the WTO, has been supported by commentators[25] and by the majority of the industrialized WTO members, notably the United States. After the *Asbestos* case,[26] the Appellate Body has adopted specific rules and time limits to prevent abuses and undue delays in the dispute settlement procedure.[27]

Acting upon the WTO example, petitions for *amicus curiae* participation have been filed and admitted in investment arbitration, both under NAFTA Chapter 11 and ICSID. NAFTA tribunals have allowed *amici* briefs in three cases: *Methanex*,[28] *UPS*,[29] and *Glamis*.[30] The first two cases have been decided on the merits. The third is still pending. Although it is unclear to what extent the *amici curiae* participation has influenced, or may influence, the arbitral decision, their briefs have certainly helped to integrate important environmental and social perspectives in investment disputes involving complex public policy interests.[31] In *Glamis*, the NAFTA tribunal has allowed the application for participation as *amicus curiae* by a tribal community – the Quechan Indians. The social group is directly affected by a Canadian company's contested mining investment in Northern California in a desert conservation area near their tribal lands, which includes sacred and ancestral sites. In these cases, presentation of *amici curiae* briefs has been accepted in spite of the absence of specific authorizing provisions in NAFTA. Further, this practice has been endorsed by a formal statement of the NAFTA Free Trade Commission on non-disputing party participation of 7 October 2003.[32]

As far as ICSID arbitration is concerned, like in NAFTA, no express provision on non-disputing party participation was contained in the 1965 World

[25] L Boisson de Chazournes, 'Transparency and Amicus Curiae Briefs' (2004) JWIT 333.
[26] See WTO Panel Report, 'European Communities – Measures Affecting Asbestos and Asbestos-Containing Products', WT/DS135/R, adopted 18 September 2000; and WTO Appellate Body Report, 'European Communities – Measures Affecting Asbestos and Asbestos-Containing Products', WT/DS135/AB/R, adopted 12 March 2001.
[27] For a full account of this practice, see E Baroncini, 'Società civile e sistema OMC di risoluzione delle controversie: gli *amici curiae*' in Francioni et al (eds), *Organizzazione Mondiale del Commercio e diritto della Comunità Europea nella prospettiva della risoluzione delle controversie* (2005) 75–113.
[28] *Methanex v United States of America*, Final Award, 3 August 2005, (2005) 44 ILM 1345.
[29] *United Parcel Service of America Inc (UPS) v Canada*, Award on the Merits, 24 May 2007, (2007) 46 ILM 922.
[30] *Glamis Gold Ltd v the Government of the United States of America*, Notice of Arbitration, 9 December 2003, available at http://www.state.gov/documents/organization/27320.pdf.
[31] The petitioners in the *Methanex* case were the International Institute for Sustainable Development, Communities for a better Environment, and Earth Island Institute; in *UPS* they were the Canadian Union of Postal Workers and the Council of Canadians.
[32] Statement of the North American Free Trade Commission on Non-Disputing Party Participation of 7 October 2003, available at http://www.ustr.gov.

Bank Convention or in the ICSID arbitration rules.[33] In the early case of *Agua del Tunari v Bolivia, amicus curiae* submission was denied based on the absence of authorization provisions and on a strict interpretation of the 'consensual nature' of ICSID arbitration.[34] However, in several subsequent cases,[35] ICSID tribunals have changed position and have admitted *amici* participation in the arbitration proceedings on the basis of a liberal interpretation of Article 44 of the ICSID Convention which allows residual discretionary powers to the tribunal on procedural questions not explicitly covered by the Convention or the Arbitration Rules. This jurisprudential development has led to a formal amendment of the ICSID Arbitration Rules,[36] with the adoption in 2006 of a specific enabling provision, the new Rule 37(2), which reads as follows:

After consulting both parties, the Tribunal may allow a person or entity that is not a party to the dispute . . . to file a written submission with the Tribunal regarding a matter within the scope of the dispute. In determining whether to allow such a filing, the Tribunal shall consider, among other things, the extent to which: (a) the non-disputing party submission would assist the Tribunal in the determination of a factual or legal issue related to the proceeding by bringing a perspective, particular knowledge or insight that is different from that of the disputing parties; (b) the non-disputing party submission would address a matter within the scope of the dispute; (c) the non-disputing party has a significant interest in the proceeding. The Tribunal shall ensure that the non-disputing party submission does not disrupt the proceeding or unduly burden or unfairly prejudice either party, and that both parties are given an opportunity to present their observations on the non-disputing party submission.

This amendment was accompanied by a modification also of Rule 32(2) which allows the presence of external observers at the arbitration hearings. These developments in arbitral practice and the formal opening in the ICSID Rules of Arbitration to the participation of representatives of civil society, experts, and NGOs is certainly not a panacea to cure all of the existing defects and limits of access to justice in the context of investment arbitration. Yet, it has the unquestionable merit of having permitted the emergence in international law of the idea of civil society as an important participant in the resolution of

---

[33] Convention on the Settlement of Investment Disputes between States and Nationals of Other States, 575 UNTS 159. The Convention entered into force on 14 October 1966.

[34] *Agua del Tunari SA v Bolivia*, ICSID Case No ARB/02/3, Decision on Jurisdiction, 21 October 2005. The reasons for the denial of the admissibility of amicus briefs are explained in a letter from the President of the Tribunal attached to the award as Annex III.

[35] *Aguas Argentinas SA, Suez Sociedad General de Aguas de Barcelona SA and Vivendi Universal SA v Argentina*, ICSID Case No ARB/03/19, Order, 19 May 2005; *Aguas Provinciales de Santa Fé SA, Suez Sociedad General de Aguas de Barcelona SA and Interagua Servicios Integrales de Agua SA v Argentina*, ICSID Case No ARB/03/17, Order, 17 March 2006; and *Biwater Gauff v Tanzania*, ICSID Case No ARB/05/22, Procedural Order, 2 February 2007. It is interesting to note how all of these cases concerned foreign investments in essential public services such as the provision of water.

[36] The Amended Rules and Regulations came into effect on 10 April 2006 and are available at <http://www.worldbank.org/icsid/basicdoc/CRR_English-final.pdf>.

investment disputes.[37] Such participation is independent both of the interests of the investor and, in principle, also of the disputing state, and it is capable of giving voice to the interests of specific groups or communities especially affected by the investment or, conversely, to the general interests of the international community that transcend the policy concerns of the host state.

IV. Access to Justice for the Protection of Extraterritorial Investors

The third and final aspect to be examined on the role of the right of access to justice in the context of international investment law is the extent to which it may affect state immunity in the event of suits brought before domestic courts by extraterritorial investors. The paradigmatic case is the default on bonds placed on the global market by a state which later faces an economic and financial crisis and the consequent necessity of rescheduling and reorganizing its public debt with consequent injury to the foreign bond holders.

Default on public debt has a long history in international law. In the 19th century such default was deemed to justify resort to force by the capital exporting state against the defaulting state. The Drago-Porter Convention of 1907[38] was the first international instrument to place some restraint on such use of force.[39] Later, with the UN Charter and the development of international law in the post World War II period, the use of force in international relations became unlawful, including for the purpose of recovering money. Therefore, in contemporary international law access to courts or other remedial process such as arbitration is essential for the protection of rights of private individuals or entities who have invested their money in financial instruments issued by foreign governments who need to resort to the global market to finance their economic development.

However, when the governments default, the availability of effective remedies by national courts is hindered by the doctrine of sovereign immunity. This doctrine has been invoked in cases of moratoria or rescheduling of foreign debt by Nigeria,[40] Mexico,[41] Argentina,[42] and many other countries, and has been

---

[37] On the concept of civil society and its impact on the development of international law, see PM Dupuy and L Vierucci (eds), *NGOs in International Law: Efficiency in Flexibility?* (2008).

[38] Hague Convention II on the Limitations of the Employment of the Use of Force for the Recovery of Contract Debts, signed on 18 October 1907, 36 Stat 2241; Treaty Series 537.

[39] The Convention did not rule out the use of force for the recovery of money loaned to another country, but made its use conditional upon the refusal of the debtor state to accept international arbitration or upon its failure to enforce an arbitral decision on the matter.

[40] See the landmark case of *Trendex v Central Bank of Nigeria*, British Court of Appeals, Civil Division, 13 January 1977, 1983 ILR 112 ff.

[41] See the famous case of *Callejo v Bancomer*, US Court of Appeals for the Fifth Circuit, 8 July 1985, 764 F2d 1101.

[42] US Supreme Court, *Argentina v Weltover*, 12 June 1992, 504 US 607.

revived in relation to the worldwide series of litigations surrounding the spectacular default on the Argentine bonds following that country's economic crisis of 2001 to 2002. Thousands of persons who had invested their savings in the defaulted bonds faced the prospect of a transaction with the Argentine Government that would have entailed the repayment of a fraction of the value of their investment capital, or to seek justice at the international or domestic level.

At the international level, the remedies available were diplomatic protection by the national state of the investor or resort to arbitration. The first avenue presented serious obstacles because of the very special feature of the Argentine bonds dispute. First, the claimants, who never set foot on Argentine soil, had bought the bonds through their banks and were scattered all over the world, could have been required to exhaust whatever local remedies were available in Argentina as a condition of admissibility of the diplomatic claim under customary international law. This would have presented formidable difficulties and unfair hardship for the claimants. Second, even if the claim were held admissible, on the merits the claimant state would have to prove that the bond default constitutes an international wrongful act by Argentina under the classical rules on the treatment of aliens. But are such rules applicable to a situation of extraterritorial injury? And if so, could not Argentina invoke financial distress and necessity as a circumstance excluding wrongfulness, as provided by Article 25 of the 2001 ILC Articles on State Responsibility? The answer to these questions is far from clear, given also the uncertainty that emerged in arbitral practice with regard to the admissibility of the 'necessity' plea advanced by Argentina in several investment disputes brought before ICSID tribunals.[43]

Given these difficulties, it is not surprising that diplomatic protection has not been forthcoming in the case of the Argentine bonds. Instead, several international arbitration claims have been brought by Italian investors before the ICSID.[44] The claims are based on the 1991 Argentina-Italy treaty on economic cooperation[45]

---

[43] In *CMS Gas Transmission Co v Argentina*, ICSID Case No ARB/01/08, Award, 12 May 2005, the Tribunal held that the defence of necessity was not admissible because the measure adopted by Argentina with regard to the investment was not the only available response to the economic crisis and because the government had significantly contributed to the materialization of the financial crisis. In *LG&E Energy Corp, LG&E Capital Corp and LG&E International Inc v Argentina*, ICSID Case No ARB/02/1, Decision on Liability, 3 October 2006, instead, the Tribunal conceded the state of necessity, but concluded that such state does not exclude the obligation to compensate the injured investor, because necessity is only temporary and the duty to provide reparation revives as soon as necessity is terminated. Both awards are available at <http://www.worldbank.org/icsid/>.

[44] *Italian Holders of Argentine Sovereign Bonds v Argentina*, ICSID Case No ARB/07/5, registered 7 February 2007; *Giordano Alpi and ors v Argentina*, ICSID Case No ARB/08/9, registered on 28 July 2008; and *Giovanni Alemanni and ors v Argentina*, ICSID Case No ARB 07/8, registered on 27 March 2007.

[45] 'Accordo fra la Repubblica Italiana e la Repubblica Argentina sulla promozione e protezione degli investimenti', 3 June 1988, available at <http://www.sice.oas.org/Investment/BITSbyCountry/BITs/ARG_Italy.pdf>.

and are currently pending. Although the avenue of international arbitration is more promising than diplomatic protection because of the direct access of injured individuals to an international redress mechanism, it is not clear whether it will yield effective remedies. For one thing, it may be open to dispute whether purchase of bonds outside of the territory of the issuing state constitutes an investment under terms of the ICSID Convention and of the relevant bilateral treaty. Further, questions of double nationality may render some claims inadmissible. At the substantive level, the defence of necessity remains a potential obstacle.

This brings us back to the question of access to courts and state immunity. In this respect, the fate of bond holders' actions against Argentina has been different in different jurisdictions. In Italy, where, ironically, a very large number of private investors have been injured, the courts have consistently declined to exercise jurisdiction on the ground that Argentina was entitled to sovereign immunity under international law. The Italian Court of Cassation in an important decision of 27 May 2005 in plenary session (*Sezioni Unite*)[46] sealed this jurisprudential approach by recognizing that the conduct of the Argentine Government had the 'public purpose ... of protecting the primary need of economic survival of the population in a historical context of very serious national emergency'. On the contrary, in the United States, following the pivotal decision in *Republic of Argentina v Weltover*,[47] the Supreme Court has consistently held that global bonds issued by Argentina fall within the commercial exception to sovereign immunity.[48] Furthermore, the case law of German courts stands in contrast with the Italian jurisprudence so deferential to sovereign immunity: the *Frankfurth Landgericht* in a judgment of 14 March 2003 denied immunity on the basis of a careful reconstruction of the customary rule of restrictive immunity and dismissed the plea of 'necessity' on the basis of the argument that, as a norm of customary international law, it may not be applied to the relations between a state and private individuals.[49] Although the latter conclusion by the German Court is open to question – since necessity as a circumstance excluding wrongfulness is to be correctly characterized as a 'general principle of law', in the terms of Article 38.1(c) of the ICJ Statute, and as such applicable to the relations between governmental as well as private entities – its restrictive interpretation of the customary law of immunity, as well as the similar interpretation followed in the US judicial practice, is correct. Both the 2004

[46] Decision No 11225, reproduced in *Rivista di diritto internazionale privato e processuale* (2005) 1094.   [47] See n 42 above.

[48] For reference to the vast number of US judicial decisions on this matter, see B Bonafé, 'State Immunity and the Protection of Private Investors: The *Argentine Bonds* case before Italian Courts'(2006) XVI Italian Yearbook of International Law 165, 177.

[49] Frankfurth Langerich am Main, *Argentinianleihen-Urteil*, 14 March 2003, No 294/02, cited in Bonafé, n 49 above, 179.

UN Convention on State Immunity[50] and the European Convention on the same subject[51] include 'commercial transactions' among the exceptions to immunity. The preparatory work of the UN Convention clearly indicates that the issuance of government bonds was considered by the ILC to be unquestionably part of the commercial activities of states.[52] Further, there is no basis in international law for holding that an inherently 'commercial transaction' may *ex post* be absorbed within the category of *acta jure imperii* by the adoption of subsequent governmental measures frustrating the rights of the investors on grounds of public requirements. If this were true, the distinction between *acta jure gestionis* and *acta jure imperii* would be deprived of any useful effect. Finally, it suffices to observe that in the prevailing case law of national courts the characterization of an act of the defendant state as 'commercial' or 'sovereign' depends on the objective nature of the act and not on the purpose underlying its adoption.[53] Again, if this was not true, the customary norm on restrictive immunity would lose its value.

The conclusion one can draw from the still unresolved saga of the Argentine bonds is that access to justice by foreign investors who have been injured by payment default of a foreign government requires a more constructive dialogue between courts of different jurisdictions in order to determine what is the correct balance to be struck between the respect for the foreign state's jurisdictional immunity and the need to ensure effective judicial remedies to innocent peoples who may have been ruined by that state's financial policies. This dialogue has been conspicuously absent in the case of the Argentine bonds. It is submitted that such dialogue is all the more necessary at this advanced stage of development of international investment law.[54] This is for two reasons: first, because it may help to clarify the content and scope of the investors' right of access to justice under international law to the benefit of investment arbitrators who often have to grapple with what is the precise meaning of the 'minimum standard of justice' in the treatment of the alien's economic interest. Second, and more pertinently for the case under discussion, even if the ICSID tribunal were to uphold the claim of the thousands of bond holders, the question of sovereign immunity would inevitably re-emerge at the moment the claimants tried to enforce the award in the national courts of the appropriate jurisdiction.

---

[50] United Nations Convention on Jurisdictional Immunities of States and Their Property, UNGA Res A/59/38 (2004), 2 December 2004.

[51] European Convention on State Immunity, signed in Basle on 16 May 1972, CETS No 74.

[52] See Report of the International Law Commission on the Work of its Fifty-first Session, 1999, UN Doc A/54/10, at 160.

[53] For a comprehensive survey of such case law, see Bonafé, n 49 above, 169.

[54] On 'judicial dialogue' in international investment law, see, for instance, V Vadi, 'Towards Arbitral Path Coherence and Judicial Borrowing: Persuasive Precedent in Investment Arbitration' (2008) 5 Transnational Dispute Management.

V. Conclusion

The impressive development of investment arbitration in contemporary international law has helped to consolidate access to justice as a principle that partakes both of human rights law and of investment law. This development has furthered the process of emancipation of individuals and private entities from the tutelage of the state by allowing the latter to bring claims directly against a state before an international dispute settlement mechanism. The great success of investment arbitration has also raised the question of whether the extensive penetration of foreign investment guarantees into areas of national regulation hitherto reserved to domestic jurisdiction should require a corresponding opportunity for access to justice and participation in arbitral proceedings by representatives of civil society of the host state. The conclusion reached in this chapter is that such concern can be met, at the substantive level, by the application in arbitral proceeding of the law of the disputing state, to the extent that it pursues legitimate public policy objectives, and by the full application of the fair and equitable standard to the benefit of both the investor and of the population affected by the investment. At the procedural level, the current trend toward a more expansive construction of civil society's access to justice is supported by the increasing acceptance of *amici curiae* participation in arbitration proceedings.

With regard to the specific problem of access to justice of extraterritorial investors – as in the case of the Argentine bonds – this chapter has emphasized the importance of a dialogue between national courts as a condition for a common understanding of the scope and limits of sovereign immunity as a persistent obstacle to the effective exercise of the right of access to justice.

4

Human Rights and International Investment Arbitration

Clara Reiner and Christoph Schreuer

I. Introduction

Investment arbitration has emerged as the most effective means of resolving investor-state disputes. The popularity of arbitration for this purpose has not only led to a rapid increase in the caseload of arbitration institutions, but has brought with it an array of new issues. As a consequence, investment law is presently being challenged by interactions with other, non-investment, obligations.[1] These are raised by investors, states, and non-party actors alike. In addition to environmental and labour-related issues, references to human rights in the domain of investment arbitration are appearing, yet they remain sparse and infrequent.

It is not impossible for investment protection treaties, such as bilateral investment treaties (BITs), to provide for human rights, but this would be highly unusual. The Model BITs of China (2003), France (2006), Germany (2005), the United Kingdom (2005), and the United States (2004) do not mention them explicitly. Mention of human rights is equally absent from the North American Free Trade Agreement (NAFTA) and the Energy Charter Treaty (ECT), two important multilateral investment treaties.[2] The ICSID Convention (Convention on the Settlement of Investment Disputes between States and Nationals of Other States) covers procedural and not substantial issues and hence does not address human rights. The most important print source for decisions on international investment law, the ICSID Reports, does not even include the term 'human rights' in its index.

---

[1] See U Kriebaum, 'Privatizing Human Rights. The Interface between International Investment Protection and Human Rights' in A Reinisch and U Kriebaum (eds), *The Law of International Relations – Liber Amicorum Hanspeter Neuhold* (2007) 165–189.

[2] See R Dolzer and C Schreuer, *Principles of International Investment Law* (2008) 314 (ECT), 330 (NAFTA), 352 (Chinese Model BIT), 360 (French Model BIT), 368 (German Model BIT), 376 (British Model BIT), 385 (US Model BIT). In its Arts 12 and 13, the US Model BIT does, however, address environmental and labour law.

This suggests that the present role of human rights in the context of investment arbitration is peripheral at best. This contribution will attempt to throw some light on the role of human rights in international investment arbitration, focusing more particularly on the issues relating to jurisdiction, the applicable law, and the invocation of human rights during proceedings.

II. Jurisdiction over Human Rights Issues

The system of investment arbitration does not generally require the exhaustion of local remedies and places the investor and the state on an equal footing, thus supplanting diplomatic protection. This is somewhat of an anomaly in the larger context of international law. Established on a case-by-case basis, arbitral tribunals draw their jurisdiction to make binding rulings on a dispute solely from the consent of the parties. The tribunal's jurisdiction is consequently both based on and limited to that agreement. Hence, the mere allegation of a human rights violation would not suffice to confer jurisdiction on a tribunal. To determine whether an investment tribunal is competent to decide on human rights issues, the clause establishing jurisdiction is decisive.

It is thus the formulation of the compromissory clause in the treaty or contract which will reveal the breadth of the tribunal's jurisdiction. In many cases, it will be 'restricted to "investment disputes" ... or to alleged violations of the substantive rights in the investment treaty'.[3] In the case of NAFTA, Article 1116 effectively delimits NAFTA's applicability to alleged breaches of Section A, namely to breaches of NAFTA obligations. Similarly, Article 26(1) and (2) of the ECT provides that only breaches of obligations contained in its Part III are arbitrable. These restrictions of jurisdiction to disputes originating from the breach of a treaty obligation coupled with the fact that these treaties contain no substantive human rights standards suggest that arbitral tribunals will lack the competence to rule on human rights issues as far as the NAFTA and the ETC are concerned. However, certain human rights violations, such as those related to the protection of the investor's property, may at the same time constitute a breach of a particular treaty obligation and hence fall within the realm of the tribunal's competence, thus providing access to investment arbitration.

In the case of *Biloune v Ghana*,[4] the Syrian investor, Biloune, had been arrested and held in custody for 13 days without charge and finally deported from Ghana to Togo. In the ensuing proceedings, the claimant also sought

---

[3] LE Peterson and KR Gray, 'International Human Rights in Bilateral Investment Treaties and Investment Treaty Arbitration' (2005), International Institute for Sustainable Development, at 10, available at <http://www.iisd.org>.

[4] *Biloune and Marine Drive Complex Ltd v Ghana Investments Centre and the Government of Ghana* (UNCITRAL), Award on Jurisdiction and Liability, 27 October 1989, 95 ILR 184.

redress for these alleged violations of his human rights. The UNCITRAL arbitration was based on Article 15(2) of the agreement between the investor and the host state, which provided that '[a]ny dispute between the foreign investor and the Government in respect of an approved enterprise ... may be submitted to arbitration'.[5]

The tribunal affirmed that customary international law requires states to accord foreign nationals a minimum standard of treatment and that international law endows all individuals, regardless of nationality, with inviolable human rights. However, it held that these rules do not imply that the tribunal is competent to rule upon every type of departure from the minimum standard or violation of human rights. Basing its reasoning on the wording of the consent clause in the agreement, the tribunal ruled that its competence is limited to disputes 'in respect of' the foreign investment and that hence the 'Tribunal lacks jurisdiction to address, as an independent cause of action, a claim of violation of human rights'.[6]

The tribunal's reasoning, based on the interpretation of the agreement's compromissory clause which limits jurisdiction to disputes 'in respect of an approved enterprise', declared that an independent claim for violation of human rights fell beyond the scope of its competence. Yet, while it may indeed not be competent for an independent claim, human rights violations cannot per se be excluded from its jurisdiction. If and to the extent that the human rights violation affects the investment, it will become a dispute 'in respect of' the investment and must hence be arbitrable.

III. Human Rights Law as Applicable Law

In considering the role of human rights in international investment arbitration, it does not suffice to establish the tribunal's jurisdiction over alleged violations of human rights, since the analysis and evaluation of the breaches will depend upon the applicable substantive standards.

It is not impossible that BITs or multilateral investment treaties contain human rights provisions, but this would be quite exceptional.[7] In the absence of specific human rights norms in investment treaties and given the parties' freedom to select the applicable law, human rights provisions are applicable to the extent to which they are included in the parties' choice of law. It depends on the choice of law provisions whether human rights norms of international or domestic law will be applicable to the case.

Numerous BITs contain composite choice of law clauses, typically including treaty rules, host state law, and customary international law. Under

---

[5] Ibid., at 188.   [6] Ibid., at 203.   [7] Peterson and Gray, n 3 above.

these provisions, human rights, as a component of international law, are part of the applicable law. For instance, Article 9 of the Chinese Model BIT (2003) provides for the settlement of disputes between investors and a contracting party (namely, the host state) and determines that '[t]he arbitration award shall be based on the law of the Contracting Party to the dispute including its rules on the conflict of laws, the provisions of this Agreement as well as the universally accepted principles of international law'.[8] The US Model BIT (2004) provides that, in certain cases, 'the tribunal shall decide the issues in dispute in accordance with this Treaty and applicable rules of international law',[9] whereas in others, international law shall be applicable alongside the law of the respondent state only when the parties do not otherwise agree.[10]

Certain multilateral investment instruments also provide for the applicability of international law, so that relevant human rights rules may also be pertinent in arbitrations based on these instruments. Article 1131 of the NAFTA determines that '[a] tribunal established under this Section shall decide the issues in dispute in accordance with this Agreement and applicable rules of international law'.[11] Furthermore, the ECT disposes that '[a] tribunal ... shall decide the issues in dispute in accordance with this Treaty and applicable rules and principles of international law'.[12]

Article 42(1) of the ICSID Convention establishes that in the absence of an agreement of the parties on the applicable law, 'the Tribunal shall apply the law of the Contracting State party to the dispute (including its rules on the conflict of laws) and such rules of international law as may be applicable'.[13] The Report of the World Bank Executive Directors specifies that 'the term "international law" as used in this context should be understood in the sense given to it by Article 38(1) of the Statue of the International Court of Justice, allowance being made for the fact that Article 38 was designed to apply to inter-State disputes'.[14]

The UNCITRAL Arbitration Rules of 1976 do not envisage the application of international law, giving priority to the parties' agreement. In the event that such an agreement is lacking, they state that 'the arbitral tribunal shall apply the law determined by the conflict of laws rules which it considers applicable'.[15] This peculiarity may be explained by the fact that UNCITRAL is primarily an instrument for the settlement of commercial disputes between private actors and hence less prone to applying public international law.

---

[8] Chinese Model BIT (2003), n 2 above, Art 9(3).
[9] US Model BIT (2004), n 2 above, Art 30(1).   [10] US Model BIT (2004), Art 30(2).
[11] NAFTA, n 2 above, Art 1131(1).   [12] ECT, n 2 above, Art 26(6).
[13] ICSID Convention, Art 42(1).
[14] See Report of the Executive Directors of the Convention on the Settlement of Investment Disputes between States and Nationals of other States, 1 ICSID Reports 31, para 40.
[15] Art 33(1) of the UNCITRAL Arbitration Rules 1976, available at <http://www.uncitral.org>.

IV. Corporate Social Responsibility

When considering whether and to what extent states are bound by human rights duties, it would be inconsistent to disregard obligations that might be incumbent upon the investor. Foreign investment has not always harvested praise, and concern about the role played by multinational enterprises in the protection of fundamental rights has grown. As a response to this, the concept of (international) corporate social responsibility has emerged, endeavouring to apply human rights responsibilities to investors.

Before attempting to substantiate the content of such obligations, it seems necessary to question whether legal persons such as corporations can be bearers of human rights responsibilities. After all, these are traditionally considered to pertain to the domain of states alone. Yet, Muchlinsky comments that:

> at a moral level it would appear that there exists a widening consensus that MNEs [multinational enterprises] should observe fundamental human rights standards. This can be supported by reference to the fundamental need to protect from assaults against human dignity regardless of whether their perpetrators are state or non-state actors.[16]

He also emphasises that '[d]espite this strong theoretical and moral case for extending responsibility for human rights violations to MNEs, the legal responsibility of MNEs for such violations remains uncertain'.[17]

Indeed, in his Interim Report, the Special Representative of the Secretary-General on the Issue of Human Rights and Transnational Corporations and Other Business Enterprises, John Ruggie, comments that 'with the possible exception of certain war crimes and crimes against humanity, there are no generally accepted international legal principles that [directly bind businesses]'.[18] He goes on to state that 'all existing instruments specifically aimed at holding corporations to international human rights standards ... are of a voluntary nature', and that relevant instruments impose obligations on states, not companies. Yet, he also indicates that:

> under customary international law, emerging practice and expert opinion increasingly do suggest that corporations may be held liable for committing, or for complicity in, the most heinous human rights violations amounting to international crimes, including genocide, slavery, human trafficking, forced labour, torture and some crimes against humanity.[19]

---

[16] PT Muchlinski, 'Corporate Social Responsibility' in P Muchlinski, F Ortino, and C Schreuer (eds), *The Oxford Handbook of International Investment Law* (2008) 655 (footnote omitted).

[17] PT Muchlinski, *Multinational Enterprises and the Law* (2007) 517.

[18] J Ruggie, 'Interim Report of the Special Representative of the Secretary-General on the Issue of Human Rights and Transnational Corporations and Other Business Enterprises' (2006) para 60.

[19] Ibid., para 61.

In the subsequent report, the UN Special Representative notes in a similar vein that '[c]orporations increasingly are recognized as "participants" at the international level, with the capacity to bear some rights and duties under international law'.[20] However, after analysing the Universal Declaration of Human Rights, the two Covenants, and other core UN human rights treaties, the Special Representative concludes that 'it does not seem that the international human rights instruments discussed here currently impose direct legal responsibilities on corporations'.[21]

Although the current state of international law does not seem to prescribe human rights obligations for investors beyond the extent to which they are incorporated into national legislation applicable to the investor, the debate is ongoing and the conclusions reached will presumably evolve. For the time being, soft law has espoused the role of formulating and developing standards which may, at a later stage, emerge as hard law.

Several international instruments provide codes of conduct for transnational corporations. For instance, the OECD Guidelines for Multinational Enterprises (27 June 2000) are 'recommendations addressed by governments to multinational enterprises [and] provide voluntary principles and standards for responsible business conduct consistent with applicable laws'.[22] The UN Global Compact, 'a framework for businesses that are committed to aligning their operations and strategies with ten universally accepted principles in the areas of human rights, labour, the environment and anti-corruption',[23] encourages companies to adopt certain values derived from the Universal Declaration of Human Rights, the International Labour Organization's Declaration on Fundamental Principles and Rights at Work, the Rio Declaration on Environment and Development, and the United Nations Convention against Corruption.

The UN Norms,[24] which were adopted by the Sub-Commission on the Promotion and Protection of Human Rights in Resolution 2003/16 of 13 August 2003, 'comprise 23 articles ... which set out human rights principles for companies in areas ranging from international criminal and humanitarian law; civil, political, economic, social, and cultural rights; as well as consumer protection and environmental practices'.[25] There can be no doubt as to their voluntary nature, since at its 56th meeting, while taking note of the UN Norms

---

[20] J Ruggie, *Business and Human Rights: Mapping International Standards of Responsibility and Accountability for Corporate Acts* (2007) para 20 (footnotes omitted). [21] Ibid., para 44.
[22] Preface, para 1, OECD Guidelines for Multinational Enterprises, available at <http://www.oecd.org/dataoecd/56/36/1922428.pdf>.
[23] <http://www.unglobalcompact.org/AboutTheGC/index.html>.
[24] Norms on the Responsibilities of Transnational Corporations and Other Business Enterprises with Regard to Human Rights, UN Doc E/CN.4/Sub.2/2003/12/Rev.2 (2003), approved 13 August 2003 by UN Sub-Commission on the Promotion and Protection of Human Rights resolution 2003/16, UN Doc E/CN.4/Sub.2/2003/L.11 at 52 (2003), available at <http://www1.umn.edu/humanrts/links/norms-Aug2003.html>. [25] Ruggie, n 18 above, para 56.

document, the Commission on Human Rights affirmed that 'as a draft proposal' the document 'has no legal standing'.[26]

V. Invocation of Human Rights in Arbitrations

A. By the Investor

Surprisingly, human rights are rarely invoked by investors in investment arbitrations.[27] This may in part stem from the fact that in most investment arbitrations, the investors involved are not natural, but juridical persons and that only the European Convention for Human Rights provides protection for the property of juridical persons.[28] Another reason may be that the standard of protection provided by human rights instruments is typically lower than the standard contained in investment treaties and contracts.

Even in cases where human rights of the investor could have been relevant, the tribunals did not address the human rights issues. Thus, in *Biloune v Ghana*,[29] the tribunal declared that it lacked jurisdiction to examine the allegations of human rights violations.

In the case of *Patrick Mitchell v DR Congo*, the Decision on Annulment cites an extract of the (unpublished) Award, which describes the dispute as relating to:

the intervention ordered by the Military Court of the Democratic Republic of Congo and executed on March 5, 1999 when the premises housing Mr. Mitchell's firm were put under seals, documents qualified as compromising and other items were seized, the employees of the firm were forced to leave the premises and two lawyers, Mr. Risasi and Mr. Djunga, were put into prison. These individuals remained incarcerated until the day of their release by a decision of the Military Court on November 12, 1999, which also ordered the removal of the seals placed on the premises of Mr. Mitchell's firm.[30]

Clearly, the seizure of property and the incarceration of employees raise human rights issues. Yet, there is no indication that the Award considered these issues and the Annulment Decision fails to mention them at all.

---

[26] UN Commission on Human Rights, Resolution 2004/116 of 20 April 2004, see also <http://ap.ohchr.org/documents/E/CHR/decisions/E-CN_4-DEC-2004-116.doc>.
[27] The international investment arbitration cases cited are available on the ICSID homepage <http://icsid.worldbank.org> or on the Investment Treaty Arbitration homepage <http://ita.law.uvic.ca/>.
[28] For an analysis of the debate concerning the extension of human rights to juridical persons, see PT Muchlinski, *Multinational Enterprises and the Law* (2007) 509–514.
[29] *Biloune and Marine Drive Complex Ltd v Ghana Investments Centre and the Government of Ghana* (UNCITRAL), Award on Jurisdiction and Liability, 27 October 1989, 95 ILR 184.
[30] *Patrick Mitchell v Democratic Republic of Congo*, ICSID Case No ARB/99/7, Decision on the Application for Annulment of the Award, 1 November 2006, at para 1, citing para 23 of the Award, 9 February 2004 (not publicly available).

B. By the Host State

States have to date not introduced claims against investors for breaches of human rights. One of the reasons for this may be procedural: the investor's consent to arbitration is generally expressed in its request for arbitration and hence limited to the substance of the request. Another reason is that active human rights violations by the investor will most likely occur with the complicity of the host state. Moreover, as discussed above, it is uncertain to what extent non-state parties are subject to human rights obligations.

Instead, host states have relied on human rights considerations defensively to justify measures with adverse effects on the investment, arguing that their treatment of an investor was in furtherance of or necessary to protect certain international human rights commitments.[31]

Under international human rights law, the state bears obligations which include not only the prohibition of engaging in human rights violations, but also the duty to prevent the infringement of human rights by others. Failure by the host state to protect its citizens may engage its responsibility. It is in this capacity that states have invoked human rights, in particular in cases involving public utilities, yet with little success.

In *CMS Gas v Argentina*, Argentina argued that the country's economic and social crisis affected human rights and that 'no investment treaty could prevail as it would be in violation of such constitutionally recognized rights'.[32] The tribunal held that when considering the issues disputed between the parties, 'there is no question of affecting fundamental human rights'.[33]

In *Azurix v Argentina*, an ICSID case concerning water and sewage systems, Argentina raised the issue of the compatibility of the BIT with human rights treaties that protect consumers' rights and argued that 'a conflict between a BIT and human rights treaties must be resolved in favour of human rights because the consumers' public interest must prevail over the private interest of service provider [sic]'.[34] The tribunal found that the matter had not been fully argued and noted that it failed to understand the incompatibility in the specific case seeing that the services to consumers continued without interruption after the termination notice.[35]

In *Siemens v Argentina*, Argentina again claimed that given the social and economic conditions of Argentina, recognizing the property rights asserted by the claimant would disregard human rights incorporated in the Constitution.[36]

---

[31] Peterson and Gray, n 3 above, 16.
[32] *CMS Gas Transmission Co v Argentina*, ICSID Case No ARB/01/08, Award, 12 May 2005, at para 114.   [33] Ibid., at para 121.
[34] *Azurix v Argentina*, ICSID Case No ARB/01/12, Award, 14 July 2006, at para 254.
[35] Ibid., at para 261.
[36] *Siemens v Argentina*, ICSID Case No ARB/02/08, Award, 6 February 2007, at para 75.

In response to Argentina's argument, the tribunal held that the argument had not been developed and that 'without the benefit of further elaboration and substantiation by the parties, it is not an argument that, *prima facie*, bears any relationship to the merits of this case'.[37]

These awards seem to indicate the tribunals' reluctance to take up matters concerning human rights, preferring to dismiss the issues raised on a procedural basis rather than dealing with the substantive arguments themselves. In an analysis on the interactions between investment and non-investment obligations in international investment law, Hirsch notes that 'structural differences [between public international law and international investment law] have led investment tribunals to grant precedence to the contractual or consensual rules that have been agreed upon by host states and investors'.[38]

Since 'the superior position of the host state regarding influence upon the content of both domestic and international law is glaring ... investment tribunals are inclined to emphasise the obligations included in the investment agreement'.[39]

A perhaps slightly different approach is discernible in the case of *Sempra v Argentina*. Here, the tribunal acknowledged that 'this debate raises the complex relationship between investment treaties, emergency and the human rights of both citizens and property owners'. Nonetheless, it found that 'the real issue in the instant case is whether the constitutional order and the survival of the State were imperilled by the crisis, or instead whether the Government still had many tools at its disposal to cope with the situation'. It concluded that 'the constitutional order was not on the verge of collapse' and that hence 'legitimately acquired rights could still have been accommodated by means of temporary measures and renegotiation'.[40]

C. By Non-Party Actors

While invocations of human rights obligations by host states have been met with little enthusiasm, tribunals have been more willing to consider human rights issues in another context, namely that of *amicus curiae* submissions. Translated as 'friend of the court', the term *amicus curiae* is used to describe a 'person who is not a party to a lawsuit but ... has a strong interest in the subject matter'.[41]

The human rights issues involved in the participation of non-parties in the arbitration proceedings are twofold. One is procedural, the other is substantive. A procedural right of petitioners to submit *amicus curiae* briefs may be seen as

---

[37] Ibid., at para 79.
[38] M Hirsch, 'Interactions between Investment and Non-Investment Obligations' in Muchlinski, Ortino, and Schreuer, n 16 above, 154 and 173.   [39] Ibid., 179.
[40] *Sempra Energy International v Argentina*, ICSID Case No ARB/02/16, Award, 28 September 2007, at para 332.   [41] *Black's Law Dictionary* (7th edn, 1999).

emanating from their right to a fair trial, such as the one enshrined in Article 6 of the European Convention on Human Rights (right to a fair trial) or Article 14 of the International Covenant on Civil and Political Rights.

In *Aguas del Tunari v Bolivia*, the petitioners argued that international human rights principles supported their participation in the arbitration, referring to Article 14 of the International Covenant of Civil and Political Rights in support of their demand to submit briefs to the tribunal.[42] Yet, despite these arguments, the President of the tribunal refused their demand, concluding that the 'requests [of the petitioners] are beyond the power or the authority of the Tribunal to grant'. He emphasized the consensual nature of arbitration and the fact that the duties of the tribunal 'derive from the treaties which govern this particular dispute'. Since neither the applicable treaties nor the consent of the parties provided for the participation of *amici curiae*, the tribunal found that it did not 'have the power to join a non-party to the proceedings; to provide access to hearings to non-parties and, *a fortiori*, to the public generally'.[43]

It is doubtful whether the right to a fair trial is suitable to promote *amicus curiae* submissions. It confers rights upon persons 'whose rights and obligations in a suit at law are being determined by a court or tribunal'[44] and concerns the standing as a party to proceedings, rather than the possibility to submit documents and briefs as *amicus curiae*. The standing as a party for those directly concerned, such as the inhabitants of Cochabamba in Bolivia, may be desirable, yet the consensual nature of the arbitration system and its limited jurisdiction would presumably prevent it.

In a second group of cases, the admissibility of *amicus curiae* submissions were considered not so much from the point of view of the petitioners' right to a fair trail, but on substantive grounds. The human rights issues raised by the petitioners were understood to contribute to the special public interest of the arbitration and thus justified the admission of *amicus curiae* briefs.

The NAFTA case of *Methanex v United States* was the first investment arbitration in which *amicus curiae* rights were accorded. Based on an interpretation of the relevant UNCITRAL and NAFTA provisions, the tribunal concluded that 'by Article 15(1) of the UNCITRAL Arbitration Rules it [the Tribunal] has the power to accept amicus submissions (in writing) from each of the Petitioners'.[45] The tribunal noted that 'the public interest in this arbitration arises from its subject matter' and argued that 'the Chapter 11 arbitral process could benefit from being perceived as more open or transparent' so that 'the Tribunal's

---

[42] *Aguas del Tunari SA v Bolivia*, ICSID Case No ARB/02/3, NGO Petition to Participate as *Amici Curiae*, 29 August 2002, at paras 47 and 48.
[43] *Aguas del Tunari*, Letter from President of Tribunal Responding to Petition, 29 January 2003.
[44] *United Parcel Service of America v Canada* (NAFTA), Decision on Petitions for Intervention and Participation as *Amici Curiae*, 17 October 2001, at para 40.
[45] *Methanex v United States* (NAFTA), Decision on *Amici Curiae*, 15 January 2001, at para 47.

willingness to receive *amicus* submissions might support the process in general and this arbitration in particular'.[46]

In the context of NAFTA arbitration, the competence of tribunals to admit *amicus curiae* submissions was confirmed by the Statement of the North American Free Trade Commission on Non-Disputing Party Participation of 7 October 2003 which clarifies that: 'No provision of the North American Free Trade Agreement ("NAFTA") limits a Tribunal's discretion to accept written submissions from a person or entity that is not a disputing party (a "non-disputing party").'[47] Hence, in the pending *Glamis Gold v United States* (NAFTA) case, the tribunal admitted the Submission of the Quechan Indian Nation since it was of the view that 'the submission satisfies the principles of the Free Trade Commission's Statement on non-disputing party participation'.[48]

The discussion concerning *amicus curiae* evolved slightly differently in the domain of ICSID arbitrations since the Convention provided the relevant framework for procedural decisions. Yet, the NAFTA cases played a role in providing precedent for the conclusions reached by the tribunals.[49]

The tribunal in *Aguas Argentinas*[50] accepted *amicus curiae* briefs in principle since 'Article 44 of the ICSID Convention grants it [the Tribunal] the power to admit *amicus curiae* submissions from suitable nonparties in appropriate cases'.[51] It went on to say that:

Courts have traditionally accepted the intervention of amicus curiae in ostensibly private litigation because those cases have involved issues of public interest and because decisions in those cases have the potential, directly or indirectly, to affect persons beyond those immediately involved as parties in the case.

The tribunal noted that:

the factor that gives this case particular public interest is that the investment dispute centers around the water distribution and sewage systems of a large metropolitan area, the city of Buenos Aires and surrounding municipalities. Those systems provide basic public services to millions of people and as a result may raise a variety of complex public and international law questions, including human rights considerations. Any decision

[46] Ibid., at para 49.
[47] Para A.1. of the Statement of the North American Free Trade Commission on Non-Disputing Party Participation of 7 October 2003, available at <http://www.ustr.gov> and <http://www.international.gc.ca/assets/trade-agreements-accords-commerciaux/pdfs/Nondisputing-en.pdf>.
[48] *Glamis Gold v United States*, Decision on Application and Submission by Quechan Indian Nation, 16 September 2005, at para 10.
[49] See, eg *Aguas Argentinas SA, Suez, Sociedad General de Aguas de Barcelona SA and Vivendi Universal SA v Argentina*, ICSID Case No ARB/03/19, Order in Response to a Petition for Transparency and Participation as *Amicus Curiae*, 19 May 2005, at para 14; and *Aguas Provinciales de Santa Fé SA, Suez, Sociedad General de Aguas de Barcelona SA and Interagua Servicios Integrales de Agua SA v Argentina*, ICSID Case No ARB/03/17, Order in Response to a Petition for Participation as *Amicus Curiae*, 17 March 2006, at para 14.
[50] *Aguas Argentinas SA, Suez, Sociedad General de Aguas de Barcelona, and Vivendi Universal SA v Argentina*, n 49 above.   [51] Ibid., at para 16.

rendered in this case, whether in favour of the Claimants of the Respondent, has the potential to affect the operation of those systems and thereby the public they serve.[52]

The tribunal in the case of *Aguas Provinciales de Santa Fé*[53] was identical in its composition to that of *Aguas Argentinas* and the proceedings concerned the same subject matter, namely water distribution and sewage systems in an urban area. Again, the tribunal concluded that 'Article 44 of the ICSID Convention grants it [the tribunal] the power to admit amicus curiae submissions from suitable non-parties in appropriate cases'[54] and specified that water and sewage systems provide basic public services as a result of which a variety of public and international law questions, including human rights considerations, emerge and that the subject matter is hence appropriate for *amicus curiae* submissions.[55]

The case of *Biwater Guaff v Tanzania*[56] also concerned water privatization. In the Petition for *amicus curiae* status submitted on 27 November 2006, the petitioners emphasized the salient relationship of service delivery to basic human rights and needs in the water sector[57] and stressed that 'the arbitration process goes far beyond merely resolving commercial or private conflicts, but rather has a substantial influence on the population's ability to enjoy basic human rights'.[58] In its Procedural Order No 5,[59] the tribunal acceded to the *amicus curiae* petition and expressed the view that:

it [the Tribunal] may benefit from a written submission by the Petitioners, and that allowing for the making of such submission by these entities in these proceedings is an important element in the overall discharge of the Arbitral Tribunal's mandate, and in securing wider confidence in the arbitral process itself.[60]

On the basis of the reasoning provided by the tribunals, it appears that in permitting *amicus curiae* briefs, arbitral tribunals seem more moved by efforts to increase transparency and respond to public interest rather than by human rights considerations.

The revision of the ICSID Arbitration Rule 37(2) on 10 April 2006 removed all doubts over the tribunal's power to admit *amicus curiae* briefs. Rule 37(2) now provides:

After consulting both parties, the Tribunal may allow a person or entity that is not a party to the dispute (in this Rule called the 'non-disputing party') to file a written submission with the Tribunal regarding a matter within the scope of the dispute . . .

---

[52] Ibid., at para 19.
[53] *Aguas Provinciales de Santa Fé SA, Suez, Sociedad General de Aguas de Barcelona, and InterAguas Servicios Integrales del Agua*, n 49 above.   [54] Ibid., at para 16.
[55] Ibid., at para 18.
[56] *Biwater Gauff (Tanzania) Ltd v Tanzania*, ICSID Case No ARB/05/22.
[57] *Biwater Gauff*, n 56 above, Petition for *Amicus Curiae* Status, 27 November 2006, at p 7.
[58] Ibid., at p 8.
[59] *Biwater Gauff*, n 56 above, Procedural Order No 5 on *Amicus Curiae*, 2 February 2007.
[60] Ibid., at para 50.

D. By the Tribunal

The influence of human rights on investment arbitration is also demonstrated by the occasional willingness of tribunals to cite human rights documents as authority for their decisions.

In the *Tecmed* arbitration, the tribunal cited both the European Court of Human Rights and the Inter-American Court of Human Rights as authority for the existence of an indirect de facto expropriation[61] and cited the European Court of Human Rights on the principle of proportionality and the differentiation between treatment of nationals and non-nationals.[62]

In *Saipem v Bangladesh*, the tribunal relied on the European Court of Human Rights' holding that rights under judicial decisions are protected property that can be the object of an expropriation and that court decisions can amount to an expropriation.[63]

Finally, in the NAFTA case of *Mondev v United States*, the tribunal cited the European Court of Human Rights (ECtHR) as authority for the non-retroactivity of criminal legislation and on the issue of state immunity and access to courts.[64] This case deserves particular attention for its demonstration of the far-flung reach of certain human rights instruments: the arbitration involved a Canadian national and the United States, which means that although neither country involved was a party to the European Convention on Human Rights, the tribunal relied on the ECtHR's jurisprudence.

VI. Conclusion

In some respects, human rights law and investment law are very similar. Ben Hamida observes that certain substantive norms such as the prohibition of discrimination and the protection of property may be common to both investment and human rights law.[65] Moreover, both are fundamental to the process of the emancipation of the individual from the state since they both provide for proceedings between an individual and a state.[66]

In the procedural context, investment law grants more rights to the individual. Many human rights treaties still do not foresee the possibility of individual complaints by private persons, let alone juridical persons. Equally, the

[61] *Técnicas Medioambientales Tecmed, SA v Mexico*, ICSID Case No ARB(AF)/00/2, Award, 29 May 2003, at para 116.   [62] Ibid., at para 122.
[63] *Saipem SpA v Bangladesh*, ICSID Case No ARB/05/07, Decision on Jurisdiction and Recommendation on Provisional Measures, 21 March 2007, at paras 130 and 132.
[64] *Mondev International Ltd v United States of America*, ICSID Case No ARB(AF)/99/2 (NAFTA), Award, 11 October 2002, at paras 138 and 141–144.
[65] W Ben Hamida, 'Investment Arbitration and Human Rights' (2007) Transnational Dispute Management 10.   [66] Ibid., 10, referring to G Burdeau.

requirement of the exhaustion of local remedies as a condition for the exercise of jurisdiction by the international body is rare in investment law. The contrary applies to human rights law, where the necessity to exhaust local remedies is the rule.[67]

In other respects, human rights and investment law differ dramatically. The paradox of nationality as it exists in the investment context is alien to human rights law. In investment arbitration, nationality is crucial. Not only is the entire concept of BITs founded on the possession of a specific nationality, but to establish the tribunal's jurisdiction the investor must fulfil both positive and negative requirements: the investor must be a national of a state party to a particular investment instrument (be it ICSID or NAFTA). In addition, the investor must not be a national of the investment's host state. This has led to what is termed 'nationality planning'. Beyond the jurisdictional phase of proceedings, the paradoxical nature of nationality becomes apparent: discrimination on the basis of nationality is prohibited thanks to clauses mandating national and most favoured nation treatment.

By contrast, nationality is irrelevant in human rights law. Foreigners and nationals alike are guaranteed rights irrespective of any specific nationality. Transferring this approach to investment law may be possible on the basis of multilateral investment treaties with wide participation. What seems more controversial than the equal treatment of all foreigners is endowing national investors with rights against their own state, since the privileged treatment accorded to foreign investors is generally justified precisely by their quality as aliens and the desire to attract foreign investments.

The differences between the investment law and the human rights system are not restricted to matters of jurisdiction. The substantive issue of expropriation also shows great differences. In investment law, the 'all or nothing' principle is applied.[68] This means that investors are entitled to full compensation in case of an expropriation and to nothing if a legitimate regulation is found to have occurred. By contrast, the European Court of Human Rights (ECtHR) has developed a more differentiated practice based on a proportionality test which includes the amount of compensation in its considerations.[69] Rather than using the proportionality test to decide whether an expropriation has occurred, it is used to decide 'whether a suitable balancing of the State's interest to interfere and the property protection interest of the person hit by the interference has taken place'.[70] Kriebaum suggests transferring elements from the ECtHR's practice to investment law so as to integrate the level of compensation into the

---

[67] Ibid., 12.

[68] U Kriebaum, 'Regulatory Takings: Balancing the Interests of the Investor and the State' (2007) 8 Journal of World Investment and Trade 719, 720.   [69] Ibid., 730.

[70] loc cit.

proportionality test and so to prevent the dissatisfying results of an 'all or nothing' approach.[71]

The current trend seems to indicate that the role of human rights in investment arbitration will continue to increase. Whether the arbitral system is the best suited for dealing with breaches of human rights remains a controversial issue. Lack of transparency and legitimacy are perhaps inevitable reproaches[72] and it remains to be seen whether these issues can be resolved.

---

[71] Ibid., 729–743.   [72] Peterson and Gray, n 3 above, 34.

5

Investment Tribunals and Human Rights: Divergent Paths

Moshe Hirsch

I. Introduction

The topic of interactions between various branches of international law attracts widespread attention from scholars and international lawyers.[1] The spotlight has recently been directed to the interface between international investment and human rights laws.[2] The interrelationship between these two dynamic spheres is mixed. Foreign investment may promote human rights in some cases and lower their protection in others.[3]

International human rights and investment laws share some common traits, but also show some basically different characteristics. Developments in both spheres reflect a fundamental structural change in international law since World War II. Traditionally, international law mainly regulated relationships among

---

[1] M Koskenniemi, Report of the Study Group of the International Law Commission, 'Fragmentation of International Law: Difficulties Arising from the Diversification and Expansion of International Law', (2006), A/CN.4/L.682.

[2] On the ongoing arbitration proceedings between Italian investors and South Africa regarding the Black Economic Empowerment policy, see LE Peterson, 'European Mining Investors Mount an Arbitration over South African Black Empowerment', *Investment Treaty News* (14 February 2007) 2–5. On this legislation and South African investment obligations, see LE Peterson, *South Africa's Bilateral Investment Treaties Implications for Development and Human Rights*, Occasional Papers, No 26 (2006), available at <http://library.fes.de/pdf-files/iez/global/04137.pdf>.

[3] On the diverse links between human rights and investments, see, eg Report of the High Commissioner for Human Rights: 'Human Rights, Trade and Investment' of 2 July 2003, E/CN.4/Sub.2/2003/9, 8–13; K Kolben, 'Foreign Investment and Human Rights Link', *Human Rights, Trade and Investment Matters* (2006) 50–51; DL Richards et al, 'Money with a Mean Streak? Foreign Economic Penetration and Government Respect for Human Rights in Developing Countries' (2001) 45 International Studies Quarterly 219; U Kriebaum, 'Privatizing Human Rights' (2006) 3 Transnational Dispute Management 1; D Spar, 'Foreign investment and human rights – International Lessons', *Challenge*, January–February 1999, available at <http://findarticles.com/p/articles/mi_m1093/is_1_42/ai_53697782/pg_1>; LE Peterson and KR Gray, *International Human Rights in Bilateral Investment Treaties and in Investment Treaty Arbitration* (2003) 16–17; and T Weiler, 'Balancing Human Rights and Investor Protection: a New Approach for a Different Legal Order' (2004) 27 Boston College International and Comparative Law Review 429.

sovereign states (and, to some extent, among inter-governmental organisations). The rapid expansion of international investment and human rights laws highlights the growing role of non-state actors in the modern international legal system. International law rules in these spheres enhance the legal protection of individuals[4] (including foreign investors), as well as various associations and legal persons that are active in these spheres (such as non-governmental organisations and transnational corporations).

International legal rules protecting individuals and foreign investors grew from the law of state responsibility for injuries to aliens.[5] While individuals and foreign investors were primarily protected in the past by their states of nationality[6] (in accordance with the rules on diplomatic protection),[7] their protection is increasingly facilitated by various international mechanisms to which they gain direct access.[8]

One of the most fundamental features common to both international human rights and investment law is the asymmetric legal relationship between sovereign states and individuals, including foreign investors. States are in a superior position vis-à-vis individuals and foreign investors. Thus, for example, states may unilaterally change the domestic law applicable to these non-state actors, and they are in a better position to influence changes in international law (for example, through concluding international treaties).[9] Consequently, legal rules and institutions developed in these spheres strive to compensate the inferior position of individuals and investors under the domestic law by enhancing legal

[4] The expansion of international criminal law also highlights the role of non-state actors in international law. International criminal law imposes significant obligations on individuals, but by criminalizing massive and severe violations of fundamental human rights, it protects individuals. On the link between international criminal law and human rights protection, see, eg A Cassese, *International Law* (2005) 377; and RG Teitel, 'Human Rights Genealogy' (1997) 66 Fordham Law Review 301–306.

[5] On state responsibility for injuries to aliens and human rights, see, eg HJ Steiner and P Alston, *International Human Rights in Context: Law, Politics and Morals* (1996) 72–75. On state responsibility for injuries to aliens and the protection of foreign investors, see FV Garcia-Amador, 'Report on International Responsibility by Special Rapporteur' (1956) *Yearbook of the International Law Commission*, vol II, 12 ff, A/CN.4/96, available at <http://untreaty.un.org/ilc/documentation/english/a_cn4_96.pdf>; and M Sornarajah, *The International Law on Foreign Investment* (2nd edn, 2004) 89.

[6] See, eg *Nottebohm Case (Liechtenstein v Guatemala)* ICJ (1955) 4; and *Mavrommatis Palestine Concessions Case (Greece v Britain)*, 2 ILR (1924) 27.

[7] See, eg RD Bishop, J Crawford, and WM Reisman, *Foreign Investment Disputes: Cases, Materials and Commentary* (2005) 3–4; and KJ Vandevelde, *United States Investment Treaties: Policy and Practice* (1992) 7–8.

[8] Although diplomatic protection is no longer the main instrument for protecting the rights of foreign investors, states of nationality sometimes extend diplomatic protection to their investors. See, recently, *Case Concerning Diallo (Guinea v Democratic Republic of The Congo)*, ICJ (2007) 64, Preliminary Objections, available at <http://www.icj-cij.org/docket/files/103/13856.pdf>.

[9] See, eg M Hirsch, *The Arbitration Mechanism of the International Center for the Settlement of Investment Disputes* (1993) 133–134; and T Wälde, 'The Present State of Research Carried Out by the English-Speaking Section of the Centre for Studies and Research' (2007) *Hague Academy Report on Int'l Investment Law*, 76–79.

protection at the international level. While these two branches of international law address a structurally similar challenge, they have evolved along different normative and institutional paths.[10] This divergence is discussed in section IV of this chapter.

This chapter complements Chapter 4 (by C Reiner and C Schreuer). While both chapters deal with investment tribunals' approach to human rights, Chapter 4 elaborates on significant issues like jurisdiction, applicable law, and corporate responsibility, while this chapter is more focused on analysis of factors that may explain the general reluctance of investment tribunals to attach significant weight to the provisions of international human rights treaties.

Section II of this chapter briefly presents the case law of international investment tribunals that have encountered various arguments regarding the applicability and relevance of international human rights law to investment disputes. Section III briefly analyses the approach emerging from the above investment awards. Section IV discusses certain factors leading investment tribunals to adopt a reserved approach towards international human rights law, highlighting the divergence of these two legal fields along the private/public divide, as well as the employment of this approach as an instrument for evading divisive issues in international human rights law (de-politicization strategy).

II. The Case Law of Investment Tribunals

This section briefly discusses the jurisprudence of international investment tribunals that faced diverse contentions regarding the applicability and significance of international human rights instruments to investment disputes. The following awards were rendered by tribunals operating under different procedural rules (the NAFTA, ICSID, and UNCITRAL arbitration rules).

A. *Biloune v Ghana*

The dispute arose out of an investment made by Biloune (a Syrian national) and a corporation (in which Biloune was the principal shareholder) in Ghana. Biloune alleged that the Government of Ghana interfered with his investment and that by various means (including his arrest and deportation from Ghana), Ghana effectively expropriated the assets of his corporation.[11] The claimant argued, inter alia, that the above-mentioned actions of the Government of Ghana constituted a human rights violation, for which compensation was required. It was asserted that the tribunal should consider this portion of the

---

[10] On the divergent evolution of these two branches of international law, see section IV.
[11] *Biloune v Ghana*, Ad-Hoc Award, 27 October 1989 and 30 June 1990, 95 ILR (1993) 184, at 187.

claim because it was the only forum in which redress for these alleged injuries might be sought.[12]

The tribunal observed that the arbitration clause included in the investment agreement provided for arbitration of disputes between the foreign investor and the Government of Ghana in respect of an approved enterprise. Consequently, the tribunal concluded that it had jurisdiction to settle disputes regarding the alleged expropriation,[13] but not with regard to the claim for human rights violations.[14] The tribunal emphasized that its competence was limited to commercial disputes arising under the contract between the parties only in respect of foreign investment. Thus, the tribunal ruled that it lacked jurisdiction to address, as an independent cause of action, a claim of violation of human rights.[15]

B. *Mondev v USA*

The *Mondev* award includes a relatively lengthy analysis of international human rights instruments and jurisprudence. The case arose out of a commercial real-estate development contract concluded in 1978 between the City of Boston, the Boston Redevelopment Authority (BRA), and a Massachusetts limited partnership owned by Mondev International Ltd (a company incorporated under the laws of Canada). Following a dispute between the parties, Mondev filed a suit in Massachusetts' courts against the two other contracting parties in 1992. The suit was dismissed by Massachusetts' courts, inter alia, by reason of a Massachusetts statute granting the BRA immunity from suit for intentional torts.[16] Mondev subsequently brought a claim pursuant to Article 1116 of the North American Free Trade Agreement (NAFTA) for loss and damage caused to its interests. Mondev claimed that due to the above court decisions and the acts of the city and the BRA, the United States had breached its obligations under the NAFTA (particularly the clauses regarding national treatment, minimum standard, and expropriation) and sought compensation from the United States.[17]

After discussing the various arguments, the tribunal concluded that it had jurisdiction only with regard to the question of whether the conduct of the US courts in dismissing the claim against the BRA infringed the minimum

---

[12] Ibid., at 203.   [13] Ibid., at 202.   [14] Ibid., at 203.

[15] The tribunal stated in this respect: 'Long-established customary international law requires that a State accord foreign nationals within its territory a standard of treatment no less than that prescribed by international law. Moreover, contemporary international law recognizes that all individuals, regardless of nationality, are entitled to fundamental human rights (which, in the view of the Tribunal, include property as well as personal rights), which no government may violate. Nevertheless, it does not follow that this Tribunal is competent to pass upon every type of departure from the minimum standard to which foreign nationals are entitled, or that this Tribunal is authorized to deal with allegations of violations of fundamental human rights.' Ibid., at 203.

[16] See *Mondev International Ltd v United States of America*, Award, 11 October 2002, ICSID Case No ARB(AF)/99/2 (Award), 42 ILM 85, at para 1.   [17] Ibid., at para 2.

standard clause under Article 1105(1) of NAFTA.[18] In the context of the discussion as to whether the above court decisions concerning statutory immunities breached the minimum standard clause, the tribunal observed an analogy between this issue and the case law of the European Court of Human Rights (ECtHR), which interpreted Article 6(1) of the European Convention on Human Rights (dealing with access to the courts in the determination of civil rights). After discussing the case law of the ECtHR, the tribunal concluded that '[b]y parity of reasoning, there are difficulties in reading Article 1105(1) so as in effect to create a new substantive civil right to sue BRA for tortious interference with contractual relations'.[19]

On the relevance of the ECtHR's jurisprudence to this case, the tribunal explained:

These decisions concern the 'right to a court', an aspect of the human rights conferred on all persons by the major human rights conventions and interpreted by the European Court in an evolutionary way. They emanate from a different region, and are not concerned, as Article 1105(1) of NAFTA is concerned, specifically with investment protection. At most, they provide guidance by analogy as to the possible scope of NAFTA's guarantee of treatment in accordance with international law, including fair and equitable treatment and full protection and security.[20]

Consequently, the tribunal ruled that it was not persuaded that the extension of a limited immunity from suit to a statutory authority amounted in this case to a breach of Article 1105(1) of NAFTA.[21]

C. *Tecmed v Mexico*

The *Tecmed* case does not directly involve international human rights law. However, the reference made by this tribunal to the jurisprudence of the ECtHR led to further arguments and rulings by subsequent tribunals that encountered questions regarding the link between international investment and human rights law. At the heart of the dispute was the decision of Mexico's environmental agency not to renew the permit of a Spanish investor to operate a landfill of hazardous waste, citing, inter alia, environmental factors. The investor argued that this governmental measure violated the conditions on which it had made its investment as well as the 1996 bilateral investment treaty (BIT) between Spain and Mexico,[22] and that it constituted an expropriation.[23]

The *Tecmed* tribunal considered whether the decision undertaken by the Mexican agency was reasonable and proportional with regard to its goals. The tribunal emphasized the weakness of foreign investors, as the latter had reduced

---

[18] Ibid., at para 75; see also at para 92.   [19] Ibid., at para 143.   [20] Ibid., at para 144.
[21] Ibid., at para 154; see also at para 156.
[22] *Técnicas Medioambientales Tecmed, SA v Mexico*, Award, 29 May 2003, ICSID Case No ARB (AF)/00/2, (2004) 43 ILM 133, at para 40.   [23] Ibid., at para 41.

or no participation in the taking of decisions that affected them, partly because they are not entitled to exercise political rights reserved to the nationals of host states.[24] The tribunal also discussed the particular vulnerability of foreign investors to bearing an excessive share of the burden involved in the realization of public aims, and cited with approval the Judgment of the ECtHR in *James v UK*:

> Especially as regards a taking of property effected in the context of a social reform, there may well be good grounds for drawing a distinction between nationals and non-nationals as far as compensation is concerned ... non-nationals are more vulnerable to domestic legislation: ...although a taking of property must always be effected in the public interest, different considerations may apply to nationals and non-nationals and there may well be legitimate reason for requiring nationals to bear a greater burden in the public interest than non-nationals.[25]

D. *Azurix v Argentina*

The above citation of the ECtHR's decision was discussed in the *Azurix* case, which also addressed an argument regarding the relationship between investment treaties and human rights law. Azurix, a corporation established in the United States, invested in a utility that distributed drinking water and treated sewerage water in Argentina's Province of Buenos Aires. Azurix alleged that Argentina violated its obligations under the 1991 BIT between the United States and Argentina, international law, and Argentine law.[26]

One of the arguments raised by Argentina related to the consistency between the BIT provisions and international human rights law. The Government of Argentina argued that its measures leading to the termination of the investment agreement were justified by the need to protect consumers' rights. 'According to Argentina's expert, a conflict between a BIT and human rights treaties must be resolved in favor of human rights because the consumers' public interest must prevail over the private interest of a service provider.'[27] The tribunal addressed this argument briefly and noted that the matter had not been fully argued, and that it 'failed to understand the incompatibility in the specifics of the instance case'.[28]

The tribunal also discussed various arguments relating to the question of whether the measures attributed to Argentina amounted to an expropriation. Regarding the public purpose criterion, the parties referred to findings and

---

[24] Ibid., at para 122.
[25] *James and others v United Kingdom* ECHR, App No 8793/79, 21 February 1986, (1986) 8 EHRR 123, at para 50. On the ECtHR jurisprudence on the protection of property, see A Mowbray, *Cases and Materials on the European Convention on Human Rights* (2007) 895–955.
[26] *Azurix Corp v Argentina*, Award, 14 July 2006, ICSID Case No ARB/01/12, at para 3.
[27] Ibid., at para 254.   [28] Ibid., at para 261.

statements made by the tribunal in *Tecmed* with regard to proportionality between the means employed and the aim for which realization was sought. The *Azurix* tribunal referred to the above citation of the ECtHR's *James* judgment in the *Tecmed* award[29] and concluded that the elements mentioned in the *Tecmed* award provided useful guidance for the purposes of determining whether regulatory actions would be expropriatory and give rise to compensation.[30]

E. *Siemens v Argentina*

The *Siemens* award addresses arguments regarding inconsistent investment and human rights obligations, as well as the relevance of the jurisprudence of the ECtHR to investment disputes. The dispute arose from an investment made by Siemens, through a local subsidiary, in Argentina in the late 1990s. Under the investment contract between the German corporation and the Government of Argentina, Siemens had to develop a national identification control system, including supervision of the production of national identity cards. Following disputes between the parties, as well as the economic crisis, the contract was terminated by the government of Argentina in May 2001.[31]

As to the question of applicable law to the dispute, Argentina drew the tribunal's attention to international human rights instruments that had a constitutional status under the Argentine law. It was argued 'that the human rights so incorporated in the Constitution would be disregarded by recognizing the property rights asserted by the Claimant given the social and economic conditions of Argentina'.[32] The tribunal observed in this respect that the argument had not been developed by Argentina, and that without further elaboration, it was not an argument that prima facie bore any relationship to the merits of the case.[33]

The tribunal also found that Argentina's measures effectively expropriated the investment and that the latter breached several provisions of the BIT.[34] The relevance of the ECtHR's jurisprudence was addressed by the tribunal in the subsequent stage of the award that focused on the amount of compensation[35] to be paid to Siemens. Argentina argued that when a state expropriated for social or

[29] Ibid., at para 311.   [30] Ibid., at para 312.
[31] For a background to the dispute, see LE Peterson, 'Argentina liable for $217 Million in Investment Treaty Arbitration with Siemens', *Investment Treaty News* (19 February 2007).
[32] *Siemens AG v Argentina*, Award, 6 February 2007, ICSID Case No ARB/02/08, at paras 74–75.
[33] Ibid., at para 79.   [34] Ibid., at paras 273 and 309.
[35] As to the relevance of *environmental* treaties to the assessment of damages following expropriation, the tribunal in the *Santa Elena* case stated that the source of the environmental obligation which motivated the expropriation, whether domestic or international, did not alter the government's duty to compensate the investor. Similarly, the host state's international obligations did not affect the amount of compensation. *Santa Elena, SA v Costa Rica*, Award, 17 February 2000, Case No ARB/96/1, 15 ICSID Review Foreign Investment Law Journal (2000) 72, at para 71.

economic reasons, the regular 'fair market value' could not apply, because otherwise it would limit the sovereignty of a country to introduce reforms.[36] Argentina relied here on the above citation of the ECtHR in the *Tecmed* case as an example to follow in terms of considering the purpose and the proportionality of the measure taken vis-à-vis the private investor.[37]

The tribunal observed that Argentina did not develop this argument, that the consideration mentioned by the *Tecmed* tribunal was part of the latter's determination of whether an expropriation had occurred and not of its determination of compensation,[38] and emphasized the difference between the two branches of international law. The *Siemens* tribunal noted in this respect that Article I of the First Protocol to the European Convention on Human Rights (which addresses the right to property) permitted a 'margin of appreciation' not found in customary international law or the investment treaty.[39]

F. *Channel Tunnel v France and the United Kingdom*

The relevance of the provisions of the European Convention on Human Rights to investment relations was disputed between the rival parties in the *Channel Tunnel* case. The claimants, who operated the undersea rail link between France and the United Kingdom, argued that the governments of the United Kingdom and France failed to protect the tunnel ('the Fixed Link') from incursions by large numbers of clandestine migrants, and that the governments were breaching their obligations under the concession agreement and the bilateral treaty. The claimants argued, inter alia, that the obligations of France and the United Kingdom, as set out in the 1986 concession agreement, should be read in conjunction with the European Convention on Human Rights and its First Protocol regarding peaceful enjoyment of possessions.[40]

The tribunal addressed this assertion in the context of its jurisdiction and stated that:

... the Concession Agreement does not contain any contractual commitment by the States Parties that they will comply with their own or with European law....In short,

---

[36] Argentina raised also an argument regarding inconsistency between the 'fair market value' and the principle of self-determination: 'Argentina maintains that it had effectively become bankrupt, and that to maintain that an expropriation is only lawful if full market compensation is payable is incompatible with the principle of self-determination' (*Siemens*, n 32 above, at para 356 (footnote omitted).   [37] *Siemens*, n 32 above, at paras 354 and 346.

[38] Ibid., at para 354.

[39] Ibid., at para 354. On this part of the award, see L Liberti, 'The Relevance of Non-Investment Treaty Obligations in the Assessment of Compensation' (2007) 4 Transnational Dispute Management 6.

[40] *Channel Tunnel Group v Governments of the United Kingdom and France*, Partial Arbitral Award, 30 January 2007, at paras 107 and 110, available at <http://www.pca-cpa.org/upload/files/ET_PAen.pdf>.

national and European law claims against the States are to be the subject of proceedings before the appropriate national or European forums. By contrast it is for the Tribunal to deal with disputes involving the application of the Concession Agreement.[41]

Consequently, the tribunal concluded that it lacked jurisdiction to consider claims for breaches of obligations that are extrinsic to the provisions of the concession agreement and the bilateral treaty.[42]

G. *Sempra v Argentina*

The dispute arose from Sempra's investment in two natural gas distribution companies, together serving seven Argentine provinces. Sempra, a company incorporated in the United States, argued that several measures adopted by the government of Argentina in the period 2000 to 2002 resulted in breaching most of the rights it had under the regulatory framework and the investment agreement.[43] Sempra further claimed that these measures constituted an expropriation and violated the 1991 BIT between the United States and Argentina.[44]

The government of Argentina argued, inter alia, that its responsibility was excluded by the rules of international law governing the 'state of necessity' whether customary or contained in the Treaty.[45] In this context, while discussing the application of the host state's obligations in cases of emergency, the tribunal addressed Argentina's arguments regarding the need to preserve the institutional survival and constitutional order during the crisis.[46] The tribunal mentioned that during the hearing, Argentina presented the following question to a legal expert: '[W]ould Argentina have been compelled because of the Inter-American Convention [on Human Rights] to maintain its constitutional order towards the end of 2001, 2002, and afterwards?' The answer from Professor Reisman was '[y]es'.[47]

The tribunal examined whether the constitutional order and Argentina's survival were imperilled by the crisis and concluded that the constitutional order was not on the verge of collapse.[48] The tribunal explained that '[e]ven if emergency legislation became necessary in this context, legitimately acquired rights could still have been accommodated by means of temporary measures and renegotiation'.[49]

---

[41] Ibid., at para 148.
[42] Ibid., at paras 151 and 153. The tribunal also emphasized that the above statement pertained to its jurisdiction and not to the question regarding applicable law. Ibid., at para 152.
[43] *Sempra Energy International v Argentina*, Award, 28 September 2007, ICSID Case No ARB/02/16, at paras 4 and 93.   [44] Ibid., at paras 94–95.
[45] Ibid., at para 98.   [46] Ibid., at para 331.   [47] Ibid., at para 331 (footnotes omitted).
[48] Ibid., at para 332.   [49] Ibid., at para 332.

III. Investment Tribunals' Approach

An analysis of the investment awards discussed in section II of this chapter reveals a quite consistent approach undertaken by international investment tribunals with regard to the *non*-significant role of international human rights law in investment disputes. Except in the *Mondev* award in 2002, investment tribunals have declined to examine the specific provisions of international human rights instruments invoked by the parties, notwithstanding the various arguments that were raised during different stages of litigation (liability and remedies) by different parties.

Investment tribunals that encountered such arguments presented diverse explanations for their *un*enthusiastic attitude towards resorting to human rights instruments. Those reasons included lack of sufficiently elaborated arguments by the parties (the *Azurix* and *Siemens* cases), lack of jurisdiction (the *Biloune* and *Euro-Tunnel* cases), and the difference between the two branches of international law (the *Siemens* case). The *Sempra* award did not elaborate the reasons for this approach.

Three investment tribunals were ready to examine the impact of the European human rights law on investment disputes (the *Mondev*, *Tecmed*, and *Azurix* awards). Two of the three investment tribunals cited the case law of the ECtHR (the *James* case) in order to emphasize the vulnerability of investors in foreign countries (the *Tecmed* and *Azurix* cases). A later attempt by Argentina to apply the same ECtHR judgment was dismissed by the *Siemens* tribunal, emphasizing the inconsistency between the European Convention's rules regarding the 'margin of appreciation'[50] and international investment law.[51] A more balanced analysis of the case law of this Human Rights Court was undertaken by the *Mondev* tribunal.[52]

The general attitude that emerges from investment tribunals' awards with regard to international human rights law is more reserved than the approach adopted by investment tribunals regarding international environmental law.[53] Generally, investment tribunals that addressed arguments regarding inconsistencies between investment and environmental treaties did not hesitate to examine carefully the environmental treaties' provisions (such as the Basel

---

[50] On the margin of appreciation doctrine under international law and the European Convention on Human Rights, see A Mowbray, *European Convention on Human Rights* (2007) 629–633; S Shany, 'Toward a General Margin of Appreciation Doctrine in International Law?' (2006) 16 European Journal of International Law 907; and E Benvenisti, 'Margin of Appreciation, Consensus, and Universal Standards' (1999) 31 New York University Journal of International Law and Politics 843.   [51] See section II E.

[52] See section II B.

[53] For a detailed examination of investment tribunals regarding the relevance of international environmental treaties, see M Hirsch, 'Interactions between Investment and Non-Investment Obligations in International Investment Law' in C Schreuer, P Muchlinski and F Ortino, *Oxford Handbook of International Law on Foreign Investment* (2008) 262.

Convention on Hazardous Wastes and the UNESCO World Heritage Convention). This detailed examination of the international environmental instruments was intended to find whether the relevant international instruments contradict each other.[54]

It should be noted that investment tribunals have not sought to develop a consistent body of rules regarding the relationships between human rights and investment instruments, and that their jurisprudence is still in a formative period.

IV. International Investment and Human Rights Law: Divergent Paths

Several factors may explain the general reluctance of investment tribunals to attach significant weight to the provisions of international human rights treaties.[55] This section highlights the different normative and institutional concepts that underlie these two branches of international law, as well as the employment of the above reserved approach as a method to evade controversial issues in international human rights law.

As discussed above, international investment and human rights laws address asymmetric legal relations between sovereign states and individuals (including corporations). States are in a superior position vis-à-vis individuals and foreign investors. Sovereign states may, for example, change the domestic law applicable to individuals and corporations, and are in a better position to influence changes in international law.[56] Consequently, legal rules and institutions developed in those spheres strive to compensate individuals and investors that are in an inferior position under the domestic law by enhancing their legal protection at the international level. As elaborated below, while international investment and human rights laws aim to cope with a structurally similar challenge and both have grown from the rules of state responsibility for injuries to aliens, they have evolved along radically divergent paths.

A. The Public/Private Divide – Normative Features

Generally, international human rights law has evolved within the public law sphere and it primarily applies to the relationship between individuals (including legal

---

[54] This approach was undertaken by the tribunals in *SD Myers v Canada*, (2001) 40 ILM 1408, at paras 205–209, 213–215; and *SPP (ME) v Egypt*, (1994) 19 Yearbook Commercial Arbitration 51, at para 78. This approach was not undertaken where the environmental instrument was invoked with regard to the host state's obligations following *expropriation* of property. *Santa Elena v Costa Rica*, n 35 above, at para 71.

[55] On several explanations for the general reserved attitude of investment tribunals to non-investment treaties, see M Hirsch, 'Conflicting Obligations in International Investment Law: Investment Tribunals' Perspective' in Y Shany and T Broude, *The Allocation of Authority in International Law I* (2008) 323–344.   [56] See section I of this chapter.

persons) and the state.[57] Under the individual/state divide, different freedoms, rights, authorities, and obligations have been assigned to individuals and states. Keeping in mind the original inferior position of individuals, human rights law has established an impressive list of individual rights and freedoms to protect weaker parties in their relations with sovereign states.

Aiming to cope with a parallel dilemma of asymmetric relations, international investment law followed a distinctive route and focused on the private law aspects of the relations between host governments and foreign investors. Thus, investment tribunals are predisposed to attach considerable weight to reciprocal promise-based obligations (arising, for instance, from the investment contract) and reliance-based obligations (arising, for instance, from the host state's regulatory framework) that are primarily formed during the negotiations and the 'entry stage'.

During the negotiations towards a contract and the 'entry stage', the gap between the parties' legal capacities is relatively smaller. Following this stage, and during most stages of the implementation of the investment, the superior position of the host state regarding its influence upon the content of both domestic and international law is glaring. In light of this asymmetric state of affairs, investment tribunals are inclined to level the normative field and emphasize the obligations included in the investment agreement and presentations made during the 'entry stage', as well as various circumstances prevailing at this critical stage, such as the information available to both parties in this phase.

Obligations, promises, and presentations undertaken by host states and foreign investors are protected by various concepts in contemporary international investment law, such as 'umbrella clauses' in BITs that elevate various undertakings incurred vis-à-vis the investor to international law obligations,[58] 'stabilization clauses' that guard against legislative changes,[59] and 'fair and equitable

---

[57] The distinction between *jus privatum* (private law) and *jus publicum* (public law) is attributed to the Roman jurist Ulpian, who drew a distinction between laws which govern relations between citizens and the government, and the principles which govern the relations of citizens with one another. T Rowland, 'Private Law' in Garland Publishing Vol II, *The Philosophy of Law: An Encyclopaedia* (1999) 687. For an insightful analysis of the history of the public-private divide, see MJ Horwitz, 'The History of the Public/Private Distinction' (1982) 130 University of Pennsylvania Law Review 1423–1428. On this distinction, see also section V of this chapter.

[58] On 'umbrella clauses' in BITs, see, for instance, K Yannaca-Small, 'Interpretation of the Umbrella Clause in Investment Agreements', OECD Working Papers on International Investment, No 2006/3 (2006), available at <http://www.oecd.org/dataoecd/3/20/37579220.pdf>; and *Eureko v Poland*, Partial Award, 19 August 2005, at paras 78–85, available at <http://www.eureko.net/press/eureko/archives/2005-09-05.asp>.

[59] On 'stabilization clauses' in international investment law, see *Letco v Liberia*, (1987) 26 ILM 647, at 666–667; *AGIP v Congo*, (1982) 21 ILM 726, at 734–735; *MINE v Guinea* (Annulment), (1990) 5 ICSID Review (1990) 95, at para 11; T Waelde and G Ndi, 'Stabilizing International Investment Commitments: International Law versus Contract Interpretation' (1996) 31 Texas International Law Journal 216; and P Weil, 'The State, the Foreign Investor and International Law' (2000) 15 ICSID Review Foreign Investment Law Journal 401.

treatment' that protects the parties' legitimate expectations formed during the 'entry stage'.[60] International investment law (both investment treaties and tribunals' jurisprudence) largely aims to protect various private law undertakings that are made between the host state and the foreign investor.

Thus, facing mixed sovereign-individual relationships, modern international investment law inclines to 'lower' these relationships to the private law level (by emphasizing the private-law nature of the relevant undertakings), and to 'elevate' their protection to the international level (to enhance their protection).

The public/private divide between international human rights law and investment law arises also from the different scope of application, as well as the cogent and non-reciprocal nature of the rules applicable in these spheres. While investment obligations primarily bind the host state and the foreign investor *inter-se*, international human rights obligations reflect fundamental values of the international community[61] and have *erga-omnes* application (that is, states undertake international human rights obligations vis-à-vis the international community as a whole).[62] This difference, which is of major importance as regards the identity of the states that are permitted to intervene in cases of violation of the relevant obligations,[63] is emphasized by the International Court of Justice's decision in the *Barcelona Traction* case, which dealt with an investment dispute.[64]

---

[60] On the role of legitimate expectations and legal certainty in international investment law, see *Tecmed v Mexico*, n 22 above, at para 154; and *Thunderbird v Mexico*, Award, 26 January 2006, UNCITRAL, at paras 74–75. See also the comprehensive analysis of this topic in the Separate Opinion, at paras 17–43, available at <http://www.iisd.org/pdf/2006/itn_separate_opinion.pdf>; *Saluka v the Czech Republic*, Partial Award, 17 March 2006, at paras 300–308, 420–425, available at <http://www.pca-cpa.org/upload/files/SAL-CZ%20Decision%20jurisdiction%20070504. pdf>; and A Lowenfeld, *International Economic Law* (2002) 475–476.

[61] See, for instance, the Preamble to the Institute of International Law Resolution on Obligations *Erga Omnes* in International Law (2005) (hereinafter Resolution on Obligation *Erga Omnes*), available at <http://72.14.221.104/custom?q=cache:GIqqQm7n3QcJ:www.idi-iil.org/idiE/resolutionsE/2005_kra_01_en.pdf+self-determination&hl=ca&ct=clnk&cd=2&lr=lang_en| lang_es|lang_ca&ie=UTF-8>.

[62] See the definition of *erga omnes* obligations in Art 1 of the Resolution on Obligation *Erga Omnes*.   [63] See, eg Art 2 of the Resolution on Obligation *Erga Omnes*.

[64] The International Court of justice stated in this decision as follows:

33. When a State admits into its territory foreign investments or foreign nationals, whether natural or juristic persons, it is bound to extend to them the protection of the law and assumes obligations concerning the treatment to be afforded them. These obligations, however, are neither absolute nor unqualified. In particular, *an essential distinction should be drawn between the obligations of a State towards the inter-national community as a whole, and those arising vis-a-vis another State in the field of diplomatic protection. By their very nature the former are the concern of all States.* In view of the importance of the rights involved, *all States can be held to have a legal interest in their protection; they are obligations erga omnes.*

34. Such obligations derive, for example, in contemporary international law, *from the ... principles and rules concerning the basic rights of the human person,* including protection from slavery and racial discrimination ...

(Case concerning the *Barcelona Traction, Light and Power Co* (Belgium v Spain), 1970 ICJ Reports 3 (emphasis added)).

The public nature of international human rights law conspicuously arises from the mandatory character of these rights. In contrast to private *jus dispositivum* obligations, some fundamental human rights[65] are considered as *jus cogens*, namely, rules from which no derogation is permitted.[66] In addition, unlike the emphasis on reciprocal obligations in investment law, the compelling nature of human rights obligations results in the prohibition to operate countermeasures that infringe fundamental human rights.[67]

B. The Public/Private Divide – Institutional Features and Methods of Protection

An examination of the institutional traits of human rights and investment laws also reveals the public/private split between these two spheres. Investors' rights are primarily protected by arbitral tribunals, which are mainly established by bilateral or trilateral investment treaties. Diplomatic protection, exercised by the investors' states of nationality, plays only a secondary role in the settlement of investment disputes. Investment arbitral tribunals are regularly established on an ad hoc basis, and they incline to adopt the *inter-partes* model, which characterizes international commercial arbitration.[68] Thus, investment tribunals tend to focus on the particular facts of the disputes, as well as the reciprocal rights and obligations of the rival parties before them. This inclination to follow the *inter-partes* model is illustrated, inter alia,[69] by the prevalent confidential features of most

---

[65] On the peremptory nature of fundamental human rights, see, eg T Koji, 'Emerging Hierarchy in International Human Rights and Beyond' (2001) 12 European Journal of International Law 917, 927; and T Meron, 'On a Hierarchy of International Human Rights' (1986) 80 AJIL 1.

[66] See Art 53 of the Vienna Convention on the Law of Treaties, (1969) 8 ILM 679. See also R Jennings and A Watts, *Oppenheim's International Law* (1996) 7–8; and Damrosch et al, *International Law* (2001) 105–106.

[67] See Art 50(1)(b) of the International Law Commissions rules on Responsibility of States for Internationally Wrongful Acts (2001), available at <http://untreaty.un.org/ilc/texts/instruments/english/draft%20articles/9_6_2001.pdf>.

[68] See, for instance, T Wälde, 'The Present State of Research Carried Out by the English-Speaking Section of the Centre for Studies and Research', *Hague Academy Report on International Investment Law* (2007) 75–76; and G Van Harten, *Investment Treaty Arbitration and Public Law* (2007) 5–6, 58.

[69] private law adjudication, see Van Harten, n 68 above/private law adjudication, see Van Harten, n 68 above, 153–175. On the private nature of enforcement mechanisms in international investment law (and a comparison with international trade law), see A Sykes, 'Public vs. Private Enforcement of International Economic Law: Of Standing and Remedy', University of Chicago Law and Economics, Olin Working Paper No 235 (2005), available at <http://papers.ssrn.com/sol3/papers.cfm?abstract_id=671801>.

investment arbitral proceedings[70] and their occasionally inconsistent case law.[71]

International mechanisms developed to protect human rights are fundamentally different from those established in international investment law. Unlike investors' rights, which are primarily protected by ad hoc arbitral tribunals, states are often pressured to comply with their human rights obligations[72] by inter-governmental organizations (such as the United Nations or International Labour Organization),[73] special supervisory bodies established by international conventions,[74] and non-governmental organizations (NGOs).[75] International adjudicatory bodies play a significant role only in certain regional human rights regimes (mainly in Europe and in America).[76]

Unlike ad hoc investment arbitration, human rights tribunals (like the European and Inter-American courts of human rights) present clear public features: they are permanent courts and their proceedings are regularly open to the public. In contrast to the enforcement of investment obligations, exposure of human rights violations to the public is a major instrument

---

[70] For a detailed analysis of transparency clauses in the arbitration rules of UNCITRAL, ICSID, and NAFTA, see C Knahr and A Reinisch, 'Transparency versus Confidentiality in International Investment Arbitration' (2007) 6 International Courts and Tribunals 97, 98–103; and J Delaney and DB Magraw, 'Procedural Transparency' in C Schreuer, P Muchlinski, and F Ortino (eds), *Oxford Handbook of International Law on Foreign Investment* (forthcoming).

[71] See, for instance, the recent string of inconsistent decisions rendered by investment tribunals regarding the defence of 'necessity' under rules of state responsibility; *CMS Gas Transmission v Argentina*, Final Award, 12 May 2005, ICSID Case No ARB/01/08, (2005) 44 ILM 1205, at paras 304–394; and *LG&E International v Argentina*, Decision on Liability, 3 October 2006, 21 ICSID Review Foreign Investment Law Journal 155 (2006), at paras 201–266. See also A Reinisch, 'Necessity in International Investment Arbitration – An Unnecessary Split of Opinions in Recent ICSID Cases?' (2007) 8 Journal of World Investment and Trade 191; and AK Bjorklund, 'Emergency Exceptions to International Obligations in the Realm of Foreign Investment: The State of Necessity and Force Majeure as Circumstances Precluding Wrongfulness' in C Schreuer, P Muchlinski and F Ortino (eds), *Oxford Handbook of International Law on Foreign Investment* (2008) 459.

[72] Although both realist and social-constructivist approaches may explain compliance with international human rights norms, it seems that the important role of international public opinion and social pressure in the field of human rights points out that social constructivist explanations are more persuasive in this sphere. On the realist (rational-choice) and social constructivist (sociological) approaches to compliance with international law, see M Hirsch, 'Compliance with International Norms in the Age of Globalization: Two Theoretical Perspectives' in E Benvenisti and M Hirsch (eds), *The Impact of International Law on International Cooperation* (2004) 166.

[73] On inter-governmental enforcement of human rights, see Steiner and Alston, n 5 above, 347 ff.

[74] See, for instance, on the committee established by the 1966 International Covenant on Civil and Political Rights, Steiner and Alston, n 5 above, 500–556.

[75] On the significant role of NGOs in international human rights law, see T Risse and K Sikkink, 'The Socialization of International Human Rights Norms into Domestic Practices: Introduction' in T Risse, S Ropp, and K Sikkink (eds), *The Power of Human Rights* (1999), 1, 17 ff; and Steiner and Alston, n 5 above, 456–499.

[76] On these regional regimes, see Steiner and Alston, 563 ff.

for inducing states to respect their international obligations ('the politics of shame').[77]

C. Private Tribunals and Public Policy Issues

The predominantly private character of investment tribunals, and their emphasis on the private-commercial aspects of disputes between sovereign states and private investors, may well explain those tribunals' ingrained inclination to overlook public policy issues (such as human rights obligations) that are involved in investment disputes. Two of the three investment tribunals that did refer to human rights jurisprudence cited the case law of the ECtHR in order to protect investors' rights.[78] This approach of the *Tecmed* and *Azurix* tribunals[79] may be explained by the general perception of private investors as being the weaker parties in investment relations. A more balanced analysis of the case law of the ECtHR is undertaken in the *Mondev* case.[80]

The emphasis on the private law aspects of investment disputes enables investment tribunals to evade controversial legal issues in international law. Most international investment rules are included in bilateral or trilateral treaties, and the lack of dense global rules in this field is explained by various factors, prominently disagreements between developing and developed countries.[81] Legal-ideological controversies are even more conspicuous in the sphere of international human rights, and particularly with regard to the human rights of foreign investors.

Fundamental disputes regarding the content and implementation of international human rights law have often evolved along political and ideological lines (for example, East/West states, developing/developed states, Christian/Islamic states).[82] Thus, for instance, the East-West divide during the Cold War led to the bifurcation of major human rights treaties between civil and political rights on the one hand, and economic, social, and cultural rights on the other

---

[77] See, for instance, JH Lebovic and E Voeten, 'The Politics of Shame: The Condemnation of Country Human Rights Practices in the UNCHR' (2006) 50 International Studies Quarterly 861.

[78] As discussed in section III of this chapter, a later attempt by Argentina to apply the same case law of the ECtHR (*James* case) was dismissed by the *Siemens* tribunal, emphasizing the inconsistency between the European Convention's rules regarding 'margin of appreciation' and international investment law.   [79] See sections II C and II D.

[80] See section II B.

[81] See, eg MJ Trebilcock and R Howse, *The Regulation of International Trade* (2005) 457–461; M Matsushita, TJ Schoenbaum, and PC Mavroidis, *The World Trade Organization: Law, Practice And Policy* (2006) 836–838; and AB Zampetti and P Sauve, 'International Investment' in A Guzman and A Sykes (eds), *Research Handbook in International Economic Law* (2007) 211, 249–251.

[82] J Gordon, 'The Concept of Human Rights: The History and Meaning of its Politicization' (1998) 23 Brooklyn Journal of International Law 691; MW Mutua, 'Politics and Human Rights: An Essential Symbiosis' in M Byers (ed), *The Role of International Law in Politics* (2000) 149; Steiner and Alston, n 5 above, 226; and Cassese, n 4 above, 378–381. On Islamic-Christian disputes regarding the scope of the freedom of religion, see M Hirsch, 'Freedom of Proselytism under the Fundamental Agreement and International Law' (1998) 47 Catholic University Law Review 407.

hand.[83] Questions regarding the human rights of foreign investors have had particularly divisive effects among states. Disagreements between Western and Socialist countries regarding compensation for expropriations precluded the inclusion of the right to property in the 1966 human rights Covenants.[84] Thus, the focus of investment tribunals on the private law aspects of investment disputes, and on the specific legal provisions set out in the particular investment agreement or treaty, enables these tribunals to avoid highly controversial issues regarding international human rights law. In this sense, the focus on private law aspects of investment relations also constitutes a de-politicizing strategy[85] employed by investment tribunals: they are concerned that rulings on divisive issues might impair their legitimacy.

The more intensified legal-ideological controversies that often accompany international human rights disputes explain why states are more amenable to consenting to international adjudication in the investment sphere (as compared to international human rights).[86] In light of the opposition of numerous states to granting jurisdiction to international adjudicatory bodies in the human rights sphere, arbitral investment tribunals that are premised on the parties' consent[87] (particularly in the commercial sphere)[88] are cautious not to address directly human rights issues that are involved in investment disputes.

V. Concluding Remarks

The preceding analysis of investment tribunals' awards reveals a quite consistent approach: with one exception (the *Mondev* case), investment tribunals have declined to examine specific provisions of international human rights instruments invoked by the parties. This general attitude of investment tribunals is more reserved than the approach adopted by investment tribunals regarding international environmental law. While various factors may explain the general

---

[83] See, for instance, Gordon, n 82 above, 706–721.

[84] Cassese, n 4 above, 382–383; and L Damrosch et al, n 66 above, 601, 663, 672, 676. On the controversy regarding the right to property, see also Sornarajah, n 5 above, 367–371; and F Martin et al, *International Human Rights & Humanitarian Law* (2006) 911–937.

[85] It is interesting to note that channelling investment disputes to international tribunals established by BITs was designed, inter alia, to de-politicize foreign investment disputes, and reduce the tensions that often accompany intervention of governments in such disputes. KJ Vandervelde, *United States Investment Treaties: Policy and Practice* (1992) 21–25.

[86] On the opposition of states to jurisdiction of international tribunals regarding human rights issues, see, for instance, Cassese, n 4 above, 386, 388.

[87] See, for instance, the following statement regarding the jurisdiction of ICSID tribunals: 'Consent of the parties is the cornerstone of the jurisdiction of the Centre', *Report of The Executive Directors on the Convention on the Settlement of Investment Disputes Between States and Nationals of other States* (1965), available at <http://www.worldbank.org/icsid/basicdoc/partB-section05.htm>.

[88] On the central role of the parties' consent in international commercial arbitration, see, for instance, GB Born, *International Commercial Arbitration* (2001) 2–3; A Tweeddale and K Tweeddale, *Arbitration of Commercial Disputes* (2005) 33–36; and Van Harten, n 68 above, 58–59.

reluctance of investment tribunals to attach significant weight to the provisions of international human rights treaties, this chapter focuses on the fundamental public/private features that divide these two branches of international law. Both investment and human rights laws aim to cope with asymmetric relations between sovereign states and private individuals or corporations. Legal rules and institutions developed in those spheres strive to compensate the inferior position of individuals and investors under domestic law by enhancing their legal protection at the international level. While these two branches of international law address a structurally similar challenge, they have evolved along different normative and institutional paths.

International human rights law presents strong features of public law and international investment law emphasizes the private law aspects of the relations between host governments and foreign investors. Consequently, investment tribunals are predisposed to attach considerable weight to reciprocal promise-based obligations and reliance-based obligations that are primarily formed during the negotiations and the 'entry stage'. Facing mixed sovereign-individual relationships, modern international investment law inclines to 'lower' these relationships to the private law level and 'elevate' their protection to the international level. The predominant private character of investment tribunals, and their emphasis on the private-commercial aspects of investment disputes, may well explain the ingrained inclination of these tribunals to overlook human rights issues that are involved in investment disputes.

While the public/private divide is not expected to be dramatically changed, some public elements within international investment law may be strengthened in the future. Historical analysis of the public/private distinction in some domestic systems revealed that the balance between the public and private poles followed historical events (such as the rise of totalitarian regimes) and ideological trends (regarding the appropriate weight of the public interest and market theory).[89] Furthermore, legal scholars have significantly criticized the belief that private law is apolitical and ideologically neutral.[90] Consequently, future ideological changes regarding the appropriate regulation of relationships between individuals and governments may change the existing balance between private and public elements in international investment law. In addition, the ongoing process of increasing exposure of investment tribunals' proceedings to the public[91] may exert more pressure on tribunals to accord greater weight to human rights issues.

---

[89] Horwitz, n 57 above, 1426–1427.

[90] Ibid., 1425–1426. For a criticism of the public/private distinction, see P Zumbansen, 'Review Essay, Sustaining Paradox Boundaries: Perspectives on Internal Affairs in Domestic and International Law' (2004) 15 European Journal of International Law 197–211 and the references therein.

[91] See, for instance, *Biwater Gauff v Tanzania*, Procedural Order No 3, 29 September 2006, at para 133, available at <http://www.worldbank.org/icsid/cases/arb0522_procedural_order3.pdf>.

6

Limits of Commercial Investor-State Arbitration: The Need for Appellate Review

Jacques Werner

The concept of human rights is a wide-ranging one – its various aspects and their interactions with investors-state arbitration are ably discussed by the contributors of this book. I would like to concentrate my contribution on what I consider a 'neglected' human right when dealing with investors-state arbitration, namely the rights of the state hosting foreign investment and the rights of the citizens of this host state, to have their political process duly respected by arbitral tribunals acting in investment cases.

As we know it, investment arbitration has been created out of the states' decision to get out of the constraints of diplomatic protection. Many arbitrations at the turn of the 20th century, like the famous *Mavrommatis*[1] case, involved claims of individuals based on diplomatic protection, which means that these disputes were not really between the two states named as parties. As a consequence of two world wars, governments became increasingly reluctant to intervene on behalf of their nationals in investment or trade disputes, considering that investors' or traders' private interests were quite often not worth an international political crisis or, worse, a *casus belli*. Another reason for their reluctance was the increased difficulty in determining the nationality of an investor in a globalizing world where large investors frequently had a diversified capital base, a diversified management, and possibly several centres of control for their operations. Drawing investment disputes outside the ambit of inter-state dealings and transferring them to a credible depoliticized dispute settlement mechanism became a definite policy goal of a number of states, to be achieved through the new generation of investment conventions.

If the expansion of investment arbitration over the last decades corresponded in the first place to the political imperatives of preventing investment disputes

---

[1] Case of the *Readaptation of the Mavrommatis Jerusalem Concessions* (Jurisdiction), 10 October 1927, PCIJ, Series A, No 11 (1927).

from turning into political disputes, it corresponded as well to an economic imperative: to facilitate the meteoric rise of the flow of world trade and investment by settling the disputes which unavoidably would arise along the way. In shaping investment arbitration mechanisms, the state drew heavily on the international commercial arbitration system, which had proved highly successful.

However, the analogy is fallacious. Commercial arbitration rests on firm ground. Its function is to oil the wheels of international commerce by removing the little stones – the disputes between contracting parties – which might cause the system to malfunction and which the national state courts are ill-positioned to deal with. Through a network of arbitral institutions, it administers several thousands of arbitral cases each year by a process which is basically a 'one-stop shop' – no recourse, except in some very limited circumstances. This is what the parties want: they know that arbitrators can err – they are just human after all – but find that bad decisions by arbitrators are a lesser evil than having a system of appellate proceedings which can drag on and on over many years, preventing the parties from putting the dispute behind them.

In disputes of investors against their host states, the frailty of the arbitral process takes on another dimension. There are not only private business interests at stake, but the actions – for instance, imposition of new taxes – taken by the legitimate and quite often democratically elected governments of host countries. These actions may be declared unlawful by an arbitral tribunal composed of three arbitrators without any elective mandate, or even the public mandate conferred on the judiciary. Any decision rendered by an arbitral tribunal disciplining a government should be convincing enough to overcome the suspicion that investment arbitration is nothing but a ploy to derail the political will of a legitimate government or, conversely, is too timid to redress the wrongs suffered by an investor for fear of confronting a powerful host country. However, there is no magic here – arbitrators in investment disputes, like arbitrators in commercial disputes, can and will err. And the consequences of their actions are different from commercial arbitration: it is not just money as in commercial arbitration which is at stake, but the public policy of the host states.

And here comes the fallacy: while it makes eminent sense for commercial arbitration to be a 'one-stop shop', it is a highly dangerous proposition for investment arbitration to follow that pattern. The absence of a meaningful appellate level is increasingly considered by host states and their political constituencies as an unjustifiable risk on their political process.

Optimists will say that the countries wishing to attract foreign investments have no choice, as evidenced by the over 2,500 bilateral investment treaties (BITs) in existence concluded by over 180 countries, and that the encroachment on national sovereignty by the arbitral tribunal is the price to pay for ensuring foreign investors' confidence in the host government's commitments. Investment arbitration is not perfect, they will say, but a better system is yet to be designed.

One of the great fallacies of international relationships is a determinist belief that economic and political circumstances in fact dictate countries' policies, leaving them with no real choice. The contrary is true: countries, like people, always have choices, even if some are more difficult and painful than others, and countries dissatisfied with the way in which investment arbitration functions can opt out of it. And they prove it: Argentina flatly refuses to pay the CMS award[2] as long as the award has not been upheld by the local Argentine courts – in obvious violation of the ICSID Convention. Bolivia and Ecuador have withdrawn from ICSID Convention. And Venezuela has denounced its BIT with the Netherlands, which was used by scores of investors as a route for their investment in Venezuela.

Human rights of the citizens of the states concerned require that the decisions taken by their government be not annulled by an arbitral tribunal without a possible recourse to an appellate instance which could decide de novo both on the facts and the law of the case. The investment arbitration system as a whole would gain much in credibility and acceptability. To be convinced of this, it suffices to look at the WTO. Under the former GATT system, panel decisions without recourse were often the targets of political attacks. The fact that three panelists could condemn a state's action was hard to swallow. Since the WTO has instituted an Appellate Body, the decisions have greatly gained in respectability and hence acceptability. This is certainly the way to go.

---

[2] *CMS Gas Transmission Co v Argentina*, Award, 12 May 2005, ICSID Case No ARB/01/08, (2005) 44 ILM 1205; Decision of the Ad-Hoc Committee on the Application for Annulment of the Argentine Republic, 25 September 2007, ICSID Case No ARB/01/8, 44.

7

Transnational Investment Arbitration: From Delegation to Constitutionalization?

Alec Stone Sweet and Florian Grisel

The arbitral world is at a crucial point in its historical development, poised between two conflicting conceptions of its nature, purpose, and legitimacy. The larger questions raised in this volume are revealing. To what extent are arbitrators agents of contracting parties, and to what extent are they agents of a larger global community? Should ICSID, or any other arbitration house that claims to offer effective resolution of contractual disputes, resist its own judicialization? Or is judicialization, and the consequent accretion of arbitral 'governance', now inevitable? Should, or must, arbitrators recognize, interpret, and apply overarching – 'constitutional' – norms whose source is public international law? Should, or must, arbitrators balance the rights of investors against public goods, such as the protection of health, the environment, and other human rights when they assess state measures that are allegedly expropriatory, and when fashioning remedies?

In this chapter, we address such questions from the standpoint of delegation theory. In part I, we introduce the basic 'principal–agent' framework (P–A) used by social scientists to explain why actors create new institutions, and we discuss how P–A has been applied to the study of courts. We then use delegation theory to frame a response to the main themes of this book (part II). The arbitral world, we demonstrate, has a choice between two models of its own structure and function, indeed, its very identity. In part III, we focus on the judicialization of investment arbitration. In particular, we consider the extent to which it can be argued that the International Centre for the Settlement of Investment Disputes (ICSID) is developing in a judicial, perhaps even constitutional, direction.

Two caveats deserve mention in advance. First, our objectives are theoretical and explanatory: we seek to provide an account of the current state of affairs from the perspective of delegation theory. This account can be read through normative lenses – readers may support or oppose judicialization, for example – but we take no stand here on the various normative issues raised. Second, this chapter does not constitute a claim that delegation theory is superior to other analytical frameworks, or that it should replace other methods of proceeding. The 'judicialization' and 'constitutionalization' of investor-state arbitration described in parts II and III illustrate factual and legal developments that deserve wider scholarly attention and analysis.[1]

I. Principals and Agents

Over the past three decades, P–A emerged as a standard approach to research on institutions as diverse as the firm,[2] state organs,[3] and international regimes.[4] In economics, it is the dominant paradigm for analysing problems of corporate governance and industrial organization; in political science, it is associated with 'rational choice' approaches to government. Although scholars use it for varied purposes, P–A is popular for three main reasons. First, it explains the origin and persistence of institutions – or modes of governance,[5] if one prefers – in light of the specific functional demands of actors who need governance. Second, it offers ready-made, appropriate concepts that the analyst can adapt easily to virtually any governance situation. Third, it helps to organize empirical research on the dynamics of delegated governance, allowing the analyst to derive testable propositions about the consequences, *ex post*, of delegating in a particular form, *ex ante*. We outline a highly simplified version of the framework here, highlighting relevant features that are agreed upon among scholars who use it, and apply it to courts.

The P–A approach dramatizes the relationship between principals and agents, against the background of a particular set of governance problems. *Principals* are those actors who create *agents*, through a formal act in which the former confers upon the latter some authority to govern, that is, to take authoritative, legally binding decisions. The agent governs to the extent that this authority is exercised in ways that impact upon the distribution of values and resources in the relevant domain of the agent's competence. By assumption, the principals are initially in control, in the strict sense that they have unconstrained discretion to constitute

---

[1] We are grateful to Ulrich Petersmann who, noting that delegation theory is largely unknown in the scholarly discourse on transnational investment arbitration, asked us to contribute this chapter. In our view, the P–A framework is of value to the extent that it both (1) clarifies theoretically relevant questions and (2) stimulates research on these questions. For a discussion of P–A conceptions of 'member-driven' dispute settlement practices in the WTO, see the contribution by Petersmann in this volume.

[2] J-J Laffont and D Martimort, *The Theory of Incentives: The Principal-Agent Model* (2001); and P Milgrom and J Roberts, *Economics, Organization, and Management* (1992).

[3] eg K Strom, W Müller, and T Bergman (eds.), *Delegation and Accountability in Parliamentary Democracies* (2004).

[4] eg M Pollack, *The Engines of European Integration: Delegation, Agency, and Agenda-Setting in the EU* (2003); and J Tallberg, 'Delegation to Supranational Institutions: Why, How, and with What Consequences?' 25 (2002) *West European Politics* 23–46.

[5] We define governance as 'the process through which the rule systems in place in any social setting are adapted to the needs and purposes of those who live under them', A Stone Sweet, 'Judicialization and the Construction of Governance' (1999) 32 *Comparative Political Studies* 147.

(or not to constitute) the agent. Since the principals are willing to pay the costs of delegation – which include expenditures of resources to design a new institution, and to monitor its activities *ex post* – it is assumed that the principals expect the benefits of delegation to outweigh costs, over time. Put simply, delegation takes place in so far as it is functional for (that is, 'in the interest of') principals.

The most common rationales for delegation are also functionalist. Among other reasons, principals choose to constitute agents in order to help them:

- resolve commitment problems: as when the agent is expected to work to enhance the credibility of promises made either between principals, or between principals and their constituents, given underlying collective action problems;

- overcome information asymmetries in technical areas of governance: wherein the agent is expected to possess, develop, and employ expertise in the resolution of disputes and the formation of policy in a given domain of governance;

- enhance the efficiency of rule making: as when principals expect the agent to adapt law to situations (for example, to complete incomplete contracts), while maintaining the authority to update policy in light of the agent's efforts; and

- avoid taking blame for unpopular policies: as when the principals command their agent to maximize specific policy goals that they know may sometimes be unpopular with important societal actors and groups.[6]

These logics will often overlap one another.

The principals' capacity to control the agent is a central preoccupation of the approach, bordering on obsession. The rationalist assumes that any agent may have, or will develop over time, its own interests, and these will at times diverge from those of the principals. To the extent that the agent performs its appointed tasks in ways that were unforeseen and unwanted by the principals, the agent will undermine the social legitimacy of delegation (which is based on the *ex ante* preferences of principals), while producing unwanted policy that may be costly to eradicate. These losses – which we will call 'agency costs' – inhere in the delegation of discretion. Principals thus face a dilemma. In order for them to reap the benefits of delegation, they have to grant meaningful discretionary power to an agent; but the agent may act in ways that undermine the logic of delegating in the first place.[7]

---

[6] Based on M Thatcher and A Stone Sweet, 'Theory and Practice of Delegation to Non-Majoritarian Institutions' (2002) 25 *West European Politics* 4.

[7] In some situations, the expected return to delegating to the agent will be inversely proportional to limitations placed on the agent's discretion. Principals, after all, can choose to govern themselves, without the help of an agent.

The analyst assumes that principals share this anxiety. Principals will therefore seek to incentivize the agent's work in order to maximize benefits while limiting agency costs. In designing and reforming an institution, the principals choose from a complex menu of options. Principals may give an agent more or less authority to govern in a specific domain *ex ante*; they may create procedures enabling them to monitor the agent's decisions; and they may choose to retain some or no power to undo an agent's decisions *ex post*. This point can be formalized. Any agent's 'zone of discretion'[8] is constituted by (1) the sum of delegated powers (discretion to take authoritative decisions) granted to the agent, minus (2) the sum of control instruments, available for use by the principals to constrain the agent, or overturn its decisions.

The zone of discretion can be defined and assessed without regard to the principals' preferences and policy goals. Nonetheless, one expects such preferences to be fundamental to the choices made. If the principals, for example, seek to bind their successors to a policy of low inflation, they may decide to create an independent central bank, with plenary powers over macro-economic policy, while insulating the bank's decision from interference by present and future elected officials. To take another example, if principals are uncertain about the kind of policy they want, say, in a regulatory domain characterized by technical complexity and scientific risk, they may give an agent the task of developing a regulatory framework as problems emerge and evolve, while retaining effective *ex post* controls. Generally, the more principals seek to pre-commit themselves to specific outcomes or values, the more discretion they will delegate to an agent, and the weaker will be *ex post* mechanisms of control. In contrast, the more principals seek a rich range of policy alternatives from which to select, on an ongoing basis, the more they will devote resources to monitoring the agent's activities, and the more effective will be the *ex post* mechanisms of control.

The size of the zone of discretion also has implications for the strategic relationship between the principals and their agent. The smaller the zone of discretion, one might argue, the greater the agent's interest will be in monitoring and anticipating the principal's assessment of its activities. The analyst assumes that the agent is more likely to take decisions that conform to the principals' policy preferences to the extent that the agent wishes to avoid being censured and punished, or having its decisions overturned by the principals. The larger the zone of discretion, however, the less credible is that threat. In some situations – which we will label one of *trusteeship* – it is highly improbable or virtually impossible for principals to overturn the agent's decisions. A further complication flows from the fact that, in many situations, the principals are multiple actors whose preferences may change and diverge over time. Other things equal,

---

[8] Based on Thatcher and Stone Sweet, n 6 above, 5–6.

the more the principals disagree among themselves about the nature of the agent's tasks and roles, the weaker they will be vis-a-vis the agent.

To illustrate, consider variation in the zone of discretion enjoyed by different types of courts. In a system of legislative sovereignty, the courts are agents of Parliament – the principal. Their task is to enforce the various codes and statutes adopted by the legislator. The judge in such a system operates in a relatively narrow zone of discretion: Parliament can overrule undesirable judicial decisions by amending the statute, using normal legislative procedures (majority vote). Constitutional and supreme courts govern in a much wider zone of discretion. They have the authority to invalidate infra-constitutional norms, including statutes; and the constituent power made the decision rules governing constitutional amendment more complex and restrictive than those governing the making of legislation precisely in order to insulate the constitutional judge's decisions from the reach of political majorities in Parliament. Wider still are the zones of discretion of the courts of many Treaty regimes – including the European Court of Justice, the Appellate Body of the World Trade Organization, and the European Court of Human Rights. One of the peculiarities of treaty law, relative to most national legal systems, is that the decision rule governing the revision of the basic norms is unanimity among the contracting States.

We now depart somewhat from the classic P–A framework. In our view, the framework loses much of its relevance when applied to certain types of agents, in particular, those whose decision-making is insulated, as a legal or practical matter, from *ex post* controls. We prefer to apply a model of 'trusteeship' to situations wherein the principals have conferred expansive, open-ended 'fiduciary' powers on an agent.[9] A trustee is a particular kind of agent, one that possesses authority over those who have delegated in the first place. Note that the judge, in the system of legislative sovereignty, does not govern the Parliament; he or she is an agent of the Parliament's will as expressed in statutory commands. Constitutional courts are trustee courts. They typically exercise fiduciary responsibilities with regard to the constitution; in most settings, they do so in the name of a fictitious entity: the sovereign people. The political parties in Parliament are never principals, with respect to the judge of the constitution, but are themselves subject to the constitutional law, as interpreted by the constitutional judge. Put in blunt strategic terms, in normal circumstances, a trustee court does not fear reversal on the part of a principal. The trustee may well be concerned with its own legitimacy, and the polity's compliance with its decisions, but not because it worries about being 'punished'.

[9] See A Stone Sweet, 'Constitutional Courts and Parliamentary Democracy' (2002) 25 *West European Politics*, building on the contributions of G Majone, 'Two Logics of Delegation: Agency and Fiduciary Relations in EU Governance' (2001) 2 *European Union Politics* 103; and T Moe, 'Political Institutions: The Neglected Side of the Story' (1990) 6 Journal of Law, Economics and Organization 213.

Mapping out a court's zone of discretion does not tell us how the court will actually use its powers. Some predictions are nonetheless implied. Other things equal – although conditions and context are rarely equivalent – the wider a court's zone of discretion, the more likely it will be that it will come to dominate the evolution of the system as a whole. We can expect a trustee court to do so in so far as three conditions are met. First, the court must have a case load. If actors never bring cases to the court, it will accrete no influence over the system. Second, once activated, judges must resolve these disputes and *give defensible reasons* in justification of their decisions. If they do, one output of adjudication will be the production of a case law, or *jurisprudence*, which is a record of how the judges have interpreted and applied the law. Third, those who are governed by the law must accept that meaning is (at least partly) constructed through this jurisprudence, and they must use or refer to relevant case law in future disputes. None of these conditions can be taken for granted as naturally occurring; they are, rather, part of a process called *judicialization*.

In the next section, we apply these ideas to transnational arbitration.

II. Judicialization

There is no single or best way to use delegation theory. The analyst must make choices about how to model any specific P–A relationship, and these choices will have consequences on how the analysis proceeds. In this section, we will use the P–A construct to conceptualize transnational commercial and investment arbitration in two distinct ways. We expect substantial disagreement among readers about which type of model is the (descriptively or normatively) appropriate model, given that this disagreement maps onto current debates about arbitration's underlying nature and purpose.

The first model would be constructed from the classic assumptions of freedom of contract. We use the conditional tense because we are not aware of other efforts to apply a P–A to arbitration, and what follows is a simplified and abbreviated account.

A P–A relationship is constituted when two contracting parties (the principals) confer upon an arbitrator (the agent) the authority to resolve any dispute that arises under the contract. The principals are also free to select the law governing the contract and the procedures to be used in the dispute settlement process, which are assumed to constrain the arbitrator. To be sure, arbitration has been steadily institutionalized over the past five decades. Rules and procedures have been substantially codified by the major arbitration houses;[10] it is

---

[10] All established arbitration houses have published rules that are mandatory for those who choose to use their services.

now settled doctrine that arbitral clauses are separable from the main contract;[11] in many parts of the world, the scope of judicial review of arbitral awards has been radically reduced;[12] and issues of *Kompetenz-Kompetenz* have been largely resolved in the arbitrator's favour.[13] However, these developments can be said to push in the same direction: to enhance the agent's authority to enforce the parties' commitments, in the face of a party's temptation to renege, once a contractual dispute erupts.

In this account, an arbitration clause is a commitment device that the parties use to help them resolve the various collective action problems associated with contracting. The legitimacy of arbitral power is not problematic, based as it is on an act of delegation that has been freely consented to by the parties. Further, the authority of the arbitrator is limited to the domain of activity governed by the contract itself. The arbitrator will typically interpret contractual provisions in light of some law of contract, and he or she will apply these interpretations to resolve the dispute, but to the extent that he or she makes law through interpretation, reason-giving, and application, this law-making is retrospective and particular, in that it applies only to a dispute involving a pre-existing contract between two parties. Put negatively, an 'unjust' arbitral ruling is much like a bad business deal, or a good deal gone bad: both exist only 'within the sphere of private contractual prerogative'.

A second type of model would accept as given most of the precepts and logics of the first model, but would reject the view that the arbitrator is merely the agent of the contracting parties. Instead, the analyst adds a level of law and institutional complexity to the equation in order to show that the arbitrator can be meaningfully conceptualized as an agent of the transnational commercial and investment community. Consider the case of transnational commercial arbitration in which the parties to the contract are both private firms. The parties have delegated to the arbitrator, thus constituting a standard, contract-based P–A relationship. However, we would insist, this act of delegation does not take place in a vacuum, or in anarchy, but in the context of an increasingly elaborate legal system.

With the 1958 New York Convention on the Recognition and Enforcement of Foreign Arbitral Awards, signatory States made national courts the public guarantors of private arbitral authority, with regard to recalcitrant parties

[11] That is, the validity of the arbitral clause is not affected by the legal nullity of the contract of which it is a part. In essence, the doctrine forecloses moves by one of the parties to the contract to avoid arbitration by pleading the contract's nullity.

[12] That is, the legal validity of arbitral awards, and thus their enforceability in national law, is presumed.

[13] *Kompetenz-Kompetenz* refers to the formal competence of a jurisdiction to determine its own jurisdiction, or the jurisdiction of another organ. Modern arbitration statutes and case law largely accept that the arbitrator possesses the authority to fix the scope of its own jurisdiction, subject of course to the will of the contracting parties.

seeking to quash foreign arbitral awards in national jurisdictions. In the United States, a series of judicial decisions have famously embraced this role, even so far as recognizing the legitimacy of foreign arbitral awards that apply mandatory US law. In Europe too (but primarily through changes in the relevant statutes), the public policy and inarbitrability exceptions contained in the New York Convention have been narrowed to the point of practical irrelevance. A scholarly war now rages between those who, in effect, consider national courts to be the agents of foreign arbitrators, and those who would see foreign arbitrators as, in effect, agents of States who have determined that arbitration is good for business, and therefore in the national interest. This controversy is evidence, again, of increasing systemic complexity. However, we do not have to take sides in this debate in order to make a crucial point: any transnational contract containing an arbitration clause, and any transnational commercial arbitration, is embedded in a larger system of law.

If the arbitrator is not merely the agent of two contracting principals, but an agent of the greater community, then we might ask if (or assume that) the arbitrator has a responsibility to take into account the community's interests in decisions. There is a great deal of evidence showing that this is, in fact, what is happening. More and more decisions are being published, and certain kinds of decisions are treated by subsequent litigators as having precedential value.[14] Scholars refer to the emergence of an 'arbitral common law', tailored to the needs of specific categories of traders, built as the common law has traditionally been built, through reasons given that later congeal as precedent.[15] Not surprisingly, the question of whether the creation of appellate instances for the arbitral system is being actively debated.[16] Each of the major arbitral tribunals requires that arbitrators give reasons for decisions; and some have developed mechanisms for reviewing these reasons prior to approving awards. In short, arbitrators are becoming – if with some hand-wringing and reluctance – more like courts.[17]

Thus, in contrast to the first model, the second type of model does not assume that arbitrators only make law that is retrospective and particular, or encompassed entirely in the contract. Arbitrators can and should be involved in law-making that is also general and prospective. Whereas proponents of the first model must worry that such law-making would undermine the legitimacy of the agent, advocates of the second model believe that the social legitimacy of arbitration is inextricably tied to the question of how arbitrators deal with various problems faced by the community. It is telling that the insistence on giving reasons, the accretion of precedent, and calls for supervisory or appellate review

---

[14] K Berger, *The Creeping Codification of the Lex Mercatoria* (1999) 57–74, 214–20.
[15] T Carbonneau, *Lex Mercatoria and Arbitration: A Discussion of the New Law Merchant* (1997) 16–18.   [16] See part III of this chapter.
[17] F Grisel, 'Control of Awards and Re-centralisation of International Commercial Arbitration' (2006) 25 *Civil Justice Quarterly* 166; and A Stone Sweet, 'The New *Lex Mercatoria* and Transnational Governance' (2006) 13 *Journal of European Public Policy* 641–643.

are justified in the name of 'justice'. The major houses are keenly aware that the legitimacy and viability of arbitration will heavily depend upon their capacities to provide a modicum of legal certainty (justice) for both present *and* future users of the system.

We now turn to the main topic of this volume, transnational investment arbitration, wherein one party to the arbitration is a State. As Hirsch notes,[18] the standard conception of investment arbitration closely resembles that of *inter partes* commercial arbitration (essentially our first model). Investment arbitral tribunals are established on an *ad hoc* basis, and their mandate is specifically limited to the settlement of the disputes that have been submitted to them. Tribunals take authoritative decisions whose reach is limited to the parties. Proponents of the first model must find a way to integrate public sources of law into their analysis of investor-State arbitration. Like Jacques Werner,[19] among others in this volume, we believe that the first model is doomed, to the extent that the judicialization process proceeds.[20]

Finally, one of this volume's themes revolves around the question of whether investor-State arbitration has been, or is being, 'constitutionalized'. There are a number of ways in which investment arbitration may be said to be *constitutional*. First, the ICSID is a global institution that governs by virtue of, and with reference to, constituting law that has been ratified by more than 140 sovereign States. The ICSID Convention, Regulations and Rules comprise that constitution and the scope of the Centre's authority is unrivalled in its domain of activity. Most stable, treaty-based international organizations would probably be considered constitutional under this definition.

The second, forcefully advocated by, among others, Ulrich Petersmann (in this volume) takes a systemic perspective.[21] This view acknowledges that the system is not constitutional according to standard ways of thinking drawn from national systems, in so far as there is no unified sovereign in the system, and there is no agreed-upon hierarchy of norms that securely integrates international and national legal orders. In a phrase, the system remains pluralistic. Nonetheless, proponents of this perspective seek to identify those elements that can be characterized as 'constitutional', and then argue that these elements deserve to be given special status in transnational and international legal process. The most commonly invoked elements are *jus cogens* norms, basic human rights, and

---

[18] See ch 5 above.

[19] See ch 6 above. In contrast to Werner, we think that commercial arbitration is judicializing as well, n 17 above.

[20] It deserves mention that the ICSID has been considered to be more of a 'court' than an 'arbitral body' in the classic sense. B Legum, 'La Réforme du CIRDI: Vers une Juridictionnalisation de l'Arbitrage Transnational?' in F Horchani (ed), *Où va le droit de l'investissement? Désordre normatif et recherche d'équilibre* (2006) 283.

[21] See also A Stone Sweet, 'Constitutionalism, Legal Pluralism, and International Regimes' Indiana Journal of Global Legal Studies (forthcoming 2009).

procedural guarantees associated with due process and access to justice.[22] What is being argued is that these norms constitute an overarching frame, a theoretically supposed 'constitution', within which one finds discrete hierarchies, both national and treaty-based. These systems interact with one another pluralistically, with reference to the frame. One then focuses on the dynamics of pluralist interaction – on inter-regime conflict, resistance, diplomacy, and cooperation – to find evidence that the system is indeed constitutional, and to identify mechanisms of systemic construction.

In this account, the arbitrator as agent, and the ICSID arbitrator, in particular, is bound to interpret and apply these norms when they are material to any arbitral proceeding. The duty flows from the very fact that these norms are constitutional. Furthermore, it is supplemented and reinforced by other norms, such as the call in the Preamble of the Vienna Convention on the Law of Treaties that disputes be resolved 'in conformity with the principles of justice'. Following this line of argument, the ICSID arbitrator is an agent of the contracting parties, an agent of the investment community, and, at least at times, an agent of the global legal (constitutional) order.

III. The Case of ICSID

We have argued (in part I) that the wider a court's zone of discretion is, the more likely it is that it will dominate the evolution of the system as a whole, through its case law. Investor-State arbitral tribunals pose special challenges to the P–A modeller. ICSID tribunals are *ad hoc*, and the parties choose their own procedural rules and arbitrators. Further, arbitrators take decisions in light of multiple sources of law, which will typically include the contract, the relevant BIT, ICSID rules, customary international law, and so on. Interestingly, the mix of *ex ante* and *ex post* controls available to parties to arbitration differs in comparison to adjudication in national courts. In a court, where jurisdiction is compulsory and the procedures and other rules are mandatory, the analyst's attention is usually focused on the *ex post* resources available to parties or principles (those who set up and manage the system). In arbitration, the *ex ante* resources available to the contracting parties are usually relatively more important, with one important exception: an unhappy party, *ex post*, may not choose an arbitrator, now undesirable, in a subsequent case.[23] Most important, the

---

[22] Although they might object, we read Erica de Wet and Ulrich Petersmann to be representative of this view. See E de Wet, 'The International Constitutional Order' (2006) 55 ICLQ 51; and EU Petersmann, 'Multilevel Trade Governance Requires Multilevel Constitutionalism' in C Joerges and U Petersmann (eds), *Constitutionalism, Multilevel Trade Governance and Social Regulation* (2006).

[23] A more complete model would, therefore, have to take into account the extent to which any given arbitrator, or tribunal, wishes to remain in the good graces of those who select arbitrators and, therefore, is likely to take into account the interests of present and future parties in decisions. We assume that these politics (to be modelled as 'anticipatory reactions') are a normal part of the arbitral world.

parties are capable of shaping the tribunal's zone of discretion, at the contracting moment, and at the point when they constitute the tribunal. However, they must agree to do so; failure to agree will typically translate into an expansion of the tribunal's zone of discretion. Yet the fact that the parties are in dispute will usually mean that agreement to constrain a tribunal's discretionary authority may not be forthcoming.

This last point made, ICSID arbitral tribunals are the judges of their own competence (Article 41 of the ICSID Convention) and have the power to decide on any question of procedure that has not been covered by the ICSID Convention, the Arbitration Rules, or any rules agreed by the parties (Article 44 of the ICSID Convention). At the same time, the parties have limited *ex post* control instruments at their disposal. In the case of the ICSID, parties are pushed into ICSID annulment committees (Article 52 of the ICSID Convention), with highly restricted access to challenges of awards in domestic courts (Article 54 of the ICSID Convention). Further, the ICSID meets each of the three conditions stipulated at the close of part I above: it has an important and steadily expanding case load; tribunals, which are under a duty to give reasons for their decisions (Article 52(1)(e) of the Rules) have, in fact, built a sophisticated case law; and, today, States and investors argue their cases primarily in terms of this case law, accepting its precedential status.

We have also suggested that judicialization implies a move from the first to the second model of delegation (see part II above). We can give empirical content to this claim by identifying specific indicators of judicialization. In this section, we discuss four such indicators: precedent; the use of balancing and proportionality by arbitral tribunals; the admission of *amicus* briefs; and the push for appellate supervision of arbitral awards.

A. Precedent

Investment arbitral tribunals are engaged in building a *jurisprudence*: a judge-made, precedent-grounded, law of investment arbitration. They are doing so in order to stabilize (potentially explosive) strategic environments, to entrench specific frameworks of argumentation, and to legitimize their own law-making.[24] Here we focus on ICSID practice.

ICSID tribunals must give reasons, but they are not obligated to follow the past reason-giving of their colleagues. Article 53 of the ICSID Convention states that: 'the award shall be binding on the parties', which echoes, in part, Article 59 of the Statute of the International Court of Justice: '[t]he decision of the Court has no binding force except between the parties and in respect of that particular case'. In *AES v Argentina*, the tribunal developed a nuanced theory of the role of precedent in ICSID. The tribunal denied that it was strictly bound by

---

[24] M Shapiro and A Stone Sweet, 'Judicial Law-Making and Precedent' in *On Law, Politics and Judicialization* (2002) ch 2.

past decisions in any formal sense, while suggesting why arbitrators would find prior rulings, on point, of 'real interest':

> Each tribunal remains sovereign and may retain, as it is confirmed by ICSID practice, a different solution for resolving the same problem; but decisions on jurisdiction dealing with the same or very similar issues may at least indicate some lines of reasoning of real interest; this Tribunal may consider them in order to compare its own position with those already adopted by its predecessors and, if it shares the views already expressed by one or more of these tribunals on a specific point of law, it is free to adopt the same solution.[25]

More recently, some tribunals have explicitly referred to the 'duty' of arbitrators to respect precedent. Consider *Saipem SpA v Bangladesh*:

> The Tribunal considers that it is not bound by previous decisions. At the same time, it is of the opinion that it must pay due consideration to earlier decisions of international tribunals. It believes that, subject to compelling contrary grounds, it has a duty to adopt solutions established in a series of consistent cases. It also believes that, subject to the specifics of a given treaty and of the circumstances of the actual case, *it has a duty to seek to contribute to the harmonious development of investment law and thereby meet the legitimate expectations of the community of States and investors towards certainty of the rule of law*[26] (emphasis added).

The tribunal in *Saipem SpA* justified these dicta in terms congruent with our second model, openly acknowledging that multiple forms of delegation and agency are nested within one another. In addition to resolving a discrete investment dispute, a central task of the tribunal is to enhance legal certainty for the community as a whole. It will do so through rendering something akin to formal justice – *like cases shall be decided in like fashion*. The tribunal portrays this second form of delegation as tacit, but irresistible. The social demand for precedent flows from the 'legitimate expectations' of states and investors for stability and coherence.

It is today indisputable that 'a *de facto* doctrine of precedent'[27] governs investor-State arbitration: the parties intensively argue the substance and relevance of prior ICSID rulings, which tribunals accept as persuasive authority, and then cite as supportive justification for their own rulings.[28]

---

[25] *AES Corp v Argentina*, ICSID Case No ARB/02/17, Award, 26 April 2005, at para 30.

[26] *Saipem SpA v Bangladesh*, ICSID Case No ARB/05/07, Decision on Jurisdiction and Recommendations on Provisional Measures, 21 March 2007, at para 67. The tribunal in *Victor Pey Casado et Fondation 'Presidente Allende' c République du Chili*, ICSID Case No ARB/98/2, Award of 8 May 2008, repeated the formula in French, at para 119.

[27] D Di Pietro, 'The Use of Precedents in ICSID Arbitration: Regularity or Certainty?' 3 (2007) International Arbitration Law Review 96.

[28] In 2006, a second sentence was added to Rule 48, which now reads: 'The Centre shall not publish the award without the consent of the parties. The Centre shall, however, promptly include in its publications excerpts of the legal reasoning of the Tribunal.'

B. Balancing and Proportionality

A second indicator of judicialization – or, the gradual entrenchment of investment arbitration as a stable system of governance in the field of international
investment – is the deployment, by arbitrators, of modes of reasoning and
doctrinal frameworks developed by courts. Most dramatically, tribunals are in
the process of embracing balancing and proportionality.

For sound strategic reasons, investment arbitrators have constructed the 'fair
and equitable treatment' standard (FETS)[29] as a master tool for dealing with
investment disputes. Indeed, arbitrators today use the standard as a kind of
multi-purpose, umbrella principle that allows them to invoke and apply a wealth
of sub-principles, including: good faith; access to justice and due process; regulatory transparency; non-arbitrariness, non-discrimination and reasonableness;
and the legitimate expectations of both parties. Among other functions, the
FETS allows arbitrators to consider a wider range of elements than would be
normal under the tests for expropriation or regulatory takings (indirect expropriation), as well as to tailor more appropriate remedies.[30] What is important for
our purposes is that the FETS organizes an approach to the kind of disputes in
which we are interested here, namely, those involving tensions between (1) an
investor's rights (including legitimate expectations in investment security) and
(2) the State's legitimate interest in regulating for the public good (including its
expectations that investors will be good corporate citizens). Using the FETS in
this way pushes tribunals toward balancing.

Balancing pushes arbitrators toward proportionality. Tribunals find balancing
attractive because of its scope and flexibility – it allows arbitrators to 'see' the
entire contextual field and to narrow or expand their intervention as required.
Proportionality analysis will determine what the investor and the State can
reasonably expect from the other, and what is arbitrary or unfair. Balancing
under the FETS also makes it possible for arbitrators to incorporate concerns for
third-party interests. Thus, Francioni argues that 'a progressive interpretation of
the FETS ... entails that the investor who seeks equity for the protection of his
investment must also be accountable under principles of equity and fairness,
toward the host state population affected by the investment'. Arbitrators who
take this approach end up balancing the 'interests of the investor and the
interests of individuals and social groups who seek judicial protection against

---

[29] The FETS is found in virtually every Bilateral Investment Treaty. The American and Canadian
version, found in the Model BIT, provides that: 'Each party shall accord at all times to covered
instruments fair and equitable treatment, in accordance with customary international law'. The
standard European provision (Dutch, German, and Swedish, among others) states that: 'Investors
and investments of each contracting party shall at all times be accorded fair and equitable treatment
in the territory of the other contracting state.'
[30] K Yannaca-Small, 'Fair and Equitable Treatment Standard: Recent Developments' in
A Reinisch (ed), *Standards of Investment Protection* (2008) 111–130.

possible adverse impacts of the investment on their life or their environment' or human rights.[31] Although the FETS enhances arbitral flexibility, its very elasticity raises anxieties about (1) the scope of arbitral authority – can it ever be constrained at the *ex ante* contractual moment? – and (2) the determinacy of rulings – can arbitrators always get to *any* decision they want? If one accepts that these worries are well founded, then one can also see why the adoption of proportionality would make sense, in so far as it would inject a measure of analytic, or procedural, determinacy to the balancing exercise. Moreover, proportionality, properly used, requires arbitrators to reduce the losses accruing to the loser as much as is legally possible, thus enhancing their legitimacy.[32]

Proportionality is an analytical framework first developed by administrative and constitutional courts in order to manage legal disputes of a particular structure, the paradigmatic example of which concerns a pleaded tension between a right on the one hand, and a constitutionally recognized public interest pursued by the State, on the other.[33] In investor-state disputes, a move toward balancing would entail both the recognition of an investor's property rights and a 'public interest' defence available to the State. In effect, the parties acknowledge that measures taken by the defendant State have infringed the investor's rights, but that hindrance may nonetheless be mitigated or justified to the extent that the measures taken were not arbitrary, and were meant to serve a proper public good. Arbitrators using the proportionality framework will deploy means-ends testing to evaluate the impact of the State's measures on the investment; they will weigh the investor's rights against the public interest being pleaded; and their conclusions will bear upon their dispositive ruling and remedies.

No arbitral tribunal referred to proportionality, even implicitly, before 2000. In that year, a NAFTA tribunal, in the case of *SD Myers v Canada*, gave a restrictive interpretation of the FETS contained in the NAFTA (Article 1105, on the authority of domestic entities to regulate matters within their borders):

> The Tribunal considers that a breach of Article 1105 occurs only when it is shown that an investor has been treated in such an unjust or arbitrary manner that the treatment rises to the level that is unacceptable from the international perspective. That determination must be made in the light of the high measure of deference that international law generally extends to the right of domestic authorities to regulate matters within their own borders.[34]

---

[31] See ch 3 above.

[32] This will be so to the extent that the ruling is disciplined by Alexy's 'law of balancing': 'The greater the degree of non-satisfaction of, or detriment to, one principle, the greater must be the importance of satisfying the other.' R Alexy, *A Theory of Constitutional Rights* (1986, translated into English 2002) 102 and 47 on principles as 'optimization' requirements. See also A Stone Sweet and J Mathews, 'Proportionality Balancing and Global Constitutionalism' in (2008) 47 Columbia Journal of Transnational Law 73–165. [33] Ibid.

[34] *SD Myers, Inc v Government of Canada*, UNCITRAL Partial Award, 13 November 2000, (2001) 40 ILM 1408, at para 263.

Sunsequently, in *Saluka v Czech Republic* (2006), an UNCITRAL arbitral tribunal referred to the obligation, under the FETS, to balance the interests of the parties:

No investor may reasonably request that the circumstances prevailing at the time the investment is made remain totally unchanged. In order to determine whether frustration of the foreign investor's expectations was justified and reasonable, the host State's legitimate right subsequently to regulate domestic matters in the public interest must be taken into consideration as well. [. . .] The determination of a breach of Article 3.1 by the Czech Republic therefore requires a weighing of the Claimant's legitimate and reasonable expectations on one hand and the Respondent's legitimate regulatory interests on the other.[35]

Since 2003, ICSID arbitrators have pushed further, explicitly adopting the proportionality principle while citing the European Court of Human Rights (ECtHR) and its case law as a source. The ECtHR uses, and requires national courts to use, proportionality analysis when it adjudicates the qualified rights found in Articles 8 to 11 and 14 of the European Convention on Human Rights, and when it deals with the right to property in Protocol No 1. In the case of *Tecmed v Mexico*, an ICSID (Additional Facility) tribunal expressly referred to two ECtHR rulings in assessing the State's actions in light of the public interest they pursue, then declared that: 'There must be a reasonable relationship of proportionality between the charge or weight imposed to the foreign investor and the aim sought to be realized in any expropriatory measure.'[36] In *Azurix v Argentina* (2006), another tribunal referred to ECtHR jurisprudence, *SD Meyers* and *Tecmed v Mexico*, to justify employing 'the public purpose criterion as an additional criterion to the effect of the measures under consideration'.[37]

In 2006, a new front for proportionality was opened. In four arbitrations involving natural gas transportation and distribution concessions,[38] Argentina pleaded the 'necessity' defence offered by the US-Argentina Bilateral Investment Treaty. Article XI of that Treaty states:

This Treaty shall not preclude the application by either Party of measures necessary for the maintenance of public order, the fulfillment of its obligations with respect to the maintenance or restoration of international peace or security, or the protection of its own essential security interests.

---

[35] *Saluka Investments BV v Czech Republic*, UNCITRAL Partial Award, 17 March 2006, at paras 304–306.

[36] *Técnicas Medioambientales Tecmed SA v Mexico*, ICSID Case No ARB(AF)/00/2, Award, 29 May 2003, at para 122.

[37] *Azurix Corp v Argentina*, ICSID Case No ARB/01/12, Award, 14 July 2006, at paras 310–312.

[38] *CMS Gas Transmission Co v Argentina*, ICSID Case No ARB/01/08, Award, 12 May 2005; *LG&E Energy Corp v Argentina*, ICSID Case No ARB/02/1, Decision on Liability, 3 October 2006; *Enron Corp, Ponderosa Assets, LP v Argentina*, ICSID Case No ARB/01/3, Award, 22 May 2007; and *Sempra Energy International v Argentina*, ICSID Case No ARB/02/16, Award, 28 September 2007.

Both parties agreed that Article XI should be understood in light of Article 25 of the 2001 Draft Articles on the Responsibility of States for Internationally Wrongful Acts (International Law Commission), understood to reflect the state of customary international law. Article 25 reads, inter alia:

1. Necessity may not be invoked by a State as a ground for precluding the wrongfulness of an act not in conformity with an international obligation of that State unless the act:
(a) is the only way for the State to safeguard an essential interest against a grave and imminent peril; and
(b) does not seriously impair an essential interest of the State or States towards which the obligation exists, or of the international community as a whole ...

Three tribunals dismissed Argentina's claim that 'necessity' justified the measures under review. Among other things, all three interpreted the 'only means' requirement as fatal to the necessity defence if *any other means* were available. All three held that the measures in question were not the only means available, while refusing to identify other means that were available. The tribunal in *LG&E v Argentina*, however, accepted the defence, but only for a specific 'crisis' period (December 2001 to April 2003). It did so in the following terms:

With respect to the power of the State to adopt its policies, it can generally be said that the State has the right to adopt measures having a social or general welfare purpose. In such a case, the measure must be accepted without any imposition of liability, except in cases where the State's action is obviously disproportionate to the need being addressed.[39]

The Argentina gas cases raise complex interpretive questions that are beyond the scope of this chapter. What is important is that arbitrators and scholars are now actively debating whether balancing and the proportionality principle ought to govern how such 'necessity' clauses are applied.[40]

C. Third-Party Participation

The participation of *amicus curiae* in proceedings comprises a third indicator of the arbitrator as 'Agent-of-the-Community'. *Amici* briefs, by definition, represent and articulate diffuse social interests.

---

[39] *LG&E v Argentina*, n 38 above, at para 195.
[40] Compare Alvarez and Khamsi (opposing balancing and proportionality) and Van Harten (supporting a proportionality approach based on the ECtHR's case law): J Alvarez and K Khamsi, 'The Argentine Crisis and Foreign Investors: A Glimpse into the Heart of the Investment Regime' in *Yearbook on International Investment Law & Policy* (forthcoming 2009), who argue that proportionality balancing is inappropriate to investor-state arbitrations; and G Van Harten, *Investment Treaty Arbitration and Public Law* (2007) 1–2, who proposes that arbitral tribunals should embrace the proportionality approach developed by the ECtHR.

As recently as 2003, ICSID tribunals routinely denied third parties leave to submit briefs and to otherwise participate in proceedings. In *Aguas del Tunari v Bolivia*, the tribunal invoked the core elements of our first model of delegation in explicit terms:

[I]t is the Tribunal's unanimous opinion that [requests to submit *amici* briefs] are beyond the power or authority of the Tribunal to grant. The interplay of the two treaties involved ... and the consensual nature of arbitration [locates] the control of [this] issue ... with the parties, not the Tribunal. [T]he Tribunal ... does not, absent the agreement of the Parties, have the power to join a non-party to the proceedings; to provide access to hearings to non-parties and, *a fortiori*, to the public generally; or to make the documents of the proceedings public.[41]

In 2006, two tribunals decided otherwise, on the basis of inherent discretion. In *Aguas Argentinas v Argentina* and *Aguas Provinciales v Argentina*,[42] arbitrators interpreted the last sentence of Article 44 of the Rules – 'If any question of procedure arises which is not covered by ... the Arbitration Rules or any rules agreed by the Parties, the tribunal shall decide the question' – as conferring 'residual power to the Tribunal to decide' to accept *amicus* briefs or not.[43] In response, the Rules were amended (new Rule 37(2)) to confer on tribunals the authority to allow/accept the submission of such briefs, and to allow external observers to attend hearings (amendment of Rule 32(2)). Rule 32(2) was the object of extensive interpretation in an order issued by the *Suez v Argentina* tribunal.[44] The order laid down an analytical process, replete with a series of tests, for determining admissibility of *amicus* briefs. Among other things, the tribunal held that briefs must address issues of substantial 'public interest' in a case that involves public goods. We will not dwell on this matter further, since Francesco Francioni assesses these developments in this volume noting, among other insights, that these changes will enable 'the emergence ... of the idea of civil society' in the arbitral world.[45]

---

[41] *Aguas del Tunari, SA v Republic of Bolivia*, ICSID Case No ARB/02/3, Letter from the President of the Tribunal, 23 January 2003.

[42] Art 44 of the ICSID Convention: '... If any question of procedure arises which is not covered by this Section or the Arbitration Rules or any rules agreed by the parties, the Tribunal shall decide the question.'

[43] *Aguas Argentinas, SA, Suez, Sociedad General de Aguas de Barcelona, SA and Vivendi Universal, SA v The Argentine Republic*, ICSID Case No ARB/03/19, Order in Response to a Petition for Transparency and Participation as *Amicus Curiae*, 19 May 2005, at para 10; and *Aguas Provinciales de Santa Fe SA, Suez, Sociedad General de Aguas de Barcelona SA and InterAguas Servicios Integrales del Agua SA v The Argentine Republic*, ICSID Case No ARB/03/17, Order in Response to a Petition for Participation as *Amicus Curiae*, 17 March 2006, at para 11.

[44] *Order in Response to a Petition by Five Non-Governmental Organizations for Permission to Make an Amicus Curiae Submission*, ICSID Case No ARB/03/19, 12 February 2007 (*Suez* February 2007 order/decision), laying down an analytical process and a series of tests for determining admissibility of *amicus* briefs. Among other things, the tribunal held that briefs must address issues of substantial 'public interest' in a case that involves public goods. For an excellent analysis of this order, see E Triantafilou, '*Amicus* Submissions in Investor-State Arbitration after *Suez v. Argentina*' 24 Arbitration International 571–586.   [45] See ch 3 above.

D. Appeal

A fourth indicator of judicialization is the demand for appellate supervision. Traditional features of arbitration, including the *inter partes* nature of the contract and the controlling law, the *ad hoc* scope of a tribunal's jurisdiction and composition, and the final character of decisions, militate against appeal. The first model of arbitral agency forcefully denies the need for a 'vertical system of control'[46] of arbitral awards. As a former Chief Justice of the United States has stressed, one important 'advantage of arbitration is that [the] process usually need not produce a body of decisional law which will guide lawyers and clients as to what their future conduct ought to be'.[47] As we have seen, however, ICSID tribunals are behaving increasingly like courts, building and using precedent, balancing, and considering wider collective interests of various sorts in their rulings. Cast in the light of the second model of delegation, the issue of appeal is inevitably raised.

Judicial bodies find appeal useful for two basic reasons.[48] First, it provides losing parties with cathartic opportunities to defend their interests, thereby enhancing the overall legitimacy of the system. Second, systems of appeal serve the goal of achieving legal certainty and doctrinal coherence, to the extent that hierarchy and supervision increase the consistency of decisions at first instance.

In the ICSID context, appeal may be attractive for further reasons. Investor-State arbitration is of huge significance in today's globalized world; the monetary stakes involved are typically high; the good reputations of large multi-national firms and States are at risk; and important disputes will always involve significant social interests. It may be, as a renowned practitioner has argued, that the investment community needs courageous arbitrators who are willing to think and to make law creatively, in the interest of the community, and in light of social and economic change. Brave judges 'will inevitably make mistakes', Van Vechten Veeder writes, and, given the inevitability of mistakes, '[one] needs an appellate system'.[49]

As judicialization proceeds, the demand for appeal will grow. At present, there is no shortage of proposals on the table, three of which deserve mention. A first consists in the creation of a standing court of appeal, an 'ICSID Appeals Facility',[50] or a chamber of the International Court of Justice acting as a 'Supreme Investment Court'.[51] A second aims at building on existing

---

[46] K-P Berger, *The Creeping Codification of the Lex Mercatoria* (1999) 73.

[47] W Rehnquist, 'A Jurist's View of Arbitration' (1977) 32 *Arbitration Journal* 5.

[48] M Shapiro, 'Appeal' (1980) 14 Law and Society Review 629, 631.

[49] V Van Vechten, 'The Necessary Safeguards of an Appellate System' (2005) 2 *Transnational Dispute Management* 7.

[50] ICSID Secretariat, 'Possible Improvements of the Framework for ICSID Arbitration' (22 October 2004) 14 ff.

[51] A Qureshi, 'An Appellate System in International Investment Arbitration' in P Muchlinski, F Ortino, and C Schreuer (eds), *The Oxford Handbook of International Investment Law* (2008) 1154, 1165 ff.

arrangements, modelling an appellate jurisdiction on the ICSID ad hoc annulment committees.[52] A third proposal would create a permanent body that would answer preliminary questions raised on an issue-by-issue basis by arbitrators, as the European Court of Justice does under Article 234 of the Rome Treaty.[53]

IV. Conclusions

In this chapter, we have argued that two models of arbitration are in deep tension, and that this tension is gradually being resolved in ways that will make the first model obsolete. Viewed institutionally, arbitrators now preside over the process through which the rules and principles that govern investor-State relations are elaborated and defended. This volume focuses on human rights. The development of investment arbitration is itself a powerful move to recognize certain rights, attaching to the investor, including property rights, access to justice, due process, and so on. With judicialization, arbitrators increasingly behave as courts do. Most importantly, they are now finding themselves weighing the rights of investors against the public purposes being pursued by States, which may include the various ways in which States may act to protect health, the environment, and other basic human rights. They have even begun to use some of the same techniques and procedures that administrative and constitutional judges have evolved in order to enhance legal effectiveness and political legitimacy. These facts deserve wider scholarly attention than they have received.

---

[52] B Legum, 'The Introduction of an Appellate Mechanism: the U.S. Trade Act of 2002' in E Gaillard and Y Banifatemi (eds), *Annulment of ICSID Awards* (2004) 289, 295–296.

[53] CJ Tams reviews this and other proposals in 'An Appealing Option? The Debate About ICSID Appellate Structure' (2006) *Essays in Transnational Economic Law*, No 57.

8

Constitutional Theories of International Economic Adjudication and Investor-State Arbitration

Ernst-Ulrich Petersmann

I. Introduction

How should citizens evaluate the ever-more important case law of international economic courts and their sometimes inadequate responses (for example, by investor-state arbitration) to 'the governance gaps created by globalization (which) provide the permissive environment for wrongful acts by companies of all kinds without adequate sanctioning or reparation?'[1] Human rights and democratic self-governance proceed from the assumption that citizens, as democratic 'principals' of all governance agents, ought to be in a position to judge governance decisions so as to hold governments democratically accountable and defend their constitutional rights if government agents fail to protect and promote the collective 'public interests' of citizens. In all democracies, citizens entrust limited governance functions to courts and regulatory agencies (including international organizations for the collective supply of international public goods) that necessitate expertise beyond the 'common sense' of citizens. Yet, the universal recognition of human rights, including individual and democratic self-governance, requires that citizens can understand themselves as authors, legal subjects and democratic principals also of such delegated governance powers which must be seen to protect and promote citizen rights across national borders.

A citizen-oriented evaluation of economic courts is also required from the perspective of justice as 'the first virtue of social institutions'[2] and the constitutional function of courts to interpret and apply the law 'in conformity with principles of justice' and human rights. Section II of this contribution recalls that

---

[1] J Ruggie, Special Representative of the Secretary-General on the issue of Human Rights and Transnational Corporations and other Business Enterprises, Report, 'Protect, Respect and Remedy: a Framework for Business and Human Rights', UN doc A/HRC/8/5, 7 April 2008, para 3.
[2] J Rawls, *A Theory of Justice* (1973) 3.

the customary law requirement (as codified in the Vienna Convention on the Law of Treaties) of settling 'disputes concerning treaties, like other international disputes ... in conformity with the principles of justice and international law', including 'universal respect for, and observance of, human rights and fundamental freedoms for all' (VCLT, Preamble), reflects the constitutional functions of courts to interpret and apply law in conformity with the 'rule of law', justice, and human rights as constitutional restraints on the 'rule of men' and their 'rule by law'. Section III explains why some of the governance problems of the World Trade Organization (WTO) are due to power-oriented conceptions of 'principal-agent' relationships as 'member-driven governance' without regard to the constitutional functions of WTO bodies to provide collective public goods with due respect for citizens as 'democratic principals'. Sections IV and V recall how the European Court of Justice (ECJ), the European Court of Human Rights (ECtHR), and the European Free Trade Area (EFTA) Court developed diverse 'constitutional methods' of interpreting treaties among European states as 'constitutional instruments' protecting fundamental freedoms and social rights of European producers, investors, traders, and consumers. Sections VI and VII argue that the worldwide context of international economic law (IEL) differs from multilevel European constitutionalism and requires WTO and NAFTA dispute settlement bodies and investor-state arbitral tribunals to exercise more judicial deference and respect for the diversity of constitutional principles in WTO members and their regulatory discretion. Section VIII concludes that national, regional, and worldwide economic courts should promote common conceptions of rule of law and 'constitutional justice', following the *Solange* method' of multilevel cooperation among national and international courts in Europe, in order to protect transnational 'rule of law communities' for mutually beneficial economic cooperation among citizens across frontiers.

II. The Rule of Law Depends on 'Constitutional Justice'

The legal institution of impartial judges has existed since the beginnings of legal civilization and is closely related to the ideals of justice and 'rule of law' as constitutional restraints on 'the rule of men' and their 'rule by law'.[3] The functional interrelationships between law, judges, and justice are reflected in legal language from antiquity (for example, in the common core of the Latin terms *jus, judex*, and *justitia*) up to modern times (compare the Anglo-American legal traditions of speaking of courts of justice, and giving judges the title of

---

[3] On the dialectic developments of constitutional rights and principles of justice restraining the instrumental 'governance by law', see already Aristotle, *The Politics and the Constitution of Athens* (S Everson (ed), 1996), book III, para 16, 1287 a–b. For a recent historical survey, see Lord Bingham of Cornhill, *The Rule of Law, Lectio Magistralis* on the occasion of the hc degree conferred by the Faculty of Law, University of Roma Tre, 14 March 2008.

Mr Justice, Lord Justice, or Chief Justice). Like the Roman god of doors *Janus*, justice and judges face two different perspectives: their retrospective 'conservative function' is to apply the existing law and protect the existing system of rights by treating like cases (or persons) alike so as – in the words of the ancient Greek poet Simonides – to 'give every man his due'.[4] Yet, as 'rule by law' risks being abused for the 'domination' of people[5] and law regulates the dynamic social change only in incomplete ways, there is also a prospective function of impartial justice that may require 'reasonable interpretations' of legal rules so as to protect 'principles of justice' against abuses of governance powers.[6] These 'constitutional functions' of the judiciary, namely, to protect progressively evolving principles of justice (such as independence and impartiality of judges, access to courts, due process of law, legality, state duties to protect human rights) in the judicial application and protection of 'rule of law'[7] are also reflected in the customary methods of international treaty interpretation as codified in the VCLT – for example, its requirement 'that disputes concerning treaties, like other international disputes, should be settled ... in conformity with the principles of justice and international law', including 'universal respect for, and observance of, human rights and fundamental freedoms for all'(VCLT, Preamble). Why is it that WTO dispute settlement bodies and investor-state arbitral tribunals, in contrast to European courts (like the EC Court, the EFTA Court, and the ECtHR) refer so rarely to 'principles of justice' and human rights in order to rationalize and justify their ever-more comprehensive case law?

---

[4] Plato, *The Republic* (D Lee (ed), 2003) 331e.

[5] On 'rule of men' as domination, and 'rule of law' as non-domination, see P Pettit, *Republicanism: A Theory of Freedom and Government* (1997).

[6] The historical division between common law and equity law in England, where the Court of Chancery provided additional remedies in certain situations if the common law courts failed to do so, illustrates the long-standing claim by theories of justice (for example, Aristotle, *Nicomachean Ethics* (M Ostwald (ed), 1999) 1137b–1138a) that equitable and reasonable interpretation and application of the law may require judges to address particular circumstances of the dispute justifying particular interpretations (for example, of 'rules of reason' and 'rules of recognition' in the sense of HLA Hart). For modern examples of changing legal and judicial interpretations, see Ruggie's Report (n 1 above) para 19:

> Experts disagree on whether international law requires home States to help prevent human rights abuses abroad by corporations based within their territory. There is greater consensus that those States are not prohibited from doing so where a recognized basis of jurisdiction exists, and the actions of the home State meet an overall reasonableness test, which includes non-intervention in the internal affairs of other States.

[7] According to FA Hayek, *The Constitution of Liberty* (1960) 153:

> [it is] because the lawgiver does not know the particular cases to which his rules will apply, and it is because the judge who applies them has no choice in drawing the conclusions that follow from the existing body of rules and the particular facts of the case, that it can be said that laws and not men rule.

Rule of law differs from 'rule by law' and 'rule by men' in terms of constitutional safeguards such as judicial enforcement of law vis-à-vis private persons and public authorities and judicial protection of human rights and other principles of justice.

A. Diverse Conceptions of Constitutional Justice

Similar to the criticism that, in the absence of an agreed conception of the judicial role, many judges outside Europe continue to 'muddle along' on the basis of outdated assumptions (for example, of the declaratory theory of judges as '*la bouche qui prononce les mots de la loi*' or the 'originalist meaning' of the Constitution),[8] WTO dispute settlement panelists and arbitrators in investor-state disputes are often criticized for their judicial reasoning and methodologies as if the declaratory theory of law had not been discredited. Notwithstanding diplomats' frequent scepticism or ignorance of international law and 'judicial law-making',[9] legal theory is essential for understanding and performing judicial processes and justifying judicial decisions in international relations. In principle, the whole universe of diverse concepts and principles of justice – such as conventional justice (for example, in the sense of rule-following), egalitarian justice (for example, in the sense of equal treatment of beings of the same essential category), distributive justice (for example, in conformity with basic needs), retributive justice (for example, in the sense of just punishment), commutative justice (for example, in the sense of mutual advantage), and procedural justice (for example, in the sense of due process of law) – may be relevant for judicial interpretation of rules of IEL.

Since ancient Greek philosophy, concepts of justice have been closely linked with concepts of rationality and reasonable methods of conflict resolution. In the *Republic*, Plato argued that both conflicts inside the divided minds of individuals and inside the class-divided city had to be overcome by reasoning ('reviewing', 'deliberating', 'judging', and so on) and justice. Yet, as justice and fairness in matters of substance remain always contested,[10] Plato's conception

---

[8] See EW Thomas, *The Judicial Process. Realism, Pragmatism, Practical Reasoning and Principles* (2008).

[9] cf Thomas, n 8 above, 7:

> Judges make law – endlessly ... The belief that judges do not make law is hopelessly out of date ... Judges also make policy regularly ... Legal theorists who condemn legal policy-making as an aberrant departure from the true judicial interpretative function also ignore this reality ... Once it is recognised that in the course of making law judges move beyond any sensible concept of interpretation and formulate policy, it becomes important that they have some familiarity with legal theory in order to define their judicial role.

On the inevitably law-creating dimensions of judicial interpretation and clarification of indeterminate rules, see also T Ginsburg, 'Bounded Discretion in International Judicial Lawmaking' (2005) 45 Virginia Journal of International Law 631–672.

[10] Even inside the United States, there is pervasive disagreement among conservatives and democrats on human rights and democracy. See R Dworkin, *Is Democracy Possible Here?* (2006). Dworkin's proposal – ie to base constitutionalism on two basic principles of human dignity (ie first, that each human life is intrinsically and equally valuable and, second, that each person has an inalienable personal responsibility for realizing his or her unique potential and human values in his or her own life) – illustrates how limited reasonable constitutional consensus on substantive justice might be even inside one of the most stable constitutional democracies.

of justice as harmony imposed by reason continues to be challenged by a long tradition of conceiving fairness and justice in terms of reasonable procedures and principles for conflict resolution (such as *audi alteram partem*: hear the other side).[11] In conformity with the view held by both Plato and Aristotle that the reasoning faculty constitutes the most authoritative element in the human soul,[12] the legal tradition of empowering independent, impartial judges to render reasoned decisions for the settlement of disputes over conflicting claims to justice seems to be much older than agreement among citizens and countries on principles of substantive justice (for example, as defined by human rights).

Even though the idea of formal justice has always been related to some notion of equality,[13] the numerous concrete conceptions of justice (for example, in cities, states, and international relations) continue to differ on how to define the essential characteristics for 'treating like cases alike and different cases differently'.[14] Hence, it is neither a coincidence that Roman law, the medieval *jus commune*, and law merchant (*lex mercatoria*), the common law, and modern European and international economic law have dynamically evolved in response to litigation (for example, in the EC courts, the EFTA Court, WTO dispute settlement bodies, and investor-state arbitration) and judicial administration of justice, thereby complementing general legislation and incomplete agreements by judge-made rules and principles of justice.[15] Nor is it a coincidence that also other political institutions (like assemblies, parliaments, and democracy) are based on argumentative procedures whose justice depends on transparent participation, representation of all interests affected, equal opportunities for adversary arguments, and reasoned justification of restrictions of individual freedom.

In his *Theory of Justice*,[16] Rawls used the idea of reasonableness for designing fair procedures that prompt rational and reasonable citizens (as autonomous moral agents) to agree on basic equal freedoms and other principles of justice (like the equal opportunity principle, the difference principle in favour of the

---

[11] cf S Hampshire, *Justice is Conflict* (2001).   [12] See Aristotle, n 6 above, 262 (1169a).
[13] Aristotle n 6 above, 1131a: 'all men agree that what is just in distribution must be according to merit in some sense, though they do not all specify the same sort of merit.'
[14] cf. C Perelman, *The Idea of Justice and the Problem of Argument* (J Petrie (ed), 1963), who distinguishes (at 7) the following six 'most current conceptions of justice': (1) to each the same thing; (2) to each according to his merits; (3) to each according to his works; (4) to each according to his needs; (5) to each according to his rank; and (6) to each according to his legal entitlement. Perelman defines 'formal justice' as 'a principle of action in accordance with which beings of one and the same essential category must be treated in the same way' (at 16). Yet, there is no agreement on how to define the 'essential characteristic' justifying equal or different treatment in the administration of justice.
[15] cf E-U Petersmann, 'Justice as Conflict Resolution: Proliferation, Fragmentation and Decentralization of Dispute Settlement in International Trade Law' (2006) 27 University of Pennsylvania Journal of International Economic Law 27, 273–366.
[16] See Rawls, n 2 above.

least advantaged, and the lexical priority of equal liberties that may be restricted only for the sake of protecting other equal liberties).[17]

In his later book on *Political Liberalism*, Rawls reframed his theory of justice as fairness by emphasizing the importance of the constitutional, legislative, and judicial concretization and institutionalization of the principles of justice and of the public use of reason for maintaining a stable, liberal society confronted with the problem of reasonable disagreement about individual conceptions for a good life and a just society. The constitutional establishment of an independent judiciary reflects not only the normalcy and inevitability of conflicts among free individuals or among their political representatives. As the independence and impartiality of judges differentiates judicial procedures from political, legislative, and executive decision-making processes, Rawls also emphasized that, 'in a constitutional regime with judicial review, public reason is the reason of its supreme court'; it is of constitutional importance for the 'overlapping, constitutional consensus' necessary for a stable and just society among free, equal, and rational citizens who tend to be deeply divided by conflicting moral, religious, and philosophical doctrines.[18] Rawls' theory of justice aimed at constitutionally agreed limitations of conflicts between the reasonable and the rational[19] and included also a theory of civil disobedience so as to bring about changes in the law or policies of democratic governments.[20] Yet, the Rawlsian theory of justice focuses on a just society in a constitutional democracy with law-abiding citizens, without developing a comprehensive theory of conflict resolution in courts or among people who

---

[17] Rawls defined his two principles of justice in the following way (at 60):

> First: each person is to have an equal right to the most extensive basic liberty compatible with a similar liberty for others. Second: social and economic inequalities are to be arranged so that they are both (a) reasonably expected to be to everyone's advantage, and (b) attached to positions and offices open to all.

These two principles were described as a special case of a more general conception of justice that Rawls expressed as follows (at 62):

> All social values – liberty and opportunity, income and wealth, and the bases of self-respect – are to be distributed equally unless an unequal distribution of any, or all, of these values is to everyone's advantage. Injustice, then, is simply inequalities that are not to the benefit of all.

[18] J Rawls, *Political Liberalism* (1993) 231 ff.
[19] Rawls, n 18 above, 48 ff, distinguishes the reasonable and the rational as distinct, albeit complementary ideas: 'Reasonable persons ... desire ... a social world in which they, as free and equal, can cooperate with others on terms all can accept. They insist that reciprocity should hold within that world so that each benefits along with others'. 'The rational ... applies to a single, unified agent (either an individual or corporate person) with the powers of judgment and deliberation in seeking ends and interests peculiarly its own' (at 50). Another basic difference between the reasonable and the rational is 'that the reasonable is public in a way the rational is not' (at 53). The 'two moral powers' of individuals (defined as fundamental interests and capacities for a sense of social justice and for rationally pursuing one's individual conception for a good life) may conflict with the third fundamental interest of free citizens, ie to be successful in terms of the particular conception of the good they have chosen.   [20] See Rawls, n 18 above, 363 ff.

are not assumed to be free and equal and are confronted with injustices. Rawls' later work on *The Law of Peoples* defines international justice by tolerance and political deference vis-à-vis 'decent', albeit non-democratic, peoples rather than – as it is done in European law and also in some areas of UN law (for example, regarding duties to protect people against violations of human rights) – in terms of cosmopolitan protection of human rights as a constitutional precondition for international 'democratic peace'.[21]

The UN Charter and UN human rights law proceed from the 'recognition of the inherent dignity and of the equal and inalienable rights of all members of the human family (as) the foundation of freedom, justice and peace in the world', as stated in the 1948 Universal Declaration of Human Rights and reaffirmed in numerous UN human rights conventions and other UN legal practices ever since. In international law, as in domestic legal systems, respect and protection of individual rights depend on effective judicial remedies. The progressive development of rights of access to justice, from a customary international law requirement for the treatment of aliens into human rights recognized in regional and worldwide human rights treaties, has become an essential component of national and regional systems of protection of human rights.[22] Yet, the scope of such human rights of access to justice remains limited (for example, to civil, criminal, and human rights matters). International trade and investment law provides for more effective legal and judicial remedies of states and individuals than in most other areas of international law (for example, in terms of compulsory international jurisdiction, individual access to national courts, investor-state arbitration, and regional courts). However, customary international law continues to leave a wide margin of discretion to states regarding their systems of 'effective remedies' before a national court of law guaranteeing independence, impartial procedures, and 'due process of law'. National theories about the relationships among legislative, executive, and judicial branches of governance tend to be highly contextual (for example, depending on the concrete constitutional provisions and democratic traditions) and, as explained in section VII below, offer little guidance for the constitutional design of international courts. Outside Europe, constitutional theories of international conflict resolution among states, and of transnational dispute settlement procedures, hardly exist and neglect that the dispute settlement function of international courts is part of a broader

---

[21] J Rawls, *The Law of Peoples* (1999). For my criticism of Rawls' international theory of justice, see E-U Petersmann, 'International Trade Law, Human Rights and Theories of Justice' in S Charnovitz et al (eds), *Law in the Service of Humanity. Essays in Honour of F. Feliciano* (2005) 44–57. On the normalcy and morality of conflicts, and the 'paradox of reasonable disagreement' (ie rule of law as a necessary response to disagreement and conflicts of interests depends on legal respect for reasonable disagreement and on dialogue and cooperation among legal institutions), see also S Besson, *The Morality of Conflict. Reasonable Disagreement and the Law* (2005).

[22] cf F Francioni (ed), *Access to Justice as a Human Right* (2007).

'constitutional function' to settle 'disputes concerning treaties, like other international disputes ... in conformity with the principles of justice and international law' and human rights, as stipulated in the VCLT as well as in the UN Charter (Article 1).

B. Diverse Conceptions of Procedural Justice

In contrast to unilateral and bilateral dispute settlement methods, third-party dispute settlement based on arbitral or judicial procedures – especially in international relations among states as well as in transnational relations among citizens and foreign governments – cannot rely on idealistic assumptions that the parties to the dispute will agree on a reasonable settlement of their dispute after giving and listening to reasons. The lack of effective enforcement mechanisms in many international jurisdictions increases the risk of non-compliance if judgments (for example, WTO dispute settlement rulings requiring changes in domestic legislation) are not perceived as just. Many dispute settlement procedures also fail to specify judicial remedies in case of persistent non-compliance.

For example, the WTO Dispute Settlement Understanding includes only few rules on 'mutually acceptable compensation' (DSU, Article 22.2) and alternative countermeasures 'equivalent to the level of nullification or impairment' (Articles 22.4 and 22.7); hence, the so far 10 WTO arbitrations on the calculation and design of trade sanctions in response to non-compliance with WTO dispute settlement rulings used diverse methods for calculating damages in order to determine an adequate level of compensation for WTO breach (as was done in the *US-Copyright* case) or the maximum level of countermeasures that victims of WTO violations may impose (as was done in the *Bananas* and *Hormones* arbitrations against the EC and the *FSC, Byrd Amendment, Gambling*, and *Cotton* arbitration procedures against the United States).[23] The findings by the arbitrators in *US-Byrd Amendment* – that 'it is not completely clear what role is to be played by the suspension of obligations in the DSU, and a large part of the conceptual debate that took place in these proceedings could have been avoided if a clear object and purpose were identified'[24] – explain the diversity of arbitral findings on the clarification of the unclear DSU provisions in the light of their multiple objectives (for example, compensation by means of 'rebalancing' of

[23] cf J Pauwelyn, *Optimal Protection of International Law* (2008), who analyses the WTO arbitral awards and legal literature on whether the ultimate objectives of 'compensation and suspension of concessions' (DSU, Art 22) are to rebalance the original bargain, to compensate the victim, to induce compliance with WTO obligations, and/or to punish the violator, and compares these DSU rules with other WTO rules on suspension of concessions (eg pursuant to GATT, Articles XIX and XXVIII).

[24] WTO Decision by the Arbitrator, *United States – Continued Dumping and Subsidy Offset Act of 2000 (US-Byrd Amendment) – Recourse to Arbitration by the United States Under Article 22.6 of the DSU*, WT/DS217, 234/ARB/CHL, 31 August 2004, at para 6.4.

reciprocal concessions or damages, sanctions in order to induce compliance and deter non-compliance with WTO rules) and underlying principles (for example, of reciprocity, 'security and predictability', and proportionality).

Theories of procedural justice in private litigation are based on assumptions of private party autonomy and models – such as the 'accuracy model' (assuming that the aim of civil dispute resolution is the correct application of the law to the facts), the 'balancing model' (assuming that the aim of civil procedure is to strike a fair balance between the costs and benefits of adjudication), and the 'participation model' (assuming that the very ideal of a correct outcome must be understood as a function of process that guarantees fair and equal participation)[25] – that may not fit 'public interest litigation' among states or investor-state arbitration involving public interests. For example, Solum's 'participatory legitimacy thesis' (namely, that the procedural justice of a judgment requires that those who are finally bound and incur the costs have reasonable opportunities to participate in the proceedings) may not be respected in investor-state arbitration and WTO disputes if government bureaucracies identify their 'public interests' with their bureaucratic self-interests without adequate regard to adversely affected citizen interests (for example, in terms of general consumer welfare, tax-payer interests, and rule of law). Solum's 'accuracy principle' (specifying the achievement of legally correct outcomes as the criterion for measuring procedural fairness) may be perceived differently by government actors which have self-interests in political compromises (for example, secretive 'voluntary export restraints') that prevent correct public information.

Depending on the jurisdiction, submissions by the parties, and applicable private law (for example, in investment disputes based on contract claims and commercial UNCITRAL procedures) and public law (for example, in disputes based on treaty claims and ICSID arbitration or procedures in the International Court of Justice), investor-state dispute settlement procedures may require similar judicial approaches (for example, to fact-gathering, distribution of burden of proof, and 'judicial economy') or different judicial approaches to procedural issues (such as confidentiality of procedures and awards in private commercial arbitration, and the possibility of *amicus curiae* briefs by third parties in ICSID, NAFTA, and WTO disputes) as well as to the substantive task of judges to interpret and apply the law in conformity with relevant 'principles of justice', for example:

- when distinguishing between formal, distributive, and corrective justice in the interpretation of WTO provisions for special and differential treatment of less-developed countries;

---

[25] These models are discussed by LB Solum, 'Procedural Justice', University of San Diego Legal Working Paper Series 2004. Also T Ralli, *Justice through Legal Dispute* (European University doctoral thesis, 2008) focuses on private law disputes and contract law adjudication.

- for reviewing the substantive justice of power-oriented rules (for example, in the judicial application of international law rules recognizing and sanctioning the 'lending privilege' of governments if loans were evidently diverted by corrupt bureaucracies); and
- for judicial protection of 'reasonable expectations' by private and public actors that courts will decide future disputes in conformity with past legal and judicial precedents.

Furthermore, the style of drafting dispute settlement reports tends to differ considerably depending on whether the reports are submitted to governments (for example, some WTO panel reports with more than 1,000 pages in 'WTO legalese' that is incomprehensible for most private citizens) or to private parties. The fact that, in both GATT 1947 as well as in WTO dispute settlement proceedings, complainants have tended to win more than 80 per cent of all panel proceedings differs markedly from normal success rates in private litigation or in European courts. Yet, this systemic disparity in success rates appears to be due to GATT/WTO consultations (which lead to the settlement or abandonment of more than one-half of all GATT/WTO complaints) and to the comprehensive GATT/WTO prohibitions of border discrimination (which induce respondents to replace discriminatory with non-discriminatory regulation) rather than to any legal biases in GATT/WTO dispute settlement practices.

C. The Need for Principle-Oriented and Teleological Interpretation of Indeterminate WTO Rules

The Agreement establishing the WTO is explicitly committed 'to preserve the basic principles and to further the objectives underlying this multilateral trading system' (WTO Agreement, Preamble). Yet, as discussed in the following sections, the EC courts, the EFTA Court, and the European Court of Human Rights (ECtHR) have insisted much more strongly on their judicial task of promoting 'constitutional justice' than GATT and WTO dispute settlement bodies and investor-state arbitral tribunals. GATT 1947 dispute settlement panels often perceived administration of justice in terms of managing intergovernmental disputes on the basis of narrow, textual interpretations of GATT rules, frequently without independent legal advice, without recourse to the customary methods of international treaty interpretation, and without thorough judicial analysis of explicit requirements of reasonableness, equity, or fairness in the application of GATT rules (for example, the requirement of a 'reasonable basis' and 'fair comparison between the export price and the domestic price' in anti-dumping calculations, or the prohibition of export subsidies resulting 'in that contracting party having more than an equitable share of world export trade in that product'). For example, it was only in the *EC Bed Linen* case that the Appellate Body emphasized the explicit requirement (in Article 2 of the 1979 and 1994 Agreements on Implementation of Article VI GATT) of a 'fair comparison' in order to find that, in the EC's calculation of anti-dumping duties, the EC should have 'compared the weighted average normal value with the weighted average of all comparable export transactions'.[26] In *US-Softwood Lumber V (Article 21.5-Canada)*, the Appellate Body insisted once again that 'the use of zeroing under the transaction-to-transaction methodology is difficult to reconcile with the notions of impartiality, even-handedness and lack of bias reflected in the 'fair comparison' requirement in Article 2.4' because it 'distorts' certain export price calculations and thereby 'inflates' dumping margins.[27]

The Appellate Body jurisprudence regarding the 'general exceptions' in GATT, Article XX offers another example for the need to interpret WTO rules in the light of their underlying legal principles (such as maintaining 'a balance of rights and obligations') and objectives (such as prevention of 'abuse of the exceptions'), which prompted the Appellate Body to clarify that:

> Determination of whether a measure, which is not 'indispensable', may nevertheless be 'necessary' within the contemplation of Article XX(d), involves in every case a process of weighing and balancing a series of factors which prominently include the contribution made by the compliance measure to the enforcement of the law or regulation at issue, the importance of the common interests or values protected by that law or regulation, and the accompanying impact of the law or regulation on imports or exports.[28]

Interpreting the contested meaning of WTO provisions 'in conformity with principles of justice', as required by the customary methods of treaty interpretation, calls for more systematic clarification of the objectives and principles underlying WTO rules through judicial reasoning and its intergovernmental criticism in the WTO Dispute Settlement Body (DSB), with due regard to the

---

[26] WTO Appellate Body Report, *EC-Bed Linen*, WT/DS141/AB/R, adopted 12 March 2001, at para 55. This interpretation of the 'fair comparison' requirement, which was subsequently confirmed by the Appellate Body in five additional rulings, had been rejected by an earlier GATT panel report (*EC-Audio Cassettes*, ADP/136 of 28 April 1995, not adopted, at para 356) on the basis of the argument that:

> if the existence and extent of dumping and the imposition of duties had been conducted on a transaction-to-transaction basis, the EC would have been entitled to impose a duty with respect to dumped transactions, where injury existed, irrespective of the prices at which other un-dumped transactions occurred.

Such narrow, textual interpretations of rules without regard to their underlying principles (such as the requirement of a 'fair comparison' in the inevitable aggregation and averaging of multiple price comparisons) was characteristic of many 'bureaucratic interpretations' of GATT 1947 and the 1979 Tokyo Round Agreements at the insistence of GATT diplomats and GATT officials who, even after the establishment of a GATT Legal Division in 1983, often continued to prevent GATT panellists from receiving independent legal advice.
[27] WTO Appellate Body Report, *US-Softwood Lumber V (Article 21.5-Canada)*, WT/DS264/AB/RW, adopted 1 September 2006, at paras 138–140.
[28] WTO Appellate Body Report, *Korea-Measures Affecting Imports of Fresh, Chilled and Frozen Beef*, WT/DS/161/AB/R, WT/DS/169/AB/R, adopted in January 2001, at para 164.

broader 'public reason' voiced in academic and civil society analyses of WTO dispute settlement practices.

Many international economic courts tend to disregard the customary law requirement of interpreting treaties and settling international disputes 'in conformity with principles of justice' and human rights (VCLT, Preamble), which requires judges to review their traditionally state-centred conceptions of public international law – for example, by judicial 'balancing' among competing principles, rights, and other rules of law. This chapter argues (in sections III and VI) that – contrary to the claims of legal positivism that courts have broad discretionary powers – WTO dispute settlement bodies rightly emphasize their 'objective assessment standard of judicial review' and increasingly clarify indeterminate WTO rules by referring to WTO objectives and the more than 40 'principles' identified in WTO law (for example, in GATT, Articles III, VII, X, XIII, XX, and XXXVI; GATS, Preamble and Article X; and TRIPS Agreement, Articles 8 and 62). European courts have successfully demonstrated that such 'constructivist interpretations' of economic law may be warranted in order to reduce legal insecurity and 'governance gaps' resulting from rapid market integration, provided courts respect the legitimate diversity of approaches to the interpretation of economic law as well as the diverse constitutional traditions of states (section IV). Sections V and VI argue that the European '*Solange* method' of judicial cooperation 'as long as' other courts respect constitutional principles of justice should be supported by citizens, judges, civil society, and their democratic representatives also in judicial cooperation with worldwide dispute settlement bodies and investor-state arbitration. Sections VII and VIII conclude that citizen-oriented conceptions of IEL are not only a precondition for maintaining an 'overlapping consensus' on legal and judicial protection of the rule of law in mutually beneficial, transnational economic cooperation among citizens: they also require clarification of the 'constitutional functions' of multilevel judicial governance (including investor-state arbitration) for protecting individual rights and the rule of law in mutually beneficial cooperation among citizens across national frontiers.

III. From 'Principal-Agent Theory' to Constitutional Theory in International Trade Governance and the WTO Dispute Settlement System

When I joined, in 1981, the GATT Secretariat as the first 'legal officer' ever employed by the GATT, abuses of trade policy powers by governments were ubiquitous. For example:

- governments undermined GATT law through dozens of unpublished 'voluntary export restraints' (for example, for textiles, steel products, and cars) which redistributed billions of US dollars to powerful interest groups – without parliamentary control, democratic discussion, and judicial review;

- GATT dispute settlement panels often refused to apply the customary methods of treaty interpretation so as to accommodate better the political and bureaucratic pressures (for example, from GATT diplomats and GATT bureaucrats) for 'realistic approaches' to the management of trade disputes;

- trade diplomats argued against judicial accountability for their non-transparent, welfare-reducing trade restrictions by urging national courts and international dispute settlement bodies to exercise 'judicial deference'.[29]

Political scientists and diplomats argue that, in intergovernmental organizations like GATT 1947 and the WTO, international dispute settlement bodies must respect their limited, delegated powers as 'agents' that remain subject to the control and oversight by Member States as the 'principals'. Yet, identification of 'the principals' with diplomats or the executive branch of governments rather than citizens, and neglect for the existence of multiple principals with constitutionally protected 'preference heterogeneity' are inconsistent not only with the universal recognition of human rights and of citizens as 'democratic principals' of governments with constitutionally limited governance powers;[30] application of power-oriented 'principal-agent delegation' metaphors to independent courts checking the legality of government decisions also risks undermining the rule of law and the international judicial review of whether multilevel governance complies with multilateral rules for mutually beneficial cooperation among citizens.[31] The more than 500 formal invocations of GATT/WTO

[29] On the controversial relationship between the 'Charming Betsy doctrine' of consistent interpretation and the 'Chevron doctrine' of judicial deference in US law, see A Davies, 'Connecting or Compartmentalizing the WTO and United States Legal Systems? The Role of the Charming Betsy Canon' (2007) 10 Journal of International Economic Law 117. Whereas US courts often exercise judicial deference without regard to the WTO obligations of the United States and to WTO dispute settlement findings on US trade regulations, a recent NAFTA Article 1904 panel reviewing US anti-dumping calculations concluded that 'zeroing seems inconsistent . . . with both the underlying principle of the Charming Betsy canon and the United States' Uruguay Round negotiating goal of obtaining an effective dispute-resolution system' (NAFTA Arbitral Tribunal (Ch 19), *In the matter of Carbon and Certain Alloy Steel Wire Rod from Canada*, 1904-4, 28 November 2007, at 38). The EC's legal advocates claim long since that European courts should not apply the 'WTO law in the books' as ratified by parliaments, but the 'WTO law in action' as determined by trade diplomats, see PJ Kuijper, 'WTO Law in the European Court of Justice' (2005) 42 Common Market Law Review 1313, 1332–1334.
[30] cf A Stone Sweet, 'Constitutional Courts and Parliamentary Democracy' (2002) 25 West European Politics 77–100. On the tensions between 'constitutional democracy', 'parliamentary democracy', and 'presidential democracy' in the United States, see B Ackerman, *The Failure of the Founding Fathers: Marshall and the Rise of Presidential Democracy* (2005).
[31] While many political scientists continue to describe 'monarchical paradigms' of 'foreign policy management' as being 'realistic', some – like KJ Alter, 'Delegation to International Courts and the Limits of Re-Contracting Power' in D Hawkins, D Lake, D Nielson, and M Tierney (eds), *Delegation and Agency in International Organizations* (2006) 337 – admit that 'starting from PA theory to understand judicial behaviour may be simply unhelpful'. Alter's description of international courts as 'trustee agents' whose independent decision-making powers help governments to limit their collective action problems, corresponds to constitutional conceptions of international law (as discussed below).

dispute settlement procedures by GATT/WTO members since 1948 demonstrate the lack of agreement among the 'principals' over the correct interpretation of many GATT/WTO rules that were drafted in deliberately vague terms so as to enable political agreement based on 'constructive ambiguity' and empowerment of independent courts to 'complete the contract' by judicial *ex post* clarification of the rules. Moreover, the universal recognition of inalienable human rights and of corresponding obligations of all UN and WTO Member States entails that the interests of citizens, as the 'democratic principals' of governments and main actors in consumer-driven markets and trade transactions, must no longer be disregarded in the judicial task of 'providing security and predictability to the multilateral trading system' (DSU, Article 3) – for example, by clarifying GATT/WTO legal restraints with due regard to general citizen interests in the rule of law and the promotion of consumer welfare.

A. Constitutional Problems of the WTO Dispute Settlement System

The DSU emphasizes the systemic nature of 'the dispute settlement system of the WTO' as 'a central element in providing security and predictability to the multilateral trading system' (DSU, Article 3.2). Yet, the detailed DSU rules on consultations, conciliation, mediation, panel procedures, appellate review, adoption of dispute settlement reports by the DSB, countermeasures, and arbitration leave open many legal questions concerning procedures (for example, preliminary rulings, burden of proof, and *amicus curiae* briefs), applicable law, and the role of precedents. In the recent Appellate Body report on *US-Zeroing*,[32] the AB offered a teleological interpretation of the dispute settlement system by stating:

Ensuring 'security and predictability' in the dispute settlement system, as contemplated in Art. 3.2 DSU, implies that, absent cogent reasons, an adjudicatory body will resolve the same legal question in the same way in a subsequent case.

This finding, which reflects basic principles of justice and of rule of law (such as treating like cases alike), was further specified by clarifying that:

The relevance of clarification contained in adopted Appellate Body reports is not limited to the application of a particular provision in a specific case ... [the] Panel's failure to follow previously adopted Appellate Body reports addressing the same issues undermines the development of a coherent and predictable body of jurisprudence clarifying Members' rights and obligations under the covered agreements as contemplated under the DSU.[33]

---

[32] WTO Appellate Body Report, *United States – Measures Relating to Zeroing and Sunset Reviews – AB-2006-5*, WT/DS322/AB/R, 9 January 2007.
[33] WTO Appellate Body Report, *US-Final Anti-Dumping Measures on Stainless Steel from Mexico*, WT/DS344/AB/R, 30 April 2008, paras 160–161.

Another constitutional problem of the WTO dispute settlement system relates to the question of whether WTO panels and the Appellate Body enjoy judicial discretion whenever they have to settle disputes over the interpretation and application of indeterminate WTO rules. Legal-positivist theories of adjudication (like that of HLA Hart) expose judges as law-makers by arguing that, whenever legal rules are indeterminate, judges do not apply positive rules of law, but exercise judicial discretion in deciding disputes.[34] During the Uruguay Round negotiations leading to the 1994 Agreement establishing the WTO, the US government insisted on inserting a 'judicial deference clause' into Article 17.6 of the WTO Agreement on Anti-Dumping reflecting the 'Chevron doctrine' of judicial deference by US courts vis-à-vis 'reasonable' administrative agency interpretations of ambiguous statutory provisions.[35] Yet, there is broad agreement among lawyers that domestic standards of judicial review of administrative agencies are based on national assumptions (such as respect for 'administrative efficiency' and Congressional oversight) that cannot be transferred to WTO law and its quasi-judicial dispute settlement system limiting national policy discretion in 153 WTO members with diverse legal systems and political preferences.[36] While the 'Hart-Dworkin debate' about the nature of common law systems (for example, whether law contains principles as well as rules, whether judges have 'discretion' to decide 'hard cases' in the absence of applicable rules) has continued for now more than four decades,[37] numerous international law rules, including WTO provisions and WTO dispute settlement reports, explicitly refer to 'principles' as an ever-more important element in the interpretation and judicial clarification of indeterminate rules. The 1994 'Decision on Review of Article 17.6 of the Agreement on Implementation of Article VI of GATT 1994' requiring WTO members to review whether the 'standard of review in paragraph 6 of Article 17 of the Agreement on Implementation of Article VI of GATT

---

[34] HLA Hart, *The Concept of Law* (1961) ch 7.

[35] Article 17.6(ii) of the WTO Agreement on Anti-Dumping, states, inter alia:

> Where the panel finds that a relevant provision of the Agreement admits of more than one permissible interpretation, the panel shall find the authorities' measure to be in conformity with the Agreement if it rests upon one of those permissible interpretations.

In the United States, the *Chevron* doctrine continues to be criticized as a 'counter-*Marbury* for the administrative state' that unduly favours agency autonomy over independent judicial review, eg of 'consistent' interpretation of domestic law in conformity with constitutional law and international legal obligations. International courts have not recognized judicial deference standards similar to those of the *Chevron* preference for political rather than judicial accountability of administrative agencies. Yet, the EC Court often reviews compliance of state measures with EC law more strictly than compliance of EC measures with EC law.

[36] cf M Oesch, *Standards of Review in WTO Dispute Settlement* (2006); and SP Croley and J Jackson, 'WTO Dispute Panel Deference to National Government Decisions. The Misplaced Analogy to the US Chevron Standard-of-Review Doctrine' in E-U Petersmann (ed), *International Trade Law and the GATT/WTO Dispute Settlement System* (1997) 203 ff.

[37] cf SJ Shapiro, 'The "Hart-Dworkin" Debate: A Short Guide for the Perplexed', Michigan Public Law and Legal Theory Working Paper No 77 (2007).

1994 ... is capable of general application',[38] led to no follow-up in view of the WTO Appellate Body jurisprudence supporting an 'objective assessment standard' of judicial review and judicial clarification of rules in the light of WTO principles and objectives that exclude more than one 'permissible interpretation'.[39] The WTO provisions on adoption by the WTO political bodies of WTO dispute settlement reports and of 'authoritative interpretations' (compare WTO Agreement, Article IX) reserve sovereign rights of WTO members and define the constitutional limits of the WTO dispute settlement system. Yet, WTO members have provided compulsory and quasi-judicial jurisdiction to WTO panels, the WTO Appellate Body, and WTO arbitrators for clarification of WTO rules subject to approval by the DSB. The quasi-automatic adoption of WTO dispute settlement rulings 'unless the DSB decides by consensus not to adopt the report' (DSU, Articles 16, 17), confirms the quasi-judicial function of WTO judges for clarifying and deciding disputes over the interpretation and application of WTO rules 'in conformity with principles of justice and international law' (VCLT) even against the views expressed by WTO members. Hence, Dworkin's conception of law as a matter of principle, legal coherence, judicial interpretation and principle-oriented clarification, and 'integrity' of law seems to fit the WTO legal system better than positivist theories of law as consisting merely of rules and of discretionary law-making powers of judges to fill 'gaps' in the rules so as to decide 'hard cases'.[40] Yet, as Dworkin's 'constructivist theory' of interpretation fails to offer precise methods for clarifying rules in the light of related legal principles, rights, and treaty objectives, judges must explain their judicial reasoning in transparent and democratically accountable ways (for example, as suggested in R Alexy's theory of interpreting rules in the light of relevant principles as 'optimization requirements' requiring judicial 'balancing' of relevant rules, rights, and principles)[41] enabling citizens and governments (for example, in the DSB) to challenge judicial clarification of rules.

---

[38] cf WTO, *The Result of the Uruguay Round of Multilateral Trade Negotiations: The Legal Texts* (1994) 453.

[39] On the incomplete WTO rules on standard of review, the 'irrelevance of domestic standard-of-review concepts', the Appellate Body case law on full *de novo* judicial review of legal interpretations, and the absence of any WTO dispute settlement findings of 'two permissible interpretations' (in the sense of Anti-Dumping Agreement, Art 17.6), see Oesch, n 36 above. On 'judicial balancing', see A Stone Sweet and J Mathews, 'Proportionality Balancing and Global Constitutionalism' (forthcoming, 2008) Columbia Journal of Transnational Law 47.

[40] cf R Dworkin, *Taking Rights Seriously* (1978); *A Matter of Principle* (1985); and *Law's Empire* (1986). According to Dworkin, 'rules' are applicable in an all-or-nothing fashion ('if, then') and require the judge to decide a case in the way dictated by an applicable rule. 'Principles' (defined as rights) and policies (defined as goals) have the dimension of weight or importance, providing one reason for deciding a case in a particular way that has to be weighed against other reasons and principles. Judges have no discretion; they must find the right judicial decision that fits best with the legal rules, institutions, legal principles, and policies, treating citizens as equals on the basis of principles of justice, fairness, procedural due process, and 'law as integrity'.

[41] On Alexy's theory of legal argumentation, see R Alexy, *A Theory of Constitutional Rights* (2002) 369 ff.

The WTO requirements (for example, in GATT, Article X; GATS, Article VI; TRIPS, Articles 41 ff; Anti-dumping Agreement, Article 13; and Subsidy Agreement, Article 23) of providing legal and judicial remedies also inside WTO members in relations between private economic actors, governments, and certain non-governmental organizations (like 'pre-shipment inspection agencies' regulated by the WTO Agreement on Pre-shipment Inspection) suggest that WTO rules must protect 'security and predictability' also for producers, investors, traders, and consumers engaged in international trade. Some WTO rules explicitly require domestic courts (compare Agreement on Government Procurement, Article XX) or commercial arbitration inside the WTO (compare Pre-shipment Inspection Agreement, Article 4) to settle disputes in conformity with the relevant WTO obligations or to protect individual trading rights and property rights (for example, as specified in the TRIPS Agreement and in the WTO Protocols on the Accession of China, Vietnam, and other countries). Yet, other questions about the interrelationships between the private, national, and international legal dimensions of the WTO dispute settlement system remain to be clarified by domestic and WTO legal practices. For example, does WTO law require domestic courts and WTO dispute settlement bodies to interpret domestic trade rules in conformity with the WTO obligations of the country concerned? Should WTO dispute settlement bodies interpret WTO requirements of 'independent' and 'impartial' domestic tribunals in conformity with international human rights obligations of access to justice? How should WTO dispute settlement bodies cooperate with other jurisdictions if, for example, in an investment dispute covered by GATS commitments, the respondent WTO member invokes the prohibition in Article 27 of the ICSID Convention of exercising diplomatic protection for investors who already submitted the dispute to investor-state arbitration? Can WTO panels refrain from exercising their jurisdiction if, for example, the respondent WTO member (for example, China, the EC) claim that complaints by certain other WTO members (for example, Taiwan, EC Member States) must be settled through domestic courts rather than through WTO panels?

B. Constitutional Problems of Multilevel Governance

Is it legally significant that DSU, Article 3 describes the 'dispute settlement system of the WTO' as a 'central element' of the broader 'multilateral trading system'? In the Uruguay Round negotiations from 1986 to 1994, the GATT Secretariat's reputation for independence and expertise prompted GATT contracting parties and the Uruguay Round negotiating groups to entrust many Secretariat experts with providing relevant facts, independent legal advice, preparing negotiating texts, chairing sessions of negotiating groups, and facilitating consensus-building on many Uruguay Round agreements (including the DSU). In subsequent WTO dispute settlement proceedings, WTO diplomats voiced concern that their governments' interpretations of WTO rules (for example, GATS schedules of market access commitments) were challenged by WTO dispute settlement bodies on the basis of legal texts and legal advice provided by the GATT/WTO Secretariat in the drafting of the legal commitments concerned (for example, Guidelines for the drafting of GATS commitments).[42] Confidence in the independence and 'public interest functions' of the Secretariat was occasionally undermined by political interferences, for instance when – at the request of US Trade Representative Carla Hills – the GATT/WTO Secretariat's Legal Affairs Division was prevented from offering independent legal advice in GATT/WTO dispute settlement proceedings challenging anti-dumping measures and the GATT/WTO Secretariat's Anti-dumping Division was 'packed' with lawyers from the US Department of Commerce and the US International Trade Commission.[43] As soon as Secretariat officials were suspected of defending protectionist interest group positions (for example, on 'zeroing' in calculations of anti-dumping duties) rather than the collective interests in liberal trade and consumer welfare, WTO negotiations became more 'member-driven' without recourse to independent Secretariat advice and mediation. Even though WTO rules have important global public good features (for example, in the sense that open markets and rule of law also benefit non-members) and the role of independent secretariats can be crucial for reducing 'collective action problems', the WTO Doha Round negotiations since 2001 differ from the previous Uruguay Round negotiations by the deliberate exclusion of WTO Secretariat experts from many 'member-driven' negotiations.

The slow progress in the Doha Round negotiations since 2001 reflects the 'constitutional problems' of WTO governance. On the one side, power-oriented trade policies and inadequate democratic support from parliaments and civil society[44] undermine consensus-building on additional WTO commitments and prompt conclusion of ever-more trade agreements outside the WTO. On the other side, the 'internationalization of constitutional law' (for example, resulting from the universal recognition of inalienable human rights and of national

---

[42] In many WTO disputes over GATS commitments (such as WTO Panel Report, *Mexico-Measures Affecting Telecommunications Services*, WT/DS204, adopted 1 June 2004, and WTO Appellate Body Report, *US-Gambling*, WT/DS285/AB/R, adopted 20 April 2005), WTO dispute settlement bodies confirmed GATS commitments on the basis of Secretariat Guidelines for the scheduling of GATS Commitments notwithstanding claims by the defendant countries that they had never intended to make such GATS commitments.

[43] The widespread distrust among WTO delegates vis-à-vis the WTO Secretariat's 'Rules Division' in charge of anti-dumping rules was reflected in the criticism in the WTO Appellate Body Report, n 33 above, that panel reports (drafted by the 'Rules Division') continued 'to depart from well-established Appellate Body jurisprudence clarifying the interpretation of the same legal issues' (ie the illegality of the use of 'zeroing' during reviews of anti-dumping orders). The Appellate Body corrected the Panel's 'misguided understanding of the legal provisions at issue' and affirmed, for the third time, that zeroing during reviews is illegal; it also emphasized (at paras 160–161) that – even if 'Appellate Body reports are not binding, except with respect to resolving the particular dispute between the parties' – 'the legal interpretation embodied in adopted panel and Appellate Body reports becomes part and parcel of the *acquis* of the WTO dispute settlement system': see n 33 above.

[44] On the continuing ineffectiveness of parliamentary control of WTO rule-making, see the European Parliament documents on *The Parliamentary Dimension of the WTO* (2006); and *Role of Parliaments in Scrutinising and Influencing Trade Policy* (2005).

constitutions) and the 'constitutionalization of international law' (for example, by international *jus cogens* rules, international organizations with hierarchical legal systems, international courts with supranational powers, and constitutional methods of interpretation) induce ever-more international lawyers to acknowledge that international rules and institutions for the collective supply of international public goods can serve 'constitutional functions' for limiting 'governance failures' (like national power politics, welfare-reducing protectionism) and for protecting human rights (for example, through humanitarian interventions and international criminal courts). For instance, 'constitutional functions' of certain WTO guarantees are recognized in view of:

- the comprehensive rule-making, executive and (quasi-) judicial powers of WTO institutions for protecting rule of law in international trade;[45]

- the 'constitutionalization' of WTO law resulting from the jurisprudence of the WTO dispute settlement bodies and their quasi-judicial clarification and protection of legal principles underlying WTO rules;[46]

- the *domestic* 'constitutional functions' of GATT/WTO rules for limiting welfare-reducing border discrimination by reciprocal reinforcement of constitutional principles (like freedom, non-discrimination, rule of law, proportionality of government restrictions, legal limitation of protectionist interest group politics) for the benefit of transnational cooperation among free citizens;[47]

- the *international* 'constitutional functions' of WTO rules, for example, for the promotion of 'international participatory democracy' (for example, by holding governments internationally accountable for the 'external effects' of their national trade policies, by enabling countries to participate in the policy-making of other countries)[48] and of the enhancement of 'jurisdictional competition among nation states'[49] and 'the allocation of authority between constitutions';[50]

- in view of the necessity of 'constitutional approaches' for a proper understanding of the transformation of states and national legal systems by the law of international organizations that use constitutional terms, methods, and

---

[45] See JH Jackson, *The World Trade Organisation: Constitution and Jurisprudence* (1998).

[46] See DZ Cass, 'The Constitutionalization of International Trade Law: Judicial Norm-Generation as the Engine of Constitutionalization' (2001) European Journal of International Law 39.

[47] See JO McGinnis and ML Movsesian, 'The World Trade Constitution' (2000) 114 Harvard Law Review 511–605; PM Gerhart, 'The Two Constitutional Visions of the World Trade Organisation' (2003) 24 University of Pennsylvania Journal of International Economic Law 1, contrasts the 'inward-looking, economic vision of the WTO' in helping member countries addressing internal political failures with the 'external, participatory vision of the WTO' helping WTO members to address concerns raised by policy decisions in other countries.

[48] See, eg PM Gerhart, 'The WTO and Participatory Democracy: The Historical Evidence' (2004) 37 Vanderbilt Journal of Transnational Law 897.

[49] See JO McGinnis, 'The WTO as a Structure of Liberty' (2004) 28 Harvard Journal of Law and Public Policy 81.

[50] J Trachtman, 'The WTO Constitution: Toward Tertiary Rules' (2006) European Journal of International Law 623.

principles for more than 50 years (see, for example, the 'Constitutions' of the ILO, WHO, Food and Agriculture Organization (FAO), and EU) and are ever-more important for coordinating national and international levels of governance for the collective supply of international public goods.[51]

Of course, similar to the diverse constitutional cultures inside nation states, the constitutional transformations of certain fields of international law differ depending on their institutional context: for example, intergovernmental institutions like the WTO differ from tripartite institutions like the ILO; supranational political institutions like the UN Security Council differ from supranational courts; and the 'bottom-up constitutionalism' of multilevel human rights law (for example, in the sense of authorizing higher standards of human rights protection at national and regional levels than in UN human rights law) differs from the 'top-down constitutionalism' of multilevel trade law (for example, in the sense of WTO rules prescribing higher standards of trade liberalization than in most autonomous, national trade laws). Multilevel trade governance and WTO law build on the 'morality of law' which, for centuries, has proven necessary for guiding social behaviour of traders, producers, investors, and consumers.[52] Yet, WTO law does not guarantee its legal consistency with human rights and other 'principles of justice'. Whereas WTO rules are interpreted as intergovernmental rights and obligations for the promotion of market access and 'sustainable development' (WTO, Preamble), the intergovernmental market freedoms in European economic law are judicially protected as fundamental freedoms of citizens, thereby recognizing the constitutional primacy of equal basic freedoms and other 'principles of justice' over government obligations to promote 'the good' and utilitarian happiness rather than 'the right'.[53]

Regardless of the diverse, but complementary, constitutional conceptions of IEL[54] and of alternative conceptions of 'global administrative law' (focusing

---

[51] cf E-U Petersmann, *Constitutional Functions and Constitutional Problems of International Economic Law* (1991); N Walker, 'The EU and the WTO: Constitutionalism in a New Key' in G de Búrca and J Scott (eds), *The EU and the WTO: Legal and Constitutional Issues* (2001); and T Cottier and M Hertig, 'The Prospects of 21st Century Constitutionalism' (2003) 7 Max Planck Yearbook of United Nations Law 261.

[52] Fuller identifies eight moral requirements as being constitutive of 'rule of law' (ie generality, clarity, promulgation, stability, consistency of rules and social behaviour, non-retroactivity and non-contradictory nature of rules which must also not require the impossible). See L Fuller, *The Morality of Law* (2nd edn, 1969) ch 2. WTO law seems to meet all of these requirements as well as additional requirements (such as judicial independence, judicial review, and fair hearings) stipulated by J Raz, *The Authority of Law* (1979) 214 ff.

[53] On the priority of justice, liberty, and rights over ethical conceptions of the good life in theories of justice from Kant to Rawls, see Rawls n 2 above, 31 ff, 243 ff; and Rawls n 18 above, 294 ff.

[54] The WTO *World Trade Report 2007* offers an excellent summary and systematization of economic, political, and 'constitutional conceptions' of the WTO legal system at 35–110. On the more general argument that collective supply of international public goods (including an open, rules-based world trading system) requires multilevel constitutional restraints of multilevel governance, see E-U Petersmann, 'Multilevel Trade Governance Requires Multilevel Constitutionalism' in C Joerges and E-U Petersmann (eds), *Constitutionalism, Multilevel Trade Governance and Social Regulation* (2006) 5–57.

on 'constitutional nationalism' rather than on 'multilevel constitutionalism'), national administrative law approaches offer no convincing model for clarifying the legitimate functions of WTO judges in WTO disputes among WTO members about contested interpretations and application of WTO rules and principles in domestic laws and policies. The diverse 'constitutional approaches' developed by European courts (see sections IV to VI) and investor-state arbitral tribunals (see section VII) to the interpretation of IEL confirm the need for reconsidering (in section VIII) the legitimate scope of judicial powers and procedures in IEL, notably the relevance of 'constitutional methods' of judicial interpretation, of 'constitutionalism' as a legal method for resolving conflicts of interests (rather than only as a legal method for constituting states), and, more generally, the constitutional preconditions for 'rule of international law'.

IV. Constitutional Pluralism: Diversity of 'Constitutional Interpretations' of IEL by European Courts

An ever-larger number of empirical political science analyses of the global rise of judicial power, and of 'judicial activism' by supreme courts and international courts in Europe, confirms the political impact of judicial interpretations on the development of national and European law and policies.[55] The 'multilevel judicial governance' in Europe – notably by the EC Court, its Court of First Instance, the EFTA Court, the ECtHR and national courts – succeeded because their judicial cooperation was justified as multilevel protection of constitutional citizen rights based on 'European public reason' that was accepted as 'just' by judges, citizens, and parliaments. Multilevel, judicial protection of fundamental freedoms was the driving force in the progressive transformation of the intergovernmental EC and European Economic Area (EEA) treaties and the European Convention on Human Rights (ECHR) into constitutional instruments protecting citizen rights and community interests across national frontiers by different kinds of 'multilevel constitutionalism':

- Multilevel judicial governance in the EC among national courts and European courts remains characterized by the supranational structures of EC law and the fact that the fundamental freedoms of EC law and related social guarantees go far beyond the national laws of EC Member States (below section IV A).

- Multilevel judicial governance in the field of human rights differs fundamentally: the ECtHR asserts only subsidiary constitutional functions

---

[55] See, for instance, A Stone Sweet, *Governing with Judges. Constitutional Politics in Europe* (2000), who describes how much third-party dispute resolution and judicial rule-making have become privileged mechanisms of adapting national and intergovernmental rule-systems to the needs of citizens and their constitutional rights.

vis-à-vis national human rights guarantees, with due respect for the diverse traditions in the 47 ECHR member countries in the field of economic regulation (below section IV B).

- The multilevel judicial governance among national courts and the EFTA Court has extended the EC's common market law to the three EEA members (Iceland, Liechtenstein, and Norway) through intergovernmental modes of cooperation that promoted the EC's constitutional principles of legal primacy, direct effect, and direct applicability of the EC's common market law only in indirect ways. Yet, this different kind of multilevel judicial cooperation (for example, based on voluntary compliance with legally non-binding preliminary opinions by the EFTA Court) effectively protects the EC's market freedoms and fundamental rights in all EEA member countries (below section IV C).

A. Multilevel Judicial Protection of EC Law Has Extended the Constitutional Rights of European Citizens

A citizen-driven common market with free movement of goods, services, persons, capital, and payments inside the EC can work effectively only to the extent that the common market and competition rules are applied and protected in coherent ways in national courts in all 27 EC Member States. As the declared objective of an 'ever-closer union between the peoples of Europe' (Preamble to the EC Treaty) was to be brought about by economic and legal integration requiring additional law-making, administrative decisions, and common policies by the European institutions, the EC Treaty differs from other international treaties by its innovative judicial safeguards for the protection of rule of law – not only in intergovernmental relations among EC Member States, but also in the citizen-driven market transactions as well as in the EC's common policies. Whereas most international jurisdictions (like the ICJ, the Permanent Court of Arbitration, the Law of the Sea tribunal, and WTO dispute settlement bodies) remain characterized by intergovernmental procedures, the EC Treaty provides unique legal remedies also for EU citizens and EU institutions as guardians of EC law and of its 'constitutional functions' for correcting 'governance failures' at national and European levels:

- The citizen-driven cooperation among national courts and the EC Court in the context of preliminary rulings procedures (Article 234 EC) has uniquely empowered national and European judges to cooperate, at the request of EC citizens, in the multilevel judicial protection of citizen rights protected by EC law.
- The empowerment of the European Commission to initiate infringement proceedings (Article 226 EC) rendered the ECJ's function as an

intergovernmental court much more effective than would have been possible under purely inter-state infringement proceedings (Article 227 EC).

- The Court's 'constitutional functions' (for example, in case of actions by Member States or EC institutions for annulment of EC regulations), as well as its functions as an 'administrative court' (for example, protecting private rights and rule of law in response to direct actions by natural or legal persons for annulment of EC acts, failure to act, or actions for damages), offered unique legal remedies for maintaining and developing the constitutional coherence of EC law.

- The EC Court's teleological reasoning based on communitarian needs (for example, in terms of protection of EC citizen rights, consumer welfare, and of undistorted competition in the common market) justified constitutional interpretations of 'fundamental freedoms' of EU citizens which governments had never accepted before in intergovernmental treaty regimes.

The diverse forms of judicial dialogues (for example, on the interpretation and protection of fundamental rights), judicial contestation (for example, of the scope of EC competences), and judicial cooperation (for example, in preliminary ruling procedures) emphasized the need for respecting common constitutional principles deriving from the EC Member States' obligations under their national constitutions, under the ECHR (as interpreted by the ECtHR) as well as under the EC's constitutional law. Judicial respect for 'constitutional pluralism' promoted judicial comity among national courts, the ECJ, and the ECtHR in their complementary, multilevel protection of constitutional rights, with due respect for the diversity of national constitutional and judicial traditions. Arguably, it was this multilevel judicial protection of common constitutional principles underlying European law and national constitutions which enabled the EC Court, and also the ECtHR, to transcend progressively the intergovernmental structures of European law by focusing on the judicial protection of individual rights in constitutional democracies and in common markets rather than on state interests in intergovernmental relations.

B. Multilevel Judicial Enforcement of the ECHR: Subsidiary 'Constitutional Functions' of the ECtHR

The ECHR, like most other international human rights conventions, sets out minimum standards for the treatment of individuals that respect the diversity of democratic constitutional traditions of defining individual rights in democratic communities. The 14 Protocols to the ECHR and the European Social Charter (as revised in 1998) also reflect the constitutional experiences in some European countries (like France and Germany) with protecting economic and social rights as integral parts of their constitutional and economic laws. For example, in order to avoid a repetition of the systemic political abuses of economic regulation prior to 1945,[56] the ECHR also includes guarantees of property rights and rights of companies. The jurisdiction of the ECtHR for the collective enforcement of the ECHR – based on complaints not only by Member States, but also by private persons – prompted the Court to interpret the ECHR as a constitutional charter of Europe[57] protecting human rights across Europe as an objective 'constitutional order'.[58] The multilevel judicial interpretation and protection of fundamental rights, as well as of their governmental restriction 'in the interests of morals, public order or national security in a democratic society' (Article 6), are of a constitutional nature. However, ECtHR judges rightly emphasize the subsidiary functions of the ECHR and of its Court:

These issues are more properly decided, in conformity with the subsidiary logic of the system of protection set up by the European Convention on Human Rights, by the national judicial authorities themselves and notably courts of constitutional jurisdiction. European control is a fail-safe device designed to catch the breaches that escape the rigorous scrutiny of the national constitutional bodies.[59]

The Court aims at resisting the 'temptation of delving too deep into issues of fact and of law, of becoming the famous "fourth instance" that it has always insisted it is not'.[60] The Court also exercises deference by recognizing that the democratically elected legislatures in the Member States enjoy a 'margin of appreciation' in the balancing of public and private interests, provided the measure taken in the general interest bears a reasonable relationship of proportionality both to the aim pursued and the effect on the individual interest affected. Rather than imposing uniform approaches to the diverse human rights problems in ECHR Member States, the ECtHR often exercises judicial self-restraint, for example:

- by leaving the process of implementing its judgments to the Member States, subject to the 'peer review' by the Committee of Ministers of the Council of Europe, rather than asserting judicial powers to order consequential measures;

- by viewing the discretionary scheme of ECHR, Article 41 for awarding just satisfaction 'if necessary' as being secondary to the primary aim of the

---

[56] For example, the wide-ranging guarantees of economic regulation and legally enforceable social rights in Germany's 1919 Constitution for the 'Weimar Republic' had led to ever more restrictive government interventions into labour markets, capital markets, interest rates, as well as to expropriations 'in the general interest' which – during the Nazi dictatorship from 1933 to 1945 – led to systemic political abuses of these regulatory powers.

[57] See ECtHR, *Ireland v United Kingdom*, 18 January 1978, (1979) 2 EHRR 25.

[58] See ECtHR, *Loizidou v Turkey* (preliminary objections), 23 March 1995, at para 75, referring to the status of human rights in Europe.

[59] L Wildhaber, 'A Constitutional Future for the European Court of Human Rights?' (2002) 23 Human Rights Law Journal 161.   [60] Ibid., 161.

ECtHR to protect minimum standards of human rights protection in all Convention states;[61]

- by concentrating on 'constitutional decisions of principle' and 'pilot proceedings' that appear to be relevant for many individual complaints and for the judicial protection of a European public order based on human rights, democracy, and rule of law; and

- by filtering out early manifestly ill-founded complaints because the Court perceives its 'individual relief function' as being subsidiary to its constitutional function.

Article 34 of the ECHR permits individual complaints not only 'from any person', but also from 'non-governmental organizations or groups of individuals claiming to be the victim of a violation' of ECHR rights by one of the state parties. The protection of this *collective dimension* of human rights (for example, of legal persons that are composed of natural persons) has prompted the ECtHR to protect procedural human rights (for example, under ECHR, Articles 6, 13, 34) as well as substantive human rights of companies (for example, under ECHR, Protocol 1, Articles 8, 10, 11)[62] in conformity with the national constitutional traditions in many European states as well as inside the EC (for example, the EC guarantees of market freedoms and other economic and social rights of companies). Similar to the constitutional and teleological interpretation methods used by the EC Court, the ECtHR – in its judicial interpretation of the ECHR – applies principles of 'effective interpretation' aimed at protecting human rights in a practical and effective manner. These principles of effective treaty interpretation include a principle of 'dynamic interpretation' of the ECHR as a 'constitutional instrument of European public order' that must be interpreted with due regard to contemporary realities so as to protect 'an effective political democracy' (which is mentioned in the Preamble as an objective of the ECHR).[63] Limitations of fundamental rights of economic actors are being reviewed by the ECtHR as to whether they are determined by law, in conformity with the ECHR, and whether they are 'necessary in a democratic society'. Governmental limitations of civil and political human rights tend to be reviewed by the ECtHR more strictly (for example, as to whether they maintain an appropriate balance between the human right concerned and the need for 'an effective political democracy') than governmental restrictions of private economic activity that tend to be reviewed by the Court on the basis of a more lenient standard of judicial review respecting a 'margin of appreciation' of governments.

---

[61] Ibid., 164–165.

[62] cf M Emberland, *The Human Rights of Companies. Exploring the Structure of ECHR Protection* (2006).

[63] On the Court's teleological interpretation of the ECHR in the light of its 'object and purpose', see Emberland, n 62 above, 20.

Article 1 of Protocol 1 to the ECHR protects 'peaceful enjoyment of possessions' (paragraph 1); the term 'property' is used only in paragraph 2. The
ECtHR has clarified that Article 1 guarantees rights of property not only in
corporeal things (rights *in rem*), but also intellectual property rights and private
law or public law claims *in personam* (for example, monetary claims based on
private contracts, employment and business rights, pecuniary claims against
public authorities).[64] Even though the ECtHR respects a wide margin of
appreciation of states to limit and interfere with property rights (for example, by
means of taxation) and to balance individual and public interests (for example,
in case of a taking of property without full compensation), the Court's expansive
protection – as property or 'possessions' – of almost all pecuniary interests and
legitimate expectations arising from private and public law relationships reveals
a strong judicial awareness of the importance of private economic activities
and economic law for effective protection of human rights and personal self-
realization in the economy and civil society. The Court's review of governmental
limitations of, and interferences with, property rights is based on 'substantive
due process' standards that go far beyond the 'procedural due process' standards
applied by the US Supreme Court since the 1930s. In a few cases challenging
government interferences with property rights of foreigners, investors opted for
parallel proceedings before arbitral tribunals and the ECtHR.[65]

C. Diversity of Multilevel Judicial Governance in Free Trade Agreements: The Example of the EFTA Court

The 1992 Agreement between the EC and EFTA states (Iceland, Liechtenstein,
and Norway) establishing the European Economic Area (EEA)[66] is the legally
most developed of the more than 250 FTAs (in terms of GATT, Article XXIV)
concluded after World War II. The EFTA Court illustrates the reasonable
diversity of judicial procedures and approaches to the interpretation of international trade law, and confirms the importance of 'judicial dialogues' among
international and domestic courts for the promotion of rule of law in international trade. In order to promote legal homogeneity between EC and EEA
market law, Article 6 of the revised EEA Agreement provides that:

---

[64] cf A Riza Coban, *Protection of Property Rights within the European Convention on Human Rights* (2004).

[65] On these few cases, and the respective advantages of property protection under investment law (eg no requirement of prior exhaustion of local remedies, full compensation for expropriation under BITs and ICSID arbitration) compared with protection of property under the ECHR (eg only exceptional protection of rights of shareholders, more flexible compensation standards), see ch 11 below. The ECtHR has so far never found that a foreigner had been expropriated in the sense of Art 1 of Protocol No 1 of the ECHR. However, many interferences with property rights of foreign investors were held to be 'other interferences' requiring less than full compensation.

[66] Agreement Establishing the European Economic Area (EEA), signed 2 May 1992, in force 1 January 1994, [1994] OJ EC L-1/3.

[W]ithout prejudice to future developments of case-law, the provisions of this Agreement, in so far as they are identical in substance to corresponding rules of the [EC and ECSC Treaties] and to acts adopted in application of these two Treaties, shall, in their implementation and application, be interpreted in conformity with the relevant rulings of the Court of Justice of the EC given prior to the date of signature of the agreement.

The EFTA Court's jurisprudence suggests, however, that 'it does not seem that the EFTA Court has treated the ECJ case-law differently depending on when the pertinent judgments were rendered'.[67] Out of the 62 cases lodged during the first 10 years of the EFTA Court, 18 related to direct actions against decisions of the EFTA Surveillance Authority, 42 concerned requests by national courts for advisory opinions, and two related to requests for legal aid and suspension of a measure. In its interpretation of EC law provisions that are identical to EEA rules (for example, concerning common market and competition rules), the EFTA Court has regularly followed ECJ case law and has realized the homogeneity objectives of EEA law in terms of the outcome of cases, if not their legal reasoning.

The EC Court, in its Opinion 1/91, held that the Community law principles of legal primacy and direct effect were not applicable to the EEA Agreement and were 'irreconcilable' with its characteristics as an international agreement conferring rights only on the participating states and the EC.[68] In spite of this restrictive interpretation, the EFTA Court, in its *Restamark* judgment of December 1994, followed from Protocol 35 (on achieving a homogenous EEA based on common rules) that individuals and economic operators must be entitled to invoke and claim at the national level any rights that could be derived from precise and unconditional EEA provisions if they had been made part of the national legal orders.[69] In its 2002 *Einarsson* judgment, the EFTA Court further followed from Protocol 35 that such provisions with quasi-direct effect must take legal precedence over conflicting provisions of national law.[70] Already in 1998, in its *Sveinbjörnsdottir* judgment, the EFTA Court had characterized the legal nature of the EEA Agreement as an international treaty *sui generis* that had created a distinct legal order of its own; the Court therefore found that the principle of state liability for breaches of EEA law must be presumed to be part of EEA law.[71] This judicial recognition of the corresponding EC law principles was confirmed in the 2002 *Karlsson* judgment, where the EFTA Court further held that EEA law – while not prescribing that individuals and economic operators be able to rely directly on non-implemented EEA rules before national

---

[67] V Skouris, 'The ECJ and the EFTA Court under the EEA Agreement: A Paradigm for International Cooperation between Judicial Institutions' in C Baudenbacher, P Tresselt, and T Orlygsson (eds), *The EFTA Court. Ten Years On* (2005), 123, 124.

[68] ECJ, Opinion 1/91, *EEA Agreement*, [1991] ECR I-6079, at para 28.

[69] *Restamark* (Case E-1/94), [1994–1995] EFTA Court Reports, 15.

[70] *Einarsson* (Case E-1/01), [2002] EFTA Court Reports, 1.

[71] *Sveinbjörnsdottir* (Case E-7/97), [1998] EFTA Court Reports, 95.

courts – required national courts to consider relevant EEA rules, whether implemented or not, when interpreting international and domestic law.[72]

V. Lessons from the European '*Solange* Method' of Judicial Cooperation Beyond Europe?

The judicial protection of fundamental freedoms and economic rights of citizens by national and international courts throughout Europe offers citizens direct judicial remedies that appear economically more efficient, legally more effective, and democratically more legitimate than the politicization of similar disputes through intergovernmental dispute settlement procedures among states at worldwide levels (for example, in the ICJ and the WTO). The fact that the EC Court has rendered only three judgments in international disputes among EC Member States since the establishment of the ECJ in 1952 illustrates that many intergovernmental disputes (for example, over private rights) could be prevented or settled in domestic courts if governments would not prevent their domestic courts from applying relevant IEL rules. In order to limit their own judicial accountability for non-compliance with their WTO obligations, both the EC and US governments requested their respective domestic courts to refrain from applying WTO rules at the request of citizens or of NGOs.[73] US courts even claim that WTO dispute settlement rulings 'are not binding on the US, much less this court';[74] also the EC Court has refrained long since – at the request of the political EC institutions who have repeatedly misled the ECJ about the interpretation of WTO obligations – from reviewing the legality of EC measures in the light of the EC's GATT and WTO obligations. The simultaneous insistence by the same trade politicians that WTO rules are enforceable at their own request in *domestic courts* vis-à-vis violations of WTO law by states inside the EC and the United States, and the effective cooperation among national courts and investor-state arbitral tribunals in the field of international investment law,[75] illustrate the political rather than legal nature of Machiavellian objections against judicial accountability of governments for their own violations of IEL.

This section suggests that the '*Solange* method' of conditional cooperation by national courts with European courts 'as long as' (which means 'solange' in German) European courts protect common constitutional principles (sections V A and B below), as well as the judicial self-restraint by the ECtHR vis-à-vis

---

[72] *Karlsson* (Case E-4/01), [2002] EFTA Court Reports, 240, at para 28.

[73] cf E-U Petersmann, *The GATT/WTO Dispute Settlement* System (1997) 19.

[74] US Court of Appeals for the Federal Circuit, *Corus Staal BV and Corus Steel USA Inc v Department of Commerce and ors*, Judgment, 21 January 2005, available at <http://caselaw.lp.findlaw.com/data2/circs/fed/041107p.pdf>.

[75] On the recognition and enforcement of investor-state arbitration awards in domestic courts, see RD Bishop, J Crawford, and M Reisman, *Foreign Investment Disputes* (2005) 1515.

alleged violations of human rights by EC institutions 'as long as' the EC Court protects the human rights guarantees of the ECHR (section V C below), should serve as a model for 'conditional cooperation' among international courts and national courts also in international economic, environmental, and human rights law beyond Europe (section VI). Such multilevel judicial cooperation and 'judicial dialogues' among courts for the protection of individual rights could contribute not only to citizen-oriented conceptions of rule of law in international civil society cooperation, but also to constitutional protection of 'participatory', 'deliberative', and 'cosmopolitan democracy' in the worldwide division of labour and its legal regulation.

A. The '*Solange* Method' of Judicial Cooperation among Constitutional Courts and the EC Court in the Protection of Fundamental Rights: The Example of the German Constitutional Court

The EC Court, the EFTA Court, and the ECtHR have – albeit in different ways – interpreted the intergovernmental EC, EEA, and ECHR treaties as objective legal orders protecting also *individual rights* of citizens. All three courts have acknowledged that the human rights goals to empower individuals and effectively protect human rights, including the objective of international trade agreements to enable citizens to engage in mutually beneficial trade transactions under conditions of rule of law and non-discriminatory competition, call for 'dynamic judicial interpretations' of treaty rules with due regard to the need for judicial protection of citizen rights in the economy as well as in the polity. These citizen-oriented interpretations of the EC and EEA Agreements were influenced by the long-standing insistency by constitutional courts in ever more EC countries on their constitutional mandates to protect fundamental rights and constitutional democracy also vis-à-vis abuses of EC powers. The '*solange* jurisprudence' of the German Constitutional Court, like similar inter-actions between other national constitutional courts and the EC Court,[76] contributed to the progressive extension of judicial protection of human rights in Community law:

- In its *Solange I* judgment of 1974, the German Constitutional Court held that 'as long as' the integration process of the EC does not include a cata-logue of fundamental rights corresponding to that of the German Basic Law, German courts could, after having requested a preliminary ruling from the EC Court, also request a ruling from the German Constitutional Court regarding the compatibility of EC acts with fundamental rights and

---

[76] cf FC Mayer, 'The European Constitution and the Courts' in A v Bogdandy and J Bast (eds), *Principles of European Constitutional Law* (2006) 281–334.

the German Constitution.[77] This judicial insistence on the more comprehensive scope of fundamental rights protection in German constitutional
law was instrumental for the ECJ's judicial protection of human rights as
common, yet unwritten constitutional guarantees of EC law.[78]

- In view of the emerging human rights protection in EC law, the German
  Constitutional Court held – in its *Solange II* judgment of 1986[79] – that it
  would no longer exercise its jurisdiction for reviewing EC legal acts 'as long
  as' the EC Court continued generally and effectively to protect fundamental rights against EC measures in ways comparable to the essential
  safeguards of German constitutional law.

- In its *Maastricht* judgment (*Solange III*) of 1993, however, the German
  Constitutional Court reasserted its jurisdiction to defend the scope of
  German constitutional law: EC measures exceeding the limited EC com-
  petences covered by the German Act ratifying the EU Treaty ('*ausbrechende
  Gemeinschaftsakte*') could not be legally binding and applicable in
  Germany.[80]

- Following GATT and WTO dispute settlement rulings that the EC import
  restrictions of bananas violated WTO law, and in view of an ECJ judgment
  upholding these restrictions without reviewing their WTO inconsistencies,
  several German courts requested the Constitutional Court to declare these EC
  restrictions to be ultra vires (namely, exceeding the EC's limited competences)
  and illegally to restrict constitutional freedoms of German importers. The
  German Constitutional Court, in its judgment of 2002 (*Solange IV*),[81]
  declared the application inadmissible on the ground that it had not been
  argued that the required level of human rights protection in the EC had *generally* fallen below the minimum level required by the German Constitution.

- In its judgment of 2005 on the German Act implementing the EU
  Framework Decision (adopted under the third EU pillar) on the European
  Arrest Warrant, the Constitutional Court held that the automatically
  binding force and mutual recognition in Germany of arrest orders from
  other EU Member States were inconsistent with the fundamental rights
  guarantees of the German Basic Law.[82] The limited jurisdiction of the EC
  Court for third-pillar decisions concerning police and judicial cooperation
  might have contributed to this assertion of national constitutional jurisdiction for safeguarding fundamental rights vis-à-vis EU decisions in the
  area of criminal law and their legislative implementation in Germany.

---

[77] BVerfGE 37, 327.
[78] The ECJ's judicial protection of human rights continues to evolve dynamically since 1969
(Case 29/69 *Stauder v City of Ulm* [1969] ECR 419; and Case 11/70 *Internationale Handelsgesellschaft* [1970] ECR 1125).   [79] BVerfGE 73, 339, at 375.
[80] BVerfGE 89, 115.   [81] BVerfGE 102, 147.   [82] BVerfGE 113, 273.

B. Progressive Extension of Fundamental Rights Protection by the EC Court

The expanding legal protection of fundamental rights in EC law in response to their judicial protection by national and European courts – vis-à-vis restrictions by EC institutions, EC Member States, intergovernmental organizations (including UN Security Council decisions), non-governmental organizations (for example, trade unions exercising their right to strike in order to prevent companies from exercising their 'market freedoms' under EC law), and individuals (for example, demonstrators blocking imports or transit of goods protected by EC 'market freedoms') – illustrates how judicial cooperation has been successful in Europe far beyond economic law. The following six 'stages' in the case law of the EC Court on protection of human rights may be distinguished:[83]

- In the supra-national, but functionally limited, European Coal and Steel Community (ECSC), the Court held that it lacked competence to examine whether an ECSC decision amounted to an infringement of fundamental rights as recognized in the constitution of a Member State.[84]

- Since its *Stauder* judgment of 1969, the EC Court has declared in a series of judgments that fundamental rights form part of the general principles of Community law binding the Member States and EC institutions, and that the EC Court ensures their observance.[85]

- Since 1975, the ever-more extensive case law of the EC courts explicitly refers to the ECHR and protects ever more human rights and fundamental freedoms in a wide array of Community law areas, including civil, political, economic, social, and labour rights, drawing inspiration from 'the constitutional traditions common to the Member States and from the guidelines supplied by international treaties for the protection of human rights on which the Member States have collaborated or of which they are signatories'.[86]

- Since 1989, the ECHR has been characterized by the EC Court as having 'special significance' for the interpretation and development of EU law[87] in view of the fact that the ECHR is the only international human rights convention mentioned in Article 6 EU.

- In the 1990s, the EC courts have begun to refer to individual judgments of the ECtHR[88] and have clarified that – in reconciling economic freedoms

---

[83] cf A Rosas, 'Fundamental Rights in the Luxembourg and Strasbourg Courts' in Baudenbacher, Tresselt, and Orlygsson, n 67 above, 163, 169.

[84] Case 1/58 *Storck v High Authority* [1959] ECR 43.   [85] n 78 above.

[86] See, eg Opinion 2/1994 [1996] ECR I-1759, at para 33.

[87] Joined Cases 46/87 and 222/88 *Hoechst* [1989] ECR 2859, at para 13.

[88] Case 13/94 *P v S* [1996] ECR I-2143, at para 16.

guaranteed by EC law with human rights guarantees of the ECHR that admit restrictions – all interests involved have to be weighed 'having regard to all circumstances of the case in order to determine whether a fair balance was struck between those interests', without giving priority to the economic freedoms of the EC Treaty at the expense of other fundamental rights.[89] The EC courts have also been willing to adjust their case law to new developments in the case law of the ECtHR,[90] and to differentiate – as in the case law of the ECtHR – between judicial review of EC measures,[91] state measures,[92] and private restrictions of economic freedoms in the light of fundamental rights.[93]

• In a series of judgments, the EC Court of First Instance protected human rights also against EC measures implementing UN Security Council sanctions against alleged terrorists. Yet, in the appeal against the *Kadi* judgment[94] that the Community courts should assess the listing and sanctioning of terrorists by the UN Security Council only in the light of UN human rights guarantees of a *jus cogens* nature, the ECJ and Advocate-General Poiares Maduro convincingly argued that – in accordance with the ECJ findings that 'measures which are incompatible with the observance of human rights ... are not acceptable in the Community'[95] – it is up to the Community courts to protect European human rights also vis-à-vis European measures implementing UN Security Council sanctions.[96]

---

[89] Case C-112/00 *Schmidberger* [2003] ECR I-5659. The judicial balancing by the ECJ refutes the claim that the ECJ gives priority to economic freedoms at the expense of other human rights.

[90] In Case C-94/00 *Roquette Frères* [2002] ECR I-9011, at para 29, for example, the ECJ referred explicitly to the new case law of the ECtHR on the protection of the right to privacy of commercial enterprises in order to explain why – despite having suggested the opposite in its earlier judgment, *Hoechst* – such enterprises may benefit from ECHR, Art 8.

[91] cf, eg the ECJ cases listed in n 78 above.

[92] cf, eg Case C-36/02 *Omega* [2004] ECR I-9609, in which the ECJ acknowledged that the restriction of market freedoms could be necessary for the protection of human dignity despite the fact that the German conception of protecting human dignity as a human right was not shared by all other EC Member States.

[93] In Case C-438/05 *Viking Line*, Judgment, 11 December 2007, not yet reported, the ECJ confirmed that trade unions – in exercising their social rights to strike (eg in order to prevent relocation of the shipping line *Viking* to another EC Member State) – are legally bound by the EC's common market freedoms that have to be reconciled and 'balanced' with social and labour rights.

[94] Case T-315/01 *Kadi v Council and Commission* [2005] ECR II-3649, Judgment of the Court of First Instance, 21 September 2005. In its judgment of 3 September 2008, the ECJ reversed the finding of the Court of First Instance and annulled the EC's implementing Regulation No 881/2002 on the ground that the Regulation violated the fundamental right to be heard, the right to effective judicial review and the right to respect for property (Joined Cases C-402/05 P and C-415/05 P, not yet reported).   [95] *Schmidberger*, n 89, at para 73.

[96] See n 94 and opinion of AG Poiares Maduro in Case C-402/05 *Kadi v Council*, Opinion of 16 January 2008, not yet reported.

C. 'Horizontal' Cooperation among the EC Courts, the EFTA Court, and the ECtHR in Protecting Individual Rights in the EEA

Judicial cooperation between the EC courts and the EFTA Court was legally mandated in the EEA Agreement (for example, Article 6) and facilitated by the fact that the EEA law to be interpreted by the EC and EFTA courts was largely identical with the EC's common market rules (notwithstanding the different context of the EC's common market and the EEA's free trade area). In numerous cases, EC court judgments referred to the case law of the EFTA Court, for example by pointing out 'that the principles governing the liability of an EFTA state for infringement of a directive referred to in the EEA Agreement were the subject of the EFTA Court's judgment of 10 December 1998 in *Sveinbjörnsdottir*'.[97] In its *Ospelt* judgment, the EC Court emphasized that:

One of the principal aims of the EEA Agreement is to provide for the fullest possible realization of the four freedoms within the whole EEA, so that the internal market established within the European Union is extended to the EFTA states.[98]

The case law of the EFTA Court evolved in close cooperation with the EC courts, national courts in EFTA countries, and with due regard also to the case law of the ECtHR. In view of the intergovernmental structures of the EEA Agreement, the legal homogeneity obligations in the EEA Agreement (for example, Article 6) were interpreted only as *obligations de résultat* with regard to the legal protection of market freedoms and individual rights in EFTA countries. Yet, the EFTA Court effectively promoted '*quasi*-direct effect' and '*quasi*-primacy' (C Baudenbacher) as well as full state liability and protection of individual rights of market participants in national courts in all EEA countries.[99] In various judgments, the EFTA Court followed the ECJ case law also by interpreting EEA law in conformity with the human rights guarantees of the ECHR and the judgments of the ECtHR (for example, concerning ECHR, Article 6 on access to justice and Article 10 on freedom of expression). In its *Asgeirsson* judgment, the EFTA Court rejected the argument that the reference to the EFTA Court had unduly prolonged the national court proceeding in violation of the right to a fair and public hearing within a reasonable time (ECHR, Article 6); referring to a judgment by the ECtHR in a case concerning a delay of two years and seven months due to a reference by a national court to the ECJ (pursuant to Article 234 EC), the EFTA Court shared the reasoning of the

---

[97] Case C-140/97 *Rechberger* [1999] ECR I-3499, at para 39.
[98] Case C-452/01 *Ospelt* [2003] ECR I-9743, at para 29.
[99] cf the EFTA Court President C Baudenbacher, 'The EFTA Court Ten Years On' and HP Graver, 'The Effects of EFTA Court Jurisprudence on the Legal Orders of the EFTA States' in Baudenbacher et al, n 67 above, respectively at 13 and 97. As Graver highlights: 'Direct effect of primary law, state liability and the duty of the courts to interpret national law in the light of EEA obligations have been clearly and firmly accepted in national law by Norwegian courts.'

ECtHR that adding the period of preliminary references (which was less than six months in the case before the EFTA Court) could undermine the legitimate functions of such cooperation among national and international courts in their joint protection of the rule of law.

The ECtHR has frequently referred in its judgments to provisions of EU law and to judgments of the ECJ. In *Goodwin*, for example, the ECtHR referred to Article 9 of the EU Charter of Fundamental Rights (right to marry) so as to back up its judgment that the refusal to recognize a change of sex for the purposes of marriage constituted a violation of ECHR, Article 12.[100] In *Dangeville*, the ECtHR's determination that an interference with the right to the peaceful enjoyment of possessions was not required in the general interest took into account the fact that the French measures were incompatible with EC law.[101] In cases *Waite and Kennedy v Germany*, the ECtHR held that it would be incompatible with the purpose and object of the ECHR if an attribution of tasks to an international organization or in the context of international agreements could absolve the contracting states of their obligations under the ECHR.[102] In the *Bosphorus* case, the ECtHR had to examine the consistency of the impounding by Ireland of a Yugoslavian aircraft on the legal basis of EC regulations imposing sanctions against the former Federal Republic of Yugoslavia; the ECtHR referred to the ECJ case law according to which respect for fundamental rights is a condition of the lawfulness of EC acts, as well as to the ECJ preliminary ruling that 'the impounding of the aircraft in question ... cannot be regarded as inappropriate or disproportionate'; in its examination of whether compliance with EC obligations could justify the interference by Ireland with the applicant's property rights, the ECtHR proceeded on the basis of the following four principles:[103]

(a) a Contracting Party is responsible under Article 1 of the Convention for all acts and omissions of its organs regardless of whether the act or omission in question was a consequence of domestic law or of the necessity to comply with international legal obligations;

(b) State action taken in compliance with such legal obligations is justified as long as the relevant organization is considered to protect fundamental rights, as regards both the substantive guarantees offered and the mechanisms controlling their observance, in a manner which can be considered at least equivalent to that for which the Convention provides;

---

[100] *Goodwin v United Kingdom*, Judgment, 11 July 2002, Reports of Judgments and Decisions 2002-VI, at paras 58 and 100.

[101] *SA Dangeville v France*, Judgment, 16 April 2002, Reports of Judgments and Decisions 2002-III, at paras 31 ff.

[102] *Waite and Kennedy v Germany*, Judgment, 18 February 1999, Reports of Judgments and Decisions 1999-I, at para 67.

[103] *Case of Bosphorus Hava Yollari Turizm v Ireland*, Judgment, 30 June 2005, [2006] 42 EHRR 1, at paras 153 ff.

(c) If such equivalent protection is considered to be provided by the organization, the presumption will be that a State has not departed from the requirements of the Convention when it does no more than implement legal obligations flowing from its membership of the organization.

(d) However, any such presumption can be rebutted if, in the circumstances of a particular case, it is considered that the protection of Convention rights was manifestly deficient. In such cases, the interest of international cooperation would be outweighed by the Convention's role as a 'constitutional instrument of European public order' in the field of human rights.

After examining the comprehensive EC guarantees of fundamental rights and judicial remedies, the ECtHR found:

that the protection of fundamental rights by EC law can be considered to be, and to have been at the relevant time, 'equivalent' ... to that of the Convention system. Consequently, the presumption arises that Ireland did not depart from requirements of the Convention when it implemented legal obligations flowing from its membership of the EC.

As the Court did not find any 'manifest deficiency' in the protection of the applicant's Convention rights, the relevant presumption of compliance with the ECHR had not been rebutted.[104]

VI. Conditional '*Solange* Cooperation' for Coordinating Competing Jurisdictions in International Trade and Environmental Law beyond Europe?

Competing multilateral treaty and dispute settlement systems with 'forum selection clauses' enabling governments to submit disputes to competing jurisdictions (with the risk of conflicting judgments) continue to multiply also outside economic law and human rights law – for example, in international environmental law, maritime law, criminal law, and other areas of international law. Proposals to coordinate such overlapping jurisdictions through hierarchical procedures (for example, preliminary rulings or advisory opinions by the ICJ) are opposed by most governments. Agreement on exclusive jurisdiction clauses (as in EC Treaty, Article 292; DSU/WTO, Article 23; and Law of the Sea Convention, Article 282) may not prevent submission of disputes involving several treaty regimes to competing dispute settlement fora. For example, in the dispute between Ireland and the United Kingdom over radioactive pollution from the MOX plant in Sellafield (United Kingdom), four dispute settlement bodies were seized and used diverging methods for coordinating their respective jurisdictions, as detailed below.

---

[104] *Case of Bosphorus Hava Yollari Turizm*, n 103 above, at paras 165–166.

A. The OSPAR Arbitral Award of 2003 on the MOX Plant Dispute

In order to clarify the obligations of the United Kingdom to make available all information 'on the state of the maritime area, on activities or measures adversely affecting or likely to affect it' pursuant to Article 9 of the Convention for the Protection of the Marine Environment of the North-East Atlantic (OSPAR), Ireland and the United Kingdom agreed to establish an arbitral tribunal under this OSPAR Convention.[105] Even though Article 35.5(a) of the Convention requires the tribunal to decide according to 'the rules of international law, and in particular those of the Convention', the tribunal's award of July 2003 was based only on the OSPAR Convention, without taking into account relevant environmental regulations of the EC and of the 1998 Aarhus Convention on Access to Information, Public Participation in Decision-making, and Access to Justice in Environmental Matters (ratified by all EC Member States as well as by the EC).[106] The OSPAR arbitral tribunal decided in favour of the United Kingdom that the latter had not violated its treaty obligations by not disclosing the information sought by Ireland.[107]

B. The UNCLOS 2001 Provisional Measures and 2003 Arbitral Decision in the MOX Plant Dispute

The UN Convention on the Law of the Sea (UNCLOS)[108] offers parties the choice (in Articles 281 ff) of submitting disputes to the International Tribunal for the Law of the Sea (ITLOS), the ICJ, arbitral tribunals, or other dispute settlement fora established by regional or bilateral treaties. As Ireland claimed that the discharges released by the MOX Plant contaminated Irish waters in violation of UNCLOS, it requested the establishment of an arbitral tribunal and – pending this procedure – requested interim protection measures from the ITLOS pursuant to UNCLOS, Article 290. The ITLOS order of December 2001, after determining the prima facie jurisdiction of the Annex VII arbitral tribunal to decide the merits of the dispute, requested both parties to cooperate and consult regarding the emissions from the MOX plant into the Irish Sea, pending the decision on the merits by the arbitral tribunal. The arbitral tribunal suspended its proceedings in June 2003 and requested the parties to clarify

[105] Convention for the Protection of the Marine Environment of the North-East Atlantic (OSPAR), opened for signature on 22 September 1992 and entered into force on 25 March 1998, (1993) 32 ILM 1072.

[106] Aarhus Convention on Access to Information, Public Participation in Decision-making, and Access to Justice in Environmental Matters, opened for signature on 25 June 1998, and entered into force on 30 October 2001, (1999) 38 ILM 517.

[107] cf T McDorman, 'Access to Information under Article 9 OSPAR Convention (Ireland v UK), Final Award' (2004) AJIL 98, 330.

[108] UN Convention on the Law of the Sea (UNCLOS), opened for signature on 10 December 1982 and entered into force on 16 November 2004, 1833 UNTS 397.

whether, as claimed by the United Kingdom, the EC Court had jurisdiction to decide this dispute on the basis of the relevant EC and EURATOM rules, including UNCLOS as an integral part of the Community legal system.[109]

C. The EC Court Judgment of May 2006 in the MOX Plant Dispute

In October 2003, the EU Commission started an infringement proceeding against Ireland on the ground that – as the EC had ratified and transformed UNCLOS into an integral part of the EC legal system – Ireland's submission of the dispute to tribunals outside the Community legal order had violated the exclusive jurisdiction of the EC Court under Article 292 EC and Article 193 of the EURATOM Treaty.[110] In its judgment of May 2006, the Court confirmed its exclusive jurisdiction in view of the fact that the UNCLOS provisions on the prevention of marine pollution relied on by Ireland in its dispute relating to the MOX plant 'are rules which form part of the Community legal order' which offered (for example, in Article 227 EC) effective judicial remedies for Ireland's complaint.[111] The Court followed from the autonomy of the Community legal system and from UNCLOS, Article 282 that the system for the resolution of disputes set out in the EC Treaty must in principle take precedence over that provided for in Part XV of UNCLOS. As the dispute concerned the interpretation and application of EC law within the terms of Article 292 EC, 'Articles 220 EC and 292 EC precluded Ireland from initiating proceedings before the Arbitral Tribunal with a view to resolving the dispute concerning the MOX plant'.[112] By requesting the arbitral tribunal to decide disputes concerning the interpretation and application of Community law, Ireland had violated the exclusive jurisdiction of the Court under Article 292 EC as well as the EC Member States' duties of close cooperation, prior information, and loyal consultation of the competent Community institutions as prescribed in Article 10 EC.

D. The 2004 Ijzeren Rijn Arbitration between the Netherlands and Belgium

The Ijzeren Rijn arbitration under the auspices of the Permanent Court of Arbitration concerned a dispute between Belgium and the Netherlands over Belgium's right to the use and reopening of an old railway line leading through a

---

[109] cf Y Shany, 'The First MOX Plant Award: The Need to Harmonize Competing Environmental Regimes and Dispute Settlement Procedures' (2004) Leiden Journal of International Law 17, 815.

[110] Treaty Establishing the European Atomic Energy Community (EURATOM Treaty), 25 March 1957, 298 UNTS 167.

[111] Case C-459/03 *Commission v Ireland* [2006] ECR I-4635, at paras 84, 121, 128.

[112] Ibid., at para 133.

protected natural habitat and the payment of the costs involved.[113] The arbitral tribunal was requested to settle the dispute on the basis of international law, including if necessary EC law, with due respect to the obligations of these EC Member States under Article 292 EC. The tribunal agreed with the view shared by both parties that there was no dispute within the meaning of Article 292 EC because its decision on the apportionment of costs did not require any interpretation of EC law (for example, the Council Directive on the conservation of natural habitats).

E. The '*Solange* Method' as Reciprocal Respect for Constitutional Justice

The above-mentioned examples for competing jurisdictions for the settlement of environmental disputes among European states raise questions similar to those regarding overlapping jurisdictions for the settlement of human rights disputes,[114] criminal proceedings in national and international criminal courts, or trade disputes over related claims in the WTO, NAFTA, the EC, and the Mercado Comun del Sur (Common Market of South America – MERCOSUR). The UNCLOS provisions for dispute settlement by regional courts (Article 282) or on the basis of 'this Convention and other rules of international law not incompatible with this Convention' (Article 288) prompted the ITLOS to affirm prima facie jurisdiction in the MOX Plant dispute. The Annex VII arbitral tribunal argued convincingly, however, that the prospect of resolving this dispute in the EC Court on the basis of EC law risked leading to conflicting decisions which, bearing in mind considerations of mutual respect and comity between judicial institutions and the explicit recognition of mutually agreed regional jurisdictions in UNCLOS, Article 282, justified suspending the arbitral proceeding and enjoining the parties to resolve the Community law issues in the institutional framework of the EC.

WTO law recognizes similar rights of WTO members to conclude regional trade agreements with autonomous dispute settlement procedures. Yet, WTO law lacks provisions corresponding to UNCLOS, Article 282 enabling WTO dispute settlement bodies to decline jurisdiction on WTO disputes in favour of other, bilaterally or regionally agreed jurisdictions; nor does WTO law include a provision similar to UNCLOS, Article 288 explicitly authorizing WTO dispute settlement bodies to decide WTO disputes also on the basis of 'other rules of international law not incompatible with this Convention'. The quasi-automatic establishment of WTO dispute settlement panels at the request of

---

[113] cf N Lavranos, 'The MOX Plant and IJzeren Rijn Disputes: Which Court is the Supreme Arbiter?' (2006) Leiden Journal of International Law 19, 1–24.

[114] cf L Helfer, 'Forum Shopping for Human Rights' (1995) University of Pennsylvania Law Review 148, 285 ff.

any WTO member entails that WTO dispute settlement bodies must respect the 'right to a panel' of WTO members even if the respondent WTO member would prefer to settle the dispute in the framework of another jurisdiction. Hence, WTO panels have accepted jurisdiction also for complaints by NAFTA and MERCOSUR Member States notwithstanding arguments by the defending country that essentially the same legal complaint (for example, challenging the legality of import restrictions on poultry imposed by Argentina, or duties imposed by the United States on lumber imports from Canada) had already previously been rejected in MERCOSUR or NAFTA dispute settlement proceedings. Under which conditions could WTO dispute settlement bodies exercise 'judicial comity' in favour of regional jurisdictions similar to the judicial comity exercised by the arbitral tribunal under the Law of the Sea Convention in favour of the EC Court in the *MOX Plant* case? For example, how should the WTO Dispute Settlement Body decide if an EC Member State (for example, Germany) would request a WTO dispute settlement ruling on the EC's WTO-inconsistent banana restrictions[115] in view of the EC Court's persistent refusal to ensure compliance by the EC institutions with their WTO obligations? Should it refuse WTO jurisdiction in view of Article 292 EC even if the WTO member concerned would have no alternative judicial remedy against EC majority decisions violating the WTO obligations of the EC and of EC Member States, as confirmed in WTO non-compliance proceedings pursuant to DSU, Article 21:5? Or should the WTO respect the 'right to a panel' of every WTO member (including EC Member States) 'as long as' the EC and the EC Court do not offer EC Member States effective legal and judicial remedies (equivalent to those offered by WTO law) against the notorious EC violations of WTO law entailing the international legal responsibility also of every EC Member State?[116] The lack of a treaty provision similar to UNCLOS, Article 282 might also have prompted the OSPAR arbitral tribunal to decide on the claim of an alleged violation of the OSPAR Convention, without any discussion of Article 292 EC and without prejudice to future dispute settlement proceedings in the EC Court based on EC law. The Ijzeren

---

[115] In two WTO non-compliance panel reports (under DSU, Art 21:5) of 7 April and 19 May 2008, the WTO confirmed, once again, that the EC restrictions on importation, sale, and distribution of bananas continue to violate Arts I and XIII GATT (WT/DS27). These two reports had been preceded by about a dozen of previous GATT and WTO dispute settlement findings since 1993 on legal inconsistencies of the import restrictions by the EC and EC Member States on bananas.

[116] Such challenges in the WTO by EC Member States of EC acts violating WTO law have never occurred so far and would violate the EC duty to cooperate pursuant to Art 10 EC. Community lawyers (like Lavranos, n 113 above, 10–11) argue that not only from the point of view of Community law, but also 'from the point of view of international law, the supremacy of Community law within the EC and its member states must be accepted' (ibid., 10–11). Yet, it is arguable even from the point of view of Community law that the duty of loyalty (Art 10 EC) applies only 'as long as' the ECJ offers effective judicial remedies against obvious violations by EC institutions of their obligations (eg under Arts 220, 300 EC) to respect the rule of law and protect EC Member States from international legal responsibility for EC majority decisions violating mixed agreements.

Rijn arbitral tribunal examined, as requested by the parties, the legal relevance of Article 292 EC and decided the dispute without prejudice to EC law.

The *'solange* principle' makes respect for competing jurisdictions conditional on regard for constitutional principles of human rights and rule of law. It has also been applied by the EC Court itself, for instance when – in its Opinion 1/91 – the EC Court found the EEA provisions for the establishment of an EEA Court to be inconsistent with the 'autonomy of the Community legal order' and the 'exclusive jurisdiction of the Court of Justice' (for example, in so far as the EEA provisions did not guarantee legally binding effects of 'advisory opinions' by the EEA Court on national courts in EEA Member States).[117] The *'solange* principle' can explain the jurisprudence of both the EC Court[118] and the EFTA Court[119] that voluntarily agreed, private arbitral tribunals are not recognized as courts or tribunals of Member States (within the meaning of Article 234 EC and the corresponding EEA provision) entitled to request preliminary rulings by the European courts. The fact that international arbitral tribunals (like the OSPAR and Ijzeren Rijn arbitral tribunals mentioned above) are likewise not entitled to request preliminary rulings from the European courts may justify judicial self-restraint and deference to the competing jurisdiction of European courts in disputes requiring interpretation and application of European law. To the extent that conflicts of jurisdiction and conflicting judgments cannot be prevented by means of exclusive jurisdictions and hierarchical rules, international courts should follow the example of national civil and commercial courts and European courts and resolve conflicts through judicial cooperation and 'judicial dialogues' based on principles of judicial comity and judicial protection of constitutional principles (like due process of law, *res judicata*, and human rights) underlying modern international law.[120] The cooperation among national and international courts with overlapping jurisdictions for the protection of constitutional rights in Europe reflects the constitutional duty of judges to protect 'constitutional justice'; it should serve as a model for similar cooperation among national and international courts with overlapping jurisdictions in other fields of international law,[121] notably if the intergovernmental rules protect cooperation among citizens across

---

[117] *EEA Draft Agreement*, Opinion 1/91 [1991] ECR I-6079.
[118] Case C-125/2004 *Denuit/Cordenier v Transorient* [2005] ECR I-923.
[119] Case E-1/94 *Restamark* [1994–1995] EFTA Court Reports 15.
[120] cf Y Shany, *Regulating Jurisdictional Relations Between National and International Courts* (2007) 166 ff.
[121] cf N Lavranos, 'Towards a *Solange*-Method between International Courts and Tribunals?' in T Broude and Y Shany (eds), *The Allocation of Authority in International Law. Essays in Honour of Prof. R. Lapidoth* (2008) 217 ff:

> if the *Solange*-method would be applied by all international courts and tribunals in case of jurisdictional overlap, the risk of diverging or conflicting judgments could be effectively minimized, thus reducing the danger of a fragmentation of the international legal order … One could argue that the *Solange*-method, and for that matter judicial comity in general, is part of the legal duty of each and every court to deliver justice.

national frontiers, such as the settlement of transnational trade, investment, and environmental disputes. Especially in those areas of intergovernmental regulation where states remain reluctant to submit to review by international courts (for example, as in the second and third pillars of the EU Treaty), *national courts* must remain vigilant guardians of rule of law so as to protect citizens and their constitutional rights from inadequate judicial remedies at the international level of multilevel governance.

F. Judicial Self-Restraint: The Example of WTO Dispute Settlement Practices

The WTO dispute settlement system differs from all other international dispute settlement systems by its uniquely institutionalized review and adoption of all WTO panel, appellate, and arbitral reports by WTO members in the Dispute Settlement Body (DSB). Notably in the field of trade-related environmental measures, WTO dispute settlement reports and the DSB have referred to the WTO objectives of 'sustainable development' (WTO, Preamble) and to multilateral environmental agreements for justifying differential treatment (for example, of imports of shrimps depending upon whether their harvesting methods protected sea turtles) on grounds of environmental protection.[122]

Yet, the WTO Panel Report on the EC's restrictions on genetically modified organisms interpreted VCLT, Article 31(3)(c) narrowly as applying only to international law rules binding all parties of the treaty concerned.[123] This narrow interpretation of the customary rules of treaty interpretation was supported by WTO members as protecting state sovereignty and limiting the relevant context of WTO rules (there are hardly any other multilateral treaties ratified by all 153 WTO members, including customs territories like Hong Kong, Macau, Taiwan, and the EC). In the *Mexico-Soft Drinks* dispute, the WTO Panel and Appellate Body declined jurisdiction for claims based on the North American Free Trade Agreement (NAFTA) and interpreted the general exception in GATT, Article XX(d) narrowly as not covering 'laws and regulations' which Mexico had adopted as countermeasures in order to respond to alleged violations of NAFTA obligations by the United States.[124] According to the Appellate Body, NAFTA obligations are not 'laws and

---

[122] WTO Appellate Body Report, '*US-Import Prohibition of Certain Shrimp and Shrimp Products*', WT/DS58/AB/R, adopted 6 November 1998.

[123] Cf WTO Panel Report, '*EC Measures Affecting the Approval and Marketing of Biotech Products*', WT/DS/291-293/R, adopted in November 2006, at paras 7.65 ff.

[124] Cf WTO Appellate Body Report, '*Mexico – Tax Measures on Soft Drinks*', WT/DS308/AB/R, adopted 24 March 2006. The Appellate Body upheld the Panel finding that Mexico's measures, which sought to secure compliance by the United States with its obligations under the NAFTA, did not constitute measures 'to secure compliance with laws or regulations' within the meaning of GATT, Art XX(d).

regulations' within the meaning of GATT, Article XX(d) because they are not part of the domestic legal order.[125] The reasoning by the Appellate Body – namely, that it 'would have to assess whether the relevant international agreement had been violated' in order to examine the applicability of Article XX(d), and 'this is not the function of panels and the Appellate Body as intended by the DSU'[126] – would presumably have led to similar judicial self-restraint in the *Swordfish* dispute between the EC and Chile in the WTO:[127] WTO dispute settlement bodies would refrain from examining the Chilean claim that Chile's violations of GATT obligations were justified countermeasures in response to preceding violations by the EC of environmental obligations under the Law of the Sea Convention. Even if – as permitted by the Law of the Sea Convention (Article 280) as well as by the DSU (for example, Articles 7 and 25) – Chile, the EC, and the DSB would request a WTO panel to examine the dispute in the light of both WTO law and the Law of the Sea Convention, the narrow interpretation of GATT, Article XX is likely to prevail, namely that GATT, Article XX does not justify unilateral departures from GATT obligations in response to violations of non-WTO agreements.

In the increasing number of WTO dispute settlement proceedings where complainants or defendants refer to related judicial proceedings in national courts (for example, Brazilian court injunctions authorizing imports of retreaded tyres), in regional jurisdictions (for example, MERCOSUR arbitral findings against Brazilian import restrictions on remoulded tyres, NAFTA Panel findings on US import restrictions on Canadian lumber, EC Court findings on EC import restrictions on bananas and genetically modified organisms), or in worldwide jurisdictions (for example, ICJ and ITLOS proceedings related to measures under review in WTO dispute settlement proceedings), mutually incoherent national and international judgments are ever-more frequent – for example, if national and regional courts do not examine justifications of the trade restrictions under WTO law (for example, in the Brazilian court and MERCOSUR arbitration cases mentioned above where the Brazilian government did not invoke GATT, Article XX as a legal justification). WTO dispute settlement bodies might also have to examine whether WTO findings on jurisdiction, evidence, burden of proof, judicial procedures (like inherent powers of courts to make preliminary rulings, 'comity' among courts), and other judicial principles (like the *litispendens* and *res judicata* principles, prohibition of abuse of rights, 'balancing' among competing principles) are consistent with the 'common law of

---

[125] Ibid., at para 56.   [126] Ibid., at paras 69 ff.
[127] WTO, *Chile-Measures Affecting the Transit and Importation of Swordfish, Request for consultations by the EC*, WT/DS193/1, 26 April 2000 (the WTO complaint by the EC, and the related Chilean complaint against the EC in the International Tribunal for the Law of the Sea, were suspended).

international adjudication' that is emerging from the increasingly common approaches adopted in multilevel judicial governance.[128] The WTO Appellate Body findings on Brazil's import restrictions of retreaded tyres[129] may imply that, in order to bring its restrictions into conformity with its WTO obligations, Brazil may have to adopt legislation overruling the preceding Brazilian court judgments authorizing such imports, as well as the MERCOSUR arbitral award on the inconsistency of the import restrictions with Brazil's MERCOSUR commitments. Yet, these incoherencies between national, MERCOSUR, and WTO dispute settlement findings concerning imports of retreaded tyres into Brazil may have been due to incoherent legal defences by the Brazilian government rather than to incoherent judgments or to inconsistencies between Brazilian law, MERCOSUR law, and WTO law. As illustrated by the '*solange* cooperation' among courts in Europe, multiple proceedings in national and international courts may mutually reinforce cooperation among courts and their multilevel judicial protection of constitutional rights – for instance, if courts assert jurisdiction, or refrain from exercising jurisdiction, depending on whether other courts offered effective legal and judicial remedies. Similar to the '*solange* cooperation' among courts with competing jurisdictions, the 'proportionality principle' for the judicial balancing of competing rights claims of governments (for example, market access rights of WTO members versus their rights under WTO exception clauses) and of individuals (for example, economic freedoms versus human rights and social rights under EC law and national laws), or for delimiting individual rights and public interest provisions, illustrate not only an increasing 'constitutionalization' and progressive development of IEL through judicial interpretations; the justification of judicial reasoning by references to constitutional principles can also rationalize and legitimize judicial findings (for example, by demonstrating the suitability, necessity, and proportionality of government restrictions for protecting constitutional rights or other public interests).[130]

---

[128] cf C Brown, *A Common Law of International Adjudication* (2007); see also Shany, n 120 above.

[129] WTO Appellate Body Report, *Brazil-Measures Affecting Imports of Retreated Tyres Measures*, WT/DS332/AB/R, adopted in February 2008.

[130] cf R Dworkin, *Taking Rights Seriously* (1977) xxi: 'judicial decisions based on arguments of principle are compatible with democratic principles'. According to R Alexy, n 41 above, 47 ff, principles are norms of relatively high generality and 'optimization requirements' which require something be realized to the greatest extent possible given the legal and factual possibilities; by contrast, rules are norms which are either fulfilled or not ('a conflict between rules can only be resolved in that either an appropriate exception is read into one of the rules, or at least one of the rules is declared invalid'). Dworkin's 'absolutist' concept of rights as 'trumps', and Alexy's more relativistic concept of rights, entail different methods for the balancing of competing rights, principles, and policy goals. Judicial interpretations of 'proportionality balancing' also tend to be influenced by the respective legal cultures and contexts. The EC Court, for example, applies a 'manifestly inappropriate' standard for reviewing whether EC measures are consistent with fundamental freedoms, but a more stringent 'necessity' and 'less restrictive alternative' test for its judicial review of the compatibility of national restrictions of fundamental freedoms with EC law.

VII. The Need for a Constitutional Theory of Judicial Review of IEL: The Example of Investor-State Arbitration

Politicians and diplomats like to defend their discretionary policy powers by claiming that the task of courts is 'to apply the law, not to make it'. Yet, there is broad agreement among lawyers today that judicial rulings can rarely be justified on purely syllogistic reasoning (rules + facts = judgment). Legal-constructivist theories of adjudication (like that of R Dworkin) reject the alleged link between indeterminacy of rules and judicial discretion by arguing that judicial reasoning on the basis of fundamental rights, general principles of law, and 'due process of law' tends to lead judges to one single right answer.[131] According to Dworkin's 'adjudicative principle of integrity', judges should interpret law in conformity with its objectives of legality and rule-of-law as expressing 'a coherent conception of justice and fairness':

> Law as integrity asks judges to assume, so far as this is possible, that the law is structured by a coherent set of principles about justice and fairness and procedural due process, and it asks them to enforce these in the fresh cases that come before them, so that each person's situation is fair and just according to the same standards.[132]

Power-oriented political scientists often reject such legal models of judicial decision-making as being outside politics as ideology. The increasing political science literature on the expansion of judicial power and on 'judicial governance' refers, for example, to the political selection of Supreme Court judges as confirming the widespread belief that the judges' political preferences influence the decisions of Supreme Courts.[133] Proponents of 'institutional theories' analyse judicial decision-making as 'collegial games' or as a function of the interaction of courts with other institutions (for example, the legislature, the executive, or other courts).[134] A few political philosophers (like J Waldron) even argue against judicial review on the ground that constitutional language is often indeterminate and leaves judges too much political discretion (as reflected by the frequent disagreements among judges).[135] The absence of political and judicial control mechanisms has been criticized especially in international investment law where decisions are made ever-more frequently by ad hoc tribunals without appellate review and without much regard to the consistency of arbitral awards among each other, or with international law and human rights. Judicial approaches and applicable rules in investment disputes in the International

---

[131] R Dworkin, n 130 above, 31–39, 68–71.
[132] R Dworkin, *Law's Empire* (1986), 225, 243.
[133] L Epstein and J Knight, *The Choices Justices Make* (1998).
[134] cf A Stone Sweet, *The Judicial Construction of Europe* (2004).
[135] J Waldron, *Law and Disagreement* (1999).

Court of Justice (ICJ), investor-state arbitration based on ICSID rules and procedures, commercial arbitration, or domestic courts may differ enormously, thus setting incentives for 'forum shopping' and 'judicial comity' so as to avoid mutually incoherent judicial reasoning and judgments.

A. Legitimate Diversity of Constitutional Conceptions of Judicial Review

The controversies over whether constitutional review is best performed as part of the normal court system (as in the United States), by independent constitutional courts (as in many European states), or by politically more accountable parliamentary bodies (as in England and some British Commonwealth countries) illustrate that the functional interrelationships between human rights, democratic procedures, and the design of judicial review may be interpreted in diverse ways. Hence, theories about the legitimate functions of courts differ among jurisdictions depending on their respective conceptions of democracy and constitutionalism. For example:

- conceptions of democracy as rule by present majorities have criticized judicial review as a 'deviant institution in the American democracy' whose 'counter-majoritarian difficulty' requires constitutional justification – for example, by the legitimacy of judicial protection of constitutional minority rights;[136]

- proponents of democratic self-governance by collective decisions of citizens have warned that judicial review risks to entail paternalistic rule by 'a bevy of Platonic Guardians';[137]

- defenders of human rights counter that judicial discourse is better capable than political discourse among periodically elected politicians to find the right answers for the interpretation of constitutional rights and human rights;[138]

- supporters of rights-based constitutional democracy justify the judicial function by the judicial protection of the constitutional rights of 'the governed' and of other constitutional principles vis-à-vis their encroachment by governments;[139]

---

[136] cf AM Bickel, *The Least Dangerous Branch: The Supreme Court at the Barr of Politics* (2nd edn, 1986) 16, 23.   [137] L Hand, *The Bill of Rights* (1958) 73.
[138] cf MJ Perry, *The Constitution, the Courts and Human Rights: An Inquiry into the Legitimacy of Constitutional Policymaking by the Judiciary* (1982).
[139] cf AS Rosenbaum (ed), *Constitutionalism: The Philosophical Dimension* (1988) 4: 'A "democratic" constitution embodies a conception of the fundamental rights and obligations of citizens and establishes a judicial process by which rights claims may be litigated.' B Ackerman, *We the People: Foundations* (1991) 262:

> If the Court is right in finding that these politicians/statesmen have moved beyond their mandate, it is furthering Democracy, not frustrating it, in revealing our representatives as mere 'stand-ins' for the People, whose word is not to be confused with the collective judgment of *the People themselves*.

- if democracy is defined by the aim 'that collective decisions be made by political institutions whose structure, composition and practices treat all members of the community, as individuals, with equal concern and respect', then judicial review can be viewed as a necessary 'forum of principle' enhancing constitutionally limited democracy and protecting equal citizen rights;[140]
- proponents of deliberative constitutional democracy argue that, 'in a constitutional regime with judicial review, public reason is the reason of its supreme court';[141] constitutional review can ensure that the procedural conditions of democratic legitimacy – basic rights to private and public autonomy – have been fulfilled.[142]

The design of international courts should not depend on contested conceptions of constitutional review inside democracies. Yet, there are clear interrelationships between 'principles of justice' and international dispute settlement procedures and processes. As international court decisions are legally binding and assert legal precedence over domestic law, justification of their constitutional legitimacy is important. Governments and international courts can enhance the legitimacy of judicial review not only by promoting due process of law, transparent and inclusive judicial procedures (for example, admitting *amicus curiae* briefs by adversely affected third parties), and by institutionalizing dialogue between legislative and judicial branches (as in the WTO Dispute Settlement Body's review and approval of all WTO dispute settlement reports) as well as with civil society (as in the WTO's annual public *fora* with civil society representatives). But constitutional justice may also require promoting citizen-oriented interpretations of intergovernmental guarantees of human rights, economic freedom, non-discrimination, and rule of law in international cooperation among citizens. Judges may lack competence to declare intergovernmental guarantees (for example, of human rights, private 'trading rights' and intellectual property rights protected in WTO law, and investor rights protected in bilateral investment treaties) to have 'direct effect' for the benefit of individual economic actors and for interpreting

---

[140] cf R Dworkin, *Freedom's Law: The Moral Reading of the American Constitution* (1996) 21 ff, 344:

> Individual citizens can in fact exercise the moral responsibilities of citizenship better when final decisions involving constitutional values are removed from ordinary politics and assigned to courts, whose decisions are meant to turn on principle, not on the weight of numbers or the balance of political influence.

[141] Rawls, n 18 above, 231 ff.

[142] cf J Habermas, *Between Facts and Norms: Contributions to a Discourse Theory of Law and Democracy* (1996) 279:

> If one understands the constitution as an interpretation and elaboration of a system of rights in which private and public autonomy are internally related (and must be simultaneously enhanced), then a rather bold constitutional adjudication is even required in cases that concern the implementation of democratic procedure and the deliberative form of political opinion- and will-formation.

corresponding citizen rights inside domestic legal systems. However, judges can prevent and settle international economic disputes by interpreting domestic laws in conformity with international legal obligations of the country concerned. From a human rights perspective, both national and international judges should – as prescribed in the VCLT – interpret IEL 'in conformity with principles of justice' and human rights, with due respect for the legitimate diversity of national and international legal systems which often define 'principles of justice' and human rights in diverse ways.[143] Both national and international judges may have to review whether 'general justice' (for example, in the sense of rule-following and precedent-following) needs to be tempered by principles of 'particular justice' (for example, in the Aristotelian sense of 'distributive justice' and 'corrective justice' depending on the particular circumstances).[144] Just as constitutional law and theories of justice tend to be highly contextual,[145] judges should clarify the 'principles' underlying the applicable law in their respective jurisdictions, the possible tensions between 'formal justice' (for example, in the sense of impartial and consistent administration of laws whatever their substantive principles) and 'distributive justice' (for example, in the sense of reasonable justifications of treating different cases differently), and the conditions for comity and cooperation among different courts. As the universal recognition of inalienable human rights has constitutionally limited the power-oriented premises of the Westphalian 'international law among states', international economic courts should examine – like European courts – the potential impact of human rights and other 'principles of justice' (for example, of non-discrimination, necessity, and proportionality) on the interpretation of economic rules and on judicial justifications of judgments.[146]

---

[143] Due to the diversity of national constitutional traditions, domestic implementation of international rules is likely always to remain diverse. For example, should fundamental rights be interpreted and applied by way of balancing (as 'optimization precepts' as proposed by R Alexy) or should they be considered as 'trumps' (R Dworkin) and definitive rules which cannot be overruled in certain situations by public policies and public goods? Are individual 'market freedoms' and other fundamental freedoms necessary consequences of respect for human liberty (as recognized in EU law), or are they 'Kitsch' (M Koskenniemi) that should be replaced by more flexible utilitarianism? On the diversity of domestic legislation and adjudication implementing international economic rules, see M Hilf and E-U Petersmann (eds), *National Constitutions and International Economic Law* (1993). On the diverse conceptions of constitutional rights, see M Kumm, *Political Liberalism and the Structures of Rights* in G Pavlakos (ed), *Law, Rights and Discourse* (2007) 131–165.   [144] cf. Aristotle, n 6 above, 1130b.

[145] cf R Post, *The Social Domains of Constitutional Law – Democracy, Community and Management* (1995). J Rawls' *Theory of Justice* (revised edn, 1999) 8, 216, distinguishes between 'ideal theory' (eg based on the assumption of 'strict compliance') and 'non-ideal theories' (eg elaborating principles for meeting injustices and responding to only 'partial compliance', eg by 'compensatory justice principles').

[146] The literal meaning of the Latin word 'justificare' – ie to make just – underlines the importance of judicial justifications for the administration of justice. The WTO Appellate Body report on *US-Zeroing*, n 32 above, rightly emphasized (at paras 160, 161) the obligation of courts and WTO panels to treat like cases alike and, hence, promote coherent interpretation and application of the law in order to meet the legitimate expectations of governments and individuals in rule of law.

B. Dispute Avoidance through Constitutional Approaches: Failures of Investor-State Arbitration

International investment law, like international trade law, is no longer defined only by governments, but increasingly also by judgments of national and international courts at the request of citizens and non-governmental organizations which call for adapting trade and investment law so as to protect human rights of individuals and communities more effectively. The constitutional dimensions of international investment law are illustrated by the commitments of ever more countries (for example, under approximately 2,500 bilateral investment treaties (BITs) and a few regional trade and investment agreements) to transnational investor-state arbitration which makes national and international guarantees of investor rights and property rights enforceable through international arbitration and national judicial enforcement measures throughout the world. Similar to WTO disputes, investor-state arbitration under BITs or under ICSID jurisdiction is usually an alternative to domestic litigation which is often perceived as biased and inadequate (for example, because domestic judges risk disregarding the relevant international law rules); international judicial remedies may also be resorted to in parallel with domestic litigation or after the exhaustion of domestic remedies. By the end of 2007, about 120 investor-state arbitration proceedings were pending under the jurisdiction of ICSID, in addition to numerous additional investor-state arbitration proceedings pending in other jurisdictions. Even though foreign investments often affect public interests, investor-state arbitrations are often submitted to commercial and confidential arbitration procedures (for example, based on UNCITRAL rules) in which public law and public interest considerations, including human rights, play little if any role.[147] As in most trade disputes, the parties to investor-state arbitration focus their arguments on economic rights (as protected by investment law) and related obligations of states. In the few investor-state disputes where human rights were invoked by investors, host states, third parties, or by the arbitrators themselves, the arbitral tribunals tended to interpret their jurisdiction, the applicable law, and the 'corporate social responsibilities' of foreign investors narrowly,[148] without ensuring that

---

[147] cf *Ruggie's Report*, n 1 above, para 37.
[148] In *Biloune and Marine Drive Complex Ltd v Ghana Investments Centre and the Government of Ghana*, Award, 1993 (95 ILR 184), for example, the tribunal concluded that its jurisdiction was limited to the alleged expropriation and did not extend to additional claims of violation of human rights. On state duties to protect citizens against human rights abuses by third parties (including business), the corporate responsibility to respect human rights, and the need for more effective access to judicial remedies, see *Ruggie's Report*, n 1 above.

investment law is interpreted and applied in conformity with human rights obligations of the governments concerned.[149]

The more than 40 ICSID cases initiated against Argentina for its 'emergency measures' taken in response to the 2001/2002 financial crises have led to arbitral awards that have been widely criticized for their lack of coherent reasoning, contradictory legal findings, and disregard for human rights – for example, in cases of privatizations of essential water services. In three recent ICSID arbitration procedures about failed water privatizations in Argentina and Bolivia, none of the arbitral decisions considered human rights of access to water, and adversely affected third parties were not allowed to intervene or submit *amicus curiae* submissions.[150] True, prior to the – legally not binding – General Comment No 15 on 'The Right to Water' adopted by the UN Committee for Economic, Social, and Cultural Rights in November 2002,[151] the legal status of rights of access to water at affordable prices (for example, as constitutional, legislative or human rights) was contested.[152] If Argentina and Bolivia – in their concession contracts with private water companies – had acknowledged their human rights obligations to protect access to water by including such obligations in the concession contracts, the subsequent investment disputes over price increases, insufficient investments, and inadequate water quality controls might have been avoided.

It was only in the more recent ICSID complaint by *Aguas Argentinas SA* requesting compensation for the alleged damage caused by Argentina's economic emergency measures adopted in 2002 that an ICSID tribunal granted the request by civil society organizations to apply for leave to make *amicus curiae* submissions on the public health and human rights dimensions of the dispute;[153] the

---

[149] In *Mondev International Ltd v United States of America*, Award, 11 October 2002 (42 ILM 85), the tribunal referred to human rights guarantees of access to courts in interpreting the minimum standard clause of NAFTA, Art 1105(1). In *Técnicas Medioambientales Tecmed, SA v Mexico*, 29 May 2003 (43 ILM 133), the tribunal cited a judgment of the ECtHR to the effect that, 'as regards a taking of property in the context of a social reform, there may well be good grounds for drawing a distinction between nationals and non-nationals as far as compensation is concerned'. For empirical analyses of the increasing tendency in the legal reasoning of ICSID tribunals to interpret investment law in conformity with other areas of international law, see OK Fauchald, 'The Legal Reasoning of ICSID Tribunals – An Empirical Analysis' (2008) 19 European Journal of International Law, 301–364. On the duties of host states to take state action in the form of legislation, regulation, monitoring, and enforcement to ensure that domestic and foreign company activities do not negatively impact the enjoyment of human rights, see *Ruggie's Report*, n 1 above; the report also emphasizes (eg at para 56) the responsibilities of companies to become aware of, prevent, and address adverse human rights impacts.

[150] *Compañía de Aguas del Aconquija, PA & Compagnie Générale des Eaux v Argentina*, ICSID Case No ARB/97/3; *Azurix Corp v Argentina*, ICSID Case No ARB/01/12; and *Aguas del Tunari SA v Bolivia*, ICSID Case No ARB/02/3. In *Azurix*, the tribunal mentioned that it failed to understand the relevance for this case of Argentina's argument that conflicts between a BIT and human rights treaties must be resolved in favour of human rights.

[151] UN CESCR, *General Comment 15* (2002) UN doc E/C.12/2002/11.

[152] cf R Eibe and P Rothen (eds), *The Right to Water* (2006).

[153] *Aguas Argentinas SA v Argentina*, ICSID Case No ARB/03/19.

tribunal's order explicitly acknowledged that the investment dispute centred around water distribution and sewage systems affecting millions of people and raising 'complex public and international law questions, including human rights considerations'.[154]

The *Tecmed* case seems to have been the first ISCID award in which the tribunal included human rights considerations in its proportionality analysis (which it had explicitly borrowed from an ECtHR judgment that pollution caused by a private waste treatment plant had violated the human rights to respect for one's home and private family life); the ICSID tribunal found that the refusal to renew an operating permit for a landfill was disproportional to its stated aim (namely, protection of public health and the environment) and constituted an expropriation in violation of Mexico's BIT obligations.[155] In view of the rapid expansion of investor-state arbitration from fewer than 10 published arbitral awards in the mid-1990s to now more than 300 known cases, there is increasing concern about the overall coherence of this rapidly evolving case law.[156]

VIII. Conclusion: Judicial Protection of Rule of Law Depends on Respect for 'Constitutional Justice'

Constitutional democracies and UN human rights law, like modern theories of justice, proceed from the constitutional assumption that the legitimacy of national and international law depends on respect for human rights and democratic constitutionalism. Citizen-driven markets constitute one of the most

---

[154] See *Aguas Argentinas*, n 153 above, Order, 19 May 2005 in response to a Petition for Transparency and Participation as *Amicus Curiae*, at para 19. This order was cited with approval in subsequent investor-state arbitrations like *Biwater Gauff v Tanzania*, ICSID Case No ARB/05/22, Procedural Order, 2 February 2007, noting that the *amicus curiae* can submit arguments addressing broad policy issues concerning sustainable development, environment, human rights, and governmental policy (at paras 52, 64).   [155] *Tecmed*, n 149 above, at para 133.
[156] In response to the criticism that the diverse commercial, national, transnational, and international jurisdictions for investment disputes, their often confidential proceedings and reports contribute to a lack of coherence of investment jurisprudence, a recent ICSID arbitration award of 21 March 2007 emphasized that:

> [The tribunal] must pay due consideration to earlier decisions of international tribunals. It believes that, subject to compelling contrary grounds, it has a duty to adopt solutions established in a series of consistent cases. It also believes that, subject to the specifics of a given treaty and of the circumstances of the actual case, it has a duty to seek to contribute to the harmonious development of investment law and thereby to meet the legitimate expectations of the community of States and investors towards certainty of the rule of law.

See *Saipem SpA v Bangladesh*, ICSID Case No ARB/05/07, Decision on Jurisdiction, ICSID IIC 280 (2007), at para 67. The recent trend of submitting investor-state arbitration to the stricter confidentiality requirements in UNCITRAL arbitration (compared with ICSID arbitration) raises issues of government accountability and democratic rights to basic information about government conduct affecting public interests.

'powerful forces capable of generating economic growth, reducing poverty, and increasing demand for the rule of law, thereby contributing to the realization of a broad spectrum of human rights.'[157] International economic courts, notably in Europe, have played a crucial role in adjusting state-centred economic and human rights agreements to the democratic demand by citizens for more effective legal protection of traders, producers, investors, consumers, and other citizen interests.

A. Judges as Guardians of the 'Overlapping Consensus' on Human Rights

The disputes in the EC Court of Justice challenging EC sanctions against alleged terrorists identified in UN Security Council Resolutions[158] illustrate that power-oriented international law rules (including UN Security Council resolutions) may lack democratic legitimacy and risk being disregarded in domestic courts if the rules are perceived as being inconsistent with human rights and other constitutional principles. UN law (for example, the human rights commitments of all 192 UN Member States under the UN Charter) and its 'rules of recognition' (as formulated in Article 38 of the Statute of the ICJ) offer ample scope for interpreting international law and its 'general principles of law recognized by civilized nations' (ICJ Statute, Article 38) 'in conformity with the principles of justice and international law' and human rights, as required not only by human rights law and democratic constitutions, but also by the customary methods of treaty interpretation. While political governance bodies often prefer interpreting international law with due regard to its underlying power realities (like the power of the US Congress to disregard international law, the legal privileges of permanent members in the UN Security Council to veto Security Council resolutions), this article has demonstrated that independent courts increasingly insist on respect for constitutional principles as preconditions for applying international rules (for example, interpretation of general international law by WTO dispute settlement bodies in conformity with basic principles of WTO law, interpretation of UN law and WTO law by EC courts in conformity with EC constitutional principles, interpretation of EC law and EEA law by national courts in conformity with common constitutional principles, and interpretation of EC law by the ECtHR in conformity with common human rights guarantees). The universal recognition of human rights, and their 'bottom-up constitutionalism' justifying more effective legal and judicial protection at national and regional levels than at worldwide levels (for example, in the UN Security Council and WTO bodies), call for judicial interpretations of

---

[157] cf *Ruggie's Report*, n 1 above, para 2.   [158] See above nn 94 and 96.

international rules 'in conformity with principles of justice' – for example, by resorting to universal principles of human rights and of non-discriminatory treatment as constitutional justifications for 'treating like cases alike and different cases differently', or by offering additional guarantees of access to justice in domestic courts.

Similar to human rights courts, also national constitutional judges increasingly argue that constitutional democracies are premised on 'active liberty'; the exercise of individual rights to participate in democratic self-government (including consumer-driven economic markets) may serve as a 'source of judicial authority and an interpretative aid to more effective protection of ancient and modern liberty alike'.[159] Notwithstanding the diverse methodological approaches to identifying 'just rules' (such as Kantian reasonableness, Rawlsian contractarianism, and Habermas' 'deliberative democratic discourse'), legitimacy no longer derives only from (inter)governmental *fiat*, but also from democratic and judicial justification of the relevant rules as being *just*.[160] The independence, impartiality, and constitutional function of judges to protect constitutional rights against abuses of power legitimize adjudication as a necessary component of constitutional democracy – for instance, by defending general constitutional rights against majority politics (including the adoption of constitutional and legislative rules by past political majorities that have not taken into account the interests of all people living at present) and against 'originalist interpretations' that are no longer consistent with the human rights of the living citizenry. Hence, the equal individual rights and democratic consensus to be protected by the courts may have to be viewed over time, with due regard to the present concerns of citizens and of deliberative democracy.[161]

As explained by John Rawls, it is unreasonable for democratic constitutions and international law regulating cooperation among people and free citizens with diverse moral, religious, and political conceptions of justice to prescribe comprehensive political doctrines of justice. Just as human rights tend to prescribe only minimum standards which may be implemented in diverse ways in national and international legal systems, so must democratic constitutionalism and international law limit themselves to protecting an 'overlapping consensus' of reasonably diverse moral, religious, and political conceptions that are likely to

---

[159] cf US Supreme Court Justice S Breyer, *Active Liberty: Interpreting Our Democratic Constitution* (2005). For a criticism by another US federal judge, see MW McConnell, 'Active Liberty: A Progressive Alternative to Textualism and Originalism?' (2006) 119 Harvard Law Review 2387 ff.

[160] On the rational Kantian, contractarian Rawlsian, and discursive Habermasian methodological approaches to identifying just rules, see, eg CS Nino, 'Can There be Law-Abiding Judges?' in M Troper and L Jaume (eds), *1789 et l'invention de la constitution* (1994) 275, 286 ff.

[161] Self-government in constitutional democracies should therefore be conceived dynamically as a 'continuous process of tacit legislation, as has been pointed out by thinkers like Hobbes who said: "the legislator is he, not by whose authority the laws were first made, but by whose authority they now continue to be laws" ', Nino, n 160 above, 293.

endure over time in democratic societies.[162] Constitutional laws and their legal protection of human rights in the economy tend to be highly contextual (for example, depending on the democratic preferences and experiences of the people concerned). Similarly, citizen-oriented 'constitutional interpretations' of international law may legitimately differ in areas of mutually beneficial cooperation among citizens (as in IEL) compared with areas of intergovernmental 'high politics' (for example, in the UN Security Council and international border disputes in the ICJ).[163] The ever-increasing number of national, regional, and worldwide courts and their increasing references (notably in Europe) to human rights reflect the emerging consensus that the dynamically changing, national and international systems of rules require judicial clarifications, settlement of disputes, and incremental 'judicial lawmaking' in order to protect citizen rights more effectively.

B. 'Constitutional Justice' Requires Judicial Protection of Rule of Law in Mutually Beneficial Economic Cooperation Among Citizens

The 'legalization' and 'judicialization' of IEL demonstrate that it is also no longer reasonable for governments and domestic courts to ignore the general consensus among economists that liberalizing trade and investments is more important for alleviating unnecessary poverty than reliance on redistributive foreign aid. Even though trade liberalization will produce winners and losers, it tends to increase national wealth inside each of the trading partners in ways benefiting also the poor (for example, by increasing their real income and choice through more, better, and lower-priced goods and services, enhancing competition and productivity, and enabling governments to use the 'gains from trade' for helping import-competing producers to adjust to import competition). This mutually beneficial character of trade liberalization in terms of global and national welfare and poverty reduction (for example, as a result of trade

---

[162] J Rawls, n 18 above, 154 ff.

[163] Many politicians assert that international courts can only be effective in areas which do not affect the security and existence of states. The essence of 'political disputes' is related to claims that the relevant legal rules should not be applied and cannot be effectively enforced by courts (eg in revolutionary situations challenging the legal foundations of existing law, neither the French courts in 1789 nor the Permanent Court of International Justice in 1938 could adjudicate the real issues in dispute). International commercial arbitration has, however, become an effective system of transnational dispute resolution and domestic legal enforcement, cf V Gessner and AC Budak (eds), *Emerging Legal Certainty: Empirical Studies on the Globalization of Law* (1998); and T Carbonneau, *Lex Mercatoria and Arbitration: A Discussion of the New Law Merchant* (1998). The ever-larger number of international criminal courts prosecuting international war crimes, aircraft hijacking, and crimes against humanity is another illustration that 'political question doctrines' often reflect 'constitutional failures' of disregard for international law as an indispensable instrument for the collective supply of international public goods demanded by citizens.

liberalization in India and China since the 1990s) offers additional, utilitarian justifications of IEL and of its potential 'constitutional functions' for limiting protectionist 'governance failures' and 'constitutional failures' inside states.[164] Yet, the legal legitimacy of IEL depends on respect for human rights and their constitutional protection rather than on utilitarian welfare arguments. State-centred theories of delegation of governance powers to international organizations must take into account that human rights, democratic constitutionalism, and justice require limiting all legislative, executive, and judicial power through human rights and constitutional principles of justice; hence, in conformity with the perennial functions of law and courts as guardians of justice vis-à-vis abuses of governance powers, international judges should perceive themselves not only as agents of the parties to the dispute (as in the case of private law and commercial arbitrators), but also as independent guardians of 'constitutional justice' (for example, taking into account legitimate interests of third parties affected by their judicial decisions). The less parliamentary control and democratic representation remain effective in intergovernmental decision-making processes in distant worldwide organizations, the more individual and democratic self-governance must be protected by constitutional, participatory, deliberative, rights-based democracy, and other compensatory forms of democratic empowerment and justice (for example, in terms of rule of law and reasoned justification by governments as well as by courts of restrictions of individual rights).[165] The disregard for human rights, for instance by WTO dispute settlement bodies, investor-state arbitral tribunals and most regional economic dispute settlement systems outside Europe may be only of marginal, practical relevance (as illustrated by the very few EC Court judgments justifying trade restrictions on grounds of human rights over the past 50 years). Yet, as individual and democratic self-governance remains illusionary without judicial protection of rule of law and of constitutional rights, the customary law requirements of settling 'disputes concerning treaties, like other international disputes ... in conformity with the principles of justice and international law', including 'universal respect for, and observance of, human rights and fundamental freedoms for all' (VCLT, Preamble), should prompt judges to explain their decisions with due respect for the human rights foundations of modern national and international law.

The alternative Westphalian conception of 'international law among states' as an instrument for advancing *national* interests in an anarchic world continues to prompt many international diplomats and state-centred lawyers to argue that effective international tribunals must remain 'dependent' tribunals staffed by ad

---

[164] cf Joerges and Petersmann, n 54 above.

[165] cf E-U Petersmann, 'State Sovereignty, Popular Sovereignty and Individual Sovereignty: From Constitutional Nationalism to Multilevel Constitutionalism in International Economic Law?' in W Shan, P Simons, and D Singh (eds), *Redefining Sovereignty in International Economic Law* (2008) 27–60.

hoc judges closely controlled by governments, for example through their power of reappointment and threats of retaliation. Independent international courts are perceived with suspicion because independent judges risk allowing moral ideals and interests of third parties to influence their judgments; the domestic ideal of rule of law is seen as inappropriate for the reality of international power politics: 'dependent tribunals' are more likely to 'render judgments that reflect the interests of the states at the time that they submit the dispute to the tribunal'.[166] Similar power-oriented conceptions of international adjudication are also advanced for the WTO dispute settlement system by legal advocates of the major trading powers – for instance, if they suggest that EU judges should review only whether EC Member States – but not whether the EC Commission and the EC Council – comply with their GATT and WTO legal obligations.[167] The often one-sided focus of WTO and investor-state arbitrators on governmental and producer interests is reflected by the fact that human rights arguments have never been made in WTO dispute settlement proceedings and, only recently, in investor-state arbitration proceedings and arbitration awards. Yet, as long as international economic courts are perceived to neglect general citizen interests as protected by human rights and other constitutional rules, governments and domestic courts may legitimately refuse domestic implementation of international judicial decisions (for example, of WTO and NAFTA dispute settlement panels and investor-state arbitration). Different kinds of challenges to the independence of international adjudication are reflected in the increasing number of requests for disqualification of individuals who serve as arbitrator in

---

[166] See E Posner and JC Yoo, 'Judicial Independence in International Tribunals' (2005) 93 California Law Review 1, 6, who define the function of international tribunals as providing states with neutral information about the facts and the law in a particular dispute. For the liberal criticism of the 'billiard ball model of public international law among egoist states' underlying such power-oriented and utilitarian approaches to international law, see, from political as well as legal perspectives, RO Keohane, A Moravcsik, and AM Slaugther, 'Legalized Dispute Resolution: Interstate and Transnational' in (2000) 54 International Organization 457 ff.

[167] See the advice by the EC's legal advocate PJ Kuijper, n 29 above. Since the 1972 *International Fruit Co* case concerning GATT 1947, the EC courts justify their refusal to review the legality of EC restrictions on the basis of precise and unconditional GATT/WTO obligations of the EC and of all EC Member States (including legally binding GATT/WTO dispute settlement rulings) by relying on misleading interpretations of GATT/WTO rules suggested by the EC Commission (cf most recently the Opinion by AG Poiares Maduro of 20 February 2008, Joined Cases C-120/06 P and C-121/06 P, at paras 47 and 52, who misinterprets DSU, Art 22 regarding countermeasures as protecting a 'freedom' of the EC lawfully to disregard WTO dispute settlement rulings requiring termination of EC violations of WTO obligations). As the 'Fediol' and 'Nakajima' exceptions to this WTO case law have never been applied by the EC Court, this 'political question doctrine' undermines the rule of law and judicial remedies both in the WTO and inside the EC by condoning the EC's longstanding GATT and WTO violations (eg the more than a dozen of GATT/WTO dispute settlement findings, since 1993, confirming the illegality of the EC's import restrictions on bananas). The lack of legal and judicial remedies of EC citizens and EC Member States against welfare-reducing EC restrictions that obviously and persistently violate GATT/WTO law runs counter also to the rule of law inside the EC (cf Art 300:7 EC).

one case and as counsel in another investment dispute: can an arbitrator be expected to rule independently against the very arguments he or she is making as legal counsel (and often also as partner of a multinational law firm working for foreign investors) in another dispute on the same legal issue? Application of the model of private ad hoc commercial arbitration to investor-state disputes is increasingly criticized for its lack of adequate judicial accountability (for example, due to lack of appellate review), lack of transparency (for example, due to absence of public notifications of commercial arbitration, closed arbitral proceedings, lack of public access to documents, and to final awards), and incoherent judicial reasoning without adequate public law constraints for final judicial decisions on how legislatures and governments may lawfully regulate foreign investments:

> as merchants of adjudicative services, arbitrators have a financial stake in furthering the system's appeal to claimants and, as a result, the system is tainted by an apprehension of bias in favour of allowing claims and awarding damages against governments.[168]

C. 'Constitutional Justice' Must Be Seen to Be Part of 'Public Reason'

As long as supervision of arbitral awards (for example, by ICSID annulment committees, or by domestic courts in the seat of commercial arbitration or enforcement) remains essentially limited to jurisdictional errors, procedural improprieties, and serious violation of *ordre public*, the absence of an appeals process to resolve contradictions in the legal reasoning of arbitral awards hinders the development of an international 'common law' on investment protection.[169] It is to be welcomed that WTO dispute settlement panels, the WTO Appellate Body, and increasingly also arbitral tribunals established under ICSID procedures[170] admit *amicus curiae* briefs by non-governmental organizations that may assist in a more inclusive balancing of all interests affected by trade and investment disputes – for example, if foreign investors and the host government were complicit in human rights violations and the tribunal considers rejecting legal claims that are inconsistent with international public policy (*ordre public*). For, in contrast to private commercial arbitration that remains organized and controlled by party autonomy, WTO and investor-state arbitration often involves

---

[168] G Van Harten, *Investment Treaty Arbitration and Public Law* (2007) 152–153.

[169] The proposals for establishing international appeals mechanisms for international investment disputes seem to have led, so far, only to changes in the recent practice of BITs concluded by the United States, cf KP Sauvant (ed), *Appeals Mechanisms in International Investment Disputes* (2008).

[170] The Revised ICSID Arbitration Rules that went into effect on 1 April 2006, and the new model BITs by Canada and the United States, allow in principle written submissions by a person that is not a party to the dispute, yet subject to various conditions. Rule 37 of the revised ICSID Arbitration Rules seems to recognize only a right to file a petition requesting that a brief may be submitted, without any broader right to disclosure of documents and information.

important public interests and broader constitutional issues that may justify *amicus curiae* briefs affording the tribunal additional arguments from adversely affected third parties.

The widespread perception of lack of legitimacy and bias – for example, 'that many awards narrow the object and purpose of investment treaty arbitration to that of investor protection'[171] – could be overcome best by judicial review of investor rights and of regulatory powers of host states with due regard to the constitutional principles underlying human rights and IEL. Just as European economic and human rights courts derived their legitimacy from promoting 'constitutional justice' (for example, in the sense of justifying the legal precedence of their judgments vis-à-vis domestic laws in terms of respect for human rights and common constitutional principles of European states), so should international trade and investment judges act as 'exemplar of public reason' (J Rawls) and independent guardians of respect for equal citizen rights by settling IEL disputes in conformity with the human rights obligations of governments and the constitutional principles of citizen-driven self-governance. Similar to Chief Justice John Marshall's justification – in *Marbury v Madison* – of the US Supreme Court as the most legitimate interpreter of US constitutional law and independent guardian of constitutional rights in disputes over constitutional interpretations, multilevel judicial governance based on cooperation among national and international courts offers more impartial guarantees of 'constitutional justice' in IEL than national judges focusing on national interests without regard to international law, its 'principles of justice', and human rights obligations.[172] Even though there is no evidence that such 'constitutional interpretations' of GATT and WTO rules would have changed the final results of any of the hundreds of GATT and WTO dispute settlement reports, they would have changed the perception of 'public reason', 'constitutional justice', and legitimacy in the WTO.

The ultimate value of governments, courts, and law, including IEL, derives from respect for justice as defined by constitutional rights protecting the equal status of citizens in their individual and democratic self-development and mutually beneficial economic cooperation. The universal human rights obligations of all 192 UN Member States justify (re-)interpreting IEL for the benefit of citizens and their human rights, as required by the customary methods of international treaty interpretation. Hence, if international tribunals protect equal rights of citizens and explain to the people the 'principles of justice' underlying their judgments, they can assert also democratic legitimacy and may

---

[171] See Van Harten, n 168 above, 174.

[172] The VCLT's explicit requirements of treaty interpretation 'in conformity with principles of justice' and human rights may be construed in the sense of Dworkin's theory that judicial decisions must not only 'fit' the ongoing practice of the law (eg by taking into account precedents and consistency); they must also justify that practice as the best interpretation of the principles of justice underlying the judicial practice (cf Dworkin, n 130 above, ch 7).

enhance individual self-government, participatory democracy as well as deliberative democracy under the rule of law, in the international economy as well as
in the polity. Yet, hopes for a 'global community of courts' protecting judicial
settlement of conflicts and international rule of law at national and international
levels inside citizen-driven 'transnational legal communities'[173] risk remaining a
distant dream unless national and international courts develop common constitutional conceptions of IEL beyond Europe and engage more actively in
transnational judicial dialogues and citizen-oriented re-interpretation and protection of IEL in domestic courts. American proposals for replacing the rule of
international law by some undefined 'international rule of law'[174] risk being
abused by hegemonic power politics – for example, if domestic laws are enforced
without adequate regard to international law (as an indispensable instrument for
the collective supply of international public goods). Just as constitutional guarantees of justice and human rights have proven necessary for the collective
supply of *national* public goods as well as for maintaining an 'overlapping
constitutional consensus' among citizens with diverse conceptions of a good life,
so does the ever-larger citizen-demand for *international* public goods require
'constitutionalizing' IEL by its legal re-interpretation and judicial protection in
conformity with human rights and other 'principles of justice', as illustrated by
the ever-more comprehensive state duties to implement IEL and judgments of
international courts in domestic legal systems and protect human rights at home
and abroad (including, as *ultima ratio*, humanitarian intervention protecting
citizens against gross human rights violations by their own governments).[175]

---

[173] cf AM Slaugther, 'A Global Community of Courts' (2003) 44 Harvard International Law Journal 191 ff.
[174] cf CJ Ikenberry and AM Slaugther (eds), *Forging a World of Liberty Under Law. US National Security in the 21st Century* (2006).
[175] cf 'A More Secure World: Our Shared Responsibility', Report of the UN High Level Panel (2004).

PART III

JUDICIAL 'BALANCING' OF ECONOMIC LAW AND HUMAN RIGHTS IN REGIONAL COURTS

9

Balancing of Economic Law and Human Rights by the European Court of Justice

Bruno De Witte

I. Introduction

Investment law and human rights law meet each other also within the confines of the EU legal order, although the conditions under which that meeting takes place are very different, almost unrecognizably so, from what occurs in international law generally. In the relations between EU Member States, international investment is effectively 'multilateralized' and now governed almost exclusively by EU law. The internal market includes a self-executing right for companies from one Member State to invest in the other Member States without being subject to any kind of discrimination, except in very narrowly defined circumstances. These legal guarantees for foreign investment come under the heading of *freedom of establishment* (covering the setting up of business in another Member State or the acquisition of a firm in another Member State) and *free movement of capital* (covering the acquisition of a limited participation in a company based in another Member State).

The existence of this clear non-discrimination standard for market access does not exclude other human rights issues from arising in connection with cross-border economic activity in the European Union. These issues are considered, in this chapter, from the perspective of the role played by the European Court of Justice (ECJ) in using human rights principles in the application and interpretation of *economic Community law*. The subject matter is, thus, larger than that of investment and includes other forms of economic activity. The reason for this is that the typical judicial balancing undertaken by the ECJ applies to all domains of economic regulation. The main distinction, in its approach, is not based on the nature of the economic activity, but on the identity of the authority or organization that seeks to regulate and limit that activity. We will therefore examine three different legal constellations:

- when the Court is called to examine economic regulation by the EU legislator in the light of fundamental rights;
- when the Court is called to examine economic regulation by the Member States in the light of fundamental rights; and
- when the Court examines private interference with economic activities in the light of fundamental rights.

I will examine these three constellations in turn, giving each time one or more examples of how the ECJ operates in such cases. The latter two situations are, in fact, those that are more directly related to the core subject of this volume, namely human rights issues arising in investment disputes, because they deal with cross-border situations; but the way in which the Court generally reviews economic interventionism by the EU legislator also provides instructive material for thinking about the role of human rights in international investment disputes. It should be added, however, that the analysis will be limited to *internal EU law*, without considering investment-related legal questions arising in the *external* relations of the Union, such as the position of the EU in the context of the WTO, the role of the EU's free trade agreements,[1] or the division of powers between the EU and its Member States in concluding investment treaties with third (non-EU) countries.[2]

Before embarking on the analysis, a quick reminder is in order about the general development of fundamental rights protection in the European Union. The ECJ's progressive development of a kind of unwritten bill of rights for the European Community was gradually given express recognition within the founding Treaties of the European Union. In particular, Article 6 of the EU Treaty now declares that respect for fundamental rights and freedoms constitutes one of the basic principles on which the Union is founded, and Article 7 provides a mechanism for sanctioning Member States which violate these principles in a grave or persistent manner. Nevertheless, these and other provisions were grafted on to a set of Treaties which, despite the broad range of powers and policies covered, were for a long time very largely focused on economic aims and objectives with little reference to other values. This legacy remains significant since, despite its constantly changing and expanding nature, the European Union's dominant focus remains an economic one, and the debate over the appropriate

---

[1] On this question, see ch 24 below.

[2] On this issue, see, eg B Poulain, 'Quelques interrogations sur le statut des traités bilatéraux de promotion et de protection des investissements au sein de l'Union européenne' (2007) *Revue générale de droit international public* 803–827. See also the Opinion of AG Poiares Maduro of 10 July 2008 in the double dispute pending before the ECJ, Case C-205/06 *Commission of the European Communities v Austria* and Case C-249/06 *Commission of the European Communities v Sweden*.

scope of its 'human rights role' remains lively and contested even after the adoption, in 2000, of an EU Charter of Fundamental Rights and Freedoms. One major element of contestation is precisely the legal status of that Charter. It was originally adopted as a non-binding instrument, although it is increasingly referred to in the institutional practice of the European Union, and it would acquire binding legal status only if and when the Treaty of Lisbon enters into force.[3]

II. The Role of Fundamental Rights in the Court's Control of the European Union's Economic Regulation

EU regulatory measures often have a direct legal impact on private economic and commercial interests. In the late 1960s already, firms began to claim legal protection for fundamental property and commercial rights which were given specific protection within certain Member State constitutions (particularly in Germany). Thus, the first steps taken by the ECJ in the field of fundamental rights protection concerned economic rights such as the right to property and the freedom to pursue a trade or profession.

The assertion that protection for fundamental human rights is part of the general principles of EC law appeared for the first time in 1969, in the final paragraph of the European Court's *Stauder* judgment.[4] Mr Stauder had brought a claim before the German courts that the implementation of an EC scheme constituted an infringement of his right to dignity. In particular, he challenged a scheme to reduce the surplus of butter, in accordance with which social security recipients would be eligible to receive subsidized butter from national traders. He argued that the requirement that beneficiaries must reveal their names and addresses constituted an infringement of the basic right to dignity protected under German constitutional law, and a reference was made by the German court to the ECJ in order to address that issue. The ECJ did not reject the applicability of human rights principles, but neither did it accept the claim that the Commission's butter scheme infringed such a right. Instead, the Court interpreted the Commission decision by looking at different language versions of the text and concluding that it was unnecessary for a recipient of subsidized butter to be identified by name, so that any potential infringement of the right to human dignity could be avoided.

In developing its own EU law standard of protection of fundamental rights, the ECJ has found inspiration both in international human rights law and in national constitutional law. A good example of the latter, 'comparative constitutional approach' to the protection of human rights was given in the *Hauer*

---

[3] For an excellent general discussion of the development of human rights protection in the EU legal order, see P Craig and G de Búrca, *EU Law - Text, Cases and Materials* (4th edn, 2008) ch 11. See also A Rosas, 'The Legal Sources of EU Fundamental Rights: A Systemic Overview' in N Colneric et al (eds), *Une communauté de droit. Festschrift für Rodriguez Iglesias* (2003) 87–102.

[4] Case 29/69 *Stauder v City of Ulm* [1969] ECR 419.

case of 1979,[5] in which the ECJ referred not only to the European Convention of Human Rights (ECHR), but also to specific provisions of particular national constitutions. In that case, which typically (for that period of European integration) dealt with the European Community's common agricultural policy, the applicant was refused national authorization to undertake the new planting of vines on a plot of land which she owned. When she objected, she was told that the authorities had acted in application of an EC regulation prohibiting the new planting of vines in that region. She appealed against the refusal, pleading the incompatibility of the Council regulation with the German Constitution. The *Verwaltungsgericht* referred the case to the ECJ, stating that if it were incompatible with fundamental German constitutional rights, the regulation might be inapplicable in Germany. The ECJ stated the following:

As the Court declared in its judgment of 17 December 1970, *Internationale Handelsgesellschaft* [1970] ECR 1125, the question of a possible infringement of fundamental rights by a measure of the Community institutions can only be judged in the light of Community law itself. The introduction of special criteria for assessment stemming from the legislation or constitutional law of a particular Member State would, by damaging the substantive unity and efficacy of Community law, lead inevitably to the destruction of the unity of the Common Market and the jeopardizing of the cohesion of the Community.

The Court also emphasized in the judgment cited, and later in the judgment of 14 May 1974, *Nold* [1974] ECR 491, that fundamental rights form an integral part of the general principles of the law, the observance of which it ensures; that in safeguarding those rights, the Court is bound to draw inspiration from constitutional traditions common to the Member States, so that measures which are incompatible with the fundamental rights recognized by the Constitutions of those States are unacceptable in the Community, and that, similarly, international treaties for the protection of human rights on which the Member States have collaborated or of which they are signatories, can supply guidelines which should be followed within the framework of Community law.[6]

The Court then referred to the right to property protected within the First Protocol to the ECHR and to the restrictions on the exercise of the right envisaged by that provision. It also made specific reference to provisions of the German, Italian, and Irish Constitutions, and to the fact that in all Member States there were legislative provisions restricting the use of real property in order to promote various public interests.

Examination of the Court's case law over the years suggests that despite the Court's recognition of fundamental rights as part of Community law and as grounds for annulment of Community measures, the impact of this development on the outcome of cases claiming a breach of fundamental rights may be minimal, even though such claims are regularly made. In *Hauer*, where the applicant claimed that the refusal of permission to grow vines on her land

---

[5] Case 44/79 *Hauer v Land Rheinland-Pfalz* [1979] ECR 3727.   [6] Ibid., at paras 14–15.

infringed her rights to trade and to property, the Court simultaneously acknowledged these rights as part of Community law, but denied that the restriction imposed upon them was disproportionate to the objectives of the Community's structural policy in this area. This pattern has repeated itself many times since. In fact, the ECJ normally shows great deference to general legislative measures adopted by the Community, only very rarely annulling such measures, whether for breach of fundamental rights or otherwise.

Occasionally, a piece of economic legislation is contested not on the basis of an economic fundamental right (such as the right to property and the right to conduct one's business), but on the basis of a classical civil or political right. Thus, in a high-profile case decided in 2006, an EC directive banning advertising for tobacco products was attacked by Germany on a series of grounds, including that it would entail a disproportionate restriction of freedom of expression (in this case, commercial expression).

The plea was rejected by the ECJ in the following terms:

... the discretion enjoyed by the competent authorities in determining the balance to be struck between freedom of expression and the objectives in the public interest which are referred to in Article 10(2) of the ECHR varies for each of the goals justifying restrictions on that freedom and depends on the nature of the activities in question. When a certain amount of discretion is available, review is limited to an examination of the reasonableness and proportionality of the interference. This holds true for the commercial use of freedom of expression in a field as complex and fluctuating as advertising.

... It must therefore be found that the Community legislature did not, by adopting such measures, exceed the limits of the discretion which it is expressly accorded.

It follows that those measures cannot be regarded as disproportionate.[7]

Beyond those leading cases, one can say, in general terms, that human rights have not often been used by the ECJ in order to declare EU economic legislation to be invalid. However, human rights play a role not only when the Court is called to assess the *validity* of an act adopted by the EU institutions (as in the cases mentioned above), but also in the *interpretation* of EU law. In some recent judgments, the ECJ seems to accept that economic and non-market objectives that are simultaneously present in a piece of internal market law do not necessarily have to be consistent with one another and that there may be an internal tension between those objectives that requires a balanced interpretation. Thus, in *Bodil Lindqvist*, the Court stated that the EU directive on the free movement of personal data seeks to ensure not only the free flow of such data within the European market, but also the safeguarding of the fundamental rights of individuals; it then added that 'those objectives may of course be inconsistent with

---

[7] Case C-380/03 *Germany v Parliament and Council* [2006] ECR I-11573, at paras 155–158. This was the second *Tobacco Advertising* judgment, after the Court had, in a judgment of 2000, annulled the first version of the Directive, already then in an action brought by Germany – but the Court had not dealt with the fundamental rights issue in that first judgment.

one another', and that the directive contains the 'mechanisms allowing these different rights and interests to be balanced'.[8] A further twist occurred in a recent case dealing with the interpretation of the same directive, where the Court held that the right to privacy had to be reconciled with the right to freedom of expression, which may justify in some cases that normally protected data be published by a newspaper.[9] In this case, we can observe that a question which seems on first view to be merely about the interpretation of an internal market directive turns out to be about reconciling two conflicting human rights. Human rights are thus embedded within economic regulation rather than being an external standard for that regulation.

III. Member State Interference with Common Market Freedoms and the Fundamental Rights Dimension

The common market freedoms (free movement of goods, services, persons, and capital) have since the creation of the European Community in the 1950s been the key principles of the 'economic constitution' of the EC. In recognition of this key role, the ECJ has often called them fundamental freedoms. Due to the principles of primacy and direct effect of EC law, these fundamental freedoms can be directly enforced by their beneficiaries (individuals and business firms) before national courts, and be used by them in order to challenge Member State laws and regulations that violate those fundamental freedoms.

A question that arose in this context is whether Member States can justify a restriction of the free operation of the common market in order to protect the fundamental rights of their citizens and residents. The EU law parameters applying in such situations were spelled out in the *Omega* judgment of the ECJ of 2004, in which it held that a Member State may legitimately invoke the protection of human dignity in order to curtail cross-border economic activities that are not illegal in other Member States. The police authorities in Bonn had issued an order against the company Omega forbidding it from operating the 'laserdrome' game, which involves shooting at human targets with a laser pistol, which could be perceived as 'playing at killing'. The game had been imported from the United Kingdom, so that Omega could argue that the prohibition involved an unjustified restriction of the free movement of goods and services. The case went up all the way to the German supreme administrative court, which held that, as a matter of German law, the police measure was justified in order to protect the right to human dignity recognized by the German Basic Law, but since it had doubts as to whether this interpretation was in conformity with Community law, it referred the case to the ECJ.

---

[8] Case C-101/01 *Bodil Lindqvist* [2003] ECR I-12971, at paras 84–90.
[9] Case C-73/07, *Tietosuojavaltuutettu*, Judgment, 16 December 2008.

The ECJ held[10] that the protection of fundamental rights was a legitimate interest that could justify a restriction of EC fundamental freedoms, provided that the restriction was proportional. With regard to this particular case, it held that the restriction could indeed be seen by the German authorities as necessary for the protection of human dignity, despite the fact that the same game was legally played in most other countries of the European Union. In other words, the Court did not require that the fundamental rights conception used by the Germans was shared by all Member States; there is no European common denominator in this matter, but a large amount of discretion left to each state – larger, arguably, in the case of fundamental rights than when the Member States invoke other public policy interests in order to restrict the economic freedoms of the common market.

A similar solution was found in a more recent judgment of 2008, in the case *Dynamic Medien*, dealing with German legislation that restricted the sale by mail order of video cassettes with the stated purpose of protecting children against injurious media material. This legislation caused a restriction of the free movement of goods on the European internal market, but the Court found it to be justified in the light of international human rights instruments for the protection of children's rights.[11] It specified, as in *Omega*, that:

> ... it is not indispensable that restrictive measures laid down by the authorities of a Member State to protect the rights of the child ... correspond to a conception shared by all Member States as regards the level of protection and the detailed rules relating to it ... As that conception may vary from one Member State to another on the basis of, inter alia, moral or cultural views, Member States must be recognised as having a definite margin of discretion.[12]

IV. Private Interference with Economic Activity and the Role of Fundamental Rights

The third dimension of our analysis involves a rather new but highly topical theme in EC law. It attracted much media attention recently with the two judgments given by the ECJ in the final weeks of 2007 in the *Laval* and *Viking Line* cases.[13]

The common market freedoms, according to their wording in the EC Treaty, are binding on the Member States (which includes all state organs at all

---

[10] Case C-36/02, *Omega Spielhallen- und Automatenaufstellungs-GmbH v Oberbürgermeisterin der Bundesstadt Bonn* [2004] ECR I-9609, at paras 34–38.

[11] Case C-244/06, *Dynamic Medien*, Judgment, 14 February 2008, at paras 39–48.

[12] Ibid., at para 44.

[13] Case C-341/05 *Laval un Partneri Ltd v Svenska Byggnadsarbetareförbundet and ors*, Judgment, 18 December 2007; and Case C-438/05, *Viking Line*, Judgment, 11 December 2007.

territorial levels, as is illustrated by the *Omega* case above), but not on private individuals or firms. However, there has been a gradual 'privatization' of free movement law in two ways: first, the ECJ has construed state duties to protect the common market freedoms against private interference; and, secondly, it is gradually tending to give direct horizontal effect to those economic freedoms.

The first approach is illustrated by the case *Commission v France* of 1997 – also known as the '*Spanish strawberries*' case – in which the Court used the concept of state duties to protect common market freedoms against private conduct.[14] At issue in that case were repeated violent acts committed by French farmers in order to prevent the sale of Spanish strawberries. The French authorities had never done anything to stop them, and the ECJ held that France, by not taking any action to protect the free movement of goods against private action, had itself violated that fundamental freedom – thus defining a qualified duty for the Member States to ensure compliance with the common market principles in relations between private parties.

Some years later, the Court added an interesting twist to this case law by accepting that this duty of the Member States could be tempered when their inactivity is justified by the wish to protect fundamental rights. In *Schmidberger* (2003),[15] the ECJ accepted that a restriction of the free movement of goods (in this case, the interruption of the Brenner motorway in Austria for almost 30 hours by demonstrations for the protection of the environment) may be justified by the need to protect the fundamental rights of assembly and expression. Here again, the Court construed the restriction of free movement as an action of the Member States: it was not the action of the demonstrators itself that was examined by the Court, but the failure of the Austrian Government to ban the demonstration (and the Brenner road block) from taking place. Therefore, this technically speaking appeared as a traditional free movement case, involving the restriction of a common market freedom (in the case at hand, the right of Mr Schmidberger, a German transporter, to take his goods unhindered from Germany to Italy through Austria) by Member State authorities. In this case, unlike in the *Spanish strawberries* case, the Member State was not held in breach of EC law precisely because it had sought to respect the exercise of fundamental rights by the demonstrators, and had found a fair balance between the fundamental rights of the demonstrators and the fundamental freedom of Mr Schmidberger and other users of the Brenner motorway.

The Court used the following general formula (which is very close to what it was going to hold one year later in the *Omega* case):

Since both the Community and its Member States are required to respect fundamental rights, the protection of those rights is a legitimate interest which, in principle, justifies a

[14] Case C-265/95 [1997] ECR I-6959.
[15] Case C-112/00 *Schmidberger v Austria* [2003] ECR I-5659.

restriction of the obligations imposed by Community law, even under a fundamental freedom guaranteed by the Treaty such as the free movement of goods.[16]

In contrast with what happened in *Spanish Strawberries* and in *Schmidberger*, the Court was squarely faced with the question of the horizontal effect of the common market freedoms in *Laval* and *Viking Lines*. Both cases concerned the extent to which trade unions are able to use industrial action to resist what they consider to be social dumping in the operation of the internal market. In the judgments, the Court held, without much reasoning, that trade unions are bound directly by the common market freedoms, and that therefore private firms can rely directly on the EC Treaty in economic and social disputes pitting them against the trade unions.

The facts of these two cases were quite complex, but, in a nutshell, they were as follows. Laval un Partneri is a Latvian building company. In 2004, the company created a subsidiary in Sweden, and posted some of its workers there, in order to perform a building contract it had obtained for the construction of a school in the city of Vaxholm. The Swedish Building Workers Union requested that the company should conclude a collective labour agreement with it, in order to fix minimum wages and other labour conditions, but Laval refused. Thereupon, the union decided to start a blockade of the construction work; the Electricians' Union, through a solidarity action, managed to block the electrical installation work at the building site. Laval had to stop the building activity and its Swedish subsidiary, which had been set up for the purpose, was declared bankrupt. The company brought legal action before a Swedish Labour Court which referred the case to the ECJ for a preliminary ruling asking whether the action of the trade unions constituted an unlawful interference with the freedom of establishment and freedom to provide services of the Latvian building company.

The *Viking* case reached the ECJ upon a reference from the English Court of Appeal. Viking is a Finnish ferry operator owning a ship, the *Rosella*, which sails between Helsinki and Tallinn. Faced with stiff competition on that route from cheaper Estonian shipping lines, Viking decided to re-register the ferry in Estonia so that it could also employ a cheaper crew, subject to Estonian employment conditions. The International Transport Workers Federation (ITWF), based in London, planned to take industrial action against Viking in order to prevent the firm from re-flagging the *Rosella* in Estonia. Viking applied successfully before the High Court (ITWF being based in London) for an injunction to stop the action. The High Court order was appealed before the Court of Appeal, which decided to refer the case to the ECJ.

Both cases, therefore, dealt with the same basic tension between the fundamental right to strike or take other industrial action, and the freedoms of

---

[16] Ibid., at paras 74–93.

establishment and services. Having accepted, as we mentioned before, that those Treaty freedoms impose direct obligations on certain private parties (namely the trade unions), the ECJ could not avoid expressing its views on the substantive question, a question which is closely related to the general theme of this volume, namely the role of human rights considerations in investment disputes (whereby it must be remembered that the term 'investment' is not used in the language of EU internal market law, but that, instead, a right of investment in the internal market is expressed, depending on the situation, by 'freedom of establishment', 'free movement of capital', and 'freedom to provide services'). The use of fundamental rights arguments operates in two economic directions in those two cases. In *Viking Line*, the trade unions invoke fundamental social rights in order to prevent relocation, that is, investment abroad. In *Laval*, on the other hand, fundamental social rights are invoked in order to justify action that prevents inward investment by a foreign company (even though the investment is on a temporary basis, for the purpose of executing a building contract).

In *Viking Line*, the Court found that the rights of workers to associate and take collective action were fundamental rights recognized by the EU legal order. Such collective action may legitimately restrict the right of establishment of an undertaking that intends to relocate to another Member State, in order to protect the workers of that firm. However, the Court added that the restriction should not be disproportionate, and should not make intra-Community relocation of the firm impossible, which was precisely the intention of the trade unions. Although the ECJ left it in final instance to the referring court to strike the balance, the implication of its judgment is that the right of trade unions to exercise their collective fundamental right is very seriously hampered by the application of internal market law, a fact which was duly noted in the comments of the judgment.[17] In *Laval*, the Court developed similar considerations. It again found that trade unions had been exercising a fundamental right to take collective action, recognized by the EU legal order, but that its practical exercise had led to barriers to inward investment which were disproportionate.

In both cases, the Court uses the term 'balancing', although the impression one gets is that it gave rather more weight to the economic freedoms invoked by the companies in these cases than to the human rights invoked by the trade unions. A particular quirk of the EU judicial system is that the outcome of the balancing does not always have to be decided by the ECJ itself. The preliminary reference mechanism may create a situation where it is not the international court itself (in this case, the ECJ) that decides on the balance to be struck, in a

---

[17] See, eg J Malmberg and T Sigeman, 'Industrial Action and EU Economic Freedoms: The Autonomous Collective Bargaining Model Curtailed by the European Court of Justice' (2008) CML Rev 1115–1146.

given case, between economic objectives and human rights, but the national court where the case originates – albeit under the guidance of general guidelines formulated by the ECJ. This is different from what the European Court of Human Rights is called to do in similar cases: it has to decide individual applications itself and cannot refer the case back to domestic courts for 'fine-tuning'.[18]

---

[18] See, for the role of the ECtHR, ch 10 below.

10

Economic and Non-Economic Values in the Case Law of the European Court of Human Rights

Pasquale De Sena[*]

I. Opening Remarks

Some clues about the relationship between human rights and investment law can be drawn from the case law of the European Court of Human Rights (ECtHR), and in particular from the decisions relating to Article 1 of the Additional Protocol No 1 to the Convention, which establishes the right of every natural or legal person 'to the peaceful enjoyment of his possessions' (paragraph 1, first sentence). According to this provision, in fact: 'No one shall be deprived of his possessions except in the public interest and subject to the conditions provided for by law and by the *general principles of international law*' (paragraph 1, second sentence; emphasis added). In the well-known decisions in the cases of *James* and *Lithgow v United Kingdom,* the ECtHR stated that 'the conditions provided by the general principles of international law' apply *only* to non-nationals, on account of their position being different from that of citizens.[1] This conclusion has been criticized in the light of both Articles 1 and 14 (principle of non-discrimination) of the European Convention on Human Rights (ECHR).[2] In any case, it does *not* imply that the principles of international law on the taking of property

---

[*] The author would like to thank Dr Andrea Saccucci for his skilful, invaluable comments and suggestions on an earlier draft of this chapter. This chapter was completed and basically updated in January 2008.

[1] *James and ors v United Kingdom*, 21 February 1986 (App No 8793/79), at para 60; and *Lithgow and ors v United Kingdom*, 8 July 1986 (App No 9006/80; 9262/81; 9263/81; 9265/81; 9266/81; 9313/81; 9405/81), at para 112.

[2] According to Article 1 of the ECHR, the rights and freedoms provided for by the Convention have to be secured for '*everyone*' (italics added) within the jurisdiction of the contracting states; moreover, discriminations on grounds of *nationality* are forbidden both by ECHR, Art 14 and the relative case law of the ECtHR; on this basis – and for the purpose of securing the right to compensation (provided for by customary rules concerning the expropriation of foreign assets) also for citizens – it has been argued that the above-mentioned conditions should apply to citizens, too

must be applied to foreigners *in all cases*; in other words, even if *more favourable* principles could be deduced from the ECHR or from the relevant case law of the ECtHR. If it did, this would amount to a violation of the very rationale of the above provision, given that the reference to international law serves precisely – according to the Court – to guarantee the possibility of a treatment *more favourable* to the economic interests of non-nationals than nationals, especially with regard to the question of compensation.[3] Moreover, the principles set out by the Convention (or the case law of the ECtHR) are certainly applicable to foreigners when it comes to questions that *do not* concern the taking of property, given that the scope of application of the principles of international law is restricted to this latter case.

This clearly means that the stances of the case law of the ECtHR are (potentially) liable to affect the evolution of international investment law, not only influencing *from the outside* the case law of other courts dealing with foreign investments, but also helping *directly* to modify this legal regime.

That said, what stances genuinely deviating from the traditional trends on the subject of foreign investments can be deduced from the case law of the ECtHR? What aspects are affected by these stances? And how, within their scope, are economic and other values intertwined?

II. Economic and Non-Economic Values in the Evolution of the Notions of 'Possession' and 'Interference'

'Property' is, as we know, already a very broad concept in international investment law, given that it includes both 'corporeal property' and all of those rights that, despite not having a 'corporeal dimension', 'have a pecuniary or monetary value'.[4] Moreover, an analogously broad definition of 'investment' can easily be found in many bilateral investment treaties as well as in regional multilateral treaties and in the recent case law of investment tribunals.[5]

(see L Condorelli, 'Commentaire de l'article 1 du premier protocole additionnel' in L-E Pettiti, P-H Imbert, and E Decaux, *La Convention Européenne des Droits de L'Homme* (1999) 971, 986 rightly points out that this question has lost its importance, given that in the case law of the Court citizens are guaranteed the right to compensation in the framework of the assessment of proportionality: below, section IV).

[3] According to the Court:

... non-nationals are more vulnerable to domestic legislation: unlike nationals, they will generally have played no part in the election or designation of its authors nor have been consulted on its adoption. Secondly, although a taking of property must always be effected in the public interest, different considerations may apply to nationals and non-nationals and there may well be legitimate reason for requiring nationals to bear a greater burden in the public interest than non-nationals.

(see *James*, n 1 above, at para 63).
[4] See, eg *Liamco v Libya*, 12 April 1977, (1981) 20 ILM 103.
[5] On this aspect, see C Schreuer and U Kriebaum, 'The Concept of Property in Human Rights Law and International Investment Law' in S Breitenmoser et al, *Menschenrechte, Demokratie und*

The text of Article 1 of Protocol No 1 to the ECHR does not make reference to the concept of property, but instead to the more vague concept of 'possession'.[6] According to the ECtHR, the concept of possession covers not only an *actual* monetary or pecuniary right, but also a 'legitimate' and well-founded 'expectation' of realizing an economic interest.

This idea, which the decision on the *Pin Valley* case established,[7] was subsequently consolidated in ECtHR case law, and it was even extended to cases in which the 'substantive economic interest' of the applicant *was not* found to be accompanied by a *specific* 'legitimate expectation'.[8] What must be underlined here is that it has evolved not only in relation to the protection of *purely economic* interests, but also in close relation to the protection of *other interests*. One needs only think of the decision of the ECtHR Grand Chamber in the *Öneryildiz* case, from which it can be deduced that the infringement of a mere expectation may amount to a violation of Article 1 of Protocol No 1, if such an infringement is accompanied by a violation of the *right to life* (ECHR, Article 2).[9]

Furthermore, the notion of 'property' has been extended due to the need to protect interests of great *social* importance. Recently, in the *Stec* case, the Grand Chamber stated in fact that even 'a right to a non-contributory benefit' – and thus to a welfare benefit based on criteria of social solidarity – 'falls within the

Rechtsstaat: liber amicorum Luzius Wildhaber (2007) 743, 750 ff, as far as the recent case law of the ICSID tribunal is concerned.

[6] On the 'background' to the right of property under the ECHR, see A Riza Çoban, *Protection of Property Rights within the European Convention on Human Rights* (2004) 123; for detailed descriptions of the progressive 'extension' of the scope of application of this concept in the case law of the Court, see W Peukert, 'Artikel 1 des 1. ZP (Schutz des Eigentums)' in W Peukert and JA Frowein, *Europäische Menschenrechtskonvention* (1996) 763, 766; and Condorelli, n 2 above, 976.

[7] In this case the Court established that an Irish judgment retrospectively declaring void an 'outline planning permission' – on the basis of which the applicants had purchased a piece of land – could be deemed an interference under Art 1 of the Protocol, given that 'that permission amounted to a favourable decision ... which could not be reopened by the planning authority', and that since the decision had been rendered 'the applicants had at least a legitimate expectation of being able to carry out their proposed development', see *Pin Valley Developments Ltd and ors v Ireland*, 29 November 1991, App No 12742/87, at para 51.

[8] In *Beyeler v Italy*, 5 November 2000, App No 33202/96, the ECtHR was, in fact, required to determine whether the legal position of the applicant – a famous Swiss gallery owner, who had purchased in Italy and (subsequently) taken possession of a painting by van Gogh, before being subjected to the exercise of a right of pre-emption by the Italian Ministry of Culture – could be deemed to constitute possession under Art 1 of the Protocol, notwithstanding the lack of any *specific* basis in Italian law; see paras 100–106, concerning both the identification of the substantive economic interest at stake and the affirmative resolution adopted by the Court.

[9] *Öneryildiz v Turkey*, 30 November 2004, Grand Chamber, App No 48939/99, relating to the destruction of an *illegally* built slum dwelling, provoked by a methane explosion at a neighbouring rubbish tip, which caused the deaths of 12 of the applicant's relatives. In spite of the illegality of the above-mentioned building, the Court ruled that the Turkish authorities had not fulfilled their positive obligations, both under Art 2 of the Convention and Art 1 of the Protocol, since they had not done everything within their power to protect the applicants' lives and proprietary interests, see paras 117–118, concerning Art 2, and paras 133–138, concerning Art 1.

scope of Article 1 of Protocol No. 1'.[10] Overcoming the distinction drawn in its previous case law between contributory and non-contributory benefit, the Grand Chamber asserted that 'if ... a Contracting State has in force legislation providing for the payment as of right of a welfare benefit – whether conditional or not on the prior payment of contributions – that legislation must be regarded as generating a proprietary interest'.[11]

On the other hand, what we can glean in relation to the notion of 'interference' has little relevance to the purposes of the present analysis. This notion is, without any doubt, broader than the traditional notions of expropriation and nationalization, given that it covers, according to the Court, not only the taking of property (first paragraph, second sentence of the aforementioned Article 1) and the enforcement of legislative measures aimed at controlling 'the use of property in accordance with the general interest or to secure the payment of taxes or other contributions or penalties' (second paragraph) – but also *any other* interference with the right of property provided for by Article 1 (first paragraph, first sentence).[12] Furthermore, it is equally certain that this extension has coincided closely with the extension of the concept of property, mentioned earlier.[13] Nevertheless, the increased importance of *non*-economic interests in the Court's case law *cannot* be ascribed to the extension of the notion of 'interference' *as such*, but, rather, to the way in which the assessment of the proportionality of these interferences is carried out (below, section IV).[14]

---

[10] *Stec v United Kingdom* (adm.), 6 July 2005, Grand Chamber, App Nos 65731/01 and 65900/01, at paras 51–55; for previous case law of the ECtHR on this subject, see Peukert, n 6 above, 772; and Condorelli, n 2 above, 977.

[11] *Stec*, n 10 above, at para 54; on the previous case law on this subject, see Riza Çoban, n 6 above, 157 ff, as well as Peukert, n 6 above, 772; and Condorelli, n 2 above, 977. For a general overview of the Court's case law extending the protection afforded by the ECHR to the field of social security, see A Gómez Heredero, *Social Security as a Human Right* (2007).

[12] See, eg *Naumenko v Ukraine*, 9 November 2004, App No 41894/98, in which an interference with the peaceful enjoyment of the pension rights and state privileges of the applicant (a Chernobyl relief worker) was considered as a result of the lack of fairness of the proceedings in her case and the unreasonable length of time taken to enforce a judgement given in her favour (para 104).

[13] This aspect is underlined by M Pellonpä, *Concurring Opinion, Pressos Compañia Naviera and ors v Belgium*, 20 November 1995, App No 17849/91; and by ML Padelletti, *La tutela delle proprietà nella Convenzione europea dei diritti dell'uomo* (2003) 153; it can be deduced from the case law of the ECHR that some substantive economic interests *cannot* be subjected to an out-and-out *expropriation*, but only to a slighter interference by virtue of Art 1, para 1. Given that pecuniary rights, too, appear to be included among such interests, see *Stran Greek Refineries and Stratis Andreadis v Greece*, 9 December 1994, App No 13427/87, at para 66, in which a judicial decision rendering void a state pecuniary obligation towards the applicant was at stake; more recently, see also *Bruncrona v Finland*, 16 November 2004, App No 41673/98, at paras 79 ff; concerning a state interference with the long-term lease of some small Finnish islands (starting from 1720) provoked by the granting of fishing rights to third parties, it could be said – on a purely theoretical level – that the Court tends to frame expropriation in narrower terms than those emerging from the *Liamco* decision (n 4 above).

[14] This also explains why a specific analysis of the Court's case law relating to the hypothesis of interference does not seem necessary.

III. Public Utility and Non-Discrimination in International Law on Foreign Investments and in the European Convention

Different remarks can be made with regard to the two classic legal requirements for expropriation and nationalization according to general international law: the principle of 'public utility' and the principle of 'non-discrimination'.

As regards the first condition, what immediately emerges is that only in the French text of Article 1 of Protocol No 1 is there mention of the concept of 'public utility' ('*utilité public*') in relation to expropriation (first paragraph), whereas the English text refers to 'public interest' (first paragraph) and 'general interest' (second paragraph) as conditions for the lawfulness of interferences. The fact that this formulation differs from the expression 'public utility' in international law on foreign investments is not particularly significant, since (in the absence of common European legal standards on the subject) the ECtHR has regularly stated that the assessment of this aspect falls within the 'margin of appreciation' of the states parties to the Convention.[15] This means that the control exercised by the Strasbourg organs is *strictly* restricted – to this level – in order to prevent states from exercising arbitrary interferences,[16] in line with the similar function fulfilled traditionally by the concept of 'public utility' in international investment law.[17]

As far as the principle of non-discrimination is concerned, more significant observations can be made, in theory at least.

This principle *is not* expressly referred to in the text of Article 1 of Protocol No 1, not even with regard to the expropriation of non-nationals, in relation to whom it is commonly held to operate in the framework of international investment law. This is not particularly significant, however, given that the right provided for by Article 1 of Protocol No 1 – and indeed all of the other rights protected by the European Convention – are subject to the principle of non-discrimination provided for by Article 14 of the Convention itself. What must be pointed out here is that Article 14 has a *broader* scope than the

---

[15] For a catalogue of relevant policy choices held by the Court as being legitimate aims under the Convention, see Riza Çoban, n 6 above, 202.

[16] On the role played by the 'public interest' in preventing cases of arbitrary interference or '*detournement de pouvoir*' in the case law of the ECtHR, see P Van Dijk et al, *Theory and Practice of the European Convention on Human Rights* (2006) 631; it must be added that in the context of the ECHR, the *non*-arbitrariness of the interferences is also guaranteed by the 'principle of legality', according to which: (1) they must have a *legal basis*, eg provision must be made for them by a domestic act (not necessarily a law in the strict sense of the word) that is 'sufficiently accessible, precise and foreseeable', see *Beyeler*, n 8 above, at para 109; and (2) they must be *lawful* (*Iatridis v Greece*, 25 March 1999, App No 31107/96, at para 58).

[17] On the condition of public utility, see, in general, R Higgins, *The Taking of Property by State: Recent Developments in International Law*, Recueil des cours (1982) III, 288, and, with specific regard to bilateral investment agreements, M Sornarajah, *The International Law on Foreign Investment* (2004) 317.

traditional rule as applied in the field of foreign investments, since it prohibits *all* forms of discrimination, not only discrimination on grounds of nationality.[18] With specific regard to foreigners, this could entail a greater degree of protection, determined by *non*-economic reasons, even though no specific decisions on this subject can be found in the case law of the Strasbourg organs. As a topical illustration of this point, Article 14 of the Convention could prove significant in cases of discriminatory interferences with foreign properties or investments which are dictated more by the need to contrast certain *political or religious* opinions than by any real public order or national security needs (for example, in the framework of the 'fight' against terrorism).[19]

That said, it is worth noting that, in the framework of the Court's case law, the principle of non-discrimination has played a significant role in broadening the interpretation of the notion of 'possession' under Article 1 of Protocol No 1 (first sentence, paragraph 1).[20] Indeed, given that Article 14 of the ECHR can be invoked only in conjunction with other substantial rights protected by the Convention, the Court has felt compelled to extend the scope of application *ratione materiae* of Article 1 of Protocol No 1 for the purpose of establishing its competence to review the compatibility of certain interferences with the said principle.[21] A clear-cut example of this approach and of its long-term effects on the interpretation of property rights may be found in the development of the Court's case law concerning the applicability of Article 1 to contributory and non-contributory social welfare benefit.[22]

---

[18] Discriminations on grounds of nationality have traditionally occurred in the field of foreign investments, but see the legal examination of the racial grounds of both the German expropriations (of Jewish properties) and the Ugandan expropriations (of Indian properties) carried out by Sornarajah, n 17 above, 318 ff.

[19] Art 14 has been applied to a case of discrimination (albeit *not* concerning the right of property) by the House of Lords in the framework of this 'fight': s 23 of the Antiterrorism Act 2001 provided for the detention of suspected international terrorists who were *not* UK nationals but *not* for the detention of suspected international terrorists who were UK nationals; see *Opinions Of the Lords of Appeal for judgment in the case A (FC) and others (FC) (Appellants) v Secretary of State for the Home Department (Respondent) X (FC) and another (FC) (Appellants) v Secretary of State for the Home Department (Respondent)*, adopted 16 December 2004, available at <http://www.publications. parliament.uk/pa/ld200405/ldjudgmt/jd041216/a&oth-1.htm>, at paras 45–73, 134–138, 157– 159; see also the decision adopted by the ECtHR in *A and ors v UK*, 19 February 2009, App No 3455/05.   [20] See section II above.

[21] In this respect, see A Saccucci, 'Il divieto di discriminazione nella Convenzione europea dei diritti umani: portata, limiti ed efficacia nel contrasto a discriminazioni razziali o etniche' (2005) 3 *I diritti dell'uomo, cronache e battaglie* 11, notably at 15; and F Sudre, 'La perméabilité de la C.E.D.H. aux droits sociaux' in *Pouvoir et liberté. Etudes offertes à Jacques Mourgeon* (1998) 467.

[22] In addition to the *Stec* case, n 10 above, at para 2, see, among others, *Gaygusuz v Austria*, 16 September 1996, App No 17371/90, in which the Court held that the right to emergency unemployment benefit was a pecuniary right under Art 1, Protocol No 1, and that the distinction made between nationals and non-nationals was in breach of ECHR, Art 14; *Wessels-Bergevoet v the Netherlands*, 4 June 2002, App No 34462/97, concerning the discriminatory nature of the

IV. Economic and Non-Economic Values in the Framework of the 'Assessment of Proportionality'

Compensation is not *specifically* provided for, in Article 1, as a condition of the lawfulness of interferences with the right of property. As we know, the ECtHR does not consider this question independently, but instead by assessing the *proportionality* of a given interference (with the right of property) to the aims pursued by public authorities. In other words, compensation is one of the elements taken into consideration by the Strasbourg organs when making this assessment.[23]

That said, as far as the assessment of proportionality is concerned,[24] it is necessary to underline the clear emergence – in three respects at least – of a rationale that is *not* purely economic.

First, interference with the right of property has sometimes been accompanied by the violation of *other*, *non*-economic rights protected by the Convention, and this violation, in turn, has, *from the outside*, influenced the assessment of proportionality in favour of the existence of a violation of Article 1. This is precisely what happened in the *Chassanogou* case, in which the fact that the interference at stake was (also) found to be in breach of Article 11 of the Convention proved to be a *decisive* factor in the Court's assessment of this interference as 'disproportionate' with the right of property.[25] In other words, in situations in which the state action affecting the enjoyment of property rights also gives rise, *at the same time*, to the violation of another (non-economic) right protected by the Convention, the Court tends to deem the aforementioned restriction wrongful on the basis that it lacks a reasonable relationship of proportionality to the aim

reduction of the applicant's old-age pension on the basis of her married status; *Willis v United Kingdom*, 11 June 2002, App No 36042/97, where the refusal to pay the applicant benefits equivalent to those to which a widow would have been entitled was held to amount to a violation of Art 14 read in conjunction with Art 1, Protocol No 1.

[23] It is precisely for this reason (and not in view of a heightening of the economic aspect of the right of property compared to traditional international law on expropriation) that the Court has considered the aspect of compensation even when assessing forms of interference less serious than expropriation: see *Chassagnou and ors v France*, 28 April 2004, App Nos 25088/94, 28331/95, and 28443/95, at paras 80–85.

[24] An overview of the proportionality test regarding interferences with Art 1, Protocol No 1 is provided by Riza Çoban, n 6 above, 204; comprehensive analyses of the crucial role played by the principle of proportionality in balancing human rights and public interests in the case law of the ECtHR have recently been carried out by YA Takahashi, *The Margin of Appreciation Doctrine and the Principle of Proportionality in the Jurisprudence of the ECHR* (2002); and S van Drooghenbroeck, *La proportionalité dans le droit de la convention européenne des droits de l'homme* (2001).

[25] In this judgment (n 23 above), the Court stated that 'compelling small landowners to transfer hunting rights over their land so that others can make use of them' was a disproportionate interference with their right of property, because they were obliged to do something that was 'totally incompatible with their beliefs', given their aversion to hunting; in fact, the Court concluded that compelling small landowners to transfer hunting rights to a municipal hunters' association was equivalent to forcing them to join such an association (para 117).

pursued. This was shown by the decision in the *Öneryldiz* case, which we have already mentioned with regard to the evolution of the idea of 'possession'.[26]

Secondly, *non*-economic interests, of both a *collective* and an *individual* nature, have played, sometimes, an important role *within* the assessment of proportionality.

By *collective* interests, we mean those alleged by states to justify interferences with the right of property. With regard to these interests, the ECtHR *has never* affirmed that they can completely exclude the duty of compensation, except in 'exceptional circumstances'.[27] On the contrary, the relevant case law does embody the principle that 'fair' compensation must bear a 'reasonable relationship' to the market value of the 'possession' which is subject to the state interference, regardless of whether this interference took the form of expropriation, nationalization, or some less drastic measure.[28] For all that, collective interests may call for something *less* than reimbursement of the full market value,[29] not only in the case of measures that are part of large economic reforms,[30] but also in that of interferences imposed by 'fundamental changes to a country's constitutional system, such as the transition from a monarchy to a republic',[31] the incorporation of a state into another[32] as well as, *a fortiori*, the transition towards a democratic regime.[33]

While it is true that, with regard to the above-mentioned interests, the ECtHR has basically confined itself to 'adapting' international principles on foreign investments to its own frame of reference, from the perspective of the influence of *individual* interests of a *non*-economic nature its case law appears much more interesting. In this regard it is worth noting that the availability of individual 'procedural remedies' to prevent the arbitrary exercising of state discretion has played a highly significant role within the scope of the Court's assessment of proportionality. More specifically, the availability of these remedies has constituted – as has rightly been pointed out[34] – an element for

---

[26] *Öneryildiz*, n 9 above, at para 1.

[27] *James and ors*, n 1 above, at para 54; this has never occurred in ECtHR case law.

[28] This takes place, eg when 'the situation is akin to a taking of property', *Beyeler*, n 8 above, at para 114; see also *Lithgow*, n 1 above, at paras 50–51.

[29] *Scordino v Italy*, 29 March 2006, App No 36813/97, at para 97.

[30] *Lithgow*, n 1 above, whereby a nationalization of companies engaged in the aircraft and shipbuilding industries was at stake.

[31] *The Former King of Greece and Ors v Greece*, 23 November 2000, App No 25701/94, at para 88.

[32] *Forrer-Niedenthal v Germany*, 20 February 2003, App No 47316/99, at para 48, where the interference with the right of property originated from a situation of exceptional nature carrying wide implications (the reunification of the German Democratic Republic (GDR) and the Federal Republic of Germany), which required a legislative intervention capable of resolving, in a uniform manner and in conformity with the reunification agreements, potential patrimonial disputes relating to assets located in the territory of the former GDR.

[33] *Broniowsky v Poland*, 22 June 2004, App No 31443/96, at para 182; and, more recently, *Velikovi and ors v Bulgaria*, 15 March 2007, App Nos 4327/98 ff, at para 172, where the Court stated expressly that in the specific context of the transition to a democratic society 'the underlying public interest . . . is to restore justice and respect for the rule of law'.

[34] Padelletti, n 13 above, 242.

evaluating the compatibility of these interferences with the Convention that has, at times, been *decisive*.[35]

Third, an equally significant role has been played by individual *non*-economic interests *within* the assessment of compensation. This is the case of some disputes in which the properties involved came to the fore not only and not so much for their economic value as for the fact that they were crucial to the realization of *other* individual interests of some *social* importance. In *Lallement v France*, the compensation awarded to the applicant – a small French farmer – was in fact deemed unreasonable because it did not take into account that the expropriated land was his 'working instrument', that it would have been impossible for him to find in the same area another, similar piece of land, and that, as a result of this, he would have been unable to provide an adequate living for his family.[36] A similar line of reasoning was followed in the ambit of the 'Czech Cases' – in particular, *Pincová and Pinc v the Czech Republic*[37] – as well as in the recently decided *Velikovi and ors v Bulgaria*.[38] Although the right of housing is not a right expressly protected under the Convention, the ECtHR, in both of these cases, did in fact take into account, in the assessment of the compensation, the severe housing problems faced by the applicants following the implementation of the so-called Restitution Laws, adopted by the defendant governments within the framework of the transition towards democracy.[39]

V. Final Remarks

To sum up the main points of this analysis, it can be said that the relationship between ECtHR case law relating to Article 1 of Protocol 1 and the traditional principles of international law on foreign investments swings between a tendency to apply these principles, *adapting* them to the frame of reference of the Convention, and a tendency to *overcome them*.

The first tendency emerges in relation to the right of property, viewed in its *specific* and traditional dimension, as an *economic* right, expressly protected by the ECHR. It is mainly from this point of view that we can explain, for example,

---

[35] *Hentrich v France*, 22 September 1994, App No 13616/88, at para 49; see also, more recently, *Bruncrona v Finland*, n 13 above, at para 87, where the Court stated 'that the *procedure of terminating the applicants' proprietary interest* [a long-term lease of some small Finnish islands] ... was incompatible with the general right to the peaceful enjoyment of their possessions as guaranteed in the first sentence of the first paragraph of Article 1 of Protocol No. 1' (emphasis added), adding that, 'although Article 1 of Protocol No. 1 contains no explicit procedural requirements, the proceedings at issue must also afford the individual a reasonable opportunity of putting his or her case to the responsible authorities for the purpose of effectively challenging the measures interfering with the rights guaranteed by this provision' (para 69).

[36] *Lallement v France*, 11 April 2002, App No 46044/99, at para 18.

[37] *Pincová and Pinc v Czech Republic*, 5 November 2002, App No 36548/97.

[38] *Velikovi*, n 33 above.

[39] *Pincová and Pinc*, n 37 above, at paras 62–63; and *Velikovi*, n 33 above, at para 225.

the development of the idea of 'legitimate expectation'[40] through which the Court, in accordance with its constant endeavour to promote the broadest realization of the rights guaranteed by the Convention ('evolutive interpretation') has brought about the evolution of the concept of property. The importance that is attributed to the needs of the democratic transitions of the countries of Eastern Europe within the framework of the assessment of proportionality can be regarded in the same way – namely, as a sort of adaptation of the traditional principles. On the other hand, it must not be forgotten that the *traditional* principles of international economic law are firmly enshrined in the 'legal culture' of the ECtHR, if one considers the way in which they were applied – still with regard to the right of property – in the *Agrotexim v Greece* case.[41] It is well known, in fact, that in this decision, the Court stated that a shareholder cannot be identified with its company for the purpose of the 'victim requirement' (ECHR, Article 34), referring expressly to the 'corporate veil' principle affirmed by the International Court of Justice in the *Barcelona Traction* case,[42] even though contemporary treaty law on foreign investments tends to give an 'independent standing to shareholders'.[43] Moreover, it has to be stressed that the Court's most recent case law concerning the amount of compensation to be awarded in cases of expropriation tends to apply to nationals the traditional standard of 'prompt, adequate and effective' compensation, by stating – in principle – that, in the event of 'distinct expropriations', 'only full compensation can be regarded as reasonably related to the value of the property'.[44]

In a great many instances, the legal situations found in ECtHr case law have been somewhat *complex*, either because the violation of Article 1 was accompanied by violations of *other* rights protected by the Convention or because of the considerable *social* importance of the rights concretely asserted. For precisely this reason, the Court has, both with regard to the extension of the concept of 'property' and in the framework of the assessment of the proportionality of interference, displayed a tendency to *overcome* the principles of international law on foreign investments.

With regard to the first of these aspects, the Court has, in one way, linked *social* interests with the concept of 'property', as in the case of the *non-contributory* welfare benefits[45] mentioned earlier; and, in another, it has also deemed that the infringement of 'simple expectations' amounted to a violation

---

[40] Above, para 1.   [41] *Agrotexim and ors v Greece*, 24 October 1995, App No 14807/89.
[42] *Case concerning Barcelona Traction, Light and Power Co (Belgium v Spain)*, ICJ Reports (1970), at para 66: according to the Court, 'the piercing of the "corporate veil" or the disregarding of a company's legal personality *will be justified only in exceptional circumstances*, in particular when it is clearly established that it is impossible for the company to apply to the Convention' (emphasis added); see M Emberland, 'The Corporate Veil in the Case Law of the European Court of Human Rights' (2003) 63 *Zeitschrift für ausländisches öffentliches Recht und Völkerrecht* 945, also for some references to the subsequent case law.
[43] Schreuer and Kriebaum, n 5 above, 754, also for an accurate description of this tendency and of the relevant case law.   [44] See *Scordino and ors*, n 29 above, at paras 256–257.
[45] See *Stec v United Kingdom*, n 10 above, at para 2.

of Article 1, in a case in which such infringement was accompanied by the violation of *another right* protected by the Convention.[46]

As far as the assessment of proportionality is concerned, the Court has tended, similarly, to judge disproportionate those interferences with the right to property that *also* lead to the violation of *other* (non-economic) *rights* protected by the Convention.[47] Furthermore, *within* this assessment, both the availability of *procedural* guarantees for the victims of these interferences[48] and the *social* importance of the individual interests involved (with specific regard to the assessment of 'reasonable compensation')[49] have – as we have said – played an independent and often decisive role.

[46] That is to say, the right to life, see, *Öneryildiz v Turkey*, n 9 above.
[47] See *Chassagnou*, n 23 above, at para 4; and *Öneryildiz*, n 9 above, at para 2.
[48] See *Hentrich*, n 35 above; and *Bruncrona v Finland*, n 13 above, at para 4.
[49] See *Velikovi*, n 33 above; and *Pincová and Pinc*, n 37 above.

11

Is the European Court of Human Rights an Alternative to Investor-State Arbitration?

Ursula Kriebaum

I. Introduction

In 1986, the European Court of Human Rights (ECtHR) for the first time decided a case concerning an interference with property rights of a foreigner (*Agosi v United Kingdom*[1]). Yet, it was only in the new millennium that cases of foreign investors containing facts typical for investment arbitration have been decided by the ECtHR.[2] In a few cases investors opted for parallel proceedings before arbitral tribunals and the ECtHR.[3] Therefore, the question arises: are the international mechanisms for the protection of human rights an alternative to investor-state arbitration?

There are several indicators which can be looked at to assess whether mechanisms for the protection of human rights can be an alternative to investor-state arbitration. Some are linked to jurisdictional questions, others concern substance, and a last group concerns procedural aspects, namely the accessibility of the protection system, the composition of the deciding organ,

---

[1] ECtHR, *Agosi v United Kingdom*, Judgment, 22 September 1986, Series A No 108.
[2] ECtHR, *Sovtransavto Holding v Ukraine*, No 48553/99, Judgment, 25 July 2002, ECHR 2002-VII; *Rosenzweig and Bonded Warehouses Ltd v Poland*, No 51728/99, Judgment, 28 July 2005; *Zlínsat, Spol SRO v Bulgaria*, no 57785/00, Judgment, 15 June 2006; *Bimer SA v Moldova*, No 15084/03, Judgment, 10 July 2007; and *Marini v Albania*, No 3738/02, Judgment, 18 December 2007.
  Ruffert in 2000 therefore still had to note that no foreign direct investment case had been decided by the Court (M Ruffert, 'The Protection of Foreign Direct Investment by the European Convention on Human Rights' (2000) 43 German Yearbook of International Law 119).
[3] ECtHR, *Neftyanaya Kompaniya Yukos v Russia*, No 14902/04 – the case was declared admissible by the ECtHR on 29 January 2009. (In parallel arbitration was started based on the Energy Charter Treaty.) *Elekkroyuzhmontazh v Ukraine*, No 655/05 – the case is registered with a chamber, but no further procedural steps have been taken so far (in parallel a claim was filed with the Arbitration Institute of the Stockholm Chamber of Commerce under the Energy Charter Treaty – *Limited Liability Co AMTO v Ukraine*, SCC Case No 080/2005 (ECT), Award, 26 March 2008) and *Nomura and Saluka v Czech Republic*, No 72066/01. The case was declared inadmissible by the ECtHR on 4 September 2001. An UNCITRAL tribunal based on the Czech Republic–Netherlands BIT found a violation of the fair and equitable treatment standard of this BIT.

the possibility to obtain interim measures as well as the enforcement of awards. This chapter focuses on the jurisdictional and substantive aspects of protection to analyse in which cases the European Convention on Human Rights (ECHR) offers a meaningful alternative to international arbitration for investors.

II. Jurisdiction

A. Jurisdiction *Ratione Personae*

The first indicator is the jurisdiction *ratione personae* of investment tribunals and of the ECtHR. Two issues are of considerable importance: nationality and the protection of shareholders.

1. Nationality

As far as investment protection is concerned, it is limited to the protection of *foreign* investors. How important it is for a corporation to have the right nationality under the customary international law protection of investments has been strikingly shown by the International Court of Justice's (ICJ) judgment in the *Barcelona Traction* case.[4] However, most international investment cases today are based on investment protection treaties, typically bilateral investment treaties. In such cases, protection only exists for certain 'privileged' foreigners, nationals of states parties to these treaties.[5] The investor must be a national of a state which is a party to a treaty with the state which interfered with the property rights of the investor. The investor's nationality is decisive for the jurisidiction of an arbitral tribunal[6] as well as for the applicablilty of the substantial protection standards.

For example, the BIT (bilateral investment treaty) between the United Kingdom and China[7] provides the following in this regard:

Article 2: Promotion and Protection of Investment

. . .

(2) Investments of nationals or companies of either Contracting Party shall at all times be accorded fair and equitable treatment and shall enjoy the most constant protection and security in the territory of the other Contracting Party. . . .

---

[4] *Barcelona Traction, Light and Power Co Ltd (Belgium v Spain)*, ICJ Reports (1970) 4.
[5] On nationality issues see, eg A Sinclair, 'The Substance of Nationality Requirements in Investment Treaty Arbitrations' (2005) 20 ICSID Review Foreign Investment Law Journal 357–388; R Wisner and R Gallus, 'Nationality Requirements in Investor-State Arbitration' (2004) 5 Journal of World Investment and Trade 927-945; C Schreuer, *The ICSID Convention: A Commentary* (2001) 265–294; C McLachlan, L Shore, and M Weininger, *International Investment Arbitration* (2007) 131–162; and R Dolzer and C Schreuer, *Principles on International Investment Law* (2008) 46–54.
[6] On the relevant rules contained in Art 25 of the ICSID Convention, see Schreuer, n 5 above, 141–144, 162–166.
[7] Agreement between the UK Government of the United Kingdom of Great Britain and Northern Ireland and the Government of the People's Republic of China concerning the Promotion and Reciprocal Protection of Investments, Treaty Series No 33 (1986).

Article 3: Treatment of Investment
(1) Neither Contracting Party shall in its territory subject investments or returns of
nationals or companies of the other Contracting Party to ...

The offer of consent to arbitration in Article 7 of the BIT limits the jurisdiction of arbitral tribunals to the nationals of the two contracting states: '(1)
A dispute between a national or company of one Contracting Party and the
other Contracting Party concerning ... shall be submitted to international
arbitration.' The same approach is taken in multilateral investment protection
treaties.[8]

Additionally, if a dispute is to be arbitrated under the ICSID Convention,[9]
the investor must not have the nationality of the state party which interfered
with the property rights of the investor.[10] Furthermore, both states have to be
parties to the ICSID Convention. Article 25(1) of the ICSID Convention[11]
provides in its relevant parts as follows:

The jurisdiction of the Centre shall extend to any legal dispute arising directly out
of an investment, between a Contracting State ... and a national of another
Contracting State, which the parties to the dispute consent in writing to submit to
the Centre ...

Article 25(2) of the ICSID Convention defines 'National of another Contracting State' as:

(a) any natural person who had the nationality of a Contracting State other than the
State party to the dispute on the date on which the parties consented to submit such
dispute to conciliation or arbitration as well as on the date on which the request was
registered ... but does not include any person who on either date also had the nationality
of the Contracting State party to the dispute; and
(b) any juridical person which had the nationality of a Contracting State other than the
State party to the dispute on the date on which the parties consented to submit such
dispute to conciliation or arbitration and any juridical person which had the nationality
of the Contracting State party to the dispute on that date and which, because of foreign
control, the parties have agreed should be treated as a national of another Contracting
State for the purposes of this Convention.

Therefore, the nationality of the investor is of crucial importance for the protection of the investment against interferences by a state and for the jurisdiction
of a tribunal in case of a dispute.

---

[8] See, eg NAFTA, Arts 1(7), 10, 13, 26; ECT, Articles 1101, 1102, 1103, 1104, 1105,
1110, 1116.
[9] Convention on the Settlement of Investment Disputes between States and Nationals of other
States, 575 UNTS 1966, 159.
[10] Schreuer, n 5 above, 270–272, 275–276; see, eg *Champion Trading Co, and ors v Egypt*,
Decision on Jurisdiction, 21 October 2003, 10 ICSID Reports, 400, 404–410; and *Waguih Elie
George Siag and Clorinda Vecchi v Egypt*, Decision on Jurisdiction, 11 April 2007, at paras
142–201.   [11] Schreuer, n 5 above, 265–334.

By contrast, in the human rights protection system a certain nationality is not a requirement for the protection of property under the ECHR.[12] The necessary link for protection is not the nationality of the person to be protected, but the fact that the interfering state is a party to the ECHR. In order to establish that the supervisory organs of the human rights treaties have jurisdiction, the person concerned has to be under the jurisdiction of the interfering state.[13]

Articles 1 and 34 of the ECHR and Article 5 of the Additional Protocol provide in this regard:

Article 1: Obligation to respect human rights
The High Contracting Parties shall secure to everyone within their jurisdiction the rights and freedoms defined in Section I of this Convention.

Article 34: Individual applications
The Court may receive applications from any person, non-governmental organization or group of individuals claiming to be the victim of a violation by one of the High Contracting Parties of the rights set forth in the Convention or the protocols thereto. The High Contracting Parties undertake not to hinder in any way the effective exercise of this right.

Article 5: Relationship to the Convention
As between the High Contracting Parties the provisions of Articles 1, 2, 3 and 4 of this Protocol shall be regarded as additional articles to the Convention and all the provisions of the Convention shall apply accordingly.

Therefore, the nationality of the claimant is irrelevant for the question of whether it is eligible to present its claim before the Court.

It follows that the ECHR may offer a remedy in case of an interference by a state party with rights of an investor who is not covered by an investment protection treaty between the state of his or her nationality and the interfering state providing access to an international arbitral tribunal.

2. Corporations and Shareholders

An important issue when assessing whether human rights protection can be an alternative to investor-state arbitration is the protection of corporations and shareholders.[14]

---

[12] Convention for the Protection of Human Rights and Fundamental Freedoms (ECHR), 4 November 1950, ETS No 5, 213 UNTS 222; and Protocol to the Convention for the Protection of Human Rights and Fundamental Freedoms, 20 March 1952, ETS No 9. See on this issue: U Kriebaum, 'Nationality and the Protection of Property under the European Convention on Human Rights' in I Buffard et al (eds), *International Law between Universalism and Fragmentation* (2008) 649–666.

[13] See L Zwaak, 'General Survey of the European Convention' in P van Dijk et al, *Theory and practice of the European Convention on Human Rights* (2006) 13.

[14] See on this issue SA Alexandrov, 'The "Baby Boom" of Treaty-Based Arbitrations and the Jurisdiction of ICSID Tribunals: Shareholders as "Investors" and Jurisdiction *Ratione Temporis*' (2005) 4 Law and Practice International Courts and Tribunals 19; C Schreuer, 'Shareholder

The protection of shareholders' rights raises a number of issues. The most basic one is whether shareholding qualifies as a protected right at all. Another one concerns the position of shareholders in relation to the company. In particular, does a minority shareholder have the right to pursue a claim independently of the company? Finally, are shareholders entitled to pursue a claim only in respect of their ownership of the shares or also for diminution of the value of the company? In international investment law it is not disputed that corporations are protected, if only they have the right nationality, and the same is true for shareholders. The nationality requirement in international investment law mentioned above would deprive a large portion of foreign investment of international protection if shareholders were not protected separately from the corporations. The protection of shareholders would depend on the nationality of the corporation. In case the local law requires a locally incorporated company as a precondition for the investment, no protection would be available at all.[15] Therefore, most contemporary investment protection treaties give independent standing to shareholders. The issue is different as far as diplomatic protection is concerned.[16]

Protection in International Investment Law' in P-M Dupuy, B Fassbender, and MN Shaw et al, *Völkerrecht als Wertordnung, Festschrift für Christian Tomuschat* (2006) 601–619; C Schreuer and U Kriebaum, 'The Concept of Property in Human Rights Law and International Investment Law' in S Breitenmoser, *Liber Amicorum Luzius Wildhaber, Human Rights Democracy and the Rule of Law* (2007) 752–758; and Dolzer and Schreuer, n 5 above, 56–59.

[15] ICSID Convention, Art 25(2)(b) foresees the possibility of an agreement between the investor and the host state to treat a locally incorporated company as a foreign investor because of foreign control.

[16] Based on customary international law, the ICJ has adopted a restrictive approach in this regard. In the *Barcelona Traction* case, it held that the state of nationality of the majority shareholders of a company (Belgium) was unable to pursue claims against the interfering state (Spain) for damages done to the company incorporated in Canada. (*Barcelona Traction*, n 4 above, at 4); in the *Diallo* case (*Diallo (Guinea v DR Congo)*, 24 May 2007, available at <http://www.icj-cij.org/docket/files/103/13856.pdf>, at paras 86–94), the ICJ denied the possibility of the state of nationality of the shareholders (Guinea) to exercise diplomatic protection against the state of incorporation (DR Congo). It noted the difference between investment protection under bi- and multilateral treaties and customary international law in this regard. The ILC (<http://untreaty.un.org/ilc/texts/instruments/english/commentaries/9_8_2006.pdf>) in its draft articles on Diplomatic Protection of 2006 was inspired by the judgment of the ICJ in *Barcelona Traction*. Article 11 of the draft articles only allows for two situations in which a state of nationality of shareholders in a corporation may exercise diplomatic protection in case of injury to the corporation. That is the case if the corporation has ceased or if the corporation has the nationality of the host state and this was a requirement for the investment in the host state:

Article 11
Protection of shareholders
The State of nationality of shareholders in a corporation shall not be entitled to exercise diplomatic protection in respect of such shareholders in the case of an injury to the corporation unless:
(a) The corporation has ceased to exist according to the law of the State of incorporation for a reason unrelated to the injury; or
(b) The corporation had, at the date of injury, the nationality of the State alleged to be responsible for causing the injury, and incorporation in that State was required by it as a precondition for doing business there.

Article 17 of the draft articles on Diplomatic Protection provides that this provision is not applied in cases where they are inconsistent with a provision of investment protection treaties.

Treaties include shareholding or participation in a company in their definitions of 'investment'. For instance, the BIT between the United States and Argentina provides the following on investment:

Article 1

1. For the purposes of this Treaty,

a) 'investment' means every kind of investment in the territory of one Party owned or controlled directly or indirectly by nationals or companies of the other Party, such as equity, debt, and service and investment contracts; and includes without limitation:

. . .

(ii) a company or shares of stock or other interests in a company or interests in the assets thereof . . . [17]

Under such a treaty the shareholder may then pursue claims for adverse action by the host state against the local company that affects its value and profitability. Arbitral practice on this point is extensive and uniform.[18]

In *Alex Genin v Estonia*,[19] the claimants, US nationals, were the principal shareholders of EIB, a financial institution incorporated under the law of Estonia. The tribunal rejected the respondent's argument that the claim did not relate to an 'investment' as understood in the BIT. It said:

The term 'investment' as defined in Art. I(a)(ii) of the BIT clearly embraces the investment of Claimants in EIB. The transaction at issue in the present case, namely the Claimants' ownership interest in EIB, is an investment in 'shares of stock or other interests in a company' that was 'owned or controlled, directly or indirectly' by Claimants.[20]

---

[17] Treaty between the United States of America and the Argentine Republic Concerning the Reciprocal Encouragement and Protection of Investment, entered into force on 20 October 1994, available at <http://www.unctad.org/sections/dite/iia/docs/bits/argentina_us.pdf>.

[18] See, eg *Antoine Goetz and ors v Burundi*, Award, 10 February 1999, 6 ICSID Reports 5; *Emilio Augustín Maffezini v Spain*, Decision on Jurisdiction, 25 January 2000, 5 ICSID Reports 396; *Compañia de Aguas del Aconquija, PA & Compagnie Générale des Eaux v Argentina* (the *Vivendi* case), Decision on Annulment, 3 July 2002, 6 ICSID Reports 340 (hereinafter, *Vivendi*); *Azurix Corp v Argentina*, Decision on Jurisdiction, 8 December 2003, 43 ILM 259 (2004); *LG&E Energy Corp v Argentina*, Decision on Jurisdiction, 30 April 2004; *AMT v Zaire*, Award, 21 February 1997, 5 ICSID Reports 11; *Alex Genin v Estonia*, Award, 25 June 2001, 6 ICSID Reports 241; *CME Czech Republic BV (The Netherlands) v Czech Republic*, Partial Award, 13 September 2001, 9 ICSID Reports 121; *Camuzzi v Argentina*, Decision on Jurisdiction, 11 May 2005, at paras 12, 78–82, 140–142; *Gas Natural v Argentina*, Decision on Jurisdiction, 17 June 2005, at paras 32–35, 50–51; *AES Corp v Argentina*, Decision on Jurisdiction, 26 April 2005, at paras 85–89; *Compañia de Aguas del Aconquija, SA & Vivendi Universal SA v Argentina (Vivendi II)*, Decision on Jurisdiction, 14 November 2005, at paras 88–94; and *Continental Casualty v Argentina*, Decision on Jurisdiction, 22 February 2006, at paras 51–54, 76–89. Decisions of investment tribunals that have not yet appeared in print are available at <http://ita.law.uvic.ca>.   [19] *Alex Genin*, n 18 above.

[20] Ibid., at para 324.

Minority shareholders too have been accepted as claimants and have been granted protection under the respective treaties:[21] in *CMS v Argentina*,[22] jurisdiction was based on the BIT between Argentina and the United States. The claimant owned 29.42 per cent of TGN, a company incorporated in Argentina. Argentina argued that CMS, as a minority shareholder in TGN, could not claim for any indirect damage resulting from its participation in the Argentinean company.[23] The tribunal rejected this argument,[24] saying:

> The Tribunal therefore finds no bar in current international law to the concept of allowing claims by shareholders independently from those of the corporation concerned, not even if those shareholders are minority or non-controlling shareholders.[25]

Furthermore, it held that: 'There is indeed no requirement that an investment, in order to qualify, must necessarily be made by shareholders controlling a company or owning the majority of its shares.'[26]

This practice has also been extended to indirect shareholding through an intermediate company.[27] The same technique has been employed where the affected company was incorporated not in the host state, but in a third state.[28]

This shareholder protection extends not only to ownership in the shares, but also to the assets of the company. Adverse action by the host state in violation of treaty guarantees affecting the company's economic position gives rise to rights by the shareholders.[29] In *GAMI v Mexico*,[30] the claimant, a US registered corporation, held a 14.18 per cent equity interest in GAMI, a Mexican registered

---

[21] See, eg *AAPL v Sri Lanka*, Award, 27 June 1990, 4 ICSID Reports 250; *Lanco v Argentina*, Decision on Jurisdiction, 8 December 1998, 5 ICSID Reports 367; *Vivendi v Argentina*, Decision on Annulment, 3 July 2002, 6 ICSID Reports 340; *CMS Gas Transmission Co v Argentina*, Decision on Jurisdiction, 17 July 2003, 42 ILM 788; *Champion Trading Co and Ameritrade International Inc v Egypt*, Decision on Jurisdiction, 21 October 2003; *GAMI Investments, Inc v Mexico*, Award, 15 November 2004 (hereinafter, *GAMI v Mexico*); *LG&E Energy Corp v Argentina*, Decision on Jurisdiction, 30 April 2004, at paras 50–63; *Sempra Energy v Argentina*, Decision on Jurisdiction, 11 May 2005, at paras 92–94; and *El Paso Energy v Argentina*, Decision on Jurisdiction, 27 April 2006, at para 138.

[22] *CMS Gas Transmission Co v Argentina*, Decision on Jurisdiction, 17 July 2003, 42 ILM 788.
[23] Ibid., at paras 36, 37.   [24] Ibid., at paras 47–65.   [25] Ibid., at para 48.

[26] Ibid., at para 51. To the same effect, see *Enron Corp and Ponderosa Assets, LP v Argentina*, Decision on Jurisdiction, 14 January 2004, at paras 39, 44, 49 (hereinafter, *Enron v Argentina* (Jurisdiction)) and Decision on Jurisdiction (Ancillary claim), 2 August 2004, at paras 21, 22, 29, 39 (hereinafter *Enron v Argentina* (Ancillary)).

[27] See, eg *Siemens AG v Argentina*, Decision on Jurisdiction, 3 August 2004, 44 ILM 138 (2005); *Enron v Argentina* (Jurisdiction), n 26 above; *Camuzzi*, n 18 above, at para 9; and *Gas Natural*, n 18 above, at paras 9, 10, 32–35.

[28] *Ronald S Lauder v Czech Republic*, Award, 3 September 2001, 9 ICSID Reports 66; and *Waste Management v Mexico*, Award, 30 April 2004, 43 ILM 967 (2004).

[29] *CMS Gas Transmission*, n 22 above, at paras 59, 66–69; *Azurix*, n 18 above, at paras 69, 73; *Enron v Argentina* (Jurisdiction), n 26 above, at paras 35, 43–49, 58–60; *Enron v Argentina* (Ancillary), n 26 above, at paras 17, 34–35; *Siemens v Argentina*, n 27 above, at paras 125, 136–150; *GAMI v Mexico*, n 21 above, at paras 26–33; *Camuzzi*, n 18 above, at paras 45–67; *Sempra Energy*, n 21 above, at paras 73–79; *Continental Casualty v Argentina*, Decision on Jurisdiction, 22 February 2006, at para 79; and *Bogdanov v Moldova*, Award, 22 September 2005, at para 5.1.   [30] *GAMI*, n 21 above.

corporation. Mexico had expropriated a number of mills belonging to GAMI. The tribunal said:

> The fact that a host State does not explicitly interfere with share ownership is not decisive. The issue is rather whether a breach of NAFTA leads with sufficient directness to loss or damage in respect of a given investment.[31]
>
> ...
>
> GAMI's shareholding was never expropriated as such. GAMI contends that Mexico's conduct impaired the value of its shareholding to such an extent that it must be deemed tantamount to expropriation.[32]

It follows that in international investment law as far as protection by investment treaties is concerned, shareholders are protected separately from the corporations. Shareholding is considered an investment. For the independent protection of the shareholder, the nationality of the shareholder and not the nationality of the corporation is decisive.

Under the ECHR it is well established that ownership of shares is protected, in principle, by Article 1 of the First Protocol.[33] *Bramelid & Malmström v Sweden*[34] concerned the forced sale of shares to the majority owner. The Commission said:

> A company share is a complex thing: certifying that the holder possesses a share in the company, together with the corresponding rights (especially voting rights), it also constitutes, as it were, an indirect claim on company assets. In the present case, there is no doubt that the NK shares had an economic value. The Commission is therefore of the opinion that, with respect to Art. 1 of the First Protocol, the NK shares held by the applicants were indeed 'possessions' giving rise to a right of ownership.[35]

The ECtHR has confirmed this position in a number of cases.[36] It has pointed out that a share certifies that the holder possesses a portion of the company together with the corresponding rights. This was not just an indirect claim on the company's assets, but also covered other rights like voting rights and the right to influence the company. The shares undoubtedly had an economic value and constituted 'possessions' within the meaning of Article 1 of the First Protocol.[37]

---

[31] Ibid., at para 33.   [32] Ibid., at para 35.

[33] See C Schwaighofer, 'Legal Persons, Organisations, Shareholders as Applicants (Article 25 of the Convention)' in M de Salvia and ME Villiger, *The Birth of European Human Rights Law/ L'éclosion du Droit européen des Droits de l'homme, Liber Amicorum Studies in honour of – Mélanges en l'honneur de Carl Aage Nørgaard* (1998) 321–331; P van den Broek, 'The Protection of Property Rights under the European Convention on Human Rights' (1986) Legal Issues of European Integration 1, 66; P Mittelberger, *Der Eigentumsschutz nach Art. 1 des Ersten Zusatzprotokolls zur EMRK im Lichte der Rechtsprechung der Strassburger Organe* (2000) 40; Schreuer and Kriebaum, n 14 above, at 752–754; and U Kriebaum, *Eigentumsschutz im Völkerrecht, Eine vergleichende Untersuchung zum internationalen Investitionsrecht sowie zum Menschenrechtsschutz* (2008) 76–77.

[34] ECommHR, *Bramelid & Malmström v Sweden*, Nos 8588/79, 8589/79, Decision on Admissibility, 29 DR 64 (1982).   [35] Ibid., at 81.

[36] See, eg *Lithgow and ors v United Kingdom*, Judgment, 8 July 1986, Series A No 102; and *Marini v Albania*, No 3738/02, Judgment, 18 December 2007.

[37] ECtHR, *Sovtransavto Holding v Ukraine*, No 48553/99, Judgment, 25 July 2002, ECHR 2002-VII, at para 9; and *Marini v Albania*, No 3738/02, 18 December 2007, at para 164.

At the same time, the ECtHR and the Commission have adopted a restrictive attitude towards shareholders who acted independently of the company in pursuit of claims arising from acts that adversely affected the company. In some cases, claims by majority shareholders were admitted on the ground that the claimants had carried out their own business through the medium of the companies and were hence directly affected. The fact that it was not their shareholding as such that was affected, but rights of the company which in turn led to a loss in the value of the shares, did not affect the standing of these shareholders.[38]

On the other hand, claims by minority shareholders were declared inadmissible even though the value of their shares had been affected.[39] However, majority shareholding in itself will not be decisive for an independent standing of shareholders. In *Agrotexim Hellas SA et al v Greece*, none of the applicants held a majority of the shares, but jointly they owned 51.35 per cent. The Commission said:

> ... the question whether a shareholder may claim to be victim of measures affecting a company cannot be determined on the sole criterion of whether the shareholder holds the majority of the company shares. This element is an objective and important indication but other elements may also be relevant. ... [I]t [the Commission] has previously taken into account the fact that an applicant shareholder was carrying out its own business through the medium of the company and that he had a personal interest in the subject matter of the complaint ... It has also considered whether it was open to the company itself, being the direct victim, to lodge an application with the Commission.[40]

The ECtHR agreed that the decisive criterion was the impossibility of an application by the company itself. The Court said:

> ... the piercing of the 'corporate veil' or the disregarding of a company's legal personality will be justified only in exceptional circumstances, in particular where it is clearly established that it is impossible for the company to apply to the Convention institutions through the organs set up under its articles of incorporation or – in the event of liquidation – through its liquidators ... This principle has also been confirmed with regard to the diplomatic protection of companies by the International Court of Justice (Barcelona Traction, Light and Power Company Limited, judgment of 5 February 1970, Reports of judgments, advisory opinions and orders 1970, pp. 39 and 41, paras. 56–58 and 66).[41]

It follows from the above practice that under the European system an independent right of shareholders under Article 1 of the First Protocol is subsidiary

---

[38] ECommHR, *X v Austria*, No 1706/62, Decision, 4 October 1966, 9 YearBook 1966, 112; and *Kaplan v United Kingdom*, No 7598/76, Report adopted on 17 July 1980 pursuant to Art 31, 21 DR 5, at p 23.

[39] ECommHR, *Yarrow Plc and ors v United Kingdom*, No 9266/81, Decision, 28 January 1983, 30 DR 155, at p 185.

[40] ECommHR, *Agrotexim Hellas SA and ors v Greece*, No 14807/89, Decision, 12 February 1992, 72 DR 148, at pp 155 and 156.

[41] ECtHR, *Agrotexim and ors v Greece* (1), Judgment, 24 October 1995, Series A No 330-A, at para 66.

to the right of the company itself and will be recognized only in exceptional cases. This would be the case, in particular, where the company itself did not have the possibility to pursue the claim.

In comparison to the investment protection system, there are considerable disadvantages in the protection system of the ECHR concerning the protection of legal persons and shareholders: shareholders are (subject to narrow exceptions) only protected against the expropriation of their shares as such. Protection for diminution of the value of the company and the piercing of the 'corporate veil' or the disregarding of a company's legal personality is justified only in exceptional circumstances, namely:

- if the claimants had carried out their business through the medium of the companies and were hence directly affected; or
- where it is clearly established that it is impossible for the company to apply to the Convention institutions through the organs set up under its articles of incorporation or – in the event of liquidation – through its liquidators, a piercing of the corporate veil is possible.

Therefore, the European Convention on Human Rights does not protect shareholders in case of indirect damages.

Hence, there are advantages and disadvantages in both systems. Nationality planning is only an issue in international investment protection. Indirect damages usually cannot be obtained under the ECHR property protection system. Therefore, for shareholders, the ECHR protection system will often not be an option.

B. Exhaustion of Local Remedies

Traditionally, before an international claim on behalf of a national may be raised before an international court or tribunal, the national must have exhausted the local remedies in the injuring state. This requirement has been developed in the field of diplomatic protection, but is also a common prerequisite in human rights law.[42] Therefore, customary international law requires that an investor exhausts all local remedies available before its home state may bring a claim on its behalf by exercising diplomatic protection.[43]

In international investment law, exhaustion of local remedies is in principle not a requirement for the admissibility of a claim or the jurisdiction of a tribunal.[44] Article 26 of the ICSID Convention explicitly provides that an exhaustion of local remedies is not required. It allows for an exception to this

---

[42] CF Amerasinghe, *Local Remedies in International Law* (2004).

[43] Dolzer and Schreuer, n 5 above, 215; Amerasinghe, n 42 above, 1; AK Bjorklund, 'Waiver and the Exhaustion of Local Remedies Rule in NAFTA Jurisprudence' in Weiler, *NAFTA Investment Law and Arbitration: Past Issues, Current Practice, Future Prospects* (2004) 253; and I Brownlie, *Principles of Public International Law* (2003) 472.

[44] See, eg C Schreuer, 'Calvo's Grandchildren: The Return of Local Remedies in Investment Arbitration' (2005) 1 The Law and Practice of International Courts and Tribunals 1.

rule, if it is expressly mentioned in the instrument containing the consent of the state – for example, a BIT or FTA, which is practically never the case. Some BITs require an investor to make use of the domestic remedies for a certain period of time before it can bring the dispute before an international tribunal.[45] Arbitral practice both in ICSID and non-ICSID cases indicates that the exhaustion of local remedies is not required for the admissibility of a claim.[46]

Only in certain cases have investment tribunals required in the merits phase that an attempt be made to rectify the measures complained of by submitting the case to the local courts.[47] Such a requirement would be incorporated into the substantive standard and would not be an issue of jurisdiction. However, the issue is far from settled.

This direct access of investors to international tribunals for dispute settlement provided for by investment protection treaties is certainly an important advantage compared to requirements of general international law and the human rights protection system.

The ECHR as well as other human rights treaties which allow for complaints against states for violations of human rights require the prior exhaustion of local remedies.

ECHR, Article 35(1)[48] provides: 'The Court may only deal with the matter after all domestic remedies have been exhausted, according to the generally recognised rules of international law ...'. The requirement is not an absolute one.[49] The ECtHR said that:

[45] For examples, see Schreuer, n 5 above, 392; and Schreuer, n 44 above, 3–5.
[46] See, eg *Compañía de Aguas del Aconquija, SA & Compagnie Générale des Eaux v Argentina*, Award, 21 November 2000, 5 ICSID Reports 299, at para 81; *Lanco v Argentina*, Decision on Jurisdiction, 8 December 1998, (2001) 40 ILM 457, 469–470, at para 39; *CME v Czech Republic*, Final Award, 14 March 2003, 9 ICSID Reports 264, at paras 412, 413; *Yaung Chi Oo v Myanmar*, Award, 31 March 2003, (2003) 42 ILM 540, 547–548; *Generation Ukraine v Ukraine*, Award, 16 September 2003, 10 ICSID Reports 240, at paras 13.1–13.5; *Nykomb Synergetics Technology Holding AB, Sweden ('Nycomb') v Latvia*, Award, 16 December 2003, printed in C Ribeiro, *Investment Arbitration and the Energy Charter Treaty*, AP1-3, para 2.4b; *IBM World Trade Corp v Ecuador*, Decision on Jurisdiction, 22 December 2003, at paras 79, 80, 84, 85; *Waste Management Inc v Mexico*, n 28 above, at para 116; *AES Corp v Argentina*, Decision on Jurisdiction, 26 April 2005, 12 ICSID Reports 312, at paras 69, 70; *Jan de Nul NV Dredging International NV v Egypt*, Decision on Jurisdiction, 16 June 2006, at para 121; *Saipem SpA v Bangladesh*, Decision on Jurisdiction, 21 March 2007, at para 151; *Eastern Sugar BV v Czech Republic*, Partial Award, 27 March 2007, at paras 141, 218; and *RosInvestCo UK Ltd v The Russian Federation*, Decision on Jurisdiction, October 2007, at paras 151–156.
[47] *Generation Ukraine*, n 46 above, at para 20.30; *Waste Management Inc v Mexico*, n 28 above, at para 97; *EnCana v Ecuador*, Award, 3 February 2006, (2006) 45 ILM 901, at para 194; and *Parkerings-Compagniet AS v Lithuania*, Award, 11 September 2007, at paras 448–454. See, eg U Kriebaum, 'Local Remedies and the Standards for the Protection of Foreign Investment' in C Binder et al (eds), *Investment Law for the 21st Century, Essays in Honour of Christoph Schreuer* (2009) 417–462.
[48] L Zwaak, 'The Procedure before the European Court of Human Rights' in P van Dijk et al, *Theory and practice of the European Convention on Human Rights* (2006) 125–161.
[49] Zwaak, n 48 above, 127; and C Grabenwarter, *Europäische Menschenrechtskonvention* (2008) 60.

... the only remedies which that Article (art. 26) [now 35(1)] requires to be exhausted are those that relate to the breaches alleged and at the same time are available and sufficient. The existence of such remedies must be sufficiently certain not only in theory but also in practice, failing which they will lack the requisite accessibility and effectiveness ...

Therefore, the rule allows for certain limited exceptions, such as:

- if the victim is denied access to the remedies;
- if the victim has been prevented from exhausting them; or
- with regard to remedies which are certain not to be effective or adequate.[50]

The requirement of the ECHR to exhaust local remedies is an important disadvantage for investors seeking relief from an interference with property rights, since it adds considerably to the time which passes from the occurrence of an interference until a judgment from the ECtHR can be obtained.

The case of *Nomura & Saluka v Czech Republic* illustrates the consequences of the different approaches on the issue of exhaustion of local remedies and shareholders' rights in international investment law and the human rights system. The case was taken to the ECtHR as well as to UNCITRAL arbitration. The case arose in the context of the forced administration and forced sale of IPB and other interferences in IPB's property rights. IPB was a Czech commercial bank, which was placed under forced administration and later sold against the wish of Saluka to another bank. Saluka held a substantial shareholding in IPB. Nomura held a beneficial interest in Saluka.

The ECtHR declared the application inadmissible in a very short decision because of lack of exhaustion of local remedies by the applicant:

The Court has examined the application and finds that the applicant failed to raise before national authorities the complaint that is being made to the Court. The applicant has therefore not exhausted the domestic remedies available under Czech law in respect of his complaint, as required by Article 35 §1 of the Convention. It follows that the application must be rejected, in accordance with Article 35 §4.[51]

The applicant Saluka, as shareholder of the directly injured company, might have claimed that there were no effective domestic remedies existing for shareholders as a matter of Czech law. The ECtHR did not make any comments on the issue, but declared the application inadmissible.

The arbitral proceedings under the UNCITRAL rules had two important advantages for Saluka. First, in investment law, shareholders have standing independently from the company. Secondly, there is no requirement to exhaust

---

[50] See, eg ECtHR, *Vernillo v France*, Judgment, 20 February 1991, Series A No 198, at para 27; *Dalia v France*, Judgment, 19 February 1998, RJD 1998-I, at para 38; and *Horvat v Croatia*, Judgment, 26 July 2001, RJD 2001-VIII, at para 38. For further examples, see Zwaak, n 48 above, 136–148; and Grabenwarter, n 49 above, 60.

[51] ECtHR, *Nomura & Saluka v Czech Republic*, No 72066/01, Inadmissibility Decision, 4 September 2001.

local remedies. Therefore, the UNCITRAL tribunal accepted that it had jurisdiction. The issue of non-exhaustion was not even raised. The tribunal said:

The Tribunal's Conclusions as to Jurisdiction

243. Having thus considered the various challenges to its jurisdiction which the Respondent has advanced, the Tribunal concludes that the Claimant's shareholding of IPB shares is an 'investment' within the meaning of the Treaty, and that the Claimant is in respect of that investment an 'investor' within the meaning of the Treaty. Accordingly, the Tribunal is satisfied that it has jurisdiction to hear the claims brought before it by the Claimant under the arbitration procedure provided for in Article 8 of the Treaty.

244. In reaching that conclusion, however, the Tribunal wishes to emphasise that, in accordance with the Treaty, its jurisdiction is limited to claims brought by the Claimant, Saluka, in respect of damage suffered by itself in respect of the investment represented by its holding of IPB shares.[52]

C. Jurisdiction *Ratione Materiae*

One of the decisive requirements for the jurisdiction of an investment tribunal is the existence of an investment. The existence of an 'investment' in international investment law is required for two purposes.[53] If a case is to be decided under the ICSID Convention, the existence of an investment is a jurisdictional requirement under Article 25(1) of the ICSID Convention. Article 25(1) states that the jurisdiction of tribunals established within its framework is limited to disputes 'arising directly out of an investment'. No definition is given for the term 'investment', but tribunals have adopted a list of descriptors that they find typical for investments. These descriptors include a substantial contribution, certain duration, an element of risk, and significance for the host state's development.[54]

Furthermore, an 'investment' is the object of protection in the instrument containing the consent to jurisdiction of an arbitral tribunal. This can be: a national law, an ad hoc agreement, or a bilateral or multilateral investment treaty. Where the jurisdiction of a tribunal is based on a bilateral investment

[52] UNCITRAL, *Saluka Investments BV v Czech Republic*, Partial Award, 17 March 2006, at paras 243, 244.
[53] See, eg Schreuer and Kriebaum, n 14 above, 743–762, 744; and Dolzer and Schreuer, n 5 above, 60–71.
[54] *Fedax NV v Venezuela*, Decision on Jurisdiction, 11 July 1997, (1998) 37 ILM 1378, at para 43; *Salini Costruttori SpA et Italstrade SpA c/ Royaume du Maroc*, Decision on Jurisdiction, 23 July 2001, Journal de Droit International 196 (2002), (2003) 42 ILM 609, at para 53; *SGS v Pakistan*, Decision on Jurisdiction, 6 August 2003, 8 ICSID Reports 406, at para 133 FN 113; *Joy Mining Machinery Ltd v Egypt*, Award on Jurisdiction, 6 August 2004, at paras 53, 57, 62; *AES Corp v Argentina*, Decision on Jurisdiction, 26 April 2005, at para 88; *Bayindir v Pakistan*, Decision on Jurisdiction, 14 November 2005, at paras 130–138; *Patrick Mitchell v Democratic Republic of the Congo*, Decision on the Application for Annulment of the Award, 1 November 2006, at paras 27–47; *Malaysian Historical Salvors Sdn, Bhp v Malaysia*, Decision on Jurisdiction, 17 May 2007, at paras 43–45, 48–147; Schreuer and Kriebaum, n 14 above, 744–745; Schreuer, n 5 above, 140;

treaty (BIT), the definition of the term 'investment' contained in the treaty is relevant in addition to the requirement under Article 25(1) of the ICSID Convention. Most BITs contain broad definitions of 'investment'.[55] Typical of these comprehensive definitions is the one contained in the BIT between Argentina and the United States:

'investment' means every kind of investment in the territory of one Party owned or controlled directly or indirectly by nationals or companies of the other Party, such as equity, debt, and service and investment contracts; and includes without limitation:
(i) tangible and intangible property, including rights, such as mortgages, liens and pledges;
(ii) a company or shares of stock or other interests in a company or interests in the assets thereof;
(iii) a claim to money or a claim to performance having economic value and directly related to an investment;
(iv) intellectual property which includes, inter alia, rights relating to:
literary and artistic works, including sound recordings, inventions in all fields of human endeavor, industrial designs, semiconductor mask works, trade secrets, know-how, and confidential business information, and trademarks, service marks, and trade names; and
(v) any right conferred by law or contract, and any licenses and permits pursuant to law ...

Similarly, broad definitions of 'investment' are contained in regional multilateral treaties such as the Energy Charter Treaty (ECT)[56] and the North American Free Trade Agreement (NAFTA).[57]

Because of the double function of 'investment', it is possible that a right of an investor is covered by the investment definition of a BIT, but the overall operation of the relevant investor does not qualify as investment under Article 25 of the ICSID Convention. In such a case, the substantial protection by the BIT is not lost, but it cannot be enforced in an ICSID proceeding. Other arbitral tribunals may be available under the dispute settlement clause of the BIT. Otherwise, diplomatic protection remains the only option. In the latter case, the investor has no direct access to an international investment tribunal.

As opposed to investment law, Article 1 of the First Additional Protocol to the ECHR does not speak of 'investments', but of 'possessions' and 'property'.[58] Therefore, property rights are protected independently from a specific economic usage. Article 1 does not contain a definition of these terms, whereas BITs

---

N Rubins, 'The Notion of "Investment" in International Investment Arbitration' in N Horn, *Arbitrating Foreign Investment Disputes* (2004) 283 ff; F Yala, 'The Notion of "Investment" in ICSID Case Law: a Drifting Jurisdictional Requirement? Some "Un-Conventional" Thoughts on Salini, SGS & Mihaly' 1 Transnational Dispute Management issue 4, October 2004; and S Manciaux, *Investissements étrangers et arbitrage entre États et ressortissants d'autres États* (2004) 37 ff.

[55] Schreuer and Kriebaum, n 14 above, 744–745; and Dolzer and Schreuer, n 5 above, 62–65.
[56] See ECT, Art 1.   [57] See NAFTA, Art 1139.
[58] Every natural or legal person is entitled to the peaceful enjoyment of his possession. No one shall be deprived of his possessions except in the public interest and subject to the conditions provided for by law and by the general principles of international law.

usually contain definitions of investment. The European Court of Human Rights has refrained from offering a general definition. However, it has generally adopted a broad concept of property in its case law on this provision.[59] The Court stressed in its judgement in *Gasus v The Netherlands*[60] concerning a security right *in rem* that the notion 'possession' is not limited to physical goods:

> The Court recalls that the notion 'possessions' (in French: biens) in Article 1 of Protocol No. 1 (P1-1) has an autonomous meaning which is certainly not limited to ownership of physical goods: certain other rights and interests constituting assets can also be regarded as 'property rights', and thus as 'possessions', for the purposes of this provision (P1-1).

The ECtHR has furthermore adopted an autonomous interpretation of the term 'possessions' which is independent of domestic law. In *Beyeler v Italy*, it said 'possessions in the first part of Article 1 has an autonomous meaning which is not limited to ownership of physical goods and is independent from the formal classification in domestic law . . . '.[61]

Immovable and other tangible property as well as claims and rights to performance, shareholding, concessions, social security rights, good will, and so on have been found to be protected by Article 1.[62] The essential element for the Court appears to be the economic value of the right or interest. The Grand Chamber of the Court held, for example, in *Anheuser-Busch*[63]: 'These elements taken as a whole suggest that the applicant company's legal position . . . came within Article 1 of Protocol No. 1, as it gave rise to interests of a proprietary nature.'[64]

> The preceding provisions shall not, however, in any way impair the right of a State to enforce such laws as it deems necessary to control the use of property in accordance with the general interest or to secure the payment of taxes or other contributions or penalties.

The French text speaks of '*biens*' and of '*propriété*'. The ECtHR has made it clear that it treats these terms as synonyms: ECtHR, *Marckx v Belgium*, Judgment, 13 June 1979, Series A No 31, at para 63.

[59] See, eg H Ruiz Fabri, 'The Approach Taken by the European Court of Human Rights to the Assessment of Compensation for "Regulatory Expropriations" of the Property of Foreign Investors' (2003) 11 NYU Environmental Law Journal 148–173, 153; A van Rijn, 'Right to the Peaceful Enjoyment of One's Possessions (Article 1 of Protocol No. 1)' in P van Dijk et al, *Theory and Practice of the European Convention on Human Rights* (2006) 865–872; and Schreuer and Kriebaum, n 14 above, 743–762.

[60] ECtHR, *Gasus Fördertechnik GmbH v The Netherlands*, Judgment, 23 February 1995, Series A No 306-B.

[61] ECtHR, *Beyeler v Italy* [GC], Judgment, 5 January 2000, ECHR 2000-I, at para 100; see also *Matos e Silva Lda v Portugal*, Judgment, 16 September 1996, Reports 1996-VI, at para 75; *Former King of Greece v Greece*, Judgment, 23 November 2000, ECHR 2000-XII, at para 60; *Tsirikakis v Greece*, No 46355/99, Judgment, 17 January 2002, at para 53; *Forrer-Niedenthal v Germany*, No 47316/99, Judgment, 20 February 2003, at para 32; *Broniowski v Poland* [GC], No 31443/96, Judgment, 22 June 2004, at para 129; and *Öneryildiz v Turkey* [GC], No 48939/99, Judgment, 30 November 2004, at para 124.

[62] See on this issue, eg van Rijn, n 59 above, 865–872; and Schreuer and Kriebaum, n 14 above, 743–762.

[63] ECtHR, *Anheuser-Busch Inc v Portugal* [GC], No 73049/01, Judgment, 11 January 2007.

[64] Ibid., at para 78.

Therefore, international investment law only protects 'investments'. The European Convention on Human Rights protects 'property'. There are certain differences between the two concepts,[65] but only rarely will typical claims of investors only be protected by Article 1 of the First Protocol and not qualify as investment under the applicable BIT or other investment protection treaties.

More important is the different treatment of shareholders in the two systems, the double function of 'investment' in investment protection treaties, and the totally different role of nationality in the two systems.

III. Merits

A. Object of Protection

In international investment law, it is essential to distinguish between the jurisdictional requirement of an investment and the object of protection. For the establishment of jurisdiction, an arbitral tribunal will have to take the overall operation of the investor into consideration. Once jurisdiction is established, the tribunal will have to assess whether the particular right which allegedly has been interfered with is protected under the definition of investment in the applicable investment protection treaty.

In that way, the tribunal in *EnCana Corp*[66] distinguished between the jurisdictional requirement of an investment and the question of whether the particular claim was covered by the investment definition of the BIT:

... the Tribunal accepts that EnCana did not, as such, invest in certificates entitling it to VAT refunds. But this is not an end of the matter. An investment is widely defined to include 'claims to money' (Article I(g)(iii)) ... Thus claims to money held through a third State investor can constitute an investment. Moreover the protection of Article VIII also extends to 'returns' which are widely defined as ...
'all amounts yielded by an investment and in particular, though not exclusively, includes profits, interest, capital gains, dividends, royalties, fees or other current income.' (Article I(j))
It is hard to imagine a broader definition ...
In the Tribunal's opinion, a law which cancels a liability the State already has to an investor, including an investor of a third state which is owned or controlled by an investor of a State Party, is capable of amounting to expropriation. The right under the law of the host State to refunds of VAT in respect of the past acquisition of goods and services is a material benefit, and it does not matter whether refunds take the form of tax credits or rights to actual payment of the amount due.[67]

Therefore, the tribunal answered the question of whether the VAT (value added tax) refund claim was covered by the property protection clause of the BIT in

---

[65] For a detailed analysis, see U Kriebaum, *Eigentumsschutz im Völkerrecht, Eine vergleichende Untersuchung zum internationalen Investitionsrecht sowie zum Menschenrechtsschutz* (2008) 172–180.
[66] *EnCana Corp v Ecuador*, Award, 3 February 2006, 12 ICSID Reports 427.
[67] Ibid., at paras 181–183.

the affirmative. At the same time, it stressed that the VAT refund claim was not an investment under Article 25 of the ICISD Convention. This was not necessary since the overall operation qualified as investment.

Some tribunals had difficulties with this differentiation.[68] The *Joy Mining* tribunal, for instance, denied jurisdiction since the actual claim – and not the overall operation which should have been looked at – did not qualify as investment.[69]

Under the ECHR, the jurisdictional requirements for the applicability *ratione materiae* of Article 1 of the First Protocol are identical with the object of protection. Therefore, no such problems as described in investment law arise.

B. Expropriation and Other Forms of Interferences

A very important difference between investment protection and property protection under the European Convention on Human Rights are the interferences covered.[70]

In international investment law, there is no uniform answer. Which interferences are covered depends upon the applicable law,[71] the standards provided for in the applicable law, and the clause on jurisdiction in the instrument of consent.[72]

Treaties for the protection of investments typically provide for protection against direct and indirect expropriation[73] without compensation. Most treaties

---

[68] *Joy Mining Machinery Ltd v Egypt*, Award on Jurisdiction, 6 August 2004, 19 ICSID Review Foreign Investment Law Journal (2004) 486, at paras 43–47. The case concerned a bank guarantee and the BIT covered in Art 1 '(i) movable and immovable property and any other property rights such as mortgages, liens or pledges'. See on this N Gallus, 'Joy Mining v. Egypt: No Joy for British Mining Equipment Company at the ICSID' 1 Transnational Dispute Management 2004 (issue 4) 5; and *Occidental Exploration and Production Co v Ecuador*, Award, 1 July 2004, 12 ICSID Reports 59. The case concerned a tax refund claim. The tribunal held '[h]owever broad the definition of investment might be under the Treaty, it would be quite extraordinary for a company to invest in a refund claim' (para 86).

[69] *Joy Mining*, n 68 above, at paras 43–47.

[70] See on the differences in more detail Kriebaum, n 65 above, 227–429.

[71] Dolzer and Schreuer, n 5 above, 265–271.   [72] Ibid., 244–247.

[73] Ibid., 89–119; and McLachlan, Shore, and Weininger, n 5 above, 290–297.

On indirect expropriation see, eg V Lowe, 'Regulation or Expropriation?' (2002) 55 Current Legal Problems 447–466; R Dolzer, 'Indirect Expropriations: New Developments?' (2003) 11 NYU Environmental Law Journal 64–93; WM Reisman and RD Sloane, 'Indirect Expropriation and its Valuation in the BIT Generation' (2003) 74 British Year Book of International Law 115–150; GH Sampliner, 'Arbitration of Expropriation Cases Under U.S. Investment Treaties – A Threat to Democracy or the Dog That Didn't Bark?' (2003) 18 ICSID Review Foreign Investment Law Journal 1–43; J Paulsson and Z Douglas, 'Indirect Expropriation in Investment Treaty Arbitration' in N Horn and S Kröll, *Arbitrating Foreign Investment Disputes: Procedural and Substantive Legal Aspects* (2004) 145–158; LY Fortier and SL Drymer, 'Indirect Expropriation in the Law of International Investment: I Know It When I See It, or Caveat Investor' (2004) 19 ICSID Review Foreign Investment Law Journal 293–327; D Clough, 'Regulatory Expropriations and Compensation under NAFTA' (2005) 6 Journal of World Investment and Trade 553–584; A Newcombe, 'The Boundaries of Regulatory Expropriation in International Law' (2005) 20

also require fair and equitable treatment (FET)[74] of the investor and contain a clause promising full protection and security.[75] Furthermore, such treaties provide for national treatment[76] and usually contain an MFN (Most Favoured Nation) clause.[77] Sometimes the international minimum standard[78] is guaranteed. Some investment protection treaties also cover contract claims[79] or provide for an umbrella clause.[80] The interpretation of MFN clauses and umbrella clauses is currently quite contested.[81]

ICSID Review Foreign Investment Law Journal 1–57; and U Kriebaum, 'Regulatory Takings: Balancing the Interests of the Investor and the State' (2007) 8 Journal of World Investment and Trade 717–744.

[74] See, eg S Vasciannie, 'The Fair and Equitable Treatment Standard in International Investment Law, and Practice' (1999) 70 British Yearbook of International Law 99–164; P Dumberry, 'The Quest to Define "Fair and Equitable Treatment" for Investors under International Law, The Case of the NAFTA Chapter 11 Pope & Talbot Awards' (2002) 3 Journal of World Investment and Trade 657–691; C Schreuer, 'Fair and Equitable Treatment in Arbitral Practice' (2005) 6 Journal of World Investment and Trade 357–386; B Choudhury, 'Evolution or Devolution? Defining Fair and Equitable Treatment in International Investment Law' (2005) 6 Journal of World Investment and Trade 297–320; Dolzer and Schreuer, n 5 above, 119–149; and I Tudor, *The Fair and Equitable Treatment Standard in the International Law of Foreign Investment* (2008).   [75] Dolzer and Schreuer, n 5 above, 149–153.

[76] Ibid., 178–186; and R Dolzer and M Stevens, *Bilateral Investment Treaties* (1995) 63–65.

[77] See E Gaillard, 'Establishing Jurisdiction Through a Most-Favored-Nation Clause' (2005) 233 New York Law Journal 105; DH Freyer and D Herlihy, 'Most-Favored-Nation Treatment and Dispute Settlement in Investment Arbitration: Just How "Favored" is "Most-Favored"?' (2005) 20 ICSID Review Foreign Investment Law Journal 58–83; R Teitelbaum, 'Who's Afraid of Maffezini?: Recent Developments in the Interpretation of Most Favored Nation Clauses' (2005) 22 Journal of International Arbitration 225–237; Y Radi, 'The Application of the Most-Favoured-Nation Clause to the Dispute Settlement Provisions of Bilateral Investment Treaties: Domesticating the "Trojan Horse"' (2007) 18 European Journal of International Law 757–774; and Dolzer and Schreuer, n 5 above, 186–191, 253–257.

[78] A Falsafi, 'The International Minimum Standard of Treatment of Foreign Investor's Property: A Contigent Standard' (2007) 30 Suffolk Transnational Law Review 317–363.

[79] See, eg Italy/Morocco BIT, Art 8(1), UNCTAD (*Tutte le controversie o divergenze ... in relazione ad un investimento ...*); Germany/Argentina BIT, Art 10 (*(1) Las controversias que surgien ... en relación con las inversiones en el sentido del presente Tratado ... (3) La controversia podrá ser sometida a un tribunal arbitral internacional en cualquiera de las circunstancias siguientes*); China/Czech Republic BIT, Art 9 (1. Any dispute which may arise between an investor of one Contracting Party and the other Contracting Party in connection with an investment in the territory of that other Contracting Party shall be ... 2. ... the investor shall be entitled to submit the case, at his choice, for settlement to ...).

[80] SA Alexandrov, 'Breaches of Contract and Breaches of Treaty – The Jurisdiction of Treaty-Based Arbitration Tribunals to Decide Breach of Contract Claims in SGS v Pakistan and SGS v Philippines' (2004) 5 JWIT 555–578; C Schreuer, 'Travelling the BIT Route. Of Waiting Periods, Umbrella Clauses and Forks in the Road' (2004) 5 Journal of World Investment and Trade 231–256; AC Sinclair, 'The Origins of the Umbrella Clause in the International Law of Investment Protection' (2004) 20 Arbitration International 411–434; T Wälde, 'The "Umbrella" Clause in Investment Arbitration: A Comment on Original Intentions and Recent Cases' (2005) 6 JWIT 183–236; B Kunoy, 'Singing in the Rain: Developments in the Interpretation of Umbrella Clauses' (2006) 7 JWIT 275–300; K Yannaca-Small, 'Interpretation of the Umbrella Clause in Investment Agreements' (2006) OECD Working Papers on International Investment, 2006/3; and Dolzer and Schreuer, n 5 above, 119–149.

[81] Favourable decisions: *Maffezini v Spain*, Decision on Jurisdiction, 25 January 2000, at paras 38–64; *Siemens*, n 27 above, at paras 32–110; *Gas Natural*, n 18 above, at paras 24–31, 41–49; *Suez, Sociedad General de Aguas de Barcelona SA, and Interaguas Servicios Integrales del Agua SA v*

In international investment law, it is widely accepted that an interference with property must lead at least to a substantial deprivation, in order to amount to an expropriation. Measures that affect an investment without amounting to a 'taking' in this sense but merely reduce its value or profitability are usually not seen as expropriatory. For an expropriation to exist, the investment must have been essentially destroyed.[82] For a substantial or total deprivation to occur it is, however, not required that an investor is deprived of its installations.[83] Rather, the economic use of the investment has to become impossible as a consequence of the state interference.[84]

Non-discrimination is one of the prerequisites of a legal expropriation in international investment law.[85]

If no expropriation is found in international investment law, the investor has to rely on other available investment protection standards of the investment protection treaty to be able to obtain redress for a state interference with its investment. These standards are not comprehensive, although FET is very

---

Argentina, Decision on Jurisdiction, 16 May 2006, at paras 52–66; *National Grid Plc v Argentina*, Decision on Jurisdiction, 20 June 2006, at paras 53–94; *Suez, Sociedad General de Aguas de Barcelona SA, and Vivendi Universal SA and AWG Group Ltd v Argentina*, Decision on Jurisdiction, 3 August 2006, at paras 52–68; *AWG Group v Argentina*, Decision on Jurisdiction, 3 August 2006, at paras 52–68; and *RosInvestCo*, n 46 above, at paras 130–132.

Decisions denying the applicability of MFN clauses to dispute settlement:

Salini v Jordan, Decision on Jurisdiction, 29 November 2004, at para 119; *Plama v Bulgaria*, Decision on Jurisdiction, 8 February 2005, 44 ILM 721, at paras 183, 184, 223, 227; *Berschader v Russian Federation*, Award, 21 April 2006, 159–208; and *Telenor v Hungary*, Award, 13 September 2006, at paras 90–100.

See also R Dolzer and T Myers, 'After Tecmed: Most-Favored-Nation Clauses in Investment Protection Agreements' (2004) 19 ICSID Review Foreign Investment Law Journal 49–60; J Kurtz, 'The MFN Standard and Foreign Investment – An Uneasy Fit'? (2004) 6 JWIT 861–886; L Hsu, 'MFN and Dispute Settlement – When the Twain Meet' (2006) 7 JWIT 25–38; W Ben Hamida, 'MFN Clause and Procedural Rights: Seeking Solutions from WTO Experiences' (2008) Transnational Dispute Management, February 2008; and Y Banifatemi, 'The Emerging Jurisprudence on the Most-Favoured-Nation Treatment in Investment Arbitration' in AK Bjorklund, IA Laird, and S Ripinsky, *Investment Treaty Law: Current Issues III, BIICL* (2008).

[82] See, eg *Técnicas Medioambientales Tecmed, SA v Mexico* (Spain/Mexico BIT), Award, 29 May 2003, 10 ICSID Reports 134, at para 102; and *Compañía de Aguas del Aconquija SA and Vivendi Universal v Argentina (Vivendi II)* (France/Argentina BIT), Award, 20 August 2007, at para 7.5.34.

[83] See, eg *Técnicas Medioambientales Tecmed*, n 82 above, at paras 35, 95, 151; and *Metalclad Corp2 v Mexico* (NAFTA), Award, 30 August 2000, 5 ICSID Reports 212, at paras 30, 45, 107.

[84] See U Kriebaum, 'Partial Expropriation' (2007) 8 Journal of World Investment and Trade 69–84, 71.

The problems of regulatory takings and the different strands of case law in investment arbitration will not be discussed here, see on that issue with further references: Kriebaum, n 73 above, 717–744.

[85] JH Herz, 'Expropriation of Foreign Property' (1941) 35 AJIL 243–262, 249; GG Fitzmaurice, 'The Juridical Clauses of the Peace Treaties' (1943) 73 Recueil des Cours (1943-II) 259, 349; M Domke, 'Foreign Nationalisations, Some Aspects of Contemporary International Law' (1961) 55 AJIL 585, 600–603; R Jennings and A Watts, *Oppenheim's International Law, Vol I* (1992) 920, 932; G White, *Nationalisation of Foreign Property* (1961) 5, 119–144; I Brownlie, *Principles of Public International Law* (2003) 514 ff; K Hobér, *Investment Arbitration in Eastern Europe: Recent Cases on Expropriation* (2007) 40; and Dolzer and Schreuer, n 5 above, 91.

broad.[86] Each of these standards provides for its own application requirements. It is therefore possible that an interference is neither an expropriation nor covered by one of the other available standards. Not all of the treaties contain the full range of protection clauses. Furthermore, some BITs only provide for jurisdiction in case of an expropriation and not for breaches of other standards contained in the BIT.[87] Investment protection does not provide for a comprehensive protection covering all possible interferences with an investment. Many cases will, however, be covered by the other treatment standards provided for in investment treaties.

The property protection clause in the ECHR, by contrast, provides for a differentiated concept of interference comprising expropriation, the control of the use of property and a comprehensive clause (called: 'other interference' in the case law of the ECHR).[88] Therefore, in contrast to international investment law, all interferences with property rights are covered by Article 1 of the First Protocol. Hence, when examining whether a violation has occurred, all interferences have to be tested against the requirements set forth in the Article.

For an expropriation to occur under Article 1, a total deprivation of the property is required; de facto expropriations are possible, but there must not

---

See, eg IUSCT, *Amoco International Finance Corp v The Government of Iran and ors*, Partial Award No 310-56-3, 14 July 1987, 15 IUSCTR 189; *Libyan American Oil Co (LIAMCO) v Government of Libya*, Award, 12 April 1977, 62 ILR 1982, 141–219, at 194; *Liberian Eastern Timber Corp (LETCO) v The Government of Liberia*, Award, 31 March 1986, 89 ILR 1992, 313.

[86] See on fair and equitable treatment eg I Tudor, n 74 above.

[87] See, eg Art XII 2(b) Agreement between the Government of Australia and the Government of the People's Republic of China on the Reciprocal Encouragement and Protection of Investments of 11 July 1988, Australian Treaty Series 1988, No 14.

In the case of *Plama v Bulgaria* (Decision on Jurisdiction, 8 February 2005) the BIT only provided for jurisdiction of an arbitral tribunal in cases of dispute with regard to the amount of the compensation for an expropriation (Ibid, paras 26, 186). Although the BIT contained an MFN clause, the tribunal did not allow for incorporating dispute resolution provisions from other treaties (Ibid, para 207). Therefore, it was not possible to obtain jurisdiction for other property protection standards by using the MFN clause (Ibid, paras 223, 227).

In the case of *EnCana v Ecuador*, the arbitral tribunal had with regard to tax measures only jurisdiction in case of an expropriation and not for the other protection standards contained in the Canada/Ecuador BIT like 'fair and equitable treatment', see *EnCana Corp*, n 66 above, at paras 149, 166–168.

The BIT in *ADC v Hungary* also contained a jurisdiction clause which limited the jurisdiction of the tribunal to expropriation. The arbitral tribunal did not have jurisdiction for the 'fair and equitable treatment' – and 'full protection and security' – standards also contained in the Cyprus/Hungary BIT (*ADC Affiliate Ltd and ADC & ADMC Management Ltd v Hungary*, Award, 2 October 2006, at para 295).

[88] See, eg A van Rijn, 'Right to the Peaceful Enjoyment of One's Possessions (Article 1 of Protocol No. 1)' in P van Dijk et al, *Theory and Practice of the European Convention on Human Rights* (2006) 872–878.

See, eg ECtHR, *Sporrong and Lönnroth v Sweden*, 23 September 1982; *Beyeler*, n 61 above, at para 106; *Sovtransavto Holding v Ukraine*, No 48553/99, Judgment, 25 July 2002, ECHR 2002-VII, at para 93; *SA Dangeville v France*, Judgment, 16 April 2002, ECHR 2002-III, at para 51; *Broniowski*, n 61 above, at para 136; and *Piven v Ukraine*, No 56849/00, Judgment, 29 June 2004, at para 49.

remain any possible use or economic value of the property.[89] The investor also has to be deprived of its installations, otherwise there is no expropriation.[90]

Discrimination with regard to an interference with property rights is a violation under Article 1 of the First Protocol and ECHR, Article 14.[91]

C. Consequences of an Established Interference

An important difference between the two systems is the consequence of an established expropriation. The answer to the question 'When does a duty to compensate in case of an expropriation occur and to what extent has the expropriated person to be compensated?' is different in the two systems.

In international investment law, the duty to compensate is linked to the fact of an expropriation. The existence of the expropriation alone attracts the obligation to compensate. The goal of the decision on the lawfulness is only to decide whether damages or compensation are due.[92] In case of an expropriation, the expropriating state has to pay compensation or damages. Either way, the indemnification has to be full. If there was no expropriation, there is no right to any indemnification unless some of the other treaty standards have been violated. The decisive question, therefore, is not whether an expropriation was lawful or unlawful, but whether or not it has occurred. One can therefore speak of an all-or-nothing approach in international investment law.[93]

Since the indemnification in case of an expropriation always has to be full no matter how legitimate the causes for the expropriation are,[94] it has become difficult to convince tribunals that an expropriation has occurred. If another protection standard, in particular FET (fair and equitable treatment), is

---

[89] For de facto expropriations see, eg ECtHR, *Papamichalopoulos v Greece*, Judgment, 23 June 1993, Series A No 260-B; *Vasilescu v Rumania*, Judgment, 22 May 1998, ECHR 1998-III; *Brumarescu v Rumania*, [GC], No 28342/95, Judgment, 28 October 1999, ECHR 1999-VII; *Zwierzynski v Poland*, Judgment, 19 June 2001, ECHR 2001-VI; *Karagiannis and ors v Greece*, No 51354/99, Judgment, 16 January 2003; and *Popov v Moldavia* (No 2), No 19960/04, Judgment, 6 December 2005.

For cases where the Commission or the Court denied the existence of a de facto expropriation, see eg ECommHR, *Pinnacle Meat Processors Co and 8 ors v United Kingdom*, No 33298/96, Decision, 21 October 1998; ECtHR, *Tre Traktörer Aktiebolag v Sweden*, Judgment, 7 July 1989, Series A No 159; *Mellacher v Austria*, Judgment, 19 December 1989, Series A No 169; *Fredin v Sweden* (no 1), Judgment, 18 February 1991, Series A No 192; *Pine Valley Developments Ltd ao v Ireland*, Judgment, 29 November 1991, Series A No 222; *Chassagnou and ors v France*, Judgment, 29 April 1999, ECHR 1999-III; and *Hutten-Czapska v Poland*, [GC], No 35014/97, Judgment, 19 June 2006. [90] See, eg ECommHR, *Pinnacle Meat Processors*, n 89 above.

[91] See, eg ECtHR, *Marckx v Belgium*, Judgment, 13 June 1979, Series A No 31; *Koua Poirrez v France*, No 40892/98, Judgment, 30 September 2003, ECHR 2003-X; and *Driha v Romania*, No 29556/02, Judgment, 21 February 2008.

[92] In order to be lawful, the following requirements have to be met: the expropriation has to be for a public purpose, non-discriminatory, compensation has to be paid, and, depending on the applicable treaty, due process has to be respected; U Kriebaum, n 65 above, 719.

[93] See on this 'all or nothing approach': Kriebaum, n 65 above, 719–720.

[94] Kriebaum, n 73 above, 719–720.

available, tribunals often prefer to opt for a violation of this standard instead of finding that an expropriation has occurred.[95] Expropriation is the only investment protection standard where the interference with property rights is in principle legal, but requires compensation, without which the interference becomes illegal. Interferences with the other treaty standards automatically lead to violations of international law obligations and damages are due.[96]

No such all-or-nothing approach exists in international human rights law with regard to expropriations. In the human rights protection system, the existence of an expropriation does not automatically lead to a duty to full compensation. Only if an *unjustified* expropriation has occurred is compensation required. In case of an unjustified expropriation, the amount of compensation must in principle, but not under all circumstances, be reasonable related to the value of the property taken.[97]

Under the European Convention on Human Rights, three requirements have to be fulfilled for an expropriation to be justified. The expropriation has to be in the public interest, lawful, and proportional. Often the key question is that of the proportionality of the interference. The amount of compensation already paid is taken into consideration when assessing whether the expropriation was proportional – that is, did not place an individual and excessive burden on the person concerned.[98] The state's interference with property rights has to strike a fair balance between the demands of the general interests of the community and the requirements of the protection of the complainant's property rights.[99]

[95] See, eg *Sempra Energy v Argentina*, Award, 28 September 2007; *Enron v Argentina*, Award, 22 May 2007; *Eastern Sugar BV v Czech Republic*, Partial Award, 27 March 2007; *PSEG Global, Inc, The North American Coal Corp, and Konya Ingin Electrik Uretim ve Ticaret Ltd Sirketi v Turkey*, Award, 19 January 2007; *LG&E Energy Corp v Argentina*, Award, 3 October 2006; *Azurix v Argentina*, award, 14 July 2006; and *Saluka Investments BV v Czech Republic*, Partial Award, 17 March 2006.
[96] See I Marboe, 'Compensation and Damages in International Law, The Limits of "Fair Market Value"' (2006) 7 Journal of World Investment and Trade 725–759.
[97] See, eg ECtHR, *James and ors v United Kingdom*, Judgment, 21 February 1986, Series A No 98, at para 54; *Lithgow* n 36 above, para. 121; *The Holy Monasteries v Greece*, Judgment, 9 December 1994, Series A No 301-A, at para 71; *Pressos Compañia Naviera SA and ors v Belgium*, Judgment, 20 November 1995, Series A No 332, at para 38; *Former King of Greece*, n 61 above, at para 18; *Motais de Narbonne v France*, No 48161/99, Judgment, 2 July 2002, at para 19; *Pincová and Pinc v Czech Republik*, Judgment, 5 November 2002, ECHR 2002-VIII, at para 53; *Broniowski*, n 61 above, at para 176; *Jahn and ors v Germany* [GC], Nos 46720/99, 72203/01 and 72552/01, Judgment, 30 June 2005, at para 94; *Strain and ors v Rumania*, No 57001/00, Judgment, 21 July 2005, at para 52; and *Draon v France* [GC], No 1513/03, Judgment, 6 October 2005, at para 79.
[98] See, eg ECtHR, *Sporrong*, n 88 above, at paras 69 and 73; *James and ors*, n 97 above, at para 50; *Lithgow*, n 36 above, at para 120; *Brumarescu*, n 89 above, at para 78; *Zwierzynski v Poland*, Judgment, 19 June 2001, ECHR 2001-VI, at para 71; *Lallement v France*, No 46044/99, 11 April 2002, at para 18; *Jahn and ors*, n 97 above, at para 95; and *Evaldsson and ors v Sweden*, No 75252/01, Judgment, 13 February 2007, at para 55; see also Ruiz Fabri, n 59, 148–173.
[99] ECtHR, *Sporrong and Lönnroth*, n 88 above, at para 69; *James and ors*, n 97 above, at para 50; *Lithgow*, n 36 above, at para 120; *Brumarescu*, n 89 above, at para 78; *Former King of Greece*, n 61 above, at para 89; *Lallement*, n 98 above, at para 23; *Jahn and ors*, n 97 above, at para 93; and *Evaldsson*, n 98 above, at para 55.

Under the ECHR, a number of factors are taken into consideration to assess whether a reasonable relationship exists between the goal and the effects of the interference. These are factors such as the severity of the interference, legitimate expectations of the complainant, the suitability of the interference to reach the public purpose, the priority of the public purpose, and a special public interest to pay less than full compensation as well as the amount of any compensation already paid.[100]

The main difference between the human rights approach and the investment law approach is that in the human rights system the proportionality test is not used to decide whether an expropriation has occurred. It is used to decide in case of an expropriation whether a suitable balancing of the state's interest to interfere and the property protection interest of the person hit by the interference has taken place.

The proportionality test in the human rights system can lead to a situation where a property owner receives less compensation than the fair market value. This will in general be the case if there is a special interest of the state to interfere and at the same time if this causes no excessive burden for the individual.[101]

However, this exception to the requirement to pay fair market value will generally not be applied by the Court in case of an expropriation of a foreigner. If a foreigner is expropriated, a reference to general principles of international law will be activated.[102] So far the Court has never found that an expropriation of a foreigner had occurred.[103] The case law nevertheless points to the direction that in case of an expropriation, there are reasons for drawing a distinction between nationals (who might get less than full compensation) and foreigners as far as the amount of compensation is concerned.

With regard to foreigners, the Court stated in the *James*[104] and *Lithgow*[105] judgments that in cases of a taking of property in the context of large-scale social or economic reforms there can be reasons for a distinction between nationals and foreigners. Both judgments concerned nationals. In both cases the Court found that the takings occurred in a situation justifying an exception to the rule that the amount of compensation must be reasonably related to the value of the

---

[100] Kriebaum, n 73 above, 731–742 with further references.

[101] For cases where the Court found that there is such an exceptional situation, see, eg ECtHR, *James and ors*, n 97 above, at para 54; *Lithgow*, n 36 above, at para 121; *Former King of Greece*, n 61 above, at para 78; and *Senkspiel v Germany*, No 77207/01, Decision, 12 January 2006.

In the case of *Jahn and ors*, n 97 above, the lack of legitimate expectations of the applicants with regard to the continuity of their ownership position concerning the expropriated land together with the exceptional circumstances prevailing in the unique context of German reunification in combination with the fact that the expropriation had been taken for reasons of social justice surprisingly led the Court to the conclusion that the lack of any compensation was justified.

For cases where the Court found the compensation to be disproportionately low, see, eg ECtHR, *Platakou v Greece*, Judgment, 11 January 2001, ECHR 2001-I, at paras 56, 57; *Pincová and Pinc*, n 97 above, at para 61; and *Scordino v Italy* (no 1) [GC], No 36813/97, Judgment, 29 March 2006, at paras 103, 104.   [102] Kriebaum, n 12 above.

[103] Ibid.   [104] *James and ors*, n 97 above.   [105] *Lithgow*, n 36 above.

property taken. The Court justified the distinction between nationals and foreigners, by observing that foreigners are more vulnerable since they are not
involved in the political process. Furthermore, there may be legitimate reasons
for imposing a greater burden in the public interest on nationals than on
foreigners:

> Especially as regards a taking of property effected in the context of a social reform [or an
> economic restructuring],[106] there may well be good grounds for drawing a distinction
> between nationals and non-nationals as far as compensation is concerned. To begin with,
> non-nationals are more vulnerable to domestic legislation: unlike nationals, they will
> generally have played no part in the election or designation of its authors nor have been
> consulted on its adoption. Secondly, although a taking of property must always be
> effected in the public interest, different considerations may apply to nationals and non-
> nationals and there may well be legitimate reason for requiring nationals to bear a greater
> burden in the public interest than non-nationals.[107]

The most recent mention of the fact that foreigners enjoy a special protection
under Article 1 of Protocol No 1 of the ECHR can be found in the dissenting
opinion of Judges Caflisch and Cabral Barreto in *Anheuser-Busch v Portugal*.[108]
The Grand Chamber of the European Court of Human Rights held that no
interference in property rights occurred although a trade mark was not registered.[109] Therefore, no violation had taken place.[110] The reasoning of the
majority is not very convincing though. In their dissenting opinion, Judges
Caflisch and Cabral Barreto stressed that the fact that the applicant is a foreigner
and therefore protected by the 'general principles of international law' should
not be disregarded. They hinted to the applicability of the principle of non-
discrimination and the rule requiring prompt, adequate, and effective compensation, which were in the opinion of the dissenters disregarded in the *Anheuser*
case by the Grand Chamber.[111]

Since the Court so far never found that a foreigner had been expropriated, it
never applied the reference to the general principles of international law in
practice. The case law built up so far by the ECtHR on this issue is not very
developed.

Nevertheless, it can be assumed that the exception from the principle that the
amount of compensation in case of an expropriation must be reasonably related
to the value of the property which is applicable to nationals in exceptional circumstances would either not apply at all, or only to a lesser extent apply to
foreigners. A reduction of the compensation in case of an expropriation is
therefore less likely with regard to a foreigner. The same is not true with regard
to the two other types of interferences (control of use/other interference). No

---

[106] The formula in squared brackets was only used in *Lithgow*.
[107] *James and ors*, n 97 above, at para 63; and *Lithgow*, n 36 above, at para 116.
[108] *Anheuser-Busch*, n 63 above.   [109] Ibid., at paras 79–87.   [110] Ibid., at para 87.
[111] Ibid., pp 30–32 HUDOC version.

difference between nationals and non-nationals is foreseen in that context. States enjoy a larger margin of appreciation of what is necessary to achieve the public interest in case of a control of use or other interference than in case of an expropriation.

Because of the high threshold for the existence of an expropriation (total deprivation) under Article 1 of the First Protocol, many interferences with property rights of foreign investors have been considered to be only 'regulations of use' or 'other interferences' and therefore the investor could not benefit from the privileged position as foreigner. In case of 'regulations of use' or 'other interferences', Article 1 offers a strong protection in case of unlawful interferences.[112] The ECtHR repeatedly held in such cases that 'the reparation should aim at putting the applicant company in the position in which it would have been had the violation not occurred'.[113] This is the standard applied by the PCIJ in its judgment in *Chorzów Factory*, which is by now the accepted standard of reparation in cases of a violation of international law.[114] Therefore, there is no difference between the case law of the European Court of Human Rights and general international law on this issue. By contrast, in case of lawful 'regulations of use' or 'other interferences', the margin of appreciation left to the states concerning the amount of compensation under Article 1 is even larger than in cases of expropriation. There is a high risk for an investor in such a case not to get full compensation.

The threshold for the existence of an expropriation is lower in international investment law than under Article 1 of the First Protocol. The privilege in Article 1 to full compensation under all circumstances for foreigners exists only with regard to expropriations.

If an investor can convince an arbitral tribunal that the challenged interference was an expropriation although the interference did not lead to a total deprivation of the property, the investor will be better off in investment arbitration than in the European human rights system since it does not risk getting less than full compensation.

In cases where the investment protection treaty only provides for jurisdiction for expropriation, the human rights protection system can be a meaningful alternative, if under investment law standards no expropriation has occurred, especially if the interference with property rights was unlawful.

---

[112] See, eg *Zlínsat, Spol SRO v Bulgaria*, No 57785/00, Judgment on Just Satisfaction, 10 January 2008; and *Bimer SA v Moldova*, No 15084/03, Judgment, 10 July 2007.

[113] See, eg *Zlínsat, Spol SRO*, at para 39.

[114] There the PCIJ held that: 'The essential principle contained in the actual notion of an illegal act – a principle which seems to be established by international practice and in particular by decision of arbitral tribunals – is that reparation must, as far as possible, wipe out all the consequences of the illegal act and re-establish the situation which would, in all probability, have existed if that act had not been committed' (PCIJ, *Case Concerning the Factory at Chorzów* (Indemnity), Judgment no 13, 1928 PCIJ, Series A No 17, Order, 13 September 1928, p 47); see, Marboe, n 96 above, 732 ff.

D. Amount of Compensation and Costs

The amounts awarded in international investment law are usually higher than in the human rights system, often in the hundreds of millions.[115] Investment awards often contain extensive discussion on the methods to be applied for measuring the harm caused.[116]

The highest sums awarded in human rights awards involving the protection of property are in the range of €24 million.[117] In *Bimer SA v Moldova*, one of the few cases before the ECtHR involving foreign investments, the claimant was awarded €520,000. This sum was in between the calculations of the experts of the claimant and the state. In *Zlínsat, Spol SRO v Bulgaria*, the claimant was awarded €300,000. In *Zlínsat*, the ECtHR undertook a thorough examination of all of the submitted expert reports on the calculation of damages and gave detailed reasons for its calculations of the amount of damages.[118] The filing of expert reports on issues of calculation of damages in the field of investment cases before the ECtHR is getting more common and the Court examines them thoroughly.

It follows that although amounts awarded in the human rights field can be substantial, they are still far below typical awards in investment cases. However, the amounts awarded primarily depend on the cases brought to the two systems and do not necessarily reflect the attitudes of decision makers.

Not only the compensation granted in awards, but also the costs in international investment arbitration are quite high. In many cases, the investor is not reimbursed for its own lawyers' fees, even if it wins the case. 'Cost follows the event' is not universally applied. Practice varies. In *PSEG v Turkey*,[119] the costs were over US$20 million. They were split in the ratio 65 per cent (loser) to 35 per cent (winner).

Before the ECtHR the applicant has to pay its lawyers' fees, but can, in case he or she wins, be reimbursed those costs which have been necessarily incurred and which were reasonable as to the quantum claimed. There are no Court fees.

Therefore, with regard to the costs, the human rights system will usually be the cheaper option.

IV. Conclusions

Although not originally designed as a body for the settlement of investment disputes, the ECtHR today must be counted among these bodies. The property protection offered under the ECHR, however, has a number of disadvantages

---

[115] *Siemens AG v Argentina*, Award, 6 February 2007, at para 403: approximately US$220 million.   [116] See Marboe, n 96 above, 725–759.

[117] *Stran Greek Refineries and Stratis Andreadis v Greece*, Judgment, 9 December 1994, Series A No 301-B: approximately €24.3 million; and *Papamichalopoulos v Greece*, Judgment on just satisfaction, 31 October 1995, Series A No 330-B: approximately €23 million.

[118] *Zlínsat, Spol SRO*, n 112 above, at paras 38–45.   [119] *PSEG Global*, n 95 above.

compared to international investment protection. The biggest comparative disadvantages of the human rights system for investors are: first, that the ECHR in principle offers no protection for indirect damages of shareholders; second, the compulsory requirement to exhaust local remedies; and third the possibility to be awarded less than full compensation in case of a violation of the Convention. Furthermore, the issue of awarding compensation could be further improved under the ECHR both in terms of the ECtHR's methodology and the reasons given.

The biggest advantage of the ECHR is the absence of the nationality requirement found in international investment law. Therefore, an investor who has no BIT or other investment protection treaty providing for the jurisdiction of an arbitral tribunal at its disposal and has invested in one of the states parties to the ECHR and its Additional Protocol can rely on the property protection offered by the Convention.

Furthermore, where the investment protection treaty only provides for jurisdiction in case of an expropriation and no expropriation has occurred, the comprehensive property protection of the ECHR is an option. Especially in cases where the interference was unlawful, there is a good chance to obtain redress before the ECtHR.

A further asset is the proportionality approach developed by the ECtHR in its case law to balance property protection interests of applicants with the state's interest to interfere with property rights for a public purpose. Investors therefore do not risk getting 'all' or 'nothing' in case of an interference with their property rights.

Ultimately, the two systems are not really alternatives, since they do not exclude each other. In typical investment cases, investment arbitration offers clear advantages. However, the human rights system can serve as a useful complement. Furthermore, the two systems could and should cross-fertilize each other.[120]

---

[120] For a comparison of the two systems and certain suggestions on cross-fertilization, see, eg Kriebaum, n 65 above.

12

Balancing of Human Rights and Investment Law in the Inter-American System of Human Rights

Pedro Nikken

I. Introduction

The legal framework and organizational structure of the Inter-American system of human rights (IASHR) are both rather complex.[1] There are indeed two systems that overlap in several ways. The oldest and less compulsory regional system is based on the Charter of the Organization of the American States (OAS Charter) and on the American Declaration of the Rights and Duties of Man (the American Declaration), both adopted in May 1948 (six months before the Universal Declaration of Human Rights). This system's sole body of international protection is the Inter-American Commission on Human Rights (the Commission) and has jurisdiction over all OAS Charter Member States, especially those that are not parties to the American Convention on Human Rights (the Convention).[2] Another system, more complete and modern, is based on the Convention and is applicable only to the states parties to it.[3] Its bodies of protection are the Commission and the Inter-American Court of Human Rights (the Court or the Inter-American Court).

The IASHR has been rather a Latin American system. All Latin American countries are parties to the Convention and have accepted the compulsory

---

[1] See H Faúndez, *The Inter-American System for the Protection of Human Rights. Institutional and procedural aspects* (2008); L Hennebel, *La Convention américaine des droits de l'homme Mécanismes de protection et étendue des droits et libertés* (2007); J Pasqualucci, *The Practice and Procedure of the Inter-American Court of Human Rights* (2003); T Buergenthal et al, *International Human Rights* (2002) 221–281; and P Nikken, 'Le système interaméricain des droits de l'homme' (1990) 2 Revue universelle des droits de l'homme 3, 97–109. See also 'Basic Documents Pertaining to Human Rights in the Inter-American System' (updated to January 2003) OEA/Ser.L/V/I.4 Rev.9 31 January 2003 (2003).

[2] Antigua and Barbuda, The Bahamas, Belize, Canada, Cuba, Guyana, St Kitts and Nevis, St Lucia, St Vincent and the Grenadines, Trinidad and Tobago, and the United States.

[3] Argentina, Barbados, Bolivia, Brazil, Chile, Colombia, Costa Rica, Dominica, Dominican Republic, Ecuador, El Salvador, Grenada, Guatemala, Haiti, Honduras, Jamaica, Mexico, Nicaragua, Panama, Paraguay, Peru, Suriname, Uruguay, and Venezuela.

jurisdiction of the Court. Therefore, most cases submitted to the Commission and to the Court come from Latin America. The United States and Canada have not ratified the Convention and the approach of the Caribbean countries has been rather hesitant.[4] As a result, many factors shaping the Latin American experience of the protection of human rights explain the issues that are analysed in this chapter concerning the relationship between human rights and foreign investments.

The first factor that has shaped the protection of human rights in the Americas is the struggle against the bloody repression carried out by the military dictatorships that ruled most Latin American countries until the 1990s. Given that context, the protection of property rights or other mainly economic topics appears to many in the human rights community as something too sophisticated, even frivolous.

The second factor is the long-standing mistrust regarding the international protection of foreign economic interests in Latin America. After all, Latin America gave birth to the Calvo Doctrine. This historical apprehension might explain the different degrees of reluctance that the Commission and the Court have shown when tackling topics where economic issues overlap with human rights.

This chapter will address two areas in which economic matters intersect with the protection of human rights in the inter-American system. We will first examine the general legal framework concerning the possible protection of private economic interests within the regional system of human rights. We will then analyse some cases in which the Commission and the Court have found a clash between the standards of protection of foreign investments and the standards of protection of human rights.

II. General Legal Framework

The object and purpose of the Convention and the other components of the IASHR is to protect and promote the rights inherent to the human being, not to assure private economic interests. However, the system does offer an environment that favours private economic activity. The system also encompasses the protection of some individual rights connected to economic interests. From this point of view, we will first analyse the approaches to investment protection that can be found in the inter-American system. We will then examine an important practical obstacle to protecting rights related to economic undertakings, such as the restriction of legal persons to access the system under Article 1.2 of the Convention and the Commission's particularly restrictive interpretation in this matter.

---

[4] Only six of the 14 members of CARICOM are parties to the Convention and only three (Barbados, Haiti, and Suriname) have accepted the compulsory jurisdiction of the Court. Trinidad and Tobago had accepted it, but later denounced the Convention.

A. Approaches to the International Protection of Investments in the Inter-American System of Human Rights

The general framework of the system offers, as a matter of principle, a favourable environment for guaranteeing investments. The system is essentially based on the principles of representative democracy and the rule of law. The Preamble to the OAS Charter proclaims, as a condition for 'American solidarity', 'the consolidation on this continent, within the framework of democratic institutions, of a system of individual liberty and social justice based on respect for the essential rights of man'. Article 2 of the Charter sets forth, among the 'essential purposes' of the OAS Charter, the promotion and consolidation of 'representative democracy, with due respect for the principle of non-intervention'. Within the inter-American system of human rights, democracy has been associated with the rule of law.[5] Along the same lines, the Inter-American Democratic Charter, adopted on 11 September 2001, proclaims that rule of law and independence of the branches of government are '[e]ssential elements of representative democracy' (Article 3).

Rule of law and the existence of an independent judiciary are essential conditions for the stability, predictability, and security that are generally acknowledged as standards for the international protection of investments. The inter-American system, therefore, theoretically offers a favourable environment for international investors regarding these standards.

Furthermore, the system guarantees the right to property. The American Declaration includes a clause on property: 'Article XXIII. Every person has a right to own such private property as meets the essential needs of decent living and helps to maintain the dignity of the individual and of the home.'

This article reveals a tendency towards a concept of property as a social right, which requires each individual to hold sufficient property to satisfy his or her essential needs and those of his or her family. Article XXIII does not refer to property as a means to accumulate wealth nor can it be directly related to activities linked to investments. Article XXIII remains the term of reference of the Inter-American Commission when processing cases regarding states that, being OAS Member States, are not parties to the Convention.

The American Convention also guarantees the right to property. The first draft of the Convention[6] covered civil and political rights as well as economic, social, and cultural rights. Chapter II of Part I of that draft (Articles 20 to 33) referred to the latter and included the right to property. Six years later, Chile and

---

[5] See I/A Court HR *Habeas corpus in Emergency Situations*, Advisory Opinion, 30 January 1987, Series A No 8, at para 24.

[6] Approved by the Fourth Meeting of the Inter-American Council of Jurists, Santiago, Chile, September 1959. On the background of Art 21 of the American Convention, see V Marroquin-Merino, 'The Protection of Property Rights in the Inter-American System: Banco de Lima Shareholders v Peru' (1991) 1 University of Miami Yearbook of International Law 218, at 223–226.

Uruguay presented alternative drafts,[7] which also included the right to property in the chapter on economic, social, and cultural rights.

The Convention adopted in 1969 partially abandoned the concept of the drafts that covered economic, social, and cultural rights. Articles 4 to 25 set forth civil and political rights, while only Article 26 (the sole article of Chapter III, Part I of the Convention) contains a very general commitment of the states 'to adopt measures ... with a view to achieving progressively ... the full realization of the rights implicit in the economic, social, educational, scientific, and cultural standards set forth in the Charter of the [OAS]'.

Nevertheless, the Convention maintained the guarantee of property, but placed it among the civil and political rights (Article 21):

1. Everyone has the right to the use and enjoyment of his property. The law may subordinate such use and enjoyment to the interest of society.
2. No one shall be deprived of his property except upon payment of just compensation, for reasons of public utility or social interest, and in the cases and according to the forms established by law.
3. Usury and any other form of exploitation of man by man shall be prohibited by law.

The wording of Article 21 and the placement of property among civil and political rights, as well as its exclusion in the Protocol of San Salvador (1988), reveal that in the inter-American system the concept of property prevails as an individual right, which may be perceived prima facie as favouring the idea of protection of investment as property. The practice of the Commission and the Court will thus be examined to verify whether it confirms this perception. We will first examine the *scope of property* as it has been dealt with in the decisions of the Court and the Commission. We will then review the criteria, particularly of the Court, used to determine *reparations* for violations to the right to property, which will show what the prevailing concept is in the system in this area. Finally, we will examine the *context* in which the Commission and the Court have handled cases of violations of the right to property, which will help us to understand the limitations that have characterized the protection of this right.

1. The Scope of Property

The case law of both the Court and the Commission has embraced a broad standard with regard to the scope of property, independent of domestic laws. The Court's first case regarding the protection of property was the *Ivcher Bronstein* case. A naturalized Peruvian citizen who was the major shareholder in a company that held a licence for a television channel had his nationality arbitrarily revoked, which prevented him, under Peruvian law, from being the owner

---

[7] Rio de Janeiro 1965, docs 35 and 49, no 11 at 275, 298.

of a television channel. The Court found that Peru had violated several articles of the Convention, including Article 21.

With regard to the protection of the rights of shareholders of a corporation, the Court started from a broad concept of property, as a right protected by the Convention:

'Property' may be defined as those material objects that may be appropriated, and also any right that may form part of a person's patrimony; this concept includes all movable and immovable property, corporal and incorporeal elements, and any other intangible object of any value.[8]

Regarding the participation of Mr Ivcher Bronstein as a major shareholder, the Court specified that '*as such, that participation constituted a property* over which Mr. Ivcher had the right to use and enjoyment'[9] (emphasis added).

In subsequent cases, the Court has decided that a pension right provided under domestic law implies that 'the pensioners acquired a right to property related to the patrimonial effects of the right to a pension'.[10] Copyright has also been considered a right to property by the Commission[11] and by the Court.[12]

According to the aforementioned concepts, the Commission and the Court identified property with every economic interest of an individual, even though it does not imply legal power over a corporal object. This is a broad conceptualization of property, similar to that adopted by the European Court of Human Rights.[13]

With regard to violations of Article 21 of the Convention, the Court has also set a broad standard. Although it has not developed the concept of *interference* applied by the European Court, it has affirmed that harm to property is based more on facts than on formalities. According to this interpretation, every legal or factual situation that deprives the owner of the use and enjoyment of property may be considered an indirect expropriation provided that 'the real situation behind it'[14] proves it. In this context, creeping expropriation – as it is known in investments law – should be considered a violation of property.

Those broad approaches to property and expropriation may be understood as another favourable sign extending to investments the protection offered by the inter-American system. However, among other relevant aspects, the practice of the Commission and the Court is far from this initial impression. The first important discrepancy arises with regard to reparations for a violation of human rights.

---

[8] *Ivcher-Bronstein v Peru*, 6 February 2001, Series C No 74, at para 122.
[9] Ibid., at para 123.
[10] *Five Pensioners v Peru*, 28 February 2003, Series C No 98, at para 103.
[11] *Alejandra Marcela Matus Acuña and ors v Chile*, 24 October 2005, Report No 90/05, at para 51. On this case, 'the Commission decided by unanimous vote of the six voting members, not to put the case before the Court' (para 63).
[12] *Palamara-Iribarne v Chile*, 22 November 2005 Series C No 135, at paras 102–106.
[13] See RG van Banning, *The human rights to property* (2001) 63.
[14] *Ivcher Bronstein*, n 8 above, at para 124.

2. Reparation

Under Article 63.1 of the Convention:

If the Court finds that there has been a violation of a right or freedom protected by this Convention, the Court shall rule that the injured party be ensured the enjoyment of his right or freedom that was violated. It shall also rule, if appropriate, that the consequences of the measure or situation that constituted the breach of such right or freedom be remedied and that fair compensation be paid to the injured party.

From its first decision regarding reparations,[15] the Court affirmed that Article 63.1 sets forth a general international rule, expressed by the International Court of Justice in *Factory at Chorzów* and *Reparation for Injuries Suffered in the Service of the United Nations*, and, therefore, by the rule of *restitutio in integrum*. Since then, its decisions normally have a paragraph similar to the following, taken from a recent decision:

The reparation of the damage flowing from a breach of an international obligation calls for, if practicable, full restitution (*restitutio in integrum*), which consists in restoring a previously-existing situation. If not feasible, the international court will then be required to define a set of measures such that, in addition to ensuring the enjoyment of the rights that were violated, the consequences of those breaches may be remedied and compensation provided for the damage thereby caused.[16]

These principles strictly conform to international customary law, set forth in the ILC Articles on State Responsibility (Articles 35 to 36) and to the universal standards on reparations for violations to human rights, found in the 'Basic Principles and Guidelines on the Right to a Remedy and Reparation for Victims of Gross Violations of International Human Rights Law and Serious Violations of International Humanitarian Law' (Principles 18 to 19).[17] When applying these principles to violations of Article 21 of the Convention, the Court has been rigorous in prioritizing restitution, but has been flexible and even reluctant regarding compensation.

The relevance of restitution has been especially evident regarding the ancestral property of indigenous communities. In one case, the Court ordered restitution through 'measures required to create an effective mechanism for delimitation, demarcation, and titling of the property of indigenous communities, in accordance with their customary law'.[18] In other cases, the Court has decided that the

---

[15] *Velásquez-Rodríguez v Honduras.* Compensatory damages (American Convention on Human Rights, Art 63(1)), 21 July 1989, Series C No 7, at para 26.
[16] *La Cantuta v Peru*, 29 November 2006, Series C No 162, at para 201. See, eg *Goiburú and ors v Paraguay*, 22 September 2006, Series C No 153, at para 142; *Case of Montero-Aranguren and ors (Detention Center of Catia) v Venezuela*, 5 July 2006, Series C No 150, at para 117; and *Ximenes-Lopes v Brazil*, 4 July 2006, Series C No 149, at para 209.
[17] Adopted by General Assembly Resolution 60/147 of 16 December 2005.
[18] *Mayagna (Sumo) Awas Tingni Community v Nicaragua*, 31 August 2001, Series C No 79, at para 164.

land taken from the indigenous community is to be returned[19] or if restoration 'is not possible on objective and sufficient grounds, the State shall make over alternative lands, selected upon agreement with the aforementioned Indigenous Community'.[20] The Commission, for its part, decided a case by arriving at the same conclusion on the grounds of Article XXIII of the American Declaration.[21]

Nevertheless, some of the Court's decisions on compensation for the violation of the right to property do not always conform to the more usual international standards. When the Court has concluded that the value of the property harmed has not been proven, but that the damage may be presumed, it has decided to set the amount of compensation 'in fairness' (*'en equidad'* in Spanish)[22] or 'on grounds of equity'.[23] Granting compensation in this manner does not seem to reflect a concept of international law on this area. It must be recognized, however, that the Court has used this formula in cases in which damage may be presumed, but its extension and amount have not been proven. The most important difference with certain principles of general international law has arisen when setting the amount of compensation, especially when the amount might be considered very high.

In the *Ivcher Bronstein* case, the Court held that the shares of a corporation were arbitrarily expropriated.[24] However, instead of directly ordering the payment of compensation for damages caused by the deprivation of their use and enjoyment, the Court concluded that:

[T]he State should facilitate the conditions to enable Baruch Ivcher Bronstein to take the necessary steps to recover the use and enjoyment of his rights as majority shareholder of *Compañía Latinoamericana de Radiodifusión S.A.*, as he was until August 1, 1997, *under the terms of domestic legislation.* With regard to the recovery of dividends and other amounts that he would have received as majority shareholder and officer of that company, *domestic law should also apply.* To this end, *the respective claims should be submitted to the competent national authorities*[25] (emphasis added).

In that case, an arbitral tribunal constituted under domestic law decided that the state should pay a compensation of US$6,200,000 to the shareholder.[26]

---

[19] *Moiwana Community v Suriname*, 15 June 2005, Series C No 124, at para 209; and *Indigenous Community Yakye Axa v Paraguay*, 17 June 2005, Series C No 125, at para 242(6).
[20] *Sawhoyamaxa Indigenous Community v Paraguay*, 29 March 2006, Series C No 146, at para 212.
[21] *Maya Indigenous Communities of the Toledo District v Belize*, Report 40/04, 12 October 2004, at para 197(2).
[22] See *Plan de Sánchez Massacre v Guatemala*, 19 November 2004, Series C No 116, at para 74; *Tibi v Ecuador*, 7 September 2004, Series C No 114, at para 237(e); and *Palamara-Iribarne v Chile*, n 12 above, at para 242.
[23] *Moiwana Community v Suriname*, n 19 above, at para 187; and *Ituango Massacres v Colombia*, 1 July 2006, Series C No 148, at para 373.   [24] *Ivcher Bronstein*, n 8 above, at paras 122–131.
[25] Ibid., at para 191(8).
[26] See *Ivcher-Bronstein v Peru. Monitoring Compliance with Judgment*, Order, 21 September 2005, at para 14 (*vistos*) (only in Spanish).

In the *Five Pensioners* case, the Court maintained this interpretation of due compensation for the arbitrary deprivation of pensions and decided that '[they] should be established by the competent national organs, as provided for in the domestic legislation'.[27]

In the *Cesti Hurtado* case, large claims were made for material damages and consequential damages (more than US$10,000,000) caused to a family corporation in which the victim was general manager and legal representative. The Court expressed its reluctance to grant compensation for this kind of damage in the following terms:

Taking into consideration the specificity of the reparations requested and also the characteristics of commercial and company law and the commercial operations involved, the Court considers that this determination corresponds to the said national institutions rather than to an international human rights tribunal.[28]

The Court suggested that the amount claimed should not be granted by an international human rights tribunal. Under the judgment, that amount was submitted to arbitration according to domestic law. The arbitral tribunal decided on a payment of US$3,065,000.[29] This decision, however, 'was appealed and the higher court annulled the proceedings'.[30]

These decisions do not seem to conform to the rule of *restitutio in integrum* under general international law. Article 63.1 of the Convention empowers the Court to grant reparations, without limiting the amount of the reparation or considering the complexity of the domestic law connected to the case. On the contrary, leaving these issues to the domestic authorities of the denounced state equals allowing one of the parties to the procedure to fix the amount of damages, which does not conform to due process. It is rather an issue of judicial policy in which the Court finds the payment of a large compensation for material damages to be inconvenient in the context of human rights cases. Whatever is the basis of this decision, it is far from the *restitutio in integrum* guaranteed in the international system of human rights since the matter will be decided by domestic authorities applying domestic rather than international law. It is true that the Court continues to supervize the case until the decision is complied with, but it is also true that this practice does not guarantee a full protection to the victim.

In conclusion, the Court's practice is not to grant large economic compensations for violations of human rights even in cases of expropriation or other interferences with the right of property. It is obviously a practice on which an investor cannot base positive expectations.

---

[27] *Five pensioners*, n 10 above, at para 178.

[28] *Cesti-Hurtado v Peru Reparations*, 31 May 2001, Series C No 78, at para 46.

[29] See *Cesti-Hurtado v Peru. Monitoring Compliance with Judgment Order*, 17 November 2004, at para 22.

[30] *Cesti-Hurtado v Peru. Monitoring Compliance with Judgment Order*, 22 September 2006, at para 14.

3. The Context

Cases concerning the violation of property rights in the inter-American system are complex either because property is not the only right whose violation is being denounced or because the violation of the right to property is framed in a particular political pattern.

The Commission has decided some cases against Nicaragua, originating in times of the Sandinista Revolution, in which only violations of property rights were at stake, but within the context of a governmental policy regarding assets that belonged to persons linked to the Somoza dictatorship. According to the claimants, that policy was applied to them arbitrarily and the Commission recommended restitution measures.[31]

However, in other cases decided by the Commission, the violation of property took place in a framework of several human rights violations. That was what happened in *Charles v Haiti*[32] (a former mayor illegally deprived of his freedom and his offices were vandalized), in which the violation of the right to property took place together with a violation of personal freedom. In *Cayard v Haiti*[33] (persecution of a rebel colonel and the vandalizing of his homes and his printing plant by the political police), the right to property was violated together with due process. In *Alejandra Marcela Matus Acuña and ors v Chile*[34] (confiscation of a book), property was violated together with freedom of speech.

The Court has not decided a single case in which the violation of the right to property has been autonomous or independent, since it has been always connected, to a greater or lesser degree, to the guarantee of other human rights.

In the aforementioned case of *Ivcher Bronstein*,[35] the violation of the right to property took place in the framework of violations of the right to a nationality (Article 20), to due process (Article 8), to judicial protection (Article 25), and to freedom of speech (Article 13). In the *Five Pensioners* case,[36] the protection of retired workers against an arbitrary reduction of their pensions was connected to the right to social security to the point that the Court suggested that the decision was also based on Article 5 of the Protocol of San Salvador.[37] In the *Plán de Sanchez Massacre*[38] and *Ituango Massacres*[39] cases, the massive executions (Article 4) took place together with the vandalizing of the victims' property.

---

[31] See *Martinez Riguero v Nicaragua*, Resolutions No 20/86, 10 April 1986, and 2/87, 27 March 1987; and *Martin v Nicaragua*, Report No 12/94, 1 February 1994. On the right to property in Nicaragua, in general, see: 'Annual Report 1994' in *Inter-American Yearbook on Human Rights 1993* (1993) 762–788.   [32] *Charles v Haiti*, Resolution No 46/82 of 9 March 1982.
[33] *Cayard v Haiti*, Resolution No 15/83 of 30 June 1983   [34] See n 11 above.
[35] See n 8 above.   [36] See n 10 above.
[37] Ibid., at para 116; see also separate opinion of Garcia Ramirez J at paras 2–3.
[38] See n 22 above.   [39] See n 23 above.

In cases involving indigenous lands,[40] the protection of property has been connected to the preservation of identity and socio-cultural values of the affected peoples, for whom restitution is particularly important. We will return to this point later.

The cautious approach of both the Commission and the Court in protecting the right to property is a warning against expectations of what role the system might play in conflicts regarding expropriation and other interferences to investments. Another obstacle, mainly practical, comes from the limitation that exists for legal persons to access the protection offered by the system.

B. Restrictions for Legal Persons to Access the Inter-American System for Human Rights

Legal persons may file claims before the Commission, but they may only invoke in a limited way the protection offered by the Convention. Article 44 of the Convention provides that '[a]ny person or group of persons, or any non-governmental entity legally recognized in one or more member States of the Organization, may lodge petitions with the Commission'. Article 1.2, on the other hand, provides that '[f]or the purposes of this Convention, "person" means every human being'. This contrasts with Article 1 of Protocol 1 to the European Convention on Human Rights, which provides that '[e]very natural or legal person is entitled to the peaceful enjoyment of his possessions'.

Construing *a contrario sensu* Article 1.2 (and also on the grounds of the Pre-amble to the Convention), the Commission has concluded that it 'lacks the competence *ratione personae* to examine claims which concern the rights of jur-idical persons'[41] because they 'are legal fiction and do not enjoy real existence in the material order'.[42] This interpretation has been applied regarding the right to property set forth in Article 21 of the Convention:

... in the inter-American system, the right to property is a personal right. The Commission is empowered to vindicate the rights of an individual whose property is confiscated, but is not empowered with jurisdiction over the rights of juridical beings, such as corporations or as in this case, banking institutions.[43]

In my opinion, the Commission's interpretation is too formalistic and by exaggeratedly construing *a contrario sensu* Article 1.2, it does not necessarily con-form to 'the ordinary meaning' that should 'be given to the terms' of Article 1.2, particularly keeping in mind the 'object and purpose' of the American

---

[40] *Awas Tingni Community*, n 18 above; *Moiwana Community*, n 19 above; *Community Yakye Axa*, n 19 above; and *Sawhoyamaxa Community*, n 20 above.

[41] *Tomás Enrique Carvallo Quintana v Argentina*, 14 June 2001, Report No 67/01, at para 55.

[42] *MEVOPAL, SA v Argentina*, 11 March 1999, Report No 39/99, at para 17.

[43] *Banco de Lima v Perú*, 22 February 1991, Report No 10/91. On the critique of the Commission's ruling in this case, see Marroquin-Merino, n 6 above, 250.

Convention, pursuant to Article 31.1 of the Vienna Convention on the Law of Treaties (VCLT). Article 1.2 only limits the protection of the Convention to human beings, but it should not be understood that the Convention denies that some individual rights are exercised through juridical persons and, sometimes, only through them. Judge Buergenthal suggested some time ago, with regard to the literal interpretation of Article 2.1 of the UN Covenant on Civil and Political Rights, that '[m]easures against a juridical entity ... can constitute violations of the Covenant insofar as they can be characterized as deprivations of an individual's right'.[44]

If Article 1.2 is interpreted taking into account the object and purpose of the protection system established by the Convention, general conclusions should not be possible in every case of harm to protected rights involving a juridical person. According to that article, what is relevant is to determine whether the main interest at stake involves rights of the 'human being'. Based on a case-by-case interpretation, according to each particular context, some human rights violations involving juridical persons should be dealt by the Commission and, if applicable, by the Court.

For example, the suppression or discrimination of a trade union, an NGO, or a political party is a breach that goes beyond the freedom of association of each of their members. The same may be said of churches regarding freedom of religion. Trade unions, churches, NGOs, and political parties are institutions whose collective function for exercising individual rights and public freedoms is more than the sum of their members' or affiliates' rights. They are entities that express the values of a democratic society, which is embedded in the Convention. A state acting arbitrarily against one of these entities, denying it the protection it requires on the basis of an interpretation *a contrario sensu* of Article 1.2 of the Convention, would imply distorting reality. Suppressing or discriminating against a trade union, a church, or a political party is an event much more serious and of a different dimension in a democratic society than depriving the right of an individual to be part of a union, a church, an NGO, or a political party. By illegally attacking any of these entities, harm is done not only to their members, but also to the right of every person who would freely join the union, the NGO, the political party, or the church in the future. Thus, if the collective entity invokes international protection, the benefits involve not only their current members, but also 'all persons subject to [the] jurisdiction' of the State, pursuant to Article 1.1 of the Convention. Moreover, in such a situation harm is done to the collective value of a democratic society and not only to the individuals who are members of the juridical person at the time of the harmful act.

---

[44] T Buergenthal, 'To Respect and to Ensure: State Obligations and Permissible Derogations' in L Henkin (ed), *The International Bill of Rights – The Covenant on Civil and Political Rights* (1981) 72–73. See also M Nowak, *U.N. Covenant on Civil and Political Rights* (2005) 829–832.

Juridical persons are legally recognized by law in order to give autonomy to collective interests, in areas as different as altruistic and commercial, including all the variety of public legal persons. As has been noted by the International Court of Justice, a legal person is 'an entity which in particular allows operation in circumstances which exceed the normal capacity of individuals'.[45] Not every juridical person has material goals and some of them can play a functional role vis-à-vis certain human rights. This circumstance has finally led to a softening of the Inter-American Commission's position and has allowed a different interpretation by the Court.

The Commission's strict interpretation is not explained solely by the text of the Convention. The Commission has also had reasons of a practical and judicial policy nature. It has avoided becoming a forum where issues related to private economic interests, normally organized through legal persons, are debated. However, that motivation has not prevented a certain degree of flexibility regarding the *locus standi* of legal persons.

The Court touched on the subject in the *Cantos* case. Mr Cantos was the main shareholder of a corporation, which was subjected to arbitrary measures by the Argentine Government. In the domestic procedures and before the Commission, Mr Cantos filed the claim on his own behalf and on behalf of his corporations. The Commission admitted the petition and submitted the case to the Court. Argentina made preliminary objections on the grounds of Article 1.2 and on previous decisions of the Commission. The Court rejected these objections because 'in general, the rights and obligations attributed to companies become rights and obligations for the individuals who comprise them or who act in their name or representation'.[46] Moreover, in rejecting the Argentine objection, the Court had a different interpretation from the Commission: 'Having demonstrated that the interpretation of Article 1(2) of the American Convention *is based on an invalid reasoning*, the Court considers that it must reject the objection filed on lack of competence'[47] (emphasis added).

On the other hand, according to the inter-American practice, the shareholder of a corporation is not excluded from international protection with regard to the property of his shares. In the *Ivcher Bronstein* case, as has been shown, the Court acknowledged that the property of corporate shares falls under the protection offered by Article 21 of the Convention. On the basis of this precedent, in *Tomás Enrique Carvallo v Argentina*, the Commission maintained its interpretation of Article 1.2 of the Convention, but specified that:

This does not mean that the rights of individuals with respect to their private property as shareholders in a corporation are excluded from the protection of the Convention.

---

[45] *Barcelona Traction, Light and Power Co, Ltd*, ICJ Reports (1970) 3, at para 39.
[46] *Cantos v Argentina*, Preliminary Objections, 7 September 2001, Series C No 85, at para 27. The Court made specific reference to the case law of the European Court of Human Rights in *Pine Valley Developments Ltd and ors*, 29 November 1991, Series A No 222   [47] Ibid., at para 31.

Rather, the foregoing criteria provide a means to distinguish when the rights of a corporation are at issue, and when the rights of an individual are at issue. *The investment of a shareholder in the capital assets of a corporation is part of that individual's property*, and susceptible to valuation and protection in principle under the American Convention[48] (emphasis added).

The *locus standi* of legal persons was also considered by the Commission and the Court from different points of view in the *Herrera Ulloa* case. A Costa Rican journalist and the newspaper *La Nación* were sued for libel. The Costa Rican courts found Mr Herrera guilty of a criminal felony and he was also found guilty in a civil action together with the company that owned the newspaper. The Costa Rican decision made Herrera himself and Mr Fernán Vargas Rohrmoser, the legal representative of *La Nación*, comply with the civil court decision. The claim was filed before the Commission, which concluded that, in addition to the journalist, Mr Vargas was a victim since he was required to comply with the sentence, with the warning that failure to do so might amount to committing the crime of contempt of court.[49] Maintaining its traditional stand, however, the Commission warned that Mr Vargas was not considered a victim because he was a representative of the newspaper *La Nación*, but rather because of the personal risk that he ran as the representative.[50]

In deciding this case, the Court did not agree that Mr Vargas was a victim because:

... the subsidiary civil penalties established in the criminal judgment are directed against the newspaper *La Nación* S.A., whose legal representative vis-à-vis third parties is Mr. Vargas Rohrmoser. Those penalties were not targeted at Mr. Vargas Rohrmoser as a private subject or individual.[51]

Nevertheless, the Court's decision not only benefited Mr Herrera, formally the sole victim, but also the newspaper *La Nación*, since the Court held that 'the State must nullify that judgment and all the measures it ordered, *including any involving third parties*'[52] (emphasis added).

In the end, the Commission has had to soften its traditional interpretation. In 2003, it granted provisional measures to a television station owned by a Venezuelan company (*Globovisión*).[53] *Globovisión* is a juridical person, which would not be granted protective measures of its human rights according to the Commission's traditional interpretation of Article 1.2 of the Convention. This can be

[48] See n 41 above, at para 56.
[49] *Demanda de la Comisión Interamericana de Derechos Humanos ante la Corte Interamericana de Derechos Humanos en el Caso 12.367 'La Nación' Mauricio Herrera Ulloa y Fernán Vargas Rohrmoser contra la República de Costa Rica* (I/A Court HR Records), at para 105.   [50] Ibid., at para 98.
[51] *Herrera-Ulloa v Costa Rica*, 2 July 2004, Series C No 107, at para 100.
[52] Ibid., at para 195.
[53] *Globovisión v Venezuela* (precautionary measures), Annual report IACommHR (2005), at paras 345–346.

partially explained, because in the inter-American system it has been constantly emphasized that freedom of expression has a social dimension that includes 'the right to receive opinions and news from others'.[54] However, reality also shows that attacks to freedom of expression are no less damaging due to the mere fact that the immediate target of those attacks is a media corporation, since often, especially when it concerns a television station, these companies are the only actual means of disseminating information and ideas. To deny them protection could mean denying protection to freedom of expression as such. It is perhaps the starting point of a review of the Commission's traditional stand on the possibility of extending the protection offered by the Convention to legal persons through which human rights are exercised.

Nevertheless, predicting that the Commission will be more flexible in its position on the admission of claims regarding legal persons does not mean that petitions of a mainly economic nature are going to be admitted. Both the Court and the Commission, through their practice, agree that arbitrariness against private economic activity is not perceived as a subject of human rights. Another question, however, may be asked: does the protection of human rights constitute a legitimate limitation to the due protection for investments? The Court's jurisprudence offers some clues to answer this question.

III. Conflicts between International Protection of Human Rights and the Protection of Investments

A conflict may arise between the international protection of human rights and the international protection of investments. One could allege that, before a tribunal established within the framework of the international protection of investments, the claim of plaintiff contradicts certain international obligations regarding human rights. This type of conflict, of course, does not happen in the inter-American system of human rights and, therefore, will not be dealt with here. The same may be said about the application of some human rights standards, such as non-discrimination, in the context of protection of investments.

On the other hand, international obligations regarding the protection of investments might be invoked before a body for the protection of human rights and would be violated if the claim of the plaintiff, namely, the victim, proceeds. Is it acceptable for a state to defend itself against a claim regarding human rights

---

[54] *Compulsory Membership in an Association Prescribed by Law for the Practice of Journalism*, Advisory Opinion, 13 November 1985, Series A No 5, at paras 30–33; *'The Last Temptation of Christ' (Olmedo-Bustos and ors) v Chile*, 5 February 2001, Series C No 73, at paras 65–67; *Ivcher Bronstein*, n 8 above, at paras 146–149; *Herrera Ulloa*, n 51 above, at paras 108–111; *Ricardo Canese v Paraguay*, 31 August 2004, Series C No 111, at paras 77–80; and *Palamara Iribarne*, n 12 above, at para 69.

by arguing that the alleged violation originated in meeting its international obligations to protect investments?

The American Convention (Article 32.2) provides that '[t]he rights of each person are limited by the rights of others'. The language of this provision mentions, in general, 'the rights of others' and not 'the human rights of others'. Do the rights of investors fall within this article? Can it be understood that the rights of investors under international law are 'rights of others' capable of legitimately limiting human rights? To what extent could an international human rights tribunal recognize that an investor's rights protected by a treaty are legitimate limitations to human rights?

The matter has been raised, although incidentally, in several cases before the Inter-American Court, which has not given a general answer, but has offered some clues that would permit some speculation.

A. The *Claude Reyes* Case and the Conflict with the Standard of Fair and Equitable Treatment

The facts referred to Chile's refusal to provide Marcel Claude Reyes and others with all of the information that they requested from the Foreign Investment Committee (a state agency) on the forestry company Trillium (a foreign investor) and the Río Condor Project. This deforestation project was to be executed in Chile's Region XII and had potential prejudicial effects on the environment and on Chile's sustainable development. The state refused to furnish information on some topics requested by the petitioners.

The state never notified the petitioners on the reasons for its refusal to furnish all the information requested by them. However, in the hearing before the Court, the Executive Vice President of the Foreign Investment Committee at the time when the information was requested stated that he had not provided the requested information, inter alia, because '[it] was not reasonable that foreign companies applying to the Foreign Investment Committee should have to disclose ... financial information ... that could be very important to them in relation to their competitors'.[55] He added that:

information regarding third parties, such as commercial information, copyrights and trademarks, use of technology and, in general, the specific characteristics of the investment projects that foreign investors wished to develop were confidential ... since this was data of a private nature, belonging to the investor, that could harm his legitimate business expectations if it were made public, and there was no legal source that permitted disclosure.[56]

The Court disregarded this line of reasoning, emphasizing that 'it was only during the public hearing ... that the [witness] explained the reasons why he did

---

[55] *Claude Reyes and others v Chile*, 19 September 2006, Series C No 151, at para 57(20a).
[56] Ibid., at para 57(21).

not provide the requested information'.[57] The Court found that the refusal to provide the information requested was a restriction of the right to seek information granted by Article 13 of the Convention (freedom of speech) and that such restriction 'did not comply with the parameters of the Convention',[58] because, among other reasons, it 'was not based on a law'[59] and because the responsible authority, 'which would have provided information regarding the reasons and norms on which he based his decision not to disclose part of the information in this specific case', did not adopt a duly justified written decision.[60] Consequently, the Court concluded that Chile had violated Articles 13 (freedom of speech) and 8 (due process in law) of the Convention.

Although Chile did not invoke it, the reason for protecting the confidentiality of the information given by the investor to the state could be related to the standards of fair and equitable treatment or of protection of investments. The state did not present it that way, since a middle-ranking officer mentioned it more as an explanation of his actions than as a formal defence. The Court, on the other hand, simply ruled out that reasoning for formal considerations, without analysing whether, in the specific case, access to confidential information was in conflict with the right of a foreign investor to a certain standard of treatment, which could involve respect for the confidentiality of some financial information that it had given to the government since the Convention also protects the right to privacy (Article 12). The Court simply analysed the forms and not the possible conflict between the foreign investor's rights and the Convention.

B. The Conflict between the Ancestral Property of Indigenous Communities and Individual Private Property

The Court has invoked Article 21 of the Convention in deciding several cases related to the ancestral or communal property of indigenous peoples,[61] as has been already mentioned, or of tribal peoples who live in strict adherence to their customs.[62] It has also granted provisional measures in this area, applying Article 63.2 of the Convention.[63] For its part, the Commission has issued a report based on Article XXIII of the American Declaration.[64] The protection of indigenous peoples' property offers several particularities, either considered as such or especially when it conflicts with individual private property.

The Court's starting point (and that of the Commission) for analysing cases of violations of the ancestral property of indigenous peoples is its special function at

[57] Ibid., at para 97.   [58] Ibid., at para 98.   [59] Ibid., at para 94.
[60] Ibid., at para 122.
[61] *Awas Tingni Community v Nicaragua*, n 18 above; *Community Yakye Axa*, n 19 above; and *Sawhoyamaxa Community*, n 20 above.   [62] *Moiwana Community*, n 19 above.
[63] *Matter of Pueblo indigena de Saravaku regarding Ecudor*, Provisional measures order of I/A court HR, 6 July 2004 (only in Spanish); *Matter of Pueblo indigena de Saravaku regarding Ecudor* Provisional measures order of I/A court HR, 6 June 2005 (only in Spanish).
[64] *Maya Indigenous Communities of the Toledo District*, n 21 above.

the social, cultural, and religious levels. This consideration has been present in each and every case related to property in indigenous territories; disregarding the fact that the ancestral right of the members of the indigenous communities to their territories could affect other basic rights, such as the right to cultural identity and to the very survival of the indigenous communities and their members.[65] For such peoples, their communal nexus with the ancestral territory is not merely a matter of possession and production, but rather consists in material and spiritual elements that must be fully integrated and enjoyed by the community, so that it may preserve its cultural legacy and pass it on to future generations.[66]

The states must take into account that indigenous territorial rights encompass a broader and different concept that relates to the collective right to survival as an organized people, with control over their habitat as a necessary condition for reproduction of their culture, for their own development, and to carry out their life aspirations. Property of the land ensures that the members of the indigenous communities preserve their cultural heritage.[67]

This special concept of property and its function for the community explains why the Court has always granted restitution as a means of reparation for a deprivation of property suffered by indigenous peoples. Due to its nature, the indigenous peoples' property is a non-fungible asset, with regard to its economic value, so the payment of compensation in the event of an expropriation does not repair in any way the damage caused to the cultural assets that are part of the property:

[T]he restitution of traditional lands ... is the reparation measure that best complies with the *restitutio in integrum* principle, therefore the Court orders that the State shall adopt all legislative, administrative or other type of measures necessary to guarantee the members of the Community ownership rights over their traditional lands, and consequently the right to use and enjoy those lands.[68]

The Court has also ordered the restoration of the lands, their demarcation and titling,[69] or, in cases where this was not possible, the handing over, with the consent of the affected community, of lands that can substitute for those that have been taken.[70]

The tendency to favour indigenous property may also be detected in the resolution of conflicts of property, that is in cases of indigenous lands where there are also individual property titles obtained under domestic law.

---

[65] *Community Yakye Axa*, n 19 above, at para 147. Also, *Awas Tingni Community*, n 18 above, at para 149; *Sawhoyamaxa Community*, n 20 above, at para 131; and *Comunidad Indígena Sarayaku Medidas Provisionales* (Spanish only), 17 June 2005, at para 9.

[66] *Moiwana Community*, n 19 above, at para 131.

[67] *Community Yakye Axa*, n 19 above, at para 146.

[68] *Sawhoyamaxa Community*, n 20 above, at para 210.

[69] *Moiwana Community*, n 19 above, at para 233.3. See also *Maya Indigenous Communities of the Toledo District v Belize*, n 21 above, at para 197(1).

[70] *Community Yakye Axa*, n 19 above, at para 217; and *Sawhoyamaxa Community v Paraguay*, n 20 above, at para 212.

The Court has held that it should not decide those conflicts because they are a matter of domestic law. At the same time, however, it has affirmed its competence to determine whether, as a result of conflicts between forms of property and owners, the state has failed to fulfil its international human rights obligations with regard to indigenous peoples:

[T]he Court cannot decide that the Sawhoyamaxa Community's property rights to traditional lands prevail over the right to property of private owners or *vice versa*, since the Court is not a domestic judicial authority with jurisdiction to decide disputes among private parties. This power is vested exclusively in the Paraguayan State. Nevertheless, the Court has competence to analyze whether the State ensured the human rights of the members of the Sawhoyamaxa Community.[71]

Along these lines, the Court's jurisprudence has avoided defining a general standard on which property prevails in clashes between them suggesting that 'the States must assess, on a case by case basis, the restrictions that would result from recognizing one right over the other'.[72]

The Court, however, has implicitly tended to favour indigenous communities' property in case of conflict. This is because it has suggested that the function of individual private property is purely economic and that in case of conflict with indigenous property, the particular function of the latter could be the basis of legitimate restrictions to the former, according to values prevailing in a democratic society:

[R]estriction of the right of private individuals to private property might be necessary to attain the collective objective of preserving cultural identities in a democratic and pluralist society, in the sense given to this by the American Convention; and it could be proportional, if fair compensation is paid to those affected pursuant to Article 21(2) of the Convention.[73]

This is also because it has favoured the restitution of ancestral lands to indigenous communities that have been taken from them and that were in private hands. In the first case before the Court concerning indigenous peoples, an international corporation had obtained a concession to exploit the ancestral lands of the Awas Tingni Community in Nicaragua. The Court decided that the concession violated the indigenous property and ordered that:

Nicaragua must abstain from acts which might lead the agents of the State itself, or third parties acting with its acquiescence or its tolerance, to affect the existence, value, use or enjoyment of the property located in the geographic area where the members of the Awas Tingni Community live and carry out their activities.[74]

---

[71] *Sawhoyamaxa Community* n 20 above, at para 136.
[72] *Community Yakye Axa*, n 19 above, at para 146.   [73] Ibid., at para 148.
[74] *Awas Tingni Community*, n 18 above, at para 164.

Moreover, the Court has favoured the expropriation of indigenous lands that had also been titled as private property, as a means to assure the restitution of the former: 'If the traditional territory is in private hands, the State must assess the legality, necessity and proportionality of expropriation or non-expropriation of said lands to attain a legitimate objective in a democratic society'.[75]

The caution of the Court exhibited in this dictum does not mean that it cannot be read as a clear suggestion to resolve the conflict through expropriation, favouring indigenous property. It is not, in fact, an absolute rule. Rather, it is a tendency that favours indigenous property, but it does not mean that it will prevail in every case of conflict with private property since the Court has acknowledged that it may be impossible for the state, for justified reasons, to adopt measures to return lands in private hands to the indigenous community. In that case, however, 'the compensation granted must be guided primarily by the meaning of the land for them'.[76]

Furthermore, in such a situation, the state 'must surrender alternative lands of equal extension and quality, which will be chosen by agreement with the members of the indigenous peoples, according to their own consultation and decision procedures'.[77] This tendency of the Court, however, is far from ambiguous: unless justified reasons prevent it, when individual owners also have title over ancestral indigenous lands, the first obligation of the state is to adopt all necessary measures to return them to the indigenous people, including by expropriation, which, in this context, is 'a lawful purpose in a democratic society'.[78]

An expropriation may be legitimate if it complies with the requirements of international law: namely, that it is in the public interest or benefit, that it is not discriminatory, that it complies with due process, and that the expropriated owner is paid a fair compensation. Nevertheless, expropriation, per se, destroys the property right of whoever is harmed by it. Therefore, even though the Inter-American Court has affirmed that it is not empowered to decide which property right prevails in case of conflict, in fact, it has done so. If the solution to be applied, unless justified reasons prevent it, is the expropriation of the individual owner and the restitution to indigenous peoples of their ancestral lands, it is because the latter prevails. In the last analysis, where two properties are in conflict, one prevails – the indigenous – while the private owner has no other right than that of a fair compensation for the loss suffered. The solution is fair. The indigenous property, because of its social and cultural nature, is not the equivalent of money, which is not the case of property in a purely economic dimension. The Court, although it clearly favours this formula to resolve the conflict between properties, when doing so it has stated that it is not empowered to make such decision. Is this a voluntary contradiction that pays homage to prudence?

[75] *Community Yakye Axa*, n 19 above, at para 217; and *Sawhoyamaxa Community*, n 20 above, at para 212.   [76] *Community Yakye Axa*, n 19 above, at para 149.
[77] *Sawhoyamaxa Community*, n 20 above, at para 135.   [78] Ibid., at para 212.

It is undoubtedly a matter that is difficult to resolve by means of a general rule since the reason to prefer indigenous property over private property is the irreplaceable function of the former. Property is a 'modal' right and may have multiple functions, many of them related to human rights and may be determined *intuitu rei*, as may happen, for example, in the case of a church with regard to freedom of religion. Therefore, the deprivation of private property cannot always be fully compensated by the payment of an amount of money, but only through restitution, as the Court has ordered in the case of indigenous lands. That is why the Court and not only the states 'must assess, on a case by case basis, the restrictions that would result from recognizing one right over the other'.[79]

Notwithstanding this conclusion, it is possible to admit that, in general, direct expropriation or other forms of interference with investments and, in particular, foreign investments, may be compensated with the payment of a monetary amount. An investment implies the use of property and other patrimonial rights toward a determined economic goal and, therefore, the function of property in this area is mainly economic and has a monetary value. In addition, the expropriation of investments is not illegitimate per se and one condition of its legality is, precisely, the payment of an adequate compensation that reflects the capital value of the property taken. Therefore, if a conflict arises between the ancestral property of indigenous or tribal peoples and a foreign investor, it is predictable that the Court will order the restitution of the former and indicate that the state should consider the expropriation of the latter.

C. A Possible Conflict between the American Convention and a Bilateral Treaty to Promote and Protect Investments

The *Sawhoyamaxa Community* case is the most interesting that has been filed before the Court regarding a possible conflict between indigenous property and foreign investment. In the hearing before the Court, the respondent state (Paraguay) argued that the lands were registered as private property 'for a long time' and that the owner of the claimed lands refuses to sell them. The state also maintained that those lands were being adequately exploited and that a bilateral treaty with Germany to promote and protect capital investments (BIT)[80] protected the owner.

The Court dismissed the claim based on private property over the disputed lands: first, because under domestic law, the indigenous communities 'have the right to claim restitution of their traditional lands even though said lands may be privately held'; and second, because if the existence of a title to private property over the lands may be 'in itself' an objective and reasoned ground for dismissing

---

[79] *Community Yakye Axa*, n 19 above, at para 146.
[80] *Sawhoyamaxa Community*, n 20 above, at paras 115(b), 137.

prima facie the claims ... 'restitution rights become meaningless and would not entail an actual possibility of recovering traditional lands'.[81] Similarly, the exploitation of the lands cannot be alleged, because that would exclude per se the indigenous communities from ever recovering their ancestral lands that are in full productivity.[82] The Court, finally, dismissed the argument of a possible conflict with a bilateral treaty on investments in the following terms:

> [T]he Court has not been furnished with the aforementioned treaty between Germany and Paraguay, but, according to the State, said convention allows for capital investments made by a contracting party to be condemned or nationalized for a 'public purpose or interest', which could justify land restitution to indigenous people. Moreover, the Court considers that the enforcement of bilateral commercial treaties negates vindication of non-compliance with state obligations under the American Convention; on the contrary, their enforcement should always be compatible with the American Convention, which is a multilateral treaty on human rights that stands in a class of its own and that generates rights for individual human beings and does not depend entirely on reciprocity among States.[83]

The Court did not undertake an analysis of the treaty with Germany, nor did it establish whether it could interpret the Convention taking into account the obligations of Paraguay under the treaty by applying Article 31.3.c of VCLT. This provision, which has become relevant in international jurisprudence since the *Oil Platforms* case,[84] has been invoked several times by the Court in interpreting the Convention. In an advisory opinion regarding consular assistance, the Court affirmed that: 'Under that article, the interpretation of a treaty must take into account not only the agreements and instruments related to the treaty (paragraph 2 of Article 31), but also the system of which it is part (paragraph 3 of Article 31).'[85]

This conclusion could be explained because it took place in the framework of an advisory opinion, where the Court is competent under Article 64.1 of the Convention to interpret the Convention and 'other treaties concerning the protection of human rights in the American states', which has been given a broad interpretation by the Court.[86]

The Court's contentious jurisdiction, on the other hand, refers to the interpretation and application of the American Convention (Articles 62 to 63 of the Convention and Article 1 of its Statute). Nevertheless, in contentious cases, the Court has repeated the same dictum as grounds for using other treaties in the framework of Article 31.3 of VCLT. In the *Street Children* case, this provision

---

[81] Ibid., at para 138.   [82] Ibid., at para 139.   [83] Ibid., at para 140.

[84] ICJ Reports (2003) at 161. See C McLachlan, 'The Principle of Systemic Integration and Article 31(3)(c) of the Vienna Convention' (2005) 54 ICLQ 279.

[85] *The Right to Information on Consular Assistance in the Framework of the Guarantees of the due Process of Law*, Advisory Opinion, 1 October 1999, Series A No 16, at para 113.

[86] Cf *'Other Treaties' Subject to the Advisory Jurisdiction of the Court*, Advisory Opinion, 24 September 1982, Series A No 1, at para 52.

was cited to incorporate certain obligations of the Convention on the Rights of the Child into a very general provision of the American Convention in this area (Article 19).[87] In the *Yakye Axa Community* case, the Court held that, to interpret Article 21 of the Convention, it was 'useful and appropriate to resort to other international treaties, aside from the American Convention, such as ILO Convention No. 169, to interpret its provisions'.[88] With less conviction, in the *Plan de Sánchez* case, the Court avoided applying the Convention on the Prevention and Punishment of the Crime of Genocide, but warned of the seriousness of the massacre against the Mayan people, 'which this Court will take into account when it decides on reparations'.[89]

In the *Sawhoyamaxa Community* case, the Court did not invoke Article 31.3 of VCLT in interpreting the American Convention in conjunction with the treaty between Germany and Paraguay. It had a procedural reason for not doing so, since the state had only mentioned the treaty in the hearing and did not provide its text to the Court, which disqualified a plea based on the treaty. Nevertheless, without citing VCLT, the Court attempted a balance that gave priority to the Convention over the bilateral treaty in two ways. In the first place, because Germany's investment in Paraguay could be 'nationalized for a "public purpose or interest"', which could justify land restitution to indigenous people'. The Court thus attempted to harmonize the Convention and the treaty by applying the same principle that it applied for a conflict between private property and that of indigenous communities, repairing the interference of the former with compensation, while requiring restitution for the latter. In that context, the criterion applied by the Court is not a break with regard to its previous jurisprudence. That, however, was not the Court's only conclusion, because it went further and suggested certain bases to recognize a higher hierarchy or, at least, a preferred standard of application of the Convention over the treaty: (1) the Convention 'is a multilateral treaty on human rights'; (2) it 'stands in a class of its own'; (3) it 'generates rights for individual human beings'; and (4) it 'does not depend entirely on reciprocity among States'.

These criteria of the Court are not conclusive. The techniques applied in international law to resolve conflicts between norms are: first, that of hierarchy, according to which a rule of *ius cogens* prevails; second, that of specificity, according to which a *lex specialis* prevails over general rules; and, third, that of temporality, under which a *lex posteriori* prevails over an earlier law on the same subject. None of these techniques is present in the ideas set forth by the Court.

The American Convention is, in fact, a multilateral treaty on human rights, but this circumstance does not give it, as a whole, a special hierarchy. It cannot be said that all of the provisions of the Convention are *ius cogens*, although some

---

[87] *'Street Children' (Villagrán-Morales and ors) v Guatemala*, 18 November 1999, Series C No 63, at paras 194–196.   [88] *Community Yakye Axa* n 19 above, at para 127.
[89] *Plan de Sánchez Massacre*, n 22 above, at para 51 and vote of Cançado J at paras 25–28.

of them undoubtedly are. The specific case concerns a conflict between two rival properties and the fact that property is a right protected by the Convention. In this context, the idea of a hierarchy between the types of property can be used instead of between each treaty as such, according to which a certain priority must be given to indigenous property because of its peculiar function. It is not necessary to establish a hierarchy between different sources of international law or different treaties to arrive at this conclusion.

The Convention, it is true, stands in a class of its own, but the same may be said of the international legal system to protect investments that includes many current treaties. The Convention and these investment treaties are both *lex specialis*, or even 'self-contained regimes' in some of the senses described by the Study Group of the International Law Commission on Fragmentation of International Law.[90]

The Convention cannot be said to have a hierarchy over a BIT because the former 'generates rights for individual human beings', as suggested by the Court. One feature of modern international law regarding investments and of those treaties in particular is that they create the right for investors to sue a state directly and autonomously before an international tribunal for violating the treaty. A BIT, therefore, also 'generates rights for individual human beings'.

The Court, finally, has declared that the Convention 'does not depend entirely on reciprocity among States'. This can be more interesting if it is linked to Article 60.5 of VCLT and to the statement of the International Court of Justice in its advisory opinion *Reservations to the Convention on the Prevention and Punishment of the Crime of Genocide* on the nature of the Genocide Convention:

In such a convention the contracting States do not have any interests of their own; they merely have, one and all, a common interest, namely, the accomplishment of those high purposes which are the *raison d'être* of the convention. Consequently, in a convention of this type one cannot speak of individual advantages or disadvantages to States, or of the maintenance of a perfect contractual balance between rights and duties.[91]

These ideas were adopted by the Inter-American Court when, considering the effect of the reservations to the American Convention:

[M]odern human rights treaties in general, and the American Convention in particular, are not multilateral treaties of the traditional type concluded to accomplish the reciprocal exchange of rights for the mutual benefit of the contracting States. Their object and purpose is the protection of the basic rights of individual human beings irrespective of their nationality, both against the State of their nationality and all other

---

[90] Report of the International Law Commission 56th session (2004) A/59/10 288–293.
[91] *Reservations to the Convention on the Prevention and Punishment of the Crime of Genocide*, Advisory Opinion, 15 ICJ Reports (1951), 23.

contracting States. In concluding these human rights treaties, the States can be deemed to submit themselves to a legal order within which they, for the common good, assume various obligations, not in relation to other States, but towards all individuals within their jurisdiction.[92]

In general, human rights treaties recognize 'that these rights derive from the inherent dignity of the human person', as proclaimed in the Preambles to the two UN Covenants. Similarly, human rights are one of the bases of the modern international community and contemporary international law, as implied in the Preamble and Articles 1.3, 55.c, and 56 of the UN Charter. Even the Preamble to VCLT includes the principle 'of universal respect for, and observance of, human rights and fundamental freedoms for all'. In any case, the 'high purposes' of human rights treaties are the reason explaining that reciprocity does not apply to them.

The different objects and purposes established in treaties on the protection of investments are not equally significant. They correspond to a distinct hierarchy. The Preamble to the Convention on the Settlement of Investment Disputes between States and Nationals of Other States reveals that its adoption was due more to practical considerations than to fulfilling essential values of the international community. International private investments are declared as a 'need for international cooperation for international development' and it is also recognized that from 'time to time disputes may arise in connection with such investments' and that 'international methods of settlement may be appropriate in certain cases'. For this, it is useful to set up 'facilities for international conciliation or arbitration to which Contracting States and nationals of other Contracting States may submit such disputes if they so desire'. The long-established institution in customary international law has been to protect foreign private investments is diplomatic protection. However, such a technique has a number of disadvantages because '[t]he investor must have exhausted all local remedies in the host State' and 'depends entirely on its national government'.[93]

It is interesting that it is precisely on the basis of the social and cultural functions of indigenous property over private property that the Court has granted a certain degree of preference to protecting the former in case of conflict. However, as has been stated, the same Court has recognized that such preference is granted 'on a case by case basis'. Therefore, at least at present, there are no general conclusions on this point nor can hierarchies be established between types of property or much less between treaties based on their object and purpose.

---

[92] *The Effect of Reservations on the Entry into Force of the American Convention on Human Rights*, Advisory Opinion, 24 September 1982, Series A No 2, at para 29. See also *Austria v Italy (Pfunders Case)* (App 788/60) (1961) 4 European Yearbook of Human Rights 116, 140.
[93] CH Schreurer, *The ICSID Convention: A Commentary* (2001) 7.

Human rights treaties do not pursue 'the reciprocal exchange of rights for the mutual benefit of the contracting States', which 'do not have any interests of their own', but 'one and all, a common interest, namely, the accomplishment of those high purposes' of the convention. Those features are relevant and have important consequences for the reciprocity of obligations, which does not exist in these cases. However, in contemporary international law that particular nature is not sufficient to conclude that those treaties become, for that sole fact, *ius cogens* or that they have special hierarchy. Moreover, there is an additional difficulty in matters of property, since the property of a foreign investor cannot be excluded from the property protected as part of human rights. However, the Court's brief and arguable reasoning in the *Sawhoyamaxa Community* case expresses once more the trend in the inter-American system that the law of human rights prevails over economic rights and that pecuniary matters are treated with certain distrust.

IV. Conclusions

The cautious approach of the Commission and the Court in protecting property sheds light on the role that the inter-American system of human rights might play in conflicts concerning expropriation and other interferences with investment. The system is not the forum to protect business activity against arbitrary acts of the state. The American Convention could be the basis for developing jurisprudence on private economic matters since property is recognized as an individual right. On the other hand, the Court's jurisprudence associates property with every economic interest of a person, even though it does not imply a legal power over a material object. The jurisprudence has also maintained that property damage arises more from facts than from forms, which implies accepting concepts such as indirect expropriation and creeping expropriation, recognized in investment law.

Nevertheless, these approaches do not correspond to the practice of the Commission and the Court, which resists mixing wholly economic interests with human rights protection, even if property is involved in the conflict. A striking manifestation of this tendency is the Court's resistance to order high amounts to compensate violations of property, regardless the actual extension of damages.

Another practical limitation is the obstacle for legal persons to access the protection offered by the system of human rights. Although it may be envisaged that this practice will change, there is no basis to expect that such a change will reach the protection of economic interests of legal persons, which are perceived to be beyond the protection of human rights.

On the other hand, the Court's jurisprudence in cases of conflict between indigenous property and private property suggests that human rights prevail over economic rights. In other words, indigenous property is fully protected when it is given back to its owners because it has a function that goes beyond pure economics. In contrast, the protection of other forms of private property is limited to compensation for expropriation. The implicit rule seems to be that, in case of conflict between property realizing significant human rights and property satisfying mere economic interests, the former should prevail.

Finally, the 'high purposes' of human rights treaties and non-applicability of reciprocity in them could become new tools for the resolution of conflicts with other conventions regulating economic activity, especially BITs. Not even a state party's breach of its obligations under a human rights treaty may be invoked by another state party for terminating or suspending the treaty itself (VCLT, Article 60.5). Taking this into account, a state's obligations under investments law could hardly be invoked as lawful justification for not fulfilling its human rights obligations. The payment of adequate monetary compensation seems to be, in principle, the solution to meet investment commitments incompatible with the fulfilment of human rights obligations. However, in principle, human rights must always prevail over rights related to international business. Although broadly based on speculations from the Inter-American Court's case law, this conclusion should not be entirely dismissed because its underlying reasoning is rooted to the purpose of human rights treaties and the fundamental principles that sustain contemporary international law. Only time will confirm or dismiss this perspective.

PART IV

CASE STUDIES ON PROTECTION STANDARDS AND SPECIFIC HUMAN RIGHTS IN INVESTOR-STATE ARBITRATION

13

Balancing Property
Rights and Human Rights
in Expropriation

Jeff Waincymer

I. Introduction

This volume has sought to grapple with the dual questions as to whether there is a role for the application of human rights law in investor-state arbitration and, if so, how adjudicators should best balance economic and human rights within those processes. This chapter deals with one element of that debate, namely, the relationship between property rights and human rights in the context of disputes over alleged expropriation contrary to treaty norms. The purpose is twofold: first, to consider whether anti-expropriation norms are a barrier to human rights promotion through their content, application, or even the regulatory chill effects that might flow from expansive indirect takings norms; and, second, to consider to what extent the development of comprehensive and balanced tests at the interface of potentially conflicting international governance regimes places great responsibility on adjudicators to refine the more open-ended norms that typically arise from treaty negotiations. A subsidiary question is whether the traditionally private field of international arbitration is as well suited to perform this function as a more permanent body such as the Appellate Body of the WTO or a body with broad public international law expertise such as the International Court of Justice.

As has been noted by Clara Reiner and Christoph Shreuer in this volume,[1] while human rights claims could arise in a number of ways and from a number of sources in investor-state arbitration, most commonly they are raised as a defence by the host state in response to a claim of improper interference with the investor's rights and entitlements. That is typically the sense in which they are

---

[1] See ch 4 in this volume.

raised in expropriation claims. Ioana Knoll-Tudor in this volume notes that there could also be claims of human rights violations by the investor.[2]

Even if we limit our analysis to the first factual scenario, we must still begin with some very challenging questions as we cannot know whether human rights may validly interfere with the property rights of investors without understanding the nature and sources of those rights and how they are to be ordered.

There are a number of related questions. What are property rights and from where are they derived? Similarly, what are human rights and from where are they derived? Is a right to property itself a human right? If so, how are conflicting human rights prioritized? If they are not human rights, by what other moral imperatives are they justified? In what circumstances might human rights be a justification for interference with that notion of property rights?

The first conceptual question is whether we seek to analyse and justify both property and human rights from a purely positivist perspective or go beyond that to broader questions of philosophy, economics, and sociology. If our analysis was limited to a positivist perspective, we would seek to identify the rules which establish and/or allow interference with those rights; determine how those rules should be interpreted; and select a methodology by which to resolve conflicts between those norms. As to the sources of the rules, we would consider customary international law and multilateral treaties, bilateral investment treaties, national constitutions and statutes, and private investment agreements between nationals and host states. If one is to identify separately the sources of property rights and human rights in an international context, one also quickly faces fragmentation concerns as addressed in the contribution by Professor Dupuy.[3]

Where interpretation is concerned, a number of contributions to this volume call for processes of interpretation that give sufficient deference to human rights and ensure that commercial interests are not prioritized. Where conflicts between norms are concerned, again contributors call for constitutional prioritization, in part because of a lack of sufficient mechanisms within investment treaties and a debateable policy basis of the approach to ranking conflicting norms under the Vienna Convention on the Law of Treaties. All of these issues are highly relevant to the case study within this chapter, but will not be repeated here. Instead, this chapter concentrates on the legal and philosophical sources of property rights and the relationship of those notions to concepts of human rights as more broadly identified. The expropriation jurisprudence is then examined to see inductively if investor-state arbitration unduly ranks certain rights over others in an unjustifiable manner. The overall conclusion to be presented is that there is no discernible bias to that

---

[2] See ch 14 in this volume; M Cohn, 'The World Trade Organisation: Elevating Property Interests Above Human Rights' (2001) 29 Georgia Journal of International and Comparative Law 427; and K Bagwell and RW Staiger, *The Economics of the World Trading System* (2002).
[3] See ch 2 in this volume.

effect, although the norms and interpretations are sufficiently vague and diverse that consistency in outcomes cannot be confidently predicted. This leads on to observations about the role of adjudication.

II. The Nature of Property Rights and Human Rights

As with many of the debates as to the relationship between human rights and international economic law, proponents and critics of investment arbitration too often talk at cross purposes. Some critics might suggest that property rights are unduly preferenced, with bilateral investment treaties (BITs) giving foreign investors undue levels of protection in excess of local citizens, which in turn provides a barrier to the promotion of human rights by host states. A different discourse argues that minimum property rights are an essential human right and that ensuring such minimal holdings is the most significant practical means to alleviate world poverty. While the two observations may not be mutually exclusive, they point to the need for some conceptual analysis and hint at the need for trade-offs where the two propositions clash in a particular dispute.

From a legal perspective, when we speak of property we generally focus on the notion of property *rights* rather than the physical item itself. This helps us to understand the range of rights and entitlements of individuals and forces us to face squarely the possibility that different people will have different rights and obligations vis-à-vis the same physical item. There is then a need to define and prioritize those rights and obligations.

When we speak of rights to property, we generally consider the exclusive right to determine its use and to exchange it with other persons. While all civilized governments recognize the notion of property and some degree of property rights, there are of course great variations in who may be entitled to hold property rights and the extent of those rights, ranging from communist systems calling for common ownership to *laissez faire* free market systems advocating the broadest rights of an individual to acquire and retain property. Yet even in the most liberal economies, clashes between property rights can be expected to occur. A corporation with a right to establish a factory that then pollutes the environment is interfering with the property rights of its neighbours. Thus, the legal system has to determine how such clashes are to be resolved. In this sense, property law and property rights are simply part of the regulatory mechanisms by which societies allocate control over resources.

At the domestic level, there are differences in approach between civilian and common law systems in terms of the way in which rights are described, the ambit of rights, and the degree to which they can be dissected.[4] Each legal

---

[4] For a discussion of civilian sources of property law, see ch 19 in this volume.

system also has to grapple with emerging notions of the kinds of things over which property rights can be allocated. New technologies and the patentability or otherwise of discoveries with regard to natural phenomena are the key examples.

Within an international investment arbitration, national property law regimes may be relevant depending on the law applicable to the particular dispute. Arbitral systems generally give arbitrators broad discretions as to applicable law, but make the discretion subject to express choices of the parties. It would normally be the case in an investment context that the host state would demand that its laws apply to the transaction. Most conflicts of law systems would lead to the same conclusion if that was the methodology applied by an arbitrator with a broad discretion. This chapter does not seek to delve into the intricacies of comparative property law, but simply wishes to note that the degree of conflict between applicable property law and human rights may vary on a case-by-case basis where national property law systems are to apply. This is not only affected by the content of the law, but also by its particular source and hence status in a hierarchy of legal norms. An example would be the broader constitutional protection of property found in the German Constitution and supported by German jurisprudence.[5]

As to the international norms under a positivist methodology, Article 17 of the Universal Declaration of Human Rights indicates that: 'Everyone has the right to own property alone or as well as in association with others.' The Universal Declaration also indicates that 'no one shall be arbitrarily deprived of his property'.[6] The 2005 UN World Summit Outcome document notes the importance of 'proper contract enforcement and respect for property rights and the rule of law'. It notes disparities in ownership between different groups and stresses the importance of 'guaranteeing the free and equal right of women to own and inherit property and ensuring secure tenure of property and housing by women'.[7]

The American Declaration on the Rights and Duties of Man indicates that 'every person has a right to own such private property as meets the essential needs of decent living and helps to maintain the dignity of the individual and of the home'.[8]

Under the European Convention for the Protection of Human Rights and Fundamental Freedoms: 'every natural or legal person is entitled to the peaceful

---

[5] See DP Kommers, *The Constitutional Jurisprudence of the Federal Republic of Germany* (2nd edn, 1997).

[6] The Universal Declaration of Human Rights, Art 17, UN Doc GA Res 217A(III), UN Doc A/810 (1948) 71.

[7] UN General Assembly Resolution 60th Session A/Res/60/1, 24 October 2005.

[8] American Declaration of the Rights and Duties of Man, Art XXIII, reprinted in Basic Documents Pertaining to Human Rights in the Inter-American System, OEA/Ser.L.V/2.82 doc 6 rev 1 (1992) 17.

enjoyment of his possessions. No one shall be deprived of his possessions except in the public interest and subject to the conditions provided for by law and by the general principles of international law.'[9] However, the rights are not unlimited. The Protocol goes on to say that 'the preceding provision shall not, however, in any way impair the right of a State to enforce such laws as it deems necessary to control the use of property in accordance with the general interest or to secure the payment of taxes or other contributions or penalties'. The latter articulation raises one of the most fundamental challenges, namely, the extent to which existing property rights can be reduced for other societal goals. Other texts also seek to put limits on property rights, first noting the need for minimum property standards and second the entitlement to subordinate such rights to the needs of the broader society. The American Convention on Human Rights notes that 'everyone has the right to the use and enjoyment of his property', but also states that 'the law may subordinate such use and enjoyment to the interests of society'. It further notes that 'no one shall be deprived of his property except upon payment of just compensation for reasons of public utility or social interest and in the cases and according to the forms established by law'.[10]

A positivist approach to identifying the nature of the broader field of human rights would begin with the work of the United Nations. Human rights are referred to in the preamble and Articles 1, 55 and 56 of the Charter of the United Nations, the Universal Declaration of Human Rights,[11] the International Covenant on Civil and Political Rights (ICCPR),[12] and the International Covenant on Economic, Social, and Cultural Rights.[13]

The Universal Declaration, while not a treaty, has come to be accepted as an important legal document. As noted above, the Declaration alludes to the right to own property and the right not to be arbitrarily deprived of property. To complicate matters, however, when the two international human rights covenants were drafted, the right to property was excluded. This was apparently due to differences in view as to the content of the concept.[14]

International human rights instruments do not purport to rank rights save for those of a *jus cogens* stature. Indeed, they generally state the opposite, arguing that all rights are equal and indivisible. Article 2 of the UDHR indicates that all human rights norms are equal in importance and are interdependent.

---

[9] Protocol 2V E 213 UNTS 262, 262; European Convention for the Protection of Human Rights and Fundamental Freedoms.

[10] American Convention on Human Rights, Art 21, OAS Treaty Series No 36, 1144 UNTS 123 in force 18 July 1978.   [11] GA Res 217A(III) UN Doc A/810 (1948) 71.

[12] Open for signature 16 December 1966, 999 UNTS 171 (in force 23 March 1976).

[13] International Covenant on Economic, Social, and Cultural Rights, 993 UNTS 3, 16 December 1966.

[14] Vadi, n 4 above, citing TRG van Banning, *The Human Right to Property* (2002) 5.

Nevertheless, many argue that they vary in terms of immediate binding effect, some being better described as soft law and aspirational.

Another complication is the debate within the human rights movement as to whether the rights are limited to negative rights against improper interference or whether the rights connote positive obligations to achieve human rights goals. The debate does not matter for property rights per se as they are naturally litigated where there is claimed undue interference. Nevertheless, where broader human rights are argued to be the basis for governmental interference, this question becomes a live one.

In addition to the sources of law articulating these norms, there is also the ongoing role of the international organizations in refining them. Richard Bilder argued that in practice 'a claim is an international human right if the United Nations General Assembly says it is'.[15] Article 13 of the UN Charter empowers the General Assembly to 'make recommendations for the purpose of ... assisting in the realisation of human rights'. Of course, a mandate to make recommendations does not expressly go so far as to establish binding principles of law. Phillip Alston has also criticized the lack of rigour in assertions as to the ambit of such rights.[16] Alston has also argued for appropriate procedural standards as a means to better identify valid concepts of human rights.[17]

From a purely positivist perspective, one could at least conclude that there is no transnational norm identifying the nature and ambit of property rights and much that can be debated about the ambit of human rights, including the degree to which such rights provide for immediate binding obligations or in some cases are better described as 'soft' law. There are also fragmentation concerns, problems of ranking conflicting norms, which under the Vienna Convention on the Law of Treaties may depend on the specificity and timing of different laws, identification of the importance of legal sources, whether by reason of being *jus cogens* or constitutional norms, interpretational challenges within legal instruments, and problems of standing and adjudicatory competence. Ioana Knoll-Tudor also notes the possibility of dual jurisdiction before an arbitral tribunal and a human rights court.[18]

While these problems are significant, one might also conclude that in a non-Communist world, property as a legal institution is respected and some degree of rights as against the state are generally enshrined. While the state is usually given an overriding ability to interfere with those rights, that should not occur without some degree of just compensation and should be based on demonstrable social needs and only following a determination under fair processes. Because

---

[15] R Bilder, 'Rethinking International Human Rights: Some Basic Questions' (1959) Wisconsin Law Review 171, 163.

[16] P Alston, 'Conjuring Up New Human Rights: A Proposal for Quality Control' (1984) 78 AJIL 607.   [17] Ibid., 617.

[18] See ch 2 above.

such principles are generally expressed within BITs and other instruments controlling foreign direct investment, arbitrations would in any event consider such interpretational and factual questions as to whether the relevant action constituted an expropriation; whether it was justified under provisions allowing for it in certain circumstances; and whether any compensation was just and adequate.

The challenges grow exponentially when we seek to justify property and human rights from more theoretical bases. Philosophical views about property and human rights have varied significantly over the centuries. Legal positivism as espoused by John Austin is the justification for a positivist view of the ambit of property and human rights, although this perspective adds a further complexity given the lack of respect for international law as law under an extreme positivist jurisprudence.[19]

The natural law tradition began with religiously inspired notions of fundamental entitlement. John Locke provided a significant impetus for the eventual recognition of property rights in first generation human rights. He argued that fundamental individual rights encompassed life, liberty, and property. The proper role of government was to support those rights. In his view, a person is entitled to the product of his or her labour. That would be so in the state of nature absent any social contract. A key element of such a social contract is to protect the individual's just desserts from arbitrary and improper interference.

A question to which we will return later is whether property rights are indeed human rights. At this stage it merely needs to be noted that if property is justified as a natural right under a Lockean analysis, it is then a very small step to describe it as a human right. Such a perspective can also have distributional implications which may be relevant when investments are taxed or expropriated. For example, Robert Nozick argues that redistributive taxation is equivalent to forced labour and is inherently unjust.[20] Even the most extreme pro-property arguments, however, assert that the right only arises where it has been justly acquired. There is then much debate about what constitutes just acquisition.

Jeremy Bentham's utilitarian perspective was based on his criticism of natural law perspectives. He argued that we should order our lives so as to promote the greatest happiness of the greatest number.[21] Utilitarians justify property rights per se as a precondition for the optimization of happiness. People's happiness is in part enhanced by the things they consume, which in turn depends on their ability to work and exchange things of value. In turn, this requires certain property rights to support such activities. Absent sufficient rights, our lives would also be less secure, which in turn would diminish our happiness. What may be less obvious is that a utilitarian perspective provides for a less certain

---

[19] J Austin, *The Province of Jurisprudence Determined* (3rd edn, 1954).
[20] R Nozick, *Anarchy State and Utopia* (1974) 174.
[21] J Bentham, *An Introduction to the Principles of Morals and Legislation* (1996 reprint).

ambit of property rights and a natural basis for society's interference with such rights. Given that justice is measured by the determination of the greatest benefit for the greatest number, it is at least conceivable that the majority might benefit by the taking of property from an individual. At the extreme, therefore, a utilitarian perspective would find it hard to identify inviolate human rights. Utilitarianism does have something to say about distribution in that it can be argued that the marginal utility of wealth decreases as one gets richer, hence a more equal distribution is more likely to increase overall satisfaction. Great disparities in wealth between a small number of rich and a large number of poor are also likely to lead to lower overall satisfaction levels.[22]

A utilitarian perspective is also strongly linked to economic justifications for the allocation of property rights. Neoclassical economics argues that promoting greater total welfare is the most efficient response to the problem of having insufficient resources by which to attain all of our goals. Economics simply states that it is better to have a bigger 'cake' to divide by whatever principle of distributive justice one seeks to do so. From an economic perspective, providing for property rights gives an incentive to productive labour and allows for an exchange via a market mechanism where supply and demand can lead to the most efficient allocation of resources. From an economic perspective, property ownership also avoids the tragedy of the commons[23] and allows a basis for lines of credit in small business and for other human activities. The tragedy of the commons can be expected to occur where resources are available to all without discrete property rights. It can be predicted that in such circumstances the incentive is for individuals to exploit the resources for short-term gain and make no effort to prevent or counter long-term depletion in the value of the resources. Grazing land will be over-grazed, oceans will be over-fished, and air will be polluted to the eventual detriment of all.

The unjust taking of property in World War II has led to a greater concern for constitutional guarantees towards an individual against an authoritarian state and shows a disinclination to rely solely on utilitarian perspectives as proof of a just political system.

It is appropriate to consider other philosophical perspectives on the nature of property within the context of a philosophical analysis of human rights per se. This is because many philosophical schools of thought approach property from this perspective. Thus, arguments such as that of Hegel that a person's dignity and self-realization require private property rights would see them as human rights or a necessary precondition to minimum human rights.[24] Hegel argues that an essential aspect of humanity is the exercise of free will and property rights are an important means by which such free will may be exercised.[25] Notions of

---

[22] AR Coban, *Protection of Property Rights within the European Convention on Human Rights* (2004) 42.   [23] G Hardin, 'The Tragedy of the Common' (1968) 162 Science 1244.
[24] GWS Hegel, *The Philosophy of Rights* (1965).   [25] Coban, n 22 above, 65.

free will and autonomy also underlie the Kantian approach to the identification of human rights. Kant argued that the autonomy of the individual and individual will are the central values from which other freedoms and rights should follow.[26] These conceptions can all support property rights as a means to enhance autonomy and the meaningful exercise of free will. It does not indicate, however, how exact distributions are to occur or how competing claims to the same end are resolved.

An important aspect of this line of philosophical inquiry is whether individuals have rights to actual *levels* of property or instead merely rights to an *opportunity* to seek to do so. The former view would more readily support redistributional interference with foreign investor rights.

Another school of thought approaches the question from the perspective of liberty. While many philosophers speak of liberty, the concept covers very different schools of thought. At one extreme, people argue for an individual's rights to be free from external interference.[27] At the other extreme are those who argue that true liberty and freedom requires certain minimum resources and opportunities for all, thus justifying some redistributional goals. The debate between John Rawls and Thomas Pogge as to whether re-distributional obligations apply internationally shows how complex and disparate these theories have become.[28] At the very least, a philosophical perspective would provide legitimate criticism for rules which give significantly varied levels of property rights, in particular favouring foreigners through BIT norms as opposed to domestic citizens.

One means by which to understand the tensions within and between different philosophical schools is to consider the inspiration for individual property rights based on historical allocations and acquisitions and, conversely, distributional goals to achieve minimum property rights. In discussing the nature and development of human rights, Burns Weston distinguishes the broad philosophical underpinnings of first generation civil and political rights as against the second generation of economic, social, and cultural rights. He sees the first as being derived from liberal individualism and economic *laissez faire* principles.[29] Such foundations naturally lead to acceptance of the right to own property and the right not to be deprived arbitrarily and without just compensation. Conversely, he sees second generation rights as having their origins primarily in the socialist tradition seeking to temper the misuses of capitalist development and unconstrained conceptions of individual liberty.[30] Being claims to 'social equality',[31]

---

[26] AD Rosen, *Kant's Theory of Justice* (1993). See also J Raz, *Morality of Freedom* (1986) 400.
[27] See, eg JS Mill, *On Liberty* (1974 reprint).
[28] See J Rawls, *A Theory of Justice* (1971); J Rawls, *The Law of Peoples, With the Idea of Public Reason Revisited* (1999); TW Pogge, 'An Egalitarian Law of Peoples' (1994) 23 Philosophy and Public Affairs 195; and TW Pogge, *World Poverty and Human Rights* (2002).
[29] B Weston, 'Human Rights' (1984) 6:3 Human Rights Quarterly 257, 264.
[30] Ibid., 265.   [31] Ibid., 266.

they naturally call for redistribution and confront the essential property rights under the first generation rights.

Many of the above comments either directly or indirectly address the question of whether property rights are themselves human rights. There are a number of arguments in favour of property rights as human rights. At the foundational level, the human body should be seen as the property of the individual, inherently negating the entitlement to slavery and other gross invasions. A second and broader justification is to build on the entitlement to work and conclude that persons should have guarantees as to the ability to enjoy the fruits of their labour. This was Locke's thought process. Other arguments are economic, postulating that the minimum standard of living that human rights seeks to promote necessitates some minimum property holdings. Because many human rights are justified on the basis of human dignity, it is similarly argued that minimum levels of ownership are required for such relaxed and dignified existence. Thus, the independent High Level Commission on Legal Empowerment of the Poor launched under the auspices of the United Nations notes that its mission 'is built on the conviction that poverty can only be eradicated if governments give all citizens, especially the poor, a legitimate stake in the economy by extending access to property rights and other legal protections to populations and areas currently not covered by the rule of law'.[32]

These different perspectives will also affect how people argue for priority between norms. Burns Weston again notes that first generation proponents argue that second and third generation rights are merely derivative. Conversely, second and third generation promoters argue that first generation rights give insufficient attention to fundamental human needs.[33]

This brief philosophical discourse shows at least that there is no consensus as to the nature and scope of property rights and human rights or whether property rights can be seen as human rights. On the other hand, there are a range of different philosophical perspectives that each seeks to support some level of property rights, albeit through different forms of reasoning. The majority of philosophical schools also suggest that such rights are not inviolate. As Coban has concluded:

Since the moral reasons ... justify only prima facie property rights, other moral reasons ... can justify limitation of those rights. If appropriation, use, or alienation of property injures others' rights, it must be restrained. And since autonomy is possible only in an autonomy-supporting environment, governments may restrict property rights in order to establish and maintain and even to develop such a society. But there must be a fair balance between individuals' interests and public interest. The measure taken by government should be proportional to the aimed ends.[34]

---

[32] The High Level Commission on Legal Empowerment of the Poor.
[33] Weston, n 29 above, 267.   [34] Coban, n 22 above, 77.

III. The Problem of Expropriation

While most governments are strongly in favour of FDI, they are also concerned to maintain their right to regulate investments both directly and indirectly and change policies from time to time as they deem fit, particularly when these might only tangentially impact upon FDI. Because foreign direct investment is a longer-term commercial activity, it is more exposed to the possibility of such shifts in government policy that might adversely affect the value of the investment. Particular tensions arise when a government activity in pursuit of a broader societal value, such as environmental, cultural, or health protection, is alleged to interfere improperly with investor protection provisions.

Both government and investor must consider how to respond to this. From the investor's perspective, like any commercial endeavour, foreign investment necessitates a consideration of return as against risk. The higher the risk of losses, the higher the rate of return is required. At the extreme, the key risk with foreign direct investment is expropriation by the host state. Rather than always seek to compensate for such risks with higher prices, or cover it through insurance,[35] which in turn would add greatly to the costs to consumers and hence to the cost of development, a more efficient approach might be to provide effective investor protection mechanisms that reduce such risks to acceptable commercial levels. Such infrastructure includes the necessary substantive laws covering rights and obligations of the parties and effective dispute settlement mechanisms. From the government's perspective, such protections will help to attract FDI as it lowers the cost of investing for the foreign party. Hence, the protection can be in the government's interest. However, the government would not want the protective mechanisms to constrain its own future regulatory options unduly.

As the above philosophical discourse has implied, the central challenge in each case is to get the balance right. A key aspect is determining how to express the chosen policy norms so that they provide sufficient clarity and support consistent and reasonable interpretations and applications. Yet there are a range of reasons why this is unlikely at the international level. One should not expect any norms to be able to be drafted with sufficient clarity that they ensure particular adjudicatory outcomes in all cases. Because current agreements mix promotion and protection norms, they tend to be drafted broadly and generally, which raises added risks of unintended consequences.

Other problems arise simply because of the nature of the concepts that traditionally apply in international economic law. Particularly general obligations

---

[35] Many countries do provide political risk insurance, eg Australia's Export Finance Insurance Corporation and the US Overseas Private Investment Corporation. Insurance companies such as Lloyds may also cover certain risks, as does the World Bank through its Multilateral Investment Guarantee Agency (MIGA).

are contained in investment protection agreements such as Most Favoured Nation treatment, national treatment, anti-expropriation rules, and compliance with minimum international standards. This is to be contrasted with the many specific governmental regulatory aspirations in non-commercial fields. When the two issues are put together, there is a tension between general and specific obligations. For example, in the disputes discussed below, an adjudicatory panel might be asked to consider broad notions of national treatment and expropriation on the one hand, against such specific environmental measures as a petrol additive law on the other. An expropriation norm is asked to cover a range of government measures from complete takings of property, removal of fundamental licences, discriminatory regulations that favour locals over foreign investors, lack of adequate protections for such things as intellectual property rights to outwardly non-discriminatory measures that nevertheless impact more seriously on foreign investors.

From a drafting point of view, there is a strong incentive to define concepts such as 'measure', 'investment', and 'expropriation' as broadly as possible so that the fullest level of protection is provided and to minimize transaction costs of disputes at the margin about jurisdictional matters. For the purposes of this chapter, a crucial corollary of this aspiration is to ensure that the rules cover both direct and indirect expropriations of investments, yet this raises then a distinct problem as to the potential for unintended consequences of rules of that nature. It becomes easy for investors to say that any form of government regulatory behaviour that adds costs and/or disincentives to their commercial activities becomes an indirect expropriation requiring compensation. From a policy perspective, the difficulty is that all government activities affect the economy and, hence, the relative values of different investment activities. This will occur irrespective of whether the government's overall philosophy is in favour of deregulation or increased regulation. Deregulation will alter the competitive conditions of established and protected industries. Increased regulation in fields of environment, health, and the like can significantly interfere with particular enterprises' profitability.

In addition, a stabilization clause may be utilized whereby the parties agree that the applicable law is that in force at the time of the contract. The latter is contentious in terms of the human rights debate. Why should a foreign investor be sheltered from retroactive regulatory changes favouring human rights, when local investors are not so sheltered? The argument in favour is that the foreign investor was induced to invest on the basis of the status quo and should at least be compensated if circumstances change. In public international law, that accords with the principle *rebus sic stantibus*, which underpins non-violation nullification norms in WTO jurisprudence. In the context of this chapter, if the investor committed large sums on the basis of a law that promised no expropriation and the law was then repealed, on what principles of justice would we not have sympathy for his or her circumstance? However, the difficult policy question is how to marry an argument based on an investor's reasonable expectations against the rights of social advancement, particularly for those governments that could not afford to pay compensation.

IV. Applicable International Law and Investment Protection

A. National Constitutions, Comparative Constitutional Models, and the Protection against Expropriation

A key aspect of any BIT is the extent to which it adds to the rights of private investors in claims of expropriation. As always, that requires a consideration of the current domestic situation and an analysis of the proposed BIT provisions. For the purposes of this chapter, which concentrates on expropriation, most developed constitutions would have some form of guarantee against governmental taking of property without just compensation. This needs to be looked at in its own right as a distinct avenue of redress and also as an element of the overall sources of law question that an arbitral tribunal might be asked to deal with. Such protections are also consistent with the prescriptions of most of the philosophical schools of thought discussed above.

For the purposes of this chapter, a brief comparison is made between the Australian and the US position to explain the backdrop to the recent Australia-US Free Trade Agreement, which included investor protection provisions, but without an elaborate dispute settlement model. One possible reason for this is the significant disparity between the ambit of protection under domestic constitutional law between the two systems. As is suggested below, the US position is much broader, hence there would have been little incentive for Australia to extend comprehensive and mutual rights in the agreement. European norms also tend to be more restrictive than the US norms.

While readers of this volume are unlikely to be concerned with the position in individual countries, an examination of these diverse models is illustrative of the problems that may arise. Australian constitutional provisions are quite narrow and the jurisprudence has displayed an uncertain but relatively conservative approach to identifying when just terms are required. The Australian Commonwealth Constitution has no general provision in relation to property. Because of this, the states retain key responsibility over property regulation. The Commonwealth may affect property indirectly through other heads of power. Section 51(xxxi) of the Constitution provides that the Commonwealth Parliament may make laws with regard to 'the acquisition of property on just terms from any state or person for any purpose in respect of which the Parliament has power to make laws'.

The first question is to determine which laws fall within this head of power. Many of these questions are left to be resolved by the courts because of the generality of the concepts and the need to determine when section 51(xxxi) is intended to apply. For example, some other heads of power which obviously support the acquisition of property, such as the taxation power, would not be seen as coming within section 51(xxxi) in order to require compensation on just terms.

There does not appear to have been a clear and consistent approach by the High Court of Australia to the application of these principles.[36] A significant constraint on the obligation is provided because of the need to show that there was an 'acquisition' of property. This is much narrower than an obligation to compensate for measures that 'relate to' an investment or which substantially adversely impact on the economic value of property without any acquisition of it.

In that regard, a significant question is whether environmental policies or conservation laws could be seen as laws which would be undermined if just terms had to be provided in the same way as the taxation analogy. If so, the Court could – under pre-existing principles of Australian constitutional jurisprudence – conclude that section 51(xxxi) is not intended to apply to such laws. That is less easy to argue. An environmental measure is not necessarily affected in terms of its policy aims simply because a government might be asked to compensate a corporation which is adversely affected by the initiative.

It is possible that a court might make use of a *reasonable expectations* test in looking at the investor's rights under section 51(xxxi). On this approach, a property owner would only be entitled to compensation on just terms where the government action overrode their reasonable expectations as to the way in which the property would be treated. While there may be good policy reasons in support of such a suggestion, such a test might make it even harder to predict outcomes accurately. Reasonable expectations could depend upon the state of the economy and the regulatory landscape at the time of feasibility studies and commencement of the investment, corporate planning discussions, other comments made by bureaucrats and politicians, and the general features of the particular industry concerned.

Where the US constitutional position is concerned, the key points to note are that on the one hand, the rights of individuals tend to be broader, while on the other, the federal government and the states have taken greater steps to try and block private party rights of standing in some circumstances. The latter development presumably flows from the already broader legal entitlements of private parties.

---

[36] S Evans, 'When Is an Acquisition of Property Not an Acquisition of Property?' (2000) 11 *Public Law Review* 183.

US notions of regulatory takings allow for challenges against non-discriminatory policies for a valid public purpose, even where this does not lead to acquisition of investment property by public entities, in cases where the policies significantly affect its commercial value. The Supreme Court has sought to limit such rights to preserve government powers, but the cases show that broad claims can be and are made and that it is difficult to develop clear principles that would pre-empt undesirable claims.

The Fifth and 14th Amendments to the US Constitution deal with regulatory takings of private property and compensatory requirements. There does not appear to be a consistent approach adopted by the Court. The Supreme Court has held that government action that does not take over or encroach on property can still constitute a taking if the regulatory effect is of sufficient magnitude.[37] In *Lucas v South Carolina Coastal Council*, the Court considered that for compensation rights to apply, there must be deprivation of all economic benefit of the property.[38] Nevertheless, in *Palazzalo v Rhode Island*, the Court accepted that compensation was possible where there were partial regulatory takings.[39] One Supreme Court justice has said:

This court has generally been unable to develop any 'set formula' for determining when 'justice and fairness' require that economic injuries caused by public action be compensated by the government, rather than remain disproportionately concentrated on a few persons. Rather, it has examined the 'taking' question by engaging in essentially ad hoc, factual inquiries that have identified several factors – such as the economic impact of the regulation, its interference with reasonable investment backed expectations, and the character of the government action that has particular significance.[40]

The overriding point is that constitutional norms vary significantly and are important aspects of property rights protection.

B. The Concept of Expropriation in International Law

The traditional international law approach to FDI flowed from two broad principles of public international law. The first was notions of territorial sovereignty. Under this principle, sovereign nations were free to regulate all aspects of commerce within their borders. Hence they could choose whether to allow aliens to invest locally and, if so, on what terms. The power to take the property of private individuals for public purposes has also been accepted. Set against this principle was the right of each state to protect its nationals and their property abroad. This in turn has led to principles of state responsibility for injuries to

---

[37] *Pennsylvania Coal Co v Mahon*, 260 US 393 (1922), at para 413.
[38] *Lucas v SC Coastal Council*, 505 US 1003 (1992).
[39] *Palazzalo v Rhode Island*, 533 US 606, 617 (2001).
[40] Rehnquist J in *Kaiser Aetna v United States*, 444 US 164, 175 (1979) quoting from *Penn Central Transportation Co v New York City*, 438 US 104 (1978), at para 124.

aliens and to their property. Two broad principles were fair dealing and no expropriation without just compensation. Customary international law does not look to the intent behind the government action. This is because it is concerned with compensation for takings and not with seeking to prevent the public policy aspirations of government. Customary international law has always accepted that it may lead to greater rights for foreigners than for locals.[41]

Other complications arose depending upon the way in which FDI was conducted. Customary international law of state responsibility for injuries to aliens initially distinguished between measures affecting property and contractual rights. Higher levels of protection were afforded to property rights. State contracts were seen as a sovereign matter. The status of state contracts in respect of state responsibility on the international plane remains problematic within academic commentaries.[42] However, it can safely be said that, over time, the differences have been minimized.

Because of the sovereign rights under international law, the notion of expropriation is not primarily concerned to proscribe governmental behaviour, but rather to ensure that fair compensation is provided. As such, Christie notes that the question of whether interference with an alien's property amounts in international law to an expropriation will not hinge on disclaimers of any *intention* to expropriate by the host state, nor will the absence of an attempt to affect the *legal title* to the alien's property be a deciding factor.[43]

In its most basic iteration, 'expropriation' is seen as a government nationalizing or obliging the transfer of assets which are the subject of investment by a foreign entity. At this level, it is not a controversial concept and is clearly proscribed by customary international law. Where matters get more complex is where an investor alleges a 'creeping' or an 'indirect' expropriation. This usually occurs where an exercise of the regulatory or police powers of a state mean that a foreign investor will not realize the expected value of its investment and seeks redress through international investment law.

Such an indirect commercial impact norm cannot readily be defined with any precision and certainly not when supported under customary international law as opposed to treaty. This has two implications. First, when significant amounts

---

[41] R Higgins, 'The Taking of Property by the State' (1982) 167 *Recueil des Cours* 259.

[42] M Sornarajah, *The International Law of Foreign Investment* (1994). See also O Schachter, 'Compensation for Expropriation' (1984) 78 AJIL 121; E Lauterpacht, 'Issues of Compensation and Nationality in the Taking of Energy Investments' (1990) Journal of Energy and Natural Resources Law 241; PM Norton, 'A Law of the Future or a Law of the Past: Modern Tribunals and the International Law of Expropriation' (1991) AJIL 474; CF Amerasinghe, 'Issues of Compensation for the Taking of Alien Property in the Light of Recent Cases and Practice' (1992) 41 ICLQ 22; and JA Westberg, 'Applicable Law, Expropriatory Takings and Compensation in Cases of Expropriation: ICSID and Iran-United States Claims Tribunal Case Law Compared' (1993) 8 ICSID Review 1.

[43] GC Christie, 'What Constitutes a Taking of Property Under International Law?' (1962) British Yearbook of International Law 307, 309.

are involved, claims of regulatory taking are easily made and are seen as sensible cost-benefit commercial decisions. Second, understanding the likely differentiation between acceptable and non-acceptable practices necessitates a case-by-case analysis and inductive reasoning from the outcome in particular disputes. While judges applying customary law might develop a consistent jurisprudence over time, private arbitrators will be particularly reluctant to make sweeping statements intended to operate as effective rules of international law.[44]

There are also differences in view under customary law as to what 'adequate' compensation entails, including whether compensation is to be calculated on a fully commercial basis or some lesser standard. For example, there is the question of whether just compensation allows for a reduced obligation for developing countries, in some circumstances at least. It has been suggested that developing countries which might not be able to pay for large-scale expropriations following decolonization should be entitled to argue that just compensation would be less than full commercial value.[45] Reduced compensation might, for example, apply where a post-Colonial developing country was seeking to claw back unduly generous natural resource concessions given to foreign investors.[46] If the contract itself was sufficiently imbalanced, it might also be that claiming full profit would be seen as an abuse of rights.[47] There also remains a debate as to whether the appropriate compensation under customary international law may depend on whether the expropriation is lawful or unlawful. For example, it is not clear whether lost profits are available in cases of lawful expropriation.[48]

Customary international law looks to unreasonable interferences of property. The Harvard Draft Convention on the International Responsibility of States for Injuries to Aliens states that:

'Taking of property' includes not only an outright taking of property but also any such unreasonable interference with the use, enjoyment, or disposal of property as to justify an inference that the owner thereof will not be able to use, enjoy, or dispose

---

[44] J Paulsson and Z Douglas, 'Indirect Expropriation in Investment Treaty Arbitrations' in N Horn and S Kroll (eds), *Arbitrating Foreign Investment Disputes: Procedural and Substantive Legal Aspects* (2004) 146. Care should also be taken with jurisprudence from regimes that broaden protection beyond mere expropriation rights, eg the European Convention on Human Rights and its protection of the right to the peaceful enjoyment of one's possessions per Art 1 of the First Protocol and the jurisdiction of the Iran/US Claims Tribunal covering 'other measures affecting property rights'.   [45] O Schachter, *International Law in Theory and Practice* (1991) 324.
[46] For such circumstances, see UN Resolution 1803 on Permanent Sovereignty over Natural Resources adopted 14 September 1962, UNGA Res 1803, 17 UN GAOR Annexes Vol I, Agenda Item No 39, 59. Other norms which may be relevant in such circumstances include the Charter of Economic Rights and Duties of States, Res 3281 (XXIX); UN GA Res 3201 (S-IV) and 3203 (S-VI): Declaration and Program of Action on the Establishment of a New International Economic Order, 1974; and Res 3262 (S-VII): Development and International Economic Cooperation 1975.
[47] eg *Himpurna California Energy Ltd (Bermuda) v PT (Gersero) Perusahaan Listruik Negara*, 14 (12) Mealey's International Arbitration Report A-1 (1990) A-50.
[48] *Amoco International Finance Corp v Iran*, 15 Iran-US Claims Tribunal 189.

of the property within a reasonable period of time after the inception of such interference.

Such a statement does not indicate what constitutes an 'unreasonable' interference. The American Restatement asserts similar views about the current status of customary international law on this issue.

Another element of customary international law in this regard is what might be termed the doctrine of state responsibility. In effect, the concept defines the circumstances in which an injured state becomes entitled to redress for damage suffered.[49] To date, there is no exhaustive multilateral treaty setting out the rules of state responsibility – however, articulating a comprehensive series of provisions on the subject was on the agenda of the International Law Commission for 45 years. A measure of success was only recently achieved, following the steps taken by James Crawford as Special Rapporteur during the 1990s.[50] This difficulty seems to have arisen due to the absence of adjudicative or enforcement mechanisms prior to the 20th century.[51]

The impact of the 'Draft Articles on the Responsibility of States for Internationally Wrongful Acts' (hereinafter, the Draft Articles)[52] on the doctrine of state responsibility has yet to be fully assessed: however, early indications are that they are perceived by the international community as a useful codification of customary international law.[53]

Subjects covered by the Draft Articles include the general principles of state responsibility, attribution of conduct to a state, breaches of international obligations, responsibility of a state in connection to an activity of another state, defences to breaches of international obligations, the implementation and content of a state's international responsibility, legitimate responses to breaches of international obligations (known as 'countermeasures'), and the matter of reparations.

There is a clear North/South aspect to the questions canvassed above. Developing countries have not readily conceded that customary international law provides for the same limitations on expropriation as are asserted by Western lawyers. A number of developing country host states applied the Calvo Doctrine named after an Argentine jurist.[54] The Calvo Doctrine called for the

---

[49] J Currie, C Forcese, and V Oosterveld, *International Law: Doctrine, Practice and Theory* (2007) 761.

[50] D Caron, 'The ILC Articles on State Responsibility: The Paradoxical Relationship between Form and Authority' (2002) 96 AJIL 857; and J Crawford, *The International Law Commission's Articles on State Responsibility: Introduction, Text and Commentaries* (2002).

[51] See *Case Concerning the Factory at Chorzów (Claim for Indemnity) (Germany v Poland), Merits* (1928) PCIJ (Ser A) No 13, at para 29.

[52] Available at <http://untreaty.un.org/ilc/texts/instruments/english/draft%20articles/9_6_2001.pdf> accessed 14 June 2008.

[53] See Responsibility of States for Internationally Committed Wrongful Acts, UNGA Res 59/35, UN GAOR, 59 Sess, UN Doc A/Res/59/35, commending the Draft Articles and soliciting submissions on potential improvements.

[54] C Calvo, *Le Droit International Théoretique et Pratiqué* (5th edn, 1896).

same treatment for foreign and domestic investors.[55] In 1974, similar principles were included in the New International Economic Order requiring that the courts of the host country should determine compensation with regard to expropriations.[56]

C. Treaty Descriptions of Expropriation Norms

Because of the differing views under customary law, it would be natural to try and clarify the meaning of expropriation within treaty instruments. However, the opposing interests are inevitably aiming for differing effects and ambit of the norms. Hence, no optimal models have been developed. Different treaty instruments adopt different articulations of the expropriation norm. Many simply refer to the concept without further articulation. A treaty will generally indicate that investments should not be expropriated or nationalized either directly or indirectly. It might broaden the proscription to 'measures tantamount to expropriation or nationalization'. BITs will also commonly indicate that the expropriation may only be for a 'public purpose'; it must be in accordance with 'due process of law'; it must apply in 'a non-discriminatory manner'; and must be based 'upon payment of prompt, adequate and effective compensation'. The reference to adequate, effective, and prompt compensation, known as the Hull Formula, can be traced to a number of early awards.[57]

While it is difficult to negotiate optimal definitions, another approach is to utilize a unilateral declaration or understanding at the time of acceding to or ratifying a convention. It may be difficult to determine whether a particular statement is merely a declaration or in fact constitutes a reservation. If it is merely a declaration, there is then a question of what legal implications it has. While there is uncertainty, it is unlikely that a unilateral declaration has any significant legal effect. Agreed Understandings, as recently used by the United States, would either have direct status as legal norms or would be evidence of intended meanings under a purposive approach to interpretation as allowed for under the Vienna Convention. Their importance would be enhanced where the Treaty expressly outlines their status as integral. Article 15.26 of the US-Singapore FTA is an important provision allowing for limitations on expropriation powers. It indicates that letters exchanged on the day of conclusion of the agreement shall form an integral part of the

---

[55] K Lipstein, 'The Place of the Calvo Clause in International Law' (1945) British Yearbook of International Law 130.

[56] Charter of Economic Rights and Duties of States, Art 2(2)(c), GA Res 3281, UN GAOR, 29th Sess, Supp (No 1) 3, 5, UN Doc A/9 559 (1974). These principles do not have the force of law and the proposition was not accepted in *Texaco Overseas Petroleum Co v Libya International Arbitral Tribunal*, Award on the Merits, 19 January 1977, (1978) 17 ILM 1.

[57] US-Norway Arbitration Award, 13 October 1922 (1918) 1 RIAA 307; and *Case Concerning German Interests in Upper Silesia*, PCIJ Series A, Nos 7, 9, 17, 19 (1926–9).

agreement. Letters were exchanged in relation to customary international law and expropriation, amongst other things.

Where the letter exchanges are concerned, the letter exchange of 6 May 2003 indicates that the expropriation Article is intended to reflect customary international law. It further indicates that an action or a series of actions by a party cannot constitute an expropriation unless it interferes with a tangible or intangible property right or property interest in an investment. This would be important to ensure that claims cannot be made about *potential* investment interests.

Comments are also made about indirect expropriation. The letter indicates that this requires a case-by-case, fact-based inquiry. Factors to be considered include:

- the economic impact of the government action, although the fact that an action or series of actions by a party has an adverse effect on the economic value of an investment, standing alone, does not establish that an indirect expropriation has occurred;
- the extent to which the government action interferes with distinct, reasonable investment-backed expectations; and
- the character of the government action.

Except in rare circumstances, non-discriminatory regulatory actions by a party that are designed and applied to protect legitimate public welfare objectives, such as public health, safety, and the environment, do not constitute indirect expropriation.

The expropriation provision in the US-Singapore FTA is also limited, in the sense that it only applies to a covered investment, which means an existing investment. Potential access to a market would not fit within the US-Singapore FTA definition of covered investments. The Article does not apply to compulsory licences or certain other intellectual property rights under the WTO TRIPS Agreement.

V. Analysis of the Jurisprudence and Its Human Rights Implications

As has been noted, two conflicting factors need to be reconciled in finding some consistent approach to the notion of regulatory takings. On the one hand, general tax and regulatory measures not specific to a particular investment must be available to governments from time to time. All persons operating within a particular market accept this as an inevitable risk of business. On the other hand, the decision to make longer-term and expensive investments inevitably arises after significant negotiations and discussions where reasonable expectations may arise either expressly or impliedly about likely future behaviour. In addition, such negotiations are conducted against a backdrop of traditional government practices that also impact on these expectations as to likely future conduct.

It is important to consider the jurisprudence in terms of the principles postulated, the outcomes, and also the trends in reasoning and methodology. It is important that this historical context is understood as it greatly impacts on an analysis of the position of expropriations in international law. In addition, because the decisions of any investment arbitration might be based on one of many thousands of treaties together with the interplay of the treaty with other sources of law, the line distinguishing whether an arbitral award is *lex specialis* or *lex generalis* is a blurry one. When combined with tribunal decisions to the effect that the interpretation of such provisions requires the interpretation of customary international law at the time when the treaty came into effect,[58] this has the outcome that the technical impact that a treaty decision might have on the broader meaning of terms is extremely complex.[59]

To some, *Methanex* has restored an appropriate balance. In analysing the various hypotheses, this section will turn first to some general observations, outline the results in key cases prior to *Methanex* and some scholarly observations about them, examine the impact of *Methanex*, if any, on subsequent jurisprudence and then make some concluding observations.

Before addressing the cases in the context of human rights issues, it is important not to confuse the question of compensation with the question of whether investor rights prevent governmental policy making for just outcomes. For wealthy developed countries at least, as long as they are willing to pay the compensation, they are free to regulate as they wish, even if an expansive approach is taken with regard to the expropriation norms. It may be different where developing countries are concerned, if the inability to pay compensation leads to regulatory chill effects. Some comments are primarily concerned with the compensation question and should be seen in that context. For example, Paulsson and Douglas postulate as a non-exhaustive guiding principle that 'the prohibition against indirect expropriation should protect legitimate expectations of the investor based on specific undertakings or representations by the Host State upon which the investor has reasonably relied'.[60] However, the presence of a legitimate expectation by a private individual may be a valid reason for compensation, but would never be a reason to bar governments from meritorious legislative activities. There are also difficult evidentiary questions with legitimate expectations tests. By what evidence is this to be determined, subjective or objective or both? What would make such expectations reasonable or otherwise?

---

[58] *Mondev International Ltd v United States*, ICSID Case No ARB(AF)/99/2, Award, 11 October 2002, 42 ILM 85 (2003).

[59] S Subedi, 'The Challenge of Reconciling the Competing Principles within the Law of Foreign Investment with Special Reference to the Recent Trend in the Interpretation of the term Expropriation' (2006) 49 International Lawyer 121, 132.

[60] Paulsson and Douglas, n 44 above, 157.

For example, in a world that is becoming ever more concerned with climate and environmental issues, when would it ever be reasonable to presume that future governments will not raise environmental standards in a way that diminishes the value of investment decisions?

Here there is some degree of convergence in practice between ECJ,[61] WTO, and investment arbitration practices. Article XX of the GATT 1994 Agreement provides that measures are required to be 'necessary' and non-discriminatory. Non-violation, nullification, and impairment norms in WTO jurisprudence look to legitimate expectations.[62] What is less clear in the WTO context is whether the dividing line is based on proportionality and appropriate balancing of trade and environmental norms or whether there is a trade bias in the jurisprudence.

Where the arbitral experiences of NAFTA are concerned, while they are not large in number, they have been highly contentious, in many cases dealing with environmental measures that are asserted to have significantly affected the commercial viability of actual or prospective investments. It is still relatively early in the development of that jurisprudence. It is also difficult to be fully appraised of the experiences as arbitration is essentially confidential and there is no reliable source from which to identify the number of claims that have been made where these are not fully pursued. As always, the mere potential for bringing claims has political significance. The amounts sought as damages are extremely large and the types of state laws being challenged go to the very heart of traditional state regulatory behaviour.

With these caveats in mind, the reality is that treaty jurisprudence refers to itself extensively, so in tracing the meaning of 'expropriation' we may accept that these decisions are of significance. Some of the literature implies that until *Methanex*, discussed below, there was a trend towards allowing indirect takings claims.[63] Much of the commentary tended to be about NAFTA claims. Critical perspectives raised the hypothesis that this was detrimental to the promotion of human rights as it impacted on governmental regulatory powers.

Human-rights-focused NGOs, notably Oxfam, have characterized the current pattern of growth in both international trade and FDI, in particular that underpinned by the presence of BITs, as anathema to the freedom of developing

---

[61] See Case 78/77 *Luhrs v Hauptzollamt Hamburg-Jonas* [1978] ECR 169. See also the Court of First Instance, Case T-94/00 *Rica Foods (Free Zone) NV v Commission* [2002] ECR I-901; and Case C-334/99 *Germany v Commission* [2003] ECR I-1139.

[62] TP Stewart (ed), *The GATT: Uruguay Round: A Negotiating History (1986–1992), Vol. II: Commentary* (1993) 2785–2786.

[63] See, eg *Metalclad Corp v Mexico*, ICSID Case No ARB (AF)/97/1, Final Award, 30 August 2000, 40 ILM 36; and *SD Myers v Canada*, Final Award on the Merits, 40 ILM 1408. See also J Lawrence, 'Chicken Little Revisited: NAFTA Regulatory Expropriations after Methanex' (2006) 41 Georgia Law Review 261, 280.

countries' governments to set optimal policy for the promotion of genuine development and, thus, the protection of economic and social human rights:

Bilateral investment treaties undermine the ability of host governments to effectively regulate foreign direct investment (FDI) to support economic development ... Developing countries are entering new agreements in the expectation that FDI will increase as a result, but there is no evidence that this is the case ... African countries have between them signed over 1,000 bilateral investment treaties, but receive less than four per cent of global FDI ...

FTAs and BITs have upset this balance [between the prohibition on direct expropriation and the ability of governments to make routine policy] by radically extending the rights of foreign investors and severely undermining the rights of governments and their citizens.[64]

Organizations like the International Institute for Sustainable Development (IISD) are less equivocal in their position regarding the impact of BITs on developing countries' capacity to pursue domestic policy objectives:

Certainly, there is significant scope for foreign investors to challenge human rights inspired measures imposed by host states. Host states which face such disputes should note that the arbitration process will often permit them to advert to their other international legal obligations, notably international human rights treaties, in an effort to defend against investor claims.[65]

The debate between human rights, free trade, FDI, and development discourses is far from simple. The human rights critiques of FDI growth do not enjoy a position undisturbed by critical interrogation themselves. As such, a prudent consideration of the human rights/FDI interface needs to maintain an awareness of this multi-faceted interplay of values and discourses. For example, as noted above, Phillip Alston takes issue with what he sees as an ongoing malaise within the push to recognize ever more and varied interests as human rights. This malaise is characterized by a lack of procedural regularity and rigour in the recognition of interests as human rights with the effect of devaluing the human rights currency, rather than 'enrich[ing] significantly the overall coverage provided by existing rights'.[66]

As one example of these tensions, Alston sees the critical response of the human rights community to the Millennium Development Goals as a rejection of the most significant current development initiative, and says that this

---

[64] E Jones, 'Signing Away the Future: How Trade And Investment Agreements Between Rich And Poor Countries Undermine Development', Oxfam Briefing Paper (March 2007), available at <http://www.oxfam.org/en/files/bp101_regional_trade_agreements_0703/download> accessed 14 June 2008.
[65] LE Peterson and K Gray, 'International Human Rights in Bilateral Investment Treaties and in Investment Treaty Arbitration', International Institute for Sustainable Development (2003), available at <http://www.iisd.org/pdf/2003/investment_int_human_rights_bits.pdf>.
[66] P Alston, 'Conjuring Up New Human Rights: A Proposal for Quality Control' (1984) 78 AJIL 607, 614.

approach fails to recognize the common objectives of both agendas. Alston suggests that this is the result of an overly prescriptive attitude of the human rights community and its failure to prioritize its concerns and effectively engage with the development agenda.[67]

For Koskenniemi and Leino, the often antipathetic relationship between the human rights community and international economic bodies and the attendant institutional struggle which pits two distinct universalist logics against one another is symptomatic of the competing efforts to reshape the international institutional hierarchy in the face of the increasing fragmentation of international law.[68]

Yet, against this backdrop, to regard the trend of expansion of investor rights as a steady one would be mistaken. Even within the confines of a single treaty such as NAFTA and even within a relatively short space of time under it, the definitions of what may or may not be expropriation were potentially irreconcilable.

A number of cases are illustrative. In *Metalclad*, the tribunal awarded damages to that company when the Mexican Government blocked its operation of a waste treatment facility through additional permit requirements that were refused and through designation of the relevant area as an ecological protection zone. Establishing new permit requirements breached the duty of fair and equitable treatment, while the establishment of the zone was held to constitute an expropriation.[69] The reasoning was contentious as it basically relied on a view that the provincial authority had exceeded its powers. The tribunal awarded Metalclad US$16.7 million, being the value of its investment plus interest. The *Metalclad* decision concluded that:

expropriation under NAFTA includes not only open, deliberate and acknowledged takings of property, such as outright seizure or formal or obligatory transfer of title in favour of the Host State, but also covert or incidental interference with the use of property which has the effect of depriving the owner, in whole or in significant part, of the use or reasonably-to-be-expected economic benefit of property even if not necessarily to the obvious benefit of the Host State.[70]

Mexico challenged the award before the Supreme Court of British Columbia in the arbitral situs. The Court overturned the tribunal's finding as to Article 1105. In the Court's view, there was no transparency obligation under Article 1105. The Court overturned one aspect of the expropriation finding, but upheld the conclusion that the ecological decree amounted to expropriation. Although

[67] P Alston, 'Ships Passing in the Night: The Current State of the Human Rights and Development Debate Seen Through the Lens of the Millennium Development Goals' (2005) 27 Human Rights Quarterly 755.
[68] M Koskenniemi and P Leino, 'Fragmentation of International Law? Postmodern Anxieties' (2002) 15 Leiden Journal of International Law 553, 570.   [69] *Metalclad*, n 63 above.
[70] Ibid., at para 103.

the Court thought that the definition extracted above was extremely broad, it was a question of law not reviewable.[71]

Similarly, in *Myers v Canada*, a tribunal awarded damages where the Canadian Government imposed an export ban on the claimant who was seeking to export certain waste products to a US processing facility. One possible justification for the decision was evidence to the effect that the intent was to favour Canadian competitors rather than environmental protection. The tribunal in the *Myers v Canada* case even went so far as to place the burden on the state to defend the necessity of its regulations before the tribunal.[72] In a practical sense, if there is no obvious and reasonable environmental benefit, at the very least the onus on the state should be higher.

In *Azinian v Mexico*, a tribunal sought to limit the ambit of the expropriation norm when rejecting a claim. DESONA was a Mexican corporation with American shareholders. The Mexican city of Naucalpan entered into a contract with DESONA in relation to the treatment of the city's solid waste. A dispute arose as to the performance of DESONA under the agreement. The contract was cancelled. Challenges were made before Mexico's State Administrative Tribunal, which upheld the city's right to cancel the contract. Appeals to the Superior Chamber of the Administrative Tribunal and to the Federal Circuit Court affirmed the decision. The American shareholders then sought compensation under NAFTA arguing breaches of Articles 1105 and 1110, claiming US\$20 million. The panel rejected the claim. The panel held that the city was entitled to rely on the *decisions of the Mexican courts* unless those decisions could be disregarded at the international level, that is, unless the decisions violated NAFTA – for example, by denial of justice.

The tribunal also made a number of comments seeking to limit the ambit of the expropriation provision. It suggested that expropriations tend to involve the deprivation of ownership rights. Regulations generally provide for a lesser interference. It considered that such a distinction 'screens out most potential cases of complaints concerning economic intervention by a state and reduces the risk that governments will be subject to claims as they go about their business of managing public affairs'. The tribunal said that:

it is a fact of life everywhere that individuals may be disappointed in their dealings with public authorities and disappointed yet again when national courts reject their complaints ... NAFTA was not intended to provide foreign investors with blanket protection from this kind of disappointment, and nothing in its terms so provides.[73]

Similarly, in *Pope & Talbot, Inc*, a tribunal found that regulatory measures taken by the Canadian Government did not amount to expropriation under NAFTA,

---

[71] *Mexico v Metalclad Corp*, 2001 BCSC 664.   [72] *SD Myers*, n 63 above.

[73] *Robert Azinian and ors (DESONA de CV) v Mexico*, Award, 1 November 1999, (2000) 39 ILM 537, at para 83; and *SD Myers*, n 63 above, at para 266.

stating: 'While it may sometimes be uncertain whether a particular interference with business activities amounts to an expropriation, the test is whether that interference is sufficiently restrictive to support a conclusion that the property has been "taken" from the owner.'[74]

While the expropriation claim was rejected, the tribunal agreed that access to the US market was a property interest protected under NAFTA. The claimant conceded that the action was not an expropriation, but was a 'measure tantamount to expropriation'. The tribunal referred to section 712 of the Third Restatement of the Foreign Relations Law of the United States in rejecting a Canadian argument that all regulatory measures should be outside Article 1110. The Restatement indicates that a state is responsible for expropriation in the following circumstances:

[State responsibility] applies not only to avowed expropriations in which the government formally takes title to property, but also to other actions of the government that have the effect of 'taking' the property, in whole or in large part, outright or in stages ('creeping expropriation'). A state is responsible as for an expropriation of property under Subsection (1) when it subjects alien property to taxation, regulation, or other action that is confiscatory, or that prevents or unreasonably interferes with, or unduly delays, effective enjoyment of an alien's property ...

The tribunal considered that the determination 'may rest on the degree of interference with the property interest ... the degree to which the government action deprives the investor of effective control over the enterprise' and whether the measure renders it 'impossible for the firm to operate at a profit'.[75] The *Pope & Talbot, Inc* tribunal was not prepared to adopt a blanket exception for police powers:

Regulations can indeed be exercised in a way that would constitute creeping expropriation ... Indeed, much creeping expropriation could be conducted by regulation, and a blanket exception for regulatory measures would create a gaping loophole in international protections against expropriation.[76]

The current leading attitude toward expropriation is represented in the 2005 decision of *Methanex*, again under NAFTA. It is suggested that this decision confirms a return to a more conservative interpretation of what actions constitute an illegal expropriation. Further, it expressly recognizes the police powers of states to regulate environmental and public health concerns and attempts to provide a guiding test that might deter more extreme claims.

The case arose when the state of California banned the use of a petroleum additive of which Methanex manufactured a component. The additive (MTBE) was regarded as a potential groundwater contaminant; Methanex brought an

---

[74] *Pope & Talbot, Inc v Canada*, Interim Award, 26 June 2000, (2002) 122 ILR 316, at para 102.   [75] Ibid., at para 99.
[76] Ibid.

action for some US$970 million, alleging that this was a regulatory expropriation of their assets, relying heavily on the reasoning in the *Metalclad* and *SD Meyers* decisions referred to above.[77] The tribunal dismissed the claim thus:

[A]s a matter of general international law, a non-discriminatory regulation for a public purpose, which is enacted in accordance with due process and, which affects, inter alios, a foreign investor or investment is not deemed expropriatory and compensable unless specific commitments had been given by the regulating government to the then putative foreign investor contemplating investment that the government would refrain from such regulation.[78]

The tribunal distinguished the *Metalclad* case on the facts, the latter being based on a finding that there was such a commitment and also because the process of promulgating the legislation in *Metalclad* was seen as decidedly suboptimal.

When viewed alongside *Azinian* and *Pope & Talbot*, the better view is that *Methanex* in fact forms part of a string of such cases in recent times coming out of the international investment tribunals which peel back the extensive privileges that had been granted to foreign investors. The Iran-US Claims Tribunal in *Sedco, Inc v Iran*[79] recognized a 'police powers' exception thus: '[It is a] principle of international law that a state is not liable for economic injury which is a consequence of bona fide "regulation" within the accepted police powers of states.'

A similar exception was recognized in *Tecmed v Mexico*[80]:

[T]he principle that the state's exercise of its sovereign powers within the framework of its police power may cause economic damage to those subject to its powers as administrator without entitling them to any compensation whatsoever is undisputable.

Another method through which a fairer balancing of rights is to be achieved besides a blanket carve-out for police powers is the greater emphasis of *proportionality* in considering whether a regulatory measure is an expropriation. The tribunal in *Tecmed* stated:

[We must] consider, in order to determine if [regulatory measures] are to be characterized as expropriatory, whether such actions or measures are proportional to the public interest presumably protected thereby and to the protection legally granted to investments, taking into account that the significance of such impact has a key role upon deciding the proportionality.

---

[77] K Dougherty, 'Methanex v. United States: The Realignment of NAFTA Chapter 11 with Environmental Regulation' (2007) 27 Northwestern Journal of International Law and Business 735, 746.   [78] *Methanex v US*, ICSID Case No ARB/98/3, Pt IV, ch D, 7.
[79] *Sedco, Inc v Iran*, 9 Iran-US Claims Tribunal Reports 248, at para 275.
[80] *Técnicas Medioambientales Tecmed SA v Mexico*, ICSID Case No ARB(AF)/00/2, Award, 29 May 2003, (2004) 43 ILM 133, at para 119.

In determining whether a measure was proportional, the tribunal took into account several factors[81]:

- the legitimate expectations of the investor at the time they made the investment;
- the importance of the interest that the regulations seek to protect;
- the impact of the regulations; and
- whether the measure will impact unfairly on a particular investor or group of investors and thus violate the requirement for fair and equal treatment.

Jurisprudence subsequent to *Methanex* primarily shows deference to these norms and, in the context of this volume, allows for the conclusion that arbitral tribunals will not generally interpret and apply anti-expropriation norms in a way in which unduly interferes with human rights. On the other hand, there is still sufficient divergence in views between tribunals, which promote at least uncertainty and suggest that it may still be some time until settled principles are broadly accepted and would be accepted as customary law. Further, all of the problems of standing and applicable law, where human rights proponents are concerned, are not resolved by this line of principle.

Turning to the subsequent cases, in *Vivendi v Argentina*[82] the tribunal made the statement that the intent of the state in instituting a regulatory measure is of secondary importance to the effect that it has on the investor. It quotes the decision in *Tecmed* extensively and with approval (although not on any directly relevant points). In *Parkerings-Compagniet AS v Republic of Lithuania (Lithuania)*,[83] the tribunal offers its own definition of indirect expropriation.

De facto expropriation (or indirect expropriation) is not clearly defined in treaties, but can be understood as the negative effect of government measures on the investor's property rights, which does not involve a transfer of property but a deprivation of the enjoyment of the property.[84]

It goes on to quote the *Metalclad* definition extracted above with approval. It should be noted that the case dealt not with the introduction of regulatory measures, but with a government's breach of contract with a company.

The tribunal in *MTD Equity Sdn Bhd (Malaysia) v Chile*[85] offers some criticism of the *Tecmed* decision thus:

---

[81] S Shill, 'Do Investment Treaties Chill Unilateral State Regulation to Mitigate Climate Change?' (2007) 24(5) Journal of International Arbitration 469, 473.

[82] *Compania de Aguas de Aconquija SA and Vivendi Universal v Argentina*, ICSID Case No ARB/97/3-20, Award, 20 August 2007.

[83] *Parkerings-Compagniet AS v Lithuania*, ICSID Case No ARB/05/8, Award, 11 September 2007.   [84] Ibid., at para 437.

[85] *MTD Equity Sdn Bhd & MTD Chile SA v Chile*, ICSID Case No ARB/01/7, Decision on Annulment of the ad hoc committee, 21 March 2007.

[T]he TECMED Tribunal's apparent reliance on the foreign investor's expectations as the source of the host State's obligations (such as the obligation to compensate for expropriation) is questionable. The obligations of the host State towards foreign investors derive from the terms of the applicable investment treaty and not from any set of expectations investors may have or claim to have. A tribunal which sought to generate from such expectations a set of rights different from those contained in or enforceable under the BIT might well exceed its powers, and if the difference were material might do so manifestly.[86]

The trouble with this logic is that it fails to note that the relevance of the expectations arguably emanate from the treaty itself, simply because that is seen as a possible limit on the plain meaning of indirect expropriation, if the latter term covers diminution in worth as well as physical taking. This is not to say that *Tecmed* is correct, but the criticism in *MTD* is simplistic.

Siemens AG v Argentina[87] contains extensive and technical commentary on when a series of actions can be aggregated to form a 'creeping expropriation' – these are not included owing to length and specificity to the facts of the case. It also states that the intention of a government is irrelevant to whether or not an action is expropriation.[88]

In *Saluca*, the tribunal held that 'a State does not commit an expropriation and is thus not liable to pay compensation to a dispossessed alien investor when it adopts general regulations that are commonly accepted as within the policy power of States'.[89] Similarly, in *Sedco, Inc v Iran*,[90] the tribunal stated: '[It is a] principle of international law that a State is not liable for economic injury which is a consequence of bona fide "regulation" with the accepted police powers of States.'

The trend back via *Methanex* has been suggested to be a consequence of the sudden realization by developed nations, which have a disproportionate share of the power in BIT negotiations, that the broad rights they have advocated for foreign investors could be equally restrictive on their own ability to self-regulate as they are in developing nations.[91] NAFTA allowed for significant disputes between developed country interests. Even if this is the cause, governments concerned for their own unconstrained policy space act as proxies for human rights advocates, although not necessarily in an optimal fashion.

Another possible explanation is that the different outcomes and comments arise either through different biases by arbitrators for and against more or less expansive norms and, secondly, through factual distinctions between cases where legitimate expectations were found in favour of the investor and those where this was not the case. At times, the distinctions themselves will be open to criticism.

---

[86] Ibid., at para 67.

[87] *Siemens AG v Argentina*, ICSID Case No ARB/02/08, Award, 6 February 2007.

[88] Ibid., at para 270. See also the discussion of *Saluka* in ch 19 in this volume, citing TRG van Banning, *The Human Right to Property* (2002) 5.

[89] *Saluka Investments BV v Czech Republic* (*Saluka* case), PCA, UNCITRAL, Partial Award, 17 March 2006, paras 284, 302.   [90] *Sedco*, n 79 above, at 275.

[91] Subedi, n 59 above.

For example, Paulsson and Douglas note that the tribunal in *Feldman*[92] rejected the challenge to a tax change, holding that tax laws are generally subject to change. The tribunal in *Goetz*[93] took a contrary decision where the investor had sought express confirmation that its mining activities qualified for tax and customs exemptions. The authors rightly note that a confirmation of existing application is not in any way a promise of continuance of such regimes.[94]

Comments by authors such as Wälde and Kolo point to the arbitration biases being more about the system per se than about the nature of the adjudicator and their view as to the essential character of investment arbitration. To the extent that it is seen as private consent-based arbitration within a commercial context, there is more likelihood of compensation being awarded. To the extent that foreign investment is seen as an activity with inherent risks of changes in governmental regulatory practices, there would be a greater tendency to leave that to the investor and its avenues of political risk insurance. Wälde and Kolo suggest that international arbitrators tend towards providing compensation in the face of new environmental regulations, whereas traditionally the European Court of Human Rights and the European Court of Justice gave greater degrees of deference to state public policy and safety concerns.[95] The authors' comments follow early NAFTA Chapter 11 practice in *Metalclad* and *Myers v Canada*. They indicate that the proper test for compensation following expropriation should be whether the regulation is proportionate and necessary for a legitimate purpose, whether the law and its application is discriminatory, whether there is a breach of an agreement, investment treaty, or legitimate investment-backed expectations, and whether interference with legitimate expectations is based on a reasonable adjustment of the regulations to evolving and accepted environmental standards.

Paulsson and Douglas also rightly point out that comments by tribunals may be nothing more than indications of the potential application of norms rather than elaboration of any dividing test.[96] They also argue that tribunals have wrongly conflated two distinct questions: first, whether there is in fact a taking, and, second, whether it meets the legal standards of expropriation as defined in the particular treaty norm.[97] Such analysis also confuses questions of fact and law.[98]

While the latter is important, of more significance for the purposes of this chapter is the need for the jurisprudence to find core principles that establish sensible criteria to distinguish between acceptable and unacceptable interference with

---

[92] *Feldman v Mexico*, ICSID Case No ARB(AF)/99/1, Award, 16 December 2002, 7 ICSID Reports 341.
[93] *Goetz v Burundi*, ICSID Case No ARB/95/3, Award, 10 February 1999, 6 ICSID Reports 5.
[94] Paulsson and Douglas, n 44 above, 155–156.
[95] See generally T Wälde and A Kolo, 'Environmental Regulation, Investment Protection and Regulatory Taking in International Law' (2001) 50 ICLQ 811.
[96] Paulsson and Douglas, n 44 above, 149.   [97] Ibid., 148.
[98] Ibid. citing BH Weston, '"Constructive Takings" under International Law: A Modest Foray into the Problem of "Creeping Expropriation"' (1975) 16 Virginia Journal of International Law 103, 112.

investments so that governments have a clear and appropriate legislative mandate. While recent cases have still made potentially conflicting statements, the subsequent jurisprudence suggests that the *Methanex* test will be largely followed, save for the tendency of individual tribunals to add their own nuances and critical comments from time to time. At the very least, the extreme criticisms of the adverse impact of expropriation norms on human rights should be confidently rejected.

VI. Exceptions for Human Rights and Related Purposes

There are a number of environmental exception models that have been utilized. For example, NAFTA Article 1114.1 indicates that:

Nothing in this Chapter shall be construed to prevent a Party from adopting, maintaining or enforcing any measure otherwise consistent with this Chapter that it considers appropriate to ensure that investment activity in its territory is undertaken in a manner sensitive to environmental concerns.

The phrase 'otherwise consistent with this Chapter' is highly problematic. If a measure is consistent with the Chapter, why is there a need for Article 1114.1? Is it to operate as an exception or is it simply a matter of general clarification?

One substantive possibility is a public interest exception supporting regulatory interference with investment rights. The advantage of this is that it would give a state government a wide field of potential action. The disadvantage is that the concept is vague and hard to apply in concrete-fact situations. Private arbitrators would be asked to rule on the public interest.

The negotiating parties could also indicate that laws and regulations of general application do not constitute expropriation. Another possibility is to exempt fully particular categories of regulatory endeavour such as environment and resource conservation. Another approach is to look at the intent of the regulation and provide that measures are only open to challenge if their aim and effect is to discriminate, expropriate, or otherwise adversely affect foreign investors. That would be a significant shift in legal principles. There is currently a mismatch between a policy ideal which might try and distinguish between protectionist measures and those undertaken for legitimate non-commercial reasons and the jurisprudence in NAFTA, which in some cases says that motive for a measure is not a relevant consideration – a view consistent with customary international law.

VII. The Role of Adjudication

As is often the case in international economic law, it is impossible to draft rules with such precision that they will provide absolute 'bright line' guidance at the margins. Instead, reliance must be placed to some degree on sensible responses by adjudicators to the treatment of such rules. Where this occurs, however, a number of other problems arise. If adjudicators cannot apply consistent principles, that is itself a problem, as consistency is a desirable aspiration of any system of justice. It also has an efficiency value as it helps to reduce transaction costs by giving clear signals to prospective investors and governments. Yet even a consistent response may not be a fair one and it may be inefficient for other reasons – for example, if it encourages a consistent misallocation of resources.

If the adjudicator is forced to take a key role, other major questions arise. Proper notions of separation of powers imply that the adjudicator must not be in effect making the rules, but simply finding a fair balance in the rules already agreed upon. That concern is heightened where international economic law is concerned as governments who cede certain rights through treaty negotiations do not wish to see adjudicators expand their obligations beyond those intended. In addition, only common lawyers are used to judges having the power to develop the law in significant ways through their rulings.

In some cases, the rules might verge on indeterminacy because there will be a difficulty in identifying the comparative benchmark. For example, particular problems may arise where an expropriation claim is based on what is alleged to be abusive taxation. Because there is no agreed base notion of an ideal tax, it is hard to determine when a fiscal measure could be described as abusive.[99] To exclude all fiscal measures simply because they are presumed to be just and necessary expropriations would allow scope for abusive behaviour. Nevertheless, attempts to distinguish between acceptable and non-acceptable practices are problematic.

Where international adjudication is concerned, there is also the problem of finding an adjudicatory model that is sufficiently neutral and respected to deal with cross-border disputes that typically bring together people with different legal cultures and even differing evidentiary, interpretative, and procedural values within dispute settlement regimes. These differences in values will be noticeable when cases deal with the more extreme arguments about indirect takings. It is difficult to establish a mechanism for this purpose that does not at least appear to be biased towards one end of the spectrum or the other, either pro-investment or pro-governmental restrictions. Any such biases, if evident, will impact significantly upon state rights to regulate in the face of investment protection obligations.

There is also a need to consider the likely magnitude and impact of cases. This depends in part on the legal culture of the other country involved in a bilateral arrangement. There is also the obvious question of whether challenges are likely to be successful. It should be expected that most extreme challenges would fail, although any dispute settlement system will inevitably see instances of unmeritorious or at least contentious results. While the likelihood of success is important, even unsuccessful claims can be politically damaging and costly from a political perspective. Uncertainty can easily deter governments from undertaking desired policy measures for fear of legal claims by foreign investors. This is commonly described as regulatory chill.

---

[99] G Alvarez and W Park, 'The New Face of Investment Arbitration: NAFTA Chapter 11' (2003) 28 (2) Yale Journal of International Law 365, 390.

This is potentially increased by an important difference between private party rights and inter-state actions. For example, where WTO type norms are concerned, these tend to call merely for prospective changes to the offending measure, although it is true that full reparation is the general norm in public international law. Private party rights lead to retrospective damages for the offending behaviour in nearly all cases. Governments which know that at worst they need to change an offending policy would feel less constrained on initial implementation than in cases where they know they could be liable for significant damages claims. This adds to the problem of regulatory chill.

These questions remind us that the ultimate utility of legal protection is generally dependent on the quality of legal mechanisms for establishing rights and the effectiveness of enforcement provisions dealing with resultant adjudicatory decisions.[100]

While private commercial arbitration is a natural response to problems of litigation against a sovereign, it raises potential problems. In the context of this chapter, perhaps the most significant is the ability of private and consent-based arbitral models to deal adequately with public law and public policy aspects of governmental regulation of investment practices. This is particularly so when there is a need to find a fair balance between the right to regulate, including the right and indeed obligation on governments to protect and promote human rights, and the right of private individuals to have investments not undermined by indirect means. It is particularly problematic when private arbitrators are asked to pass judgments on whether or not governmental fiscal measures are abusive. When arbitrators are asked to sit in judgment as to the circumstances when regulations become compensable takings, inevitably they are asked to consider questions as to the reasonableness of the policy and its proportionality to the area of concern. They are, thus, sitting in judgment on governmental policy development and initiatives.

This raises a question as to whether private adjudicators selected through arbitration processes are best suited to deal with these complex public-private issues, particularly where they impact upon human rights. Arbitration as a system emanated from a private consent-based paradigm, where the parties concerned were already in a commercial relationship and wished to resolve any future disputes speedily and in confidence, with adjudicators that they themselves saw as best suited to the task. That model does not sit easily with disputes which wholly or in part deal with alleged negative externalities on society at large or on significant disadvantaged groups within society, as is inevitably the case with human rights issues. More often than not, the proponents of human rights interests have no direct standing to represent their perspective, at most relying on the host state to act as proxy.

---

[100] On the other hand, it is important not to overrate the value of law within the political context of investor-state dispute resolution, particularly in countries that do not have a strong respect for the rule of law.

There is also the question of whether eminent arbitrators, who have developed their reputation in the field of private corporate disputes dealing primarily with contract and construction claims, are best suited to deal with non-discriminatory norms, fair dealing, and expropriation elements of international treaties together with the jurisdictional complexities as to the various international, national, and contract-based sources of law discussed in the following section. Of course, the ability of the parties to select appropriate experts enables them to deal with these concerns. However, the lack of standing for human rights proponents means that they are not part of that selection process. If human rights law is a key incidental element of the claims, the selections made might not have given enough weight to this area of expertise.

VIII. Conclusion

Human rights norms would rarely, if ever, call for expropriation without just compensation. Thus, the key question is what unintended impact FDI protection might have. Where states are involved in investment arbitration, it will inevitably be the case that political decisions are taken from time to time. Investors will respond to such behaviour by shifting their spheres of investment. Public condemnation of failure to follow the rule of law should add to the disincentives against such behaviour. While such instances are significant for the countries involved, a more systemic question is the degree to which international commercial arbitration per se can cope with the interplay of public and private norms and values in the setting of investment arbitration. Recent jurisprudence suggests that it can. Alvarez and Park also suggest that none of the Chapter 11 arbitrations has departed from traditional notions of customary international law.[101]

The jurisprudence from *Methanex* is to be preferred. Definitions merely based on investor expectations such as that applied in the *Metalclad* case create difficulties as they do not make reference to necessity, proportionality, or reasonableness. They do not address the balancing of competing entitlements. They have been criticized as going so far as to require a government to stand guarantor for the investor's return, something which clearly falls beyond the purview of a state's responsibilities.[102] 'Police-powers'-based definitions take into account a broader range of factors and are more likely to lead to a fair decision which adequately balances the interests of investors with those of state sovereignty.[103]

---

[101] Alvarez and Park, n 99 above, 379.   [102] Subedi, n 59 above, at 131–132.
[103] It is also interesting to compare this jurisprudence with the way in which WTO jurisprudence deals with the trade and human rights interface under the chapeau of GATT 1994, Art XX as mentioned above. Cases suggest that a reasonableness test should be imposed which in turn calls for some consideration of proportionality as a subset of a reasonable regulatory response.

On the other hand, the newer tests call for complex and contentious decisions on what is reasonable government policy by private arbitrators. When the protections are directed towards foreigners only, it is certainly contentious to have private arbitrators, deciding on the rights of private foreigners, to, at times, make across-the-board comments about the desirability of the policy. The key remains the compensation. Investment arbitration, unlike WTO norms, does not call for the measures to be removed. It simply calls for compensation. The human rights concern arises when a government cannot afford the compensation without cutting other important spending initiatives.

The point has previously been made that it is not only concluded cases or even actual cases that should raise concerns. Concerns about actual or potential experiences under investor-state dispute settlement can also impose a chilling effect on national initiatives. Even if tribunals will generally adopt conservative interpretations, in the short term at least, misguided corporate perceptions should be a cause of concern.

In addition, because of the ultimate need to resort to domestic courts for enforcement purposes, arbitration cannot effectively overcome extreme problems of political ill-will, corruption, and lack of respect for the rule of law.

An analysis of the NAFTA experiences suggests that the contentious cases brought did not depend on indirect expropriation being seen as a different concept to measures tantamount to expropriation, even though that was argued at times. The important issue to identify from an examination of NAFTA language and experiences is that, if there is a broad definition of investment, an understandable reference to indirect and equivalent measures in a world where government regulatory practices inevitably impact upon market values of investments, all coupled with private rights of action, the potential exists for similar claims being brought under other FTAs and BITs.

The same is even more so where investment is concerned, particularly given the NAFTA experiences in the expropriation disputes. It is inconceivable that all NAFTA parties would have signed that agreement in its current form if they were aware of the types of cases that were to be brought and the types of rulings that tribunals were to make. Those experiences and the NAFTA parties' attempts to make binding interpretive rulings all suggest that negotiators should work together to find mutually satisfactory mechanisms to ensure that, on the one hand, there are adequate protections for private investors, but, on the other, that the mechanisms do not unduly interfere with legitimate governmental aspirations either through actual cases, through threats of cases, or simply through the chilling effect of that potential.

14

The Fair and Equitable
Treatment Standard
and Human Rights Norms

Ioana Knoll-Tudor

I. Introduction

The fair and equitable treatment (FET) clause is found in most of the 2,000 bilateral investment treaties (BITs) signed between more than 170 countries in the world as well as in some multilateral and regional conventions. The clause came into the public spotlight when investors started to use the arbitration system relying on the FET in their claims. The arbitral tribunals were obliged to respond to claims in their awards; this, in turn, contributed to rendering public the discussion on the FET.[1] Given the generality of the clause, it was thought for a long time that the standard would be able to accommodate any claim that could not be qualified in a more specific manner. In time and with practice, however, arbitral tribunals managed to shape this standard to the extent that today FET is clearly attached to a number of situations, and more will certainly be added by future practice.

Recently, a new question arose in connection to the FET standard: how do human rights (HR) norms influence the FET? The question arose from existent case law where investment norms and HR norms complemented each other. The question arose therefore from practice; it is far from being a purely academic or hypothetical issue. This book is meant to contribute from different angles to the discussion on the recent and already very controversial relationship between investment law and HR norms.

This contribution will focus specifically on the FET standard and the scenarios in which it may interact with HR norms. It will discuss both situations that have already been encountered in case law, and constellations that may arise

---

[1] Although it is the *AAPL v Sri Lanka* award that made it procedurally possible for investors to bring a state in front of an international arbitral tribunal, claims under NAFTA popularized this type of claim. *Asian Agricultural Products Ltd v Sri Lanka* (*AAPL*), ICSID, ARB/87/3, Award, 27 June 1990.

in the future. Before proceeding with these situations, we will first analyse the FET standard in detail. The first part of this contribution will inquire into the conventional basis of the FET, studying the various drafting formulations found in the existing agreements and the situations in which the FET standard has already been applied. A survey of the standard would not be complete without a brief comment on the compensation awarded in the event of the state breaching the FET obligations. The compensation phase is important, in our opinion, because it represents more than a procedure to calculate the damages suffered by the investor: at this stage all interests at stake are rebalanced. The second part of this contribution will highlight the relationship between FET and HR norms by focusing on the applicability of HR norms in an arbitral context. Since other contributions to this book examine this in more depth, we will only provide a number of ideas regarding this aspect. The final part of this contribution will develop on the possible scenarios where FET and HR norms are likely to overlap, and on the options that arbitrators have when required to rule on them.

II. Diversity of Formulations in FET Clauses

The first treaties to refer to international law in connection with the protection of aliens and their property were the US treaties on Friendship, Commerce, and Navigation (FCN) signed in the post-World War I period. The terms 'equitable' and 'fair and equitable' treatment appeared in certain US FCN treaties[2] only after the failure of the negotiations on the Havana Charter. Most commentators believe that the provisions of the Havana Charter, although never ratified, served as an inspiration to many national and regional investment provisions.[3] The first modern bilateral investment treaty was signed between the Federal Republic of Germany and Pakistan in 1959.[4] Until the late 1980s, the Federal Republic of Germany was the leading state in the bilateral treaties' signature movement. Switzerland followed close behind, signing its first BIT in 1961 with Tunisia and now being among the countries that have the most well-developed web of BITs.

The FET standard is generally held to be a clause repeated identically in all BITs: this is a questionable perception that is not verified in practice. The 2003 UNCTAD 'World Investment Report' (WIR), while observing that 'the scope

---

[2] US FCN treaties with Ireland (1950), Greece (1954), Israel (1954), France (1960), Pakistan (1961), Belgium (1963), and Luxembourg (1963) contained express assurances that foreign persons, properties, enterprises, and other interests would receive 'equitable treatment', while others, including those with the Federal Republic of Germany, Ethiopia, and the Netherlands used the terms 'fair and equitable treatment' for a similar set of items involved in the foreign investment process.

[3] See RR Wilson, *United States Commercial Treaties and International Law* (1960) 120.

[4] The sensitivity of the Federal Republic towards investment protection is allegedly due to German investors losing their assets, in a number of countries, as the consequence of the two world wars.

and content of the BITs have become more standard over years',[5] adds that given the increasing number of BITs, 'the formulations of individual provisions remain varied'. The 2004 UNCTAD WIR is even more sceptical about the uniformity of BITs, since it reports that 'not all BITs are identical although they have much in common'.[6] An empirical research conducted on 358 BITs revealed that the existing FET clauses contain a number of variations that assign different meanings to the FET standard.[7]

FET appears in the body of the conventional text and sometimes also in its preambles. Without adding any substantive rights to those specifically stipulated in the operative paragraphs, the presence of FET in the preamble of a convention underlines the general tone of the treaty and reinforces its role in the body of the treaty. The most common drafting of a preamble that contains a FET reference creates a link between the standard and a stable framework for investment, the stimulation of the capital flow, and the intensification of economic cooperation. A sample of such a preamble is the one found mostly in the BITs signed by the United States and it reads: 'Agreeing that fair and equitable treatment of investment is desirable in order to maintain a stable framework for investment and maximum effective use of economic resources'.[8] The BITs signed by Argentina illustrate a different version of a FET mentioning preamble: 'Desiring to intensify economic cooperation to the mutual benefit of both countries and to maintain fair and equitable conditions for investments by investors of one Contracting Party in the territory of the other Contracting Party'.[9] These are the most significant variations in the drafting formulas of the FET preambles.

Concerning the body of these BITs, out of the 358 reviewed BITs, only 19 did not mention the FET standard either in their preambles or in their body-texts.

[5] UN Conference on Trade and Development (UNCTAD), 'World Investment Report, FDI Policies for Development: National and International Perspectives' (2003) 89.
[6] UN Conference on Trade and Development (UNCTAD), 'World Investment Report: The Shift towards Services' (2004) 224.
[7] In order to have the most accurate perception of these clauses, one has to survey more than 2,500 existing BITs and that is certainly a long and difficult task. We conducted a study on the basis of 358 BITs signed by 10 states (Argentina, Australia, Bangladesh, Canada, France, Japan, Romania, Saudi-Arabia, Switzerland, and the United States) representing an *échantillon* of the existing treaties. The research included BITs signed by: two developing countries, a developing country and a developed one, members of regional arrangements, such as NAFTA or MERCOSUR, Argentina, which is currently involved in a growing number of ICSID disputes, Eastern European countries that have recently become an important destination for foreign direct investment, and also, increasingly, respondents in ICSID disputes. See I Tudor, *The Fair and Equitable Treatment Standard in the International Law of Foreign Investment* (2008).
[8] This phrasing can be found in the following BITs that were part of our study: US-Argentina, US-Armenia, US-Bulgaria, US-Czech and Slovak Republics, US-Democratic Republic of Congo, US-Ecuador, US-Estonia, US-Grenada, US-Jamaica, US-Kazakhstan, US-Kyrgyzstan, US-Latvia, US-Mongolia, US-Moldova, US-Romania, US-Sri Lanka, US-Tunisia, US-Turkey, US-Lithuania, US-Cameroon, US-Poland, and US-Russian Federation, and France-Dominican Rep.
[9] This phrasing can be found in the BITs signed by Argentina with Finland, the Netherlands, New Zealand, and Sweden and also in the Romania-Sweden BIT.

However, five out of the 10 countries studied did sign at least one BIT without a FET clause, which shows that the absence of a FET clause is not an isolated phenomenon.[10]

The BITs that contain a FET clause may be divided into three main categories: the first category is composed of the BITs that mention the FET standard alone, the second of those that mention FET in combination with a reference to international law, and the third of those that mention the FET together with other standards of treatment, mainly the Most Favoured Nation and/or the National Treatment, but also the 'full protection and security' obligation.

The first category of drafting formulations is the one mentioning the FET alone, without any further indication, as in the Argentina-Australia BIT: 'Each Contracting Party shall at all times ensure fair and equitable treatment to investments.'[11] Some FET clauses contain engagements from the contracting parties to 'ensure' or 'guarantee' a treatment in accordance to FET. In other words, the host state undertakes to apply all of the necessary measures in order to allow investors to enjoy their rights not only de jure but also de facto.

The second category of formulations is the one where the FET obligation is complemented by a reference to international law. The standard provision of this category is the one found in the Canadian BITs:

Each Contracting Party shall accord investments or returns of investors of the other Contracting Party:

(a) fair and equitable treatment in accordance with principles of international law, and

(b) full protection and security.[12]

The combination of the FET obligation with the respect of international law adds a useful guideline for the interpretation of FET and justifies the frequent reliance by the parties and by arbitrators on provisions of general international law. As previously mentioned, only Canadian treaties contain a reference to both the FET standard and international law, without any other mention. In addition to this category, the reference to international law is found also combined with examples of acts contrary to the FET and together with a reference to 'full protection and security'. The decision of the contracting parties to offer in their BIT a

---

[10] Japan and Romania, for example, signed more than one BIT without a FET clause. This is the case for the BITs signed by Romania with China, Denmark, Egypt, Germany, Ghana, Indonesia, Pakistan, Senegal, Turkey, Albania, and Cameroon. The BITs signed between Japan and Bangladesh, China, Pakistan, Sri Lanka, the United States, and Turkey do not contain a FET clause either. Finally, the BIT between France and Tunisia also lacks a FET clause.

[11] Argentina-Australia BIT, Art 4. Most of the BITs signed by Australia contain this type of clause.

[12] This formulation is to be found in the BITs signed by Canada with Armenia, Barbados, Costa Rica, Croatia, Czech Republic, Ecuador, Egypt, El Salvador, Hungary, Latvia, Lebanon, Panama, Philippines, Poland, Russia, South Africa, Thailand, Trinidad and Tobago, Ukraine, Uruguay, and Venezuela.

non-exhaustive list of examples of what amounts, in their view, to a violation of the FET standard is not commonly encountered. The France-Guatemala BIT provides for such a FET clause in which the contracting parties agree that:

...sont considérées comme entraves de droit ou de fait au traitement juste et équitable, toute restriction à l'achat et au transport de matières premières et de matières auxiliaires, d'énergie et de combustibles, ainsi que de moyens de production et d'exploitation de tout genre, toute entrave à la vente et au transport des produits à l'intérieur du pays et à l'étranger, ainsi que toutes autres mesures ayant un effet analogue.

The examples concentrate mainly on allowing the foreign investor freely to exploit the investment, and protect him or her from potentially damaging actions by the state. It may prove useful to have clauses drafted on this model more often because they provide for a better delimitation of FET's meaning. This category should include the FET clauses that prohibit any 'arbitrary or discriminatory' measures limiting the 'management, maintenance, use, enjoyment or disposal thereof, as well as the acquisition of goods and services or the sale of their production'.[13]

The third and last category of FET clauses is the one that refers to a series of other standards of treatment or protection. The most commonly encountered standards are the national treatment and the MFN, but also 'full protection and security'. There are two possible connections between these standards. The FET, NT, and MFN standards may be treated as equivalent or minimum levels of treatment, as it is the case in the Romania-Czech Republic BIT:

Each Contracting Party shall in its territory accord investments and returns of investor of the other Contracting Party treatment which is fair and equitable and not less favourable than that which it accords to investments and returns of its own investors or to investments and returns of investors of any third State whichever is more favourable.

In this formulation, it clearly appears that FET should be equivalent or higher (because 'not less favourable') than the 'most favourable' level offered by the national and the MFN treatments. The link among the different standards of treatment is achieved by sentences like 'the FET should not be less favourable than the MFN/NT' or 'the FET should be at least as favourable as the MFN/ NT'. In such treaties, the MFN and/or national treatment are used so as to indicate the minimum level of the FET.

The second type of clause is the one in which the FET standard is in the same clause with the mention of 'full protection and security'. The combination between the two standards is a frequent drafting formulation, the prototype

---

[13] eg the FET clause of the Bangladesh-Philippines BIT is drafted as follows:

Investments and returns of investors of each Contracting Party shall at all times be accorded fair and equitable treatment and shall enjoy full protection and security in the territory of the other Contracting Party. Neither Contracting Party shall in any way impair by unreasonable or discriminatory measures the management, maintenance, use, enjoyment, extension or disposal of such investments.

provision of this category is spelled out in the Japan-Hong Kong BIT: 'Investments and returns of investors of each Contracting Party shall at all times be accorded fair and equitable treatment and shall enjoy full protection and security in the area of the other Contracting Party.' These two standards are not interconnected in the same way as the previous ones because there is no hierarchical-type relation between them; they are always situated at the same level.

From the examined BITs, it appears that the wide web of BITs signed across the world presents a diversity of formulations of FET clauses that is also found in the regional and multilateral investment treaties.

At a regional level,[14] the provisions on the treatment of investment are more often included in agreements that cover a broader range of areas than investment as such. The number of regional agreements grew considerably in the last decade,[15] and the geographical organization of investment rules is slowly becoming an important feature in the analysis of foreign direct investment. In this context, a clear line may be drawn between the European and American approaches to investment rules; other such geographical distinctions may emerge in the future.[16] A relatively recent example of a FET clause that occupies an important place in a regional agreement is the one of the Energy Charter Treaty. The Charter contains a FET clause that is particularly long and detailed, accompanied by a number of annexes and reservations which offer a possibility for each contracting party to almost tailor '*sur mesure*' clauses.[17]

At a multilateral level there are more non-binding texts that serve rather as recommendations than binding ones; the cause for this situation is the difficulty of reaching a consensus in presence of an important number of states.[18] These

[14] The regional instruments reviewed for this survey are: the Fourth APC-EEC Convention (Lomé IV); the Energy Charter Treaty; the Economic Agreement of Bogotá; the Treaty of Cologne for Reciprocal Promotion and Protection of Investments in MERCOSUR; the Treaty establishing the Common Market for East and Southern Africa (COMESA); the 11th Chapter of NAFTA; the Agreement for Investment of Arab capital; the ASEAN Agreement on Promotion and Protection of investment; and the CARICOM and Cuba agreement.
[15] One of the reasons for the reinforcement of the regional level negotiations is the weak result of the multilateral level initiatives.
[16] The UNCTAD 'World Investment Report' (2004) reports that there are three main geographical approaches: the Western Hemisphere, the European approach, and the South-South approach. See UNCTAD, n 6 above.
[17] There is certainly a trend towards more detailed or more carefully drafted FET clauses which may be attributed to the fast-growing arbitral system that involves the greatest number of countries than ever before.
[18] The texts reviewed for this survey are: the Havana Charter; the International Code of Fair Treatment for Foreign Investments; the Abs-Shawcross Draft Convention on Investments Abroad; the Code of Liberalization of Capital Movements; the OECD Draft Convention on the Protection of Foreign Property; the Draft International Code of Conduct on the Transfer of Technology; the set of multilaterally agreed equitable principles and rules for the control of restrictive business practices; the United Nations General Assembly Resolution 3281 (XXIX): Charter of Economic Rights and Duties of States; the UN Code of Conduct on Trans-national Corporations; the Declaration on International Investment and Multinational Enterprises; the Convention establishment the MIGA; the Guidelines for International Investment; and the Multilateral Agreement on Investment.

three drafting categories of the FET clauses are also present at the multilateral level. The evolution of the FET standard shows that it first appeared in international investment agreements before being introduced in bilateral level treaties, where consensus is more easily reached. The first mention of a notion close to the FET is found in the 1948 Havana Charter.[19] A direct antecedent of the term 'fair and equitable treatment' as used in many international investment agreements is the 1967 OECD Draft Convention on the Protection of Foreign Property.[20] Following the failure of this OECD initiative, the United Nations elaborated a Code of Conduct.[21] It contained a FET clause that provoked numerous discussions between the negotiating parties and numerous variations of this clause were proposed. The Code was never adopted. The 1997 OECD Draft Multilateral Agreement on Investment[22] also contained the obligation to accord fair and equitable treatment to Member States' investors. The MAI was subject to intense discussions, but was not adopted.

The study of the bilateral, regional, and multilateral levels leads to the conclusion that there are different levels of treatment corresponding to a FET standard, not a single, uniform one. The level of treatment and the exact meaning of the FET depend on the wording of each clause and it is the arbitrator's task to respect the wording of the treaty and of the clause referring to FET. Finally, FET may be drafted in such a way as to be combined with other standards of treatment. Our empirical research does not confirm the thesis of a FET clause identically repeated in all BITs; on the contrary, it shows that there is a diversity of formulations that are worth examining. Confronted with these different formulations, can one conclude that there is only one FET standard or should it be assumed that there is more than one? Is it possible to conceive under a same label, that of the FET, a variety of concepts? The answer to these questions is far from simple.

A. One Single Principle or More?

One of the possible answers to the previous questions may be found by looking for a smallest common denominator of all of these variations. All states which agree to sign a treaty containing a FET clause agree, at the very least, to accord FET to foreign investors on their territories, during the entire period of their

---

[19] Chapter 3 of the draft Havana Charter, in its Art 11, contained the possibility for the organization to make recommendations for and promote bilateral or multilateral agreements on measures designed 'to assure just and equitable treatment for the enterprise, skills, capital, arts and technology brought from one Member country to another'. International Trade Organization, *The Havana Charter* (1948).

[20] OECD, 'Draft Convention on the Protection of Foreign Property' (April 1967), available at <http://www.oecd.org>.

[21] UNCTAD, Draft International Code of Conduct on the Transfer of Technology (1985 version), available at <http://www.unctad.org>.

[22] OECD, Draft Multilateral Agreement for Investment (1998), available at <http://www.oecd.org>.

investment operations, posterior to the entry phase. There are two questions which should be asked in this context: the first one concerns the relationship between the FET and the International Minimum Standard (IMS). Is the FET standard more than the customary IMS? If this first question is answered affirmatively, then the second question should be: is there enough material to support the customary character of a FET standard, independent from the IMS?

There is a practical reason behind discussion concerning the customary character of FET: given the numerous incomplete formulations of the FET clauses, some referring to international law, some not, some BITs not even referring to the FET, a customary character of FET would provide an answer to these shortcomings. However, to justify and bring enough proof as to the customary character of FET is a challenging operation with few chances of success.

A reference to international law is encountered in an important number of the FET clauses reviewed and is directly linked to the discussion on the customary character of the FET standard. To believe that the treaty is not linked to international law unless there is a specific reference to it represents a voluntarist reading of the situation. The FET standard may be simply a vague standard which the parties feel should be consolidated on each and every occasion, in each and every investment convention. This is true today and will certainly be even more so in two years from now, since the context and very specific wording of the FET clause has to be taken into account and the number of BITs is growing fast. Moreover, given the popularity of the FET standard in investors' claims, states have started to pay attention when drafting their FET clauses.[23]

The letter of submission of the US BIT to the Senate contains a brief explanation of the provisions contained in the treaty. Concerning the article that provides for fair and equitable treatment and full protection and security, the letter mentions that it:

... sets out a minimum standard of treatment based on standards found in customary international law. The obligations to accord 'fair and equitable treatment' and 'full protection and security' are explicitly cited. The general reference to international law also implicitly incorporates other fundamental rules of customary international law regarding the treatment of foreign investment. However, this provision does not incorporate obligations based on other international agreements.[24]

Despite this letter of submittal, it is difficult to read the sentence 'Investments shall at all times be accorded fair and equitable treatment, shall enjoy full protection and security and shall in no case be accorded treatment less than that required by international law' and not see that while the basic requirement of the clause is the respect of international law, the two standards go beyond it, creating a different standard of treatment.

---

[23] Some states even started considering the termination of a number of their BITs as a consequence of the different arbitral proceedings they have been involved in.

[24] *Letter of submittal to the US Senate*, at IX, US 1 Table.

There is actually no theoretical obstacle to the existence of a customary FET since the existence of a conventional basis does not cancel the customary one. Moreover, there is a real relevance of a customary basis, independently from the conventional one, in the case of FET. Even *jus cogens* principles can find their expression in conventional sources. Some authors, such as Judge Schwebel, establish a firm linkage between conventional and customary bases: he contends that it is precisely this network of 2,500 BITs which contributed to the emergence of a customary FET.[25] Moreover, Article 42 of the ICSID Convention and Article 38 of the ICJ Statute both refer to customary international law. Article 31.3.c of the ICJ Statute refers to all customary international law. For all these reasons, FET is an almost codified standard.

B. The Content of the Standard

Most of the definitions of the standard contain a series of elements that, gathered under the same umbrella, give a complete picture of what is commonly understood by a *standard*: a broad behavioural direction or an indeterminate concept; a large margin of manoeuvre left to the arbitrator/judge and a very flexible character, which adapts to a variety of circumstances; a link between law and society; the reference point of which is an average social conduct; a reference to the conformity between national law and international law.

The role of the judge in the application of the standard is not only central, but also necessarily creative. The judge may appreciate the law on the basis of logical standards or he or she may take into account the average values and behaviours of a society at a given moment in time. The arbitral tribunal in *Mondev* underlined the existence of a high margin of appreciation in the hands of the arbitrators, claiming that 'a judgment of what is fair and equitable cannot be reached in the abstract; it must depend on the facts of the particular case. It is part of the essential business of courts and tribunals to make judgments such as these.'[26] In the presence of a standard, the judge becomes the vehicle through which the legal norm is applied to the dispute. Therefore, the social or economic fact acquires a normative character. This freedom of the judge to adapt the law does not reach unanimity among scholars. Al Sanhoury admits that there is an obvious risk that the judge applies the standard arbitrarily. However, he considers that in the absence of standards, the judge may be obliged to model and shape the meaning of a rule in order to fit the normative context; this might not be a better option.[27] The other criticism formulated against the role of the judge is that his or her

[25] SM Schwebel, 'The Influence of Bilateral Investment Treaties on Customary International Law' (2005) 2(5) Transnational Dispute Management 27.

[26] *Mondev International Ltd v United States of America* (hereinafter, *Mondev*), ICSID, ARB(AF)/99/2, Final Award, 11 October 2002, at 118.

[27] A Sanhoury, *Les restrictions contractuelles à la liberté individuelle de travail dans la jurisprudence anglaise, Contribution à l'étude comparative de la règle de droit et du standard juridique* (1925).

quasi-legislative role undermines the separation of powers in the state's system. Maury, for instance, expresses strong doubts as to the important role played by empirical considerations while determining the standard, because he considers that the empirical method results in more legal uncertainty.[28] He takes as an example the doctrine of equity that undermines the indispensable certainty of a legal system. Maury does not take into account, however, that it is the legislator who establishes the normative content of the standard and the guidelines to be respected, locking the judge into a certain perimeter that he or she may not cross. Therefore, the *marge de manoeuvre* of the judge is perfectly controlled and is conscientiously delegated by the legislator to perform a specific task. The supporters of the standard believe in a perfect judge-legislator relationship. The legislator provides the judge with the spirit of the law, its finality, and applicable standards, but leaves their application to the discretionary power of the judge. This structure of the law allows an individualization of justice.

The first and most important conclusion of the previous section is that the reference to equity alongside fairness, in the case of FET, does not give to the tribunal the power to take a decision *ex aequo et bono*. This conclusion is by now generally accepted and was recently reaffirmed by the tribunal in the *Saluka* case. The tribunal held that 'this does not imply, however, that such standards as laid down in article 3 of the Treaty [FET] would invite the Tribunal to decide the dispute in a way that resembles a decision *ex aequo et bono*'.[29]

The direct translation in the FET standard of the individual meanings of fairness and equitableness was rarely accepted by arbitral tribunals. There is only one award that refers to such an incorporation; the tribunal estimated that 'l'obligation de traitement juste et équitable n'aurait pas un contenu prédéterminé et renverrait aux notions de justice et d'équité entendues objectivement mais en tenant compte des circonstances de faits de l'espèce'.[30] No other tribunal went so far as to consider that the content of FET has to be, directly and exclusively, derived from the meanings of these two notions. Today, after an important number of cases in which the standard has been interpreted by various arbitrators, a consensus seems to have been reached by tribunals: FET has a technical legal content of its own which is independent from the two notions that compose it. In my view, the notions of fairness and equitableness did inspire the arbitrators in their search for content of the FET. Although this inspiration did not manifest itself through a direct transposition of the meaning of these two concepts into FET, but through a more subtle type of inspiration, it is not possible to contest the importance of these two concepts in the understanding of

---

[28] Maury, 'Observations sur les modes d'expression du droit: règles et directives' in *Recueil Lambert* (1938).
[29] *Saluka Investments BV v Czech Republic* (hereinafter, *Saluka*), PCA, UNCITRAL, Partial Award, 17 March 2006, at para 284.
[30] *Consortium RFCC v Morocco (hereinafter, RFCC), ICSID, ARB/00/6, Award, 22 December 2003*, at para 51.

FET. The factual situations in which the FET standard has been applied do comply with the notions of fairness and equitableness, even though the arbitral tribunals do not refer to them as *source of inspiration*.

In *Waste Management*, the tribunal held that 'the standard is to some extent a flexible one which must be adapted to the circumstances of each case'.[31] The standard has an ability to cover an extensive list of factual situations through its 'open-ended' nature.[32] In *GAMI*, the arbitrators declared that 'the challenging task ... is to apply these abstractions [the FET clause]'.[33] As discussed above, the arbitrators have an important role to play in the awakening process of the standard, since its evolutionary character implies that a series of factual circumstances have to be taken into account by the arbitrator, when deciding upon a FET-based claim. In *Pope & Talbot*, the tribunal considered that NAFTA Article 1105 incorporated an evolutionary standard, which allowed subsequent practice, including treaty practice, to be taken into account. When considering the meaning and implications of the NAFTA Free Trade Commission's (FTC) interpretation, the United States expressed the view, in the *ADF Group* case, that the reference to customary international law of NAFTA Article 1105(1) is not 'frozen in time'[34] and that the minimum standard of treatment is subject to evolution. Canada joined the United States on the evolutionary character of the standards of treatment. In the same case, it noted that:

Canada's position has never been that the customary international law regarding the treatment of aliens was 'frozen in amber at the time of the Neer decision'. Obviously, what is shocking or egregious in the year 2002 may differ from that which was considered shocking or egregious in 1926. Canada's position has always been that customary international law can evolve over time, but that the threshold for finding violation of the minimum standard of treatment is still high.[35]

In *Mondev*, the tribunal added that:

a reasonable evolutionary interpretation of article 1105(1) is consistent both with the *travaux*, with the normal principles of interpretation and with the fact that ... the terms 'fair and equitable treatment' and 'full protection and security' had their origin in bilateral treaties in post-war period. In these circumstances the content of the minimum standard today cannot be limited to the content of customary international law as recognized in arbitral decisions of the 1920s.[36]

---

[31] *Waste Management Inc v Mexico (hereinafter, Waste Management)*, ICSID Case ARB(AF)/00/3, Award, 30 April 2004, at para 99.   [32] *Mondev*, n 26 above, at para 127.

[33] *GAMI Investments Inc v Mexico* (hereinafter, *GAMI*), UNCITRAL, Final Award, 15 November 2004, at para 92.

[34] *ADF Group Inc v United States of America* (hereinafter, *ADF*), ICSID Case ARB(AF)/00/1, Final Award, 9 January 2003, at para 179.

[35] Second Submission of Canada Pursuant to NAFTA Art 1128, 19 July 2002, para 33, in *Pope & Talbot Inc v Government of Canada* (hereinafter, *Pope & Talbot*), UNCITRAL.

[36] *Mondev*, n 26 above, at para 123.

The circumstances to be taken into account by the arbitrator at this stage, namely, the determination of the content of the standard to be applied, are essentially linked to the general situation of the state. The arbitrator's aim, in an initial phase, is to appreciate the situation of the state in order to situate it in a group of similar states and identify the average type of treatment that a reasonable state in similar conditions would offer to its investors. This rather abstract operation is necessary in order to determine the threshold at which FET has to be applied in a particular case. It aims at establishing a threshold which is anchored in reality and follows the logical path of the current world: an investor may not invest in Romania, acting and hoping to be treated as if he or she were in Switzerland.[37] Already at this stage of the procedure, the capacity of the state is a determinant element alongside other factual elements that are specific to the case.

C. Situations

The content of the FET is difficult to determine because the FET is a standard. This lack of a fixed content is not a weakness; on the contrary, it constitutes the strength of the FET. One strategy of analysing the FET standard is to determine a list of factual situations in which it has already been applied. In *Mondev*, the tribunal confirmed that the standard 'applies to a wide range of factual situations, whether in peace or in civil strife, and to conduct by a wide range of State organs or agencies'.[38] This list of factual situations found in the existing case law is not exhaustive and it is meant to evolve with the future cases.[39] However, these factual situations are a prime source of information about the content of the FET standard. We will focus on nine such circumstances: the non-respect of the obligation of vigilance and protection, denial of due process and/or of procedural fairness, non-observance of the investor's legitimate expectations, coercion and harassment by the organs of the host state, failure to implement

---

[37] *Noble Ventures, Inc v Romania* (hereinafter, *Noble*), ICSID Case ARB/01/11, Final Award, 17 October 2005.

[38] *Mondev*, n 26 above, at para 95. Further in the award, the tribunal added that 'a judgement of what is fair and equitable cannot be reached in the abstract; it must depend on the facts of the particular case' (at para 118).

[39] The factual situations could be classified in two categories. The first category is that of the factual situations that are sufficient to create obligations for the state or, *a contrario*, those whose breach, alone, may engage the state's responsibility. They are, in a way, *self-sufficient*. In the second category, there are those situations that may be called accessories, because they have to be associated with a *self-sufficient* situation in order to have an influence on the breach of the FET. The type of influence that these situations may have on the main one may be characterized either as *circonstances aggravantes* or as complementary obligations. This is the case when the host state failed to implement its legislation. As such, a government's failure to implement its own law will not automatically lead to the violation of the FET obligation because '[m]uch depends on context'. See *GAMI*, n 33 above, at para 91.

and/or enforce national laws, unjustified enrichment, evidence of bad faith, absence of transparency, and arbitrary and discriminatory treatment.

1. Non-Respect of the Obligation of Vigilance and Protection

The obligation of vigilance and protection is similar to an obligation of due diligence that the state has in its relationship to the foreign investors. Due diligence is 'nothing more nor less than the reasonable measures of prevention which a well-administered government could be expected to exercise under similar circumstances'.[40] The responsibility of the state is engaged by 'the mere lack or want of due diligence',[41] there is no need to establish negligence. In his separate opinion in the *AAPL* case, Judge Asante observed that:

> the requirement as to the fair and equitable treatment, full protection and security and non-discrimination treatment all underscore the general obligation of the host State to exercise due diligence in protecting foreign investment in its territories, an obligation that derives from customary international law.[42]

In *Lauder*, the tribunal clearly accepted that FET 'is related to the traditional standard of due diligence'.[43] However, this obligation of due diligence is to be seen within certain limits. For example, it may not imply the obligation of the state to intervene in a dispute between two companies. The only duty of the state is 'to keep its judicial system available for the Claimant and any entities he controls to bring their claims, and for such claims to be properly examined and decided in accordance with domestic and international law'.[44] It seems that there is an obligation within FET to treat foreign investors in such a way as to allow them to conduct their activity in the most hospitable environment. This obligation requires from the state a similar behaviour as the one required by the more specific standard of 'full protection and security'.[45]

2. Denial of Due Process and/or of Procedural Fairness

There are two different concepts to which FET has been applied: denial of due process and denial of procedural fairness. Denial of due process refers to the more specific notion of denial of justice, whereas procedural fairness refers to all types of procedures in which the investor may be involved with the organs of the state, namely, administrative procedures. Both the actions and the omissions of the state qualifying under these two categories have been found to violate the FET standard.

---

[40] A Freeman, 'Responsibility of States for Unlawful Acts of Their Armed Forces' (1956) 88 Recueil des Cours de l'Académie de Droit International 15–16.

[41] CF Amerasinghe, *State Responsibility for Injuries to Aliens* (1967) 281–282.

[42] Asante opinion in *AAPL case*, n 1 above, at para 639.

[43] *Ronald S Lauder v Czech Republic* (hereinafter, *Lauder*), UNCITRAL, Award, 3 September 2001, at para 292.   [44] Ibid., at para 314.

[45] The full protection and security standard has been interpreted as focusing on physical protection.

Denial of justice[46] is an important notion of international law which has inspired a rich set of scholarly writings.[47] There are two major issues to be developed in connection with the claim for denial of justice: the issue of local remedies against administrative procedures and the procedure before the national courts. The tribunal in *Loewen* declared that the procedure conducted in front of the national courts did not amount to a violation of 'fair and equitable treatment' by the United States because it had not been established that the United States had failed to make adequate remedies reasonably available to the complainants, namely, the possibility of appeal. The tribunal concluded that Loewen had failed to demonstrate that those remedies, in particular resorting to the US Supreme Court, were not reasonably available to it.[48] In *Metalclad*, the tribunal evaluated the procedure that led to the denial of a construction permit to the investor: 'the permit was denied at a meeting of the Municipal Town Council of which Metalclad received no notice, to which it received no invitation, and at which it was given no opportunity to appear'.[49] Thus, one of the elements examined by tribunals in order to appreciate if foreign investors were offered due process is the availability of local remedies and the possibility to benefit from a standard of review of the decisions that concern them directly.

However, tribunals have been careful in analysing the actions and decisions taken in the frame of municipal and national systems in order to avoid any interference with national sovereignty. In *Loewen*, for example, the tribunal declared '(w)hether the conduct of the trial amounted to a breach of municipal law as well as international law is not for us to determine'.[50] The reluctance of the tribunal to recognize, in this case, that the due process obligation was violated contrasts with the very severe terms used by the arbitrators to describe the procedure in the local courts. The reason for this contrast is, as declared by the tribunal itself, that 'too great readiness to step . . . into the domestic arena . . . will

---

[46] For a definition of the notion of denial of justice, see AO Adede, 'A Fresh Look at the Meaning of the Doctrine of Denial of Justice under International Law' (1976) 14 Canadian Yearbook of International Law 72, 91. Adede defined denial of justice as an 'improper administration of civil and criminal justice as regards an alien, including denial of access to courts, inadequate procedures, and unjust decisions'. Also, in the *Loewen* case, Professor Greenwood, while defining denial of justice as the obligation to 'maintain and make available to aliens, a fair and effective system of justice', considers that this obligation is part of customary international law. *Loewen Group Inc and Raymond L Loewen v United States of America* (hereinafter, *Loewen*), ICSID, ARB(AF)/98/3, Final Award, 26 June 2003, at para 129, quoting Professor Greenwood's Second Opinion, at para 79.

[47] The literature on the denial of justice is rich and the issues to be discussed in connection with this notion are numerous. For more comprehensive studies on this notion, see JW Garner, 'International Responsibility of States for Judgements of Courts and Verdicts of Juries amounting to Denial of justice' 10 British Yearbook of International Law 181 (1929); A Freeman, *The International Responsibility of States for Denial of Justice* (1938); J Paulsson, *Denial of Justice in International Law* (2005); and ch 2 in this volume. [48] *Loewen*, n 46 above.

[49] *Metalclad Corp v United States of Mexico* (hereinafter, *Metalclad*), ICSID Case ARB (AF)/97/1, Final Award, 30 August 2000, at para 91. [50] *Loewen*, n 46 above, at para 34.

damage ... the viability of NAFTA itself'.[51] Tribunals may be reluctant to go further in their condemnation of the proceedings in front of local courts.

Also in *Loewen,* the tribunal noted: 'the whole trial [in local courts] and its resultant verdict were clearly improper and discreditable and cannot be squared with minimum standards of international law and fair and equitable treatment'.[52] The positive obligation of the host state under international law is 'to provide a fair trial of a case to which a foreigner is a party'.[53] A fair trial is one in which there is no discrimination against the foreign litigant or in which this one does not become the victim of sectional or local prejudice. The general position of tribunals as to the treatment of foreign investors in the procedures before the national courts is that this treatment should respect the characteristics of fair trial and due process of law.

Now, the question to be answered is what exactly constitutes denial of justice. 'Manifest injustice in the sense of a lack of due process leading to an outcome which offends a sense of judicial propriety is enough'[54] to constitute a breach of NAFTA Article 1105. However, the error of a national court is not sufficient to breach the due process obligation: what is required is 'manifest injustice' or 'gross unfairness',[55] 'flagrant and inexcusable violation',[56] or 'palpable violation' in which 'bad faith not judicial error seems to be the heart of the matter'.[57] In the *Azinian* case, the tribunal offered another situation which qualifies for disrespect of the due process obligation by the host state: 'the clear and malicious misapplication of the law'.[58]

Even though the denial of justice appears at first sight as a very broad notion, it has also a series of limitations. The investor who relies on the national courts of the host states and receives a negative answer may not subsequently address

---

[51] *Loewen,* at para 42. Needless to say that this reluctance of the *Loewen* tribunal has been criticized by a great many of the commentators. Wallace justifies it by 'fear, exaggerated in my view, of the expected reactions from political leaders in the United States, from the NGOs and others – which light jeopardize the very continuation of Chapter 11 and perhaps even the NAFTA'. D Wallace, 'Fair and Equitable Treatment and Denial of Justice: *Loewen* v. *US* and *Chattin* v. *Mexico*' in T Weiler (ed), *International Investment Law and Arbitration: Leading Cases from the ICSID, Nafta, Bilateral Treaties and Customary International Law* (2005).

[52] *Loewen,* n 46 above, at para 137. These severe terms are not isolated in this decision; the tribunal qualified the award of the national court in such terms at various stages of the reasoning. For example, the tribunal said 'the conduct of the trial by the trial judge was so flawed that it constituted a miscarriage of justice amounting to a manifest injustice as that expression is understood in international law' (at para 54). Further in the award, the arbitrators reiterated their surprise affirming that 'by any standard of measurement the trial ... was a disgrace ... By any standard of evaluation, the trial judge failed to afford Loewen the process that was due' (at para 119).

[53] Ibid., at para 123.   [54] Ibid., at para 132.

[55] Garner, 'International Responsibility of States for Judgements of Courts and Verdicts of Juries amounting to Denial of Justice' (1929) 10 British Yearbook of International Law 181, 183.

[56] J de Arechaga, 'International Law in the Past Third of a Century' (1978) 159 Recueil des Cours de l'Académie de Droit International 282.

[57] O'Connell, *International Law* (1970) 498.

[58] *Robert Azinian v Mexico* (hereinafter, *Azinian*), ICSID Case ARB(AF)/97/2, Final Award, 1 November 1999, at para 103.

the arbitral tribunal seeking a revision of the domestic courts' decision. The tribunal in *Mondev* noted that if investors seek local remedies 'and lose on the merits, it is not the function of NAFTA tribunals to act as courts of appeal'.[59] This interpretation was also followed by other tribunals, namely *Azinian*. In this case, the tribunal declared that 'the possibility of holding a State internationally liable for judicial decisions does not, however, entitle a claimant to seek international review of the national court decisions as though the international jurisdiction seized has plenary appellate jurisdiction'.[60] The claim before an international arbitral tribunal posterior to the use of local remedies must be grounded on real legal issues, not on the refusal of the investor to accept a negative answer to its claim since 'NAFTA was not intended to provide foreign investors with blanket protection from this kind of disappointment, and nothing in its terms so provides'.[61]

In *Middle East Cement*, the tribunal applied the provisions of the BIT between Greece and Egypt concerning fair and equitable treatment and full protection and security to a situation concerning the seizure and auction of a ship without prior notification to the owner. The tribunal considered that a 'matter as important as the seizure and auctioning of a ship of the Claimant should have been notified by a direct communication',[62] which would have been possible. A prior notification was necessary 'irrespective of whether there was a legal duty or practice to do so'.[63] It is not surprising that the tribunal decided that, even in the absence of a legal duty, the investor should have been notified. The tribunal evaluated the behaviour of the state according to the FET standard, which is based on international law, not domestic law, and found that the host state violated its FET obligation. This decision confirms a rather consistent ruling of the tribunals that, in the presence of serious procedural shortcomings, the FET standard is violated. The treatment of the investor does not have to fall below 'the level that is unacceptable from the international perspective'[64] in order to violate FET.

The obligation of procedural fairness is read in a broad manner, including all types of procedures engaged in by the investor with the organs of the state, not only the judicial procedures. The host state may not justify a procedure because it respects domestic law, because the fair and equitable treatment provides for a 'basic and general standard which is detached from the host State's domestic law'.[65] It is precisely the fact that the threshold at which the FET is applied is determined by reference to international law, not national law, that characterizes this standard.

---

[59] *Mondev*, n 26 above, at para 126.   [60] *Azinian*, n 58 above, at para 99.
[61] Ibid., at para 83.
[62] *MTD Equity Sdn Bhd and MTD Chile SA v Chile* (hereinafter, *MTD*), ICSID Case ARB/01/7, Award, 25 May 2004, at para 143.   [63] Ibid., at para 143.
[64] *SD Myers Inc v Government of Canada* (hereinafter, *SD Meyers*), UNCITRAL, First Partial Award, 13 November 2000, at para 134.
[65] *Alex Genin v Estonia* (hereinafter, *Genin*), ICSID Case ARB/99/2, Final Award, 25 June 2001, at para 367.

3. Non-Observance of the Investor's Legitimate Expectations

The term 'legitimate expectations' is well known to the international law of foreign investment.[66] Back in 1920, in the *Expropriated Religious Properties* arbitration, the tribunal referred to the notion of legitimated expectations by reference to the FET standard when it declared that the case in front of it 'apparaît comme juste et équitable et de nature à satisfaire les légitimes préten-tions respectives des parties'.[67] More recently, the tribunal in the *Generation Ukraine* case confirmed that the protection of the investors' legitimate expecta-tions 'is a major concern of the minimum standards of treatment contained in bilateral investment treaties'.[68]

A foreign investor should be aware of a certain number of elements con-cerning the host state when he or she decides to make an investment. These elements should be taken into account by the investor not only when he or she decides to invest in one country rather than in another, but also in the every-day contact with the state and its administration. If evaluated correctly, these ele-ments contribute to the formation of a set of expectations which is legitimate and only these *legitimate* expectations receive protection from international law.

The respect by the host state of the investor's legitimate expectations is the perfect illustration of how fairness spreads its content into FET. In *Tecmed*, the arbitral tribunal observed with reference to the FET clause that:

in the light of the good faith principle established by international law, [it] requires the Contracting Parties to provide to international investments treatment that does not affect the basic expectations that were taken into account by the foreign investor to make the investment.[69]

These expectations of the investors may be qualified as 'legitimate', 'justified', 'basic',[70] 'reasonable', or fundamental; these adjectives are used indistinctively to refer to legitimate expectations.

---

[66] The notion of legitimate expectations is not applied exclusively in the context of the FET standard. It is also used in relation to indirect expropriation. It is possible to envisage a future autonomy of the concept; since in the context of indirect expropriation the concept operates with a different set of qualities and requirements than in the context of the FET, which shows that it has enough resources to adapt to diverse situations. Moreover, the notion of 'legitimate expectations' is a well-known concept in the legal system of England and Wales, frequently used in the area of administrative law.

[67] *Expropriated Religious Properties* (case between France, Great Britain, Spain, and Portugal), Award, 4 September 1920 (1920) I RIAA 7, at 12.

[68] *Generation Ukraine Inc v Ukraine* (hereinafter, *Generation Ukraine*), ICSID Case ARB/00/9, Final Award, 16 September 2003, at para 20.37

[69] *Técnicas Medioambientales Tecmed SA v Mexico* (hereinafter, *Tecmed*), ICSID Case ARB(AF)/00/2, Final Award, 29 May 2003, at para 154.

[70] *CME Czech Republic BV v Czech Republic* (hereinafter, *CME*), SCC, UNCITRAL, Partial Award, 13 September 2001, at para 611; and *Eureko BV v Poland* (hereinafter, *Eureko*), Ad hoc Tribunal, Partial Award, 19 August 2005, at para 232.

Two recent cases confirmed that the protection of the legitimate expectations of investors is an integral part of the FET standard. In *Saluka*, the tribunal held that '(t)he standard of "fair and equitable treatment" is therefore closely tied to the notion of legitimate expectations which is the dominant element of the standard'.[71] Furthermore, in *CME*, the tribunal concluded that the host state breached the FET 'by evisceration of the arrangements in reliance upon which the foreign investor was induced to invest.'[72]

The difficulty with applying the legitimate expectations doctrine comes from the fact that the notion is very broad. A number of criteria have been developed in order to narrow down its scope. The most complete definition of legitimate expectations was given in the *Thunderbird* case:

... the concept of 'legitimate expectations' relates, within the context of the NAFTA framework, to a situation where a Contracting Party's conduct creates reasonable and justifiable expectations on the part of an investor (or investment) to act in reliance on said conduct, such that a failure by the NAFTA Party to honour those expectations could cause the investor (or investment) to suffer damages.[73]

The general criteria followed until now by most arbitral tribunals that had to examine this concept are the following: the type of conduct necessary to generate expectations that become legitimate by an authority of the host state; the level of the expectations have to be reasonable and justifiable in the light of the conduct; and there has to be a causal link between the failure to respect these expectations and the damage suffered by the investor.

As to the first criterion, the type of action that can create legitimate expectations, there is a general understanding that this action has to be directly attributable to the government.[74] The disagreement between investors and states arises as to the type of action that legitimates the expectations of the investor: may a lack of action or an unclear declaration, for example, create legitimate expectations? In the *Thunderbird* case, Mexico argued that the investor required a licence or permit in order to create legitimate expectations. The tribunal took a broader approach and considered that legitimate expectations can arise from other actions of the government as well, not necessarily from a licence or permit. The tribunal also looked at the behaviour of the authorities during the course of their relationship with the investor. The authorities have different opportunities to correct an eventual misrepresentation of the investor. Mexico acted repeatedly in a way that led the investor to believe that he was respecting the laws: therefore, the tribunal decided that the

---

[71] *Saluka*, n 29 above, at para 302.   [72] *CME*, n 70 above, at para 155.

[73] *International Thunderbird Gaming v Mexico* (hereinafter, *Thunderbird*), UNCITRAL, Award, 26 January 2006, at para 147.

[74] In *Metalclad*, the tribunal considered that the expectations of the investor were legitimate because they were built on 'the representations of the federal government'. *Metalclad*, n 49 above, at para 87.

same authorities could take a measure sanctioning this behaviour, without violating the legitimate expectations of the investor.[75]

Concerning the second criterion, the expectations of the investors have to be reasonable and justifiable in the light of the circumstances of the case.[76] As the *Waste Management* tribunal formulated it, 'it is relevant that the treatment is in breach of representations made by the host State which were reasonably relied on by the claimant'.[77] What is reasonable? There is no easy answer to this question in the existing case law. The *Saluka* tribunal gives an example of what is not reasonable: expecting 'that the circumstances prevailing at the time the investment is made, remain totally unchanged'[78] and not taking into account the host state's legitimate right to regulate domestic matters.

Except for the fact that the expectation of the investor has to be commensurate with the behaviour of the authorities, there are also other elements taken into account by tribunals with regard to the investor's behaviour. In *Metalclad*, the tribunal acknowledged that the investor had completed his construction before being refused the additional necessary construction permit.[79] On the contrary, the arbitral tribunal in *Noble* took into account the fact that the investors did not invest a single dollar in the host country, while building high expectations as to the treatment to be received from the Romanian Government.[80]

The tribunal in *Metalclad* summed up these first two criteria by finding that:

Metalclad was entitled to rely on the representations of federal officials and to believe that it was entitled to continue its construction of the landfill. In following the advice of these officials, and filling the municipal perit application on November 15, 1994, Metalclad was merely acting prudently and in full expectation that the permit would be granted.[81]

This same view was adopted by the tribunal in the *Waste Management* case.[82] The legitimate expectations concept 'requires a weighing of the Claimant's legitimate and reasonable expectations on the one hand and the Respondent's legitimate regulatory interest on the other'.[83]

As to the third criterion, the investor has to be able to prove that the damage suffered is a direct consequence of the action of the state. There are expectations that are presumed legitimate. In *Saluka*, the tribunal noted that 'the expectations of the foreign investor certainly include the observation by the host State of such well-established fundamental standards as good faith, due process, and non-discrimination'.[84] A link may be drawn between the concept of legitimate

---

[75] The tribunal specifically underlined the fact that the investor constructed the landfill 'openly and continuously, and with the full knowledge of the federal, state and municipal government'. Ibid., at para 87.   [76] *Saluka*, n 29 above, at para 304.
[77] *Waste Management*, n 31 above, at para 99.   [78] *Saluka*, n 29 above, at para 305.
[79] *Metalclad*, n 49 above, at para 90A.   [80] *Noble*, n 37 above.
[81] *Metalclad*, n 49 above, at para 89.   [82] *Waste Management*, n 31 above, at para 98.
[83] *Saluka*, n 29 above, at para 306.   [84] Ibid., at para 306.

expectations and transparency on the one hand and the good faith principle on the other. The non-observance of the investors' legitimate expectations is often a result of a lack of transparency or of good faith of the host state.

4. Coercion and Harassment by the Organs of the Host State

In general, the claims of the investors on the basis of coercion or harassment usually go hand in hand with an additional claim that the treatment received is more severe than the one received by nationals or other foreign investors. This type of claim is rarely successful since the investor has to be able to prove that the treatment received amounts to harassment. In *Genin*, for example, the investor argued that he had been threatened with criminal charges by the Estonian authorities, as well as with deportation and refusal to extend his residency permit, which amounted to harassment. However, the tribunal considered that the investor did not bring sufficient proof to sustain that the contacts between the investor and the authorities amounted to harassment.[85] In *Eureko*, the alleged harassment of the investors by the Polish authorities was dealt with under the 'full protection and security' standard. The tribunal dismissed the investor's claim on this ground due to the lack of proof that the state was the author or instigator of the actions in question, but maintained that an action has to be 'repeated and sustained' in order to engage the state's responsibility.[86] Finally, the tribunal in *Saluka* held that according to the FET, the host state 'must grant the investor freedom from coercion or harassment by its own regulatory authorities'.[87]

5. Failure to Implement and/or Enforce National Laws

A successful foreign investment operation relies in great part on a stable legal and administrative framework offered by the host state. Studies that analysed the elements taken into account by a foreign investor, when deciding upon the location of its investment, have uniformly confirmed that a stable legislative and administrative framework is essential for a positive decision of the investor in favour of a specific location. The stability requirement is a prominent characteristic of the FET standard and is present in all of the factual situations examined above. However, together with the obligation of due process, the obligation to implement and/or enforce national law as well as the obligation to control local authorities illustrate, in the clearest way, the stability factor of FET.

It was the *GAMI* arbitral tribunal that had the task of deciding whether the failure to implement and enforce national laws constituted a violation of the FET obligation. Naturally, Mexico argued that an ICSID tribunal does not have the mandate to examine the application of national laws by national authorities. The tribunal admitted that the role of international law is certainly not to

---

[85] *Genin*, n 65 above, at para 347.   [86] *Eureko*, n 70 above, at para 237.
[87] *Saluka*, n 29 above, at para 308.

evaluate the content of a national regulatory programme, but precisely to inquire whether 'the State abided by or implemented that programme'.[88] The tribunal added that 'it is no excuse that regulation is costly. Nor does a dearth of able administrators or a deficient culture of compliance provide a defense. Such is the challenge of governance that confronts every country.'[89]

The discussion over the content of the national laws and the capacity of the international tribunals to have a say in it had been discussed previously in the *SD Meyers* case. The tribunal in this case considered that governments are free to make their own choices and:

in doing so, they may appear to have made mistakes, to have misjudged the facts, proceeded on the basis of a misguided economic or sociological theory, placed too much emphasis on some social values over others and adopted solutions that are ultimately ineffective or counterproductive. The ordinary remedy, if there were one, for errors in modern governments is through internal political and legal processes, including elections.'[90]

This paragraph illustrates the limit of the arbitral tribunals' mandate. The content of a national law and the reasoning behind it are part of a political choice of the host state and may not be discussed in front of an arbitral tribunal. Therefore, the mere failure to implement national law does not automatically mean that the host state breached the FET standard. The context in which this failure takes place is determinant for the final decision of the tribunal as to the breach of FET. The facts in the *GAMI* case are illustrative of the type of context needed to reach a violation of FET: 'the imposition of a new licence requirement may for example be viewed quite differently if it appears on a blank slate or if it is an arbitrary repudiation of a pre-existing licensing regime upon which a foreign investor has demonstrably relied.'[91]

The *Olguín* case brings an interesting development to the discussion on the failure to implement national law. The tribunal could not, in this case, establish a violation of the FET obligation on this basis, given the absence in the BIT of 'strict rules that impose economic sanctions on States that fail to closely monitor their financial entities'.[92] However, the tribunal judged such rules to be 'desirable' since they do not exist in Paraguay, but also in the majority of the countries in the region. The type of situation in which the state could be held responsible on the basis of the FET concerns the obligation to maintain a coherent legislative, but also administrative, framework.

6. Unjustified Enrichment

It is not surprising that unjust enrichment has been among the situations to which FET has been applied: first, because it is a broad equitable concept, fitting

---

[88] *GAMI*, n 33 above, at para 91.   [89] Ibid., at para 94.
[90] *SD Meyers*, n 64 above, at para 261.   [91] *GAMI*, n 33 above, at para 91.
[92] *Eudoro A Olguín v Paraguay* (hereinafter, *Olguín*), ICSID Case ARB/98/5, Final Award, 26 June 2001, at paras 70, 74.

perfectly the inherent balancing objectives of FET; and, second, because the commercial and financial transactions are areas of law predisposed for the enrichment of one person at the cost of another, under perfectly legal circumstances. The principle has mostly been used in claims for compensation following an instance of nationalization.[93] In the recent *Saluka* case, the claimant invoked the unjustified enrichment principle in order to argue the violation of the FET standard. The tribunal underlined the novelty of such a use for this principle. It added that such an assimilation between the principle and the standard implied that 'an investor would therefore also be protected by this standard against unjust enrichment by the host State'.[94] After analysing the facts of the case, the tribunal dismissed the claim on this point, because it was based on a legally incorrect application of the unjustified enrichment principle. The tribunal ruled that 'the notion of one party being an accessory to an unjustified transfer between two other parties is not part of the concept of unjust enrichment'.[95]

Despite the dismissal of this claim on the basis of unjustified enrichment, the tribunal in *Saluka* did not hold that the assimilation between the standard and the principle was unfounded; it dismissed the case on this point only because the facts did not support the legal basis. The assimilation, if better justified in a future claim, may be successful.

7. Evidence of Bad Faith

The *bona fide* obligation implies that the entire relationship between the state and the foreign investor is to be performed in respect of this requirement. Traditionally, good faith occupies an important place in the development of international economic relations.[96] The ICJ acknowledged that the good faith principle is 'one of the basic principles governing the creation and performance of legal obligations'.[97] However, the Court has also been very explicit in not recognizing the good faith as 'a source of obligation where none would otherwise exist'.[98] Good faith relates to the manner in which already established international obligations are being performed; it does not, usually, constitute an individual substantive obligation.[99] The

[93] In the field of investment law, the concept of unjust enrichment has received different interpretations. On the one hand, it has been used to justify the payment of compensation in cases of expropriation and, on the other hand, it has been used against foreign investors to condemn the exploitation of natural resources based on an unbalanced relationship between the host state and the foreign investor. With its application, in the field of the FET, the unjust enrichment receives a third function. For a discussion on the principle of unjust enrichment in international law, see C Schreuer, 'Unjustified Enrichment in International Law' (1974) 22 AJCL 282.
[94] *Saluka*, n 29 above, at para 450.   [95] Ibid., at para 455.
[96] The Charter of economic rights and duties of states, for example, mentions the good faith principle in ch 1, s j.
[97] ICJ, *Nuclear Tests Case*, ICJ Reports (1974), at 268, para 46; and at 473, para 49.
[98] ICJ, *Borders and Transborder Armed Actions Case*, ICJ Reports (1988), at 105, para 94.
[99] In the introduction of this section, we mentioned a possible classification of the factual situations in two groups: those that contained an obligation on their own and those that could not create an obligation alone.

arbitral tribunal in the *ADF* case concluded that there is no additional substantive content brought by the good faith principle, since 'an assertion of breach of a customary law duty of good faith adds only negligible assistance in the task of determining or giving content to a standard of fair and equitable treatment'.[100]

Furthermore, the tribunal in *Mondev* declared that 'a State may treat foreign investment unfairly and inequitably without necessarily acting in bad faith'.[101] Confirming the previous awards, the tribunal in *Loewen* estimated that bad faith or malicious intention is not an essential element of unfair and inequitable treatment or denial of justice amounting to a breach of international justice.[102] This is to say that a lack of due process leads to a breach of the international obligation of the state to ensure a necessary judicial system even without the need to demonstrate that this breach was done with a bad faith or malicious intention. In *Tecmed*, the tribunal decided that 'the commitment of fair and equitable treatment ... is an expression and part of the bona fide principle recognised in international law, although bad faith from the State is not required for its violation'.[103]

To conclude, bad faith is usually an additional element to a substantive obligation: it is rarely an obligation on its own. However, there are cases when an action accomplished in bad faith is a sufficient ground to recognize a breach of the FET obligation. In *Genin*, the arbitrators found that the acts violating the FET 'include acts showing a wilful neglect of duty, an insufficiency of action falling far below international standards, or even subjective bad faith'.[104]

8. Absence of Transparency

In *Metalclad*, the tribunal defined the host state's obligation of transparency[105] as:

the idea that all relevant legal requirements for the purpose of initiating, completing and successfully operating investments made, or intended to be made, under the Agreement should be capable of being readily known to all affected investors of another Party. There should be no room for doubt or uncertainty on such matters.[106]

The tribunal added that the investors should be able to act, on the basis of the existing legal framework, 'in the confident belief that they are acting in accordance with all relevant laws'.[107] The tribunal concluded that Mexico violated its obligation to create a transparent and predictable framework for Metalclad's investment operations and therefore failed to treat Metalclad in a fair and equitable manner according to NAFTA Article 1105. In another case, the tribunal interpreted the lack of transparency connected to procedures involving a

---

[100] *ADF*, n 34 above, at para 191.   [101] *Mondev*, n 26 above, at para 116.
[102] *Loewen*, n 46 above, at para 132.   [103] *Tecmed*, n 69 above.
[104] *Genin*, n 65 above, at para 367.
[105] For a general study on the notion of transparency, see United Nations Conference for Trade and Development (UNCTAD), *Transparency* (2004).   [106] *Metalclad*, n 49 above, at para 76.
[107] Ibid., at para 76.

loan transaction as incompatible with the host state 'commitment to ensure the investor a fair and equitable treatment'.[108]

The transparency obligation is closely linked to the notion of legitimate expectations, since the investor, acting in accordance with the laws and regulations made available to him or her by the host state, believes that he or she is acting legally. In this situation, any damage suffered by the investor as a result of a law that was not applied, or which was applied but to which he or she did not have access, engages the responsibility of the state. In the *Metalclad* case, the tribunal took into account the information made available to the investor and which contributed to the formation of an expectation; the tribunal declared that 'Metalclad was led to believe'[109] and further noted that Metalclad relied 'on the representations of the federal government'.[110]

In the existing case law, the obligation of transparency was applied mainly in connection to the host state rules and regulations and their availability to the investors. The tribunal in *Tecmed* broadened this obligation of transparency, applying it to 'the goals of the relevant policies and administrative practices or directives'[111] which should also be made available to the foreign investors. This view was also confirmed in *GAMI*.[112] The transparency obligation has to be seen in the light of the usually long investment relationship between the state and the investor. The investor is entitled to:

expect that the government's actions would be free from any ambiguity that might affect the early assessment made by (him) of its real legal situation or the situation affecting its investment and the actions the investor should take to act accordingly.[113]

9. Arbitrary and Discriminatory Treatment

The arbitrary and discriminatory character of an action or omission of the host state is usually dealt with by tribunals once the specific wrong-doing of the state is established. In the *GAMI* case, this two-step operation is perfectly illustrated.[114]

Determining the discriminatory character of a measure is usually easier than determining its arbitrary character. Discrimination is established either in comparison with the treatment accorded to national investors (national treatment) or to

[108] *Emilio Augustín Maffezini v Spain* (hereinafter, *Maffezini*), ICSID Case ARB/97/7, Final Award, 13 November 2000, at para 83.   [109] *Metalclad*, n 49 above, at para 85.
[110] Ibid., at para 87. The Supreme Court of British Columbia partially cancelled the NAFTA award, arguing that the tribunal relied on the lack of 'transparency' in order to find a violation of Art 1105, whereas transparency should be based on NAFTA ch 18 and only claims under ch 11 are for an arbitral tribunal to deal with (Art 1116-1 allowing investors to bring complaints on the basis of ch 11 exclusively).   [111] *Tecmed*, n 69 above, at para 154.
[112] *GAMI*, n 33 above. In this case, the actions of the state in the field of sugar production were determined by two parameters: the national consumption and production. The state made this policy public and the investor was aware of it; therefore, the arbitrators decided that a sudden measure taken by the state following a change in one of these parameters that it cannot control could not be considered as a violation of the FET, on the basis of non-transparency.
[113] *Tecmed*, n 69 above, at para 167.   [114] *GAMI*, n 33 above, at para 25.

other foreign investors in similar circumstances. The tribunal in *Saluka* laid down three conditions for a measure or a conduct of the state to be considered discriminatory: 'if (i) similar cases are (ii) treated differently (iii) and without reasonable justification'.[115] The tribunal in *Lauder* created an interesting link between FET and discrimination, declaring that 'it will also prevent discrimination against the beneficiary of the standard, where discrimination would amount to unfairness or inequity in the circumstances'.[116]

As to the arbitrary character of a measure, tribunals refer either to the definitions of the legal dictionaries or they propose their own definition. The tribunal in *Lauder*, for example, used the definition of the *Black's Law Dictionary*: 'arbitrary means 'depending on individual discretion ... founded on prejudice or preference rather than on reason or fact'.[117] In *Tecmed*, the tribunal defined an arbitrary action as:

> presenting insufficiencies that would be recognised '... by any reasonable and impartial man', or although not in violation of specific regulations, as being contrary to the law because ... [it] shocks, or at least surprises, a sense of juridical propriety.[118]

Many tribunals relied on the ICJ definition of arbitrariness given in the *ELSI* case and according to which it 'is not so much something opposed to a rule of law ... it is wilful disregard of due process of law, an act that shocks, or at least surprises a sense of judicial propriety'.[119] The ICJ considered the notion of arbitrariness under a specific provision of a BIT, but noted also that the Chamber's discussion 'is nevertheless instructive as to the standard of review that the international tribunal must employ when examining whether a State has violated the international minimum standard'. The main idea was, in this context, that 'of arbitrary action being substituted for the rule of law'.[120]

It appears that arbitrary and discriminatory measures amount to violations of the FET standard. In *MTD*, for example, after having analysed the FET, the tribunal was confronted with an additional claim of unreasonable and discriminatory measure and decided that 'this claim has been considered ... as part of the fair and equitable treatment'.[121] Moreover, the majority of tribunals treated these two issues

---

[115] *Saluka*, n 29 above, at para 313.

[116] *Lauder*, n 43 above, at para 292. The tribunal did not find in this case that the measures of the host state were discriminatory and arbitrary (ibid., at para 293). Two other cases provide for an interesting development on the discriminatory character of a host state measure: *Methanex Corp v United States of America* (hereinafter, *Methanex*), UNCITRAL, Final Award, 3 August 2005, at para 26 at 274; and *Waste Management*, n 31 above, at para 98.

[117] *Lauder*, n 43 above, at para 221. The tribunal was extremely brief in exploring the claimant's argument on arbitrariness, lacking an argumentative depth and simply repeating the wording of the dictionary definition, on the negative. Ibid., at para 231.

[118] *Tecmed*, n 69 above, at para 154.   [119] *Loewen*, n 46 above, at para 131.

[120] The Chamber considered that mere domestic illegality did not equate to arbitrariness at international law. ICJ, *Case Concerning Elettronica Sicula SpA* (hereinafter, *ELSI*) (*United States of America v Italy*), Decision, 20 July 1989, ICJ Reports 15 (1989), at paras 120–130.

[121] *MTD*, n 62 above, at para 196.

together. The tribunal in *Lauder* considered that a measure of the state has to be cumulatively arbitrary and discriminatory in order to violate the provision of a BIT. The tribunal justified this finding by the fact that 'the plain wording of the provision ... uses the word "and" instead of the word "or" '.[122] The *RFCC* tribunal, faced with these two obligations, judged that they were 'incontestablement le reflet l'un de l'autre'.[123] Host states must 'accept liability if its officials fail to implement or implement regulations in a discriminatory or arbitrary fashion'.[124] In conclusion, one of the best definitions of what is arbitrary and discriminatory is a treatment that is different from the ordinary treatment without a reasonable justification.[125]

III. HR and FET

The discussion about the role of HR norms may at first sight seem unusual in the context of investment law cases, and even more so with regard to claims based on the FET standard. It should be remembered, however, that the expansion of BITs coincided with that of international HR norms. Both types of norms are meant to protect non-state actors from the actions of the state, and both provide for an individualized mechanism of enforcement. In addition, states delegate to private investors more and more of the responsibilities that were once considered to lie within their exclusive competence. It is then perhaps natural, when attributions are transferred from the public to the private scene, that issues concerning the responsibilities of foreign investors emerge. This means that even though originally it was the exclusive obligation of the state to protect HR, the potential for liability of investors under international HR law may be created or expanded.[126]

Inserting HR claims in an investment arbitration procedure is a complex matter. The questions arising out of such an insertion are numerous and include the following:

- To what extent may an arbitral tribunal declare itself competent to examine the issue without breaching its mandate?

- What happens in the event of conflict between a human rights obligation and an investment obligation of the host state?

- Is the arbitrator's role to solve such a conflict? Does an arbitrator possess enough HR expertise to decide on HR claims?

---

[122] *Lauder*, n 43 above, at para 219.   [123] *RFCC*, n 30 above, at para 51.
[124] *GAMI*, n 33 above, at para 94.   [125] *Saluka*, n 29 above, at para 498.
[126] McLachlan, Shore, and Weiniger wrote that 'some elements of human rights law may furnish a source of general principle from which the obligation of fair and equitable treatment may be given contemporary content'. C McLachlan, L Shore, and M Weiniger, *International Investment Arbitration* (2007) 206.

As the debate over HR and the FET standard is relatively recent, the following discussion may raise more questions than yield answers.

A. Can HR Norms be Applied in International Investment Law Cases?

FET claims that rely to some extent on HR violations must be first discussed from the perspective of the applicable law. Can the arbitrator apply human rights norms? As the arbitrator's mandate is to solve an investment dispute, questions arise about his or her competence to rule on HR claims. The question of competence is of high importance as it may trigger the annulment of the award: if an arbitrator declares him- or herself competent to hear an HR claim, the award may be annulled for an excess of power, since it may be estimated that the arbitrator went beyond what was specified in his or her mandate.[127] The inclusion of *excès de pouvoir* among the limited existent grounds for annulment shows the extent to which it is important for the arbitrator to confine him- or herself to act within the mandate given to him or her by the parties and the applicable conventional basis.

Having said this, the arbitral tribunal, as all international tribunals, is expected to apply general international law. The existence of self-contained regimes in international law, although a fashionable argument a couple of years ago, has never received the full support of international lawyers. According to the theory of the self-contained regimes, there are areas of law that have become so specialized that they create their own legal norms and survive in a hermetically sealed environment, outside general international law. WTO law, investment law, European Communities law, and human rights law are some of the examples given by the supporters of the self-contained regime theory.[128] Time and practice has shown that all of these areas of law, although creating norms tailored for their specific needs, form an integral part of general international law and use general international law whenever necessary.[129]

From a conventional perspective, it is interesting to investigate whether existent BITs or other investment treaties contain references to HR norms and obligations. The answer is no: generally there is no clear mention of HR obligations of the state or of the investors in the existent conventional framework. Some BITs do make reference in their preambles to the respect of the

---

[127] ICSID Convention, Art 52. *Excès de pouvoir* of the arbitrator is one of the very few cases in which an arbitration award may be annulled.

[128] See, notably, E Canal-Forgues, 'Sur l'interprétation dans le droit de l'OMC' (2001) 105 Revue Générale de Droit International Public 11; JI Charney, 'Is International Law Threatened by Multiple International Tribunals?' (1998) 271 Recueil des Cours (1998) 219; and G Marceau, 'A Call for Coherence in International Law: Praises for the Prohibition Against "Clinical Isolation" in WTO Dispute Settlement' (1999) 33 Journal of World Trade 110.

[129] For a development on the self-contained regime theory as it was applied to the WTO law and investment law, see I Tudor, 'Droit de l'OMC et droit de l'investissement: regards croisés' in J Chaisse and T Balmelli (eds), *Essays on the Future of the World Trade Organisation* (2008) 171.

environment and health, and some FET clauses also refer to the respect of international law, including, therefore, HR norms that have become customary international law. The FET clauses that refer to the respect of international law are usually formulated as follows: 'Each Contracting Party shall accord investments or returns of investors of the other Contracting Party a fair and equitable treatment in accordance with the principles of international law . . .'[130]

The existent investment case law shows that arbitrators have recourse to general international law to find methods of interpretations or applicable principles and rules in cases where the applicable conventional instruments are silent on certain points. Relying on general international law is, however, limited to the basic sources of general international law – namely, customary norms and general principles of international law. Therefore, the arbitral tribunals concentrate their decisions primarily on the existent conventional norms and, when applicable, on the contractual provisions binding between the parties.

According to the above, when a claim based on customary HR norms is brought, the arbitrator should take them into account. At this point it would be interesting to summarize the discussion on which international HR norms have become customary, but such an investigation would exceed the limits of this contribution and would not, moreover, answer the main question of whether arbitrators would possess enough expertise to rule on a claim based on customary HR norms.

Beyond the jurisdictional competence, which may always be legally justified by new drafting formulations or even become a generally accepted practice, the reality is that HR law is becoming a very technical area of law, is evolving at a fast pace, and deserves extensive preparation in order to master it. Arbitrators are usually nominated by the parties, on the grounds of their knowledge and experience in the field of investment law, which is also fast evolving and very technical. Therefore, in practice, one will rarely find an arbitrator who will be an expert both in investment and HR law. The technicality and rapid evolution of these two areas of law results in norms whose contents are not yet stabilized or, as in the case of the FET standard, leave a substantial margin of appreciation to the arbitrators. In such a situation, could one recommend HR norms to be ruled upon and discussed in front of non-specialized tribunals when international law is equipped with regional and international courts created exclusively in order to decide on HR claims?

Moreover, precisely because these HR courts exist, is there then a risk of forum shopping, in the sense that the same HR claim could then be brought both in front of an arbitral tribunal and in front of an HR court? For example, if the party who brings the HR claim in front of the arbitral tribunal does not

---

[130] A number of the BITs signed by Canada contain such a FET clause.

338   *Case Studies on Protection Standards and Specific Human Rights*

receive satisfaction, it can always start a new additional procedure in front of an HR court.[131] Such a situation would merely serve to multiply the number of jurisdictions able to rule over HR claims, with the obvious risk of not being able to control the number of proceedings and to unify the rulings of these different courts on the same norms. From this perspective, it appears more prudent to allow each area of law to be ruled upon by the appropriate courts, which have not only jurisdiction over the matter, but also are composed of competent judges.

Finally, from a practical perspective, an arbitrator who would be competent to rule over both an investment claim and an HR claim may find him- or herself in the situation where these two norms are in conflict. In order to respect its FET obligation, the state would have had to violate an HR obligation. Is the arbitrator in a position to rule over such a conflict and decide which obligation should prevail? As opposed to an integrated body of supranational rules such as the EU *acquis*, investment law in its current state does not contain the appropriate norms that would allow the arbitrator to deal with such a conflict.

To conclude, it appears that the current drafting formulations of the FET clauses do not give arbitrators a straightforward competence over HR claims. Strictly interpreted, only the FET claims referring to international law principles may give arbitrators the authority to decide over customary HR norms. Having said this, the lack of experience and expertise of most arbitrators in the field of HR, as well as the technicality and rapid evolution of HR norms, makes it very difficult in practice for arbitrators to adjudicate HR claims that are brought in connection with an investment case. These considerations are not always followed by arbitral tribunals. The remaining part of this work will analyse arbitral case law in order to establish the manner in which various tribunals have dealt with HR claims, and the type of HR claims that have already been brought in front of them.

B. HR Claims and Arguments in a FET Claim Context

In an arbitral proceeding initiated by the investor, an argument based on human rights would mostly be made by the host state, as an argument in its defence.[132] While the existent arbitral case law does not contain many examples of how

---

[131] In the ongoing *GLAMIS* case, for example, the Quechuan Indian Nation has already declared that in the event that the arbitral tribunal rules in favour of the investor, they would start a new proceeding in front of the Inter-American Court of Human Rights. This new proceeding would be opened against the United States of America. See Notice of Intent of Glamis, submitted on 21 July 2003. See also ch 16 in this volume.

[132] Generally, when it is an investor who decides to complement its request by an HR argument, the issue at stake concerns taking of property or expropriation, not FET.

states have used HR-based arguments,[133] two situations seem to be the most frequent:

- The first situation is one in which the host state argues that its behaviour, which is believed to have breached the FET standard, was necessary in order to respect an international human rights obligation. In other words, the violation of the FET obligation is justified, because otherwise the state would have violated one of its human rights obligations. This is a situation where two obligations of the state are in conflict.

- In the second situation, the state justifies its violation of FET by alleging that the investor has violated an HR – therefore, in order to put an end to this human rights violation, the state had to take a measure or act in a way which resulted in the violation of FET. In this second scenario, the investor contributes directly to the violation of FET because of his or her behaviour.

The main difference between the two situations is the existence or not of a wrongdoing by the investor.

In law, as mentioned above, there are few examples of tribunals' rulings on HR arguments to allow us to establish a trend or pattern. However, the type of HR violation that has been raised in the existent investment law procedures concerns the conditions of labour of the host country employees, the environment,[134] the rights of indigenous people,[135] public health,[136] sustainable development, or the right to water.[137]

So far, there have been three main approaches adopted by arbitral tribunals that had to decide on a claim or an argument based on non-investment treaty obligations, such as HR:

- The tribunal denied the relevance of the non-investment treaty obligation. The tribunal in the *Santa Elena* case decided, for instance, that 'the fact that the expropriation was made with the aim of protecting the environment does not have any impact on the legal character of expropriation or the amount of compensation'.[138]

---

[133] As a general remark, it is to be noted that even the few times that HR arguments were made in the existent case law, they were not developed and argued enough. The best example of an underdeveloped HR argument is the *Siemens v Argentina* case. The lack of focus on these arguments exists because the states themselves do not firmly believe in the relevance of such arguments in front of an arbitral tribunal. A better-argued HR claim may have a chance to engage the tribunal in a more sophisticated discussion on HR.

[134] *Compañia del Desarrollo de Santa Elena v Costa Rica* (hereinafter, *Santa Elena*), ICSID Case ARB/96/1, Award, 17 February 2000; and *Azurix Corp v Argentina* (hereinafter, *Azurix*), ICSID Case ARB/01/12, Award, 14 July 2006.

[135] *Glamis Gold Ltd v the Government of the United States of America*, n 131 above.

[136] *Azurix*, n 134 above.

[137] *Aguas del Tunari SA v Bolivia*, ICSID Case ARB/02/3, Decision on respondent's objections to jurisdiction, 21 October 2005.   [138] *Santa Elena*, n 134 above, at para 71.

- The tribunal affirmed the relevance of the non-investment treaty obligations *in abstracto*, but did not recognize it *in concreto*. In the *Siemens* case, the tribunal, without rejecting the HR argument as such, ruled that the respondent did not develop this argument well enough.[139] Also, in the *Azurix* case, the tribunal did examine the claim of the state that it took the measure in order to protect public health, and ruled that 'governments have to be vigilant and protect the public health of citizens but the statements and actions of the provincial authorities contributed to the crisis rather than assisting in solving it'.[140]

- The tribunal recognized the non-investment treaty argument and took it into account in the calculation of compensation. In the *MTD* case, for example, the compensation awarded to the investor, by virtue of a FET breach by the host state, was diminished by 50 per cent because the investor's own actions increased the transactions' risks and, as experienced businessmen, 'Claimants should bear the consequence of their own actions'.[141]

These three approaches show that there is hardly a consensus among arbitrators on how to approach obligations unrelated to the investment as such. As mentioned above, both from a practical and a legal perspective, having the arbitrator rule over an HR claim is not generally accepted. However, in practice, when confronted with a violation of HR by the investor, the arbitrator may choose to be vigilant with respect to such behaviour. Conversely, the argument of a state that it did not comply with its FET obligation because it had to comply with another conflicting obligation is not acceptable either. Therefore, in the specific case of the FET, the last scenario, where the non-investment obligations are taken into account at the stage of compensation, appears to be promising. Compensation is a strategic stage of the arbitral award as concerns a FET claim, since investors aim not only at putting an end to the wrongful act of the state, but also at receiving reparation for the damages suffered as a result of the wrongful act. Case law shows that, when ruling on a FET claim, the arbitrators account for a number of elements, such as the specific economic and political situation of the state, or a wrongdoing of the investor that has allegedly contributed to the violation of FET. Although there is no uniformity in the arbitral awards reviewed, one can detect a number of common approaches: some tribunals decide to take these elements into account at the moment of establishing the liability of the state,[142] while others decide to take them into account only at the stage of calculating the compensation due to the investor.[143]

---

[139] In this case, Argentina's argument was that the protection of the investor's property rights had resulted in the violation of international HR law norms.

[140] *Azurix*, n 134 above, at para 144.   [141] *MTD*, n 62 above, at para 178.

[142] See, eg the *Genin* award, n 65 above, at para 348; *Generation Ukraine* case, n 68 above, at para 20.37; or *Olguín*, n 92 above, at para 65.

[143] See, eg the separate opinion of Brownlie in *CME*, n 70 above, at para 117; and *MTD*, n 62 above, at para 178.

Although the FET obligation is not, as such, a reciprocal obligation between the state and the investor, the standard itself encapsulates a concept of balance and aims at giving each one of these two parties what is due. The inherent concepts of fairness and equity would not be served if FET resulted in the calculation of damages without taking into account the behaviour of the investor that may have contributed to the losses he or she claims to be reimbursed for. This may include behaviour on the part of the investor that breaches national or international labour standards which the state is obliged to uphold. It appears, therefore, that, as much as it would be difficult to find a legal justification to the decision of an arbitral tribunal to accept a claim of the state that it violated its FET obligation in order to safeguard an HR obligation (the conflict of obligations scenario), the behaviour of an investor who has violated a customary HR may not be deliberately overseen by the arbitrators. Moreover, from the perspective of the 'clean hands' doctrine,[144] it is difficult to argue that an investor receives full compensation for a situation to which he or she contributed. Many tribunals have already taken this view in the more general context of a wrongdoing of the investor.[145]

As regards the scenarios in which two obligations conflict, the difficulty lies clearly in balancing a violation of the FET by the state against its violation of another obligation.[146] In practice, arbitrators who find that the FET was violated should clearly establish this and order the state to pay compensation to the investor. However, should the investor continue its activity and the state comply with its FET obligation, the state would be in violation of an HR obligation and it may be brought in front of an HR court by those whose rights are violated. In order to avoid such a situation, it may be envisaged that the state and the investor reach an agreement following which the investment of the investor ends, putting also an end to the violation of the HR, and compensation is paid by the state (including, for example, the lost profits of the investor). As a general rule, states have to analyse each of the situations very carefully before signing a contract or giving permits and licences to foreign investors.[147]

[144] The 'clean hands' doctrine is an equity principle that dates back to the 18th century, when a British barrister gathered several cases where the plaintiffs were denied remedy because of their inequitable conduct. According to this principle, a person coming to court with a lawsuit or petition for a court order must be free from unfair conduct (have 'clean hands') with regard to the subject matter of his or her claim. [145] For an example of such cases, see n 138 above.
[146] The *GAMI* tribunal found, eg that the difficulty and high costs of implementing the national legislation may not be an excuse for the state to violate FET. *GAMI*, n 33 above, at para 94. In the same way, the necessity to comply with a different obligation may not be an excuse to violate the FET obligation.
[147] Such a situation resembles a situation of legal expropriation for a public interest with payment of compensation. The state realizes that it is in a position where it has to violate an HR obligation in order to comply with its FET obligation; therefore, it decides to put an end to the investor's presence on its territory. Unless such a situation has a presumption of legality once the HR obligation is documented, investors may refuse such an arrangement.

To sum up the possible impact HR norms may have on a FET claim, it appears that, despite the fact that arbitral tribunals may declare themselves competent to rule over a customary HR claim, such a claim should under no circumstance have an influence over the decision of the arbitrators on the merits of the case. The decision on a violation of the FET obligation by a state should only be taken on the basis of both the conventional and customary FET basis and the actions and measures taken by the state. The only stage where a human rights claim may impact upon a FET claim is the compensation stage. The tribunal, after considering a human rights claim, may conclude that the compensation of the investor has to be reduced proportionally to the investor's violation of HR. The risk, of course, is that the tribunal, even though it finalized the discussion on the merits, has to reopen it because it has first to determine whether there was indeed a violation of human rights by the investor, and then include its findings in the calculation of the compensation. Such a mixture between the compensation stage and a second merits stage may, in practice, result in a difficult and long procedure.

Those states that decide to include an HR argument in their claims must, by the intermediary of their counsels, make sure that they bring enough documentary proof and legal basis in support of their claim. The lack of experience of arbitrators in the field of HR may lead them to discard a claim unless the evidence in front of them is complete. In such cases, argumentation as to the customary character of the invoked HR norm, as well as rulings of various HR courts on this same norm, is advisable to be included in the state memorial.

One effect of the inclusion of HR claims in investment cases is that states will start to close legal gaps. Some states opt for an amendment of their BIT provisions in order to include a reference to HR. The 2004 US Model BIT, for instance, in its Article 13, introduced a reference to labour law: 'The Parties recognize that it is inappropriate to encourage investment by weakening or reducing the protections afforded in domestic labour laws.' One cannot exclude the possibility that, faced with frequent HR arguments, states will decide to renegotiate the terms of their BITs and include a clear provision on this issue.

IV. Conclusion

The FET obligation, which is generally criticized for resulting in an unbalanced relationship between the investor and the host state,[148] appears, after a thorough study of the existing BITs and relevant case law, to be a standard that brings a

---

[148] The critics of the FET standard are traditionally the NGOs and the developing countries which receive foreign investment but which are rarely exporting investment. However, with an increasing number of states generating investment and with developed countries finding themselves in the position of respondents in investment cases, it is difficult to define precisely the critics of the FET standard.

measure of equity to this relationship. Far from being a cause of imbalance, the FET allows investors and host states to have a relationship based on international law standards that creates a stable and predictable framework for investment. The introduction of HR-based arguments and claims in the adjudication of a FET claim has to be considered by the arbitral tribunals at the stage of calculating the compensation, not at the stage of establishing the liability of the state: if the HR claim is included in the discussion of compensation only, the liability of the state on the basis of FET is established solely on the analysis of its behaviour. Arguments based on HR violations by an investor may only reduce the compensation, but the breach of the FET obligation by the state remains. The existent BITs, in their current stage of drafting, do not address this issue directly, but given the increasing frequency with which HR discussions appear in investment cases, it is likely that states will take steps towards rectifying this issue.

15

Non-Discriminatory Treatment in Investment Disputes

Federico Ortino

I. Introduction

In the pursuit of economic growth and development, the promotion and protection of foreign investment has constituted, in the last 40 years, one of the core
objectives of economic cooperation among states.[1] International investment
agreements (IIAs), principally bilateral investment treaties (BITs), and free trade
agreements (FTAs) have focused in particular on protecting foreign investors
through a few basic treatment guarantees principally against discriminatory,
unfair, and expropriatory conduct by host states.[2] Modern IIAs include, in one
form or another, the principle of non-discrimination on the basis of the
nationality of the investor ('national treatment' and 'most-favoured nation
treatment' standards), absolute standards of treatment (such as the principle of
'fair and equitable treatment' and 'protection and security'), and guarantees
against expropriation.

As these guarantees may directly restrain states' legislative, administrative, or
judicial measures taken to implement a host of public policies (industrial, fiscal,
environmental, labour, health, etc), their potential impact (whether positive or
negative) on human rights is not difficult to perceive. Take, for example, the
right to water as implicit in a number of international human rights treaties
(such as, for example, the International Covenant on Economic, Social, and
Cultural Rights (ICESCR)).[3] Investment protection norms *may* have positive
spillovers both in the sense of attracting foreign capital and know-how necessary

---

[1] In 1959, in the first of the bilateral investment agreements (BITs) of modern times, Germany
and Pakistan expressly recognized 'that an understanding reached between the two States is likely to
promote investment, encourage private industrial and financial enterprise and to increase the
prosperity of both the States'.

[2] More recently, these agreements have also aimed at liberalizing investment flows through the
reduction of market access barriers.

[3] See Arts 11 and 12 of the International Covenant on Economic, Social, and Cultural Rights,
adopted by General Assembly resolution 2200A (XXI) of 16 December 1966.

to develop or improve host states' water infrastructure and distribution services and in the sense of imposing certain good governance standards (non-discrimination, transparency, reasonableness, due process) on host states' regulatory authorities in charge of administering water services. On the other hand, investment protection norms *may* also have a negative impact on the right to water in the sense of limiting host states' policy space to change or correct previous measures (such as privatization programmes or concession agreements) 'with a view to achieving progressively the full realization' of the right to water, as these changes may be perceived by foreign investors as violations of the non-discrimination principles, the fair and equitable principle, or the guarantees against expropriation.[4]

Given the general and undefined nature of these investment norms, their meaning and import can only be elucidated by arbitration, the chosen mechanism for the settlement of investment disputes.[5] Most investment norms should, in fact, be characterized as instruments of 'judicial integration' as the role of the judiciary (arbitral tribunals, in our case) is central in defining and implementing these norms.[6] It follows that, in order to evaluate the impact of investment norms on human rights, it is indispensable to focus on the manner in which these norms have actually been interpreted by arbitral tribunals. The raw material is not lacking: on the basis of a complex network of more than 2,500 IIAs, the last decade has witnessed an increased number of investor-state disputes (380), generating an impressive growing body of jurisprudence (approximately 180 decisions) touching upon several procedural and substantive aspects of international investment law.

Based on an examination of this growing body of jurisprudence, this chapter argues that there still exists a wide margin of inconsistency in the way in which arbitral tribunals interpret the national treatment standard even in the same IIA. Although it is still early to determine the full extent of the impact of the national treatment standard in IIAs on human rights, there is ample scope for treaty makers and arbitral tribunals to ensure that international investment law is drafted and interpreted in accordance with human rights law. In this sense, this chapter emphasizes that the diversity of treaty language and the diversity of the interpretation of this language may represent a very useful learning ground for policy makers in the field. In other words, international law on foreign investment is still in its formative years and rules, institutions, and stakeholders are still being identified and formed.

[4] See, eg the well-known investment disputes in *Vivendi Universal v Argentina*, ICSID Case No ARB/97/3; and *Agua del Tunari v Bolivia*, ICSID Case No ARB/02/3.
[5] See the Convention on the Settlement of Investment Disputes between States and Nationals of Other States signed on 18 March 1965 (hereinafter, 'the ICSID Convention').
[6] F Ortino, *Basic Legal Instruments for the Liberalisation of Trade* (2004) 24–27.

Section 1 briefly describes the several non-discrimination provisions in IIAs. Section II delineates a few features of the national treatment concept. Section III examines the interpretation of the national treatment standards by arbitral tribunals. On the basis of the findings in section III, section IV draws the lessons on the impact of the national treatment standard on human rights.

II. Non-Discrimination Provisions in IIAs

There may be several types of non-discrimination provisions in IIAs, including the national treatment (NT) standard, the most-favoured nation (MFN) treatment standard, and the prohibition of arbitrary and discriminatory treatment.[7] In general, the NT standard requires that a nation treat within its own borders foreign investors in the same manner as it treats national investors. By requiring that each member treats investors of other members at least as well as it treats its own investors, the NT standard provides for a 'relative' standard of treatment.[8] It does not guarantee a specific level of protection or that foreign investors will receive a 'fair' or 'reasonable' treatment. The NT standard simply guarantees against states affording foreign investors less favourable treatment compared to that granted to domestic investors.[9] For example, Article 1102(1) of the North American Free Trade Agreement (NAFTA)[10] provides that:

Each Party shall accord to investors of another Party treatment no less favorable than that it accords, in like circumstances, to its own investors with respect to the establishment, acquisition, expansion, management, conduct, operation, and sale or other disposition of investments.[11]

---

[7] Equally, the Fair and Equitable Treatment (FET) standard and the provisions on expropriation contain non-discrimination elements as well. See C Schreuer, 'Protection against Arbitrary or Discriminatory Measures' (2008) Transnational Dispute Management.

[8] SH Seid, *Global Regulation of Foreign Direct Investment* (2002) 44; and PE Comeaux and NS Kinsella, *Protecting Foreign Investment under International Law: Legal Aspects of Political Risk* (1997) 44, 106. Cf M Sornarajah, *The International Law on Foreign Investment* (2004); and P Muchlinski, *Multinational Enterprises and the Law* (1999).

[9] By contrast, the 'fair and equitable treatment' principle provides for an 'absolute' standard of treatment by requiring states to recognize to foreign investors a certain (minimum) level of treatment, the determination of which does not have to depend on the treatment afforded to domestic investors.

[10] The North American Free Trade Agreement signed in December 1992, available at <http://www.nafta-sec-alena.org>.

[11] The second paragraph of NAFTA, Art 1102 affords NT protection to 'investments' of investors. It states as follows:

Each Party shall accord to investments of investors of another Party treatment no less favorable than that it accords, in like circumstances, to investments of its own investors with respect to the establishment, acquisition, expansion, management, conduct, operation, and sale or other disposition of investments.

The MFN treatment standard seeks to prevent discrimination against investors from foreign countries on grounds of their nationality. In other words, it requires that a host country extend to investors from one foreign country treatment no less favourable than it accords to investors from any other foreign country in like cases. For example, Article 10(7) of the Energy Charter Treaty (ECT)[12] provides that:

Each Contracting Party shall accord to Investments in its Area of Investors of other Contracting Parties, and their related activities including management, maintenance, use, enjoyment or disposal, treatment no less favourable than that which it accords to Investments ... of the Investors of any other Contracting Party or any third state and their related activities ...

Although they include both an NT and MFN obligation, many IIAs also add an additional non-discrimination requirement. For example, Article II(3)(b) of the US-Estonia BIT[13] provides that:

Neither Party shall in any way impair by arbitrary or discriminatory measures the management, operation, maintenance, use, enjoyment, acquisition, expansion, or disposal of investments. For purpose of dispute resolution under Articles VI and VII, a measure may be arbitrary or discriminatory notwithstanding the fact that a Party has had or has exercised the opportunity to review such measure in the courts or administrative tribunals of a Party.

Some IIAs also regulate so-called 'performance requirements', that is stipulations imposed on foreign investors to act in ways considered beneficial for the host state. The most common performance requirements relate to local content, export performance, domestic equity, joint ventures, technology transfer, and employment of nationals. Their purpose is to induce foreign investors to do more to promote local development – by raising local content, creating linkages, transferring managerial techniques, employing nationals, investing in less-developed regions, strengthening the technological base, and promoting exports. These requirements can be mandatory or voluntary, they can be applied to all companies (local and foreign), or they can discriminate between companies by ownership or even by particular nationality.[14]

Increasingly, IIAs expressly regulate discriminatory performance requirements. For example, Articles 8 and 9 of the 2004 US-Uruguay BIT[15] read in part as follows:

---

[12] The Energy Charter Treaty opened for signature on 17 December 1994, available at <http://www.encharter.org>.

[13] Bilateral Investment Treaty between the United States and Estonia signed on 19 April 1994, available at <http://www.unctad.org/iia>.

[14] UNCTAD, 'World Investment Report 2003 – FDI Policies for Development: National and International Perspectives' (2003) 119–123.

[15] Bilateral Investment Treaty between Uruguay and the United States signed on 7 September 2004, available at <http://www.unctad.org/iia>.

Article 8: Performance Requirements

1. Neither Party may, in connection with the establishment, acquisition, expansion, management, conduct, operation, or sale or other disposition of an investment of an investor of a Party or of a non-Party in its territory, impose or enforce any requirement or enforce any commitment or undertaking:

(a) to export a given level or percentage of goods or services;

(b) to achieve a given level or percentage of domestic content;

(c) to purchase, use, or accord a preference to goods produced in its territory, or to purchase goods from persons in its territory;

(d) to relate in any way the volume or value of imports to the volume or value of exports or to the amount of foreign exchange inflows associated with such investment;

(e) to restrict sales of goods or services in its territory that such investment produces or supplies by relating such sales in any way to the volume or value of its exports or foreign exchange earnings;

(f) to transfer a particular technology, a production process, or other proprietary knowledge to a person in its territory; or

(g) to supply exclusively from the territory of the Party the goods that such investment produces or the services that it supplies to a specific regional market or to the world market.

. . .

Article 9: Senior Management and Boards of Directors

1. Neither Party may require that an enterprise of that Party that is a covered investment appoint to senior management positions natural persons of any particular nationality.

2. A Party may require that a majority of the board of directors, or any committee thereof, of an enterprise of that Party that is a covered investment, be of a particular nationality, or resident in the territory of the Party, provided that the requirement does not materially impair the ability of the investor to exercise control over its investment.

Despite the existence of several non-discrimination rules in IIAs, this chapter focuses on the NT standard as being one of the most recurrent grounds for claims brought by foreign investors on the basis of IIAs.

III. National Treatment Standard: Delineating the Concept[16]

While the underlying objective of the NT standard is the promotion of foreign investment, its basic function has focused more strictly on protecting foreign investors from internal regulation affording more favourable treatment to domestic investors. What does one mean by granting NT or, in other words, prohibiting discrimination based on the (foreign) nationality of the investor (or investment)? And if a measure has a detrimental impact (or adverse effect) on foreign compared to domestic investors, can it be said to discriminate even though, on balance, it is a sensible measure? In order to answer these two related

---

[16] This section is partly based on F Ortino, 'From Non-Discrimination to Reasonableness: A Paradigm Shift in International Economic Law?' Jean Monnet Working Papers 1/2005.

questions, it is essential to delineate two basic features of the NT standard: 'nationality discrimination' and 'public policy justification'.

A. Different Ways of Understanding 'Nationality Discrimination'

Although there may be several ways in which the notion of nationality discrimination may be understood, one could capture most of them by focusing on four possible key features of an allegedly discriminatory measure: language, effect, inherence, and intent. Even though dimensions of all four features may be used cumulatively, disaggregation is useful in order to clarify each distinct feature.

The first concept is based on the discriminatory 'language' of the national measure under review, more commonly known as formal or de jure discrimination.[17] Formal discrimination on grounds of nationality may occur when a measure *explicitly* discriminates on the basis of the nationality of the investor. In other words, the measure is said to breach the NT standard because it employs the prohibited factor (nationality) as *the* differentiating criterion. For example, a domestic fiscal regime which requires foreign companies to pay 20 per cent corporate tax, while domestic companies need only pay 10 per cent would presumptively be caught by the prohibition of nationality discrimination since companies are subject to differential taxation expressly on the basis of their nationality.

However, formally *different* treatment may not constitute unequal treatment, if the different treatment is predicated on grounds of substantial equality between foreign and domestic investors (for example, taxing domestic and foreign companies differently in order to avoid double taxation). Similarly, formally *identical* treatment does not guarantee by itself equal treatment, if the identical treatment has a detrimental effect or impact on foreign compared to domestic investors (for example, requiring of all investors a particular qualification or authorization, only available domestically, will have, to a very large extent, the same dividing effect as a rule excluding foreign investors, although the rule formally contains no reference to the nationality of the investor). For this reason, the prohibition of nationality discrimination has been extended to cover notions of substantial or material discrimination on grounds of nationality.[18] The thorny questions surrounding the concept of material discrimination relate to the *determination* of the investors (or investments) whose treatment should be compared, as well as the *type* and *amount*[19] of detrimental effect which is necessary to establish de facto discrimination.

---

[17] It has been said that the NT principle appears to have been developed in international economic law with formal discrimination in mind. R Hudec, 'GATT/WTO Constraints on National Regulation: Requiem for an "Aim and Effects" Test' (1998) 32 International Lawyer 619, 622.

[18] See G Davies, *Nationality Discrimination in the European Internal Market* (2003) 10–11.

[19] This is where a broad interpretation of what constitutes material discrimination on grounds of nationality may equate in practical terms to the principle of equality.

While discrimination based on the mere 'detrimental impact' or 'adverse effect' on foreign investors is perhaps the concept that captures the broadest spectrum of nationality discrimination, there are other ways in which the prohibition on nationality discrimination may be understood. One is based on the *inherent* discriminatory character of the national measure under review. Regulatory measures which treat residents and non-residents differently are perhaps the best-known cases of this type of discrimination.[20] Since most residents are nationals and most non-residents are not nationals, this type of regulatory requirement or distinction may be said to be inherently discriminatory vis-à-vis foreigners. One could be inventive and include also regulatory requirements/distinctions based on language (for example, only lawyers that speak Swedish can practise law in Sweden), religion (for example, only Catholic teachers may be employed in Italian public schools), and so forth.[21] It is obvious, however, that defining when a national measure is inherently discriminatory may constitute a rather difficult task[22] and depending how rigorous or loose such concept is defined, the reach of the NT standard changes dramatically.

A further way to understand nationality discrimination is based on the discriminatory *intent* of the national legislator. This approach is premised essentially on the objective of eradicating protectionism. Although discriminatory or protectionist intent may be said to be more or less objectively identified,[23] it seems that the fundamental feature of this strand resides on attributing relevance to the policy purposes of the national measure under review. In other words, in order to detect discriminatory or protectionist intent, an inquiry over the policy reasons underlying the national measure needs to be carried out.[24] If a valid argument can be made that the measure under question has been taken to pursue a legitimate public policy, this can be used as evidence disproving the existence of protectionist intent. To take the examples given above, while a qualification requirement available only domestically may be said to have discriminatory effects (or detrimental impact) vis-à-vis foreign investors, there will not be a protectionist *intent* if the qualification is deemed to be somehow related

---

[20] See ECJ jurisprudence on free movement of services. For commentary, see P Eeckhout, 'Constitutional Concepts for Free Trade in Services' in G de Burca and J Scott (eds), *The EU and the WTO: Legal and Constitutional Aspects* (2001) 233–234, who calls this type of discrimination 'indirect' discrimination to distinguish it from a purely factual or effects-based discrimination.

[21] See also M Krawjeski, *National Regulation and Trade Liberalization in Services* (2003) 108–114.

[22] G de Burca, 'Unpacking the Concept of Discrimination in EC and International Trade Law', in G de Burca and J Scott (eds), *The EU and the WTO: Legal and Constitutional Aspects* (2001) 189.

[23] See S Lester, B Mercurio et al, *World Trade Law* (2008) 274, distinguishing between 'subjective' and 'objective' intent.

[24] On the relevance of protectionist intent, see R Hudec, n 17 above, 625–626; D Regan, 'Regulatory Purpose and "Like Products" in Article III:4 of the GATT' (2002) Journal of World Trade 443–444; and M Danusso and R Denton, 'Does the European Court of Justice Look for a Protectionist Motive under Article 95?' (1990) Legal Issues of European Integration 67 ff.

to, or justified by, the pursuit of a legitimate regulatory purpose such as consumer protection.

B. The Relationship between Nationality Discrimination and Public Policy Justification

The relationship between discrimination and the policy justification underlying the measure at issue may change depending on what one means by 'discrimination'. If one takes the effect-based notion of discrimination (does the measure have discriminatory effects, or, to be more precise, does it have detrimental impact on foreign investors?), then it might be said that the issue of justification (is the measure, nonetheless, a sensible rule?) is distinct from a finding of discrimination. This seems to be true also for the criteria based on 'inherence' and 'language'. One can deal with these types of prohibition on nationality discrimination (namely, defined on the basis of 'language', 'inherence', or 'effect') by saying that some kinds of discrimination are justified, thus adopting a two-step analysis:

Step 1	Step 2
discriminatory language or inherently discriminatory character or detrimental impact vis-à-vis foreign investors = violation of the NT standard	unless it is *justified*

However, as seen in the preceding section, if one focuses on protectionist 'intent' (is the purpose of the measure to protect domestic capital?), an inquiry over the policy reasons underlying the national measure might be said to become an almost indispensable tool in determining whether the measure discriminates on grounds of nationality. Accordingly, in the case of a national measure which, despite its disparate impact vis-à-vis imported products or foreign investors, is justified on policy grounds, one can say that discrimination does not exist at all. This is the so-called one-step analysis, where 'justification' considerations are entangled within, and are part of, an assessment of 'discrimination':

Step 1
unjustified detrimental impact on foreign investors = protectionist intent = violation of the NT standard

This is not simply a structural issue (namely, in order to appreciate detrimental effects, one does not need to take into account policy justifications, while, in order to identify protectionist intent, one does). The fundamental point in the relationship between 'discrimination' and 'justification' deals with the normative choice made by the 'legislator' when imposing, or the 'interpreter' when applying, the NT principle.

On one extreme, the prohibition of nationality discrimination may simply mean that *only* formal discrimination based on the nationality of investors is not permitted (option 1). This prohibition may either be supplemented by a clause according to which formally discriminatory measures may be justified on public policy grounds (option 1A), or be an absolute rule with no possibility to take into account public policy considerations (option 1B).

Option 1

A. NT prohibits nationality discrimination, understood as covering only 'formal discrimination', unless it is justified on public policy grounds (rule/justification)

***

B. NT prohibits nationality discrimination, understood as covering only 'formal discrimination', with no possibility of justification (absolute rule)

On the other extreme, the same prohibition may be extended to reach all national measures with mere detrimental impact on foreign investors (namely, material discrimination; this is option 2). Again, such a prohibition may either be accompanied by a justification provision (option 2A) or be an absolute rule (option 2B).

Option 2

A. NT prohibits nationality discrimination, understood as covering 'material discrimination', unless it is justified on public policy grounds (rule/justification)

***

B. NT prohibits nationality discrimination, understood as covering 'material discrimination', with no possibility of justification (absolute rule)

Options 1B and 2B (the absolute rule) stress the normative relevance of the discriminatory 'language' or 'effect' of national measures. There is no possibility of justifying such language and effect on public policy grounds. By adding a justification provision (options 1A and 2A), the normative relevance of the discriminatory 'language' and 'effect' somehow diminishes, since there are other values and interests that need to be taken into account.[25]

Three further points should be emphasized. First, on a practical level, while option 1B (absolute ban on discriminatory language) could be accepted, option 2B (absolute ban on discriminatory effect) would encounter serious legitimacy problems. As seen before, there is a great proportion of national measures with a detrimental impact on foreign interests, which are nonetheless sensible and necessary rules. Should they all be prohibited?

Second, while in option 1A (ban on discriminatory language with possibility of justification) the normative balance between 'discrimination' and 'public policy grounds' appears to remain clearly tilted in favour of the former (that is, in most cases, formal discrimination will be difficult to justify), in option 2A (ban on discriminatory effect with possibility of justification) this balance seems at least to be evenly distributed among the two competing values.

Furthermore, and fundamentally, when the NT principle is extended to cover national measures with detrimental impact (on foreign investors), the normative focus of the principle is not on the detrimental impact per se, rather on whether the measure (with detrimental impact) is related to a legitimate regulatory purpose (namely, is justified on public policy grounds).[26] The fact that the national measure has detrimental impact becomes a 'threshold' question, where the justification analysis is the real key test.

Independently of whether one defines nationality discrimination on the basis of 'effect' and thus uses the two-step approach or one defines nationality discrimination on the basis of 'intent' using the one-step approach, in both cases the relevant (normative) inquiry appears to be the determination of whether the measure at issue is justified on public policy grounds.

IV. Investment Jurisprudence Interpreting the NT Standard

The practical application of the NT standard may revolve around several key concepts. These include principally: (1) the relationship between foreign and domestic investors; (2) the meaning of 'less favourable treatment'; (3) the legitimate policy objectives justifying the national measure at issue; and (4) the relationship between the measure and the relevant policy objective. These four concepts, which might be found explicitly in the text of the NT provisions or simply stem from their interpretation by the relevant judicial bodies, may play different or multiple roles in international investment law.

---

[25] There will also be a normative difference if public policy considerations come into play as part of the finding of discrimination (one-step analysis) or at the stage of justifying such discrimination (two-step analysis).

[26] It is not relevant here whether justification is addressed separately from, or is part of, the determination of discrimination.

These four concepts may be grouped under the following two indispensable pillars of the NT standard: (1) nationality discrimination; and (2) public policy justification. Independently of its formal (textual) structure, the NT standard has so far been envisioned as a two-step analysis: the adjudicator needs to determine, first, the existence of 'nationality discrimination' and, second, the existence of a 'public policy justification'.[27] Accordingly, this is how this section is subdivided.

A. Nationality Discrimination

The jurisprudence applying the NT standard focuses around the following two key elements: 'likeness' and 'less favourable treatment'.

1. Likeness

Several IIAs explicitly provide that the NT standard involves a comparison between foreign investors/investments and domestic investors/investments that are in 'like' or 'similar' situations or circumstances (for example, NAFTA; BITs of United States and Canada).[28] However, in other investment agreements the national treatment rule is not qualified by a 'likeness' criterion (for example, Energy Charter Treaty; BITs of France and Germany).[29]

Most of the existing arbitral jurisprudence has dealt so far with NT provisions explicitly qualified by likeness. The interpretations of the meaning and function of the likeness criterion have, however, varied substantially even with regard to the same provision.

One reading of the likeness criterion has focused on the nature and extent of the *competitive relationship* between investors. According to this view, if the aim of

---

[27] As mentioned above, I will not address the arbitral decisions interpreting the investment treaty protection against 'arbitrary', 'unreasonable', or 'discriminatory' measures, which is often included in IIAs (often in addition to a national treatment provision). However, there is evidence that the legal test with regard to the non-discrimination principle is based on a two-prong test. For example, in *Plama Consortium Ltd v Bulgaria*, ICSID Case No ARB/03/24, Award, 27 August 2008, the tribunal interpreted the obligation to refrain from 'discriminatory measures' in the Energy Charter Treaty (ECT), Art 10(1) as follows: 'With regard to discrimination, it corresponds to the negative formulation of the principle of equality of treatment. It entails like persons being treated in a different manner in similar circumstances without reasonable or justifiable grounds' (at para 184). Cf Schreuer, n 7 above.

[28] Art II(1) of the United States-Ecuador BIT states in part as follows:

Each Party shall permit and treat investment, and activities associated therewith, on a basis no less favorable than that accorded in like situations to investment or associated activities of its own nationals or companies, or of nationals or companies of any third country, whichever is the most favorable . . .

[29] For example, ECT, Art 10(7) states in part as follows:

Each Contracting Party shall accord to Investments in its Area of Investors of other Contracting Parties, and their related activities including management, maintenance, use, enjoyment or disposal, treatment no less favourable than that which it accords to Investments of its own Investors . . .

the NT standard is to prohibit measures that protect domestic investors, then it is logical to focus on the comparison between foreign and domestic investors that are in competition with each other. Domestic investors may be 'protected' by the less favourable treatment accorded to foreign investors only if the domestic and foreign investors are in a competitive relationship in the marketplace. Without such relationship, no differential treatment granted to the foreign investors will have the effect of affording protection to the domestic investors. For example, several early NAFTA tribunals pointing to the potentially broad meaning of the term 'like circumstances' in Article 1102 concluded that the relevant comparison involves, first of all, investors and investment in the 'same business or economic sector'. These tribunals in particular looked, albeit in a very summary manner, at the competitive relationship between the corporate entities involved in the dispute. For example, in *Myers*, the tribunal noted that the foreign and domestic investors involved in the dispute were engaged in providing the same service (polychlorinated biphenyl (PCB) waste remediation) and that the foreign investor 'was in a position to attract customers that might otherwise have gone to the domestic operators because it could offer more favourable prices and because it had extensive experience and credibility'.[30] In *ADF*, the investor claimed that it was in like circumstances since it operated in the same sector, sold the same product, and competed for the same customers as the domestic investors. It bought the same input, treated that input the same way, and delivered the same fabricated steel to the same clients.[31]

A second reading of the likeness criterion has rejected the relevance of the competitive relationship between investors. Rejecting such a 'narrow' interpretation of the term 'in like situations' in the US-Ecuador BIT, the tribunal in *Occidental* accepted the claimant's argument that Ecuador had breached the NT obligation because a number of companies involved in the export of other goods, particularly flowers, mining, and seafood products, were entitled to receive a VAT refund, while these refunds were denied to the claimant, an oil exploration and production company.[32] The tribunal noted that:

'in like situations' cannot be interpreted in the narrow sense advanced by Ecuador as the purpose of national treatment is to protect investors as compared to local producers, and this cannot be done by addressing exclusively the sector in which that particular activity is undertaken.[33]

---

[30] The tribunal added that: 'It was precisely because SDMI was in a position to take business away from its Canadian competitors that Chem-Security and Cintec lobbied the Minister of the Environment to ban exports when the U.S. authorities opened the border.' *SD Myers, Inc v Canada*, First Partial Award, 13 November 2000, at para 251.

[31] *ADF Group Inc v United States of America*, ICSID Case No. ARB(AF)/00/1, Final Award, 9 January 2003, at para 64. See also *Feldman Karpa v Mexico*, ICSID Case No ARB(AF)/99/1, Award, 16 December 2002, at para 172.

[32] *Occidental Exploration and Production Co v Ecuador*, LCIA Case No UN3467, Award, 1 July 2004.   [33] *Occidental*, at para 173.

A third reading of the likeness criterion has taken a diametrically opposite approach. In a highly controversial NAFTA dispute between Methanex and the US Government over the legality of a Californian ban on use or sale of MTBE gasoline additive adopted on environmental protection grounds, the tribunal appears to have limited the category of domestic investors 'in like circumstances' relevant for purposes of the NT determination to those domestic investors in an 'identical' situation with the foreign investor, excluding the broader and allegedly competitive ethanol producers.[34] The tribunal noted that:

The key question is: who is the proper comparator? Simply to assume that the ethanol industry or a particular ethanol producer is the comparator here would beg that question. Given the object of Article 1102 and the flexibility which the provision provides in its adoption of 'like circumstances', it would be as perverse to ignore identical comparators if they were available and to use comparators that were less 'like', as it would be perverse to refuse to find and to apply less 'like' comparators when no identical comparators existed. The difficulty which Methanex encounters in this regard is that there are comparators which are identical to it.[35]

Similarly, the recent tribunal in *Champion Trading Co* has adopted an apparently narrow interpretation of the term 'in like situations' in the NT obligation in the US-Egypt BIT.[36] In determining whether the foreign investment was in a like situation with several domestic companies (that had allegedly received payments from the Egyptian Government), the tribunal looked beyond to whether the domestic and foreign cotton traders were operating in the same sector. The tribunal stated that:

Although both kinds of companies operate in the same industry and are subject to same kind of rules, there is a significant difference between a company which opts to buy cotton from the Collection Centres at fixed prices and a company which opts to trade on the free market, whether or not the company is privately-owned or State-owned or whether the company is national or foreign.[37]

Accordingly, despite the fact that the foreign and domestic cotton traders were operating in the same economic sector, they could be distinguished on the basis that the domestic traders were buying cotton from the Collection Centres at fixed prices. It is, however, not clear whether this difference is enough to exclude a competitive relationship between the foreign investor and the domestic traders at issue.

2. *'Less Favourable Treatment'*

Although the textual formulations of the NT standard vary with regard to the required treatment, the most commonly used formulation contemplates

---

[34] *Methanex v United States*, UNCITRAL, Final Award, 3 August 2005.

[35] *Methanex*, at para 17, Pt IV, Ch B, p 8.

[36] *Champion Trading Co, Ameritrade International, Inc, James T Wahba, John B Wahba, Timothy T Wahba v Egypt*, ICSID Case No ARB/02/9, Award, 27 October 2006.

[37] *Champion Trading Co*, at para 154.

treatment of foreign investors and investments that is 'no less favourable' than that accorded to domestic investors and investments of the host country.[38] As in the case of the likeness criterion, arbitral tribunals have differed in the test adopted for establishing whether a measure affords 'less favourable treatment' to the foreign investor. Two separate issues may be identified in this regard.

First, arbitral tribunals have differed with regard to whether the incriminated measure's *adverse effect* on foreign investors is sufficient to establish less favourable treatment or whether *discriminatory intent* is also an indispensable element in the national treatment equation. Several investment tribunals seem to rely on the measure's effects only, excluding the relevance of the measure's intent. In *Myers*, the NAFTA tribunal stated as follows:

Intent is important, but protectionist intent is not necessarily decisive on its own. The existence of an intent to favour nationals over non-nationals would not give rise to a breach of Chapter 1102 of the NAFTA if the measure in question were to produced no adverse effect on the non-national complainant. The word 'treatment' suggests that practical impact is required to produce a breach of Article 1102, not merely a motive or intent that is in violation of Chapter 11.[39]

The relevance of this statement by the majority in *Myers* should be emphasized in light of the separate opinion submitted by the third arbitrator, Dr Schwartz, which had focused primarily on an assessment of protectionist intent.[40]

In *Feldman*, the tribunal found that on balance the US investor had been treated in a less favourable manner compared to domestically owned reseller/exporters of cigarettes (that is, a de facto discrimination by the Mexican Ministry of Finance) in violation of Mexico's obligations under NAFTA, Article 1102. Such finding was based on a very simple two-pronged conclusion. First, no cigarette reseller-exporter (namely, the relevant category identified for purposes of the comparison) could legally have qualified for the tax rebates, since none would have been able to obtain the necessary invoices stating the tax amounts separately as required for the tax rebates. Second, the US investor was denied the rebates at a time when at least three other companies in like circumstances (all of Mexican nationality) were granted them.[41]

In *Occidental*, the tribunal was convinced that treatment less favourable than that accorded to national companies had 'not been done with the intent of discriminating against foreign-owned companies'. However, the tribunal noted

---

[38] Other times the national treatment obligation requires states to accord foreign investors and investment the 'same' or 'as favourable treatment as' that accorded to domestic investors and investments.
[39] *Myers*, n 30 above, at para 254. In *Pope & Talbot*, the tribunal also seems to look at the effects in determining whether the Canadian measure at issue afforded less favourable treatment to the foreign investor. See, eg *Pope & Talbot Inc v Government of Canada*, Award on the Merits (Phase 2), 10 April 2001, at para 102.
[40] See separate opinion by Dr Bryan Schwartz on 12 November 2000, which clearly (and unfortunately) constituted the basis for the drafting of the majority opinion.
[41] *Feldman*, n 31 above, at para 176.

that 'the result of the policy enacted . . . in fact has been a less favorable treatment to [the foreign investor]'.[42]

Adopting a different approach, other tribunals have relied more or less expressly on discriminatory intent in order to sustain a national treatment claim. In *Genin*,[43] the tribunal rejected the non-discrimination claim brought against Estonia, noting that:

> there is no indication that the Bank of Estonia specifically targeted EIB in a discriminatory way, or treated it less favourably than banks owned by Estonian nationals. Moreover, Claimants have failed to prove that the withdrawal of EIB's license was done with the intention to harm the Bank or any of the Claimants in this arbitration, or to treat them in a discriminatory way.[44]

Equally, in *Methanex*, the tribunal expressly required that in order to establish a violation of the NT obligation, the Canadian investor 'must demonstrate . . . that California intended to favour domestic investors by discriminating against foreign investors'.[45]

The second less controversial issue surrounding the 'less favourable treatment' test is whether nationality discrimination is established simply by showing that *one foreign* investor has been treated less favourably than at least *one domestic* investor in like circumstances, or whether a broader 'nationality imbalance' (foreign investors as a whole are treated less favourably than similar domestic investors as a whole) needs to be established by the claimant.

Most of the cases so far decided (in particular under NAFTA Chapter 11) seem to have established a violation of the NT obligation simply by showing that the national measure under review affords less favourable treatment to the foreign investor (who has brought the claim) compared to the treatment afforded to at least one domestic investor in like circumstances.[46] In *Pope & Talbot*, for example, the tribunal noted that a breach of NAFTA, Article 1102 is presumptively established 'once a difference in treatment between a domestic and a foreign-owned investment is discerned'.[47] Canada had argued in its defence that in cases of alleged de facto discrimination, a violation of the NT obligation can be found only if the measure in question 'disproportionately disadvantages' the foreign-owned investments or investors.[48] According to Canada, the tribunal must determine:

---

[42] At para 177. See also *International Thunderbird Gaming v Mexico*, UNCITRAL, Award, 26 January 2006, 'It is not expected from Thunderbird that it show separately that the less favourable treatment was motivated because of nationality. The text of Article 1102 of the NAFTA does not require such showing' (at para 177).

[43] *Genin and ors v Estonia*, ICSID Case No ARB/99/2, Award, 25 June 2001.

[44] *Genin*, at para 369.   [45] *Methanex*, n 34 above, at para 12, Pt IV, Ch B, p 6.

[46] T Grierson-Weiler and I Laird, 'Standards of Treatment' in P Muchliski, F Ortino, and C Schreuer (eds), *The Oxford Handbook of International Investment Law* (2008) 293.

[47] *Pope & Talbot, Inc v The Government of Canada*, UNCITRAL, Award on the Merits of Phase 2, 10 April 2001, at para 79.

[48] See also Canada Statement of defence in *Ethyl Corp v Canada*, Statement of Defence (Canada), 27 November 1997, at paras 80–81.

whether there are any Canadian owned investments that are accorded the same treatment as the Investor … Then, the size of that group of Canadian investments must be compared to the size of the group of Canadian investments receiving more favourable treatment than the Investment. Unless the disadvantaged *Canadian* group (receiving the same treatment as the Investor) is smaller than the advantaged group, no discrimination cognizable under Article 1102 would exist.[49]

The tribunal rejected Canada's 'disproportionate disadvantage' approach based on its unwillingness to weaken the NT obligation and the objectives of NAFTA. The tribunal noted that 'the recognition that the NT obligation can be violated through *de facto* measures has always been based on an unwillingness to allow circumvention of that right by skillful or evasive drafting' and that such a 'result would be inconsistent with the investment objectives of NAFTA, in particular Article 102(l)(b) and (c), to promote conditions of fair competition and to increase substantially investment opportunities'.[50] Furthermore, the tribunal emphasized the 'practical implications' of Canada's suggestion,[51] how 'unwieldy' it would be to show disproportionate disadvantage and 'how it would hamstring foreign owned investments seeking to vindicate their Article 1102 rights'.[52]

This interpretation seems to have also been indirectly accepted (in a dicta) by the recent *Methanex* decision. In invoking a violation of the NT provision, Methanex emphasized the word 'most' contained in the third paragraph of Article 1102, which states that:

The treatment accorded by a Party under paragraphs 1 and 2 means, with respect to a state or province, treatment no less favorable than the most favorable treatment accorded, in like circumstances, by that state or province to investors, and to investments of investors, of the Party of which it forms a part.

In other words, according to Methanex, this provision means that Methanex and other Canadian or Mexican investors and investments are entitled to the best, not the worst, treatment accorded to like domestic investors and their investments. Although the tribunal did not find a breach of the NT provision as the California ban did not differentiate between foreign and domestic like

---

[49] *Pope & Talbot*, n 39 above, at para 44.   [50] *Pope & Talbot*, at paras 69–70.
[51] The investor would need 'to ascertain whether there are any other American owned lumber producing companies among the more than 500 softwood lumber quota holders operating in Canada. If so, the treatment accorded those companies as a whole would have to be measured and then weighed against the predominant treatment, whatever that might mean, accorded Canadian companies operating in like circumstances. A violation of Article 1102 could then only be found if the differing treatment between the class of American investments and their Canadian competitors in like circumstances is "disproportionately" in favour of the domestic investments, whatever that might mean' (*Pope & Talbot*, n 39 above, at para 71).
[52] On one level, it may be argued that this approach is unconsciously spurred by the nature of the dispute settlement mechanism devised by IIAs: a mechanism that recognizes to individual investors the right to directly vindicate the obligations assumed by the three state parties. See F Ortino, 'From Non-Discrimination to Reasonableness: A Paradigm Shift in International Economic Law?' Jean Monnet Working Papers 1/2005.

investors,[53] it did recognize that Methanex's reading of Article 1102(3) was 'entirely plausible'.[54]

B. Justification on Public Policy Grounds

The analysis under the NT standard does not necessarily end with a finding of nationality discrimination. Particularly in the case where such a finding is based on the adverse effect on the foreign investor, it may be justified on public policy grounds.

Justification on public policy grounds, such as consumer protection, public health, or environmental protection, may be expressly provided for in so-called 'general exceptions' provisions of investment treaties, usually formulated on the basis of GATT, Article XX.[55] However, since the use of these general exceptions provisions in international investment treaties is not common, tribunals have given relevance to public policy justifications even when no such general exceptions provision was included in the text of the underlying treaty. For example, in the context of NAFTA Chapter 11, notwithstanding the lack of a provision expressly permitting states to justify on public policy grounds national measures that afford less favourable treatment to foreign investors, NAFTA tribunals have interpreted the 'in like circumstances' language in Article 1102 as a de facto public policy justification mechanism. Accordingly, if the less favourable treatment afforded to a foreign investor vis-à-vis a domestic one may be justified on the basis that such differentiation is related to a legitimate public policy, then there is no violation of the NT obligation. This may be seen as the *second* function of the phrase 'in like circumstances' in NAFTA, Article 1102 (the first one being the determination of the relevant comparator).[56] In *Myers*, for example, the tribunal expressly noted that 'the assessment of "like circumstances" must also take into account circumstances that would justify governmental regulations that treat them [i.e., a foreign investor and a domestic investor competing in the same business sector] differently in order to protect the public interest'. According to the tribunal, such interpretation conforms with the general principles emerging from the legal context of the NAFTA, including both its concern with the environment and the need to avoid trade distortions that are not justified by environmental concerns.[57]

---

[53] See above section on 'likeness'.   [54] *Methanex*, n 34 above, at para 22, Pt IV, Ch B.
[55] For example, Art 83 of the Singapore-Japan New Age Economic Partnership or Art 200 of the China-New Zealand FTA. Cf A Newcombe, 'General Exceptions in International Investment Agreements', presented at 2008 London WTO Conference.
[56] See above section on 'likeness'.
[57] *Myers*, n 30 above, at paras 247–250. See also the panel's decision in the *Mexican Trucking* dispute (*United States – In the Matter of Cross Border Trucking Services (Mexican Trucking)*, Award, 6 February 2001), where reference was made to the 'immediate source' for the 'in like circumstances' language, the United States-Canada FTA: 'The United States has referred to elaborating language in the FTA on the national treatment obligation to support the interpretation of the phrase used in NAFTA to permit differential treatment where appropriate to meet legitimate regulatory objectives' (para 249).

A similar approach is found in arbitral tribunals' decisions outside the NAFTA context. In *Champion Trading*, for example, the tribunal explained that Article II(2)(a) of the US-Egypt BIT requires parties not to treat investors differently on the grounds of their different nationality, if they are in like situations. More importantly, the tribunal added that 'the question would remain whether a difference of treatment in like situations could be permissible based on other objective grounds'.[58]

The two main conditions prescribed by investment tribunals for allowing such public policy justification are that: (1) the public policy is *legitimate* or *admissible*; and (2) the relation between the measure and the public policy is *reasonable*.

1. Admissible Public Policies

At least within the context of NAFTA, Article 1102, there appears to be no quantitative and qualitative limitation on the types of public policies that may be taken into account for purposes of justifying less favourable treatment vis-à-vis foreign investors.[59]

The de facto exception in NAFTA, Article 1102 being an open-ended list, the only general condition imposed with regard to the range of admissible public policies is perhaps that they be 'legitimate' or 'rational'. However, there has not been much discussion on the issue of the legitimacy of the public policies underlying a national measure affording less favourable treatment to foreign investors. In the few cases so far decided by NAFTA tribunals under Chapter 11, the following public policies have been considered 'legitimate': (1) to ensure the economic strength of the domestic PCB processing industry in order to maintain the ability to process PCBs within the country in the future[60]; (2) to remove the threat of countervailing duty actions[61] and to provide for new entrants[62] in the lumber industry; (3) to ensure road safety in the trucking services sector[63]; (4) to obtain better control over tax revenues, discourage smuggling, protect intellectual property rights, and prohibit gray market sales;[64] and (5) to ensure that the sugar industry in Mexico was in the hands of solvent enterprises.[65]

---

[58] *Champion Trading*, n 36 above, at para 134. The tribunal, however, did not answer this latter question since it found that the foreign and domestic companies at issue were not in a like situation.

[59] There is neither an exhaustive or closed list of public policies that may justify differential treatment, nor a requirement that such policies be of a non-economic character.

[60] *Myers*, n 30 above, at para 255 ('This was a legitimate goal, consistent with the policy objectives of the Basel Convention.')   [61] *Pope & Talbot*, n 39 above, at paras 87, 102.

[62] Ibid., at para 78.   [63] *Mexican Trucking*, n 57 above, at para 257.

[64] *Feldman*, n 31 above, at para 170 (dicta). Related to the issue of the admissibility of the public policies considered within an Art 1102 analysis, it is the requirement that the national policy at issue be 'not motivated by preference of domestic over foreign owned investments' (*Pope & Talbot*, n 39 above, at paras 87, 93, 103). See also *Feldman*, at para 182, where the tribunal excluded the existence of 'any rational justification' for Mexico's less favourable de facto treatment of CEMSA noting that the US investor was owned by a very outspoken foreigner, who had filed a NAFTA Chapter 11 claim against the Government of Mexico.

[65] *GAMI Investments, Inc v Mexico*, UNCITRAL, Final Award, 15 November 2004, at para 114.

2. Relation between the Measure and the Public Policy

Before a measure affording less favourable treatment in violation of the NT standard may be said to be related to, or justified on, a relevant public policy, arbitral tribunals seem to require that such relation or justification be somehow 'reasonable'. In *Pope & Talbot*, for example, the arbitral tribunal expressly required that there be a 'reasonable nexus between the measure and a rational, non-discriminatory government policy'.[66]

The relevant question in this context is defining under which condition a measure may be said to be *reasonably related to* a public policy. In NAFTA Chapter 11 case law, the intensity of the inquiry over the reasonableness of such relationship greatly varies among the existing decisions: (1) some tribunals seemed to have accepted the reasonableness of the measure simply on the basis that a non-discriminatory reason existed; (2) other tribunals have performed a 'minimal relationship test' inquiring on the *suitability* or *effectiveness* of the measure at issue to pursue its policy objective; and (3) other tribunals have imposed an even stricter test requiring that the measure under review be *necessary* to pursue its policy objective (namely, it is the 'least trade restrictive alternative').

In *GAMI*, for example, the tribunal accepted Mexico's argument that its measure (expropriating only half of the sugar mills in the country) was not in violation of NAFTA, Article 1102 because the measure was 'plausibly connected with a legitimate goal of policy'. The tribunal's argument was as follows:

> The reason [for the expropriation] was not that [the sugar mills] were prosperous and the Government was greedy. To the contrary: Mexico perceived that mills operating in conditions of effective insolvency needed public participation in the interest of the national economy in a broad sense. The Government may have been misguided. That is a matter of policy and politics. The Government may have been clumsy in its analysis of the relevant criteria for the cutoff line between candidates and non-candidates for expropriation. Its understanding of corporate finance may have been deficient. But ineffectiveness is not discrimination. The arbitrators are satisfied that a reason exists for the measure which was not itself discriminatory. That measure was plausibly connected with a legitimate goal of policy (ensuring that the sugar industry was in the hands of solvent enterprises) and was applied neither in a discriminatory manner nor as a disguised barrier to equal opportunity.[67]

It is interesting how the tribunal was not interested in analysing whether the Mexican measure was 'ineffective', 'misguided', or 'deficient' as long as there was a plausible connection with the legitimate policy goal pursued by the Mexican authorities.

An example of the second, more rigid approach may be found in *Pope & Talbot*, where the tribunal found that the application by Canada of the export control regime for softwood lumber only to certain provinces (determining differential treatment among a foreign investor operating in one of these provinces and those

---

[66] *Pope & Talbot*, n 39 above, at paras 78, 81.   [67] *GAMI*, n 65 above, at para 144.

companies operating in the non-covered provinces) was 'reasonably related' to the rational policy of removing the threat of countervailing duty (CVD) actions by the United States. Since the United States had never made a final CVD determination against producers in the non-covered provinces, there was no need for Canada to apply the control regime to those provinces.[68]

The stricter necessity test was, on the other hand, applied, for example, by the *Myers* tribunal. Having conceded that Canada was pursuing a legitimate goal (namely, to ensure the economic strength of its PCB processing industry), the NAFTA tribunal noted that there were a number of legitimate ways by which Canada could have achieved its goal and that the export ban was not one of them. The indirect motive was understandable, but the method contravened Canada's international commitments under the NAFTA. Canada's right to source all government requirements and to grant subsidies to the Canadian industry are but two examples of legitimate alternative measures. The fact that the matter was addressed subsequently and the border re-opened also shows that Canada was not constrained in its ability to deal effectively with the situation.[69] The same tribunal made reference to NAFTA, Article 104 (on the relation between NAFTA and environmental and conservation agreements), which provides that 'where a Party has a choice among equally effective and reasonably available means of complying' with environmental and conservation agreements (including the Basel Convention), the party is obliged to choose 'the alternative which is the least inconsistent with other provisions of [the NAFTA]'.[70]

V. Inconsistency of Interpretations, Human Rights, and the Emerging System of International Investment Law

The analysis of arbitral practice with regard to the national treatment standard in IIAs has evidenced substantial levels of inconsistency in the interpretation of the

---

[68] *Pope & Talbot*, n 39 above, at paras 84–88.   [69] *Myers*, n 30 above, at para 255.

[70] *Myers*, at para 215. Canada had claimed that its action was consistent with Canada's other international obligations, including the Basel Convention and Transboundary Agreement, and that these prevail over Chapter 11 obligations in the circumstances to the extent of the inconsistency (*Myers*, at para 150). For a strict version of the test, see also the *Mexican Trucking* case (n 57 above, at para 259), where the panel made reference to the NT provision in the 1988 FTA between Canada and the United States which specified the conditions for complying with such provision. Article 1202, para 3 of the 1988 FTA between Canada and the United States stated as follows:

> [T]he treatment a Party accords to persons of the other Party may be different from the treatment the Party accords its persons provided that: (a) the difference in treatment is *no greater than that necessary* for prudential, fiduciary, health and safety, or consumer protection reasons; (b) such different treatment is equivalent in effect to the treatment accorded by the Party to its persons for such reasons; and (c) prior notification of the proposed treatment has been given in accordance with Article 1803.

meaning and function of key concepts underlying the application of this standard. In particular, arbitral tribunals have differed in their understanding of the nature of the relationship between foreign and domestic investors who need to be compared in order to determine the existence of discrimination (the so-called 'likeness' concept). While the majority of tribunals seem to focus on the foreign and domestic investors operating at least in the same economic sector (if not being in competition with each other), one tribunal has taken a much wider reading of the likeness concept comparing a foreign oil exporter with a domestic flower exporter (*Occidental*) and another tribunal has taken a much stricter reading limiting the comparison to identical investors (*Methanex*).

Another substantial difference in the interpretation of the national treatment standard lies in the relevance of discriminatory intent. While several arbitral tribunals seem to rely on the measure's adverse effects on foreign investors only (*Myers, Feldman, Occidental,* and *Pope & Talbot*), a few tribunals have relied more or less expressly on discriminatory intent in order to sustain a national treatment claim (*Genin* and *Methanex*).

Equally different approaches may be detected with regard to the nature of the relationship between the host country's measure allegedly discriminating and the policy objective justifying the different treatment at issue. While a few tribunals have performed a 'minimal relationship test' inquiring on the *suitability* or *effectiveness* of the measure at issue to pursue its policy objective (*Pope & Talbot*), one tribunal has justified the different treatment at issue simply on the basis that a non-discriminatory reason for the different treatment existed (*GAMI*), and at least two other tribunals have imposed a stricter test requiring that the measure under review be the 'least restrictive alternative' available to pursue its policy objective (*Myers* and *Mexican Trucking*).

It is self-evident that the extent of the potential impact of the national treatment standard on the protection and promotion of human rights may depend on the different interpretation of the various elements of the national treatment obligation found in IIAs. A broad interpretation of the concept of 'likeness', focusing exclusively on the measure's adverse effects on the foreign investor, or requiring a high level of reasonableness between the measure and the public policy objective justifying the different treatment will impose higher restraints on the host country's ability to regulate its economy in order to protect and promote human rights. Equally, a strict reading of the 'likeness' concept, requiring the existence of discriminatory intent vis-à-vis the foreign investor, or accepting a different treatment of a foreign and domestic investor on the basis of the mere existence of a public policy objective underlying the measure under review may, on the other hand, guarantee the host country more flexibility to undertake policies in the pursuit of human rights.

The fundamental dilemma in the application of the national treatment standard lies in striking the appropriate balance between restraining governmental conduct in order to protect foreign investment, on the one hand, and allowing host states enough regulatory space to pursue human rights policies, on the other. As the analysis in this chapter shows, the flexibility of the national treatment standard is such as to permit a wide range of outcomes.

It is true that the current state of the law with regard to the national treatment standard in IIAs may appear unsatisfactory as the level of inconsistencies is relatively high. This apparent chaotic state of the law may represent a cause of concern for all parties involved, particularly the host state and the foreign investor. The lack of legal certainty may be the cause for inconsistent actions by the former (investment rules will not be able to provide clear normative benchmarks for public authorities) and inefficient actions by the latter (unclear rules will imply higher costs for the investor and the economy as a whole).

However, despite these costs, there may be some important benefits stemming from the current state of affairs in the international law of foreign investment. The diversity in interpretation (that is, the apparent chaos) also represents an immensely useful learning ground for policy makers in the field. Only by observing how these general standards have been interpreted and applied to particular cases are policy makers able to determine or improve the content of investment treaties. Given the greater flexibility in modifying most IIAs (they are mostly concluded on a bilateral basis for an initial period of 10 years), national policy makers can modify or adapt international disciplines on the basis of the rich jurisprudence now available. In this sense, within the investment context, there is a very interesting and strong dialectic that is emerging between the arbitral jurisprudence, on the one hand, and the political/legislative arm, on the other. There are plenty of examples where states have actually learned from the jurisprudence and have made changes to their investment policies and treaty-making (for example, one can look at the latest model investment agreements of the United States and Canada).[71]

It is undeniable that international law on foreign investment is still in its formative years, where the rules and institutions of the game are still being identified and formed. Within this context, the relevance of

---

[71] The benefits stemming from this apparently chaotic state of affairs in international investment law may also be emphasized by a comparison with the other major branch in international economic law, the world trading system. Under the WTO, there is a single multilateral treaty regime and there is a strong two-tiered quasi-judicial dispute settlement mechanism. One indication coming out of the WTO experience is that multilateral rules, once interpreted by a strong quasi-judicial arm, become very difficult to change at the multilateral level. One can argue that the level of dialectic between the political and judicial branches in the WTO is very low.

human rights law and policy should play an important role in shaping the interpretation and development of investment rules, including the national treatment standard. Human rights considerations appear to be essential in strengthening the legitimacy of the emerging system of international investment law.

16

Implementing Human Rights in the NAFTA Regime – The Potential of a Pending Case: *Glamis Corp v USA*

*Julien Cantegreil**

à Lia Brozgal

I. Introduction

The original purpose of the North American Free Trade Agreement (NAFTA) was twofold: eliminating tariff barriers and reducing most of the non-tariff barriers between Canada, the United States, and Mexico.[1] This comprehensive free trade agreement between industrial and developing countries has generated, as it turned out, the largest free trade area in terms of total gross domestic product. NAFTA negotiators had moreover sought to maximize the basic protective norms for cross-border investors by granting them a private right to arbitrate their investment grievances with 'any law, regulation, procedure, requirement of practice' at any level of government of another NAFTA country.[2] The extensive understanding granted to the terms of 'investment' and 'compensation' and the absence of any 'rules of origin of capital' in Chapter 11 would later reinforce this unique degree of protection towards investors.[3] This preliminary assessment would not be completed without mentioning that

* My debts are gratefully expressed to Professors J H H Weiler, A von Mehren (†), G Aguilar-Alvarez and W Michael Reisman, H H Koh, Fr Francioni and E-U Petersmann for seminars on, resp. "NAFTA and WTO" and "International Commercial Arbitration" (Harvard, 2001), "International Investment Law" and "Introduction to Transnational Law" (Yale, 2006) and "Investment and Human Rights" (E.U.I., 2007). The supportive attention of Professor Pierre-Marie Dupuy throughout these years made this possible.
[1] North American Free Trade Agreement, 17 December 1992, US-Can-Mex, 32 ILM 605 (1993).
[2] On Chapter 11, see documents at <http://www.naftaclaims.com> and <http://www.state.gov/s/l/c3439.htm> (United States). See also NAFTA Chs 4 and 14.
[3] cf for instance Prosper Weil's dissenting opinion in *Tokio Tokelés v Ukraine*, ICSID ARB No 02/18, Decision on Jurisdiction, 29 April 2004, 11 ICSID Reports 313, at 16 with the

NAFTA has also been considered as a forerunner of human rights' concerns in international investment law, with commentators calling for having its rules 'hopefully ... upheld and replicated at the ICSID/BIT level'.[4] It comes as no surprise that so many alleged achievements in usually competing directions are rather confusing when it comes to formulating a clear-cut assessment of NAFTA's specificity regarding human rights within the BIT landscape.

Scholarly research and practice complicate the matter. Although many theories have been formulated, no reliable empirical study of the economic impact of NAFTA's investment provisions exists yet. These provisions have spurred an increase in financial transactions,[5] but member countries have also been affected before and after 1994 by other factors, including national policies, changes in terms-of-trade amongst member countries, and an increase in global trade and finance flows. External macroeconomic shocks such as the Mexican financial crisis or the US stock market collapse in 2000 also played a critical role. No analysis based on a single country would provide any more guidance in this matter. Chapter 11, for instance, improved the standing of American and Canadian investors in Mexico as well as expanding the Mexican sectors in which they operate.[6] It has qualitatively shifted Mexico's exports toward manufactured goods. It has also led to a quantitative increase in merchandise trade and investment[7] as well as a substantial vertical specialization and intra-firm trade among the NAFTA partners. Yet it remains difficult to differentiate these trends from two phenomena unrelated to NAFTA: the occurrence of unanticipated effects as soon as the member countries agreed to pursue negotiations for a free trade agreement in 1991, and the fluctuation of Mexican trade driven by exogenous factors.[8]

---

understanding of potential 'market share' in the host country in *SD Myers, Inc v Canada*, First Partial Award, 13 November 2000, (2001) 40 ILM 1408, at para 232.

[4] See ch 22 in this volume. In the ICSID context, see, eg *Aguas del Tunari v Bolivia*, ARB No 02/3, Decision on Jurisdiction, 21 October 2005, 20 ICSID Review Foreign Investment Law Journal 450; and *Azurix Corp v Argentina*, ICSID ARB No 01/12, Award, 14 July 2006.

[5] Modelizations are many: see J Sachs and A Warner, 'Economic Reform and the Process of Global Integration' (1995) 2 Brookings Papers on Economic Activity 523–564; and J Frankel and D Romer, 'Does Trade Cause Growth?' (1999) 89(3) American Economic Review 379–399. In the NAFTA context, see W Easterly, N Fiess, and D Lederman, 'NAFTA and Convergence in North America: High expectations, Big Events, and Little Time' (2003) 4(1) Economía 1–53.

[6] See A Tornell, F Westermann, and L Martinez, 'NAFTA and Mexico's Less-Than-Stellar Performance', NBER Working Paper 10289 (2004).

[7] Concerning increasing foreign direct investments between Mexico and its partners until 2000, see A Cuevas, M Messmacher, and A Werner, 'Changes in the Patterns of External Financing in Mexico since the Approval of NAFTA', Central Bank of Mexico Working Paper (2002). Cf Tornell, Westermann, and Martinez, n 6 above.

[8] See A Kose, G Meredith, and C Towe, 'How Has NAFTA Affected the Mexican Economy? Review and Evidence', IMF Working Paper, WP/04/59 (2004). Cf AO Krueger, 'Trade Creation and Trade Diversion under NAFTA', NBER Working Paper 7429 (1999), with J Romalis, 'NAFTA and CUSFTA's Impact on North American Trade', University of Chicago Working Paper (2002).

Evaluating NAFTA investment's provisions proves even more challenging in the field of human rights. On the one hand, the three parties expanded the usual role of a free trade agreement[9] in signing the 'greenest trade agreement ever negotiated',[10] with the preamble and side agreements also including several human rights and sustainable development principles.[11] NAFTA tribunals have taken into consideration this broader legal framework, often not available to ICSID tribunals applying BITs or investment contracts.[12] Nevertheless, some dispositions of the agreement were crafted in a way that was explicitly favourable to the investors; others were drafted in a way that would de facto positively influence their own advantage against human rights concerns.[13] Furthermore, the lack of definition of terms such as 'expropriation' or 'measure tantamount to ... an expropriation' enabled NAFTA tribunals to formulate their own definitions in dicta,[14] which has extended the scope of expropriation and compensation in the NAFTA regime.[15] For this reason, the potential integration of investment-trade with environmental human rights concerns has, de facto, developed into a competition of contradictory trends to the disadvantage of human rights such as exemplified by the *Metalclad* and *Methanex* arbitrations. Nothing new is expected on this front until NAFTA tribunals, which have to solve conflicts between international obligations to protect both investments and human

[9] See D Esty, 'Making trade and environmental policies work together: lessons from NAFTA' in J Cameron, P Demaret, and D Geradin (eds), *Trade and The Environment: The Search For Balance* (1994) 389. NAFTA was accompanied with a North American Agreement on Labor Cooperation. Its preamble outlines the necessity to 'UNDERTAKE each of the other goals in a manner consistent with environmental protection and conservation'; 'PROMOTE sustainable development'; and 'STRENGHEN the development and enforcement of environmental laws and regulation'. These preambles are not without importance – see in the WTO context 'United States – Import Prohibition of certain Shrimp and Shrimp products', WTO Appellate Body report, AB-1998-4, especially para 121.
[10] S Charnovitz, 'The North American Free Trade Agreement: Green Law or Green Spin?' (1994) Law and Policy in International Business 26, at the introduction and fn 2.
[11] See, inter alia, NAFTA's Preamble ('public walfare'), Art 1101(4) ('social welfare ... [or] health'), and Art 1114(2) ('domestic health, safety or environmental measures').
[12] See, most clearly, *SD Meyers*, n 3 above.
[13] With regard to compensation, compare Art 1110(2)-(3)-(6) with the Hull and the 'appropriate compensation' standards. See also R Dolzer, 'Indirect Expropriations: New Developments?' (2002) 11 New York University Environmental Law Journal 73 ('when in doubt, these treaties should be interpreted *in favorem* investors, stressing and expanding his rights so as to promote the flow of foreign investment').
[14] See, inter alia, *Ethyl Corp v Canada*; *Metalclad v Mexico*, ICSID Case No ARB (AF)/97/1, Award, 30 August 2000, 5 ICSID Reports 209; *SD Myers*, n 3 above; *Pope & Talbot v Canada*, Interim Award, 26 June 2000; *Loewen v United States*, ICSID Case No ARB (AF)/98/3; and *Methanex v United States*.
[15] cf references to 'expected benefit' in the *Metalclad* award and to 'access to market' in the *Pope & Talbot* award. See also J Fowles, 'Swords Into Plowshares: Softening The Edge of Nafta's Chapter 11 Regulatory Expropriation Provisions' (2006) 36 Cumberland Law Review 83.

rights, agree at least upon a satisfactory principle of coordination of these obligations under international law.[16]

This chapter focuses on the pending *Glamis v United States* case, since it encapsulates all issues that are crucial to the protection of human rights under the NAFTA Chapter 11 provisions.[17] Its analysis will be of great help to make an assessment of NAFTA's impact on human rights. The first section of this chapter presents the non-controversial relevant factual elements of the case (II). The second section analyses the way in which human rights issues have been dealt with by the respondent, *Hearings* of the case included (III). The following section shows how human rights issues have been mischaracterized during the litigation stage (IV). The concluding remarks of this chapter serve to widen the perspective in proposing a framework to litigate such issues in order to promote human rights within the NAFTA regime (V).

II. The *Glamis* Case: An Example of Human Rights Litigation Under NAFTA Chapter 11

A. Facts of the Case

In 1994, the Canadian Corporation Glamis Gold Ltd (hereinafter, Glamis) acquired full ownership of mining claims and mill sites in the Southern California Imperial Desert through an American subsidiary.[18] Referred to as the Imperial Project, this investment of 1,650 acres of federal public land would have generated a large open-pit with a cyanide heap and a leach gold mine.[19]

---

[16] The distinction between 'incompatibilité' and 'interference' among investment and human rights international obligations is well presented by L Liberti, 'Investissement et droits de l'homme' in P Kahn and T Wälde (eds), *New Aspects of International Investment Law* (2007) ch 16, 807 ff. See also A van Aaken, 'Fragmentation of International Law: The Case of International Investment Protection', Law and Economics Research Paper Series, Working Paper No 2008-1, University of St Gallen (2008). Eg international investors are granted rights. See PM Dupuy, 'Sur les rapports entre sujets et "acteurs" en droit international contemporain' in LC Vohrah et al (eds), *Man's Inhumanity to Man. Essays on International Law in Honour of Antonio Cassese* (2003) 261 ff. Yet, their duties are extremely limited: see M Bekhechi, 'Droit international et investissement international: quelques réflexions sur des développements récents' in *Le Droit international au service de la paix, de la justice et du développement. Mélange Michel Virally* (1991) 109–124.
[17] The complexity of the case arises from the additional facts that human rights norms are poorly settled and those being the most affected by the contested measures are not 'party' to the arbitration. See the Tribunal Decision Accepting Quechan *Amicus* Application, 16 September 2005, at paras 10 ff.
[18] On the *Glamis* case, see documents available at <http://www.naftaclaims.com/disput es_us_glamis.htm>, including the hearings.
[19] See Notice of Arbitration, 9 December 2003, paras 3ff (hereinafter, Notice of Arbitration) and the description provided in the hearings, at 449.

The core legislative context of this investment is threefold. The attractive Hardrock Act of 1872 gives any US citizen the right to enter onto federal public lands and, upon proof of a valuable and marketable discovery of hardrock minerals, to acquire a property right to 20 acres of land.[20] The Federal Law Policy and Management Act of 1976 (FLPMA) creates the California Desert Conservation Area (CDCA), a zone of 25 million acres designed to protect a significantly scenic and biologically important area (this territory would later be surrounding the Imperial Project).[21] This Act grants the Department of the Interior the authority to manage and impose special protections on the federal public land within the CDCA, including those containing mining claims located under the Hardrock Act of 1872.[22] In the event that new projects in a portion of the conservation area arrive, it requires that the Bureau of Land Management (BLM) prepares and implements a comprehensive plan for operation, development, and protection of the public land.[23] Finally, the California Desert Protection Act of 1994 (CDPA) prohibits mining or development on a wilderness area on hundreds of thousands of acres of the California desert in the neighbourhood of the Imperial Project.[24]

Glamis claims to have undertaken a 'significant investment necessary to establish and begin gold mining operations' after 1994, only once being 'assured that the Imperial Project [would remain] comfortably outside of the wilderness areas designated by the CDPA'. The BLM finally approved the project in 1996 when it determined from the seventh plan of operation submitted by Glamis that 'unnecessary or undue degradation w[ould] not occur'.[25]

However, the Quechuan Indian Nation would soon claim that the proximity of the Imperial Project to alleged sacred ancestral sites would impair their spiritual and ceremonial practices, obstructing them from transmitting their culture to new generations.[26] In support of this claim, the Solicitor of the Interior Department issued a legal opinion arguing that the project could be

---

[20] 30 USC s 26 (2000). Note that according to US law, the locator of an unpatented mining claim holds only a possessory interest in the land on which its claim, which grants him or her the right to enter onto the land and extract minerals but not to extract those minerals in a particular manner nor to leave the land unreclaimed after mining, is complete: see respondent's Counter Memorial, 19 September 2006, 19–23.

[21] 43 USC s 1732(b) (1994) and also the hearings, at 323 ff.

[22] FLPMA 302(b) notes specifically that FLPMA's provision regarding the CDCA represents an amendment to the Hardrock Mining Act 1872. See R Flynn and J Parsons, 'The Right to Say No: Federal Authority over Hardrock Mining on Public Lands' (2001) 16 Journal of Environmental Law and Litigation 323 ff.

[23] See E Bluemel, 'Accommodating Native American Cultural Activities on Federal Public Land' (2005) 41 Idaho Law Review 475, 537; and M Yablon, 'Property Rights and Sacred Sites: Federal Regulatory Responses to American Indian Religious Claims on Public Land' (2004) 113 Yale Law Journal 1623, 1653 ff.   [24] 16 USC s 410aaa-410aaa-83 (2000).

[25] Notice of Arbitration, at para 6.

[26] US Counter-Memorial, 19 September 2006, at 50 ff; and the hearings, at 1549 (Quechuan position) and 981 (Imperial Project's peculiarities). It has been compared to 'churches without walls' and the Wailing Wall in Jerusalem.

denied, if it were to result in 'undue impairment' under BLM regulations. As a result, the BLM came to reverse its initial decision[27] and on January 2001, for the first time in American history, the Secretary of the Department of the Interior would deny the mining permit based on environmental and human rights concerns.[28] However, the new Presidential Administration reinterpreted FLPMA's applicability to the project differently, rescinding the former decision of denial.[29] By the end of 2002, the BLM concluded that Glamis had 'valid existing rights'.

Before the federal action could be completely corrected, the legislature of the State of California passed a law applicable to the Imperial Project and any other project that had been pending as of 12 December 2002, requiring that all metallic mining sites are to be backfilled and restored so as to achieve the approximate original contours of the land.[30] The State of California would later claim to have acted in light of the increasing environmental regulation and the known harms stemming from unreclaimed open-pit mines in California. It argues to have legally balanced competing interests and that 'the NAFTA should not be construed to prevent state parties from adopting general regulations that require persons and companies, including investors, to clean up the environmental degradation that they cause'.[31] Conversely, in 2002, Glamis claims to have invested in 2002 approximately $13 million in project development in reliance on the 1994 Congressional Act and an initial approval by local and federal government.[32] It also alleges a legitimate expectation to carry on with its project without having to comply with any further discriminatory state regulation.[33] Glamis informed the Department of the Interior of its decision to pursue new avenues of relief due to the fact that it 'would have been futile for it to continue to participate in further administrative processing'. Although Glamis maintained its

---

[27] On the timing of the measure, see the Q&A with the tribunal in the hearings, at 1299.

[28] C Knight, 'A Regulatory Minefield: Can The Department of Interior Say "No" To A Hardrock Mine?' (2002) 73 University Of Colombia Law Review 619, 622. Secretary Bruce Babitt based his decision on the cumulative adverse impacts of the project on the Quechuan religious sites; see Notice of Arbitration, at para 15. See Record of Decision for the Imperial Project Gold Mine Proposal, Imperial County, California (2001), BLM Case File No CA 670-41027, available at <http://www.blm.gov/ca/pdfs/elcentro_pdfs/Glamis_ROD_final_1-01.pdf>.

[29] See testimony of Mr Jeannes, claimant's witness in the hearings, at 197 ff, in particular at 205 and 217.

[30] This law originates in an emergency regulation by the California State Mining and Geology Board (12 December 2002), which soon memorialized into Senate Bill 22 and later a law in April 2003, Cal Pub Res Code, SS, 2770–2775 (West 2006). See comments on the unsuccessful Senate Bill 18 in B Goode, 'A Legislative Approach to the Protection of Sacred Site' (2004) 10 Hasting West-Northwest Journal of Environmental Law and Policy 169. See the press release of the Governor Davies at Notice of Arbitration, Ex A   [31] The hearings, at 1808.

[32] Notice of Arbitration, at para 10.

[33] Notice of Arbitration, at paras 15 and 20. Claimant's Memorial (5 May 2006), at 50 ff and 79 ff. Contra, see Non party submission, Quechuan Indian Nation, at 3, note 7 and the application of this law and regulation to Golden Queen Comp which, after having sought unsuccessfully an exemption from California's complete backfilling requirements, redesigned its mine Plan of Operations.

mining claims and paid royalties allegedly to retain jurisdiction in this case,[34] it quickly ceased to communicate with the Department of the Interior.[35]

B. Procedure

The options for Glamis were many under US law. It could have challenged the California regulations and law under the Fifth Amendment to the US Constitution either as a regulatory taking[36] or as a 'per se' of 'total' taking.[37] It could also have argued that environmental regulations were pre-empted by federal mining and environmental law even if the case would have probably been more difficult to argue under the precedent of *California Coastal Commission v Granite Rock Co.*[38] In any case, Glamis's interests in not pursuing the case in US domestic courts prevailed. By 9 December 2003, Glamis filed a Notice of Arbitration under Chapter 11 of the NAFTA, claiming US$50 million compensation for damages caused by the actions and inactions of the United States of America and its subordinate entity, the State of California, in an alleged violation of the rules on minimum standard of treatment (1105) and expropriation (1110).[39] The arbitral decision is currently pending.

III. The Current Litigation of Human Rights in the *Glamis* Case

As it is often the case in (indirect) expropriation matters under NAFTA, the *Glamis* case brings to the forefront issues such as the scope of 'investment',[40] the inclusion of the 'reasonably-to-be-expected economic benefits' within property,[41] and the economic valuation of the appropriate damages.[42] This section refers solely to the

---

[34] This will prove essential in a context of an exceptional rise in gold prices, from $323 an ounce in 2002 to approximately $675 an ounce at the time of the hearings, and $1,000 an ounce by 2008. Contra, see Behre Dolbear's negative valuation in the hearings, at 1222 ff.

[35] Reasons for keeping on paying these claims are uncertain; see the hearings, at 1824.

[36] See *Penn Central Transportation Co v City of New York*, 438 US 104 (1978).

[37] See *Lucas v SC Coastal Council*, 505 US 1003 (1992). Compare with *Pope & Talbot*, Interim Award, 26 June 2000, 122 ILR (2002) 316, at 317; and *Metalclad*, n 14 above, at para 33.

[38] 480 US 572 (1987), where the USSC held that states could adopt more stringent environmental regulation of hardrock mining on federal land. See J Wallace, 'Corporate Nationality, Investment Protection Agreement, and Challenges to Domestic Natural Ressources Law' (2005) 17 Geographic International Environmental Law Review 365, 378 ff.

[39] Notice of Arbitration, at para 25. See US argument in response, in US Counter Memorial, n 20 above, respectively at 216 ff and 107 ff. An ultimate assessment is in the hearings, at 144. Note that on 4 November 2006, Goldcorp, Inc announced its acquisition of Glamis Gold Ltd. For the purposes of this arbitration, the claimant will still be referred as 'Glamis'.

[40] 'Investment' has been extended to intangible economic interest, but not yet to a 'going concern'. See reference to 'market share' in *SD Myers*, Second Partial Award, 21 October 2002, at para 95

[41] See *Metalclad*, n 14 above, at para 103.

[42] Compare claimant's and respondent's witness proposals in the hearings, at 611 and 699 respectively.

conflicts between the protections of property and other environment-human-rights norms that could be dealt with by the arbitral tribunal.[43] It seeks to assess where to locate the legal issues concerning human rights that the tribunal will have to decide upon. The first part of the analysis deals with the expropriation's side of the conflict, which involves an *a priori* limitation and an *a posteriori* mitigation of propriety rights (A). The second part deals with issues related to Article 1105 (B).

A. Expropriation

In the event that the tribunal decides to deal with expropriation, it would have to deal with two issues of importance for those litigating human rights issues as respondents in expropriation cases under NAFTA.[44] The first challenge of the tribunal would be whether the idea of an 'absolute property right' makes sense under NAFTA or whether property claims, even if acquired, are only possessory interests circumscribed from their inception by the pre-existing federal, state, and local regulations.[45]

1. Inherent Limitations of Property Rights

If the tribunal was to find Glamis's federal property interest and unpatented mining claims circumscribed by 'background principles' of state law (to the extent that these latter are reasonable and not pre-empted by federal law),[46] it may conclude that the subsequent burdening of property rights constituted by the challenged California measures is not expropriatory.[47] To do so, the tribunal will first have to determine whether these 'background principles' include the right to mine in a manner that would cause the very harm that each of the legislative measures from California sought to prevent. It could also have to decide upon whether the principle expressed by the US Supreme Court in *Lucas v SC Coastal Council*[48] is a threshold inquiry under NAFTA that must be

---

[43] Many elements are either confidential or heavily contested, among which many, based on hearsay, would probably be dismissed if strict rules of evidence were applied.

[44] The respondent's strategy concerning Art 1110 is as follows. With regard to state measures, the respondent argues that Glamis has failed to show that its claim against the Californian measures is ripe, that the Californian measures deprived it of a property right it possessed, or that the California measures indirectly expropriated its investment. With regard to the Federal Government's actions in processing Glamis's plan of operations, the respondent argues that Glamis failed to show that its claim of delay is founded in fact or law, that the DOI expropriated its investment during its review of Glamis's plan of operations, or that the DOI's actions following the rescission of the Record of Decision were expropriatory.

[45] See the hearings, at 118. See US Counter Memorial, 19 September 2006, at 122–127 (with also reference to obligation under CIL).   [46] See the hearings, at 2084 ff.

[47] Both parties agree on this: see Investor's Reply Memorial, 15 December 2006, at para 50; and Respondent's Rejoinder Memorial, 15 March 2007, at 11.

[48] *Lucas*, n 37 above, at 1027. Under *Lucas*, any confiscatory regulation must rely upon a principle that 'inheres' in the background principle: see Respondent's Rejoinder Memorial, 15 March 2007, at 38, n 108.

addressed to deal with the principle of full compensation for confiscatory regulatory measures.

American law certainly recognizes that the scope of any property right is informed by the legislative and regulatory framework at the time such rights are acquired. For instance, the Court of Appeal for the Federal Circuit made no ambiguity in its *M & J Coal Co v United States* decision that the 'bundle of property rights' acquired by the claimant never included a cognizable property right to mine in the manner it proposed.[49] American law even grounds the recognition of the 'bundle of property rights' in the evolutionary nature of the legislative and regulatory framework of the right in question.[50] Should the tribunal find guidance in the fact that the federal government has been increasingly concerned by environmental issues in hardrock mining, as well as the reality that several domestic courts have increasingly recognized the protection of sacred sites,[51] it would certainly be led to recognize bundles of rights in Glamis's property.[52] However, the tribunal must ground its decision in the sole recognition by international law that where property rights are from their inception subject to a restriction, the claimant's property rights cannot include the right to engage in the activity proscribed by (or the right to be relieved from the requirements imposed by) the subsequent application of that restriction. The *Feldman* tribunal refers to a claimant being 'stymied by a longstanding requirement' under the applicable excise tax law.[53] Similarly, the *Thunderbird* tribunal denied that Mexico had expropriated a property interest that the claimant never held because of pre-existing legal limitations.[54] In the event that the

---

[49] In *M & J Coal Co v United States*, 47 F3d 1148 (Fed Cir 1995), the Court noted that the claimant's property rights being limited by pre-existing environmental and health safety standards, the Office of Surface Mining's requirement that the claimant modifies its plan of operations to prospect surface structure does not constitute a taking. On the 'bundle of rights', see *Lucas*, n 37 above, at 1027; and *American Pelagic Fishing Co v United States*, 379 F3d 1363 (Def Circ 2004), cert denied, 125 S Ct 2963 (2005). Compare also US Counter Memorial, 19 September 2006, at 127–137 with the hearings, at 1846–1849.

[50] Under US law, reinterpretations are constrained by congressional notification and reasonableness: see, respectively, *Light v US*, 220 US 523 (1911); and *United States v Riverside Bayview Homes Inc*, 474 US 121 (1985). For a rather deferential interpretation, see *Chevron USA Inc v Natural Resources Defense Council Inc*, 467 US 837 (1984); and *Babitt v Sweet Home Chapter of Communities*, 515 US 687 (1995).

[51] See *Lyng v Northw Indian Cemetery Protective Association*, 485 US 439 (1988); and case law in B Goode, 'A Legislative Approach to the Protection of Sacred Site' (2004) 10 Hasting West-Northwest Journal of Environmental Law and Policy 169, 171.

[52] See Flynn and Parsons, n 23 above, 253 ff and 271 ff. See also *Seminole Nation v United States*, 316 US 286 (1942), at 296–297. Prospective elements are examined in E Bluemel, 'Accommodating Native American Cultural Activities on Federal Public Land' (2005) 41 Idaho Law Review 475, 562.

[53] In which case the claimant never possessed the alleged 'right': see *Marvin Roy Feldman Karpa v Mexico*, ICSID No ARB(AF)/99/1, Award, 16 December 2002, 7 ICSID Reports 341, at paras 118–119.

[54] The claimant was found no right to operate gaming machines prohibited by law; see *International Thunderbird Gaming Corp v Mexico*, Award, 26 January 2006, at paras 124 and 208.

Glamis tribunal endorsed this jurisprudential recognition – that under international law the scope of property rights is informed by the legislative and regulatory framework at the time such rights are acquired – it would have to locate the pertinent legislative and regulatory framework under international law.

In this regard, Glamis has distanced itself throughout the course of the procedure from its pre-emption argument with regard to federal law.[55] Should the tribunal deal with expropriation, it would probably have to determine the validity under international law of identified state law background principles that predate Glamis's acquisition of its unpatented mining claims. Two Californian regulations are at stake: SB 22 and SMGB. The United States has disputed not that Glamis has a property right in its mining claims, but that the property rights include the rights to be free from California's reclamation requirement: absent a showing of necessity, a prohibition on causing irreparable damage to Native American sacred sites is required under the 1975 California Sacred Sites Act (SSA).[56] A requirement that mined lands be reclaimed to a 'usable condition' and pose no danger to public health and safety under the 1975 Surface Mining Reclamation Act (SMRA) is an additional legal requirement.[57] According to the respondent, SB 22 is a mere implementation of the SSA's prohibition on irreparably damaging Native American sites. Similarly, the SMGB regulations are a mere implementation of SMRA's reclamation standard. The respondent also claims that Glamis has never had a right to mine in a manner that violated the usable condition reclamation standard under SMRA and protections accorded to Native Americans under the SSA. As a result, should it decide to engage in this questioning, the issues for the tribunal would be at minimum threefold: under international law, do the SMRA or the SSA include background principles in the event, as Glamis claims, that they were purposely not universally applied or general in nature?[58] Does grandfathering provisions in the SMGB and SB 22 regulations render them, as Glamis also claims, incapable of being expressions of background

---

[55] Glamis claims that the background principles of state property law at issue here (California's constitutional authority to accommodate Native American religious practices, etc) cannot 'prevail' over its 'federal-law property interest' in its mining claim: see Reply, at 57. However, neither the SSA nor the SMRA seems to be pre-empted by federal law and therefore cannot constitute a background principle of California law which limits the rights held by Glamis in its unpatented mining claims. In any event, pre-emption being purely a question of municipal law, it could not be a valid ground for decision before an international tribunal. Under international law indeed, the particular allocation of power between the states and the Federal Government in the United States is a matter that falls within the realm of exclusive domestic authority.

[56] California Public Resources Code, para 5097.9 (2001).

[57] California Public Resources Code, para 2733 (2001). Note that according to the United States, the principle of religious accommodation is equally required under the First Amendment of the US Constitution and Art 1 of the California Constitution.

[58] On the way the SMGB regulation clarifies SMRA under the *Lucas* Framework, see the hearings, at 1083–1098 and 1846–1864. To compare SB 22 with the Californian background principles found in the SSA, see the hearings, at 1098–1141. According to Glamis, the pre-existing

principles of law? Are these regulations an objectively reasonable application of 'background principle'? As Glamis claims, they have done 'more than duplicate the result that could have been achieved in the courts', and not created an enforceable pre-existing limitation that could have been objectively applied through the courts to impose backfilling and site re-contouring obligations on the Imperial Project.[59]

2. Ex Post Limitation of Property Rights

If the 'background principle' argument could not be successful in resolving the dispute, or if the tribunal concludes that Glamis had acquired a right to mine in a manner that contravenes both the SMRA and the SSA as later specified through the amendments to the California Mining and Geology Board's reclamation regulations (SMGB) and California Senate Bill 22 (SB 22),[60] there would potentially still be a venue to litigate human rights concerns due to the 'indirect expropriation' argument.[61] Indeed, even if mining was a highly regulated industry in which regulations were evolving continually as sovereign entities seek to better protect public welfare and public resources, the tribunal would still have to evaluate the scope of a permissible regulatory activity under NAFTA through the following threefold factual inquiry.[62] If government actions are presumed to be non-expropriatory, Glamis would have the burden of proving that an indirect expropriation has occurred.

limitations identified by the United States are consistent with Lucas (See *Lucas*, n 37 above, at 1029) since they constitute 'specific legal prescription or prohibition': see Investor's Reply Memorial, 15 December 2006, at para 47. Two questions may be dealt in turn by the tribunal. First, in the event that the background principles at issue are general in nature, it remains to be known whether 'only specific legally binding restrictions . . . can limit after-acquired property interest': see Glamis Reply, at para 36; *Thunderbird*, n 54 above, at para 124 (a general ban on gambling under Mexican Law due to the 'skill character'); and *Feldman*, n 53 above, at para 119 (the tribunal did not consider the degree of specificity of the limitation). Secondly, Glamis claims that California's prior lack of complete backfilling requirement somehow created a property interest in conducting mining activities free from SMRA's reclamation standard. In this later matter, note that the *Feldman* tribunal found unavailing the claimant's 'prior use' argument (*Feldman*, at para 125). See also majority opinion in *Thunderbird*, at para 28, similarly finding that the claimant 'never enjoyed a vested right' in its prohibited gaming operations

[59] During the seventh day of the hearings, Glamis began to ground its denial of Californian measures expressing background principles in SMRA in both the fact that that Act would not apply to the Imperial Project and its reclamation to be site-specific: See the hearings, at 1647. Cf US position at the hearings, at 1852–1854.

[60] Glamis has progressively shifted its claim to the sole alleged indirect expropriation by the challenged Californian measures.

[61] Both parties agree that customary international law standard is applied as to what constitutes indirect expropriation and measures tantamount to expropriation and is informed by the US Fifth Amendment taking law. They diverge on the prioritization of these two elements. Compare Memorial, at para 147 (Glamis) and the hearings, at 101 (respondent).

[62] According to the awards *Técnicas Mediaoambientales Tecmed, SA v Mexico*, ICSID No ARB (AF)/00/2, Award, 29 May 2003, (2004) 43 ILM 133; and *Compañía del Desarrollo de Santa Elena, SA v Costa Rica*, ICSID No ARB/96/1, Award, 17 February 2000, (2000) 39 ILM 317, the environmental dimension of the measure makes no difference with regard to its expropriatory nature.

2.1 Deprivation of Value

A finding of expropriation is usually defined by the deprivation of the entire or virtually all of the economic value of the investment.[63] Beyond factual issues such as the extent to which the measures de facto impacted Glamis's property rights,[64] the tribunal could also assess further whether a nearly full deprivation is a compensable taking under international law. In doing so, its reasoning would be twofold: either balancing economic consequences in relation to the investor's reasonable investment-backed expectation (together with the nature of these measures), or focusing on the sole economic impact of the measures. In the latter option, a finding of indirect expropriation would be related to a substantial economic impact[65]; the expectations and character of the measures being taken into account would help to ascertain whether something has been taken from the investor.

2.2 Reasonable Investment-backed Expectations

Article 1110 is certainly not a remedy for an investor whose business plans are ultimately frustrated by governmental regulations or for an investor seeking compensation because of 'natural evolution' of the regulations.[66] In this regard, the *Glamis* tribunal would also probably have to make an assessment upon reasonable investment-backed expectations under NAFTA: can investors be given 'assurances' of stability? What are the conditions under which new regulations are a 'reasonably possible' extension of existing laws? To answer this question, the tribunal would most likely have to assess the precedential value of

---

[63] With regard to interference, cf *Pope & Talbot*, n 37 above, at para 102 ('sufficiently restrictive'); *CMS Gas Transmission Co v Argentina*, Award, 12 May 2005, (2005) 44 ILM 1205 ('effectiv[e] neutraliz[ation]'); and *GAMI v United States of Mexico*, Final Award, 15 November 2004, (2005) 44 ILM 545, at para 126 ('must be seen as taken'). Even when faulting Argentina for adoption of emergency economic measures, the LG&E tribunal declined to find an expropriation because there was no 'permanent severe deprivation of LG&E's rights with respect to its investment or almost complete deprivation of value of LG&E's investment': see *LG&E v Argentina*, Decision on Liability, 3 October 2006, (2007) 46 ILM 36.

[64] See US Counter-Memorial, 19 September 2006, at 161–180. The Federal Government's denial of Glamis's plan of operations was in place for a few months. It appears that the Imperial Project would have been profitable even if Glamis complied with California's reclamation requirements: see the valuation by the respondent in its Rejoinder Memorial, 15 March 2007, at 56–89 (even assuming that SB 22 and SMGB regulations were applied to Glamis, the evidence shows that the Imperial Project was worth at least US$21.5 million as of the date of the alleged expropriation, and is worth at least US$159 million in March 2007). On the financial assurance, the Singer Pit Gold, the cost per ton of backfilling the East Pit, the Swell factor and the present value of Glamis's gold mining rights, see the contradictory valuations the tribunal was provided with during the hearings, at 224, 1174–1186, 1221, 1565 ff, 1578, 1877, 1888 ff, and 1899–1908 and the last rebuttal statement by Glamis, at 2055 ff.

[65] See the Q&A between Mr Sharpe and the arbitrators, the hearings, at 1160–1266.

[66] According to the *Feldman* tribunal, 'not all Government regulatory activity that makes it difficult or impossible for an investor to carry out a particular line of business is an expropriation under Article 1110' (*Feldman*, n 53 above, at 112). See also respondent's Rejoinder Memorial, 15 March 2007, at 93–96.

some of the Argentinian and NAFTA cases underlining the importance of both the context and the agreement between the investors and the governments.[67] This assessment would enable the tribunal to determine specifically whether the vast pre-existing regulatory and statutory regimes would make it reasonably foreseeable that SMGB would not strengthen its reclamation standards in compliance with SMRA. The question is twofold. Should a reasonable investor have known that the regulatory climate throughout the United States, and particularly in California, was one that was increasingly protective of Native American cultural resources and cultural and religious freedom? Could a reasonable investor have invested in California in reliance on the belief that California would not act to protect such values? According to the state of California, only this extension of pre-existing law could ensure that mined lands would be returned to a usable condition in order to protect the public health and safety from the dangers left from hardrock open-pit mines. Conversely, Glamis argues that it was safe to assume that the Californian legislature would not require that open-pit mines near sacred sites be backfilled to return the area to its approximate original contours.

In the event that the investor received 'no specific commitment'"[68] that the regulations would not be changed in the particular manner in which they were changed,[69] the tribunal could well decide to concretize the 'bottom line' of an 'undue regulatory surprise'[70] in a highly regulated context[71]

---

[67] Concerning the *Methanex*, *Feldman*, *Thunderbird*, and *GAMI* awards, see Glamis's position in the hearings, at 29, 1279, and 1281. In the Argentine cases, note that Argentina had either fully abandoned the regulatory framework that it had agreed to (*CMS Gas*, n 63 above; and *Enron Corp and Ponderosa Assets, LP v Argentina*, ICSID No ARB/01/3, Award, 22 May 2007), refused to honour and forced renegotiation of rate adjustment provisions contained in their respective concession contracts (*Azurix*, n 4 above; and *Siemens AG v Argentina*, ICSID No ARB/02/08, Award, 6 February 2007) or revoked specific assurance that were made by all levels of the Mexican Government (*Tecmed*, n 62 above).

[68] As stated by the *Methanex* tribunal: 'as a matter of general international law, a non-discriminatory regulation for a public purpose, which is enacted in accordance with due process and, which affects, inter alios, a foreign investor or investment is not deemed expropriatory and compensable unless *specific commitments* had been given by the regulating government to the then putative foreign investor contemplating investment that the government would refrain from such regulation' (*Methanex Corp v United States*, Final Award, 3 August 2005, (2005) 44 ILM 1345 Pt IV, Ch D, at para 7). Cf Reply, at para 184; and US Counter-Memorial, at 182–183. See also *Feldman*, n 53 (dismissal of the claimant's expropriation claim in large part for lack of evidence of specific assurances that the claimant would receive certain tax treatment). On the *Feldman* award, see reply, at para 142; and US Counter Memorial, at 183–185.

[69] See US position in the hearings, at 1271 ff. On the buffer-zone language in the CDPA, upon which Glamis implies that it received assurance that California would not require complete backfilling, see the hearings, at 28 and 1292.

[70] The hearings, at 1700. On the repeatedly acknowledged principle of valid existing rights, see the exhibits 89, 96, and 112 provided in the Memorial, and the hearings, at 60–63.

[71] The *Methanex* tribunal rejected Methanex's expropriation claim, noting that 'Methanex entered a political economy in which it was widely known, if not notorious, that governmental environmental and health protection institutions at the federal and state level, operating under

under NAFTA.[72] In the absence of specific commitments that the government would refrain from enacting specific measures, an investor can have no reasonable expectation that the government will not so regulate.[73] Examples abound in international law of regulatory and legislative actions that were found to be reasonably foreseeable extensions of pre-existing rules. Such a determination would be necessary for the tribunal to decide whether Glamis could have reasonably expected that if Native American cultural roots were discovered on the territory in question, there would be no possibility that Glamis would be prevented from mining in the manner in which it had originally planned.[74] Such a determination is equally necessary for the tribunal also to decide whether it was reasonable for Glamis to expect no real possibility of additional required backfilling (if it was shown that the reclamation techniques employed at existing open-pit metallic mines in the California Desert was ineffective in assuring compliance with pre-existing law requiring the reclamation of land to usable condition).

2.3. Balancing Test

Finally, concerning the nature of the government's actions, the tribunal may decide whether the 'balancing test' to be applied[75] relates to the proportionality of the measure to its goal and to its discriminatory nature, or to the fact that measures are akin to a physical taking and therefore expropriatory (or akin to a regulation and therefore presumptively non-expropriatory).[76] Since it is uncontested that the measures at stake are of general applicability at face value

---

the vigilant eyes of the media, interested corporations, non-governmental organizations and a politically active electorate, continuously monitored the use and impact of chemical compounds and commonly prohibited or restricted the use of some of those compounds for environmental and/or health reasons' (*Methanex*, n 68 above, at para 9). In highly regulated industries such as mining, the tribunal may consider whether the investor acquired the property in reliance on the non-existence of the challenged regulation. Under US law, see *Concrete Pipe and Products of California v Construction Laboreres Pension Trust for Southern California*, 508 US 602 (1993).

[72] About liability to measures taken in response to the discovery of external facts in a context where the investor knew that the area contained resources protected by long existing laws, see in the US domestic court *Hunsiker v Iowa*, 519 NW2d 367 (Iowa, 1994).

[73] US Counter-Memorial, 19 September 2006, at 181–188.

[74] See US Counter-Memorial, at 50–58 and Rejoinder, at 90 ff for evidence of the existence, prior to Glamis's acquisition of its mining claim, that the area in which the Imperial Project is located contained Native American sacred sites. Even assuming *arguendo* that the Quechan people's sacred sites had not been discovered until after Glamis had made its investments in the project, under this line of interpretation Glamis could not have had a reasonable expectation that California would not legislate in the form SB 22 to protect those sites.

[75] See the hearings, at 1922 and 2065.

[76] Tribunals rarely question the state's own proclamation that it is enacting a non-discriminatory statute for a legitimate public purpose, especially when it is explicit in this regard. See the *Saluka Investments BV v Czech Republic*, Partial Award, 17 March 2006; the *Lauder v Czech Republic*, Final Award, 3 September 2001, 9 ICSID Reports 66; and the *SD Myers*, n 3 above, awards.

and hence of public purpose,[77] the tribunal would in any event also have to deal with the issue of discrimination, because Glamis does not consider it to be sufficient to have a facially neutral measure. Should the tribunal not render a judgment in favour of a presumption under international law that non-discriminatory regulatory measures of general application are not expropriatory,[78] it should demonstrate, following the *Whitney Benefits* case, what constitutes a discriminatory intention as well as support a review of the intentions behind the Californian measures.[79] This part of the award would be of significant importance for human rights activists: if only certain statements in the legislative and regulatory history of the Californian measures were sufficient to demonstrate the presence of discrimination, any legislation would be prejudicial towards investors since legislatures typically react to problems brought to their attention by the constituents by passing legislation that addresses such issues.[80]

B. NAFTA, Article 1105

If Glamis had sought a review of some factual determinations made by administrative agencies during the processing of its plan of operations and a *de novo* review of their legal conclusions, it could have presented its claim to a US court. Rather, it availed itself of its option under NAFTA to have its grievance arbitrated under international law.[81] Because both parties contest the scope and reach of Article 1105, this case may potentially lead the tribunal to give an interpretation of the minimum standard of treatment (MST) under customary international law (CIL).[82] In this event, the tribunal would first have to make an assessment on the legal basis of the fair and equitable standard under NAFTA. The claimant places fair and equitable treatment firmly within the minimum standard of treatment to be accorded under customary international

---

[77] The purpose of the measure was to ensure that, after the conclusion of metallic mining, open pits are reclaimed 'to usable condition which is readily adaptable for alternative land uses' (California Public Resources Code, para 2712(a) (2001)). Note that in the sole portion of *Metalclad* to survive vacatur, in which the tribunal had found that a specific ecological decree constituted an expropriation (para 109), this latter was not of general applicability.

[78] Regulatory measures had often been considered as a kind of indirect expropriation even if the takings and/or measures were adopted for environmental or public interest reasons. See the *Pyramide* award (full compensation), the *Compañia del Desarrollo de Santa Elena* award (full compensation), and the *Metalclad* award (full compensation) because the investor had been given previous assurances by the Federal Government.

[79] As stated in *Methanex*, Decision on Jurisdiction, 7 August 2002, it does not necessarily follow from the fact that a single governmental actor is motivated by an improper purpose that the motive can be attributed to the entire government.

[80] See arbitrator Caron's thoughts on SB 22 in the hearings, at 1345.

[81] See *Azurix*, n 4 above, and also *SD Myers*, n 3 above, at para 261; and *GAMI*, n 63 above, at 93. [82] See claimant's Reply, at para 204.

law,[83] whereas the respondent understands the customary international law minimum standard of treatment embodied in Article 1105 requiring something idiosyncratic and less than the 'fair and equitable treatment' under international law.

According to the United States, Glamis had the burden to establish that the purported rules on which it bases its claims derive from CIL, but also that each of the measures allegedly constituting a breach of fair and equitable treatment are individually unlawful under CIL.[84] Glamis has focused on three alleged obligations which it claims are obligations of customary international law under the minimum standard of treatment. As a result, the tribunal may have to determine whether only 'the whole set of circumstances' related to the claimant must be assessed collectively or whether interrelated measures have to be parsed separately.[85] In the latter, the tribunal may also have to consider whether each of these three rules of transparency, reasonable expectations, and proportionality have coalesced to achieve the requisite density 'in terms of uniformity, extent and representativeness'[86] of customary international law. Assuming that Glamis could elevate one factor from the direct expropriation analysis to become the sole determinant of whether there has been a violation of CIL, each of them should be evaluated.

1. Transparency

Glamis seems to allege that the minimum standard of treatment under international law requires states to provide foreign investors with ample opportunity to comment in advance on laws and regulations that may affect them. This procedure is critically referred to by the respondent as 'creating some kind of International Administrative Procedure Act'.[87] Should the tribunal act upon this statement to decide upon the transparency in the adoption of either of the two Californian measures or about the action of the Federal Government, it would first have to assess the jurisprudential value of certain cases, such as *SD Myers*,[88]

---

[83] Memorial, at 121–123; and NAFTA cases such as *Mondev, ADF*, or the US submission to the *Pope & Talbot* arbitration. Beyond NAFTA arbitration, see also the *CMS, Occidental*, and, to some extent, *Saluka* arbitrations.

[84] Glamis seems progressively no longer to maintain that any of these three purported rules alone are standing rules of customary international law, but only that they represent together a requirement of the minimum standard of treatment: see the hearings, at 1402.

[85] See *Occidental v Ecuador*, LCIA Case No UN3467, Award, 1 July 2004, where the tribunal held that the investor was not required to identify the rule of customary international law.

[86] Final Report of the International Law Association Committee on Formation of the Customary (General), International Law, Statement of Principles Applicable to the Formation of General Customary International Law, para II.C.12 cmt.b (2000).   [87] The hearings, at 1393.

[88] The separate opinion of Dr Bryan Schwartz in *SD Myers*, n 3 above, at para 254

Metalclad Corp (Supreme Court of British Columbia),[89] *Feldman*,[90] *CMS*,[91] *Maffezini*,[92] but also *Saluka*,[93] *Tecmed, ADC*,[94] and *Azurix*.[95]

1.1. Reasonable Expectations

The tribunal may have to decide whether Article 1105 requires it to weigh the laws and assurances at the time of the investment with the host state's regulatory interests.[96] As to the reach of this expectation, the tribunal will have to assess whether the frustration of an investor's expectation could form the basis of a stand-alone claim establishing a breach of customary international law and its minimum standard of treatment, or if a party must prove something beyond mere breach, such as repudiation of the contract for non-commercial reasons.[97] Even assuming that Glamis could elevate one factor from the direct expropriation analysis to become the sole determinant of whether there has been a violation of customary international law, the tribunal will have to weigh the precedential value of other NAFTA cases which have found the frustration of an investor's expectations to be actionable only when based on explicit or implicit representations made by the government which it later refused to honour.[98]

2. Arbitrary Action

It is well established that international law grants states broad discretion in making legislative decisions, and that tribunals should not undermine a determination by the state to enact economic legislations or regulations to address a matter of public concern.[99] As conceded by Glamis, state legislative and

---

[89] See *Metalclad*, n 14 above, at paras 71, 74, and 101; and *Mexico v Metalclad Corp*, Sup Ct BC, 2 May 2001, 5 ICSID Reports 236, at para 72. See Memorial, at paras 535–536 and Reply, at para 227 (Glamis contends that the British Columbia Court's decision 'has virtually no value in the international context') and also V Lowe, *Regulation or Expropriation? Current Legal Problems* (2002) 447, 454. Cf Rejoinder, at 165–166. The *Feldman* tribunal, n 53 above, at para 133 confirmed Metalclad's vacature by the Supreme Court of British Colombia for 'misstat[ing] the applicable law to include transparency obligations' in Article 1105(1)   [90] *Feldman*, n 53 above, at para 133.
[91] *CMS Gas*, n 63 above.
[92] *Maffezini v Spain*, ICSID No ARB/97/7, Award, 13 November 2000, 5 ICSID Reports 419, at para 83.   [93] *Saluka v Czech Republic*, Partial Award, 17 March 2006, at para 294.
[94] *ADC Affiliate Ltd and ADC & ADMC Management Ltd v Hungary*, ICSID No ARB/03/16, Award, 2 October 2006, at para 445.   [95] *Azurix*, n 4 above, at para 378.
[96] See *Thunderbird*, n 54 above, at para 147.
[97] On the facts, see Glamis's supporting elements, in the hearings, at 1749 ff. See the aforementioned *Saluka v Czech Republic* case, but also *Waste Management, Inc v Mexico*, Award, 30 April 2004, (2004) 43 ILM 967, according to which it also depends on representations made by the host state which were reasonably relied upon by the claimant, cf ICSID Annulment Committee in the *MTD v Chile*, ad hoc committee, at para 6.
[98] See *CMS Gas*, n 63 above, at paras 266–281, *Azurix*, n 4 above, at para 375; *ADC*, n 94 above, at para 375; and *Tecmed*, n 62 above, at para 160.
[99] See the *ADF* tribunal's reference to 'something more than simple illegality or a lack of authority under the domestic law of the State'. See also the extensive understanding of the review of state's motives by the *Tokio Tokelés* tribunal, n 3 above. Compare last statements made during the hearings – the hearings, at 72–83 (claimant) and 1765–1773 (respondent).

regulatory measures are entitled to significant deference.[100] Nevertheless, claims that bring forth issues of procedural fairness have become a vital element of the fair and equitable treatment standard.[101] As a result, the tribunal may well have to wrestle with, beyond factual questions, the existence of a rule of customary international law that prohibits this type of reclamation requirement. Whether customary international law imposes upon states the obligation to adopt only legislation that is purportedly best suited to address the problem that states seek to rectify is another important issue.

2.1. The Potential of the *Glamis* Case

NAFTA has opened the possibility for investors to challenge national, state, and local environmental and human rights policies such as Canada's phase-out of a dangerous pesticide (*Ethyl* case) or California's ban on a gasoline additive and water pollutant (*Methanex* case). NAFTA tribunals have ruled in favour of investors. Deciding that a municipal government's denial of a construction permit for the building of a toxic waste facility was expropriatory as well as a governor's later declaration of an ecological preservation of the site (*Metalclad* case), or rendering a judgment against the implementation of the Basel Conventions on the Control of Transboundary Movements of Hazardous Wastes (*SD Myers* case) or against the US-Canadian Softwood Lumber Agreement (*Pope & Talbot* case) are all historical examples of judgments in favour of investors.[102] Unsurprisingly, the primary interest in the *Glamis* case arises from the fact that, if the tribunal decides on one of the various alternatives litigated by both parties (as put forth in the previous section), its forthcoming award will probably extend the prioritization given to investors over human rights concerns in the NAFTA regime. Under this restricted reading, the Glamis award is only another precedent for carrying forward, in Dworkinian terms, the unfolding 'chainnovel' of international investment law. A proactive look at human rights within the NAFTA regime should nevertheless lead to another interpretation. It is striking indeed that when focusing on how human rights issues are channelled until the litigation stage, the *Glamis* litigation highlights

Glamis describes its claim for the first time during the hearings as a 'denial of justice' at 104 and 2108, although it usually applies in a judicial context and with a much higher threshold: see *Loewen*, n 14 above (offend a sense of judicial propriety), at para 132; and *Thunderbird*, n 54 above (shock a sense of judicial propriety); and the *Elettronica Sicula SpA* (*ELSI*) case (*United States of America v Italy*), ICJ Reports (1989) 15 (contrary to the very rule of law).

[100] The hearings, at 1731.

[101] The *CMS* tribunal stated that 'any measure that might involve arbitrariness is, in itself, contrary to Fair and Equitable Treatment'. In the *ELSI* case, the United States argued that the arbitrary actions include those which are not based on fair and equitable reasons.

[102] Following the *Ethyl* arbitration, the Canadian Government reversed its ban on Methylcyclopentadienyl Manganese Tricarbonyl (MMT) and paid US$13 million to Ethyl. Following the *Metalclad* arbitration, Mexico paid Metalclad $15.6 million in compensation. Following the *SD Myers* arbitration, Canada paid SD Myers US$4.8 million for its loss of business opportunities. Following the *Pope & Talbot* arbitration, Canada paid $582,000 in damages and legal fees.

how much can be lost in the arbitral process (III). Under this global viewpoint, the Glamis arbitration could nurture a programmatic consideration of human rights under NAFTA (IV).

IV. Some Mischaracterization of Human Rights Stakes in the *Glamis* Case

During the course of this arbitration, the primary thrust of the respondent's argument was to justify the regulatory power of the State of California on three grounds. First, the Federal Government would have diligently processed Glamis's plan, followed applicable procedures, and made reasonable and defensible legal determination. Second, Glamis would also have remained free to pursue required federal and state approvals. Finally, it would have been economically viable for Glamis to proceed with its project in compliance with California's reclamation measures. This strategy of litigation has prevailed over another form of jurisprudence, contained in an *amicus curiae* filed with the tribunal,[103] which makes the use of the regulatory power of the State of California a legitimate protection under NAFTA of cultural rights of an indigenous population.[104] The complexity of this second human rights claim arises from both the uncrystallized nature of its supportive norm (A) and the fact that it was not directly vocalized either by the federation, which does not endorse the Quechuan's concerns, or by the Quechuan people, who are not party to the arbitration and can only participate as *amicus curiae* at the discretion of the tribunal (B). The claim being partly based on the investor's alleged reliance upon a federal decision not to respect alleged sovereign rights of indigenous peoples to preserve their sacred land, it may be considered inappropriate that these indigenous peoples have no direct right to participate in the proceeding.

A. Indigenous Rights in NAFTA

The Quechuan people claim that any right granted to Glamis to exploit their land could be only enjoyed upon satisfaction, among other obligations,[105] of the international obligations owed by the respondent to take steps necessary to

---

[103] The respondent has decided not to support the Quechuan people's argument contained in an *amicus curiae* filed with the tribunal, that the United States at all levels of government is obliged under customary international law to protect the sacred places of indigenous peoples living within its borders.

[104] Should it have done so, the Glamis case could have even more obviously highlighted the emerging string of recent arbitral awards involving investments in environmentally sensitive sectors referred to by Professor Francioni in ch 3 in the present volume.

[105] On the Federal Government's obligations to protect tribes and tribal cultural resources, see the respondent's Statement of Defence, at 5–6.

protect and promote their geographical and cultural interests. Should the tribunal consider this claim as well, it would certainly have to decipher whether there is an obligation under international law to take steps to prevent or mitigate negative impacts of development activities on the territories of indigenous people,[106] as well as to consult and reach agreement with them.[107]

As a matter of treaty law, the American Convention on Human Rights and the American Declaration on the Rights and Duties of Man, which do not specifically mention indigenous people, include general human rights provisions explicitly upholding the rights to property, to physical wellbeing,[108] and implicitly affirming the right to the integrity of culture.[109] Moreover, indigenous peoples' rights to land and natural resources are increasingly well defined and recognized by a consistent pattern of international legal practice, such as the International Labour Organization Convention on Indigenous and Tribal People (ILO Convention no 169). This convention establishes an obligation to respect, protect, and take positive steps to promote the rights and interests of indigenous peoples in their ancestral land, as well as to be free from discrimination under international law.[110] This international practice is strengthened by domestic laws in each of the NAFTA countries.[111] Although the respondent is not party to the ILO Convention, the *Glamis* tribunal could affirm that the core obligations of this Convention have now constituted a norm of customary international law to recognize and protect indigenous peoples' rights

---

[106] See J Anaya, 'The Protection of Indigenous People's Rights over Lands and Natural Resources Under the Inter-American Human Rights System' (2001) 14 Harvard Human Rights Journal 33, 82 ff. From the *Eastern Greenland* decision (PCIJ, 1933) to the *Western Sahara* decision (ICJ Reports (1975) 12), the legal doctrine has certainly evolved with regard to the place of indigenous peoples: see A Gupta, *Human Rights of Indigeneous Peoples* (2005) 74 ff.

[107] See J Anaya, 'Indigenous people's participatory rights in relation to decisions about natural resources extraction' (2005) 22 Arizona Journal of International and Comparative Law 7.

[108] See in part American Declaration, Arts III and V–VI, and the American Convention, Arts 12 and 17. See Anaya, n 106 above, 49.

[109] Indigenous peoples' traditional land-use patterns are included by the UN Human Rights Committee as cultural elements that states must take affirmative measures to protect under Art 27 of the Covenant on Civil and Political Rights, regardless of whether states recognize indigenous peoples' ownership rights over lands and resources subject to traditional uses.

[110] With regard to compliance with the ILO Convention 169, see J Anaya, *Indigenous People in International Law* (2nd edn, 2004) 195 ff and 226 ff; and M Willis and T Seward, 'Protecting and Preserving Indigenous Communities in the Americas' (2006) 33 SPG Human Rights 18 and the several UNESCO recommendations.

[111] Mexico is party to the American Court of Human Rights. See, moreover, many federal laws and the Constitution of 1917, in part its Arts 4 and 27, Section VII, para 2. The Mexican Government ratified ILO's Convention 169 in 1989. Canada is not party to the American Court of Human Rights, but many bilateral agreements have been negotiated between the Canadian Government and aboriginal groups since the 1970s. See also the Common Law doctrine on aboriginals, ss 25 and 35 (Indians, Métis, and Inuit) of the Constitution Act of 1982 and the decisions *Sparrow v R*, 1990 2 SCR 1075 (Can) and *Calder v AG of British Columbia*, 34, DLR (3d), at 145 (Canadian Supreme Court, 1973). The United States are not party to the American Court of Human Rights. Nevertheless, see the restrictions introduced by *Lyng v Northwest Indian Cemetery Protection Association*, 485 US 439 (1988).

to land and natural resources in connection with traditional/ancestral use and occupancy patterns.[112]

The Inter-American Court has proactively recognized and protected indigenous people and their traditional resources as an obligation under international law.[113] In a case originated with a petition to the Commission charging Nicaragua about the alleged failure to take steps necessary to secure the land rights of the Mayagna indigenous community of *Awas Tigny*, the court concluded that Nicaragua had violated indigenous rights by granting to a foreign investor a concession to undermine the community's traditional land, relying on an extensive interpretation of the right to 'property' (so as to include the communal property of indigenous people) as defined by their customary use and tenure, notwithstanding its treatment under national law.[114] The recognition of the collective rights of indigenous communities by the Inter-American Court has influenced many cases concerning cultural practices and beliefs in relation to damages such as the *Plan de Sanchez Massacre v Guatemala* case.[115] Although this proactive adjudicatory trend is not binding, it may be referenced in support of its reasoning by the *Glamis* tribunal.[116] Furthermore, since the Commission has also progressively recognized that a *sui generis* regime of international

---

[112] In the *Mayagna Awas Tingni Community* case, the Inter-American Court did not explicitly adopt the Inter-American Commission's use of customary international law, but nevertheless applied an 'evolutionary interpretation' of the property rights provision to the American Convention. On cultural heritage, see also E Morgera, 'Significant Trend in Corporate Environmental Accountability: The New Performance Standards of the International Finance Corporation' (2007) 18(1) Colorado Journal of International Environmental Law and Policy 179.

[113] The Court has applied the American Declaration on the Rights and Duties of Man, whereby indigenous rights in ancestral lands were recognized and protected in international law. See, eg I/A Court HR, *Mayagna (Sumo) Awas Tingni Community v Nicaragua*, 31 August 2001, Series C No 79; I/A Court HR, *Yakye Axa Indigenous Community v Paraguay*, 17 June 2005, Series C No 125; I/A Court HR, *Sawhoyamaxa Indigenous Community v Paraguay*, 29 March 2006, Series C No 146; and I/A Court HR, *Yakye Axa Indigenous Community v Paraguay*, 29 March 2006, Series C No 146.

[114] It relied on Art 21 of the American Convention on Human Rights: see *Mayagna (Sumo) Awas Tingni Community*, at paras 151 and 173 on the application of norms. In *Moiwana Community v Suriname*, 15 June 2005 and *Yakye Axa Indigenous Community*, n 113 above, at para 135, the Court even extended its approach by stressing that the valuing of indigenous lands calls for criteria other than those usually applicable to private property. On this topic, see Anaya, n 106 above, fn 14; and J Anaya and C Grossman, 'The Case of Awas Tingni v. Nicaragua: A New Step in the International Law of Indigenous People' (2002) 19 Arizona Journal of International and Comparative Law 1. Note that the Inter-American Commission has also adjudicated petitions against Belize, Canada, and the United States, which, although the latter are not party to the Convention, may be judged under the American Declaration on the Rights and Duties of Man.

[115] The Court ordered the government to pay damages to the Achi Mayan survivors for communal cultural harms, including divorcing the community from customary funeral rites and other traditions, dislocating transmission of cultural practices to new generations by the murder of elders and women responsible for disseminating these practices: see I/A Court HR, Decision on reparations, 19 November 2004, Series C No 116. See also M Willis and T Seward, 'Protecting and Preserving Indigenous Communities in the Americas' (2006) Human Rights Magazine, spring.

[116] See also the *Western Shoshone* case, where the UN Committee for the Elimination of Racial Discrimination calls in 2006 for the United States to initiate dialogue to find a solution acceptable

norms protecting indigenous rights within a specific territory currently exists, this protection should be applied within the context of any international dispute.

B. *Amicus Curiae*

Should the respondent lose the *Glamis* case under NAFTA and decide to implement the award in a way not favourable to the Quechuan Indian Nations, nothing bars this party from expressing its specific human rights concerns in suing their own representative before the Inter-American Court on Human Rights, in the (improbable) case that the United States agrees to abide by the Court's jurisdiction. This ultimate procedural dimension exemplifies a paradox lying at the very heart of NAFTA's protection of human rights. The American people may be impacted by the *Glamis* arbitration as taxpayers, but the Quechuan people may also be impacted, as a tribe. Nevertheless, they cannot directly express their concern.

Under the Free Trade Commission Statement on Non Disputing Parties Participation, an *amicus curiae* may be accepted on a case-by-case basis and as long as a certain number of requirements are respected.[117] The Quechuan people noticed the relevance of Article 27 of the International Convenant on Civil and Political Rights and other International Law Instruments concerning cultural heritage. This indirect system of representation may assist the expression of human rights concerns in the final award,[118] although this engine is insufficient in itself. The Quechuan people's specific claim originating the arbitration was based in part on the investor's alleged reliance upon a federal decision denying the alleged sovereign rights of these indigenous people to preserve their sacred lands.[119] However, this indirect representation remains at the discretion of both the tribunal and the parties: one of whom wanted to conduct extensive

to the Western Shoshone, in accordance with CERD General Recommendation 23 on the rights of indigenous people to own, develop, control, and use their communal lands, territories, and resources: see <http://www2.ohchr.org/english/bodies/cerd/docs/68decision-USA.pdf>.

[117] See Letter of Acceptation, 16 September 2005, at paras 4 and 9 and the Submission of the Quechuan Indian Nation, at 3–4. See, eg in the UNCITRAL context, *Methanex Corp v United States*, Decision on Petitions from Third Persons to Intervene as *Amicus Curiae*, 15 January 2001; and *UPS v Canada*, Decision of the Tribunal on Petitions for Intervention and Participation as *Amicus Curiae*, 17 October 2001. In the ICSID context, see the denial in *Aguas del Tunari*, n 4 above. Yet, the ground-breaking 2001 decision by the *Methanex* tribunal has paved the way to analogous solutions by ICSID tribunals such as in *Aguas Argentinas SA and ors v Argentina*, ICSID ARB No 03/19, Order in Response to a Petition for Transparency and Participation as *Amicus Curiae*, 19 May 2005; *Suez, Vivendi Universal SA and Sociedad General de Aguas de Barcelona SA v Argentina*, ICSID No ARB/03/19; and also the *Biwater Gauff (Tanzania) Ltd v Tanzania*, ICSID No ARB 05/22, Procedural Order No 5, 2 February 2007, at para 59. See the new Art 37(2) of the ICSID Arbitration Rules (as of 10 April 2006).

[118] Nevertheless, the *Methanex* merits decision (n 68 above) shows that the formal acceptation may be practically of little help.

[119] See T Weiler's comments in NAFTA News Volume V, Issue 1, 20 September 2007.

mining operations on the site, while the other must act under the direction of the same administration that attempted to facilitate those wishes. This judicial paradox creates a core problem in the struggle to protect the human rights of third-party individuals. No litigation other than *Glamis* could, in this regard, better exemplify both the merits and the limits of *amicus curiae* to protect human rights in the NAFTA regime. Although welcomed by both parties, they cannot fully represent human rights concerns of a sovereign (indigenous) nation[120] allegedly protected under customary international law as well as recognized by the General Assembly of the United Nations with its declaration on the protection of property rights of indigenous peoples.

V. Elements in Support of a Proactive Adjudication Regarding Human Rights

The full implementation under NAFTA of human rights norms such as the protection of indigenous cultural rights depends on both executive and legislative domestic actions, and judicial and arbitration interpretations, or a combination of these four elements. The most efficient protection is definitively derived from domestic agencies more than from the Chapter 11 arbitration itself.[121] Should this former protection fail, options remain at the stage of arbitration as exemplified in the *Glamis* case: norms of protection of indigenous cultural rights may be well defined as norms of customary international law. The last section of this chapter will use the methodology of both the New Haven School of International Law and of the transnational legal process to frame a human rights strategy within the NAFTA regime, which would seek to enhance the internalization of international human rights norms through arbitration in order to have these human rights norms 'obeyed' (HLH Hart) within the NAFTA regime.[122] In this manner, privilege will be given to the so-called vertical strategies of interaction, interpretation, and internalization. Repetition of *interactions* among the various actors of the transnational legal process will serve well to highlight the concern at stake: to relax the requirements in order to facilitate the introduction of *amicus curiae* would, for instance, empower more actors to participate in the project of protecting human rights in the NAFTA regime. *Interaction* is aimed at producing a robust interpretation of human

---

[120] US Constitution, Art I, s 8, cl 3.

[121] See M Yablon, 'Property Rights and Sacred Sites: Federal Regulatory Responses to American Indian Religious Claims on Public Land' (2004) 113 Yale Law Journal 1623, 1658 ff.

[122] An example is given by H Koh, 'Transnational Public Law Litigation' (1991) 100 Yale Law Journal 2347, concerning the efforts of victims of human rights abuse in US federal courts to enforce norms of international human rights law against their abusers. On both the 'clarification of standpoints' and the 'focal lenses', see WM Reisman, 'View from the New Haven School of International Law' (1992) 86 American Society of International Law Proceedings 118, 120 ff.

rights norms: NAFTA arbitral panels may be used for norm-enunciation and elaboration of these standards, such as those argued for indigenous people by the Quechuan people. A legal *internalization* occurs when the international norm is incorporated into the NAFTA regime: it could be fostered by a litigation provoking an arbitral incorporation of human rights norms either implicitly, by construing existing disposition of the Treaty consistently with international human rights norms, or explicitly, through 'transnational public law litigation'.[123] Multiple strategies may be employed in relation to these three goals. There are at least two strategies available depending on the position as a lawyer (A) or an arbitrator (B).

A. The Lawyer's Perspective: Litigating in Search of an Interpretation

The existence of many factual and interpretative unsettled issues renders it impossible to predict the outcome of the case at this stage. With regard to the lawyers' side, it remains nevertheless possible to decipher three hypotheticals.

1. Hypothetical 1

The respondent may want to succeed at the bottom edge, namely, avoid paying the claimed US$50 million to Glamis and simultaneously avoid having the NAFTA tribunal acknowledging additional international law protection for indigenous people.[124] To succeed on jurisdictional grounds would be sufficient in this regard, as exemplified by the respondent's focus on the 'diversity of nationality' requirement under NAFTA.[125] Since NAFTA remains silent on the implication of dual nationality for an alleged infringement of Articles 1105 and 1110 in a claim brought pursuant to Chapter 11, the respondent bases its strategy on the test prescribed by customary international law, allegedly of direct applicability. This would allegedly bar the claimant from bringing a claim or receiving a

---

[123] There are other strategies to internalize international human rights norms, of either a social or a political nature. As shown by H Koh, the US human rights advocates failed to achieve judicial internalization of an international treaty norm in the Haitian refugee case, but achieved a political internalization in the form of a reversal of the Clinton Administration's policy in tandem with the growing social outrage about the treatment of Haitian refugees. In some cases, such as the torture case *Filartiga v Pena-Irala*, 630 F2d 876 (2d Cir 1980), it may be sufficient to launch and promote a judicial incorporation. In the latter event, it helped to push President Bush to ratify the UN Convention against Torture and the Congress to enact the Torture Victim Protection Act of 1991.

[124] Note, nevertheless, the respondent's Counter Memorial, 19 September 2006, at 33, which cites various international instruments concerning cultural heritage, in particular UNESCO recommendations.

[125] See *Amicus curiae* submission of Friends of the Earth Canada and Friends of the Earth United States, 20 September 2005, at paras 10–39. Indeed, NAFTA was never intended to allow claims by a party's own nationals against a decision of that party, which could be encouraged by abusive corporate 'inversion'. The *Loewen* tribunal refused to relax a customary rule of diplomatic protection on diversity of nationality, where no specific provision of NAFTA does so. See *Loewen*, n 14 above, Award, 26 June 2003, (2003) 42 ILM 811, at paras 223–230.

Chapter 11 remedy against the United States because it is an alleged national of the two countries.[126] This minimal strategy is also apparent in the respondent's focus on the lack of ripeness of Glamis's claims that the Federal Government failed to approve its plan of operations and that the Californian measures constitute a 'de facto ban on open-pit metallic mining'.[127]

2. Hypothetical 2

The tribes may seek to profit from this arbitration to better highlight their own specific claims and, by this interaction, increase the pressure on the Federal Government to respect their alleged rights under international law.[128] In this manner, it may be enough for the tribe to have both parties accept their sending of an *amicus curiae* to the tribunal. This middle-range strategy would let the respondent – the United States – focus on not paying compensation for the alleged expropriation. It would only let the tribe put forth a claim for violation of human rights through *amicus curiae* and not within the main counter memorial and rejoinder of the respondent. By pursuing this trajectory, the respondent would have its financial interest defended, its sub-entities satisfied, and, simultaneously, it would minimize the risk of having the tribunal acknowledge the indigenous rights of direct applicability in NAFTA.

3. Hypothetical 3

The tribe may well want a significant victory on interpretation. As sovereign people, it may indeed be more concerned with the recognition of its indigenous rights as a tribe as opposed to having the federation not pay compensation. In this regard, it would be more important for them to have the tribunal decide upon the merit of their claim and interpret the applicable norms in a manner

---

[126] The claimant identifies itself as a 'public held Canadian corporation incorporated in 1972 under the laws of the Province of British Columbia': see Notice of Arbitration, at 4. However, Glamis is also an American due to its central administration and set of operations located in the United States (see *Amicus Curiae*, n 125 above, at para 9).

[127] Glamis asserts that 'further processing of a proposed mine that faces insurmountably cost prohibitive reclamation requirement would be futile' (Investor's Reply Memorial, at para 292). See also Claimant's Memorial, at para 445. Glamis has reiterated this argument during the hearings: see the hearings, at 1821 ff and 1836 ff and the comments of Arbitrator Caron at 2143 ff. It is not clear whether once the regulation was adopted, nothing more could have been done and that the process was stopped since Glamis Gold informed the DOI in a letter from July 2003 when the NAFTA arbitration was initiated. Should the tribunal decide upon this jurisdictional issue, it would have to decide upon the appropriateness of the final decision ripeness requirement under US law, in particular the *Whitney Benefits* decision, which has found that a cognizable expropriation claim arises upon the actual application of a challenged measure to a claimant and not upon the mere enactment of such measure. See *Whitney Benefits v United States*, 926 F2d 1169, 1178 (Fed. Cir 1991); the hearings, at 1833 ff, and the rebuttal argument by Counsel for Claimant in the hearings, at 2049 ff.

[128] On the facts compare the statements in the hearings, at 242, 250, and 283.

which recognizes that the rights of indigenous people are applicable in the NAFTA regime. This last strategy is definitively a riskier option. Should the tribunal take this claim, it could eventually decide that with regard to property, any claimant is 'stymied by a longstanding requirement' to respect the indigenous people's rights – a ruling which would be of great assistance to internalize this norm within the NAFTA regime. Conversely, the tribunal may also render a limited interpretation of the human rights applicable to the NAFTA.

B. The Arbitrator's Perspective: Building a Coherent Law of Investment[129]

Arbitrators may perform their task in two ways: minimalist or maximalist. Minimalism, commonly known as the constitutional law 'passive virtues', makes sense when considering that arbitrators are appointed by parties and limited to their consent. Maximalism would alternatively refer to the arbitrators, often renowned and prestigious jurists in the NAFTA arbitration, as gatekeepers of the international investment law community.[130] Although it is well known that 'powerful pressures on the members of the tribunal to be obscure rather than explicitly rational' may also make them strategically unwilling to deal with merits of the issues at stake,[131] it may be their duty as NAFTA arbitrators, some argue, to deal explicitly with a maximal range of issues to foster a specific trend in NAFTA arbitration.[132] This never-ending debate between two conceptions of adjudicating in US domestic constitutional law is also a debate in the arbitration community.[133] First and foremost, because only a few human rights norms are referenced in the NAFTA and in BITs: what else other than an interpretative strategy provided by the arbitrators could guarantee the efficiency of human rights norms within the NAFTA context[134] (certainly not by applying the international human rights norm *principaliter*, but by reading the pertinent human rights provisions in light of both the case and the pertinent norms of international law)? According to the *Glamis* case, three reasons would call for a maximalist arbitration.

---

[129] Concerning the required 'Intellectual tasks of the Jurist', see Reisman, n 122 above, 123.

[130] To read in line with the suggestion of Ph Fouchard, 'L'arbitrage et la mondialisation de l'économie' in Frison-Roche (ed), *Philosophie du droit et droit économique. Quel dialogue? Mélange en l'honneur de Gérard Farjat* (1999) 381–395.

[131] G Alvarez and WM Reisman, *The Reasons Requirement in International Investment Arbitration: Critical Case Studies* (2008) ch 1.

[132] See, for instance, Ari Afilalo's strategy of adjudication in A Afilalo, 'Meaning, Ambiguity and Legitimacy: Judicial (Re-) Construction of NAFTA Chapter 11' (2005) 25 Northwest International Law and Business Journal 279, 313.

[133] See, for instance, G Maggs, 'The Rehnquist Court's Noninterference with the Guardians of National Security' (2006) 74 George Washington Law Review 1122.

[134] Art 1131 rules inter alia that '[a] Tribunal established under this Section shall decide the issues in dispute in accordance with this Agreement and applicable rules of international law'.

1. Expropriation

The issue of expropriation has been reduced to the question of whether the government measures at issue have destroyed all of the economic value of Glamis's investment, or interfered with it to the extent that one could conclude 'that the property has been "taken" from the owner'.[135] The norm to which this claim relates remains unclear: according to the 'sole-effect' doctrine, the crucial test for determining whether an indirect expropriation has occurred is whether the regulation had an expropriatory effect on an investment regardless of the government's intent. On the other hand, the 'police-power' doctrine balances the impact on property against the objective of the government's measures to determine whether an expropriation has occurred.[136] While the text cannot assist in deciphering between both interpretations, several awards have progressively left the sole effect's conception of expropriation under *Metalclad* to the doctrine of police powers in *Methanex* and *SD Myers*. In the absence of any interpretative note, the tribunal could begin to tackle this doctrinal trend.

1.1. Appellate Review

It is repeatedly acknowledged that NAFTA and other international investment law tribunals are not appellate courts. As stated by the *ADF* tribunal: it 'has no authority to review the legal validity of the US measures here in question under the US Internal administrative law. [It does] not sit as a court with appellate jurisdiction with respect to US measures.'[137] It comes as no surprise that the respondent claims that Glamis's claim is tantamount to a mechanism for reviewing domestic administrative procedure since it is:

… ultimately dependent upon persuading the tribunal to review de novo each and every government action that had any effect on its mining claims, then hoping that this tribunal will reach factual conclusions and make policy choices different from those made by the respective federal and state governments.[138]

---

[135] *Pope & Talbot*, Interim Award, n 14 above, at para 102; or *GAMI*, n 63 above, at para 126. See the respondent's Counter-Memorial, 19 September 2006, at 161–180, concluding that Glamis's Imperial Project mining Claims retained substantial value, both as of December 2002 and as of today. Then its claim fails as a matter of law on this basis alone. On expropriation, see J Lawrence, 'Chicken Little Revisited: Nafta Regulatory Expropriation After Methanex' (2006) 41 Georgia Law Review 261, 275.

[136] The distinction is provided, for instance, in R Dolzer and F Bloch, 'Indirect Expropriation: Conceptual Realignments?' (2003) 5 International Law Forum du droit international 155, 158.

[137] *ADF Group Inc v United States*, ICSID No ARB (AF)/00/01, Final Award, 9 January 2003, 6 ICSID Reports 470, at para 190. See also in BIT, *CME Czech Republic BV v Czech Republic*, UNCITRAL Final Award, 14 March 2003, 9 ICSID Reports 121; and *EnCana v Ecuador*, UNCITRAL Final Award, 3 February 2006, 12 ICSID Reports 427.

[138] In this regard, see the respondent's Rejoinder Memorial, 15 March 2007, at 3:
in re determination of professional archeologists that a portion of the Quechuan's sacred trail system traversed the project area were not supported by a preponderance of the evidence; the DOI violated the Administrative Procedure Act by issuing an opinion

Despite this traditional limitation, international investment law tribunals have increasingly taken direct control over acts and omissions of the 'Regulatory State' according to international minimum standard. Tribunals such as NAFTA tribunals have frequently carried out some form of domestic law judicial review of measures submitted to scrutiny under international law. The extent to which the *Thunderbird* tribunal commanded the use of domestic law in the BIT generation has been recently emphasized.[139] As clearly shown: 'the tribunal preferred to formally deny this reality and adhere to the "non Court of Appeal" doctrine. It concluded by making a full de novo finding of facts and policies on those issues'. The *Glamis* tribunal may wish to actualize its full potential as a judicial body, thus recognizing and legitimizing the influential role of domestic law in investment disputes.[140]

1.2 Reasoning

ICSID's rules, under which many NAFTA tribunals are settled, clearly stipulate that the tribunal is required to provide reasons for its opinions.[141] There is no doubt that Article 52 does not refer to *errores in devidendo*, although what constitutes a sufficient reason still remains ambiguous. As recently recalled by Reisman and Alvarez, the first series of annulment petitions under Article 52 of the ICSID which initially permitted the review system in ICSID to grapple with

interpreting an undefined term in the agency's statute without conducted rulemaking; and the California State Mining and Geology Board was obligated to review scientific studies before determining that massive open pits accompanied by large piles of waste rock leave the land in a condition unsuitable for alternate use post-mining.

[139] *Thunderbird*, n 54 above. In *Glamis*, such as in cases where the waiver of the exhaustion of local remedies rule is used, international investment law tribunals do not count with the help of domestic courts and the records resulting from their proceedings. For an analysis of this trend from the denial of justice age to the BIT generation, see Santiago Montt's thoughtful discussion that in *Thunderbird* the fair and equitable treatment claim was dismissed by tribunals on two substantive accounts, ie the illegality of the machines were illegal under domestic law and the insufficient strength of the Oficio to overcome that basic illegality and give rise to expectation on which the investor could have relied: S Montt, 'The award in *Thunderbird v. Mexico*' in G Alvarez and WM Reisman (eds), *The Reasons Requirement in International Investment Arbitration: Critical Case Studies* (2008) 261.

[140] See the classic by W Jenks, 'The Interpretation and Application of Municipal Law by the Permanent Court of International Justice' (1938) 19 British Year Book of International Law 67.

[141] In favour of the reason's requirement, see more generally Alvarez and Reisman, n 130 above. See also Art 48(3) of the Washington Convention, Art 47(1)(i) of the ICSID Arbitration Rules, Art 52(2)(i) of the ICSID Additional Facility Rules, and Art 32(3) of the UNCITRAL Arbitration Rules. The sanction under Art 52(1)(e) of the Convention for failing to comply is severe: 'either party may request annulment of the award by an application in writing addressed to the Secretary-General on one or more of the following grounds: ... that the award has failed to state the reasons on which it is based'. As stated by Alvarez and Reisman, '[t]he progress of the drafters' thinking on this issue, which is tracked in the legislative history of the Convention, indicates that requiring reasons was important for the drafters from the very genesis of the Convention'. More generally, see C Schreuer's comments in *The ICSID Convention: A Commentary* (Cambridge University Press, 2001).

this question produced two emerging juridical norms.[142] First, the ad hoc committee in *Klöckner*, which was the first application for an annulment ever lodged against an ICSID award, ushered in an 'extremely high, indeed unprecedented standard' of the ICSID review process[143] by emphasizing a formal rather than a substantive test of reasons.[144] Nevertheless, the *Amco v Indonesia* committee departed from *Klöckner* by rejecting the notion of automatic nullification as a consequence of any mechanical or technical discrepancy.[145] Both *Amco* and later the *MINE*[146] committees incorporated a lower standard: as a minimum base line standard, the explanation for an arbitration decision should permit an understanding of the reasoning of the tribunal. Reisman and Alvarez claim that this standard, as 'both a textual and a teleological interpretation of the ICSID reasons regime ... serves as a mode of control on the arbitral tribunal's discretion and a confirmation that the tribunal respected other explicit requirements in Article 52'. The ad hoc committee should concentrate on the question of whether there were any material violations in the award.[147] The *Glamis* case is governed by the UNCITRAL Arbitration Rules, this rendering it coherent with the requirement of both the UNCITRAL Arbitration Rules and the rather minimal ICSID standard[148] to stand for an explicit reasoning of the tribunal with regard to human rights issues under NAFTA.

---

[142] See the slightly different presentation by Antonio Crivellaro at the colloquium 'La Procédure arbitrale relative aux investissements internationaux: aspects récents', IHEI: Ecole normale supérieure (3 April 2008). Professor Crivellaro differentiated *Klöckner I* (*Klöckner v Cameroon*, Award, 21 October 1983, 2 ICSID Reports 9) and *Amco I* (Decision on Annulment, 16 May 1986, 1 ICSID Reports 509) with *MINE* (partial annulment), *Klöckner II* (*Klöckner v Cameroon*, Decision on Annulment, 3 May 1985, 2 ICSID Reports 95). This second award and the decision of the ad hoc committee were unpublished), and *Amco II* (The *Amco* case was retransmitted to a new tribunal, which rendered an award, whose annulment was rejected by an ad hoc committee) with *Wena* ((2002) 41 ILM 933) and *Vivendi I* (*Vivendi Universal v Argentina*, (2000) 16 ICSID Review), where Professor Shreuer says: 'the ICSID annulment process has found its proper balance. [They] show that ad hoc committees will only intervene in serious and important cases'. See the current dismissals in the cases *Repsol*, *MTD*, *Soufraki*, *Lucchetti*, and *CMS*.
[143] See *Klöckner v Cameroon*, Decision on Annulment, 3 May 1985, 2 ICSID Reports 162. See the dissenting opinion of Klöckner's party-appointed arbitrator considering the award as null due to 'important mistakes, the numerous contradictions and failures to state the grounds and the misrepresentation of contractual clauses'.
[144] The *Klöckner* committee held that as long as 'answers seem tenable and not arbitrary, they do not constitute a manifest excess of power', and in case of doubt, analysis would be in favour of the validity of the award. The *Klöckner* ad hoc committee concluded that an 'absence of reasons' would occur if a particular conclusion or decision of the arbitral tribunal was completely unsupported or explained in the award or lacked 'sufficiently pertinent' or 'reasonably acceptable' reasons: see paras 116, 126, and 130.   [145] *Amco I*, n 141 above, at 520–21.
[146] See *Maritime International Nominees Establishment (MINE) v Guinea*, Decision on Annulment, 22 December 1989, 4 ICSID Reports 79, at 88. The tribunal awarded in MINE's favour and, following the lead of *Klöckner* and *AMCO*, Guinea applied for a review, citing a failure inter alia to state reasons and to address certain allegedly pivotal questions.
[147] Alvarez and Reisman, n 130 above.
[148] cf Antonio Crivellaro's position in 'La Procédure arbitrale CARDI' in *La procédure arbitrale relative aux investissements internationaux: aspects récents*, Colloque IHEI (University of Paris II, 3 April 2008).

17

Human Rights Arguments in *Amicus Curiae* Submissions: Promoting Social Justice?

James Harrison

I. Introduction

This chapter analyses the human rights interventions of various civil society organizations in international investment arbitration through the submission of *amicus curiae* briefs. It asks what value these interventions have had in promoting social justice issues in the arbitration process.

I start by exploring the social justice issues that arise through international investment arbitration and the rationale for engaging with these issues utilizing a human rights framework. The following section then provides a brief history of the recent practice of civil society groups in submitting *amicus* briefs to investment tribunals, and how these have been viewed by the tribunal panels and by commentators on the system. I then turn to considering the human rights arguments raised in a great number of these submissions, and the impact of these human rights arguments on the tribunals. In the last two sections, I consider the benefits and limitations of this human rights approach. It will be argued that the language and legal obligations of human rights appear to have an important impact in terms of ensuring that *amicus* submissions of civil society groups are accepted by tribunals. However, there are fundamental problems inherent in this mechanism which makes it unlikely that the human rights arguments raised will have any significant role in the decision-making process of the tribunal panels. The chapter concludes with some thoughts about the wider implications of these findings for international investment law, international human rights law, and international law more generally.

II. International Investment Arbitration in a Social Justice Context

There is great political, social, and scholarly legal debate about the extent to which international economic law (IEL) rules take into account broader social justice concerns. From international trade law rules on trade in goods and services and intellectual property protection to the international monetary rules of the World Bank and the International Monetary Fund (IMF), questions are regularly raised by a range of actors about whether international economic law rules balance the interests of governments, corporations, and individuals in a way which can be seen as promoting broader conceptions of justice – including issues of importance to affected societies.[1] The dominant legal 'external' social justice critique of IEL rules has been provided by human rights. Legal scholars, organs of the United Nations, and a wide range of non-governmental organizations have sought to analyse the extent to which IEL rules adhere to the norms and standards of human rights, and as a result can be seen as promoting social justice.[2]

While social justice critiques of international economic institutions such as the World Trade Organization, World Bank, and IMF have been widespread for a number of years, it is only more recently that the social justice implications of international investment treaties and the way in which they are arbitrated has become of widespread interest to academics as well as to wider civil society. Investment treaties allow multinational companies from one state to sue for expropriation or 'indirect' expropriation of their property.[3] Indirect expropriation has been interpreted to include regulations or other activities of governments which significantly diminish the value of investments. On the basis of such a loss, foreign companies of a state which has signed a treaty can bring a claim against a state party to the same investment treaty directly before an international tribunal, bypassing the domestic court system.

---

[1] No strong normative claims are made about the term 'social justice' in this chapter. The only claim made here is that any legal system which adheres to conceptions of social justice must, at a minimum, somehow take into account (and be seen to take into account) issues of key significance to those stakeholders which are (potentially) affected by its decisions. It will be argued that the issues raised by international investment arbitration clearly raise a number of such issues. It is accepted that social justice is an extremely contested expression and that '[t]o date, political philosophers have made relatively few serious attempts to explain how a theory of social justice translates into public policy'. See the Preface of G Craig, T Burchardt and D Gordon (eds), *Social Justice and public policy: Seeking Fairness in Diverse Societies* (2008). No such attempt will be made here. Rather, the scrutiny here will be upon the extent to which human rights interventions create added value in terms of the clear social justice issues raised in international investment arbitration proceedings.

[2] eg from UN Agencies, see Office of the High Commissioner for Human Rights, 'Liberalisation of Trade and Services and Human Rights – Report of the High Commissioner' (E/CN.4/Sub.2/2002/9) (25 June 2002); and 'Human Rights, Trade and Investment, Report of the High Commissioner' (E/CN.4/Sub.2/2003/9) (2 July 2003). From NGOs, see, eg International Federation for Human Rights (FIDH), *The WTO and Human Rights* (2001). From academics, see M Darrow, *Between Light and Shadow: The World Bank, the International Monetary Fund and International Human Rights Law* (2003); and J Harrison, *The Human Rights Impact of the World Trade Organisation* (2007).

[3] The term 'expropriation' is here used in the widest possible sense to cover, eg 'nationalization', 'taking', etc, but see R Dolzer and C Schreuer, *Principles of International Investment Law* (2008) for a more detailed analysis of the legal principles.

Increased interest in the wider social impact of these treaties has arisen at a time when there is an explosion in numbers of both bilateral investment treaties and in the numbers of investment arbitration claims made under those treaties. There are now almost 2,500 bilateral investment treaties, with roughly 1,500 signed in the past 10 years.[4] Two-hundred-and-nineteen treaty-based investment claims have now been initiated, with two-thirds of those initiated since 1990.[5] There is great variety between these different investment treaties. There is also great variety between the different procedural rules under which they are adjudicated – for instance between the rules of the International Centre for Settlement of Investment Disputes (ICSID) and the ad hoc tribunals established under UN Commission on International Trade Law (UNCITRAL) Rules. However, there are unifying features of the system as a whole such that we can talk of 'principles of international investment law'[6] and the adjudicatory structure has even been described as 'an entrenched system of investment treaty arbitration designed to protect investors from the exercise of public authority' which is 'established as a general adjudicative system in the regulatory sphere'.[7]

International arbitration proceedings under Chapter 11 of the North American Free Trade Agreement (NAFTA) first focused attention on the wide-ranging areas of sensitive government regulation that could potentially be challenged through arbitration tribunals. Many of these cases appeared to have profound social justice implications, involving government regulation ostensibly aimed at, for example, protecting the environment, or ensuring a universal postal service.[8] More recently, the impact of various arbitration processes under bilateral investment treaties is being realized. Most notably, a recent estimate of the cases against Argentina arising out of its 2001–2002 economic crisis found 43 ICSID arbitrations with potential liabilities of more than US$8 billion, more than the entire financial reserves of Argentina in 2002, and with one estimate that the total value of potential claims could rise to US$80 billion.[9] The legal

---

[4] 'World Investment Report 2006 FDI from Developing and Transition Economies: Implications for Development' (United Nations 2006) 26.

[5] J VanDuzer, 'Enhancing the Procedural Legitimacy of Investor-State Arbitration Through Transparency and *Amicus Curiae* Participation' (2007) 52 McGill Law Journal 681–723, 690. See also on numbers of ICSID claims, G Van Harten, *Investment Treaty Arbitration and Public Law* (2007) 30.   [6] As in the title of Dolzer and Schreuer, n 3 above.

[7] Van Harten, n 5 above, 28. This is undoubtedly a contentious claim and many would at the very least argue that the purpose of such treaties is to protect investors against the *illegitimate* exercise of public power. The debate probably turns on the contested nature of what constitutes a legitimate exercise of power.

[8] A number of these cases will be discussed further below, but in relation to regulation which purported to protect the environment, see, eg *Methanex Corp v United States*, Final Award on jurisdiction and merits, (2005) 44 ILM 1345; and with regard to the postal service, see *United Postal Services v Canada*, Award on the Merits, (2007) 46 ILM 922.

[9] W Burke-White, 'The Argentine Financial Crisis: State Liability Under BITs and the Legitimacy of the ICSID System', University of Pennsylvania, Institute for Law and Economics Research Paper No 08-01 (24 January 2008) 1–31, 5, with references to sources for liability figures.

approach and consistency of some of the early tribunal decisions on these cases has been heavily criticized.[10] A number of the cases involve claims in relation to the running of essential services, in particular water and sanitation services where the basic welfare requirements of millions of people are at issue. Similar questions are raised in a recent case against Tanzania, where water and sanitation services were also at issue.[11] Finally, in September 2007, a case was lodged through ICSID against South Africa arguing that South African legislation setting minimum black ownership and management requirements in mining companies was discriminatory and amounted to an expropriation of the property of the mining company.[12] At the same time as all of these cases involving sensitive regulatory issues are being adjudicated upon, the debate about the economic benefits to countries of signing up to these investment treaties is becoming increasingly contested.[13]

Alongside the contentious substantive social justice issues raised, there is also significant discussion over the fairness of the procedures of international investment arbitration. Different arbitration rules have different procedures, so UNCITRAL Rules differ from those of ICSID, while NAFTA investment treaties impose certain procedural requirements not necessarily adopted in other investment arbitrations – for instance, the procedural rules for the submission of *amicus* briefs, which will be discussed later in this chapter. But do these differing international investment procedures currently correctly balance the need to protect commercial interests and confidentiality with the requirements of transparency and openness where sensitive regulatory decisions of government are at issue? At the heart of these problems, it is argued, is the difficulty of reconciling a process with routes in private arbitration with cases which involve the regulatory decisions of sovereign governments.[14]

These issues of both substantive and procedural fairness in international investment arbitration can clearly be addressed through the medium of human rights. Above and beyond other IEL rules, there appears to be an even stronger rationale for raising human rights issues in the context of investment arbitra-

---

[10] See *Gas Transmission Co v Argentina*, ICSID Case No ARB 01/08, Decision of the Ad Hoc Committee on the Application for Annulment, 46 ILM 1136 (2007); and Burke-White, n 9 above, for a discussion of the inconsistencies between the different awards of the tribunal, problems in interpretation of key terms (eg necessity), and the findings of the above Annulment Committee which are highly critical of the reasoning of the tribunal.

[11] *Biwater Gauff (Tanzania) Ltd v Tanzania*, ICSID Case No ARB/05/22, Concurring and Dissenting Opinion, 24 July 2008.

[12] *Piero Foresti, Laura de Carli and ors v South Africa*, ICSID Case No ARB(AF)/07/1. Details of the claim are reported in International Investment News, 14 February 2007, at <http://www.iisd.org/pdf/2007/itn_feb14_2007.pdf>.

[13] See, eg K Gallagher and M Birch, 'Do Investment Agreements Attract Investment? Evidence from Latin America' (2006) 7 JWIT 961; and M Hallward-Driemeier, 'Do Bilateral Investment Treaties Attract FDI? Only a Bit ... and They Could Bite' *World Bank*, June 2003.

[14] Discussing all of these issues at length, see Van Harten, n 5 above, generally and with regard to the blurring of public/private law in particular at 45 ff.

tion, which is a process by which investors are specifically enforcing their property rights. Seen through a rights-based paradigm, there are balancing rights-based claims that states need to take into account in order to ensure that they are protecting the rights of their peoples to essential services such as water, or vulnerable or otherwise disadvantaged groups (for example, indigenous peoples).[15] These are subjects which potentially engage human rights norms and standards set out in international human rights treaties and many national constitutions. Increasing numbers of academic commentators, UN Agencies, and NGOs have picked upon the human rights dimensions of many international investment cases.[16]

Claimant companies and states defending claims have rarely raised human rights arguments in proceedings, and when they have done so, arguments have tended not to be set out in any great detail.[17] On the other hand, civil society organizations, intervening in investment arbitration proceedings, have regularly raised detailed human rights arguments. In the six cases where permission to make *amicus* submissions have so far been granted, human rights arguments have been raised in five submissions by petitioners. This chapter therefore analyses this recent trend in international investment arbitration for third-party interventions which raise human rights arguments. It is important to conduct this analysis within the broader context of the overall purpose of *amicus* submissions as expressed by the tribunals themselves and commentators upon the system. The next section therefore examines these broader issues.

III. The Role of *Amicus* Submissions in Investment Treaty Arbitration

The concept of an '*amicus curiae*' was largely developed through the US courts, and was subsequently taken on by a range of other national legal systems.[18] It has been utilized in different ways in different court systems, but, generally speaking, *amicus curiae* submissions have for a long time been a mechanism by which national and international courts and tribunals have accepted interventions by third parties who are not directly involved in proceedings. At the international level, the European Court of Human Rights, the Inter-American

---

[15] See Van Harten, n 5 above, 122, 136–151 arguing that international investment arbitration concerns important issues of social policy and the regulatory powers of government, but that it tends to favour investor rights, which act as a rights based trump card.

[16] In particular, see the work conducted under the remit of the UN Special Representative, John Ruggie. There are several detailed briefing papers which summarize the main issues and much of the existing literature at <http://www.business-humanrights.org/Updates/Archive/SpecialRepPapers> (accessed on 10 September 2008).

[17] See discussion in section III below.

[18] For a history of its early development in the US courts, see E Angell, 'The *Amicus Curiae* American Development of English Institutions' (1667) 16:4 ICLQ 1017–1044.

Court of Human Rights, the European Court of Justice, the International Criminal Tribunals for the Former Yugoslavia and Rwanda, the Special Court for Sierra Leone, the World Trade Organization Dispute Settlement Body, and NAFTA and ICSID arbitration tribunals have all accepted *amicus* submissions from non-governmental bodies or independent experts.[19]

There has been extensive academic commentary upon the recent series of decisions in investment arbitration tribunals to allow *amicus curiae* submissions, within the broader context of discussions about the overall transparency and procedural fairness of the tribunal process.[20] Therefore, these developments will be briefly summarized and issues of contention highlighted, with a view to contextualizing the narrower focus on the human rights arguments raised in the *amicus* submissions which will be discussed below.

A. *Amicus Curiae* Submissions in International Investment Arbitration Cases

The opening up of investment arbitration proceedings to wider public partici- pation through the submissions of *amicus* briefs started in the *Methanex* case.[21] This involved a claim filed under NAFTA Chapter 11 in which the claimant sought US$970 million of damages because of a Californian ban on a gasoline additive. It was argued by the US Government that the rationale for this ban was that the additive was a health risk because it potentially contaminated ground-

---

[19] For a discussion of the role of *amicus curiae* in various international courts and tribunals, see L Bartheolomeuusz, 'The *Amicus Curiae* before International Courts and Tribunals' (2005) 5 Non- State Actors and International Law 209–286; and J Vinuales, 'Human Rights and Investment Arbitration: The Role of *Amicus Curiae*' (2006) 8 Revista Colomiana de Derecho Internacional 231–273, 238 ff, 245 ff for a summary of how WTO case law was extensively referred to in early decisions to accept *amicus* submissions in investment arbitration cases. On the international criminal tribunals, see S Williams and H Woolaver, 'The Role of *Amicus curiae* before Interna- tional Criminal Tribunals' (2006) 6 International Criminal Law Review 151–189.

[20] See, eg K Tienhaara, 'Third Party Participation in Investment-Environment Disputes: Recent Developments' (2007) 16:2 Review of European Community and International Environmental Law 230–242. Vinuales, n 19 above; VanDuzer, n 5 above; Knahr, 'Transparency, Third Party Participa- tion and Access to Documents in International Investment Arbitration' (2007) 23:2 Arbitration International 327–355; R Buckley and P Blyschak, 'Guarding the Open Door: Non-Party Participa- tion Before the International Centre for Settlement of Investment Disputes' (2007) 22:3 Banking and Finance Law Review 353–376; B Stern, 'Un petit pas de plus: l'installation de la société civile dans l'Arbitrage CIRDI entre Etat et investisseur' (2007) 1 Revue de L'arbitrage 3–43; L Mistelis, 'Con- fidentiality and Third Party Participation, UPS v Canada and Methanex Corporation v United States' (2005) 21:2 Arbitration International 211–231; H Mann, 'Opening the Doors, At least a Little: Comment on the *Amicus* Decision in Methanex v United States' (2001) 10 Review of European Community and International Environmental Law 241–245; and AK Bjorklund, 'The Participation of Amici Curiae in NAFTA Chapter Eleven Cases' Essay papers on investment protection – Ad Hoc Experts Group on Investment Rules (22 March 2002), available at <http://www.international.gc.ca/ trade-agreements-accords-commerciaux/disp-diff/participate.aspx?lang=en>.

[21] *Methanex*, n 8 above. For a detailed discussion of the *Methanex* submissions by the parties and the decision of tribunal on *amicus* submissions, see Vinuales, n 19 above, 251 ff.

water. There was great public interest in the case due to the potential for a government measure, ostensibly aimed at protecting public health and the environment, to give rise to such an enormous claim for damages by a private corporation. Both the US and Canadian Governments argued that public interest in the issues and the need for openness and transparency in NAFTA proceedings made it appropriate for the tribunal to accept submissions from suitably qualified *amicus curiae*.[22] In a landmark decision, the NAFTA tribunal then held that it did indeed have the power to accept submissions by *amicus curiae*.[23] This was followed in October 2003 by a statement on third-party participation issued by the Free Trade Commission of NAFTA (consisting of representatives of the governments of the states parties to NAFTA – the United States, Canada, and Mexico), stating that any person 'with a significant presence in the territory of a party' may file for leave to file a petition.[24] The tribunal should, in making its decision on whether to accept the *amicus* submission, consider the extent to which[25]:

(a) the non-disputing party submission would assist the Tribunal in the determination of a factual or legal issue related to the arbitration by bringing a perspective, particular knowledge or insight that is different from that of the disputing parties;
(b) the non-disputing party submission would address matters within the scope of the dispute;
(c) the non-disputing party has a significant interest in the arbitration; and
(d) there is a public interest in the subject-matter of the arbitration.

This procedure was adopted by the *Methanex* tribunal, which accepted briefs from a number of civil society groups concerned primarily with the potential environmental impact of the tribunal's decision.[26] Two further NAFTA tribunals operating under UNCITRAL Rules have since found that they had the power to accept *amicus* submissions, and have accepted submissions from a number of interested third parties. First, there was *UPS v Canada*, a case in which United Parcel Service (UPS), a US courier service, alleged that Canada

---

[22] *Methanex Corp v USA*, Statement of the USA Regarding Petitions for *Amicus* Status, 27 October 2000, available at <http://naftaclaims.com/Disputes/USA/Methanex/MethanexUS FirstSubReAmicus.pdf>; and Submission of the Government of Canada, 10 November 2000, available at <http://naftaclaims.com/Disputes/USA/Methanex/MethanexCanadaFirstSubReAmicus.pdf>.

[23] *Methanex Corp v USA*, Decision of the Tribunal on Petitions from Third Parties to Intervene as '*Amici Curiae*', 15 January 2001, available at <http://naftaclaims.com/Disputes/USA/Methanex/MethanexCanadaFirstSubReAmicus.pdf> (hereinafter, *Methanex Amicus* Order).

[24] NAFTA Free Trade Commission, 'Statement of the Free Trade Commission on non-disputing party participation', 7 October 2003, 44 ILM 796 (2005).

[25] Ibid., para 6. At para 7, the Free Trade Commission also states that:

The Tribunal will ensure that:
(a) any non-disputing party submission avoids disrupting the proceedings; and
(b) neither disputing party is unduly burdened or unfairly prejudiced by such submissions.

[26] See Tienhaara, n 20 above, 232.

Post used its monopoly in postal letters to compete unfairly with competitors in courier services, including UPS itself. *Amicus* submissions were accepted from the Canadian Union of Postal Workers (CUPW), the Council of Canadians, and the US Chamber of Commerce.[27] The second case was that of *Glamis Gold v USA*, which involved a claim by the firm Glamis Gold relating to mining concessions. Glamis argued that compliance with environmental regulations involving aboriginal land made the value of their investment worthless. Submissions were accepted from the Quechan Indian Nation, as well as various environmental groups and the National Mining Association.[28] These latter two cases will be discussed further below as human rights arguments were raised by *amici* in both cases.

A number of tribunals adjudicating upon bilateral investment treaties under ICSID rules have also made determinations about *amicus* submissions. Interestingly, all three cases have involved the privatization of water industries and subsequent claims by investors that their properties have been expropriated or that they have been otherwise unfairly treated as per the treaty in question. The first case was the highly infamous and controversial *Aguas del Tunari SA v Bolivia*, where there were widespread protests as a result of water rate increases imposed by Aguas del Tunari, owned by US firm Bechtel. As a result of these protests the company abandoned its concession and filed a claim for compensation through ICSID. A number of individuals and civil society organizations petitioned, inter alia, for *amicus curiae* status in the arbitration, but were refused permission at the 'jurisdictional' stage of the proceedings.[29] Pressure from international civil society continued until proceedings were eventually settled with nominal compensation paid to Bechtel.[30]

The first ICSID tribunal which decided that it had the authority to receive *amicus* submissions and to grant a non-party *amicus curiae* status was in the case of *Suez/Vivendi v Argentina*.[31] The same decision was made by the same tribunal panel in another ICSID case against Argentina – *Suez/Interaguas v Argentina*, who also found they had the power to accept petitions, although in that case the tribunal required more information about the petitioners in order to make their

---

[27] For all the various petitions, submissions and orders in relation to this case, see <http://www.naftaclaims.com/disputes_canada_ups.htm>.

[28] For all the various petitions, submissions and orders in relation to this case, see <http://www.naftaclaims.com/disputes_us_glamis.htm>.

[29] See letter from David D Caron, President of the tribunal in *Aguas del Tunari* (29 January 2003).

[30] See, eg the report by the Democracy Centre, available at <http://www.democracyctr.org/bolivia/investigations/water/bechtel-vs-bolivia.htm>.

[31] *Suez, Sociedad General de Aguas de Barcelona SA and Vivendi Universal SA v Argentina*, Order in Response to a Petition for Transparency and Participation as *Amicus Curiae*, 19 May 2005, ICSID Case No ARB/03/19 (hereinafter, *Suez/Vivendi Amicus* Order 1); and *Suez, Sociedad General de Aguas de Barcelona SA and Vivendi Universal SA v Argentina*, Order in Response to a Petition by Five Non-Governmental Organisations For Permission to Make an *Amicus Curiae* Submission, 12 February 2007, 46 ILM 439 (2007) (hereinafter, *Suez/Vivendi Amicus* Order 2).

decision regarding their participation.[32] Both of these cases arose from Argentina's economic crisis of 2001 and the decision by the Government to abandon the pegging of the peso to the dollar and to freeze public utility rates. In both of the above cases the claimants were running water and sanitation services where rates were frozen and they made claims regarding the negative impact on their businesses. Finally, a further ICSID tribunal, in another case involving privatization of water services and subsequent claims of expropriation, *Biwater v Tanzania*, also accepted an *amicus curiae* submission by a collective of national and international NGOs.[33] As under NAFTA, ICSID rules have now been changed in order to institutionalize the procedure by which tribunals should decide upon whether to accept *amicus* submissions. The criteria the tribunal should apply are very similar to that under NAFTA.[34]

There is remarkable similarity in the reasoning of all of these tribunals about the rationale for the decisions to accept *amicus* submissions in these cases. All of the tribunals (except *Glamis v USA*, where no detailed reasoning was provided) highlighted a number of factors which were key to their decision-making. First, they highlighted the public interest or public importance of the issues in question as key to them deciding to grant the petitions.[35] Second, they maintained that the expertise and perspectives which the *amici* might bring would be

---

[32] *Suez, Sociedad General de Aguas de Barcelona SA and Interagua Servicios Integrales de Agua SA v Argentina*, Order in Response to a Petition for Participation as *Amicus Curiae*, 17 March 2006, ICSID Case No ARB/03/17, available at <http://icsid.worldbank.org/ICSID/FrontServlet?requestType=CasesRH&actionVal=showDoc&docId=DC512_En&caseId=C18> (hereinafter, *Suez/ Interaguas Amicus* Order). The panel in both cases consisted of Professor Jeswald W Salacuse, (President) Professor Gabrielle Kaufmann-Kohler, and Professor Pedro Nikken. It is important to note that the constitution of the panel in *Suez/Interaguas* (17 February 2004) predated the decision to accept *amicus* submissions in *Suez/Vivendi* (19 May 2005), so no implied consent by the parties in *Suez/ Interagua* to the acceptance of third-party submissions can be assumed.

[33] *Biwater Gauff (Tanzania) Ltd v Tanzania*, Procedural Order No 5, 2 February 2007, 46 ILM 576 (2007) (hereinafter, *Biwater Amicus* Order).

[34] ICSID Rules Rule 37(2) states:

(2) After consulting both parties, the Tribunal may allow a person or entity that is not a party to the dispute (in this Rule called the 'non-disputing party') to file a written submission with the Tribunal regarding a matter within the scope of the dispute. In determining whether to allow such a filing, the Tribunal shall consider, among other things, the extent to which:
(a) the non-disputing party submission would assist the Tribunal in the determination of a factual or legal issue related to the proceeding by bringing a perspective, particular knowledge or insight that is different from that of the disputing parties;
(b) the non-disputing party submission would address a matter within the scope of the dispute;
(c) the non-disputing party has a significant interest in the proceeding.

[35] *Suez/Interaguas Amicus* Order, n 32 above, at paras 18–20; *Suez/Vivendi Amicus* Order 1, n 31 above, at paras 18–21; *Suez/Vivendi Amicus* Order 2, n 31 above, at para 9; *Methanex Amicus* Order, n 23 above, at para 49; *UPS v Canada*, Decision of the Tribunal on Petitions for Intervention and Participation as *Amicus Curiae*, 17 October 2001, available at <http://naftaclaims.com/Disputes/Canada/UPS/UPSDecisionReParticipationAmiciCuriae.pdf> (hereinafter, *UPS Amicus* Order), at para 70; and *Biwater Amicus* Order, n 33 above, at paras 51–52.

important in assisting them to come to the correct decision in the case.[36] In addition, the acceptance of *amicus* submissions by investment tribunals would also have the desirable consequence that it would improve the transparency of investor-state arbitration in cases of substantial public interest, thereby enhancing its legitimacy in the eyes of the public.[37]

B. Evaluation of the *Amicus* Submission Process

It is interesting to compare the rationales of the tribunals set out above with a more general survey of the functions of *amicus curiae* before international courts and tribunals. This survey has found four core functions: the provision of specialist legal expertise, particularly 'about matters outside the court's core competence'; the provision of factual information relevant to the case of which the court might not otherwise be aware; access to proceedings to persons who might be affected by the decision of the court or tribunal; and, finally, as a mechanism for allowing participation of those who are representing broader public interest considerations.[38] The rationale of the investment tribunals as set out above appears to include three of these core functions – *amici* will be able to represent broader public interest considerations and provide legal and possibly even factual information which will help the court in deciding the case. However, contrary to the tribunals' rationale, the survey suggests that *amicus curiae* submissions should not be viewed as a mechanism for increasing the transparency of international courts and tribunals, and that participation of *amici* 'is conceived more in terms of the interest of the court or tribunal than that of the person trying to participate'.[39]

While most commentators have viewed the acceptance of *amicus* submissions as a positive development,[40] they have differed markedly on the (potentially) negative aspects of *amicus* participation. Therefore, on the one hand, there are those who see the need to impose strict limits on the extent of non-party involvement in arbitration proceedings. It is argued that there are dangers that the acceptance of *amicus* submissions may marginalize the wishes of the parties and will also impose extra burdens upon investors (since the majority of *amicus* submissions will advance arguments that support states) in a way that will make the system less attractive to them.[41] It is also suggested that tribunals will have to remain vigilant in order to ensure that NGOs accepted as *amici* are in fact

---

[36] *Suez/Vivendi Amicus* Order 1, n 31 above, at para 24; *Methanex Amicus* Order, n 23 above, at para 48; *Biwater Amicus* Order, n 33 above, at para 50; and *UPS Amicus* Order, n 35 above, at para 62.
[37] *Suez/Interaguas Amicus* Order, n 32 above, at para 21; *Suez/Vivendi Amicus* Order 1, n 31 above, at para 22; *Methanex Amicus* Order, n 23 above, at para 49; *UPS Amicus* Order, n 35 above, at para 70; and *Biwater Amicus* Order, n 33 above, at para 54 citing *Methanex*.
[38] Bartheolomeuusz, n 19 above, 278–280.   [39] Ibid., 274, 284–285.
[40] See, eg Van Harten, n 5 above, 163; VanDuzer, n 5 above, 720 ff; and Tienharra, n 20 above, 242.
[41] Vinuales, n 19 above, 254; and Buckley and Blyschak, n 20 above, 373–374.

accountable and representative organizations.[42] Arguments are also made that it is important to limit the scope of non-party participation, including to restrict *amici*'s access to documents, in that their role is not to dispute the arguments of the parties, but simply to assist in reaching 'the correct, just decision'.[43]

On the other hand, a number of commentators have argued that the acceptance of *amicus* submissions should be seen as part of a broader positive trend towards widening participation and increasing the openness and transparency in a number of investment treaty arbitration procedures which reflects the need for investor-state arbitration to be perceived as being a legitimate form of dispute resolution.[44] In particular, recent NAFTA arbitrations have included public hearings on closed circuit television or at least transcripts of the hearings and access to a wide range of documentation relating to the proceedings. Recent US and Canadian BITs have entrenched procedures for accepting *amicus* submissions, stipulating that all hearings will be open to the public and all documents will be made public, subject to limits to protect commercial confidentiality.[45] These provisions are set in stark contrast to investment arbitration conducted under UNCITRAL Rules (other than NAFTA claims), which do not even require public notification that a claim has been lodged, where disclosure of documents is far more restricted, and no *amici* have ever been granted permission to participate. ICSID rules fall somewhere in between – with documents, hearings, and awards that are kept private without the consent of the two parties.[46] Commentators have therefore questioned the extent to which *amici* who are permitted to participate in such proceedings are able to participate effectively. For instance, in cases where *amici* do not have access to documents which contain the arguments of the parties, there has been criticism that this is likely to limit the effectiveness of *amicus* submissions.[47]

This rather divided debate reflects the wider divisions about the purposes and aims of international investment arbitration. On the one hand, strict limits to the involvement of *amicus curiae* reflects the private law origins of an arbitration process driven by the wishes of the parties, the need for confidentiality, and worries that non-parties will have agendas that will distort proceedings; parties should be able to

---

[42] Knahr, n 20 above, 348–349.
[43] Buckley and Blyschak, n 20 above, 375. See also Vinuales, n 19 above, 269–270.
[44] VanDuzer, n 5 above, 686 and 720.
[45] Tienhaara, n 20 above, 242; and VanDuzer, 720–723. But Van Harten, n 5 above, 164 states that European BITs do not contain the same form of transparency mechanisms as the BITs now regularly negotiated by Canada and the United States.
[46] For more detailed discussion of the 'transparency' of the various international arbitration rules, see OECD, 'Transparency and Third Party Participation in Investor-State Dispute Settlement Procedures', Statement by the OECD Investment Committee (June 2005), available at <http://www.oecd.org/dataoecd/25/3/34786913.pdf>.
[47] VanDuzer, n 5 above, 715; Tienharra, n 20 above, 242 and 232 specifically with regard to *Methanex*, noting that it was only when proceedings were opened up (based on consent of parties) that *amici* became aware that the United States was only defending the case on the basis of public health grounds, and on that basis submitted petition post-hearing that it should be heard on environmental grounds too.

choose to make or reject arguments as they see fit, based on an assessment of the strengths of their case as they see them, and not have arguments of *amici* foist upon them which may not suit their case. On the other hand, the fact that sovereign states are subject to such procedures, that cases can involve sensitive regulatory issues, and that judgments can potentially have important wider public impacts drives the call for greater legitimacy, of which effective participation by *amicus curiae* is perceived as being part. In the remainder of this chapter I will consider the extensive human rights issues which have been raised by various groups of *amici* in investor-state arbitration and the handling of these arguments by the tribunals. What value do these interventions bring to the international investment arbitration process? How effectively have they fulfilled the functions which the tribunals have viewed them as performing? And how well does the *amicus* process bridge the gap between the different aims and functions of international investment arbitration as viewed by different actors and commentators?

IV. Human Rights and *Amicus* Submissions

Above I have set out the details of the six tribunals who have accepted *amicus* submissions. In five of these cases, human rights arguments were raised by at least one of the parties making submissions. We now concentrate on those submissions and in particular the way in which they have been handled by the relevant tribunals. There are two important stages to this process. I first consider the rationale for the acceptance of the *amicus* submissions by the tribunals in each of these cases, and how important the human rights dimension was in such decisions. I also consider how the human rights arguments raised have affected the final awards of the tribunals in the two cases which have so far been decided and published.

A. The Rationale of Tribunals for Acceptance of *Amicus* Submissions

The first case, *UPS v Canada* (arbitrated under UNCITRAL Rules) was rather different from the others, in that it was originally the claimants who raised the human rights issue. UPS claimed that Canada's failure to respect the collective bargaining rights of Canada Post's workers were in breach of its international human rights and labour rights obligations. Therefore, this led to a breach of Canada's obligations under NAFTA, Article 1105 (minimum standard of treatment) because of the unfair competition of the lower costs of a workforce without collective bargaining rights.[48] The respondent refuted these claims on the basis that UPS had no standing to make such claims, that they were made in the wrong

---

[48] *UPS v Canada*, Investor's Memorial, 23 March 2005, available at <http://naftaclaims.com/Disputes/Canada/UPS/UPS-Merits_Memorial-23-03-05.pdf>, at paras 645–671.

forum, and that there was no rule of customary international law prohibiting the anti-competitive behaviour that resulted from the lack of collective bargaining rights.[49] The Canadian Union of Postal Workers and the Council of Canadians, in their *amicus* submission, examined in more detail the arguments for why it would be inappropriate for the tribunal to find in favour of the claimants for a breach of labour rights and human rights standards in NAFTA proceedings. They argued that UPS should not be able to claim damages through NAFTA on the basis of infringement of international labour and human rights obligations of persons who were not even represented in the proceedings and who would not benefit from the award.[50]

In the second case, *Glamis v USA*, also arbitrated under UNCITRAL rules, Glamis claimed damages in relation to a mining concession with regard to environmental regulations which imposed various obligations to clean up the mining area because it was in the vicinity of Native American sacred sites belonging to the Quechan Indian Nation. Glamis claimed that as a result of these obligations, the mining concession was now worthless. The tribunal accepted an *amicus* brief from the Quechan Indian Nation which argued, inter alia, that the tribunal is required to interpret provisions of NAFTA in accordance with relevant provisions of international law, including extensive international protections of the rights of indigenous peoples with regard to their cultural and religious rights and land rights.[51] The submission went on to argue that the tribunal was required to take into account the ways in which the US Government was required under relevant international human rights law norms to safeguard the rights and interests of the Quechan people. The tribunal gave no reasoned explanation of the grounds on which they were accepting the submission. They merely stated that it 'satisfied the principles of the Free Trade Commission's Statement on non-disputing party participation'.[52] No mention was made of the human rights arguments raised by the petitioners, other than to clarify that the acceptance of the submission did not indicate either agreement or disagreement with the substance of the submission.[53] However, given the extensive human rights arguments made by the petitioners in their application

---

[49] *UPS v Canada*, Investor's Memorial, n 48 above, at paras 946–979. Canada argued that the proper place for such arguments was before an international human rights complaints mechanism (eg the International Labour Organization or Human Rights Committee) and that the complaint would need to be made by the employees or their representatives.

[50] *UPS v Canada*, Application for *Amicus Curiae* Status by the Canadian Union of Postal Workers and the Council of Canadians, 20 October 2005, available at <http://naftaclaims. com/Disputes/Canada/UPS/UPS-CUPE_CC_Amicus_Submission-20-10-05.pdf>, at paras 26–37.

[51] *Glamis Gold v USA*, Quechan Indian Nation *Amicus* Application and Submission, 19 August 2004, available at <http://www.naftaclaims.com/Disputes/USA/Glamis/Glamis-Amicus-Quechan-01-19-08-05.pdf>, at p 8f.

[52] *Glamis Gold Ltd v USA*, Decision on Application and Submission by Quechan Indian Nation, 16 September 2005, available at <http://www.naftaclaims.com/Disputes/USA/Glamis/Glamis-Amicus-Decision-16-09-05.pdf>, at para 10.

[53] Glamis *Amicus* Order, n 52 above, at para 15.

for leave to file a non-party submission, the fact that the *amicus* submission has been accepted should indicate that the human rights framework utilized was part of 'a perspective, particular knowledge or insight that is different from that of the disputing parties' and therefore valuable to the considerations of the tribunal.[54]

The original *amicus* brief and later supplemental submission in *Glamis* both argue that the tribunal is required to interpret provisions of NAFTA in accordance with relevant provisions of international law, including extensive international protections of the rights of indigenous peoples.[55] The Supplemental Submission specifically argues that the claimant 'was silent on the applicable international standards for the protection of cultural heritage and sacred places' and that the respondent failed to address these issues fully.[56] The respondent's counter-memorial only mentions relevant UNESCO Declarations on cultural heritage, not any of the indigenous rights instruments which the *amici* claim are relevant to deciding the claim.[57] We await a decision of the tribunal in respect of this claim.

The other three cases where human rights issues have been raised through *amicus* briefs have all been arbitrated under ICSID rules. As discussed above, they have all been cases involving provision of water services by private companies. They have all involved petitions by a number of *amici* framing their entire *amicus* submissions in terms of human rights. In each of the three cases, the *amici* petitioned the tribunal on the basis that the measures taken by the government which were the subject of the action (freezing the prices of public utilities/bringing the utilities back under public ownership) were measures that engaged human rights involving access to essential services.[58] While the above NAFTA tribunals (*Glamis* and *UPS*) made no specific reference to human rights in their rationale for acceptance of *amicus* submissions, the tribunals in these cases explicitly referred to human rights in their decisions to accept the *amicus* submissions. The two ICSID tribunals with identical arbitrators arising from the Argentine economic crisis – *Suez/Vivendi v Argentina* and *Suez/Interagua v Argentina* – have explicitly stated that the raising of human rights arguments that

---

[54] Statement of the Free Trade Commission, n 24 above.

[55] Quechan *Amicus* Submission, n 51 above, at p 8f; and *Glamis Gold v USA*, Supplemental Submission of Non-Disputing Party Quechan Indian Nation, 16 October 2006, available at <http://www.naftaclaims.com/Disputes/USA/Glamis/Glamis-USA-Amicus-Quechan_Band-Submission_2.pdf>, at p 1f.

[56] Non-Party Supplemental Submission, *Glamis Gold Ltd v USA*, Submission of the Quechan Indian Nation, at p 1.

[57] *Glamis Gold Ltd v USA*, Respondent's Counter Memorial, 19 September 2006, available at <http://www.naftaclaims.com/Disputes/USA/Glamis/Glamis-USA-Counter_-Memorial.pdf>, 33–35.

[58] eg *Suez, Sociedad General de Aguas de Barcelona, SA and Vivendi Universal SA v Argentina*, ICSID Case No ARB/03/19, Petition for Transparency and Participation as *Amicus Curiae*, 27 January 2005, available at <http://www.ciel.org/Publications/SuezAmicus_27Jan05_English.pdf>.

would not otherwise be made is a strong part of the rationale for allowing the *amicus* submissions. In *Suez/Vivendi*, the tribunal states:[59]

> [T]he investment dispute centers around the water distribution and sewage systems of a large metropolitan area, the city of Buenos Aires and surrounding municipalities. Those systems provide basic public services to millions of people and as a result may raise a variety of complex public and international law questions, *including human rights considerations* (emphasis added).

As a result, the tribunal argues that there are strong public interest grounds in allowing *amicus curiae* submissions. Furthermore, the human rights expertise of the petitioners was one of the grounds for accepting that they would be able to assist the tribunal in its decision-making over the case.[60] The petitioners were a combination of national and international civil society organizations specializing in human rights, environmental law, and broader social justice issues.[61] The *Suez/Interagua* tribunal declined to accept *amicus* briefs from the petitioners on the basis that they had submitted insufficient information regarding their expertise, experience, and independence, but again the tribunal found that strong public interest, including the same human rights dimensions, made this an appropriate subject matter for *amicus curiae* submissions.[62]

Finally, the *Biwater v Tanzania* tribunal also accepted an *amicus* submission from five international and national non-governmental organizations, again specializing in a range of human rights, environmental, and broader social justice issues.[63] The *amici* in *Biwater* state their primary concerns as human rights and sustainable development.[64] The tribunal cited this human rights expertise as one of the grounds on which their petition should be accepted.[65] The *Biwater* tribunal also cited the above passage from *Suez and Vivendi*, including the importance of 'human rights considerations', as equally applying in their case,[66] and stated that the petitioners appeared to have 'the reasonable potential to assist the Arbitral Tribunal by bringing a perspective, particular knowledge or insight that is different from that of the disputing parties'.[67]

---

[59] *Suez/Vivendi Amicus* Order 1, n 31 above, at para 19. This passage and reference to the human rights issues arising was again stressed in the second order – *Suez/Vivendi Amicus* Order 2, n 31 above, at paras 17 and 18.   [60] *Suez/Vivendi, Amicus* Order 2, at para 16.

[61] Petitioners were the Centro de Estudios Legales y Sociales (CELS), Asociación Civil por la Igualdad y la Justicia (ACIJ), Consumidores Libres Cooperativa Ltda. de Provisión de Servicios de Acción ComunitariaUnión de Usuarios y Consumidores, Centre for International Environmental Law (CIEL), and the International Institute for Sustainable Development (IISD).

[62] *Suez/Interaguas Amicus* Order, n 32 above, at para 18.

[63] The petitioners were the Lawyers' Environmental Action Team (LEAT), the Legal and Human Rights Centre (LHRC), the Tanzania Gender Networking Programme (TGNP), CIEL, and IISD.

[64] *Biwater v Tanzania, Amicus Curiae* Submission, available at <http://www.ciel.org/Publications/Biwater_Amicus_26March.pdf>, at para 7.

[65] *Biwater Amicus* Order, n 33 above, at para 50, referring generically to the expertise of the *amici*, having previously referred extensively, inter alia, to their specific human rights expertise.

[66] Ibid., at para 52.   [67] Ibid., at para 50.

B. The Impact of *Amicus* Submissions on the Final Awards of Tribunals

Only two of the above cases have so far been decided and the decisions made public. In *UPS v Canada*, the panel rejected the human rights and labour rights arguments of the claimant on the basis that UPS had failed to provide a sufficient factual or legal basis to succeed in its claim.[68] The tribunal briefly mentioned the petitioners' submission, but made no mention of the human rights and labour rights arguments they raised.[69] Given that it was not the *amici* who had raised the human rights issues, and the failure of the defendants' case preceded consideration of the human rights arguments, it may seem reasonable that the tribunal did not mention their arguments.

The second case, which has been recently decided, is that of *Biwater v Tanzania*. In their judgment, the tribunal found in favour of the petitioners to the extent that an expropriation had taken place, but did not award any damages because no loss could be found to the claimant.[70] With regard to the *amicus* submission, the award included a detailed summary of the arguments in the *amicus* petition, and stated that the petitioners had provided a 'useful contribution to these proceedings', through 'their specialised interests and expertise in human rights, environmental and good governance issues locally in Tanzania' which had materially differed from the 'interests, expertise and perspectives of the two disputing parties'.[71] The tribunal reiterated that there had been no initial need to provide the petitioners with disclosure of documents filed in the dispute, as 'the broad policy issues on which the Petitioners are especially qualified are ones which were in the public domain, and about which each Petitioner was already very well acquainted'.[72]

The tribunal went on to state that the *amici*'s submissions have informed the tribunal's analysis of the claims, 'and where relevant, specific points arising from the *Amici's* submissions are returned to in that context'.[73] Specific mention is only made of their arguments twice thereafter. In determining the appropriate threshold for a violation of fair and equitable treatment (but not an expropriation), the tribunal states that it has taken into account the submissions of the petitioners including the due diligence requirements on foreign investments, the limits of legitimate expectations in a risky investment environment, and the 'relevance of the parties' respective rights and obligations as set out in any relevant investment treaty'.[74] However, it is difficult to see how the arguments of

---

[68] *UPS v Canada*, Award on the Merits, n 8 above, at para 187.   [69] Ibid., para 3.
[70] See *Biwater v Tanzania*, Concurring and Dissenting Opinion, n 11 above, but note the dissenting opinion with the alternative legal reasoning.   [71] Ibid., at para 359.
[72] At the conclusion of the merits hearing, all parties agreed that no further intervention by the petitioners was required, and so this issue was not revisited (see *Biwater v Tanzania*, Concurring and Dissenting Opinion, n 11 above, at para 368 – see also para 83).   [73] Ibid., at para 392.
[74] Ibid., at para 601.

the *amici* have in any way influenced the decision of the tribunal.[75] The process by which they have reached their decision seems to be entirely drawn from their assessment of the strengths of the far more detailed arguments put forward by the two parties in light of relevant authorities. Given that the *amici* did not have access to the documents in the case, this is hardly surprising. The second mention of the *amici* in the substance of the decision is indicative of this – refuting an argument made by them, on the basis that they did not have access to the full evidence at the time they made their submissions.[76] There is no mention of the claims of the *amici* with regard to the 'broad policy issues' which were supposed to be the basis of their submission. There is certainly no consideration of the relevance of human rights in determining the obligations and liabilities of the parties to the dispute, despite the fact that the tribunal did have opportunities when these issues could have been raised.[77]

V. Benefits and Problems of Human Rights Interventions through *Amicus* Submissions in Investment Arbitration Proceedings

As I have now set out the nature of the human rights interventions by the *amici* and their treatment by the tribunals to the extent that they have so far been considered, I will now explore the benefits of utilizing human rights in this form of intervention in order to raise social justice issues. I will then go on to examine the problems and limitations of this mechanism.

A. The Benefits of a Human Rights Approach

In five out of the six cases where *amicus* submissions have so far been accepted by international investment tribunals, at least one of the *amicus* briefs has raised extensive human rights arguments.[78] Why have such arguments been so prevalent? Partly this must be as a result of the civil society organizations which have made the interventions. This has included a number of human rights

---

[75] They are not raised in relation to any of the specific points which the tribunal decides, and are not applied in relation to the decision on expropriation at all, rather being limited to the tribunal's decision on fair and equitable treatment.

[76] *Biwater v Tanzania*, Concurring and Dissenting Opinion, n 11 above, fn 208.

[77] There are various instances where the tribunal addresses the extent to which actions of the government in, eg occupying City Water's Facilities, usurping management control of the company, or deporting its staff may have acted through necessity, emergency, or for a public purpose, but nowhere are these terms interpreted with reference to the human rights arguments made by the *amici*. See, for instance, paras 503 and 515 of the judgment. The tribunal also discusses the deterioration in City Water's performance and the potential threat this caused to a vital public service without mention of human rights. See, for instance, para 654.

[78] In all of the ICSID cases, there was only one *amicus* submission submitted to the tribunal, each of them framed utilizing human rights arguments.

organizations. However, it has also included environmental organizations, indigenous groups, trade unions, and more general social justice and legal campaigning organizations. So, human rights arguments do not appear to be inevitable as a result of the coalitions of organizations making the submissions. A strong rationale for utilizing this framework must be that human rights are international and national legal obligations through which particular values are given legal expression. A human rights framework creates primary obligations with regard to, for example, provision of essential services, the rights of indigenous peoples, or the rights of workers. It requires states to justify interference with these rights and to protect their peoples from interference with those rights by third parties. Such rights and obligations have considerable attractiveness to groups who are seeking to intervene into a system whose primary function is perceived by those groups to be the protection of the property rights of international investors.

This is not to say that investment arbitration is necessarily de-legitimized for having the primary purpose of protecting investors' property rights. International courts and tribunals must inevitably be 'differentiated and specialised in order to perform their critical function'.[79] However, their specialization makes it very difficult for them to connect with the concerns of civil society. In the context of the investment arbitration cases considered here, this 'distance' is exemplified by the nature of the primary legal issues which are the concerns of investment tribunals, such as determining whether an 'expropriation' has taken place, whether there has been 'fair and equitable treatment', and whether any 'necessity' justifies the actions of the state. The scenarios which give rise to these same legal issues are viewed by many civil society actors as involving very different factors – 'challenging corporate investor rule' and the need to take into account the welfare of the people and broader 'social justice' impacts of the investment arbitration process which do not find natural expression in the terminology of international investment law.[80] It is in light of this separation that '*amicus* briefs serve to marshal, crystallise and articulate public concerns in a form that is rendered relevant and intelligible to a specialised court'.[81] They translate these public concerns from a 'noise' to a 'signal' which is able to be heard by the tribunals.[82]

The language and obligations of human rights is the chosen method by which a great number of *amici* have chosen to frame their arguments. The noise of 'social justice' is translated into the 'signal' of human rights. These are legal obligations which tribunals find difficult to ignore – under ICSID, Article 42 and according

---

[79] R Eckersley, 'A Green Public Sphere in the WTO?: The *Amicus Curiae* Interventions in the Transatlantic Biotech Dispute' (2007) 13 European Journal of International Relations 337.

[80] See, eg 'Challenging Corporate investor Rule: How the World Bank's Investment Court, Free Trade Agreements, and Bilateral Investment Treaties have Unleashed a New Era of Corporate Power and What to Do about it', Food and Water Watch, Institute for Policy Studies (April 2007).

[81] Eckersley, n 79 above, 337.   [82] Ibid.

to many other bilateral investment treaties they are directed to apply such rules of international law as might be applicable.[83] International human rights law obligations appear to be precisely the kind of applicable international law which is relevant between the parties in disputes such as those highlighted above.[84] The success of such a strategy and the relevance of the legal obligations are demonstrated by the fact that the tribunals have found a need to accept these submissions. There must be some debate over the extent to which the human rights arguments raised by the *amici* in *Glamis* were significant issues in the tribunal's decision to accept those submissions (although it has been argued that they must have been at least a factor in their decision). However, in *Suez/Vivendi* and *Biwater*, the tribunals' reasoning appears to make it clear that the human rights expertise of the *amici* and the human rights issues involved in the litigation were important factors in their decision to accept *amicus* submissions.

From the tribunal's perspective, it is also recognition of the fact that governments are not themselves always going to raise their own human rights obligations in relation to the issues raised by the case in question. NGOs with particular human rights expertise may be better informed about the human rights legal framework and how it applies to the situation on the ground than governments, particularly those from developing countries with limited resources.[85] It also seems likely that governments will not raise relevant human rights arguments in all cases through fear that they are creating obligations for themselves in other settings. For example, an argument in an investment tribunal by a government that it has a universal obligation to provide water to its population might then be utilized by individuals litigating in domestic courts against that government for non-provision of such essential services. Therefore, allowing *amicus curiae* submissions which articulate the nature of these human rights obligations is a way of introducing arguments that the tribunal might not otherwise hear.

B. The Problems of a Human Rights Approach

In terms of access to the tribunal, for the reasons set out above, human rights language and obligations therefore appear to be a powerful 'signal' for communicating the social justice 'noise' which civil society actors feel about the potential impact of particular international investment proceedings. However,

---

[83] Arguing that international human rights law can and should be taken into account in various ways in the interpretation of international investment law, see A van Aaken, 'Fragmentation of International Law: The Case of International Investment Protection', Law and Economics Research Paper Series, Working Paper No 2008-1, available through the Social Science Research Network Electronic Paper Collection.

[84] However, the situation where one state party to the BIT in question had not ratified the relevant treaty would make the question of the applicability of human rights more complex. For a discussion of this issue in the context of international trade law, see Harrison, n 2 above, 202.

[85] Making this point with regard to environmental issues in the *Methanex* case, see Buckley and Blyschak, n 20 above, 360.

the very limited evidence of the final decisions of tribunals give rise to concerns over the extent to which that 'signal' is then being heard in the tribunal's decision-making process. In *UPS*, there was only passing mention of the *amicus* submissions.[86] Despite their extensive exposition of the *amici*'s arguments in *Biwater*, the tribunal did not engage with the human rights arguments presented by the *amici* in explaining the grounds for its decision.

It is important to stress that the tribunals are not breaching any legal obligation in failing to take into account human rights arguments. There is no general legal principle which gives rise to an obligation upon a tribunal to consider, either explicitly or implicitly, arguments made by an *amicus curiae*. WTO and NAFTA tribunals are not obliged to give any consideration to *amicus* submissions, while other international courts and tribunals have not felt the need to articulate their obligations towards *amici* once they have made their submissions.[87] It is argued that the practice of the international criminal tribunals and the ECHR suggests that they might view themselves as having stronger obligations to at least consider submissions that have been made.[88] However, as the *UPS* tribunal stated, 'international law and practice and related national law and practice have either ignored or given a very low priority to third party intervention'.[89] In fact, investment tribunals have appeared far more receptive than, for instance, WTO panels to considering the arguments of *amici*. The WTO has been far more openly dismissive of both petitions to submit *amicus* briefs and the substance of submissions which have been accepted.[90] By contrast, the attitude of the tribunal in *Biwater v Tanzania*, in setting out at length the arguments of the *amici* and saying that it had found the submission to be a 'useful contribution to these proceedings' is, superficially at least, far more engaged and respectful.[91] Beyond this, it would appear to be the prerogative of the tribunal to decide whether or not to engage with the human rights arguments received on the basis of whether or not they have actually found those arguments useful, and to signify this as they see

---

[86] The tribunal decision referred to the *amicus* briefs in its overview of the case, but not in its substantive reasoning. [87] Bartholomeusz, n 19 above, 276. [88] Ibid. [89] *UPS*, Decision on *Amicus Curiae* Petitions, n 35 above, at para 40.

[90] See, eg 'European Communities – Measures Affecting Asbestos and Asbestos-Containing Products', Report of the Appellate Body, 12 March 2001 (WT/DS135/\AB/R), at para 56 where it is stated that all 11 *amicus* submissions submitted within the requisite time limits were rejected without any reasoning for this decision and critical of the lack of reasoning; see Bartholomeusz, n 19 above, 263. See also 'European Communities – Measures Affecting the Approval and Marketing of Biotech Products', Reports of the Panel, 29 September 2006 (WT/DS291/R), at para 7.11, where *amicus* briefs were accepted from two coalitions of environmental organizations, but the panel simply stated that it 'did not find it necessary to take the *amicus curiae* briefs into account'.

[91] This may reflect the different dynamics of the two legal systems. The dispute settlement branch of the WTO has antagonized its membership far more than international investment tribunals have by accepting *amicus* submissions. This is because since WTO dispute settlement is an inter-state procedure, all *amicus* submissions in WTO cases will inevitably oppose the arguments of one state participating in any given case. Developing countries have viewed themselves as being at a disadvantage, partly as many have fewer resources to respond to *amicus* submissions and partly as most resource-rich NGOs

appropriate. However, confusion and contradiction in the rationale for accepting *amicus* submissions in the first place means that future tribunals appear unlikely to ever substantively engage with the human rights framework presented and the arguments which are being made through it.

As set out above, there are three key rationales identified by the tribunals in decisions to accept the *amicus* submissions in the cases considered. First, the tribunals highlighted the public interest or public importance of the issues in question; second, they maintained that the expertise and perspectives which the *amici* might bring would be important in assisting them to come to the correct decision in the case; and third it would also have the desirable consequence that it would improve the transparency of the arbitration process, thereby enhancing its legitimacy in the eyes of the public. But these roles are inherently problematic, and even contradictory when considering the human rights submissions of the *amici*.

With regard to the first two roles, there are dangers in the *amici* being asked to perform simultaneously both of these roles in the investment arbitration process. Investment arbitrators inevitably have limited expertise in human rights law. Therefore, the *amici* are asked to take on a key role in informing the tribunal with regard to the legal issues – the nature and relevance of the human rights obligations. They then must also argue for the consideration of issues of public importance through the medium of these same human rights obligations. It must be extremely difficult for the tribunal to make an objective assessment about the nature of the legal obligations that should be taken into account, when the 'experts' on those issues are then arguing strongly for them to be interpreted in line with the public interests they represent. It is true that there has been a blurring of this role in many other national and international courts and tribunals. However, where international courts and tribunals are dealing with issues beyond their core expertise, they appear far more likely to deal explicitly with or even adopt the approach of *amici* where the *amici* are more akin to independent experts, than being representative of public interests, and therefore advocates for a particular interpretation of the legal obligations.[92] The *Methanex*

---

are from the developed world, and they are perceived as being anti-developing countries particularly with regard to environmental issues. Most *amicus* submissions in investment arbitrations, however, tend to critique the arguments of corporations, and so states parties to the treaties in question do not feel threatened to such a degree. Further, many of the states from which the investors are most likely to come are those in favour of *amicus* briefs (eg Canada, the United States) so not that they are unlikely to come to the defence of their corporations on this issue. Discussing these issues, see Bartholomeusz, n 19 above; and Eckersley, n 79 above, 340.

[92] See, eg Bartholomeusz, n 19 above, 254, discussing the Special Court for Sierra Leone's adoption of the arguments of Professor Philippe Sands in the case of *Prosecutor v Charles Ghanky Taylor*, case no SCSL-2003-01-I, Decision on Immunity from Jurisdiction, 31 May 2004. However, see also Williams and Woolaver, n 19, 175, arguing that academics are not neutral, in that they have 'predefined views on the issues raised' which are 'often widely published and accessible'. Tribunals will therefore need to be wary about the extent of the 'independence' of any expert they call, but this does not detract from the broader point about the need to separate the roles of expert on the law and advocate of the public interest.

tribunal explicitly stated that '*amici* are not experts; such persons are advocates (in the non-pejorative sense) and not "independent" in that they advance a particular case to a tribunal'.[93] However, this is not an approach which appears to have been taken by those tribunals which have allowed submissions (at least partly) on the basis of human rights expertise.

The limitations of seeing the *amici* as human rights experts is demonstrated by the enormous variety in the level of detail and application of the relevant human rights norms and standards between the different submissions. For instance, while the *amici* in *Glamis* and *Suez/Vivendi* set out a great range of human rights obligations applying to the case, the submissions in *Biwater* have very limited detail about the relevant human rights obligations. In terms of arguments about the relevance of those human rights obligations as applicable law, the *amici* in *Suez/Vivendi* present a far more detailed and complex picture than any of the other submissions. To an extent this reflects the strengths of the human rights arguments in each of the cases, as well as other tactical considerations of the *amici*.[94] As such, it is difficult to perceive the *amici* as having sufficient independence from the public interests they seek to represent to present the nature of the human rights obligations in such a way that they can be objectively assessed by the tribunal. Furthermore, even with regard to the most detailed and complex submissions, as in *Suez/Vivendi*, it is a difficult and complex process to understand how such obligations impact upon the investment law obligations which the tribunal is primarily considering. For instance, what weight should be given to the expert interpretations of relevant rights, raised by the *amici*, such as the Committee on Economic, Cultural, and Social Rights or the UN Special Rapporteur on Housing? It has been argued with regard to international trade law, for instance, that the legal obligations created by the economic, social, and cultural rights such as the right to water are insufficiently precise to be relevant to the decision-making processes of adjudicatory bodies.[95] Similar issues plague other rights-based claims in the IEL context – for instance, what legal status does the UN Declaration on the Rights of Indigenous People have and how should it be treated in the investment arbitration process?

---

[93] *Methanex Amicus* Order, n 23 above, at para 38.

[94] For instance, Argentina has ratified ICESCR and a range other relevant human rights instruments. Section 75(22) of the Constitution confers upon these human rights conventions 'constitutional hierarchy' and provides that they 'are to be understood as complementing the rights and guarantees recognised in the Constitution itself' (see *Suez/Vivendi* petition at p 10). In relation to the *Biwater* case, Tanzania, on the other hand, has not ratified ICESCR and so the *amici* must rely on other instruments such as the International Convention on the Protection of the Child. In relation to the *Glamis* case, the *amici* make much reference to the UN Declaration on the Rights of Indigenous Peoples, but they do not address its legal status.

[95] See, eg G Marceau, 'WTO Dispute Settlement and Human Rights' (2002) 13 European Journal of International Economic Law 753–814, 786: 'What is the "right to health"? What is the "right to food", and what does such a right entail in terms of the rights and obligations of States? And why and how are they relevant to WTO obligations?'

These issues are exacerbated by the implications of the third key rationale of the tribunals for the acceptance of *amicus* submissions – their perceived positive impact on the transparency of investor-state arbitration, thereby enhancing its legitimacy in the eyes of the public. Here there is a fundamental mis-understanding of the process and its power to confer legitimacy. It is difficult to understand how the tribunals can view the acceptance of *amicus* submissions as a transparency mechanism. Holding public hearings, making tribunal documents publicly available, and publicizing decisions are all procedures that make the arbitration process more transparent, and as such are 'legitimacy'-ends in themselves. Accepting *amicus curiae* submissions is a mechanism for increasing *participation* in the arbitration process. The extent of effective participation will indeed depend upon other transparency issues, in particular the extent of access to key documents which enable the *amici* to understand the detailed arguments of the parties in the case.[96] However, if the *amicus* submissions themselves are to have any legitimizing function for the tribunal, then it is the extent to which that participation is viewed as meaningful which will determine the degree of legitimacy obtained. Such participation is only meaningful to the extent that the tribunal can demonstrate real engagement with the legal frameworks utilized by the *amici* and the arguments advanced within those legal frameworks. This is all the more so when the tribunals have specifically noted the relevance of the human rights legal frameworks which are utilized. Perceiving the role of the *amici* as merely increasing transparency suggests that no actual engagement with their arguments is necessary in order to enhance the tribunal's legitimacy, and the rationale for this is fundamentally flawed.

Overall, there are a number of mutually reinforcing problems with the role of the *amici*; the contradictory expert/advocate role; the lack of expertise among the tribunal with regard to human rights; the inherently complex task of understanding the legal obligations to which human rights give rise in an IEL context; and the mistaken view that the amicus procedure can legitimize without effective participation. These give rise to deep concerns about the extent to which *amicus* submissions are likely to be marginalized by tribunals in the future.

---

[96] See CIEL and IISD, Revising the UNCITRAL Arbitration Rules to Address State Arbitrations (CIEL/IISD, 2007), 10, available at <http://www.iisd.org/pdf/2007/investment_revising_uncitral_arbitration.pdf>:

> a non-disputing party requesting leave to submit an *amicus curiae* brief to a tribunal could not elaborate on whether its perspective, knowledge or insight is different from the disputing parties' or useful to the tribunal, if the record remains secret. Likewise, it would be impossible for a non-disputing party to prepare a submission within the scope of the dispute when access to pleadings is denied.

At the very least in such a situation, there would seem to be a greater onus on the tribunal to explain how they have utilized the arguments of the *amici*, if the *amicus* process is to in any way legitimize the decisions of the arbitration panels in a way that increases the transparency of the process.

VI. Conclusions and Broader Impact

It is difficult to draw firm conclusions about the value of human rights interventions in *amicus curiae* submissions in international investment on the basis of a small number of cases, the majority of which have not yet been finally decided. However, the reasoning of the tribunals in accepting the submissions does seem to give rise to some fundamental issues about their role and purpose, and therefore the degree to which such human rights interventions are meaningfully raising social justice issues for consideration by the tribunal.

In the second section of this chapter, I set out some of the fundamental concerns that had been raised about the legal obligations created by international investment agreements, the system by which they are arbitrated, and the level of liabilities they give rise to. This has raised some fundamental concerns about the broader social justice impact of the system. In allowing expression of broader public interests in *amicus* submissions through, inter alia, the medium of international human rights obligations, tribunals appear to be recognizing the fact that there is a need to address these concerns. However, the resulting confusion and contradiction in the role and purpose of the *amici* appears to make it unlikely that the substantive social justice issues which they raise will be appropriately taken into account in the arbitration process. The bigger question is whether this is important, if the tribunals are deciding cases on the basis of a correct application of the relevant international investment law. I finish with some brief thoughts on this issue.

From the perspective of the *amici*, it is not necessarily important in the individual cases that their human rights arguments are not substantively engaged with. In both *UPS* and *Biwater*, the 'right' decision was made from the perspective of those making the human rights arguments.[97] For many NGOs, it is argued that the publicity they receive among their own constituencies in submitting the briefs may be as important as the extent to which they are able to influence the decision-making of the tribunal.[98] From the perspective of the arbitrators and perhaps even the claimants, there may also be good reason to maintain the status quo. When the tribunal in *Aguas del Tunari SA v Bolivia* rejected a petition to submit an *amicus* brief, the result was ongoing international pressure on Bechtel from a range of civil society organizations protesting about the injustice of their action, which led to the settlement of the case for a nominal amount.[99] It may be in the

---

[97] In the *Biwater* case, human rights arguments might even be seen as the pretext to allow the *amici* to raise other more technical issues of interpretation of investment law by the tribunal.

[98] See L Butler, 'Effects and outcomes of *Amicus Curiae* Briefs at the WTO: An Assessment of NGO experiences', available at <http://socrates.berkeley.edu/~es196/projects/2006final/butler.pdf>, (accessed on 10 September 2008) 13; and Eckersley, n 79 above, 350. Making the same argument, but with no attempt at empirical analysis, see Vinuales, n 19 above, 270.

[99] See, eg the report by the Democracy Centre at <http://www.democracyctr.org/bolivia/investigations/water/bechtel-vs-bolivia.htm>.

interests of tribunal panels to appear engaged with petitions for, and the content of *amicus* submissions, while continuing to make their decisions on the basis of the international investment law principles where their expertise lies.[100]

However, the issue may become more obviously problematic when the 'wrong' decision is made, and a tribunal decides to award damages to a claimant, contrary to the human rights arguments put forward in an *amicus* submission. If the human rights arguments are also ignored by a tribunal in coming to their decision in that scenario, then questions are likely to be asked about the extent to which tribunals are failing to engage with applicable law and the interests which are expressed through that legal framework. More fundamentally, the whole *amicus* process may be questioned as failing to address the more fundamental legitimacy questions at the heart of international investment arbitration. In such a scenario, civil society organizations may utilize such tribunal decisions as evidence of the wider lack of legitimacy of the whole international investment arbitration process.

From an institutional human rights perspective, a failure by tribunals to make judgments with regard to human rights issues in international investment arbitration might be viewed positively by some actors. There are inherent dangers in experts from a particular field of international law making judgments about the applicability of another field of international law, about which they have very little knowledge and probably limited sympathy.[101] However, this kind of 'defensive' human rights model has limitations which need to be considered. It will always be investment arbitration tribunals which are making the multi-million dollar damages awards, not human rights adjudicatory mechanisms. As such, even a ruling which drew negative conclusions about the ambit or relevance of human rights might actually have long-term benefits in terms of the ability of human rights to have a positive impact upon issues of fundamental social justice. It could be the basis of a range of actions by relevant actors. At its most combative, the response from human rights advocates might be that the tribunal had erred in its findings, and utilize this as a basis for action in the national courts, or for campaigning more generally. At its most introspective, it might also encourage human rights advocates to consider what is required to

---

[100] Clearly, the identity of individual members of the tribunals is going to be very important in this decision-making process. It has already been noted how two Argentine tribunals (*Suez/Vivendi* and *Suez/Interaguas*) unsurprisingly reached identical decisions with regard to *amicus* participation in those cases. Also interesting to note is that the chairman of the tribunal in *Aguas del Tunari SA v Bolivia* (David D Caron) was also an arbitrator in *UPS v Canada*. It is interesting to speculate how his experience in the former case may have led to a change of attitude in the latter.

[101] Making this point with regard to international trade law, see P Alston, 'Resisting the Merger and Acquisition of Human Rights Law: A Reply to Petersmann' (2002) 13 European Journal of International Law 815–844. Making the point with regard to international law more generally, see ILC, 'Fragmentation of International Law: Difficulties Arising From the Diversification and Expansion of International Law: Report of the Study Group of the International Law Commission', finalised by Koskenniemi, A/CN.4/L682 (13 April 2006) para 252.

ensure that these human rights obligations have the requisite specificity and binding force to be effective in fora such as investment tribunals. For instance, is there a need to formulate more detailed indicators of, for example, the right to water, and the situations in which investors would be failing to respect those rights?[102] Finally, it might encourage the development of other forms of legal argument to be pursued by civil society groups in the knowledge that human rights obligations do not necessarily effectively address all of the social justice issues raised by international investment proceedings.[103]

From the perspective of the coherence and unity of public international law, the acceptance of *amicus* submissions raising human rights arguments by investment arbitration panels has superficial attractions. Tribunals are thereby recognizing the formal requirement to take into account other branches of international law. However, lack of engagement with the human rights arguments presented demonstrates the procedural and substantive barriers to meaningful interaction between the two legal regimes through this mechanism. In social justice terms, this reinforces the idea of an international legal system where power about 'how scarce resources should be distributed' is left in the hands of 'technical and legal experts' from one particular regime.[104] This undoubtedly weakens the edifice of international law in the eyes of those outsiders to the regime who seek to engage with it.

---

[102] Office of the High Commissioner for Human Rights, 'Report on Indicators for Promoting and Monitoring Implementation of Human Rights' (6 June 2008) HRMI/MC/2008/3 could act as a starting point for such work.

[103] This may involve a more concentrated focus on the provisions of international investment law and general international law and how legal obligations such as necessity can be interpreted in such a way as to promote key social justice issues.

[104] M Koskenniemi, 'The Fate of Public International Law, Between Technique and Politics' (2007) 70 Modern Law Review 1–30, 4.

18

'Proportional' by What Measure(s)? Balancing Investor Interests and Human Rights by Way of Applying the Proportionality Principle in Investor-State Arbitration

Jasper Krommendijk and John Morijn

I. Introduction

Human rights obligations often demand more from a state than non-inter-ference. All states hold obligations to protect, respect, and fulfil human rights for those persons and legal persons within their jurisdiction.[1] The obligation to respect requires states to refrain from interfering with individuals' enjoyment of human rights. The obligation to protect entails that states have to protect persons against violation of their human rights. The obligation to fulfil stands for positive action that the state may need to undertake in order to further the enjoyment of human rights. At the same time, states have concluded international investment agreements[2] with other states, whereby the host state commits itself to protect the investments of nationals from the other 'home' state. Those agreements only specifically explicate obligations of the host state vis-à-vis the foreign investor.

---

[1] For example, the Convention on the Rights of the Child (CRC) was signed by all states, except Somalia and the United States. The International Covenant on Economic, Social, and Cultural Rights (ICESCR) and the International Covenant on Civil and Political Rights (ICCPR) have 159 and 162 signatory states respectively (situation on 10 October 2008). In addition, the fact that, for example, the United States has only *signed* the CRC and ICESCR, and China the ICCPR, entails that these states should no longer act against the object and purpose of these treaties (VCLT, Art 18).

[2] There are three different forms of those agreements: bilateral investment treaties (BITs) of which there are currently around 2,500, regional investment treaties, and chapters on investment integrated in broader bilateral or regional agreements, addressing also issues of trade, such as NAFTA. Because of the similarities in protection, this chapter will refer to those agreements as international investment agreements. See A van Aaken, 'Fragmentation of International Law: The

The *factual* reality for most states, therefore, is that they hold various different international obligations in parallel which they are to be understood as seeking to respect simultaneously, in good faith. Yet, when a state adopts a regulatory measure in light of its international human rights obligations, foreign investor rights may be impacted in the process. Such a scenario can develop into a dispute – as indeed by now it has on a number of occasions[3] – in which obligations flowing from international investment agreements and human rights can come into tension. In aiming to solve this dispute, investment arbitrators will be required, in one way or another, to balance human rights protection imperatives against investor interests in the light of the different international obligations underlying the dispute. The core issue will then often be whether the human rights justified measure is proportional from the viewpoint of investment law.[4] For a balanced analysis, however, one may also question whether the solution found in investment arbitration is proportional from the viewpoint, and in the sense of human rights law.

Within investor-state arbitration practice there are various interconnected ways in which states' prerogatives to protect human rights can be accommodated: by (re)interpreting investment law provisions and principles, such as the fair and equitable treatment standard, to take account of parallel international obligations,[5] and by mitigating the amount of compensation awarded.[6] In this chapter we will narrowly focus on the first possibility. More specifically, we will study the application of the principle of proportionality in the course of investor-state arbitration with regard to expropriation. By addressing whether this practice has been consistent with human rights requirements, we effectively raise the question of whether solutions found by investment arbitrators have accommodated two measures of proportionality simultaneously, that of investment law *and* human rights law.

Case Of International Investment Protection', University of St Gallen Working paper No 2008-1, St Gallen (2008) 6, available at <http://papers.ssrn.com/sol3/papers.cfm?abstract_id=1097529>; and R Bachand and S Rousseau, 'International Investment and Human Rights: Political And Legal Issues', Rights and Democracy Background Paper, Ottawa (2003) 17, available at <http://www.dd-rd.ca/site/_PDF/publications/globalization/bachandRousseauEng.pdf>.

[3] For an extensive analysis of this interaction, see, for instance, ch 22 in this volume.

[4] In this chapter we will primarily refer to the proportionality principle as a legal and judicial standard to assess the reach and effect of measures taken by states or individuals. The core idea of the principle of proportionality, that measures and action taken shall not go further than what is necessary, is also visible in the public international law fields of self-defence, retaliation, countermeasures, humanitarian law, and human rights law. Xiuli has argued that with respect to those areas of international law the principle of proportionality has reached the status of customary international law: see H Xiuli, 'The Application Of The Principle Of Proportionality In *Tecmed v. Mexico*' (2007) 6(3) Chinese Journal of International Law 635–652, 637. The proportionality is sometimes also referred to in slightly different ways. It is sometimes employed as a way to analyse the standard of judicial review and the level of scrutiny afforded to judges. See M Andenas and S Zleptnig, 'Proportionality and Balancing in WTO Law: A Comparative Perspective' (2007) 20(1) Cambridge Review of International Affairs 71–92, 72–74. Another context in which proportionality plays a role concerns its use for reviewing the exercise of competences. In the context of EC law, for example, proportionality considerations demand that action by the EC shall not go beyond what is necessary to achieve the objectives of the EC treaty. [5] See ch 14 in this volume.

[6] See ch 23 in this volume.

II. Before Balancing: Assessing the Legal Relevance and Deeper Significance of Human Rights for Investor-State Arbitration

Before we can consider the way in which the proportionality principle is being applied in investor-state arbitration, and can come to be interpreted in a human rights consistent manner, we will first clarify our understanding of the legal significance of human rights to investment law. We will argue that the complexity of investor-state arbitration relates to the fact that both the interests of the state and those of the investor have human rights aspects: obligations with regard to human rights protection are relevant for both sides of the balance (section II.A.). We then indicate how at a more fundamental and principled level, human rights law may equally represent an articulation of values that are foundational to investment law: as specific articulation of the object and purpose of investment law itself in the light of which investment law provisions are to be interpreted, and investment law principles applied (section II.B.).

A. The Legal Relevance of Human Rights within Investment Law

In analysing in what way international human rights law can be seen as relevant to investment law, first of all it is important to observe that international investment agreements do not preclude rules of international law from being applicable. On the contrary, NAFTA, the Energy Charter, and numerous BITs refer explicitly to their applicability.[7] Although the question of applicability of international law is left open in the context of UNCITRAL, the Stockholm Chamber of Commerce, the International Court of Arbitration, and the London Court of International Arbitration, the principal forum of investor-state arbitration, the ICSID Convention, explicitly mentions international law as part of the applicable law.[8] This has led arbitral tribunals to conclude that international law is indeed fully applicable.[9] As a result, it is generally accepted that general

---

[7] The US Model BIT 2004 refers to the applicability of 'rules and principles of international law'. NAFTA, Art 1131, para 1 equally provides that: 'A tribunal established under this Section shall decide the issues in accordance with this Agreement and applicable rules of international law'. Article 26(6) of the Energy Charter (ECT) similarly refers to 'applicable rules and principles of international law'. Most of the BITs refer to fair and equitable treatment 'in accordance with (the rules and criteria) of international law' or 'no case ... less favourable than that required by international law'. NAFTA, Art 1105, para 1 provides for 'treatment in accordance with international law, including fair and equitable treatment'. As for the NAFTA, both the reference to 'international law' as well as 'fair and equitable treatment' makes the application of special international law possible.   [8] ICSID Convention, Art 42(1). See ch 4 in this volume.
[9] See also *Amco Asia Corp and ors v Indonesia*, ICSID Case No ARB/81/1, Decision on Jurisdiction, 10 May 1988, at para 40:

> Thus international law is fully applicable and to classify its role as 'only' supplemental and corrective seems a distinction without difference. In any event, the Tribunal believes that its task is to test every claim of law in this case first against Indonesian law, and then against international law.

rules of international law, such as those found in the Vienna Convention on the Law of Treaties (VCLT), are applicable in investor-state arbitration disputes.[10] Tribunals, indeed, have sought recourse to the VCLT to give meaning to provisions in the investment agreements.

Yet, uncertainty remains with regard to direct application of sources of non-investment law.[11] Some authors argue that special international law, and thus also human rights law,[12] could be applicable, because international law should in their view have an 'international public policy function'.[13] Van Aaken argues, on the other

---

In *CMS Gas*, the tribunal stated that 'a more pragmatic and less doctrinaire approach has emerged' allowing for the application of both domestic as international law. See *CMS Gas Transmission Co v Argentina*, ICSID Case No ARB/01/08, Award, 12 May 2005, at para 116.

[10] Van Aaken, n 2 above, 11–12.

[11] Some investment agreements contain clauses that make it possible directly to apply substantive rules of special international law, but only those that are favourable to the foreign investor. Nevertheless, this possibility of directly applying substantive rules of special international law may also be more generally taken as indicative of the fact that investment agreements and international investment law do not operate in clinical isolation from public international law. See, eg Art 3(5) of the Bilateral Investment Treaty between the Netherlands and the Czech Republic:

> If the provisions of law of either Contracting Party or obligations under international law existing at present or established hereafter between the Contracting parties in addition to the present Agreement contain rules, whether general or specific, entitling investments by investors of the other Contracting Party to a treatment more favourable than is provided for by the present Agreement, such rules shall to the extent that they are more favourable prevail over the present Agreement.

See also Art 16 of the US Model BIT 2004:

> This Treaty shall not derogate from any of the following that entitle an investor of a Party or a covered investment to treatment more favourable than that accorded by this Treaty: 1. laws or regulations, administrative practices or procedures, or administrative or adjudicatory decisions of a Party; 2. international legal obligations of a Party; or 3. obligations assumed by a Party, including those contained in an investment authorization or an investment agreement.

Finally, ECT, Art 10(1) provides: 'In no case shall such Investments be accorded treatment less favourable than that required by international law, including treaty obligations.'

[12] Human rights are barely included in international investment agreements. There are, however, a number of significant exceptions, such as the 2002 European Free Trade Area-Singapore Agreements and the Norway Model BIT. In the preamble of the European Free Trade Area-Singapore Agreement, a reaffirmation of the commitment to the principles in the UN Charter and the Universal Declaration of Human Rights is included. The preamble of the Norway Model BIT provides for a similar reaffirmation: 'Reaffirming their commitment to democracy, the rule of law, human rights and fundamental freedoms in accordance with their obligations under international law, including the principles set out in the United Nations Charter and the Universal Declaration of Human Rights.' Nonetheless, such a preambulary clause does not bring about directly any enforceable rights and obligations, but could only be relevant when interpreting other provisions. There are other provisions found in preambles referring to the environment, labour rights, and the promotion of sustainable development. Human rights are further included in the Investment Agreement for the COMESA Common Investment Area of Eastern and Southern African States that is recently agreed upon and not yet in force. In this agreement the Committee is empowered to develop minimum standards relating to investment in the area of human rights.

[13] E Gaillard and Y Banifatemi, 'The Meaning of "And" in Article 42(1), Second Sentence of the Washington Convention: The Role of International Law in the ICSID Choice of Law Process' (2004) 18(2) ICSID Review 375–411.

hand, that direct application would not be possible.[14] However, one may wonder about the significance of the distinction between taking into account human rights directly or 'only' indirectly, that is, when interpreting investment provisions through the general principle of interpretation of VCLT, Article 31(3)(c).[15] Although the difference may be interesting from a theoretical viewpoint, as a practical matter, the entry of human rights by either route seems to have the same effect. That is because:

in practice . . . there is a good chance that the two (application and interpretation) might lapse into each other – such would seem well-nigh inevitable, if only because it would be difficult to apply something without at the same time interpreting it, and to interpret a term without a context in which to apply it.[16]

As a result, applying a human rights provision directly or applying it indirectly as a source to interpret investment law does not appear likely to lead to results that are different in a relevant way.

Using non-investment law obligations, such as human rights, as a source to interpret investment law can be instrumental because of the often rather flexible, vague, and open standards laid down in investment agreements. Because most investment agreements contain behavioural obligations in general terms, tribunals are required to balance various elements and interests on a case-by-case basis.[17] International law from non-investment law sources was indeed touched upon by arbitral tribunals when states invoked it in their defence of the treatment offered to foreign investors. For example, in both *SPP v Egypt* and *Parkerings v Lithuania*, cultural rights were considered.[18] In *Maffezini v Spain*, the tribunal accepted environmental rights of citizens.[19] Furthermore, international environmental law was been taken into account in *SD Myers v Canada* and *Santa*

---

[14] Van Aaken, n 2 above, 16.

[15] VCLT, Art 31(3)(c) is viewed as embodying the principle of systemic integration within the international legal system that *regulates tensions between different international legal rules*. See M Hirsch, 'Interactions Between Investment and Non-Investment Obligations in International Investment Law', Hebrew University International Law Research Paper No 14-06, Jerusalem (2006) 11, available at <http://papers.ssrn.com/sol3/papers.cfm?abstract_id=947430>. This rule has been confirmed by the tribunal in *Saluka*:

In interpreting a treaty, account has to be taken of 'any relevant rules of international law applicable in the relations between the parties' – a requirement which the International Court of Justice ('ICJ') has held includes relevant rules of general customary international law.

See *Saluka Investments BV (The Netherlands) v The Czech Republic*, UNCITRAL, Partial Award, 17 March 2006, at para 254.

[16] J Klabbers, 'Reluctant Grundnormen: Articles 31(3)(c) and 42 of the Vienna Convention on the Law of the Treaties and the Fragmentation of International Law' in M Craven, M Fitzmaurice, and M Vogiatzi (eds), *Time, History and International Law* (2007) 144.

[17] G Marceau, 'WTO Dispute Settlement And Human Rights' (2002) 13(4) European Journal of International Law 753–814, 790. See also the WTO Appellate Body Report, 'Japan-Taxes on Alcoholic Beverages', AB-1996-2, 23 August 1996.

[18] *Southern Pacific Properties (Middle East) Ltd v Egypt*, ICSID Case No ARB/84/3, Award of the Tribunal, 20 May 1992; and *Parkerings-Compagniet AS v Lithuania*, ICSID Case No ARB/05/8, Award, 11 September 2007.

[19] *Maffezini v Spain*, ICSID Case No ARB/97/7, Award on the Merits, 13 November 2000.

Elena v Costa Rica.[20] In *CMS Gas Transmission Co v Argentina*, the tribunal looked to the customary international law rule of necessity.[21] The tribunals in all of those instances looked at the full context of the investment treaty obligations.

The conclusion that the applicable law may come to include other sources of international law is also in line with a more principled viewpoint. Even a specific subsystem of law with its own norms and remedies is not segregated from the body of general international law.[22] The regime remains an integral part of it, because it is founded upon international norms. In the context of investment law, it could be said that because international investment treaties form part of and are instruments of international law, international law would also be automatically applicable.[23] The law of this regime should not be applied and interpreted in a 'clinical vacuum',[24] nor read in 'clinical isolation from public international law', to borrow a phrase from the first dispute in the WTO context.[25] And although norms of special regimes prevail over general law, because of the rule *lex specialis derogat lex generalis*, that regime will not be entirely self-sufficient due to the inevitable lacunae and ambiguities in the wording of provisions.[26] Besides this more vertical relationship between a specialist sub regime and general international law, on a horizontal level isolation will not be feasible as well. As observed above, interaction with other sub regimes, such as human rights law, can lead to tensions.[27]

This is where analyses about the legal relevance of human rights to investment law usually stop. The way in which human rights become *specifically* relevant to a state-investor dispute is not spelt out. However, this downplays the significance of human rights in the investment law context and also the complexity that it raises. In particular, acknowledging the applicability of human rights law in investment arbitration is not the end of the discussion. We need to consider in what way human rights law comes to play into the *typical* scenario of expropriation in the context of an investor-state conflict.

A state holds different vertical international obligations simultaneously, albeit with regard to (legal) persons in different legal capacities. It holds human rights

---

[20] *SD Myers, Inc v Canada*, UNCITRAL NAFTA Chapter 11 Arbitration Tribunal, Partial Award, 13 November 2000; and *Compañia del Desarrollo de Santa Elena, SA v Costa Rica*, ICSID Case No ARB/96/1, Award on Merits, 17 February 2000.   [21] *CMS Gas*, n 9 above.
[22] P-M Dupuy, 'A Doctrinal Debate in The Globalization Era: on the "Fragmentation" Of International Law' (2007) 1(1) European Journal of Legal Studies 1–19, 4.
[23] The Deputy Secretary General of ICSID stated, for example, that 'because the treaties are instruments of international law, it should be implicit that arbitrators should have recourse to the rules of general international law to supplement those treaties'. See R Suda, 'The Effect of Bilateral Investment Treaties on Human Rights Enforcement and Realization', Global Law Working Paper No 01/05, New York (2005) fn 268, available at <http://www.nyulawglobal.org/workingpapers/GLWP0105Suda_000.rtf> (last accessed on 10 October 2008).
[24] P-M Dupuy, 'The Unity of Application of International Law at The Global Level and the Responsibility of Judges' (2007) 1(2) European Journal of Legal Studies 1–23, 23.
[25] WTO Appellate Body Report, 'United States – Standards for Reformulated and Conventional Gasoline', AB-1996-1, WT/DS2/AB/R, adopted 20 May 1996, 17.
[26] B Conforti, 'The Role of the Judge in International Law' (2007) 1(2) European Journal of Legal Studies 1–16, 2.
[27] B Simma and D Pulkowski, 'Of Planets and the Universe: Self-Contained Regimes in International Law' (2006) 17(3) European Journal of International Law 483–529, 492.

obligations towards non-nationals acting as economic operators by investing in the country, particularly with regard to the protection of their property. At the same time, a state continues to hold obligations with regard to all nationals within its jurisdiction, whatever their legal capacity. The crucial insight is that in a number of human rights law texts[28] – including, as will become clear below, those that investment arbitrators have started to draw on particularly[29] – these different legal capacities of (legal) persons are subsumed into and dealt with under the single legal discipline of human rights law. On the other hand, as a matter of investment law, foreign investors receive entitlements vis-à-vis states solely in their capacity as economic operators.

Now, from the viewpoint of human rights law, a state's continuing human rights responsibilities towards its nationals feature among the considerations on one side of the balancing act in an investor-state dispute about expropriation, while the obligation of the same state to protect the right to property of a non-national economic operator weighs in on the other side of the balance. It should be noted that while in this analysis we will focus on the complexity arising from the simultaneously applicable international obligations on states with regard to both sides of the balance, the situation is considerably more complex even from a human rights viewpoint. In particular, also private actors, including investors, are increasingly seen as obligation holders *in their own right*, both within investment law[30] and within human rights law.[31]

---

[28] Most international, regional, and national human rights documents, such as the ICCPR and ICESCR, only recognize natural persons as potential rights holders, but there are a number of significant exceptions. See P Oliver, 'Book Review: Marius Emberland, The Human Rights of Companies: Exploring the structure of ECHR Protection' (Oxford: Oxford University Press, 2006) (2006) 43(6) CML Rev 1766–1768, 1766:

> The European Convention of Human Rights stands alone amongst human rights treaties in recognising that legal persons as well as natural persons are the rightful holders of some fundamental rights ... Hence the immense importance across the human rights world of the case law of the European Court of Human Rights relating to companies' rights: this body of judgements might one day act as the model for others.

See also South African Constitution, Art 8(4): 'A juristic person is entitled to the rights in the Bill of Rights to the extent required by the nature of the rights and the nature of that juristic person.'

[29] See below section C for a discussion of ECHR case law as referred to by investment arbitrators, particularly with regard to the right to property.

[30] It is often suggested that under investment agreements, the foreign investor has no concurrent obligations or responsibilities towards the state. However, the situation is more nuanced as a matter of investment law. Although international investment agreements as such are silent on foreign investors' duties and obligations, arbitrational practice shows that those duties are taken into account in determining whether expropriation has occurred in the first place. Foreign investors have not only the duty to invest with the adequate knowledge of risk, but also a duty to conduct business in a reasonable manner and to refrain from unconscionable conduct. See, eg *Waste Management, Inc v Mexico* (No 2), ICSID Case No ARB(AF)/00/3, Final Award, 30 April 2004, at para 177. For a more elaborate discussion, see ch 22, in this volume; and P Muchlinski, '"Caveat Investor"? The Relevance Of The Conduct Of The Investor Under The Fair And Equitable Treatment Standard' (2006) 55(3) ICLQ 527–558.

[31] Companies/investors are increasingly seen as human rights obligation holders themselves. Several guidelines make clear that foreign investors and companies also have obligations. See, eg the

Human rights are thus relevant to both sides of the balance. Crucially, therefore, the difficulty in reconciling the different obligations for states does not reside in, or boil down to, some type of normative irreconcilability. It is a *practical* problem of how interpretation of multiple norms in force simultaneously can be given meaning in parallel, in this case by an investment arbitrator. On the other hand, the 'institutional isolation' of the right to property within investment law should not be translated into normative or interpretational isolation, in the sense of disconnecting the right to property from other human rights *within* investment law. This is the challenge discussed in section C below.

In other words, we argue that the implications of human rights for investment law may be more complex than it is usually presented. It is more complex than usually presented by investment lawyers, who may often downplay the relevance of international (human rights) law as applicable law, or of interpretational relevance. Yet, it is also more complex than acknowledged by many human rights lawyers, who deny that human rights play a role on both sides of the balance. They usually presume some type of normative irreconcilability and therefore *a priori* caution against dealing with human rights within investment law – without, however, closely scrutinizing the actual state of investment arbitration practice.

B. The Deeper Significance of Human Rights to Investment Law

Apart from the legal relevance of human rights to the interests of *both* parties in an investor-state dispute, and the necessity to take account of this legal reality by arbitrators when balancing their interests in a particular dispute, it is necessary to lay out two further issues here that dramatically increase the scope for human rights argumentation to be brought up in investment law disputes.

First, discussions about the relevance of human rights in investor-state arbitration often focus on the perceived danger of states potentially starting to use

Tripartite Declaration of Principles concerning Multinational Enterprises and Social Policy, the OECD Guidelines for Multinational Enterprises, and especially UN Economic and Social Council, 'Norms on the responsibilities of transnational corporations and other business enterprises with regard to human rights', paras 1 and 12. For a more detailed discussion, see ch 21 in this volume. In the latest report of the Special Representative of the Secretary-General, John Ruggie, the responsibility to respect human rights for transnational corporations and business enterprises is even considered a core principle. The problem with those guidelines and report is that it remains unclear what the exact scope and content of those corporate responsibilities is. With regard to the Draft Norms, the obligations just listed are rather vague and general, that do not shed any light on the specific responsibility corporations have with regard to certain human rights. More concrete and detailed obligations are listed with regard to only a limited number of areas. With regard to the latest report, although the responsibilities are construed in relation to all rights, it is not specified what the responsibility to respect actually entails. It is, furthermore, still doubtful whether the responsibilities go further than only moral obligations and social expectations being merely soft law that guides and suggests rather than compels. See the Report of the Special Representative of the Secretary-General on the issue of human rights and transnational corporations and other business enterprises, J Ruggie, 'Protect, Respect and Remedy: a Framework for Business and Human Rights' A/HRC/8/5 (7 April 2008).

investment law as a forum/modus to *enforce* human rights, *imposing* their standards on the company. This is, however, a very one-sided perspective. It is indeed true that the jurisdiction of investment tribunals is limited to particular disputes between a foreign investor and a host state, and that those tribunals could not be used to enforce other treaties or customs, such as the violation of human rights law.[32] For example, in an early case, the tribunal in *Biloune v Ghana* held that it was not authorized to deal with allegations of violations of human rights of the foreign investor.[33]

Nonetheless, a possibility of a state wanting to *defend* its position in terms of human rights must be added to the picture. It is in this light that the acceptance of several tribunals of NGO *amicus curiae* briefs in the proceedings should be appreciated and applauded, as a means of making space for public interest and human rights aspects.[34] States should be encouraged to invoke human rights obligations in their defence in international treaty-governed investor-state dispute settlement, as it is reflective of their good faith effort to respect different international obligations simultaneously.

Secondly, human rights also have a deeper significance for investment law because they represent a legally relevant articulation, or clarification of one of investment law's *own* objectives. One of the original motivations behind both the investment law and human rights regimes is the promotion of sustainable development. The preamble of NAFTA, which is compulsorily part of the relevant legal context of the treaty according to customary rules of treaty interpretation, refers to the determination of the parties to promote sustainable development. Furthermore, it is affirmed that flexibility to safeguard the public welfare should be preserved. The ICSID Convention also includes a similar reference with the acknowledgment that foreign investment has a role in the economic development of the host state.[35] Therefore, the ICSID Convention was originally set up not in order to protect private property as such, but with

---

[32] LE Peterson and KR Gray, 'International Human Rights In Bilateral Investment Treaties And In Investment Treaty Arbitration', International Institute for Sustainable Development Research Paper, Winnipeg (2003) 6, available at <http://www.iisd.org/pdf/2003/investment_int_human_rights_bits.pdf>.

[33] *Antoine Biloune and Marine Drive Complex Ltd v Ghana Investments Centre and the Government of Ghana*, UNCITRAL, Awards of 27 October 1989 and 30 June 1990, at para 203.

[34] See *Suez, Sociedad General de Aguas de Barcelona, SA and Vivendi Universal, SA v Argentina*, ICSID Case No ARB/03/19, Order in Response to a Petition for Transparency and Participation as Amicus Curiae, 19 May 2005, at para 19. See also *Suez, Sociedad General de Aguas de Barcelona SA, and InterAguas ServiciosIntegrales del Agua SA v Argentina*, ICSID Case No ARB/03/17, Decision on Jurisdiction, 16 May 2006, at para 18; and *Biwater Gauff (Tanzania) Ltd v Tanzania*, ICSID Case No ARB/05/22, Procedural Order No 5 on *amicus curiae*, 2 February 2007, at para 52. For a more detailed analysis, see ch 22 in this volume.

[35] See the preamble of the Convention on the Settlement of Investment Disputes Between States and Nationals of other States (ICSID): 'Considering the need for international cooperation for economic development, and the role of private international investment therein'. It should be added that in bilateral investment treaties, this connection between economic justifications for investment protection and wider objectives related to the public interest is also made in preambles. Both the France and Netherlands Model BITs have the objective 'to stimulate the transfer of capital

the broader purpose of stimulating development.[36] On the other hand, much recent work done within the United Nations also links human rights to sustainable development.[37] For these reasons, sustainable development, and human rights protection as an important articulation of that objective, should be taken into account while interpreting investment law provisions.[38]

Importantly, this argumentation has to some extent already been brought into practice. It is because of those broader aspects that tribunals have begun to reject one-sided approaches and called for a more balanced interpretation, also taking into account the state's sovereignty and responsibility to create an 'evolutionary framework for the development of economic activities'.[39] The tribunal in *Noble Ventures* held that 'it is not permissible, as is too often done regarding BITs, to interpret clauses exclusively in favour of investors'.[40] The tribunal in *El Paso* added in this regard that:

a balanced interpretation is needed, taking into account both State sovereignty and the State's responsibility to create an adapted and evolutionary framework for the development of economic activities, and the necessity to protect foreign investment and its continuing flow.[41]

The rationale for formulating the objective of the investment regime in broad terms is that the medium- and long-term benefits of investment liberalization can only be obtained in a reliable domestic regulatory context. Constraints that preclude the enactment of governmental measures to promote human rights would disrupt the achievement of the goal of sustainable development.[42] It is

and technology between the two countries in the interest of their economic development'. The Swiss Model BIT and the Peru-Paraguay BIT talk of the objective to promote the economic prosperity of both states. As a result, the rights of foreign investors are not treated solely as an end in itself, but rather as a means to an end. Cf G van Harten, *Investment Treaty Arbitration and Public Law* (2007) 140. That is to say, to promote trade and investment between the respective states. See *Loewen Group, Inc and Raymond L Loewen v United States*, ICSID Case No ARB(AF)/98/3, Award on Merits, 26 June 2003, at para 222.

[36] Van Aaken, n 2 above, 34. See also *Amco*, n 9 above, at para 23: 'to protect investment is to protect the general interest of development and of developing countries'.

[37] See, eg, UNDP, 'Integrating human rights with sustainable human development', UNDP Policy Document (1998), available at <http://www.undp.org/governance/docs/HR_Pub_policy5.htm>; and Office of the High Commissioner for Human Rights, 'Claiming the MDGs: A Human Rights Approach', OHCHR Special Issue (2008), available at <http://www2.ohchr.org/SPdocs/Claiming_MDGs_en.pdf>: 'The international human rights framework, to which all States have subscribed, must be seen as . . . the baseline commitment on development' (at iii).

[38] Bachand and Rousseau, n 2 above, 33.

[39] *Pan American Energy LLC and BP Argentina Exploration Co v Argentina*, ICSID Case No ARB/03/13, Decision on Preliminary Objections, 27 July 2006, at para 99. For one-sided approaches, see, eg *Siemens v Argentina*, ICSID Case No ARB/02/08, Award, 6 February 2007, at para 81; or *SGS Société Générale de Surveillance SA v the Philippines*, ICSID Case No ARB/02/6, Jurisdiction, 29 January 2004, at para 116.

[40] *Noble Ventures Inc v Romania*, ICSID Case No ARB/01/11, Award, 12 October 2005, at para 52.

[41] *El Paso Energy International Co v Argentina*, ICSID Case No ARB/03/15, Decision on Jurisdiction, 27 April 2006, at para 70.

[42] H Mann, 'The Right of States to Regulate and International Investment Law' (2002) 5–6, available at <http://www.iisd.org/pdf/2003/investment_right_to_regulate.pdf>.

telling in this regard that the recent Norway Model BIT 2007 explicitly connects human rights and sustainable development, by including a reference to states' obligations under the Universal Declaration of Human Rights.[43] Interpretation of investment law provisions that takes into account the broader object and purpose implies a process of balancing of simultaneously binding obligations flowing from human rights law and investment law.[44]

III. Behind Balancing: A Close Look at the Interpretation of the Proportionality Principle in Investor-State Arbitration Practice Relating to Expropriation

In aiming to give interpretational expression to the simultaneously binding obligations flowing from human rights law and investment law, we will address the way in which measures invoked with reference to human rights law are to be weighed in the context of investment arbitration. As was pointed out above, various routes exist within investment law to make the weight of human rights law felt in this context, including by applying the fair and equitable treatment principle and by mitigating the amount of compensation granted to an investor. We aim to focus on the way in which human rights law can be given its due in investment law by helping to reinterpret the investment law provisions and principles of 'police powers' and general exceptions clauses (section III.A.). To narrow down the focus further, we identify tendencies in the way in which the proportionality principle has been applied in the context of expropriation (section III.B.).

A. Entry-Points for Human Rights in Expropriation Cases and the Significance of the Proportionality Principle

With regard to the prohibition of expropriation, the two most obvious ways to integrate human rights considerations into investor-state arbitration appear to be via the concept of 'police powers' and via general exceptions clauses. In international law it is recognized that certain measures taken by a state in the exercise of its police powers do not require compensation to be paid.[45] Police powers have been defined as:

The power of a state to place restraints on personal freedom and property rights of persons for the protection of the public safety, health, and morals, or the promotion of the public convenience and general prosperity . . . the police power is the exercise of the sovereign right of a government to promote order, safety, security, health, morals and

---

[43] The Commentary makes clear that the motivation behind the drafting of the Model BIT is 'to lead the development from one-sided agreements that safeguard the interests of the investor to comprehensive agreements that safeguard the regulative needs of both developed and developing countries'. See 'Comments on the model for future investment agreements', available at <http://ita.law.uvic.ca/documents/NorwayModel2007-commentary.doc>, 10.

[44] Van Aaken, n 2 above, 36.   [45] Peterson and Gray, n 32 above, 12.

general welfare within the constitutional limits and is an essential attribute of government.[46]

'Police powers' is an international law term for what we now call 'regulatory measures by a state to protect or enhance the public welfare'.[47] In this concept lies the origin of the state's right to regulate. According to Mann, it is in this context that human rights considerations become relevant. That is to say, the closest approximation of the obligation to protect and promote human rights is the concept of the state's right to regulate.[48] Consequently, the concept of police powers seems, at first glance, to be a good entry point for human rights arguments.

However, there appear to be certain difficulties with regard to this route. First, the exact scope of the police powers doctrine is still unclear, due to the different and often opposing arbitral rulings. On the one hand, there are several decisions, often referred to as being part of the 'sole effect doctrine', that stress the economic effects of government measures on foreign investors, while societal interests and purposes are neglected. The decision in *Santa Elena* is seen by most authors as the embodiment of this approach.[49] Furthermore, in *Metalclad* the tribunal decided that the motivation and intent behind a governmental measure are irrelevant.[50] Only the economic results would be relevant. The tribunal in *Siemens* was also unwilling to consider the nature and purpose of the measure.[51]

Nevertheless, on the other hand, the existence and validity of the concept of police powers has been confirmed by several other tribunals, enabling considerations of the purpose of the measure taken.[52] In *Saluka Investments BV v Czech Republic*, the tribunal stated, for instance, that:

the principle that a State does not commit an expropriation and is thus not liable to pay compensation to a dispossessed alien investor when it adopts general regulations that are

---

[46] H Mann, 'International Investment Agreements, Business and Human Rights: Key Issues and Opportunities', International Institute for Sustainable Development, Winnipeg (2008) 18, available at <http://www.iisd.org/pdf/2008/iia_business_human_rights.pdf> (referring to *Black's Law Dictionary* (6th edn, 1990)).

[47] H Mann, 'The Final Decision in *Methanex v. United States*: Some New Wine in Some New Bottles', International Institute for Sustainable Development, Winnipeg (2005) 6, available at <http://www.iisd.org/pdf/2005/commentary_methanex.pdf>. This can be compared with the wording of GATS, Art I.3(c) that talks of 'exercise of governmental authority'.

[48] Mann, n 46 above, 17.

[49] See *Compañia del Desarrollo de Santa Elena*, n 20 above, at para 71. For a more detailed overview, see ch 22 in this volume.

[50] *Metalclad Corp v Mexico*, ICSID Case No ARB(AF)/97/1, Award, 30 August 2000, at para 110.   [51] *Siemens v Argentina*, n 39 above, at para 354. See also Mann, n 46 above, 22.

[52] The Iran-US Claims Tribunal held in SEDCO that: 'it is an accepted principle of international law that a State is not liable for economic injury which is a consequence of bona fide "regulation" within the accepted police power of states'. See Iran-US Claims Tribunal, *SEDCO Inc v National Iranian Oil Co*, ITL 59-129-3, 27 March 1986, at para 275. In *SD Myers*, a NAFTA tribunal ruled that 'the general body of precedent usually does not treat regulatory action as amounting to expropriation'. See *SD Myers*, n 20 above, at para 281. See also *Feldman v Mexico*, ICSID Case No ARB(AF)/99/1, NAFTA Chapter 11 Arbitration Tribunal, Award on Merits, 16 December 2002, at paras 100, 103, and 112; and *Methanex v United States*, UNCITRAL NAFTA Chapter 11 Arbitration Tribunal, Final Award, 3 August 2005, pt V, ch D, at para 7.

'commonly accepted as within the police power of States' forms part of customary international law today.[53]

This is the case when, 'in the normal exercise of their regulatory powers, they adopt in a non-discriminatory manner bona fide regulations that are aimed at the general welfare'.[54] This latter approach is also incorporated in the latest bilateral investment treaties. In the US Model BIT (2004), it is stated that:

except in rare circumstances, non-discriminatory regulatory actions by a party that are designed and applied to protect legitimate public welfare objectives, such as public health, safety, and the environment, do not constitute indirect expropriations.[55]

Similar provisions are found in Canada's model Foreign Investment Promotion and Protection Agreement (FIPPA).[56] Indicative in this regard is the revised Spain/Mexico BIT from 2006 which was revised as compared to the BIT on which basis the tribunal ruled in *Tecmed*.[57] Furthermore, in the regional agreement between Eastern and Southern African states bona fide police powers to protect or enhance legitimate public welfare objectives are not considered to amount to indirect expropriation.[58] What is evident from those recent

[53] *Saluka Investments*, n 15 above, at para 262.   [54] Ibid., at para 255.
[55] See US Model BIT (2004), Annex B, para 4, sub b.
[56] See FIPPA, Art 13, para 1:
   Neither Party shall nationalise or expropriate a covered investment either directly, or indirectly through measures having an effect equivalent to nationalization or expropriation (hereinafter referred to as 'expropriation'), except for a public purpose, in accordance with due process of law, in a non-discriminatory manner and on prompt, adequate and effective compensation.
See also FIPPA, Annex B.13(1), sub c:
   Except in rare circumstances, such as when a measure or series of measures are so severe in the light of their purpose that they cannot be reasonably viewed as having been adopted and applied in good faith, non-discriminatory measures of a Party that are designed and applied to protect legitimate public welfare objectives, such as health, safety and the environment, do not constitute indirect expropriation.
[57] Bilateral investment treaty Spain-Mexico 1996, Art 5(1):
   La nacionalización, expropiación, o cualquier otra medida de características o efectos similares (en adelante 'expropiación') que pueda ser adoptada por las autoridades de una Parte Contratante contra las inversiones en su territorio de inversores de la otra Parte Contratante, deberá aplicarse exclusivamente por razones de utilidad pública, conforme a las disposiciones legales, en ningún caso será discriminatoria y dará lugar al pago de una indemnización al inversor o a su causahabiente o sucesor legal conforme a los párrafos 2 y 3 del presente Artículo.
See also Bilateral investment treaty Spain-Mexico 2006, Art 5(1):
   Ninguna Parte Contratante expropiará o nacionalizará una inversión, directa o indirectamente a través de medidas equivalentes a expropiación o nacionalización ('expropiación'), salvo que sea: (a) por causa de utilidad pública; (b) sobre bases no discriminatorias; (c) conforme al principio de legalidad; y (d) mediante el pago de una indemnización conforme al párrafo 2.
[58] Common Market for Eastern and Southern Africa Investment Agreement for the COMESA Common Investment Area, Art 20.8:

developments in state practice is that in response to the interpretations by tribunals, states are doing their utmost to protect their regulatory capabilities from foreign investors' claims.[59] States do this by incorporating provisions that clarify the scope and extent of the concept of police powers, placing restrictions on too expansive interpretations of expropriation by arbitration tribunals.[60]

Secondly, apart from uncertainty about the scope of the concept of police powers, it is also not clear to what extent (all) human rights form part of the concept of policy powers. Indeed, from the viewpoint of human rights law, the wording of *police* powers may signify a particular connotation with civil and political rights. Nonetheless, with regard to the provisions highlighted above that clarify the scope and extent of the concept of police powers, it could be argued that the *public welfare* objectives listed cover a broad spectrum and are illustrative instead of exhaustive, as is implied by the wording of 'such as'.[61] In the Free Trade Agreement between the Republic of Korea and the United States, this is also made explicit in a footnote: 'For greater certainty, the list of "legitimate public welfare objectives" in subparagraph (b) is not exhaustive.'[62] Furthermore, it could be argued that because of the phrase 'except in rare circumstances', the model agreements create a presumption against the existence of regulatory takings for which compensation should be paid.[63] This would be in line with Mann, who argues that restrictions of the right to regulate, in the form of complying with investment agreements, is a departure from the general right to regulate, which is a basic feature of sovereignty.[64] Although it cannot be concluded with certainty, it seems possible to argue that the promotion and protection of human rights in principle would be covered by the phrase 'legitimate public welfare objectives' as can be found in the US Model BIT, the Canadian FIPPA, and the regional agreement between Eastern and Southern African. An additional argument for this is that states have laid down in the 1993 Vienna Declaration that

> Consistent with the right of states to regulate and the customary international law principles on police powers, bona fide regulatory measures taken by a Member State that are designed and applied to protect or enhance legitimate public welfare objectives, such as public health, safety and the environment, shall not constitute an indirect expropriation under this Article.

[59] Mann, n 46 above, 25.

[60] C McLachlan, L Shore, and M Weiniger, *International Investment Arbitration: Substantive Principles* (2007) 280.

[61] J Coe Jr, 'Emerging Dilemmas in International Economic Arbitration: The State of Investor-State Arbitration – Some Reflections on Professor Brower's Plea for Sensible Principles' (2005) American University International Law Review 929–956, 943.

[62] This footnote refers to Annex 11-b (3)b:
> Except in rare circumstances, such as, for example, when an action or a series of actions is extremely severe or disproportionate in light of its purpose or effect, non-discriminatory regulatory actions by a Party that are designed and applied to protect legitimate public welfare objectives, such as public health, safety, the environment, and real estate price stabilization (through, for example, measures to improve the housing conditions for low-income households), do not constitute indirect expropriations.

[63] Coe, n 61 above, 943.   [64] Mann, n 42 above, 5.

the protection and promotion of human rights is the *first* responsibility of governments.[65]

Where states have not incorporated a provision that serves as guidance for tribunals to interpret the scope and extent of the concept of police powers, there might prima facie exist more difficulties. Nevertheless, the concept of police powers is a flexible one, and reference to the promotion of the general welfare in the *Black's Law Dictionary* definition seems to suggest the possibility of human rights to qualify as such. In *Saluka*, the tribunal adopted even a more flexible concept, because it talks of measures 'aimed at the general welfare'. Besides, the NAFTA tribunal in *Methanex* did not refer to the concept of police powers explicitly, but only required a public purpose. Consequently, it did not have to discuss whether or not the police powers concept applied only to health measures and could not be extended to cover environmental measures, as the United States argued. In this way the tribunal adopted a modern regulatory approach to the police powers concept.[66] Such an approach leaves even more possibilities for human rights arguments to be taken into account.

A third and final difficulty with the concept of police powers is that a too wide interpretation could have negative consequences for the protection of investment. This could run counter to the reasonable expectations of the parties, who agreed on the investment agreement.[67] Construing a wide concept of police powers entails the danger of an almost unlimited regulatory capacity of states to adopt new measures in the general interest. It could cut back the protection of foreign investment against abuse or unjustified use of police powers by the host state.[68]

In the light of these three points, the significance of the application of the principle of proportionality, which will be exhaustively analysed in the next section, becomes clear. Xiuli states that the principle of proportionality that protects regulatory measures with public interest objectives exercised in good faith is perhaps the only way to deal with public and private interests which may be involved simultaneously.[69] Moreover, both the WTO and the EC adjudicative bodies use the principle of proportionality to balance private parties' interests with the public interest of complying with international human rights obligations by construing the border between legitimate governmental regulation and excessive, discriminatory, abusive, and protectionist interference with private commercial interests.[70] The principle of proportionality can therefore be

---

[65] Vienna Declaration, World Conference on Human Rights, Vienna, 14–25 June 1993, UN Doc A/CONF.157/24 (Part I) (1993) 20.

[66] Mann, n 47 above, 6.

[67] T Eres, 'The Limits of GATT Article XX: A Back Door for Human Rights?' (2004) 35(4) Georgetown Journal of International Law 597–635, 630.

[68] U Kriebaum, 'Privatizing Human Rights: The Interface Between International Investment Protection and Human Rights' in A Reinisch and U Kriebaum (eds), *The Law of International Relations* (2007) 182.   [69] H Xiuli, n 4 above, 642–643.

[70] T Waelde and A Kolo, 'Environmental Regulation, Investment Protection and "Regulatory Taking" in International Law' (2001) 50(4) ICLQ 811–848, 832.

used as a tool to constrain recourse to the concept of police powers as a justification for measures taken, and restrict its invocation to measures taken in good faith with genuine and legitimate objectives.

Next to the possibility of invoking human rights through the concept of police powers, there is also a second route to invoke human rights when investment agreements explicitly lay down general exceptions.[71] The US Model BIT contains such a general exception clause with regard to national security.[72] The Energy Charter Treaty also incorporates a provision that deals with exception in the context of the maintenance of public order and the protection of human, animal or plant life or health.[73] The Norway Model BIT even has a provision dealing with general exceptions that is applicable to the whole treaty, including expropriation.[74] The commentary makes clear that the clause on general exceptions is based on GATS, Article XIV, with certain terminological adjustments to adapt the text to investment agreements.[75] It is interesting to note here that the Norwegian Government has not entered into new BITs since the middle of the 1990s, because the government was concerned about the compatibility of, amongst other things, provisions relating to compensation for expropriation with its constitution, and the impact of the agreements upon policy-making in developing countries.

General exceptions are increasingly being included in newly negotiated or renegotiated international investment agreements. This is evidence of the

---

[71] In WTO law, the general exceptions in GATT, Art XX or GATS, Arts XIV and XIVbis constitute opening windows for the application of non-trade law through interpretation.

[72] Art 18 of the US Model BIT states:

Nothing in this Treaty shall be construed: 1. to require a Party to furnish or allow access to any information the disclosure of which it determines to be contrary to its essential security interests; or 2. to preclude a Party from applying measures that it considers necessary for the fulfilment of its obligations with respect to the maintenance or restoration of international peace or security, or the protection of its own essential security interests.

[73] See ECT, Art 24. Nonetheless, the exceptions do not apply to the prohibition of expropriation.

[74] See Norway Model BIT, Art 24:

Subject to the requirement that such measures are not applied in a manner which would constitute a means of arbitrary or unjustifiable discrimination between investments or between investors, or a disguised restriction on international [trade or] investment, nothing in this Agreement shall be construed to prevent a Party from adopting or enforcing measures necessary: i. to protect public morals or to maintain public order; ii. to protect human, animal or plant life or health; iii. to secure compliance with laws and regulations that are not inconsistent with the provisions of this Agreement; iv. for the protection of national treasures of artistic, historic or archaeological value; or v. for the protection of the environment.

The right to regulate is expressly embedded in Art 12 of the BIT:

Nothing in this Agreement shall be construed to prevent a Party from adopting, maintaining or enforcing any measure otherwise consistent with this Agreement that it considers appropriate to ensure that investment activity is undertaken in a manner sensitive to health, safety or environmental concerns.

Articles 25–27 also encompass prudential regulation, security, and cultural exceptions.

[75] See 'Comments on the model for future investment agreements', n 43 above, 10.

intention of states to enhance their control over the interpretation by tribunals of investment key provisions. Up until now, there has been very little arbitral practice related to general exceptions. In the very recent *Continental Casualty Co v Argentina*,[76] however, the tribunal ruled on the exception found in Article 11 of the US/Argentina BIT, which provides an exception for state measures to maintain public order or for the protection of its own essential security interests. Nevertheless, the majority of investment agreements does *not* (yet) provide for explicit general exceptions. This is a significant state of affairs because the inclusion of general public interest exceptions would be the most transparent and predictable way for tribunals to deal with human rights law.[77] An alternative would be to add an interpretative note clarifying the scope and extent of the concept of police powers, as in the US Model BIT. Lacking that, it is for tribunals to take up the challenge and come to a human rights consistent interpretation of investment law provisions.

B. The Practice of Proportionality Testing in Investor-State Arbitration Regarding Expropriation

The proportionality principle constitutes a legal and judicial standard to assess the reach and effect of measures taken by states or individuals. In particular, it facilitates the solution of conflicts or tensions between different rights and obligations by providing a tool to evaluate justifications for interferences with other rights and obligations. The principle is used to determine whether a measure has gone too far, in law or in fact. It helps to construe the border between legitimate governmental regulation and excessive interference with rights and obligations that states hold simultaneously. Accordingly, the principle of proportionality is applied by the ECJ, especially with regard to economic free movement law, the ECtHR, the US Supreme Court with regard to the interstate commerce clause, and the WTO Appellate Body.[78]

The proportionality principle is generally considered to be composed of three sub-elements: suitability, necessity, and proportionality.[79] *Suitability* requires that the governmental measure is appropriate or helpful to achieve its objectives. Therefore, a causal relationship should exist between the objective and the measure.[80] It further demands that the objective in itself must be just.[81] *Necessity* requires that means are necessary to achieve the end and that the state takes the least restrictive and burdensome, but equally effective, measure.[82] *Proportionality stricto sensu* demands that the effects of the measure on the investor's interest are not disproportionate or excessive compared with the public purpose.

---

[76] *Continental Casualty Co v Argentina*, ICSID Case No ARB/03/9, Award, 5 September 2008.
[77] Van Aaken, n 2 above, 20.
[78] Waelde and Kolo, n 70 above, 832.
[79] Xiuli, n 4 above, 636; and Andenas and Zleptnig, n 4 above, 74.
[80] Andenas and Zleptnig, 74.   [81] Xiuli, 636.   [82] Andenas and Zleptnig, 75.

An analysis of arbitration practice regarding expropriation shows that tribunals have adopted different approaches to the process of balancing and to the use of the proportionality principle. Sometimes, the principle is explicitly referred to, while at other times only some of its (sub) elements are mentioned in the reasoning of the tribunal. Therefore, the focus of the analysis here is not only on what tribunals have *said*, but also on what they seem to have *done*.

The first case in which an arbitral tribunal used the principle of proportionality was in *Tecmed*.[83] In this case, the US Tecmed company contested that the non-renewal of the permit to operate a landfill of hazardous waste by Mexico's environmental agency amounted to (indirect) expropriation. Mexico argued that the measure did not constitute an expropriation, but should be considered as a legitimate regulatory action to protect the environment. In this context, Mexico also referred to the social and political pressure by the local community, because of the investor's performance. In order to determine whether or not the measure would constitute expropriation, the tribunal reasoned that the proportionality of the measure in relation to the public interest should be taken into account. According to the arbitral tribunal, 'there must be a reasonable relationship of proportionality between the charge or weight imposed to the foreign investor and the aim sought to be realised by any expropriatory measure'.[84] Interestingly, in this context the tribunal referred to several rulings of the European Court of Human Rights, particularly to *James v UK*:

Not only must a measure depriving a person of his property pursue, on the facts as well as in principle, a legitimate aim 'in the public interest', but there must also be a reasonable relationship of proportionality between the means employed and the aim sought to be realised.[85]

The tribunal noted that in the resolution adopted by the Mexican authorities, no reasons of public interest or public emergency were specified and that the order was merely inspired by socio-political considerations. In the light of this intention, the resolution was deemed to be disproportional and, thus, to violate the BIT and international law. The tribunal found that there did not exist a situation of such severity that justified the deprivation or neutralization of the economic or commercial value of the investment.[86] This reasoning does imply, however, that had the situation been more serious and urgent, the proportionality analysis could have led to a different determination to the effect that no expropriation had occurred. For this reason, the *amici curiae* in *Suez*[87] refer to this *Tecmed* passage in support of their argument that the potential breakdown

[83] *Técnicas Medioambientales Tecmed, SA v Mexico*, ICSID Case No ARB (AF)/00/2, Award, 29 May 2003. [84] Ibid., at para 122.
[85] The tribunal quotes ECtHR, *James and ors v United Kingdom*, 8793/79 ECHR, 21 February 1986, at para 50. It further referred to ECtHR, *Matos e Silva, Lda, and ors v Portugal*, Judgment, 16 September 1996, 92, at p 19; ECtHR, *Mellacher and ors v Austria*, Judgment, 19 December 1989, 48, at para 24; and ECtHR, *Pressos Compañía Naviera and ors v Belgium*, Judgment, 20 November 1995, 38, at para 19. [86] *Tecmed*, n 83 above, at para 139.
[87] *Suez, Sociedad General de Aguas de Barcelona*, n 34 above.

of essential services could result in a public health emergency.[88] On the other hand, seen from the perspective of the foreign investor, this (sub-)element of necessity in the measures taken by the host state can constrain the exercise of the police powers and the use of it as justification by the state.

In *Azurix v Argentina*, the foreign investor alleged that Argentina subjected its water and sewage concession to expropriation without compensation and that Argentina further denied fair and equitable treatment and full protection and security. Azurix complained that the reaction of the provincial health authorities to the algae outbreak was insufficient, because they failed to finish the work on the systems and equipment. Azurix also accused the government of stirring up public uproar by warning customers that the tap water should be boiled and inciting consumers to refuse to pay their water bills. In this case, the tribunal approvingly referred to *Tecmed*. It did not, however, assess the underlying intentions of the governmental measure, because it found that 'the impact on the investment was not to the extent required to amount to an expropriation'.[89]

Nevertheless, the remarks of the tribunal in *Azurix* clarify the relevance of the principle of proportionality in relation to the concept of police powers. The tribunal stated that 'for the Tribunal, the issue is not so much whether the measure concerned is legitimate and serves a public purpose, but whether it is a measure that, being legitimate and serving a public purpose, should give rise to a compensation claim'.[90] It referred to the ruling in *SD Myers*[91] with regard to the criterion of bona fide regulation within the accepted police powers as being insufficient. The tribunal agreed with Judge Higgins, who criticiszed the intellectual viability of the difference between expropriation and regulation based on public purpose: 'is not the State in both cases (that is, either by a taking for a public purpose or by regulating) purporting to act in the common good? And in each case has the owner of the property not suffered loss?'[92] The tribunal therefore concluded that the public purpose criterion should be complemented and it consequently invoked *Tecmed* and the proportionality principle developed therein.[93]

Biwater forms an interesting continuation of this line of cases.[94] Tanzania privatized its water system in 2003 and transferred control to the Biwater subsidiary City Water Services (CWS). The Government, however, took control back in 2005 when it found that water and sewerage services had deteriorated under the management of CWS, because there were problems with the supply of water. Tanzania not only seized Biwater's assets, but also occupied City Water's facilities and deported part of the staff. The defendant state, Tanzania, invoked a certain margin of appreciation, thereby referring to a number of cases of the ECtHR. Tanzania's position was summarized by the

---

[88] Ibid., at para 24.

[89] *Azurix v Argentina*, ICSID Case No ARB/01/12, Award, 14 July 2006, at para 322.

[90] Ibid., at para 310.   [91] *SD Myers*, n 20 above.

[92] *Azurix*, n 89 above, at para 310.   [93] Ibid., at para 311.

[94] *Biwater Gauff*, n 34 above, Award, 24 July 2008.

tribunal as follows: 'Water and sanitation services are vitally important, and the Republic has more than a right to protect such services in case of a crisis: it has a moral and perhaps even a legal obligation to do so.'[95] This, in combination with the fact that City Water had created a real threat to public health and welfare, led Tanzania to conclude that it was not unreasonable for it to get rid of City Water's control over the water system.[96]

In solving the case the tribunal did not, however, elaborate on the margin of appreciation and the level of deference that the Tanzanian Government may have enjoyed. It merely concluded that the measures Tanzania have taken, more specific occupation of City Water's facilities, and usurpation of management control were:

unreasonable and arbitrary, unjustified by any public purpose (there being no emergency at the time), and the most obvious display of *puissance publique*. In effect, City Water was completely shut out of the Project, in violation of its rights under the Treaty, without any adequate justification.[97]

With regard to the deportation of the staff, it concluded that 'in all the circumstances, therefore, there was no necessity or impending public purpose to justify the Government's intervention in the way that took place'.[98] On this basis, amongst other things, the tribunal concluded that, on a cumulative basis, the measures taken by Tanzania amounted to an expropriation.[99] Although the principle of proportionality was not explicitly referred to, it is undeniable that some type of balancing occurred here, in which the sub-elements of the principle of proportionality were implied.

The very recent case of *Continental Casualty*[100] involved a similar approach. In this case, Continental Casualty, a provider of workers' compensation insurance, complained that the loss in the value of its investment, due to a series of emergency measures adopted by Argentina during the financial crisis of 2001 to 2002, amounted, amongst other things, to (indirect) expropriation. The measures included restrictions on capital transfers out of Argentina, restrictions on the rescheduling of cash deposits, the pesification of US dollar deposits, and the pesification and default of certain Argentine debt obligations. Argentina defended the measures by relying on Article XI in the US-Argentina BIT, which provides exceptions for measures necessary for the maintenance of public order and the protection of essential security interests.

In this case the sub-elements of the proportionality principle are also clearly reflected in the award. The tribunal dealt especially with the element of necessity and the reasonably available alternatives.[101] It further investigated

[95] Ibid., at para 434.   [96] Ibid., at para 436.   [97] Ibid., at para 503.
[98] Ibid., at para 515.   [99] Ibid., at para 519.
[100] *Continental Casualty Co*, n 76 above.
[101] Ibid., at paras 189–231. In this regard the tribunal explicitly refers to a 'process of weighing and balancing of factors', thereby relying extensively on the legal practice of the WTO/GATT Appellate Body:

The necessity of a measure should be determined through 'a process of weighing and balancing of factors' which usually includes the assessment of the following

whether the measures contributed to the realization of their legitimate aims, and were apt to make a material or decisive contribution, which is what the element of suitability requires. The tribunal concluded in this regard that the measures 'were in part inevitable, or unavoidable, in part indispensable and in any case material or decisive in order to react positively to the crisis' and that there was undoubtedly 'a genuine relationship of end and means in this regard'.[102] It also stated that the measures were applied in 'a reasonable and proportionate way' and 'were basically limited to the economic and financial aspects of the economic crisis', thereby not interfering with private contracts, nor did they entail a complete (re)nationalization.[103] In this wording, the sub-element of proportionality *stricto sensu* appears to be present, because the tribunal concluded that the measures did not go further than and were not excessive in relation to the objective pursued.

What becomes clear from those cases involving human rights interests on both sides of the balance is that an objective test is needed to evaluate the regulatory measures taken by a state in order to prevent the abuse of the police powers concept. The principle of proportionality is aimed at protecting measures taken in good faith in the public interest by differentiating them from abusive and protectionist governmental action.[104] It further avoids that measures satisfy the police powers test when they are in fact excessive in their effect.[105]

In this sense, it is significant that the United States has begun to include direct references to the proportionality standard in some of its agreements.[106] In addition, the practice of the ECtHR, the WTO Appellate Body, and the ECJ shows that measures alleged to be taken in the public interest are subject to a closer investigation that balances the public interest with private interests through the lens of the principle of proportionality.

Although relying on the proportionality principle therefore seems the most logical approach, the *amici curiae* in *Suez* argued that applying the proportionality principle would be redundant:[107] 'Considerations of proportionality are

---

three factors: the relative importance of interests or values furthered by the challenged measures, the contribution of the measure to the realization of the ends pursued by it and the restrictive impact of the measure on international commerce (para 194).

[102] Ibid., at paras 197 and 232.   [103] Ibid., at para 232.   [104] Xiuli, n 4 above, 642.
[105] Ibid.
[106] See, eg Annex 11-b (3)b of the Free Trade Agreement between the Republic of Korea and the United States of America:

Except in rare circumstances, such as, for example, when an action or a series of actions is extremely severe or disproportionate in light of its purpose or effect, non-discriminatory regulatory actions by a Party that are designed and applied to protect legitimate public welfare objectives, such as public health, safety, the environment, and real estate price stabilization (through, for example, measures to improve the housing conditions for low-income households), do not constitute indirect expropriations.

[107] The *amici curiae* only address the issue of proportionality in the alternative, when their argument that the measure is covered by the concept of police powers is rejected. See *Sociedad General de Aguas and Vivendi Universal, SA and Argentina, Amicus Curiae* Submission, n 87 above, 21.

unnecessary when the application of police powers is limited to genuine situations involving the public interest'.[108] This is an unconvincing line of argumentation. For a genuine invocation of the concept of police powers to be upheld, a more thorough investigation by the tribunal is necessary. This goes further than *merely declaring* that a measure was taken in the 'public interest' with a legitimate objective, and therefore somehow *automatically* complying with the police powers concept. In addition, the police powers doctrine in itself embodies a requirement of reasonableness.[109] Both of these substantive 'conditions' are far from clear-cut and depend upon the circumstances of the case – necessitating a consideration of proportionality. Investment law 'proportionality' is not *a priori* at odds with human rights obligations incumbent upon states, particularly because investors' interests also have human rights aspects.

A second observation relates to how in *Tecmed* the tribunal explicitly referred to the case law of the European Court of Human Rights, concerning Article 1 of the ECHR First Protocol that deals with the right to property. This Court also adopts a balancing approach in which the private wellbeing and quality of life is balanced against the general economic interests of the community.[110] Therefore, at first sight, there might seem to be no difference in the way in which the tribunal and the court apply the principle of proportionality. In *Tecmed* and *Azurix*, the arbitral tribunals have used the proportionality principle to determine whether or not an expropriation has occurred.[111] The ECtHR has used the proportionality principle to determine whether or not there has been a breach of Article 1 of Protocol No 1.[112]

Nevertheless, the investment law proportionality test cannot be directly equated to the human rights law proportionality test. The difference is due to the application of the margin of appreciation doctrine by the ECtHR.[113] The European Court has recognized that states maintain a certain margin of appreciation with regard to governmental measures taken in the public interest, inter

---

[108] Ibid., at 21 and 25–26. [109] See *Feldman*, n 52 above.

[110] See, eg ECtHR, *Lopez Ostra v Spain*, 16798/90 [1994] ECHR 46, 9 December 1994; and ECtHR, *Hatton and ors v United Kingdom*, 36022/97 ECHR, 10 February 2001 and 8 July 2003 (Grand Chamber).

[111] See *Azurix*, n 89 above, at para 312: 'The Tribunal finds that these additional elements provide useful guidance for purposes of determining whether regulatory actions would be expropriatory and give rise to compensation.' It thereby referred to *James*, n 85 above, at para 50.

[112] *James*, n 85 above, at para 72.

[113] Noteworthy in this regard is the fact that the provision in the Norway Model BIT primarily derives from ECHR, Protocol 1, Art 1, as the commentary makes clear. See Norway Model BIT, Art 6 (expropriation):

> 1. A Party shall not expropriate or nationalise an investment of an investor of the other Party except in the public interest and subject to the conditions provided for by law and by the general principles of international law. 2. The preceding provision shall not, however, in any way impair the right of a Party to enforce such laws as it deems necessary to control the use of property in accordance with the general interest or to secure the payment of taxes or other contributions or penalties.

See 'Comments on the model for future investment agreements', n 43 above, 10.

alia because national authorities are better placed to appreciate the local society and its needs.[114] As the court has adopted a wide view of the notion of public interest by referring to political, economic, and social issues which differ widely between states, it has concluded that the margin of appreciation should also be a wide one. The state's judgment should therefore be accepted, unless it is manifestly unreasonable.[115]

Something approximating a 'margin of appreciation' approach has also found its way into investment arbitration. Initially, the tribunal in *Siemens* held that the margin of appreciation that states have under the ECHR is not found in the bilateral investment treaty between Argentina and Germany, or in customary international law.[116] Nevertheless, arbitral tribunals have referred to related concepts such as 'deference' or 'restraint'. In *Tecmed*, the tribunal talked of 'due deference owing to the State when defining the issues that affect its public policy or the interests of society as a whole, as well as the actions that will be implemented to protect such values'.[117] It is, nevertheless, remarkable that the tribunal proceeded in a way quite comparable to the ECtHR.[118]

Recently, the tribunal in *Continental Casualty* explicitly dealt with the 'margin of appreciation', and stated that 'a certain deference to such a discretion . . . may well be by now a general feature of international law also in respect of the protection of foreign investment under BITs'.[119] It still remains to be seen in what way tribunals will seek to rely exactly on the concept of margin of appreciation.[120] So far, tribunals have used the concept particularly to support and

---

[114] *James*, n 85 above, at para 46.   [115] Ibid.   [116] *Siemens*, n 39 above, at para 354.

[117] *Tecmed*, n 83 above, at para 122.

[118] Ibid., at para 122:

> such situation does not prevent the Arbitral Tribunal, without thereby questioning such due deference, from examining the actions of the State in light of Article 5(1) of the Agreement to determine whether such measures are reasonable with respect to their goals, the deprivation of economic rights and the legitimate expectations of who suffered such deprivation. There must be a reasonable relationship of proportionality between the charge or weight imposed to the foreign investor and the aim sought to be realised by any expropriatory measure.

Thereby the tribunal cited the ECtHR cases *Mellacher*, and *Pressos Compañia Naviera*, both n 85 above.

[119] *Continental Casualty Co*, n 76 above, at para 181. The tribunal further recognizes that 'this objective assessment must contain a significant margin of appreciation for the State applying the particular measure: a time of grave crisis is not the time for nice judgments, particularly when examined by others with the disadvantage of hindsight'. Nevertheless, the tribunal stresses that:

> caution must be exercised in allowing a party unilaterally to escape from its treaty . . . This is especially so if the party invoking the allegedly self-judging nature of the exemption can thereby remove the issue, and hence the claim of a treaty breach by the investor against the host state, from arbitral review (para 187).

The tribunal thus proceeds almost in a similar way as in *Tecmed*, n 83 above, at para 122.

[120] In *Azurix*, the respondent Argentina invoked the principle of deference in order to define the public interest in the context of expropriation, and quoted *SD Myers* with regard to the fair and equitable treatment standard. In both instances, the tribunal did not touch this issue explicitly. See *Azurix*, n 89 above, at paras 291 and 333.

add extra argument to the police powers doctrine. From another perspective, it could be argued that by relying on the ECHR wording of 'margin of appreciation', tribunals de facto inserted a pro-regulation bias, namely, they have started measuring 'proportionality' from the perspective of non-investment law within the context of investment law itself. That could be seen as a highly significant move.

Apart from the methodological significance of human-rights-inspired proportionality testing, there are also important substantive lessons to be learnt from ECHR practice with regard to human rights issues directly relevant for investor-state arbitration about expropriation. In determining whether or not a violation of property rights has occurred, the ECtHR requires, first and foremost, a legal basis for the deprivation of property.[121] In this way, it is ensured that a measure is reasonable and foreseeable and that the state complies with the rule of law and the principle of stability and transparency.[122] Furthermore, the measures taken must be proportionate. Article 1 of the First Protocol is interpreted by the Court to constitute an obligation on the state to strike a 'fair balance' between the demands of the general interest of the community and the requirements of the protection of the individual's fundamental rights. The requisite balance will not be found if the person concerned has had to bear 'an individual and excessive burden'.[123]

Therefore, it is evident from ECtHR practice that the right to property is relative and not an absolute standard. This is because the practice of balancing implies that there may be circumstances where the public interest is valued as more important than the need to protect the individual's/investor's rights. The right to property can therefore be limited by the principle of proportionality when it is applied to strike a fair balance between the public interest and the respective human right. Moreover, the court's practice evidences a holistic view of all human rights. The court identifies the interests that are protected by the right to property in a way which reflects 'the whole of the Convention'.[124] This approach might be equally relevant for investment law – first, it may ease the possible detrimental effects of the 'institutional isolation' of the right to property within investment law and, second, it reminds us of the necessity to view human rights as reflective of the purpose of sustainable human development that also underlies investment law.

It is encouraging that these substantive lessons are by now also starting to be reflected in investment arbitration practice. Notable in this regard is the award that the tribunal rendered in *Continental Casualty*.[125] The tribunal referred to

---

[121] ECtHR, *Frizen v Russia*, 58254/00 ECHR, 24 March 2005, at para 34.

[122] OECD, '"Indirect Expropriation" and the "Right To Regulate" in International Investment Law', OECD Working Paper No 2004/4 (2004) 17, available at <http://www.oecd.org/dataoecd/22/54/33776546.pdf>.   [123] *James*, n 85 above, at para 50.

[124] *Sporrong and Lönnroth v Sweden*, 7151/75; 7152/75 ECHR, 23 September 1982, at para 69.

[125] *Continental Casualty Co*, n 76 above.

and acknowledged the ECHR and the jurisprudence of the ECtHR.[126] In addition, it stated explicitly that:

On the other hand, there are limitations to the use of property in the public interest that fall within typical government regulations of property entailing mostly inevitable limitations imposed in order to ensure the rights of others or of the general public (being ultimately beneficial also to the property affected) ... These restrictions are not therefore considered a form of expropriation and do not require indemnification, provided however that they do not affect property in an intolerable, discriminatory or disproportionate manner.

In conclusion, it may be observed that there appears to be an emerging, but still ambiguous practice of proportionality testing in investor-state arbitration. The appropriateness of expropriatory measures allegedly justified by human rights considerations is first measured from the viewpoint of investment law proportionality. More indirectly, however, arbitrators equally seem to add a measure of human rights proportionality to their balancing exercise particularly by way of references to ECtHR case law. This is a significant development that is to be encouraged. Yet, it is also just a first step toward developing an arbitration practice reflective of states' multiple international legal obligations, and of the fact that human rights weigh in on both sides of the balance of state and investor interests.

IV. Beneath Balancing: From Applicability to Invocation and Effective Interpretation of Human Rights in Investor-State Arbitration

After an overview of the relevant practice, it may be useful to point out that connecting human rights considerations to investment arbitration is still in its infancy. Several barriers are yet to be overcome – by states, human rights activists, and investors. In this section we will highlight a number of barriers that still stand in the way of the effective invocation and consistent interpretation of human rights in investment arbitration.

How are human rights to come on the agenda of the particular dispute in the first place? Logically, an occasion of balancing human rights imperatives and investor interests in investor-state arbitration hinges on human rights being invoked by one of the parties. Yet, arbitrators are unlikely to start referring to human rights law on their own motion, in a rabbit-from-the-hat fashion. Given the complex nature of expropriation cases, where human rights play a role on both sides of the balance, in theory both states as obligation holders and investors as right holders (namely, of the human right to property) could invoke human rights. Yet, the likeliest scenario is that the invocation of human rights will be done by, or

---

[126] Ibid., at paras 276 and 279, fnn 402, 405, and 408.

on behalf of, the state. The UN High Commissioner for Human Rights stressed the importance of states using human rights arguments before arbitral tribunals, given the absence of an international mechanism to consider claims about violations of economic, social, and cultural rights. The report therefore urges an interpretation of investment agreements in the light of the wider social context.[127]

Yet, often human rights argumentation has been neither sufficiently nor precisely articulated by those invoking it, such as *amici curiae*. It is insufficient for human rights defenders to merely point to 'the importance of' human rights. For example, in their brief in *Suez*, the *amici curiae* demanded that the tribunal should take into account that no government may validly contract away its treaty-based human rights obligations. This demand remained somewhat cryptic and low on specifics when they stressed that the 'tribunal may want to avoid any interpretation of the concession agreement that would lead to a direct conflict between Argentina's human rights obligations and its specific commitments to the claimants'.[128] Similarly, legally vague argumentation is visible in the report of the UN High Commissioner for Human Rights. With regard to the possibility of a clash of investment law and human rights obligations of states, the report merely states that 'taking into account the need to balance States' right to regulate with investors' rights, investment agreements will also establish certain exceptions to their application, giving States some flexibility to protect the public interest and promote development'.[129]

There is a danger that such observations will remain non-operational unless the grounds under the general exceptions are more precisely indicated and unless it is more clearly accounted for what the potential implications would be for the balancing exercise of human rights entering the picture as mere *exceptions*.

There are a number of concerns that need to be overcome when aiming to move towards a satisfactory balancing practice. It is often said that the interpretation of human rights law by arbitral tribunals could have implications for the human rights regime itself. It is in the context of the WTO that Eres addresses this issue:

> Before seeking to apply the WTO's enforcement mechanism on behalf of human rights, human rights advocates must seriously address a host of issues: What are the ramifications of empowering panels and the Appellate Body to analyse human rights law? Do human rights advocates really intend to abandon human rights law to trade specialists? What are the effects of WTO involvement on the consensus and good will underlying human rights law?[130]

---

[127] Report of the High Commissioner for Human Rights, 'Human Rights, Trade and Investment', E/CN.4/Sub.2/2003/9, 2003, paras 41, 54–55.
[128] *Suez, Sociedad General de Aguas de Barcelona, Amicus Curiae Submission*, n 87 above, 20. See above section III.B. for a rebuttal of the position of the *amici curiae* that proportionality considerations would be *a priori* alien to human rights justified measures aiming to rely on the policy powers concept. [129] Report of the High Commissioner, n 127 above, at para 25.
[130] Eres, n 67 above, 631.

These questions are equally relevant for investment law as well. The argument brought forward in the previously mentioned *amicus curiae* brief in *Suez* also pointed to a more methodological question as to whether human rights should be balanced at all. Weighing investors' rights with human rights would imply that human rights protection is negotiable.[131] Some argue that when the weight of human rights is made conditional upon the circumstances, human rights are given a 'shifting character' and could eventually be 'swallowed up' in the course of the balancing process.[132] Furthermore, it is often observed that when human rights are balanced with investors' rights they are actually made context-dependent. As a result, those human rights are subjected to utilitarian assessments of net benefit. Cali argues that this is essentially inconsistent with human rights protection.[133] She criticizes the above-mentioned 'fair balance' approach of the European Court of Human Rights, because in her view it falsely construes the idea that when a human right is upheld, the public interest is given up at the same time. Human rights reflect the interests of the whole society and not a specific person.

Although there may be a number of significant implications underlying these observations that would require deeper analysis, it is to be observed that most of these critical thoughts take international trade law as their basis. However, in the context of international trade law, the balance usually only contains *one* human right, at least from the human rights law perspective.[134] As we have seen, in the context of investment law, human rights are involved on *two* sides of the balance, because investment agreements essentially protect the foreign investor's right to property. In addition, an individual does not exercise its human rights in isolation, but in a society. This is the reason that human rights are often not absolute and therefore subject to balance.

Another methodological complication, which seems to be a more pertinent barrier, flows from the traditional focus of human rights as constraints on the use of power by the state. This focus is turned on its head by invoking human rights through concepts such as 'police powers', 'public security', and 'public morality' – notions that embody the top-down power of a state vis-à-vis individuals. Human rights protection and these notions are conceptually different and there may be a measure of legal tension to be expected to invoke one through the other.[135] If states refer to their human rights obligations through

---

[131] See, eg J Morijn, 'Balancing Fundamental Rights and Common Market Freedoms in Union Law: Schmidberger and Omega in the Light of the European Constitution' (2006) 12(1) European Law Journal 15–40, 40.

[132] B Cali, 'Balancing Human Rights? Methodological Problems With Weights, Scales and Proportions' (2007) 29(1) Human Rights Quarterly 251–272, 253.   [133] Ibid., 259.

[134] For a critical discussion of academic writings and judicial practice that consider some economic free movement rules as human rights in and of themselves, see J Morijn, 'Conflicts Between Fundamental Rights or Conflicting Fundamental Rights Vocabularies? An Analysis of Diverging Uses of "Fundamental Rights" in the Context of International and European Trade Law' in E Brems (ed), *Conflicts between Fundamental Rights* (2008) 591–617, particularly at 603–611.

[135] Morijn, n 131 above, 39.

these very notions in justifying certain measures in an investment law context, this may in fact serve to *legitimize* the very exercise of power that human rights protection typically seeks to qualify.[136]

Finally, a number of further concerns could arise when arbitral tribunals are led to interpret human rights law obligations. They have to do with the institutional setting in which the balancing is to take place. Because of the perceived lack of independence and transparency of arbitral tribunals, their competence to deal with those issues has been questioned. Especially the limited role of parties other than the state and the foreign investor has been seen as crucial. Currently, *amici curiae* are allowed to submit their observations, but whether that will change the process of balancing is, to date, still unknown.[137] Another critical aspect is the lack of judicial oversight and the confidentiality and secrecy of the proceedings, while public interests are involved. Furthermore, there are reasons to expect that arbitrators may lack expertise and may not be sufficiently qualified to interpret human rights law, a completely different field of law. Even if they are highly qualified, arbitrators are likely intuitively to appreciate human rights arguments from a different, more economical, perspective and will use a methodology of investment law to deal with human rights law. Investment law proportionality may then partly swallow up human rights law proportionality. Another concern has to do with the impartiality of arbitrators. Because arbitrators are selected by the parties themselves, there may be a professional incentive for arbitrators to rule in favour of providing wide protection to foreign investors. This is to ensure that more foreign investors will seek a remedy for alleged violations of investment agreements. Consequently, more work is created for themselves.[138] In the light of those institutional aspects, there remains uncertainty about the consequences of tribunals interpreting human rights law.

In sum, from the perspective of human rights law one needs to be aware of these issues to come to a fair assessment of the likeliness that efforts to lobby for human rights invocation will lead to a satisfactory result from a human rights viewpoint. On the other hand, the alternative of having tribunals that are simply ignoring human rights issues in the course of proceedings can be considered even less attractive. Indeed, focusing on the application of the proportionality principle entails several positive consequences as well. It not only forces states to justify the measures they have taken in relation to 'a relatively structured legal criterion', but also obliges arbitral tribunals to follow such a structured approach.[139] This in itself limits the discretion of the

[136] Cali, n 132 above, 253.   [137] Van Aaken, n 2 above, 32.
[138] S McBride, 'Reconfiguring Sovereignty: NAFTA Chapter 11 Dispute Settlement Procedures and the Issue of Public-Private Authority' (2006) 39(4) Canadian Journal of Political Science 755–775, 760; G van Harten, 'The Public-Private Distinctions in the International Arbitration of Individual Claims Against the State' (2007) 56(2) ICLQ 371–394, 393; G van Harten and M Loughlin, 'Investment Treaty Arbitration as a Species of Global Administrative Law' (2006) 17(1) European Journal of International Law 17, 121–150, 147.
[139] Andenas and Zleptnig, n 4 above, 89.

arbitrators, and makes the arbitrational process more rational, coherent, and predictable in comparison with the current situation of the often divergent approaches adopted by tribunals.

V. Conclusion

States hold different vertical international obligations in parallel, including those flowing from human rights and investment treaties, which they must seek to respect simultaneously and in good faith. When a state adopts a human rights justified measure, the rights of foreign investors under the investment treaty may be impacted in the process. In case such a scenario develops into a dispute, states' obligations flowing from international investment agreements and human rights can come into tension. The application of the principle of proportionality in the course of investor-state arbitration regarding expropriation is one of the routes through which a balancing of human rights protection imperatives and investor interests can take place. The legal question will then become whether the human rights justified measure is proportional from the viewpoint of investment law. From the viewpoint of human rights this in turn raises the question of whether solutions found in investment arbitration are 'proportional' in the sense of human rights law. In this chapter, we have addressed the latter issue.

In seeking to answer the question of whether the application of the proportionality principle in investor-state arbitration with regard to expropriation has been consistent with human rights, we first found that the complexity of investor-state disputes relates to the fact that interests on *both* sides of the balance have human rights aspects. In that light, we argued that the implications of human rights for investment law may be more complex than it is usually presented. It is more complex than usually presented by investment lawyers, who often downplay the (interpretational) relevance of international (human rights) law. We found that human rights law may in fact be seen as an articulation of one of the *own* aims of investment law, in that many investment treaties express their object and purpose in terms of sustainable development. As a matter of treaty interpretation, the object and purpose of investment law provisions need of necessity to be taken into account. Yet, it is also more complex than apparently acknowledged by many human rights activists. In these circles, it is often denied that human rights play a role *on both sides* of the balance. Moreover, it is erroneously presumed that some type of *a priori* normative irreconcilability between human rights and investment law exists. As a result, it is not seen that giving human rights a place in the investment law context is actually a *practical* problem of how multiple norms in force simultaneously can be given meaning in parallel by an investment arbitrator.

Against that background, we traced investor-state arbitration practice with regard to expropriation for evidence of how state and investor interests are being balanced. We particularly focused on the way in which states have been able to rely on the concept of 'police powers' to expropriate investors on the basis of what may be seen as human-rights-justified measures. We found that there appears to be a very recently emerging, but as yet still ambiguous practice of proportionality testing in this context. The appropriateness of human-rights-justified state measures to expropriate investors is measured first of all from the viewpoint of an investment law proportionality standard. More indirectly, however, particularly by way of references to case law of the European Court of Human Rights, arbitrators seem equally to have added a human rights proportionality measurement to their balancing exercise. By virtue of this practice of 'double proportionality' testing, it was posited that investor-state arbitration practice may be seen as merging investment and human rights law proportionality standards – a development that is to be encouraged.

Nonetheless, we argued that we are just at the beginning of these developments. In particular, we identified several remaining barriers standing in the way of effective use of human rights as accepted applicable law. States, human rights activists, investors, and arbitrators will need to overcome various further institutional and methodological hurdles to move toward a reliable practice of effective invocation and consistent interpretation that is reflective of the prime importance of human rights protection.

19

Reconciling Public Health and Investor Rights: The Case of Tobacco

*Valentina Sara Vadi**

I. Introduction

This study explores the linkage between international investment law and public health law, focusing on the specific issue of tobacco control. Since the recent inception of the WHO Framework Convention on Tobacco Control,[1] which has established cognitive and normative consensus for promoting global public health through tobacco control, states have gradually adopted a series of measures to comply with such a convention. However, international economic governance risks undermining the goal of tobacco control. International trade liberalization has significantly reduced tariff and non-tariff trade barriers, taking down the prices of tobacco products and determining an increase in cigarette smoking, particularly in low income countries.[2] Investment treaties which protect foreign assets, including trademarks and good will, have further facilitated foreign investment in the tobacco business, thus increasing competition and lowering tobacco prices. In addition, as investment treaties broadly define the notion of investment, a potential tension exists when a state adopts tobacco control measures interfering with foreign investments, as regulation may be considered as tantamount to expropriation under investment rules. As investment treaties provide foreign investors with direct access to investment arbitration, foreign investors can directly challenge national measures aimed at protecting public health and can seek compensation for the impact on their business of such regulation.

Several questions arise in this connection. Are investment treaties compatible with states' obligations to protect public health? Is investor-state arbitration a

* The author wishes to thank Professor Ernst-Ulrich Petersmann, Professor Francesco Francioni, Professor Pierre-Marie Dupuy and Dr Gus Van Harten who discussed with me some issues treated in this study and Nicola Hargreaves and Nicola Owtram for helpful comments on an earlier draft. Despite these debts, responsibility for this chapter remains hers.

[1] WHO Framework Convention on Tobacco Control, WHA Res 56.1, World Health Assembly, 56th Ass 4th plenary meeting, Annex WHO Doc A56.VR/4, 21 May 2003, (2003) 42 ILM 3, 518–539 (hereinafter, FCTC). The Convention entered into force on 27 February 2005.

[2] See World Bank/WHO, *Tobacco Control in Developing Countries* (2000).

suitable forum to protect public interests? The argument will proceed in four parts. First, the international law instruments concerning tobacco control will be sketched out. Second, an examination will be made of the regulatory framework disciplining international investment law. Third, this study will explore the conflict areas between investment governance and tobacco control, examining some recent case studies. This survey will show that, in some cases, the regime established according to investment treaties does not strike an appropriate balance between the different interests concerned. Fourth, this chapter offers a series of legal tools available to policy makers and adjudicators in order to reconcile the different interests at stake.

II. International Health Governance and Tobacco Control

Tobacco control is a fundamental aspect of contemporary public health governance. Whatever its conceptualization, be it considered a human rights issue or a mere public policy objective, it can be held that the legitimacy of such a goal is uncontested. From a legal perspective, it is important to underline the legal relevance of tobacco control not only at both national/constitutional and regional levels, but also at the international level. First, this section explores the conceptualization of tobacco control as a component of the right to health, assessing the pros and cons of this theory. Second, it scrutinizes the more neutral conceptualization of tobacco control as a fundamental policy objective and examines the relevant legal framework.

A. Linking Tobacco Control to the Right to Health

Some authors have seen tobacco control as 'a human rights issue',[3] and in particular as a component part of the right to health.[4] This argument would be based on several grounds. First, at the international level, the Committee on Economic, Social, and Cultural Rights has construed Article 12 of the International Covenant on Economic, Social, and Cultural Rights on the right to the highest attainable standard of health[5] to require states parties to implement

---

[3] See V Leary, 'Concretizing the Right to Health: Tobacco Use as a Human Right Issue' in F Coomans, F Grünfeld, I Westendorp, and J Willems (eds), *Rendering Justice to the Vulnerable: Liber Amicorum in Honour of Theo van Boven* (2000) 161.

[4] The right to health is expressly recognized in a series of international law instruments. See, for instance, WHO Constitution, 22 July 1946, preamble, 14 UNTS 185, 186–187; Universal Declaration of Human Rights GA res 217A (III), Art 25(1); Convention on the Rights of the Child, 20 November 1989, Art 24, 28 ILM 1457, 1465–1466; Convention on the Elimination of All Forms of Racial Discrimination, 21 December 1965, Art 5(e)(iv), 660 UNTS 195, 222; and Convention on the Elimination of All Forms of Discrimination Against Women, 18 December 1979, Arts 11(1)(f), 12, 1249 UNTS 13, 18–19.

[5] Art 12 of the International Covenant on Economic, Social, and Cultural Rights states:

1. The States Parties to the present Covenant recognize the right of everyone to the enjoyment of the highest attainable standard of physical and mental health.

certain tobacco control measures.[6] In particular, states are encouraged to undertake information campaigns regarding the adverse consequences of cigarette smoking.[7] By failing to undertake tobacco control initiatives, governments would violate their HR obligations to protect public health.[8] Indeed, General Comment No 14 expressly states that:

> Violations of the obligation to protect [the right to health] follow from the failure of a State to take all necessary measures to safeguard persons within their jurisdiction from infringements of the right to health by third parties. This category includes such omissions as the failure to regulate the activities of individuals, groups or corporations so as to prevent them from violating the right to health of others; the failure to protect consumers and workers from practices detrimental to health, e.g. by ... the failure to discourage production, marketing and consumption of tobacco ... the failure to discourage the continued observance of harmful ... cultural practices.[9]

Although general comments are not a primary source of law, they are deemed to be authentic or authoritative interpretations of treaty text, thus contributing to the clarification and development of the living law or *droit vivant*.[10]

Second, at the regional level, the European Court of Human Rights has affirmed the human rights dimension of tobacco control, according a wide margin of appreciation to national governments regarding the precise parameters of a tobacco regulatory regime.[11] In *Wöckel v Germany*, the European Commission on Human Rights provided guidance concerning the scope of states parties' affirmative obligations to protect non-smokers from environmental smoke.[12] In particular, as the German Government had already undertaken a public information campaign, imposed restrictions on tobacco advertising, and prohibited smoking in certain public areas, the Commission held that the applicant's right to life and respect for private and family life had not been violated, interpreting Articles 2 and 8 of the Convention as not requiring Germany to do more than it had already done. In *Novoselov v Russia*, the Court considered that the conditions

---

2. The steps to be taken by the States Parties to the present Covenant to achieve the full realization of this right shall include those necessary for: ... (c) The prevention, treatment and control of epidemic, endemic, occupational and other diseases ...
International Covenant on Economic, Social, and Cultural Rights, 16 December 1966, 993 UNTS 3, 8.

[6] UN Committee on Economic, Social, and Cultural Rights, General Comment No 14: The Right to the Highest Attainable Standard of Health (E/C.12/2000/4), 11 August 2000.

[7] General Comment No 14, para 15: 'Article 12.2 (b) also ... discourages the abuse of alcohol, and the use of tobacco, drugs and other harmful substances.'

[8] For commentary, see M Crow, 'Smokescreens and State Responsibility: Using Human Rights Strategies to Promote Global Tobacco Control' (2004) 29 Yale Journal of International Law 209–250, 211.   [9] General Comment No 14, n 6 above, para 51.

[10] Authors have stressed the extensive character of their interpretation. See G Abline, 'Les observations générales, une technique d'élargissement des droits de l'homme' (2008) Revue trimestrielle des droits de l'homme 449–479.

[11] European Convention for the Protection of Human Rights and Fundamental Freedoms, 4 November 1950, 213 UNTS 222.

[12] *Wöckel v Germany*, App No 32165/96, ECommHR 1998.

of detention had to be compatible with the prisoner's human dignity, health, and wellbeing.[13] Thus, the lack of adequate ventilation, aggravated by a general tolerance of smoking in the cell, was an element that ultimately led the Court to find a violation of Article 3 of the Convention.

Third, even national constitutional courts have adjudicated on tobacco control and linked this issue to the human rights discourse. Some courts have held that constitutional human rights norms require governments to undertake tobacco control measures.[14] For instance, in *Deora v India*, the Indian Supreme Court held that the Union of India had violated the constitutional right to health of its citizens by failing to undertake adequate tobacco control measures.[15] Similarly, the Bangladeshi Supreme Court banned the advertising of tobacco products in the mass media, to ensure protection to the right to health and human dignity, as required by the Bangladeshi Constitution.[16]

The exponents of the theory which subsumes tobacco control under the umbrella of the right to health stress that, on the one hand, this conceptualization would concretize the right to health.[17] On the other hand, it would 'contribute to advancing human well-being beyond what could be achieved through an isolated health or human rights based approach',[18] bringing 'considerable attention and rhetorical force to the issue'.[19] However, one may wonder whether such a linkage determines positive externalities for tobacco control. In other words, while there is scientific consensus on the lethal effects of tobacco smoke, there is less agreement on the need for some states to ratify the International Covenant on Economic, Social, and Cultural Rights[20] or on the customary status of the right to health.[21] Whatever the position adopted on this issue,[22] the national and regional case law shows that there is both a scientific consensus over the need of tobacco control and an increasing jurisprudential trend towards

---

[13] *Novoselov v Russia*, App No 66460/01, ECtHR, 2 June 2005, at para 39.

[14] There is an emerging jurisprudence on the scope of governments' obligations to regulate the activities of tobacco companies within their jurisdictions. For an exhaustive account of this case law, see for instance, Crow, n 8 above.

[15] *Murli S Deora v Union of India*, AIR 2002 SC 40, available at <http://www.elaw.org/node/1834>.

[16] *Nurul Islam v Bangladesh*, WP Nos 1825/99, 4521/99, 7 February 2000, available at <http://www.elaw.org/node/1768>.   [17] Leary, n 3 above, 162.

[18] Ibid., 163.   [19] Ibid., 169.

[20] Notably, the United States has signed but not ratified the International Covenant on Economic, Social, and Cultural Rights. See P Alston, 'U.S. Ratification of the Covenant on Economic, Social and Cultural Rights: The Need for an Entirely New Strategy' (1990) 84 AJIL 2, 365–393. See also CA Bradley, 'Unratified Treaties, Domestic Politics, and the US Constitution' (2007) 48 Harvard International Law Journal 2, 307–337.

[21] Some authors argue that the right to health already belongs to customary international law. See ED Kinney, 'The International Human Right to Health: What Does this Mean for Our Nation and the World?' (2001) 34 Indiana Law Review 1457.

[22] Some authors even argue that there would be an emerging human right to tobacco control. See C Dresler and S Marks, 'The Emerging Human Right to Tobacco Control' (2006) 28 Human Rights Quarterly 599–651.

linking it to the right to health. Although these cases are not formal precedents, they may have an impact on the reasoning of other courts and tribunals.[23]

B. The Framework Convention on Tobacco Control

After having scrutinized the theorization of tobacco control as a human rights issue, this section analyses the current international law instruments that discipline tobacco control. In 2003, the World Health Organization (WHO)[24] adopted of the Framework Convention on Tobacco Control (hereinafter FCTC)[25] establishing an international system of public health governance for this issue.[26] This move represents a major point break in international public health law, as the WHO had never before used the power of adopting conventions.[27]

Looking at the rationale for the change, it appears that this new approach reflects the renaissance of interest in public health law, both at the national and international level.[28] Tobacco control epitomizes a typical public health issue as it underlines the special responsibility of states in public health and requires regulation of the relationship between the state and its population and between the state and individuals who may pose a risk to the public health.[29]

More importantly, the CTC seems to be the direct result of the cognitive consensus on the lethal effects of tobacco smoke.[30] According to the WHO, tobacco consumption is the second major cause of death in the world, currently

---

[23] On judicial dialogue in HR matters, see, for instance, C McCrudden, 'Judicial Comparativism and Human Rights' in E Örükü and D Nelken (eds), *Comparative Law: a Handbook* (2007) 371–398.

[24] The WHO was established in 1948 as a specialized agency of the United Nations and was designed to promote and protect the health of all peoples. The WHO membership includes 193 countries and two associate members. See Member Country list, available at <http://www.who.int/countries/en/>. See also WHO, *Working for Health – An Introduction to the World Health Organization* (2007).

[25] See A Taylor, 'Global Health Governance and International Law' (2003) 25 Whittier Law Review 253–272, 261–262.

[26] Due to the uncertain political viability of obtaining consensus on a conventional treaty structure, the World Health Assembly opted for a *framework convention* that can be supplemented by specialized protocols. The structural basis for framework conventions is to use an incremental process in law making. This process begins with a framework convention that establishes a general consensus of the issue to be addressed and a system of governance. This is followed by the development of more specific commitments in subsequent protocols. If the treaty is implemented effectively, it could act as a possible model for tackling other health issues.

[27] WHO Constitution, Art 19.

[28] See, for instance, DP Fidler, 'A Globalized Theory of Public Health Law' in B Bennett (ed), *Health, Rights and Globalization* (2006) ch 5.

[29] Public health law studies 'the legal powers and duties of the state to assure the conditions for people to be healthy . . . and the limitations on the power of the state to constrain the autonomy . . . proprietary, or other legally protected interests of individuals for the protection or promotion of community health.' See LO Gostin, *Public Health Law: Power, Duty, Restraint* (2000) 4.

[30] K Shibuya et al, 'WHO Framework Convention on Tobacco Control: Development of an Evidence Based Global Health Treaty' (2003) 327 British Medical Journal 154–157.

responsible for the death of one in 10 adults worldwide,[31] and it has been increased by globalization. According to the World Bank, the long-term costs of treating tobacco illness would outweigh the short-term economic benefits derived from tobacco production and trade.[32]

With regard to the content of the FCTC, its main objective is to protect present and future generations from the health, social, and economic consequences of tobacco use.[33] The Convention covers a wide range of issues, including measures relating to the reduction in the demand and supply of tobacco. Among the measures relating to reducing the demand in tobacco are price and tax measures, regulation and disclosure of the contents of tobacco products, packaging and labelling, education, training and public awareness, and ban and restriction on tobacco advertising. For instance, states parties are required to take effective measures to ensure that 'tobacco product packaging and labelling do not promote a tobacco product by any means that are false, misleading, deceptive or likely to create an erroneous impression about its characteristics, health effects, hazards or emissions'. Each unit package should also carry a health warning of the prescribed size and visibility.[34] In addition, the parties are required to 'undertake a comprehensive ban on tobacco advertising, promotion and sponsorship'.[35] Among the measures aimed at reducing the supply of tobacco are the elimination of the illicit trade of tobacco products, restriction on sales to and by minors and technical and financial assistance for tobacco growers and workers to move to alternative occupations. In addition, the FCTC encourages parties to implement measures beyond those required by the Convention in order to better protect human rights.[36]

The Convention also includes a monitoring mechanism based on periodic national reporting. Where a dispute arises among states parties concerning the interpretation and application of the FCTC, the states parties should make a good faith attempt to settle it through negotiation. If negotiation fails, the parties may submit the dispute to ad hoc arbitration.[37] On the enforcement issue, the FCTC provides that the parties shall consider taking legislative action to deal with criminal and civil liability, including compensation where appropriate.[38]

As the regulation of the manufacture and advertising of tobacco products necessarily involves both free market and public health concerns, the FCTC

---

[31] Scientific evidence has unequivocally established that tobacco consumption causes disease, dependence, and death. WHO, 'Why is Tobacco a Public Health Priority?', fact sheet, available at <http://www.who.int/tobacco/en/index.html>.
[32] World Bank, *Tobacco Control Policy: Strategies, Successes and Setbacks* (2003) 10.
[33] For a general overview, see, for instance, N Devillier, 'La Convention cadre pur la lutte anti-tabac de l'Organisation Mondiale de la Santé' (2005) XXXVIII Revue Belge de Droit International 701–728. [34] FCTC, Art 11.
[35] FCTC, Art 13. [36] FCTC, Art 2(1). [37] FCTC, Art 27.
[38] See S Murphy, 'Liability and the WHO Framework Convention on Tobacco Control' (2003) 5 International Law Forum du Droit International 62–71.

provides a conflict clause to discipline its relationship with other international agreements and legal instruments:

> The provisions of the Convention and its protocols shall in no way affect the right of parties to enter into bilateral or multilateral agreements, including regional or sub-regional agreements, on issues relevant or additional to the Convention and its protocols, provided that such agreements are compatible with their obligations under the convention and its protocols.[39]

The WHO Framework Convention on Tobacco Control is one of the most widely supported treaties in the history of the United Nations.[40] It identifies and lists the existing tools of tobacco control, thus furthering a process of international harmonization. In the case of disputes concerning the linkage between tobacco control regulation and the protection of foreign investments, will international adjudicators take into account the provisions of the FCTC? If the FCTC is not applicable to the parties, it may be questioned whether its existence amounts to scientific evidence or consensus over the lethal effects of tobacco. Another interesting question is whether adjudicators would consult the WHO on the matter or would use the publicly available material edited under the auspices of the WHO and the World Bank.

III. International Investment Governance

The law of foreign investment is one of the oldest and most complex areas of international law. As there is still no single comprehensive global treaty, the investor's rights are defined by a plethora of bilateral and regional investment treaties and by customary international law.[41] Investment treaties provide an extensive protection to investors' rights to encourage foreign direct investment towards economic development.

At the substantive level, investment treaties broadly define the notion of investment, which generally covers both tangible and intangible property, thus including intellectual property, trademarks, and good will. In addition, investment treaties extensively construe the notion of compensable expropriation, including direct expropriation, *indirect expropriation*, and *measures tantamount to expropriation*.[42] Treaty provisions lack a precise definition of indirect

---

[39] FCTC, Art 2(2).

[40] The FCTC has 168 signatories and 164 parties: see <http://www.who.int/fctc/signatories_parties/en/index.html> (accessed 17 April 2009).

[41] See, for instance, JW Salacuse, 'The Treatification of International Investment Law' in JJ Norton and P Rogers (eds), *Law, Culture, and Economic Development – Liber Amicorum for Professor Roberto McLean* (2007) 241–252; SM Schwebel, 'The Reshaping of the International Law of Foreign Investment by Concordant Bilateral Investment Treaties' in S Charnovitz, DP Steger, and P van den Bossche (eds), *Law in the Service of Human Dignity – Essays in Honour of Florentino Feliciano* (2005) 241–245; and AF Lowenfeld, 'Investment Agreements and International Law' (2003–2004) 42 Columbia Journal of Transnational Law 123.

[42] See, for instance, NAFTA, Art 1110.

expropriation and their language encompasses a potentially wide variety of state activity that may interfere with an investor's property rights. Thus, regulation aimed at protecting public health and interfering with an investor's business rights may be considered to be a measure that is tantamount to expropriation.

There is no settled approach to cases where investors allege that certain regulatory measures constitute a compensable form of expropriation.[43] However, the more recent jurisprudence of arbitral tribunals reveals a remarkable tendency to shift the focus of the analysis away from the context and the purpose of the state regulation to focus more heavily on the sole effects on the owner. Thus, if there has been an expropriation, there will be an obligation to pay compensation.[44] So far, the *public purpose* of a given regulation has been subject to only limited exploration by tribunals and is not per se a defence to a claim of expropriation.[45] For instance, in *Pope & Talbot v Canada*,[46] it was underlined that regulations can indeed be characterized in a way that would constitute *creeping expropriation* even if fashioned in a non-discriminatory manner. The arbitral tribunal further held that an exception for regulatory measures would create a gap in international protection against expropriation.

Further, customary compensation rules, uniformly enshrined in investment protection treaties, do not differentiate between various public purposes of expropriations, posing instead a single standard of compensation having the characteristics of promptness, adequacy, and effectiveness.[47] For instance, in *Santa Elena*,[48] the arbitral tribunal concurred with the claimant that the particular public policy objective pursued by the expropriation could not per se affect the level of compensation. In other words, the question of compensation was not linked to the legality of taking.[49] As the *Santa Elena* tribunal held, 'where property is expropriated, even for environmental purposes, whether domestic or international, the state's obligation to pay compensation remains'.[50]

---

[43] C Brower and L Hellbeck, 'The Implications of National and International Environmental Obligations for Foreign Investments Protection Standards, Including Valuation: A Report From the Front Lines' in *International Investments and Protection of the Environment: The Role of Dispute Resolution Mechanisms* (2001) 19–28.

[44] C Schreuer, 'The Concept of Expropriation under the ECT and Other Investment Protection Treaties' (2005) 2 Transnational Dispute Management 1.

[45] J Coe and N Rubins, 'Regulatory Expropriation and the Tecmed Case: Context and Contributions' in T Weiler (ed), *International Investment Law and Arbitration: Leading Cases from ICSID, NAFTA Bilateral Treaties and Customary International Law* (2005) fn 163.

[46] *Pope & Talbot v Canada*, Interim Award, 26 June 2000, (2001) 40 ILM 258, at para 99.

[47] This rule has become known as the Hull formula, as it stems from a letter dated 21 July 1938 from Cordell Hull, the US Secretary of State, to the Mexican Government demanding compensation for the expropriation of agrarian property.

[48] *Compañia Desarrollo de Santa Elena v Costa Rica*, ICSID Case No ARB/96/1, Final Award, 17 February 2000, 15(1) ICSID Review FILJ (2000) 169–204.

[49] As Sornarajah puts it: 'It is generally accepted that a lawful taking creates an obligation to pay compensation, whereas an unlawful nationalization creates an obligation to pay restitutionary damages'. See M Sornarajah, *The International Law of Foreign Investments* (2nd edn, 2004) 345.

[50] *Santa Elena*, n 48 above, at para 72.

At the procedural level, investment agreements offer investors the possibility to bring claims before an arbitral tribunal. In this context, arbitral awards ultimately shape the relationship between the host state, on the one hand, and the foreign investors on the other[51] even in matters of public law,[52] as arbitrators determine matters such as the legality of governmental activity, the degree to which individuals should be protected from regulation, and the appropriate role of the state.[53]

While a method is needed to settle investor-state disputes, the use of arbitration, which constitutes a private model of adjudication, in this delicate field has shown some shortcomings that would need to be redressed. Because investment disputes are settled using a variety of different arbitral rules – not all of which provide for public disclosure of claims – there can be no accurate accounting of all such disputes. That some portion of the iceberg remains hidden from view should be a matter of concern given the public policy implications of such disputes. In addition, as investor-state arbitration does not grant the public a formal role in the proceedings, the question is whether more transparency should be granted. While some investment agreements have already institutionalized forms of transparency and public participation,[54] the majority of these instruments do not provide room for publicity, thus engendering questions of legitimacy.

While investment treaties are meant to protect investors from mistreatment by host states,[55] they have triggered high profile challenges by corporations against domestic regulation involving human rights considerations. With regard to the North American Free Trade Agreement (NAFTA),[56] Professor Brower has underlined that: 'Although NAFTA shares a philosophical affinity with the protection of civil and political rights, its application has determined a dramatic increase of support for economic and social rights in North America', and has also acknowledged its 'transformation into a vehicle for reconsideration of economic, social and cultural rights'.[57] After examining some relevant case studies, this chapter will put forward some policy options

[51] G Van Harten, *Investment Treaty Arbitration and Public Law* (2007) 70.
[52] G Van Harten, 'The Public-Private Distinction in the International Arbitration of Individual Claims Against the State' (2007) 56 ICLQ 371–393, 372; and Z Douglas, 'The Hybrid Foundations of Investment Treaty Arbitration' (2003) 74 British Year Book of International Law 151, 221–237.   [53] See ch 8 in this volume.
[54] See, for instance, Art 28 of the 2004 US Model BIT, which states that the arbitral tribunal shall have the authority to accept and consider *amicus curiae* submissions from a person or entity which is not a disputing party.
[55] See, for instance, ch 3 in this volume; J Paulsson, *Denial of Justice in International Law* (2005); and AK Bjorklund, 'Reconciling State Sovereignty and Investor Protection in Denial of Justice Claims' (2005) 45 Virginia Journal of International Law 4, 809–895, in particular at 810–833, 849–898.
[56] North American Free Trade Agreement between Canada, the United States, and Mexico, entered into force on 1 January 1994, (1993) 32 ILM 289.
[57] CH Brower II, 'NAFTA's Investment Chapter: Initial Thoughts About Second Generation Rights' (2003) 37 Vanderbilt Journal of Transnational Law 1533–1566.

in an attempt to reconcile public health considerations with investor rights in international investment law.

IV. Case Studies

A. *Grand River et al v United States* – US Tobacco Dispute Settlements

In 2005, Grand River, a Canadian company involved in the tobacco trade, filed a NAFTA investor-state claim, seeking compensation for the alleged violation of NAFTA Chapter 11 at UNCITRAL.[58] In this pending case, Grand River argues that the tobacco settlements between the US states and large tobacco firms have harmed its investment in the United States. As scientific evidence mounted, showing that cigarette smoking caused cancer and other diseases, the United States adopted a number of governmental policies to curb it, and most states entered into the Master Settlement Agreement (MSA).[59] The MSA required each company adhering to it to make cash payments to a central account in respect of each cigarette sold to pay state costs incurred in the treatment of indigent patients suffering from tobacco-related illnesses. In exchange for payments, the states would drop all antitrust and consumer protection lawsuits. In order to avoid free riding by competitors not participating in the initiative, opting-out firms would have to contribute a percentage of their sales to escrow accounts to pay eventual law suits against tobacco companies. Finally, states made these escrow accounts non-refundable.

In a preliminary way, petitioners argue that the market share of a product in the territory of a NAFTA party constitutes an *intangible form of property*, and business activity would thus also constitute an *investment* as defined in NAFTA.[60] In general terms, the petitioners argue that the major tobacco firms conspired to ensure that smaller businesses were covered by the settlement in an effort to force them out of business. The requirement to make payments into

---

[58] Notice of Arbitration Under the United Nations Commission on International Trade Law and the North American Free Trade Agreement between Grand River Enterprises Six Nations Ltd, Jerry Montour, Kenneth Hill, and Arthur Montour and Government of the United States of America, 3 March 2004, available at <http://www.state.gov/documents/organization/30961.pdf>.

[59] In 1998, 46 US states entered into the MSA with major tobacco companies to settle legal claims that the states had filed seeking to recoup medical expenses incurred for treating smoking-related illnesses of indigenous smokers and to pay for smoking reduction programmes. The text of the MSA is available at website of the National Association of Attorneys General, at <http://www.naag.org/backpages/naag/tobacco/msa>.

[60] On the notion of investment in international investment law, see, for instance, YGL Wolters, 'The Meaning of "Investment" in Treaty Disputes: Substantive or Jurisdictional? – Lessons from Nagel v Czech Republic and S.D. Myers v. Canada' (2007) 8 Journal of World Investment and Trade 175–185; and B Legum, 'Defining Investment and Investor: Who is Entitled to Claim?' (2006) 22 Arbitration International 4, 521–526.

state accounts would constitute an expropriation in violation of NAFTA, Article 1110, because it would raise prices by an amount that would neutralize cost advantages and prevent small companies from offering meaningful price competition.[61] In addition, the petitioners allege that they have been deprived of fair and equitable treatment under NAFTA, Article 1105, because they are bound by the terms of a settlement they did not negotiate.

Crucially, as the claimants are Native Americans, they hold that the tobacco business is their traditional activity, and that the case would involve their cultural rights.[62] According to the claimants, respect of international law protecting cultural rights of indigenous peoples in the present dispute would be required by interpretation of NAFTA, Article 1105: 'In any given case, the standard of treatment owed by a government will be informed by all sources of international law, including treaties, general principles and customary international law'.[63]

The question is whether the consideration of human rights in investment arbitration has to favour only the investors or might also favour the respondent state. Interpreting Article 1105 and the fair and equitable treatment standard in a *fair* manner, *all* international law sources would be relevant. Thus, not only would international law protecting indigenous peoples but also international health law become crucial. Will arbitrators take public international law into account? Will they define cultural phenomena, such as tobacco consumption and trade, as cultural heritage? The clash between the different interests concerned seems to require a balancing process of a quasi-constitutional nature.[64]

With regard to the first question, arbitrators have already applied *general principles of international law* in the Decision on Objections to Jurisdiction.[65] As the decision on the merits is still pending, one can wonder whether the arbitral tribunal will show the same attitude with regard to the substantive issues.

With regard to the balancing problem, a solution might be borrowed by the recent UNESCO Convention for the Safeguarding of Intangible Cultural

---

[61] *Grand River Enterprises Six Nations Ltd, and ors v United States of America*, at 11.

[62] Indeed, in their application, the claimants state:

> This arbitration is not about health protection or promotion. It is not about state rights to regulate in the interests of the public good. And it is not only about the anti-competitive measures being imposed at the behest of a few large companies in exchange for a share of their profits. This arbitration concerns and arises out of the Respondent's discrimination against a group of aboriginal investors, their traditions, businesses and livelihoods, and the expropriation of their markets, all in violation of their rights under international law.

Grand River Enterprises, Statement of Claimants' Claims Arising Directly Out of the Adoption and Implementation of the Allocable Share Amendments, 6 November 2006.

[63] *Grand River Enterprises*, Statement of Claimants, at para 97.

[64] V Vadi, 'Cultural Heritage & International Investment Law: A Stormy Relationship' (2008) 15 International Journal of Cultural Property 1–23, 16.

[65] The tribunal applied the principle of prescription to some claims not only under a specific NAFTA provision (NAFTA, Art 1116), but also invoking its validity as a *general principle of law*. *Grand River Enterprises*, ICSID, Decision on Objections to Jurisdiction, 20 July 2006.

Heritage (CSICH).[66] This Convention expressly safeguards only intangible cultural heritage[67] that is *compatible* with existing human rights instruments.[68] Thus, by way of analogy, even if smoking was deemed to be an intangible cultural heritage of the Six Nations, it could not be protected, because of its incompatibility with public health.

B. The GATT/WTO Analogy: Retrospect and Prospect

This section explores the way in which the analogous linkage between tobacco regulation and free trade has been handled in the parallel GATT/WTO framework. In particular, it does so not only looking at the well-known *Thailand-Cigarettes* case, but also briefly scrutinizing some contemporary consultations that might evolve in a WTO dispute.

The GATT *Thailand-Cigarettes* case is an interesting precedent that might be taken into account by the arbitral tribunal in *Grand River*.[69] As Thailand prohibited the importation of cigarettes, but authorized the sale of domestic cigarettes, the United States brought a case against Thailand under GATT, complaining that the import restrictions were inconsistent with GATT, Article XI:1, and claiming that they were not justified either by Articles XI:2 or XX (b).[70] By contrast, Thailand argued, inter alia, that the exception included in Article XX(b) reflected the recognition that public health protection is a basic responsibility of governments. Further, the import restrictions would be justified under this provision because chemicals and other addictives contained in US cigarettes made them more harmful than Thai cigarettes.

The panel accepted as its starting point Thailand's authority under Article XX(b) to enact measures to reduce consumption of cigarettes because cigarettes posed a serious risk to public health. However, it found that the import restrictions were inconsistent with Article XI:1 and not justified under Article

[66] Convention for the Safeguarding of Intangible Cultural Heritage signed in Paris on 17 November 2003 (UNESCO Doc MISC/2003/CLT/CH/14) and entered into force on 20 April 2006. The Convention has 111 states parties as at 17 April 2009. As neither Canada nor the United States has signed or ratified this Convention, so far it is not applicable to these countries. The country list is available at <http://www.unesco.org/culture/ich/index.php?pg=00024>.

[67] CSICH, Art 2, para 1 defines intangible cultural heritage as including:

> practices ... that communities ... recognize as part of their cultural heritage. This intangible cultural heritage, transmitted from generation to generation, is constantly recreated by communities and groups in response to their ... interaction with nature ... and provides them with a sense of identity and continuity, thus promoting respect for cultural diversity and human creativity.

[68] CSICH, Art 2, para 1.
[69] GATT Panel Report, *Thailand-Restrictions on the Importation of and Internal Taxes on Cigarettes*, adopted on 7 November 1990, BISD 375/200.
[70] GATT, Art XX(b) states in part: 'nothing in this Agreement shall be construed to prevent the adoption or enforcement by any contracting party of measures: ... (b) necessary to protect human ... life or health'.

XI:2, because they plainly discriminated against foreign products. It further concluded that the import restrictions were not necessary within the meaning of Article XX(b). The panel report is important for several reasons. First, the panel consulted with the WHO, asking it to present its conclusions on technical aspects of the case, such as the health effects of tobacco consumption.[71] The panel stated that smoking constituted a serious risk to human health and that measures designed to reduce tobacco consumption fell within the scope of Article XX(b). It noted that this provision clearly allowed contracting parties to give priority to human health over trade liberalization.[72] Second, although Thai measures were found to be discriminatory and inconsistent with the necessity test, the panel considered that Thailand could take other measures to limit the health consequences of cigarette liberalization. Acceptable measures would include taxes on tobacco products, advertising bans, labelling requirements, and so on and so forth. In conclusion, *Thailand-Cigarettes* was a landmark case, because it opened the door to inter-organizational cooperation and acknowledged the priority of public health policy over trade liberalization, showing that tobacco control policies may be consistent with international trade agreements, if implemented in a non-discriminatory fashion.[73]

However, the issues are far from being settled. Recently, in February 2008, the Philippines, a major exporter of cigarettes to Thailand, requested consultations with Thailand concerning a number of Thai fiscal and customs measures affecting cigarette imports from the Philippines.[74] In making the request, the Philippines said that while it did not dispute the sovereign right of Thailand to regulate its tobacco market, including the right to enact any public health policies that it deemed appropriate, Thailand had an obligation to treat imported cigarettes fairly, both at the border and in the internal market, and in a non-discriminatory and transparent manner. The Philippines complained that Thailand administered these measures, which inter alia included a health tax, in a discriminatory and unreasonable manner, thereby violating GATT 1994, Article X:3(a). According to the request of consulation, the Thai Tobacco Monopoly (TTM), which is the only business entity authorized by Thai law to produce cigarettes in Thailand and has a market share of approximately 80 per cent, would have 'numerous personal and institutional links between the Thai government', allegedly determining 'serious conflicts of interests in the administration of Thai fiscal and customs legislation pertaining to cigarettes', and leading 'to biased, partial, and unreasonable administration

---

[71] See *Thailand-Cigarettes*, n 69 above, at paras 50–57.   [72] Ibid., at para 73.

[73] For a similar conclusion, see World Bank, *Curbing the Epidemic: Governments and the Economics of Tobacco Control* (2000).

[74] World Trade Organization, Request for Consultations by the Philippines, *Thailand – Customs and Fiscal Measures on Cigarettes from the Philippines*, 12 February 2008, WT/DS371/1. On 20 February 2008, the European Communities requested to join the consultations.

of Thai law'.[75] In particular, Thailand would determine excessive customs values for Philippine exports of cigarettes inconsistently with the Customs Valuation Agreement, and because these customs values serve as the tax basis for imposing the health tax, Thailand would thus impose a higher tax burden on imported products than on like and/or directly competitive domestic products.[76] In addition, it is underlined that the Thai law contains no procedure for cigarette importers to claim a refund of the portion of the tax paid as a result of the excessive customs valuation.[77] By so doing, Thailand would act inconsistently with Article III:2.[78] The opacity of some tax rules which have not been published is also highlighted and deemed to be in violation of Article X:1 of the GATT 1994, which requires governments to publish trade laws and regulations of general application.[79]

The Dispute Settlement Body, on 21 October 2008, has deferred the Philippines' panel request,[80] following an objection by Thailand.[81] In particular, Thailand proposed to resolve the matter bilaterally and remained open for further consultations, but also alleged that its customs and fiscal laws were fully consistent with its WTO obligations. It is still too early to take a predictive approach to this conflict, as it is possible that the Philippines and Thailand settle the dispute by amiable means. However, this contemporary conflict highlights once more the difficulty of establishing the boundary between legitimate regulation and disguised protectionism.

C. *Feldman Karpa*

Another case that is worth analysing is *Marvin Feldman Karpa v Mexico*.[82] The case concerned the application of certain tax laws by Mexico to the export of tobacco products by CEMSA, a company owned and controlled by Marvin Feldman Karpa, an American citizen. While Mexican law imposed a tax on the production and sale of cigarettes in the domestic market, it applied a zero tax rate to cigarette exports under some circumstances. In particular, rebates were applied only to cigarette producers, but were denied to resellers, such as CEMSA. CEMSA initiated an Amparo action before the Mexican courts, alleging that these measures infringed upon the constitutional principle of tax equity. The Mexican Supreme Court of Justice ruled in favour of CEMSA, finding unanimously that measures allowing rebates only to producers and their distributors violated constitutional principles of non-discrimination. As Mexican authorities asked CEMSA to fulfil other requirements, Marvin Karpa filed an arbitration request at ICSID on behalf of his company.

---

[75] Ibid., at para 2.   [76] Ibid., at para 16.   [77] Ibid., at para 17.
[78] Ibid.   [79] Ibid, at para 18.   [80] WT/DS371/3.
[81] WTO News Items, 21 October 2008, available at <http://www.wto.org/english/news_e/news08_e/dsb_21oct08_e.htm>.
[82] *Marvin Roy Feldman Karpa v Mexico*, Award, 16 December 2002, ICSID Case No ARB(AF)/99/1, available at <http://www.state.gov/documents/organization/16639.pdf>.

The claimant alleged that Mexico's refusal to rebate taxes applied to cigarettes exported by CEMSA constituted a breach of Mexico obligations under NAFTA Chapter 11, and in particular of Articles 1102 (National Treatment), 1105 (Minimum Level of Treatment), and 1110 (Expropriation). In particular, the claimant's key contention was that the various actions of the Mexican Government in denying rebates on cigarette exports resulted in an *indirect* or *creeping expropriation* of his investment. Nor did the claimant believe that the Mexican Government policy of limiting cigarette exports was justified by public policy grounds, particularly in light of the stated purpose of the law, which was to encourage Mexican exports of tobacco products.

The arbitral tribunal questioned whether the actions of the Mexican Government constituted an expropriation or were valid governmental activity: 'if there is a finding of expropriation, compensation is required even if the taking is for a public purpose, non-discriminatory and in accordance with due process of law'.[83] However, it held that 'non-discriminatory, *bona fide* general taxation does not establish liability',[84] and 'not every business problem experienced by a foreign investor is an indirect or creeping expropriation under article 1110'.[85] Thus, the award finally dismissed the claim of expropriation, but upheld the claim of violation of national treatment.

The case is interesting in two respects. First, it theoretically distinguished between general regulation and indirect expropriation, considering good faith as a guiding principle for such an assessment:

> governments must be free to act in the broader public interest through the protection of the environment ... tax regimes ... and the like. Reasonable governmental regulation of this type cannot be achieved if any business that is adversely affected may seek compensation ...[86]

Second, it is interesting to point out that the purpose of the national law in question was to encourage Mexican exports. Indeed, the case shows a very typical practice in contemporary trade as many countries have long been tobacco growers and cigarette manufacturers. Exporting health hazards may represent a lucrative aspect of their economy and constitute a sort of *health dumping*.[87]

---

[83] Ibid., at para 98.   [84] Ibid., at para 106.   [85] Ibid., at para 112.
[86] Ibid., at para 103.
[87] *Environmental dumping* may be defined as the practice of exporting environmental risks from one country to another. It is often viewed as an instrument used by some countries in the attempt to attract foreign investments and trade. Environmental dumping would allow the delocalization of polluting firms from a country with strong environmental policies to a country with weaker environmental regulation. On environmental dumping, see, for instance, D Sturm and A Ulph, 'Environment and Trade: The Implications of Imperfect Information and Political Economy' (2002) 1 World Trade Review 235–256. *Health dumping* may be conceptualized as a parallel concept, indicating the lowering of health standards to attract foreign investments. A concrete example is offered by the tobacco trade. While the amount of tobacco products sold in industrialized countries has decreased in recent years, due to increased regulation aimed at protecting public health, tobacco companies have moved to new markets where information asymmetry has facilitated the diffusion of tobacco use. See J Mackay and M Eriksen, *The Tobacco Atlas* (2002) 50.

V. Policy Options

Having examined the conflict area between the law of foreign investment and tobacco control measures, this study argues that investment protection and public health have not to be deemed incompatible or irreconcilable. On the contrary, the different norms arising from these different treaty regimes can be reconciled through a series of policy and legal instruments. This chapter will focus on three different methods: negotiation/mediation, interpretation, and legal drafting.

Before examining each of these tools, it is important to stress that in the following analysis, reference will be made to the protection of foreign property, not only in its tangible dimension, but also in its intangible one. Indeed, while the above-mentioned investment arbitrations have mainly concerned tax measures, it is important to stress that future litigation might concern trademarks as well, as has happened before different fora, such as the European Court of Justice and the European Court of Human Rights. Due reference to the case law of these courts will also be put forward in the course of the following analysis.

A. Negotiation/Mediation

Negotiation and mediation are useful tools to reconcile opposing interests. They both constitute dispute resolution methods alternative to judicial settlement and arbitration, and are both based on cooperative and interest-based approaches. In abstract terms, negotiation generally creates a situation where both parties cooperate to reach a satisfactory result.[88] Agreement often can be reached if parties look not at their stated positions, but rather at their underlying interests to reach a decision that benefits both parties. The negotiation process may also produce more successful outcomes than the adversarial 'winner takes all' approach.[89]

Mediation may also play a useful role in this context. Where the degree of animosity between the parties is so great that direct negotiations are unlikely to lead to a dispute settlement, the intervention of a neutral third party to reconcile the parties may be a very suitable option.[90] Mediation involves the good offices of a neutral third party which facilitates communication between the discussants. Like negotiation, mediation is guided by the goal of finding a win-win situation for all parties through a creative process that focuses on the interests of the parties rather than on their positions.[91] As the mediator does not have the

---

[88] See H Raiffa, *The Art and Science of Negotiation* (1982); and A Plantey, *International Negotiation in the Twenty-First Century* (2007).

[89] See R Fisher and W Ury, *Getting to Yes: Negotiating Agreement Without Giving In* (1983).

[90] J Collier and V Lowe, *The Settlement of Disputes in International Law: Institutions and Procedures* (1999) 29.

[91] See N Alexander, 'Global Trends in Mediation: Riding the Third Wave' in N Alexander (ed), *Global Trends in Mediation* (2006) ch 1.

authority to make a binding decision and does not follow a fixed procedure, the procedure allows for flexible and dynamic dialogue. Further, mediation might involve other stakeholders' participation. In a sense, it might facilitate access to justice by affected third parties.

Successful negotiations and mediations may also have a positive impact on subsequent cases, providing a useful paradigm and creating confidence in the belief that conflicts may generate positive outcomes.[92] Time is another intrinsic advantage of these alternative dispute resolution methods, as these instruments usually achieve results in a short time frame. Importantly, they are not required to deal with the past: they ask the parties to look at their future and to reshape their duties and responsibilities towards each other. Foreign investors thus participate in the decision-making process that will ultimately affect them. All of the different interests are explored and discussed in these proceedings. In addition, experience shows that agreements entered into through a voluntary process stand out on account of their durability, because of the parties' high identification with the agreement achieved. At the national level, in some cases, negotiation has led to positive results. For instance, in the United States, the Master Settlement Agreement between states and tobacco companies has settled thousands of disputes.

At the international level, though, the advantages of alternative dispute resolution (ADR) mechanisms should not lead us to overestimate these methods. While they can be extremely useful in those situations where both contracting parties have equal or similar bargaining power – like in commercial disputes among private parties – agreements between host states and foreign investors may lead to unsatisfactory results. Critics correctly argue that mediation does not provide the procedural safeguards of more structured dispute settlement mechanisms and therefore offers no guarantees of justice, particularly where an imbalance in bargaining power exists between the parties.[93] Concretely, unbalanced negotiation or mediation may lead states to accept unnecessary limits on their regulatory power. For instance, the recent agreement between the Mexican Government and the tobacco industry which excludes graphic health warnings and conditions the disclosure of ingredients in respect of industrial secrets and confidential information has been widely criticized because it contrasts with the key articles of the FCTC which Mexico ratified and which requires graphic warnings and unconditional disclosure of ingredients.[94]

---

[92] B Depoorter, 'Law in the Shadow of Bargaining', Working paper, forthcoming: see <http://pantheon.yale.edu/~bwd8/>. The author develops a theory on the precedent value of alternative dispute settlements, stating that trial outcomes and alternative dispute settlements are not distinct categories. Instead, alternative dispute settlements would influence the path of the law.

[93] See M Cappelletti, 'Alternative Dispute Resolution Processes Within the Framework of the World-Wide Access to Justice Movement' (1995) Modern Law Review 287, 288.

[94] J Samet, H Wipfli, R Perez-Padilla, and D Yach, 'Mexico and the Tobacco Industry: Doing the Wrong Thing for the Right Reason?' (2006) 332 British Medical Journal 353–354.

As developing and least-developed countries need foreign investments to foster development and growth, these countries may have an incentive to lower health and environmental standards (that is, *race to the bottom*) to attract foreign investment flows.[95] This recently happened in Uzbekistan, where a foreign tobacco company lobbied and obtained a series of regulatory benefits as part of its investment conditions. Advertising bans were replaced by an advertising code drafted by the tobacco industry, and smoke-free restrictions were scaled back to cover only healthcare facilities, kindergartens, and schools.[96]

The existence of investment treaty obligations and the threat of an investor-state dispute by a foreign investor may have a chilling effect on policy makers. When Canadian health officials were to issue a new regulation on cigarette labeling, Philip Morris, a US tobacco company, is known to have threatened to use the NAFTA investment chapter to challenge the proposed rules on cigarette packaging.[97] In particular, the company considered filing an investment claim, alleging a potential twofold infringement of NAFTA Chapter 11. First, the company insisted that the terms *light, mild,* and *low* were incorporated into cigarette names and communicated differences of taste to consumers. Banning these descriptors would not only destroy valuable trademarks and the goodwill they represent, but would be tantamount to indirect expropriation. Second, Philip Morris argued that the Canadian regulation would violate the fair and equitable treatment standard, as tobacco companies were initially encouraged to market low-yield cigarettes.[98]

In the end, Canada adopted the labelling system, but the threat of an investment dispute might prove potent in less industrialized countries.[99] For instance, in Thailand, companies were able to stall mandatory disclosure of cigarette ingredients by affirming that this would amount to a violation of trade secret rights protected under trade and investment agreements.[100] In 2002, when Thailand considered imposing graphic warnings on the covers of cigarette packets, Philip Morris argued that the regulation would unnecessarily limit *free speech* and its right to communicate with its customers. The company also lamented that the regulation would have infringed its trademark rights.[101] While tobacco

[95] E Sebrié and SA Glantz, 'The Tobacco Industry in Developing Countries has Forestalled Legislation on Tobacco Control' (2006) 332 British Medical Journal 313–314.
[96] A Gilmore, J Collin, and M McKee, 'British American Tobacco's Erosion of Health Legislation in Uzbekistan' (2006) 332 British Medical Journal 355–358.
[97] LE Peterson, *Bilateral Investment Treaties and Development Policy Making* (2004) 37.
[98] S Chase, 'Tobacco firms Warns "Mild" and "Light" Cigarette Ban May Violate NAFTA', *Globe & Mail*, 16 March 2002.
[99] See S Grass, 'Inordinate Chill: BITs, Non-NAFTA MITs and Host-State Regulatory Freedom- An Indonesian Case Study' (2002–2003) 24 Michigan Journal of International Law 893. With regard to tobacco control, see E Sebrie et al, 'Tobacco Industry Successfully Prevented Tobacco Control Legislation in Argentina' (2005) 14 Tobacco Control 2.
[100] R Mackenzie et al, '"If We Can Just 'Stall' New Unfriendly Legislations, the Scoreboard is Already in Our Favor": Transnational Tobacco Companies and Ingredients Disclosure in Thailand' (2004) 13 Tobacco Control 79–87.
[101] See M Macan-Markar, 'Thai Authorities Have Malboro Man Fuming', *Asia Times*, 14 May 2002.

companies argue that graphic warnings constitute 'an emotional rather than a rational response to the issue of consumer awareness and information',[102] it has been proved that pictorial warnings work by also reaching people who are illiterate and cannot read the language in which the warnings are written.

In conclusion, while negotiation and mediation may represent useful means to settle disputes between foreign investors and the host state, where there is no equal bargaining power, more legal approaches are preferable. This chapter will now particularly refer to treaty interpretation and legal drafting.

B. Interpretation

Interpretation is not only a part of the implementing process of a treaty, but it also plays a fundamental role in avoiding antinomies between different treaty regimes. In a sense, interpreters clarify and reconcile the meanings of the existing provisions by applying them to the specific cases. Whatever the conception of the adjudicative function that arbitrators adopt, it is generally accepted that adjudicators are neither mere *bouche de la loi*, nor authentic law makers.[103] In a sense, arbitrators have a *maieutic* role, as they give birth to the meaning of treaty provisions, having to identify the applicable rules, to clarify their meaning, and to relate them to the specific facts of the case. According to the International Law Commission, 'the interpretation of documents is to some extent an art, not an exact science'.[104] However, to say that adjudicators' role is creative would probably go too far, because it would undermine their legitimacy.[105]

Customary rules of treaty interpretation, as restated by the Vienna Convention on the Law of Treaties,[106] offer the adjudicators the conceptual and legal framework to perform their function to settle disputes 'in conformity with the principles of justice and international law'.[107] Customary rules of treaty interpretation are applicable to investment treaties because investment treaties are international law treaties. Further, some investment treaties expressly mention these rules.[108] Notably, with regard to the governing or substantive law to be

[102] See M Macan-Markar, 'Tobacco Wars: Singapore the Picture of Health', *Asia Times*, 5 September 2005.
[103] On the different conceptions of the adjudicative function, see ch 8 in this volume.
[104] Report of the International Law Commission on its 18th session, 4 May to 19 July 1966 (A/6309/Rev.1).
[105] On the role of creative interpretation in international law, see A Szpak, 'A Few Reflections on the Interpretation of Treaties in Public International Law' (2005) 18 Hague Yearbook of International Law 59–70, 69; on creative interpretation in investor-state arbitration, see SP Subedi, *International Investment Law – Reconciling Policy and Principle* (2008) 135–137.
[106] Vienna Convention on the Law of Treaties, signed in Vienna on 23 May 1969, entered into force on 27 January 1980, 1155 UNTS 331.
[107] Vienna Convention, Preamble. For an accurate analysis, see E-U Petersmann, 'Do Judges Meet their Constitutional Obligation to Settle Disputes in Conformity with "Principles of Justice and International Law"?' (2007) 1 European Journal Legal Studies 1–38.
[108] For instance, Australia-United States Free Trade Agreement, Art 21.9.2 expressly states that the arbitral panel shall consider the agreement 'in accordance with applicable rules of treaty

applied in investment disputes, NAFTA expressly requires that '[a] Tribunal established under this Section shall decide the issue in dispute in accordance with this Agreement and applicable rules of international law'.[109] NAFTA tribunals have clarified that 'applicable rules of international law comprise the customary international rules of treaty interpretation which are reflected and codified in Articles 31 and 32 of the VCLT'.[110] In parallel, Article 42 of the ICSID Convention provides that if 'the parties cannot agree on the applicable law, the tribunal will apply the law of the host state and such rules of international law as may be applicable'.[111]

According to the *general rule of interpretation*, which comprises several subnorms, 'a treaty shall be interpreted in good faith in accordance with the ordinary meaning to be given to the terms of the treaty in their context and in the light of its object and purpose'.[112] As a matter of convenience, the following analysis will follow the order in which these subnorms generally appear.

1. Textual Interpretation

According to the principle of textuality, treaties are to be interpreted on the basis of their actual text. Looking at the literal terms of investment treaty norms, there is no black-letter norm which demands foreign investors not to take into consideration consumers' protection. To the contrary, recent free trade agreements which include chapters on investments expressly provide general clauses allowing public health measures. In a concise way, NAFTA, Article 1114(2) states that:

The parties recognize that it is inappropriate to encourage investment by relaxing domestic health, safety or environmental measures. Accordingly, a party should not waive or otherwise derogate from, or offer to waive or otherwise derogate from, such measures as an encouragement for the establishment, acquisition, expansion, or retention in its territory of an investment of an investor. If a Party considers that another party has offered such an encouragement, it may request consultations with the other party and the two parties shall consult with a view to avoiding any such encouragement.[113]

In a more detailed fashion, CAFTA, Annex 10-C(4)(b) expressly states: 'Except in rare circumstances, non-discriminatory regulatory actions by a party that are designed and applied to protect legitimate public welfare objectives, such as public health, safety and the environment, do not constitute indirect expropriations.'

With regard to intellectual property, investment treaties usually recall the relevant provisions of the TRIPS Agreement, which expressly presents a clause regulating the interface between public health protection and intellectual

interpretation under international law as reflected in Articles 31 and 32 of the Vienna Convention on the Law of Treaties'.   [109] NAFTA, Art 1131(1).
[110] *Canadian Cattlemen for Fair Trade v United States*, Award on Jurisdiction, 28 January 2008, at para 46.   [111] ICSID Convention, Art 42.
[112] Vienna Convention, Art 31.1.   [113] NAFTA, Art 1114, para 2.

property. For instance, while the Central America Free Trade Agreement[114] does not expressly include a public health exception with regard to intellectual property, it makes clear reference to the TRIPS Agreement, as it states that 'the parties affirm their existing rights and obligations under the TRIPS Agreement'.[115] Thus, such FTA incorporates the provision of TRIPS, Article 8 which is applicable or may provide guidance in the context of investment disputes. Notoriously, Article 8 states that 'members may, in formulating or amending their laws and regulations, adopt measures necessary to protect public health and nutrition, and to promote the public interest in sectors of vital importance to their socio-economic and technological development, provided that such measures are consistent with the provisions of this Agreement'. In addition, paragraph 2 of the same provision adds that: 'Appropriate measures, provided that they are consistent with the provisions of this Agreement, may be needed to prevent the abuse of intellectual property rights by right holders'.

The mentioned provision seems to provide space for reconciliation between private and public interest in intellectual property (IP) regulation. It imposes some limits though. In particular, the measures to be adopted need to be consistent with the TRIPS Agreement. Prima facie, this clause might be interpreted as to give precedence to intellectual property over other interests. However, on a closer look, it merely requires to take the whole agreement into account when adopting the necessary measures to prevent abuses of IP rights. In a sense, it reaffirms the need to interpret the treaty 'in accordance with the ordinary meaning to be given to the terms of the treaty in their context and in the light of its object and purpose'.[116]

2. Teleological Interpretation

From a functional perspective, legal rules can be considered as an instrument to realize certain legal, social, and economic goals and values. The method of teleological interpretation searches for the purpose of a norm to clarify uncertainties in its exact content. With regard to the notion of indirect expropriation, the parallel notion of property or investment represents its legal and factual contraposition, but theoretical premise. As Sornarajah underlines, 'the notion of creeping expropriation is based on the unbundling of property rights'.[117] Therefore, in order to understand the content of indirect expropriation, the notion of property must be clearly defined and delimited, also in relation to its function.[118]

---

[114] The Dominican Republic – Central America Free Trade Agreement, commonly called DR-CAFTA, encompasses the United States and the Central American countries of Costa Rica, El Salvador, Guatemala, Honduras, Nicaragua, and the Dominican Republic. The final text was signed on 5 August 2004 and is available at <http://www.ustr.gov/assets/Trade_Agreements/Bilateral/CAFTA/CAFTA-DR_Final_Texts/asset_upload_file747_3918.pdf>.

[115] CAFTA, Art 15.1.7.   [116] VCLT, Art 31.1.

[117] See M Sornarajah, *The International Law of Foreign Investments* (2nd edn, 2004) 352.

[118] The notion of indirect expropriation has been explored by a number of studies. See the pioneering study written by R Higgins, 'The Taking of Property by the State' (1982) Recueil des

The right to property is an extremely problematic notion in international law, as 'it cannot be easily classified as an exclusively civil and political right or as a social right'.[119] Indeed, such right was not included in the 1966 Covenants, because its exact content was a matter of debate,[120] and the Universal Declaration merely prohibits arbitrary deprivation of property, but does not provide for an articulated regime.[121] Many national and regional instruments build upon the well-known Justinian's Digest. However, Roman law is not only important because it is the conceptual matrix of modern legal provisions forming the foundation of modern international law,[122] but also because of its functional worth.

According to Roman law, *Dominium est jus utendi et abutendi re sua, quatenus juris ratio patitur*: the concept of property includes the use, enjoyment, or disposition of the property right within the limits established by the law. The limitation of the right by the law is not so much a limitation on the institution as an internal safeguard: what would seem to limit the nature of the right actually confirms it and preserves it by establishing its legitimacy. The Roman concept of property has been successfully transposed into modern terms by the Napoleon Code[123] and appears in most modern constitutions.[124] Looking at these instruments and regional treaties, it appears that property rights are not absolute, but their owners can enjoy them within the limits established by the law.[125] As Professor Alexander further highlights:

… property as a constitutional right may be thought to serve two quite different functions. The first is an individual, or personal function: securing a zone of freedom for the individual in the realm of economic activity … The second function that might be recognized is social and public … it is to serve the public good … Property is

Cours III, 263–392. See also A Newcombe, 'The Boundaries of Regulatory Expropriation in International Law' (2005) 20 ICSID Review FILJ 1, 1–57; R Dolzer, 'Indirect Expropriations: New Developments?' (2003) 11 New York University Environmental Law Journal 64–93; and LY Fortier and SL Drymer, 'Indirect Expropriation in the Law of International Investment: I Know When I See It, or *Caveat Investor*' (2004) 19 ICSID Review FILJ 2, 293–327.

[119] See C Krause, 'The Right to Property' in A Eide, C Krause, and A Rosas, *Economic, Social and Cultural Rights* (1995) 143. The author highlights that: 'Historically, [the right to property] is associated with civil liberties, but at the same time it has strong economic implications and is therefore often discussed in the context of social rights.' Ibid.

[120] See TRG Van Banning, *The Human Right to Property* (2002) 5.

[121] UDHR, Art 17. Universal Declaration of Human Rights (doc. UNGA Res. 217 A (III), adopted on 10 December 1948).

[122] On the connection between Roman law and international law, see A Pillet, *Les Fondateurs du droit international* (1904).

[123] Napoléon Code, Art 544. The article reads as follows: 'La propriété est le droit de jouir et de disposer des choses de la maniére la plus absolue, pourvu qu'on n'en fasse pas un usage prohibé par les lois et les réements.'

[124] See, for instance, Italian Constitution, Art 42. Art 14 of the German Basic Law inter alia states that the 'content and limits [of the right to property] shall be defined by the laws' and affirms that: 'Property entails obligations. *Its use shall also serve the public good*' (emphasis added).

[125] See JW Singer, 'The Ownership Society and Takings of Property: Castles, Investments and Just Obligations' (2006) 30 Harvard Environmental Law Review 309 ff.

individually owned … but the basic reason why the institution of property is recognized is to advance the collective good of the society which has recognized it.[126]

Turning now to IP, which is a special form of property, if we look at the very rationale of protecting IP rights, we see that IP is never absolute, but presents a highly regulated regime. The notion that IP serves a social function has wide acceptance in international law, as expressly indicated by Articles 7 and 8 of the TRIPS Agreement[127] and by Article 15 of the International Covenant on Economic, Social, and Cultural Rights.[128]

Accordingly, the state may restrain a person from enjoying his or her property if this use is harmful to others. The police power of a state stems from the concept that good governance aims at public welfare and it restrains private property for the protection of the public safety and health. Where a deprivation of property or other economic loss arises out of *bona fide* general regulation, it should be considered within the boundaries of acceptable exercise of police powers and would not be compensable. As regulation can effectively reduce or destroy the use of private property, the notion of indirect expropriation has been developed to include those state measures that, albeit not materially seizing property, still deeply diminish its value. In this context, the conceptual distinction between police power and expropriation becomes vague. Thus, the concept of police power has been rarely applied in arbitral jurisprudence, notwithstanding its theoretical value.

Looking at the arbitral jurisprudence, in the *Methanex* case, the tribunal accepted as a principle of customary international law that a state is not responsible for bona fide regulation that falls within the scope of a generally recognized *police power*.[129] Outside NAFTA, other arbitral tribunals have adopted the same line of argument. More recently, in *Saluka v Czech Republic*,[130] the arbitral tribunal accepted the principle that 'a state does not commit an expropriation and is thus not liable to pay compensation to a dispossessed alien

---

[126] GS Alexander, 'Constitutionalizing Property: Two Experiences, Two Dilemmas' in J McLean (ed), *Property and the Constitution* (1999) 88–109, 89.

[127] TRIPS, Art 7 states: 'The protection and enforcement of intellectual property rights should contribute to the promotion of technological innovation and to the transfer and dissemination of technology, to the mutual advantage of producers and users of technological knowledge and in a manner conducive to *social and economic welfare*, and to a *balance of rights and obligations*' (emphasis added).

[128] Art 15.1 of the International Covenant on Economic, Social, and Cultural Rights states:

   1. The States Parties to the present Covenant recognize the right of everyone:

       …
       (b) To enjoy the benefits of scientific progress and its applications;
       (c) To benefit from the protection of the moral and material interests resulting from any scientific, literary or artistic production of which he is the author.

[129] *Methanex Corp v United States*, Final Award on Jurisdiction and Merits, 3 August 2005, (2005) 44 ILM 1345.

[130] *Saluka v Czech Republic*, UNCITRAL Rules Arbitration, Permanent Court of Arbitration, Partial Award, 17 March 2006, available at <http://www.ita.law.uvic.ca>.

investor when it adopts general regulations that are commonly accepted as within the police power of States'.[131]

3. Subsidiary Means of Treaty Interpretation

The instrumental or functional conceptualization of property has been adopted by a variety of courts at both national and regional level. This jurisprudence should not be neglected, as it may provide a rich source of comparative understanding on the linkage between tobacco control and investment treaty regime.

Although, according to the ICJ Statute, judicial decisions are recognized only as *subsidiary* means of interpretation[132] and there is no *stare decisis* in international law, in most cases, as Professor Schreuer highlights, *conversations across cases* take place,[133] and a systematic study of the case law of international tribunals suggests the 'tendency to chart a coherent course within law'.[134] Looking at the arbitral awards, there is not only a sort of *endogenous path coherence* by which arbitrators look at previous arbitral awards, but also an increasing *eterogenous path coherence* by which arbitrators look at the jurisprudence of other international courts.[135] In particular, reference is made not only to the ICJ jurisprudence and the WTO Dispute Settlement Body case law, which have dealt respectively with the protection of foreign investments and international economic law, but also to the case law of regional human rights courts.

In this sense, a review of the jurisprudence of the ECtHR and the ECJ concerning tobacco control may provide some useful reference. The ECJ stated in the famous *Tobacco Products Judgment*[136] that the right to property, which forms part of the general principles of Community law,[137] is not absolute and that 'its exercise may be restricted, provided that those restrictions in fact correspond to objectives of general interest ... and do not constitute a disproportionate and intolerable interference, impairing the very substance of the rights guaranteed'.[138] The case concerned some provisions of Directive 2001/37, which required cigarette packets to carry indications of the levels of harmful substances

---

[131] *Saluka*, at paras 253–265.

[132] According to Art 38(1)(b) of the Statute of the International Court of Justice, the sources of international law include international conventions and international customs, as well as general principles and, as a subsidiary means of interpretation, judicial decisions and the teachings of the most highly qualified publicists of international law.

[133] C Schreuer and M Weiniger, 'Conversations across Cases – Is There a Doctrine of Precedent in Investment Arbitration?' (2008) 5 Transnational Dispute Management 1–18.

[134] C McLachlan, 'The Principle of Systemic Integration and Article 31(3)(c) of the Vienna Convention' (2005) ICLQ 279–320, 289.

[135] V Vadi, 'Towards Arbitral Path Coherence & Judicial Borrowing: Persuasive Precedent in Investment Arbitration' (2008) 5 Transnational Dispute Management 1–16.

[136] Case C-491/01 *R v Secretary of State for Health (ex p British American Tobacco Investments Ltd and Imperial Tobacco Ltd)* [2002] ECR I-11453 (hereinafter, *Tobacco Products* judgment).

[137] The right to property is a fundamental right in the Community legal order, protected by the first subpara of Art 1 of the First Protocol to the European Convention on Human Rights (ECHR) and enshrined in Art 17 of the Charter of Fundamental Rights of the European Union.

[138] *Tobacco Products* judgment, at para 149.

and warnings concerning the risks to health.[139] British American Tobacco and other tobacco companies claimed that the large size of the new health warnings required by Article 5 of the Directive constituted a serious infringement of their IP rights. These warnings would dominate the overall appearance of tobacco product packaging, thus curtailing the use of their trademarks. The companies also complained that the absolute ban on the use of terms such as *mild* or *light* would amount to a trademark infringement, as these terms are incorporated into the trademark.

The Court found that the imposed measures did not prejudice the substance of companies' trademark rights, but constituted a proportionate restriction on the use of property to ensure a high level of health protection. In particular, the prohibition on using a trademark incorporating *mild* or similar descriptors did not keep tobacco manufacturers from distinguishing their products by using other distinctive signs. The restrictions on the trademark right caused by the Directive did in fact correspond to an objective of general interest pursued by the Community and did not constitute a disproportionate and intolerable interference, impairing the very substance of that right.[140]

The claimants also maintained the infringement of of the TRIPS, Article 20, which provides that use of a trademark in the course of trade is not to be unjustifiably encumbered by special requirements such as its use in a manner detrimental to its capacity to distinguish the goods or services of one company from those of its competitors. The Court ultimately dismissed this argument, as the TRIPS Agreement does not have direct effect in the Community legal order.[141]

The ECJ decision fully conforms to the trademark protection rationale, which is to enable purchasers to know the origin of the goods, thereby protecting the public from fraud and deceptiveness.[142] Indeed, trademarks can be conceived as tools of information about ownership, origin, or quality,[143] but also as instruments of consumer protection.[144] As light cigarettes are as harmful as regular cigarettes, the use of descriptors such as *light* on tobacco product packaging would mislead smokers to believe that these products are less harmful than others. In this sense, public health considerations would help to overcome the

---

[139] Directive 2001/37 on the approximation of the laws, regulations, and administrative provisions of the Member States concerning the manufacture, presentation and sale of tobacco products, [2001] OJ L194/26.
[140] *Tobacco Products* judgment, at paras 149–153.
[141] It is only where the Community intended to implement a particular obligation assumed in the context of the WTO, or where the Community measure refers expressly to the precise provisions of the WTO agreements, that it is for the Court to review the legality of the Community measure in question in the light of the WTO rules. See also Case C-149/96 *Portugal v Council* [1999] ECR I-8395, at para 47; Case C-301/97 *Netherlands v Council* [2001] ECR I-8853, at para 53; and Joined Cases C-27/00 and C-122/00 *Omega Air and ors* [2002] ECR I-2569, at para 93.
[142] B Sodipo, *Piracy and Counterfeiting GATT, TRIPS and Developing Countries* (1997) 16.
[143] Ibid., 74.   [144] Ibid., 81.

dysfunctions of the trademark system, especially when it is used excessively and contrary to its rationale.[145]

Further, notwithstanding that the Court did not adjudicate on TRIPS, Article 20, a close investigation of this article shows that its purpose is to stop rules that *unjustifiably* require a trademark to be used with another trademark, or in a way that harms its distinctiveness. Therefore, Article 20 'presents no obstacle to the requirements to print large health warnings on cigarette packets'.[146]

In the *cause célèbre, Anheuser-Busch Inc v Portugal,* generally known as the *Budweiser* case,[147] the ECtHR concluded that registered trademarks are protected by the property right clause of the European Convention's First Protocol.[148] Therefore, the ECtHR's consistent case law on the right to property might provide useful guidance for arbitrators facing expropriation claims,[149] especially with regard to the amount of compensation that should be paid or not paid in case of regulatory measures concerning tobacco control. The theory of inherent limitation of property rights would clearly constitute the ground for

[145] See L Helfer, 'Toward a Human Rights Framework for Intellectual Property' (2006–2007) 40 University of California Davies Law Review 972–1020, 1017.

[146] D Rogers, 'The TRIPS Regime of Trademarks and Designs' (2007) European Intellectual Property Review 76–78, 77.

[147] An American investor, Anheuser Busch Inc, producing and selling beer under the brand name *Budweiser* applied to the Portuguese competent authorities to register Budweiser as a trademark. However, the trademark was not granted, as *Budweiser bier* had already been registered as a designation of origin on behalf of Czech company, Budejovicky Budvar. After a series of challenges at the national level, the American company filed a suit at the ECtHR, claiming that the registration denial amounted to a deprivation of its possessions without compensation. The Court held that Art 1 of protocol No 1 was inapplicable to the present case and could not therefore have been infringed. *Anheuser-Busch Inc v Portugal,* App No 73049/01 ECtHR, 10 October 2005, 1 HR Rep (2006). However, the Grand Chamber subsequently held that the right to property included intellectual property as well as applications to register trademarks. *Anheuser-Busch Inc v Portugal,* ECtHR, Grand Chamber, No 73049/01, 11 January 2007. For commentary, see, for instance, G Burkhart, 'Trademarks Are Possessions As Are Applications' (2007) 2 Journal of Intellectual Property Law and Practice 4, 197–198. Professor Helfer criticizes the extensive interpretation of the ECtHR, questioning whether IP deserves to be treated as a human right. See L Helfer, 'The New Innovation Frontier? Intellectual Property and the European Court of Human Rights' (2008) Harvard International Law Journal 1–52, 6.

[148] The protection of property rights was not included in the European Convention on Human Rights, but in its first optional protocol. Protocol to the Convention for the Protection of Human Rights and Fundamental Freedoms, opened for signature on 20 March 1952, 213 UNTS 262, 262. Art 1 of Protocol No 1 to the Convention provides:

> Every natural or legal person is entitled to the peaceful enjoyment of his possessions. No one shall be deprived his possessions except in the public interest and subject to the conditions provided for by the law and by the general principles of law. The preceding provisions shall not, however, in any way impair the right of a State to enforce such laws as it deems necessary to control the use of property in accordance with the general interest or to secure the payment of taxes or other contributions or penalties.

[149] E Freeman, 'Regulatory Expropriation Under NAFTA Chapter 11: Some Lessons From the European Court of Human Rights' (2003–2004) 42 Columbia Journal of Transnational Law 177–215; and H Ruiz-Fabri, 'The Approach Taken by the European Court of Human Rights to the Assessment of Compensation for "Regulatory Expropriations" of the Property of Foreign Investors' (2002–2003) 11 New York University Environmental Law Journal 148–174.

non-compensation.[150] In this regard, the Court has taken a relatively sophisticated approach to the wisdom of requiring compensation for regulation that incidentally diminishes the value of property. The Court has stated that the notion of public interest is extensive and that states have a very wide margin of appreciation to consider what is in the public interest.[151] In particular, a very important public interest will weigh in the balance to justify a control of the use of property without compensation. In assessing whether a fair balance of public and private interests has been involved, the Court looks at the nature and proportionality of the interference and at the legitimate expectations of the private owners.[152]

For instance, in *Fredin v Sweden*, the Court held that environmental legislation had a public interest goal to protect nature, and that it was thus proportionate, notwithstanding that there was no payment of compensation.[153] Similarly, in *Pinnacle Meat Processors Co v United Kingdom*,[154] the Commission denied the applicants' compensation. The case concerned a regulation aimed at preventing the possibility of contracting the human form of Bovine Spongiform Encephalopathy (BSE) from infected beef. When a law stated that meat extracted from cattle heads could no longer be sold, the applicant companies, which conducted a business that involved de-boning cattle heads, were forced out of business. In evaluating whether there was a fair balance between the protection of the public and private interest, the Commission observed that protecting people against a potentially fatal disease was a pre-eminent interest. Thus, the Commission declared the application admissible: the applicants' loss was not as expropriation.[155]

The ECJ has adopted a very similar approach, ruling that the protection of public health is a general interest which can even justify substantial adverse consequences for freedom of trade and property rights. For instance, in his opinion to the *Booker Aquaculture and Hydro Seafood* case, Advocate General Mischo stated that regulation imposing the destruction of fish when a disease is discovered does not constitute an expropriation, but an extreme case of *control of the use* of goods.[156] Consequently, it was held that the measures, even without

[150] This inherent limitation analysis was adopted by the US Supreme Court in the case *Lucas v South Carolina Coastal Council*. In *Lucas*, Justice Scalia held that 'where the State seeks to sustain regulation that deprives land of all economic beneficial use, we think it may resist compensation only if the logically antecedent inquiry into the nature of the owner's estate shows that *the proscribed use interests were not part of his title to begin with*' (emphasis added). *Lucas v SC Coastal Council*, (1992) 505 US 1003, at 2899–2900.
[151] *James v United Kingdom*, 98 ECtHR (ser A) 9, 32 (1986).
[152] H Mountfield, 'Regulatory Expropriations in Europe: The Approach of the European Court of Human Rights' (2002–2003) 11 New York University Environmental Law Journal 136–147, 142.
[153] *Fredin v Sweden*, 192 ECtHR (Ser A) (1991).
[154] *Pinnacle Meat Processors Co v United Kingdom*, App No 33298/96, 27 EHRR 217 (1998) (Commission Report).   [155] Ibid., at 223.
[156] Opinion of 20 September 2001 of AG Mischo in Joined Cases C-20/00 and C-64/00 *Booker Aquaculture and Hydro Seafood* [2003] ECR 7411.

recognizing a right to compensation, did not constitute a disproportionate and intolerable interference with the right to property.[157]

With specific regard to tobacco products, in the *Swedish Match* cases,[158] the ECJ recognized that the prohibition of the marketing of tobacco for oral use restricted free trade,[159] but stressed that such a regulation was intended to protect a high level of health, which is an objective of general interest.[160] The case concerned a Swedish manufacturer of tobacco products for oral use, called *snus*, who wished to commercialize these products in the United Kingdom. In parallel, a German trader wanted to import *snus* in Germany and place them on the German market. Both activities were prevented by national laws in accordance with a 2001 Directive.[161] The two companies thus brought actions against the decisions taken by national authorities before the English Court and the German Court respectively, claiming that the Directive breached several principles of Community law. The courts deferred a number of questions to the ECJ for a preliminary ruling.

The ECJ considered that in the exercise of the power conferred by Article 95 of the EC Treaty, the Community legislature has to take as a base a high level of health protection. As scientific evidence has shown that tobacco products for oral use can cause cancer of the mouth, and these products contain nicotine which is addictive and toxic, the Court held the legislature fully entitled to prohibit the commercialization of these new products. Further, the Court noted that the legislature had already explained the reasons for the ban in a previous 1992 Directive,[162] noting that tobacco products for oral use were particularly attractive to young people, and the risk of their developing an addiction to nicotine was high. Thus, the measure was deemed to be necessary and appropriate.

It is worth recalling that an almost identical approach was adopted by the US Supreme Court in *Austin v Tennessee*,[163] which affirmed a decision adopted by the Tennessee Supreme Court. In this old case, the Court held that the regulation of cigarette sales came within the powers of the states:

Without undertaking to affirm or deny their evil effects, we think it within the province of the legislature to say how far cigarettes may be sold or to prohibit their sale entirely . . .

---

[157] *Booker Aquaculture and Hydro Seafood*, n 156 above, at paras 85–93. For commentary, see, for instance, K Lenaerts and K Vanvoorden, 'The Right to Property in the Case Law of the Court of Justice of the European Communities' in H Van den Berge (ed), *Propriété et Droits de l'Homme – Property and Human Rights* (2006) 195–240, 237.

[158] Case C-210/03 *Swedish Match* [2003] ECR I-11893; and Case C-434/02, *Arnold André* [2004] ECR I-11825.   [159] *Swedish Match*, at para 73.

[160] *Swedish Match*, at para 74.

[161] Directive 2001/37/EC of the European Parliament and of the Council of 5 June 2001 on the approximation of laws, regulations, and administrative provisions of the Member States concerning the manufacture, presentation, and sale of tobacco products, [2001] OJ L194/26.

[162] Council Directive 92/41/EEC of 15 May 1992 on the approximation of the laws, regulations, and administrative provisions of the Member States concerning the labeling of tobacco products, [1992] OJ L158/30.

[163] *Austin v Tennessee*, 179 US 343 (19 November 1900).

and there is no reason to doubt that the act in question is designed for the protection of public health.

In conclusion, as property rights are individual rights, but also serve a social function, certain regulatory measures may be considered as their intrinsic limits or *natural boundaries*, rather than *exceptions* to their protection.

4. Systematic Interpretation

If looking at the object and purpose of the treaty does not help, another criterion of treaty interpretation requires adjudicators to take into account 'any relevant rules of international law applicable in the relations between the parties'.[164] As stated by Sinclair, pursuant to Article 31(3)(c), '[e]very treaty provision must be read not only in its own context, but in the wider context of general international law, whether conventional or customary'.[165] In this regard, the International Court of Justice has recognized in its advisory opinion on *Legal Consequences for States of the Continued Presence of South Africa in Namibia* that an adjudicator's interpretation cannot remain unaffected by subsequent developments of law and 'an international instrument has to be interpreted and applied within the framework of the entire legal system prevailing at the time of interpretation'.[166]

Coherently, with regard to the governing or substantive law to be applied in investment disputes, while only some BITs make reference to international law, NAFTA expressly requires that '[a] Tribunal established under this Section shall decide the issue in dispute in accordance with this Agreement and applicable rules of international law'.[167] According to Article 38(1)(b) of the Statute of the International Court of Justice, the sources of international law include, inter alia, international conventions and international customs.[168]

The problem is that while the national judge knows that the law that has to be applied to the case and applies it even if the parties have invoked different rules (*iura novit curia*), arbitrators generally consider only the investment agreements and the legal arguments expressly made by the parties (*secundum alligata et probata*). Further, the principle *nec ultra petita* or *nec ultra fines mandati* requires the arbitral tribunal to limit itself to the scope of power allowed. The violation of its mandate by the arbitral tribunal is widely recognized as a cause for the annulment of the international arbitral award.[169]

---

[164] Vienna Convention, Art 31(3)(c).

[165] I Sinclair, *The Vienna Convention on the Law of Treaties* (1984) 139.

[166] ICJ Advisory Opinion of 21 June 1971, *Legal Consequences for States of the Continued Presence of South Africa in Namibia (South-West Africa) Notwithstanding Security Council Resolution 276 (1970)*, ICJ Reports (1971) 16.

[167] NAFTA, Art 1131(1).   [168] Statute of the International Court of Justice, Art 38.

[169] The recognition or enforcement of an award shall be refused under the New York Convention, Art V.1(c) if the award contains decisions on matters beyond the scope of submission to arbitration.

Legal advocacy has rarely used human rights language in investment arbitration. This may be due to the limits given by the applicable law and the traditional divide between human rights and international economic law in legal discourse.[170] These two fields of law have evolved in an almost autonomous way, developing not only specific jargons or dialects, but also specific cultures.[171] However, this omission may also be due to the investor's willingness to locate the dispute in a given legal framework, in a sort of forum shopping. An investor's attorneys may wish to voluntarily pass over the human rights issues, as this would be detrimental to their client's position. The secrecy assured by certain arbitral rules is another intrinsic advantage to investors violating human rights. Crucially, the respondent state may also have an interest in not introducing human rights arguments in the course of the legal proceeding.

However, the splendid isolation of international arbitration from international law has to come to an end. First, arbitrators may be willing to take public international law into account because of international law. This is not a tautology, arbitral activism, or something which goes against arbitral ethics. On the contrary, it is a natural consequence of arbitrators' duty to interpret international law treaties according to customary rules of treaty interpretation which, inter alia, require systemic interpretation.[172]

Second, arbitrators may be willing to take public international law into account because of *reputation*. High quality awards are extremely important to build arbitrators' reputation which is a key issue in international investment arbitration. As arbitrators 'are purportedly selected for their virtue-judgment, neutrality, expertise',[173] they have an interest in maintaining and increasing the 'symbolic capital acquired through a career of public service or scholarship'.[174]

---

[170] See the well-known debate in E-U Petersmann, 'Time for a United Nations Global Compact for Integrating Human Rights into the Law of Worldwide Organizations. Lessons from the European Integration' (2002) 13 European Journal of International Law 621–650; P Alston, 'Resisting the Merger and Acquisition of Human Rights by Trade Law: A Reply to Petersmann' (2002) 13 European Journal of International Law 845–851; and E-U Petersmann, 'Taking Human Dignity, Poverty and Empowerment of Individuals More Seriously: Rejoinder to Alston' (2002) 13 European Journal of International Law 815–844.

[171] On the development of a specific 'culture' or 'theology' in international economic law (with particular regard to international trade law), see DP Steger, 'The Culture of the WTO: Why It Needs to Change' (2007) 10 Journal of International Economic Law 3, 483; on the existing 'folklore' or 'experience of arbitration specialists' to be transmitted to 'future arbitration connoisseurs', see WW Park, 'Arbitration's Protean Nature: The Value of Rules and the Risk of Discretion', the XVII Freshfields Lecture (2003) 20 Arbitration International 3, reprinted in JDM Lew and L Mistelis, *Arbitration Insights* (2007) 348. On the development of a specific human rights culture, see, for instance, A Fernandez, 'From an Idea to a Culture of Human Rights: Human Rights in the 21st Century' (2002) Finnish Yearbook of International Law 35–49. More generally, on the notion of legal culture, see also R Cotterrell, 'Comparative Law and Legal Culture' in R Cotterrell (ed), *Living Law* (2008) 281–312.

[172] D French, 'Treaty Interpretation and the Incorporation of Extraneous Legal Rules' (2006) 55 ICLQ 281–314.

[173] Y Dezalay and BG Garth, *Dealing in Virtue. International Commercial Arbitration and the Construction of a Transnational Legal Order* (1996) 8.   [174] Ibid., 8.

Third, arbitrators should acknowledge their responsibility for the charting of the contours of international law norms and, more broadly, as cartographers of the international legal order.[175] If arbitral awards are referred to as persuasive precedents, then arbitrators must realize their determinant role not only with regard to the single dispute, but also with regard to the possible influence that their reasoning may have on subsequent arbitral panels.[176]

In conclusion, interpretation is not merely an exercise of legal logic; which tools of interpretation a judge deploys is equally 'a matter of harmony with what, for want of a better world, one might term experience and common sense'.[177] While the ability of investment arbitration to function and achieve desirable adjudicatory results is clearly important, the interest of society in the legitimate exercise of authority and the maintenance of juridical values is equally important.[178]

C. Legal Drafting

1. Specific Safeguards

Having analysed the empirical or *ex post* approach to the interplay between tobacco control and international investment governance in the context of litigation, it can be asked whether an *ex ante* or legislative approach to tobacco control in investment agreements might be envisaged. In general, public health goals are more directly achievable through the political and legal processes than through litigation. For instance, at the European level, the Treaty Establishing a Constitution for Europe expressly referred to tobacco regulation.[179] Albeit the Constitution never came into force, it paved the way for the Treaty of Lisbon,[180] which similarly included a provision on tobacco control.[181] Should tobacco products be treated as an exception to the international investment rules, so that

---

[175] On the impact of Chapter 11 cases on the further development of international law, see C Brower and L Steven, 'Who Then Should Judge? Developing the International Rule of Law Under NAFTA Chapter 11' (2001) 2 Chicago Journal of International Law 193, 201.

[176] See above, section 3.

[177] V Lowe, 'The Role of Law in International Politics' in M Byers (ed), *The Politics of Law Making: Are the Method and Character of Norm Creation Changing?* (2000) 216.

[178] T Carbonneau, *Cases and Materials on the Law and Practice of Arbitration* (2003) 1205.

[179] Treaty Establishing a Constitution for Europe, 16 December 2004, 2004 OJ (C310) 1, Art III-278. The Treaty never entered into force. For commentary, see F Nicola and F Marchetti, 'Constitutionalizing Tobacco: The Ambivalence of European Federalism' (2005) 46 Harvard International Law Journal 507–525.

[180] Treaty of Lisbon Amending the Treaty on European Union and the Treaty Establishing the European Community, signed on 13 December 2007, [2007] OJ C306/135. According to Art 6 of the Treaty of Lisbon, 'this Treaty shall enter into force on 1 January 2009, provided that all the instruments of ratification have been deposited, or, failing that, on the first day of the month following the deposit of the instrument of ratification by the last signatory State to take this step'. At the time of this writing, 23 Member States deposited their ratification instruments in Rome (<http://europa.eu/lisbon_treaty/take/index_en.htm> (accessed 17 April 2009)).

[181] Treaty of Lisbon, Art 127d(iv).

investment in these products can be more easily restricted? Should tobacco products be excluded *tout court* from investment treaties?

With regard to the first question, setting up an exception to investment protection for the tobacco trade would be a feasible option. This approach has already been adopted in the context of the US-Vietnam Free Trade Agreement, which excludes tobacco from its tariff regulation and reduction scheme.[182] In parallel, investment treaties might exclude the tobacco trade from their application scope. According to the exemption, if an investor invokes dispute settlement to challenge any regulatory measure taken by the state under this provision, an arbitral tribunal will not have jurisdiction.

Should investment treaties recognize the need to promote policy regulation aimed at tobacco control? Theoretically, there is no need for such a specific provision, as protecting public health is a traditional police power of a given state. However, as the concept of expropriation in investment agreements is very broad, a detailed provision clarifying that tobacco control measures in conformity with the Framework Convention on Tobacco Control will not be considered as measures tantamount to expropriation would help arbitrators to issue consistent decisions.

2. Rethinking the Purpose of International Investment Agreements

International investment treaties have become 'constitutional charters' of rights for foreign investors, establishing fundamental principles such as non-discrimination, fair and equitable treatment, and so on and so forth.[183] So far, investment treaties have protected not only investors' property rights, but also their individual freedom to pursue an economic activity, thus paralleling human rights treaties and constitutional provisions. Some commentators have highlighted that no concomitant responsibilities or liabilities and no protection for public welfare are included in investment agreements.[184] Consequently, the central criterion for resolving investment disputes seems to have been the protection of the foreign investor. For instance, in the *Metalclad* case, the tribunal repeatedly referred to NAFTA's objective of promoting foreign investment, although the case also involved environmental concerns.[185] Similarly, in *Siemens v Argentina*, the arbitral tribunal observed that it was obliged to interpret key treaty rules through the lens of the Treaty's object and purpose, which was to 'create favourable conditions for

---

[182] Agreement Between the United States of America and the Socialist Republic of Vietnam on Trade Relations, signed on 13 July 2000, available at <http://www.ustr.gov/assets/World_Regions/Southeast_Asia_Pacific/Vietnam/asset_upload_file917_10731.pdf>.
[183] On the 'constitutionalization' of investment law, see, for instance, D Schneiderman, *Constitutionalizing Economic Globalization – Investment Rules and Democracy's Promise* (2008).
[184] H Mann, 'The Right to Regulate and International Investment Law: A Comment' in UNCTAD, *The Development Dimension of FDI: Policy and Rule Making Perspectives* (2003) 212.
[185] *Metalclad Corp v Mexico*, Award, ICSID (Additional Facility) Case No ARB(AF)/97/1, 30 August 2000, (2001) 40 ILM 36.

investments and to stimulate private initiative'.[186] This is why it has been observed that preambular statements in investment treaties 'cannot simply be conflated with a general preference for the interests of the investor over those of the host state. The overall objective in fact requires a balanced approach.'[187]

As in the interpretation of investment treaties, particular attention is given to the object and purpose of the Treaty as expressed in the preamble, it will be important for policy makers to ensure that investment treaties recognize not only the importance of a favourable investment climate, but also the importance of other policy goals, such as health promotion.[188]

The concept of sustainable development might play a crucial role in construing more balanced preambles and favouring balancing. For instance, the NAFTA preamble expressly mentions the goal of sustainable development. Literally, sustainable means that it 'meets the needs of the present generation without compromising the ability of future generations to meet their own needs'.[189] According to a restrictive interpretation, sustainable development would be an environmental law concept requiring the optimal use of the world's resources to protect and preserve the environment. However, in recent times, the principle of sustainable development, restated not only in multilateral environmental agreements, but also in trade agreements, has been broadened to include some elements of social rights. The emphasis would be put on human needs rather than wants, and on inter- and intra-generational equity. In the *Shrimp Turtle* case, the Appellate Body acknowledged that '[the concept of sustainable development] has been generally accepted as integrating economic and social development and environmental protection'.[190] Thus, social dimensions and wellbeing have come to play a role in international discourse regarding development.

Importantly, both public health and foreign investment are essential component parts of sustainable development.[191] Health is fundamental to poverty reduction, human development, and economic growth. In parallel, the

---

[186] *Siemens v Argentina*, Decision on Jurisdiction, 3 August 2004, ICSID Case No ARB/02/08, at para 81.

[187] C McLachlan, 'Investment Treaties and General International Law' (2008) ICLQ 361, 371.

[188] For, instance, the US Model BIT states in its Preamble that the 'importance of providing effective means of asserting claims and enforcing rights with respect to investment under national law as well as through international arbitration' and the desire 'to achieve these objectives in a manner consistent with the protection of health, safety, and the environment, and the promotion of internationally recognized labor rights'.

[189] *WTO Shrimp/Turtle case, Recourse to Art 21.5 by Malaysia*, fn 202.

[190] *WTO Shrimp/Turtle Case, AB Decision*, fn 107.

[191] Mann, n 184 above, 212; and SP Subedi, 'Foreign Investment and Sustainable Development' in F Weiss, E Denters, and P de Waart (eds), *International Economic Law With a Human Face* (1998) 413–428.

development dimension is a conceptual pillar in the health policy discourse. Indeed, basic levels of social welfare and economic development are of fundamental importance to the fullest attainable standard of health. As foreign direct investment is deemed generally to promote economic and social development, the linkage between foreign investment and public health may endorse positive outcomes.

In this sense, some recent Economic Partnership Agreements concluded by the European Community include a specific commitment that 'the application of this Agreement shall fully take into account the human, cultural, economic, social, health, and environmental best interests of their respective population and of future generations'.[192]

VI. Conclusions

The interplay between human rights and investor rights has attracted interesting scholarly reflections. While some authors somehow oppose the *merger and acquisition* of the two branches of public international law,[193] others propose methods for balancing conflicting interests, thus assuming a collision of rights.[194] This study, which has focused on the specific issue of reconciling a public health issue such as tobacco control with investment treaty regime, has proposed a nuanced approach, adopting a multilayered framework of analysis. With regard to treaty interpretation, the existing customary canons may help interpreters to avoid conflict of norms. As investment law is part of international law, it has to be consistent with its norms, and it has to be interpreted in accordance with the customary rules of treaty interpretation. Although examined in a separate manner, the legal canons of treaty interpretation are complementary and may be used cumulatively.

First, according to the canon of literal interpretation, there is no manifest inconsistency between the two sets of norms. On the contrary, some recent bilateral investment treaties expressly mention the need to protect public health in their treaty text. Second, according to the canon of systematic interpretation, investment treaties should not be considered as self-contained regimes, but as an important component part of public international law. Accordingly, arbitrators should adopt a holistic approach, taking human rights treaties and relevant customary law into account when they interpret relevant investment treaty provision. Third, adopting a functional or teleological interpretation, property is not an absolute right, but it has both external and inherent limits. Thus, as the

---

[192] See Art 3.1 of the Economic Partnership Agreement Between the CARIFORUM States, of the one Part, and the European Community and Its Member States of the other Part, available at <http://ec.europa.eu/trade/issues/bilateral/regions/acp/pr220208_en.htm>.
[193] See ch 14 in this volume.   [194] See ch 18 in this volume.

arbitral tribunal held in *Feldman Karpa v Mexico*, 'not every business problem experienced by a foreign investor is an indirect or creeping expropriation'.[195] On the contrary, certain types of regulation adopted to protect public health should be properly viewed as an intrinsic limit to property. Reference to subsidiary means of treaty interpretation like the case law of the ECJ and the ECtHR seem to confirm this multifaceted approach.

De lege ferenda, at a procedural level, as investor-state disputes often present a constitutional dimension, investor-state arbitration would require appropriate procedural reforms.[196] At a substantive level, introducing specific clauses in investment agreements clarifying that tobacco control measures in conformity with international standards are not to be considered as a form of expropriation would be a feasible option. Such clauses would facilitate the task of the adjudicating bodies. Finally, reshaping the purpose of investment agreement from the mere protection of foreign investment to the promotion of sustainable development would provide a more balanced conceptual framework. This chapter contends that foreign investment should not be considered an end in itself, but as one of the available tools to promote human welfare.

---

[195] *Feldman Karpa v Mexico*, n 82 above, at § 102.
[196] See A Jaksic, 'Procedural Guarantees of Human Rights in Arbitration Proceedings A Still Unsettled Problem?' (2007) 24 Journal of International Arbitration 159–172; and G Van Harten, 'A Case for an International Investment Court', Society of International Economic Law Conference Paper, 4 July 2008.

20

The Human Right to Water Versus Investor Rights: Double-Dilemma or Pseudo-Conflict?

*Pierre Thielbörger**

I. Introduction

Water is perhaps the most important topic in contemporary international investment law. At the same time it is also one of the most controversial: although the privatization of water supplies through foreign investment has globally gained more and more importance over the last years, the legal status of the human right to water remains unresolved. These two factors make it difficult to find adequate solutions for the settlement of international disputes that arise from water privatizations through foreign investments. The focus of this chapter is to characterize this difficulty, and to suggest solutions to this tension between the right to water and the rights of investors.

In a first step, this chapter outlines the current status of the right to water in international law. Is it accepted in the international legal order as much as it is claimed by civil society? And does the acceptance of a right to water exclude or promote the privatization of water supply systems? In order to throw light on the 'trendy' phenomenon of privatization, we will examine three recent prominent investment disputes related to water, and their settlement through arbitrational tribunals of the International Centre for the Settlement of Investment Disputes (ICSID). What are the typical interests that clash in these disputes? And has the right to water played a prominent role in their settlement?

With this knowledge in theory and praxis, one can then approach the question of how the clash between the right to water and the rights of investors, as typical in the case of water privatization, has been resolved in the past, and consider how it could be alternatively solved in the future.

* The author would like to thank Professor Ernst-Ulrich Petersmann, Angelos Dimopoulos and Mark Dawson for their invaluable comments on an earlier draft of this chapter.

II. The Right to Water as a Human Right

The global water crisis could not be more apparent: according to the UN Development Report 2006,[1] more than 1.2 billion people are without access to clean drinkable water, while 2.6 billion lack access to sanitation.[2] Almost 2 million children die each year for want of clean water and clean toilets.[3] Although no person and no state refutes the claim that all humans *should* have a right to water of sufficient quantity and quality,[4] there is currently still no explicit, comprehensive, and legally binding recognition of such a right in the texts of international conventions and treaties.[5]

This does not, however, mean that the right to water is a *novum* in international and human rights law. The right might not be *recognized* in a legally binding manner, but it is at least *mentioned* by name in a few, albeit important, universal and regional human rights instruments. One of the first legal fields to provide explicit protection of the right to water is international humanitarian law, which establishes the right in times of armed conflict. Geneva Convention III relative to the Treatment of Prisoners of War and Geneva Convention IV relative to the Protection of Civilian Persons in Time of War state that sufficient drinking water is to be supplied to prisoners and other detainees[6] and that they are to be provided with shower and bathing facilities.[7] The Additional Protocols to the Geneva Conventions of 1977 prohibit the destruction of 'objects indispensable to the survival of the civilian population such as ... drinking water installations and supplies and irrigation works'.[8]

Also emerging from the end of the 1970s is the Convention on the Elimination of Discrimination against Women,[9] which obliges states parties in

---

[1] UN Development Report 2006, available at <http://hdr.undp.org/hdr2006/>, released in November 2006.

[2] These figures are roughly confirmed by a similar report by the WHO: see WHO, *Global Water and Sanitation Assessment* (2000) 1–3.

[3] UN Development Report 2006, n 1 above, Foreword.

[4] See S McCaffrey, 'The human right to water' in E Brown Weiss, L Boisson de Chazournes, and N Bernasconi-Osterwalter (eds), *Fresh Water and International Economic Law* (2005) 93. McCaffrey, however, seems to address the question of a *moral* right in this statement.

[5] P-M Dupuy, 'Le droit à l'eau, un droit international?' in G Grisel (ed), *La mise en oeuvre du droit à l'eau*, Institut International de droit d'expression et d' Inspiration (2006) 277, 278, with many further references.

[6] See Geneva Convention III, Arts 21, 25, and 46 relative to the Treatment of Prisoners of War of 12 August 1949 and Geneva Convention IV, Arts 89 and 127 relative to the Protection of Civilian Persons in Time of War of 12 August 1949.   [7] See Geneva Convention III, Art 29.

[8] Protocol Additional to the Geneva Conventions of 12 August 1949, and relating to the Protection of Victims of International Armed Conflicts (Protocol I) of 8 June 1977, Art 54; and Protocol Additional to the Geneva Conventions of 12 August 1949, and relating to the Protection of Victims of Non-International Armed Conflicts (Protocol II) of 8 June 1977, Art 14. Certainly, this right is more shaped as a collective than as an individual right.

[9] GA Res 34/180 of 18 December 1979, UN Doc A/34/830.

Article 14 (2-h) to ensure to rural women the right to enjoy adequate living conditions, particularly in relation to water supply. Articles 24(1) and (2)(c) of the Convention on the Rights of the Child[10] from 1989 commits states parties to implementing children's rights to health by taking appropriate measures to combat disease and malnutrition. Furthermore, regional human rights treaties, such as the African Charter on the Rights and Welfare of the Child and the Protocol to the African Charter on Human and Peoples' Rights on the Rights of Women in Africa, offer special references to the right to water.[11] Additionally, numerous *non-binding* declarations such as the Mar del Plata Declaration of the 1977 UN Water Conference,[12] the UN General Assembly Declaration on the Principles for elderly persons,[13] and the 1992 Dublin Statement on Water and Sustainable Development[14] have called for an individual and legally binding right to water.

While this call has long existed, it has taken international judges a long time to answer it. Prominent cases like *Lake Lanoux*[15] or more recently *Gabcikovo-Nagymaro*[16] have been cornerstones of international water jurisprudence or arbitration. However, judges and arbitrators have often been reluctant to accept *subjective* rights when they dealt with the protection and distribution of water. Only recently have courts and tribunals started to develop creative and innovative approaches in recognizing a right to water – by linking the right to water to a variety of other accepted human rights. The recognition of a human right to water has therefore been termed an 'emerging trend'[17] in the jurisdiction of international courts and quasi-courts. In particular, the right to health, as for instance laid down in ICESCR, Article 12, and the right to life, as enshrined in ICCPR, Article 6, are often referred to by the courts.

[10] GA Res 44/25 of 20 November 1989, UN Doc A/Res./44/25.
[11] See Art 14(2)(c) of the African Charter on the Rights and Welfare of the Child, OAU Doc CAB/LEG/24.9/49 (1990): 'state parties ... shall take measures to ensure the provision of adequate standard of nutrition and safe drinking water' and Art 15(a) of the Protocol to the African Charter on Human and Peoples' Rights on the Rights of Women in Africa of 11 July 2003, according to which state parties shall 'provide women with access to clean drinking water'.
[12] See Preamble, Mar del Plata UN-Declaration, Argentina, 1977: 'All people ... have the right to have access to drinking water in quantities and quality equal to their basic needs.'
[13] See GA Res 46/91 16 December 1991, 'Implementation of the International Plan of Action on Ageing and Related Activities', Section Independence: 'Older persons should have access to adequate food, water, shelter, clothing and health care.'
[14] Principle No 3 of 'The Dublin Statement on Water and Sustainable Development' of 31 January 1992 of the International Conference on Water and the environment establishes 'the basic right of all human beings to have access to clean water and sanitation at an affordable price'.
[15] *Lake Lanoux, Spain v France*, Arbitrational Award, 16 November 1957, (1957) 12 Report of International Arbitrational Awards 281–317; English text at (1957) 24 International Law Reports 101-142.
[16] *Gabcikovo-Nagymaros Project, Hungary v Slovakia*, judgment, 25 September 1997, ICJ Reports 1997, p 7.
[17] J Scanlon, A Cassar, and N Nemes, 'Water as a Human Right?' in World Conservation Union Environmental Policy and Law Paper, No 51 (2004) 13 ff.

One explicit example of linkage of the right to water with the right to health is the legal reasoning of the African Commission in its Communications 25/89, 47/90, 56/91 and 100/93 (Joined) against Zaire,[18] where the Commission interlinked water issues on several occasions with the right to health as laid down in Article 16 of the African Charter on Human and Peoples' Rights.[19] It stated that the government's failure to provide basic services, such as drinking water and electricity, constituted a violation of the right to health for everyone.

To give an example for the direct derivation of the right to water from the right to life, the American Commission on Human Rights found in its Report on the Human Rights Situation in Ecuador[20] that inhabitants exposed to toxic byproducts of oil exploitation in their drinking and bathing water were subject to serious danger. It was argued that, where environmental contamination and degradation pose a persistent threat to the existence of human beings, the rights to life and to physical security and integrity were the relevant rights to be implicated.[21]

However, it is not only courts who have tried to give shape to the human right to water. In 2002, the UN Committee on Economic, Social, and Cultural Rights (CESCR) – the body responsible for the oversight of the covenant of the same name – adopted its General Comment No 15 on 'The Right to Water'.[22] This is by far the most relevant of all legal recognitions of the right to water.

The Committee interpreted the Covenant's Article 11(1) dealing with 'the right of everyone to an adequate standard of living . . . including adequate food, clothing and housing' as covering also an independent right to water for personal and domestic use. As the listed rights of food, clothing, and housing were not exhaustive due to the use of the word 'including', the Committee found that the right to water clearly fell into the category of those non-explicitly mentioned guarantees, essential for securing an adequate standard of living.[23]

---

[18] African Commission on Human and Peoples' Rights, *Free Legal Assistance Group and ors v Zaire*, Comm No 25/89, 47/90, 56/91, 100/93 (1995), para 47.

[19] Art 16 of the African Charter on Human and Peoples' Rights:

   1. Every individual shall have the right to enjoy the best attainable state of physical and mental health.
   2. State Parties to the present Charter shall take the necessary measures to protect the health of their people and to ensure that they receive medical attention when they are sick.

   Text available at <http://www.achpr.org/english/_info/charter_en.html>.

[20] Inter-American Commission on Human Rights, 'Report on the Situation of Human Rights in Ecuador', OEA/Ser.L/V/II.96, doc 10 rev 1 (1997) ch VIII, available at <http://www.cidh.oas.org/countryrep/ecuador-eng/index%20-%20ecuador.htm>.

[21] Inter-American Commission on Human Rights, 'Report on the Situation of Human Rights in Ecuador', OEA/Ser.L/V/II.96, doc 10 rev 1, Ch VIII, The Applicable Legal Framework, 2. Relevant Inter-American Law.

[22] General Comment No 15, UN Doc E/C 12/2002/11 of 26 November 2002.

[23] Ibid., Art 3.

The Committee derived this stand-alone right to water furthermore from the health provisions of the ICESCR. Article 12(1) provides everyone with the right to the highest attainable standard of health. In an earlier comment, the Committee had already stated that the underlying components of the right to health also include drinkable water.[24] In General Comment No 15, the Committee went further and elaborated a number of aspects relating to water under the right to health. It concluded that health could not be ensured effectively under unsafe or toxic water conditions.[25]

The Committee also defined the different aspects of the content of the human right to water. It claimed that everyone, on the basis of non-discrimination, had the right to sufficient, safe, physically accessible, and affordable water of an acceptable quality.[26] Therefore, states were called upon to respect, protect, and fulfil this right.[27] General Comment No 15 was the first recognition of an independent and generally applicable human right to water.

In assessing this legal situation, one could summarize that many legal documents in international law *mention* a right to water, but none of them establishes such a right in a comprehensive and legally binding manner. An explicit recognition in a separate water convention or as an addition to one of the existing human rights instruments seems, currently, out of political reach. Attempts to establish water as a human right have just recently been refused by a majority of states at the World Water Fora in Mexico City in 2006 and Istanbul in 2009.[28] Only in a '*Complementary* Ministerial Declaration',[29] signed solely by the representatives of Cuba, Bolivia, and Venezuela, was it suggested that 'access to water with quality, quantity and equity constitutes a Fundamental Human Right'.[30] Therefore, there are severe doubts about if and when a consensus on the establishment of a right to water can be achieved among states in the future. One is tempted to call this another example of the at least partial failure[31] of the institutions of contemporary international law, in particular the United Nations, to protect human rights properly.

In the absence of a successful political initiative, it has been the judges and quasi-judges who have taken action. A clear and consistent line might not be

---

[24] General Comment No 14, UN Doc E/C 12/2002/4 of 4 February 2002, Arts 11, 12, 15, 34, and 51.   [25] General Comment No 15, n 22 above, Art 8.
[26] Ibid., Art 12 (a)–(c).   [27] Ibid., Arts 20–29.
[28] See Summary Reports of the World Water Fora in Mexico City and Istanbul published by the International Institute for Sustainable Development (IISD), available at <http://www.iisd.ca/download/pdf/sd/ymbvol82num15e.pdf> and <http://www.iisd.ca/ymb/water/worldwater5/html/ymbvol82num23e.html>. For a comprehensive description of the latest 2009 World Water Forum in Istanbul, see also <http://www.worldwaterforum5.org/>.
[29] See text at <http://ministerial.worldwaterforum5.org/fileadmin/wwc/News/newsletter/synthesis_righttowater_4wwf.pdf>; see also <http://www.iisd.ca/download/pdf/sd/ymbvol82-num15e.pdf>, 11.   [30] Ibid., n 29 above, para 2.
[31] E-U Petersmann, 'The Human Rights Approach advocated by the UN High Commissioner for Human Rights and by the International Labour Organization: Is it relevant for WTO Law and Policy?' (2004) 7(3) Journal of International Economic Law 613, 614.

visible in the different judgments of different courts, with the right to water sometimes linked to civil and political rights and other times to economic, social, and cultural rights. However, the general trend towards the recognition of the right is clearly visible in international jurisprudence and arbitration. In order to act on this suggestion and at the same time to resolve the disorder of this ill-defined status[32] of the right to water, the Economic, Social, and Cultural Commission released General Comment No 15 on 'The Right to Water'.

The General Comment is a major achievement and represents significant progress towards the recognition of the right. General Comment No 15 offers a detailed account of the contours of the right to water, and is at the same time the most extensive discussion of a comprehensive right to water by an international human rights body.

However, the General Comment also contains a number of drawbacks. First, it is an authoritative interpretation of the ICESCR, but it is not legally binding.[33] The General Comment does not therefore create a comprehensive human right to water; it merely expresses the Commission's view that the right is a necessary part of other (accepted) human rights.

Second, one should not forget that the Commission, by legally connecting the right to water to the right to an adequate standard of living and to health, has somewhat implicitly ruled against connecting it to civil and political rights, in particular the right to life: an option that seemed to be on the table before. The reason for the Committee's choice is obvious: the ICESCR only supervizes the interpretation of the ICESCR; it has no control over the interpretation of the ICCPR. Therefore, the Committee did everything possible within its mandate and power. Much as we are tempted to hail this achievement, we should not forget that accepting the right as a purely socio-economic right has far-reaching consequences. The illustrated alternative attempts of international courts to connect the right to water with the right to life have become meaningless, although this approach would find some parallel also in the legal orders of some nation states.[34]

One has to conclude that the right to water and its supporters currently face a double dilemma. First, the assumption that a right to water derives from the right to an adequate standard of living and the right to health is more of a

---

[32] A Cahill, 'The Human Right to Water – A Right of Unique Status: The Legal Status and Normative Content of the Right to Water' (2005) 9(3) International Journal of Human Rights 389, 391.

[33] See ECOSOC Res 1987/5 of 26 May 1987, UN Doc E/C.12/1989/4, containing no authorization to release legally binding comments; see also E Filmer-Wilson, 'The Human Rights-Based Approach to Development: The Right to Water' (2005) 23(2) Netherlands Quarterly of Human Rights 213, 218.

[34] Most prominently this is the case in the Indian legal order: see, for instance, the famous cases *Narmado Bachao Andolan v Union of India* (2000) 10 SSC 664 (767); and *Vivrendra Gaur and ors v State of Haryana* (1995) (2) SCC 577, in which the Indian Supreme Court directly linked the right to water with the right to life.

suggestion by the CESCR than a legal ruling. The acceptance of the states, which would create the desired legal effects, is missing.

Second, even assuming that the right to water will be accepted under these rights by states in the future, this would still attach to the right to water all of the frequently bemoaned problems that economic, social, and cultural rights face in general: their contested quality as proper rights,[35] the reluctance to define the states' concrete legal obligations under these rights, and the difficulty of enforcing them in national and international courts and in arbitrational processes.

III. Three Case Studies on Water and Foreign Investment

We have, by now, established a theoretical overview of the ambiguous status of the right to water under international law. One should now turn to the question of how investment tribunals have handled the right in practice: has there been a role for the right in the settlement of international investment disputes? The three chosen examples are prominent recent cases before ICSID about failed water privatizations: a scenario in which investors' rights can typically clash with the peoples' right to water.

A. *Compañia de Aguas de Aconquija v Argentina*[36]

In one of the poorest provinces of Argentina, Tucumán, the local government decided in 1993 to privatize its dilapidated water and sewage facilities. Only one consortium, led by the Compagnie Générale des Eaux (CGE), a French corporation that later became Vivendi Universal, finally made a bid. However, this bid did not meet the province's self-made requirements: it included a reduced amount of mandatory investments for CGE and higher prices for customers than suggested by the provincial authorities. Nevertheless, Tucumán accepted a 30-year water concession with CGE's Argentine affiliate Compañia de Aguas del Aconquija (AdA). After a political upheaval in Tucumán in 1996, the newly elected governor re-negotiated the contract with AdA, seeking reduced prices for customers and higher mandatory investments through AdA. After a compromise was found, the governor of Tucumán, however, submitted a substantively altered contract to the legislature, which AdA refused to sign. In 1997, CGE and AdA finally notified the rescission of the concession contract.

---

[35] M Dennis and D Stewart, 'Justiciability of Economic, Social and Cultural Rights: Should there be an International Complaints Mechanism to Adjudicate the Rights to Food, Water, Housing and Health?' (2004) AJIL 462, 465.

[36] For the facts and the procedural history, see *Compañia de Aguas del Aconquija, SA (AdA) & Compagnie Générale des Eaux v Argentina*, ICSID Case No ARB/97/3, Award, 21 November 2000, 5 ICSID Reports 299, ss A–C.

1. Procedure and Awards

In December 1996, CGE and AdA filed a claim with ICSID against the Argentine Republic, claiming Argentina's liability for Tucumán's actions under the France-Argentina BIT and the ICSID Convention, seeking US$300 million for damages. In the subsequent award of 2000, the arbitrators had to decide whether the ICSID had jurisdiction at all, and whether the Argentine Republic should be held liable.

On the first issue, the arbitrators acknowledged that the parties had agreed in the contract to exclusively submit any arising dispute to the local courts of Tucumán.[37] However, the tribunal noted that under Article 25 of the ICSID Convention and Article 8 of the French-Argentinian BIT, its jurisdiction extended to *any legal dispute* arising directly out of an investment by a French investor in Argentina.[38] Additional arguments by Argentina stating that acts of provincial officials could not be attributed to the federal government under the Argentine constitution were declined by the well-established contrary principle in international law.[39] Therefore, the tribunal assumed its jurisdiction.

On the substantial issue, the claimants had argued that some of Tucumán's actions had resulted in a fall in the recovery rate and in a unilateral reduction of the tariff rate and that the province had acted in bad faith.[40] The tribunal concluded that Argentina could *not* be held liable under the BIT until the companies had tried to enforce their rights through the local courts of Tucumán, because a detailed interpretation and application of the concession contract would be necessary to decide on the alleged violations of the BIT;[41] this right, however, had been attributed in the contract exclusively to the jurisdiction of the Tucumán courts. As regards to the alleged violation of the 'fair and equitable treatment' provision, the tribunal more specifically stated that the company would have needed to show that the action of Tucumán's provincial government would have amounted to a breach of the BIT through *Argentina*.[42]

Following this dismissal, CGE and AdA sought partial annulment of the award, arguing in particular that the tribunal had manifestly exceeded its powers.[43] The Annulment Committee stated that the tribunal – contrary to its own assumption – did in fact have the jurisdiction to base its decision upon the concession contract. It recalled that a 'state may breach a treaty without breaching a contract, or vice versa'.[44] The arbitral tribunal should have

---

[37] Ibid., at p 2, referring to Art 16.4 of the concession contract.   [38] Ibid., at para 45.
[39] Ibid., at para 49.   [40] Ibid., at para 63.   [41] Ibid., at para 79.
[42] Ibid., at para 82.
[43] *AdA v Argentina*, Case No ARB/97/3, Decision on Annulment, at para 2.
[44] Ibid., at para 95.

examined whether the provincial authorities had breached their obligation to grant 'fair and equitable treatment'[45] under Article 3 of the BIT. If this analysis required an interpretation of the concession contract, the tribunal should have carried out that task,[46] which it had refused to do with reference to the exclusive jurisdiction of the local courts of Tucumán.

2. Analysis of the Case in Light of the Human Right to Water

What lessons can be learned from the *Aconquija* case with a view to the human right to water? One should first acknowledge that an actual water crisis (such as a water shortage or dangerous water quality) never appeared in Tucumán. In other words, it is worth noting that a violation of the right to water can already appear during the negotiation or conclusion of a concession contract. Although the Tucumán officials had undisputedly realized the need to ensure the stability of water prices and water quality, they finally decided, against their own requirements, to accept a contract which would not ensure these standards. This already constitutes a violation of the right to water: to commit oneself to a contract that most likely creates a clash between the popular obligation of the human right to water and the self-made obligation towards the investor. In order to avoid dilemmas of this kind, states must consider the requirements of the right to water already during the phases of negotiation, and insist on their inclusion within the concession contract.

Second, the most remarkable part of the award is certainly the issue of jurisdiction. As Thomas Wälde points out, '[f]oreign investors tend to be successful in international arbitration, mainly because the (BIT, contract) is largely on their side'.[47] It is therefore somewhat understandable that provinces like Tucumán have tried to grant exclusive jurisdiction over the concession contract to their local courts in the past. However, given the *Aconquija* case, it will be difficult for states in the future to bypass ICSID arbitration. The Annulment Committee made it clear that it will not accept any attempts to deprive ICSID tribunals of their jurisdiction under the ICSID Convention and the BITs, by granting exclusive jurisdiction over the interpretation of the concession contract to local courts. It will be even more important for states, rather than engaging in (ultimately unsuccessful) attempts to bypass the ICSID arbitrations, to make sure that they protect the right to water in their own actions from the very beginning. States can at least not rely on the 'mild' jurisprudence of their own local courts: the ICSID tribunals will remain the crucial instance for the

---

[45] See on this provision in general, ch 14 in this volume; and S Schill, 'Fair and Equitable Treatment under Investment Treaties as an Embodiment of the Rule of Law' (2006) 3 Transnational Dispute Management 9–30.

[46] *AdA*, Decision on Annulment, n 43 above, at para 112.

[47] TW Wälde, 'ICSID Annulment Committee' (2004) 1(1) Transnational Dispute Settlement 1135.

settlement of disputes of this kind in the future and, if necessary, this will also include the interpretation of concession contracts.

B. *Azurix Corp v Argentina*[48]

In 1999, the US-based water services firm Azurix, an Enron spin-off, paid US $438.6 million in an auction for an exclusive 30-year concession to run the water and sewage systems in the province of Buenos Aires. Already by March 2000, conflicts about water quality and water pressure arose: customers complained about very poor water pressure, and the authorities warned half a million residents that their local water supply had been intoxicated by bacteria. Customers were advised to boil their tap water, to minimize exposure to water and baths, and ultimately not to pay the water bills. Local authorities talked about the biggest water crisis in the province for at least 25 years.[49] Azurix in return countered that the province had agreed in the concession contract to complete certain repairs of the equipment and systems, but that the necessary work had never been undertaken. Azurix also claimed that the province had attempted to interfere with the water tariffs and had incited public panic. The company finally terminated the concession contract in October 2001.

1. Procedure and Awards

Following this, Azurix filed a claim under the US-Argentina BIT for more than US$550 million in compensation. After a preliminary decision on jurisdiction in December 2003, the ICSID arbitrators granted compensation to Azurix in their award of June 2006: however, this compensation amounted only to US $165 million.

In their reasoning, the ICSID tribunal found 'a total disregard for their [the Province's] own contribution to the algae crisis and readiness to blame the Concessionaires for situations that were caused by years of disinvestment, and to use the incident politically'[50] and that the local government had more contributed to the crisis than helped to resolve it.[51] The tribunal held Argentina liable for not having provided 'fair and equitable treatment' in light of the legitimate expectations of the investor,[52] as the authorities had acted unreasonably by engaging in political interference related to the tariff regime. Secondly, the arbitrators held that the obligation to provide 'full protection and security' was violated by Argentina, as this concept should go beyond a baseline level of physical police protection, but required host governments to ensure an overall

---

[48] For the facts and the procedural history, see *Azurix Corp v Argentina*, ICSID Case No ARB/01/12, Award, 14 July 2006, ss II, III, and VI.

[49] M Perin, 'Azurix Water bugs Argentina', Houston Business Journal of 5 May 2000, available at <http://houston.bizjournals.com/houston/stories/2000/05/08/tidbits.html>, quoting Ana Maria Reimers, Bahia Blanca's public health chief.   [50] *Azurix*, n 48 above, at para 144.

[51] Ibid., at para 144.   [52] Ibid., at para 316.

'stability afforded by a secure investment environment'.[53] The tribunal also held Argentina liable for subjecting Azurix to 'arbitrary measures' contrary to the BIT, explicitly preventing Azurix from collecting payment from its customers.

In some crucial aspects, however, the tribunal *rejected* Axurix's claims. First, the company had claimed that the so-called canon payment of US$438 million could justify periodic tariff increases. The tribunal, however, decided that the canon payment should *not* be considered recoverable through periodic tariff increases;[54] rather it fell to the investor to make the appropriate calculation as to the expected earning stream and to bid for the concession accordingly.[55] This finding became crucial when the tribunal quantified (the relatively low) compensation. Secondly, the tribunal also held that Argentina's actions had *not* reached the level of an 'expropriation'.[56]

The subsequent 'Decision on the Continued Stay of Enforcement', rendered in December 2007, confirmed these findings.

2. Assessment of the Case in Light of the Human Right to Water

On the issue of expropriation, Argentina had insisted that the *intentions* of the state – such as the protection of important public interests such as public health or the right to water – were critical to drawing the line between 'legitimate regulation' and 'confiscatory regulation'.[57] The arbitrators expressed support for the approach adopted by an earlier ICSID tribunal in the case of *Tecmed v Mexico*,[58] where the presiding tribunal had borrowed a *proportionality* analysis[59] from the jurisprudence of the European Court of Human Rights in *James v UK*.[60] On such an approach, a tribunal should also assess the legitimacy of the aim being pursued by the state, in addition to the degree of impact upon the foreign investor. The crucial question would then be whether means and aims were proportionate.[61] Having articulated this approach, the tribunal would go on to find that, in this particular case, the degree of impact suffered by the claimant did *not* rise to the level of an expropriation at all.[62] The tribunal consequently gave no indication as to how it might have assessed the intentions underlying the impugned government actions.

This, of course, was in the result favourable for the Argentine Republic. It is, however, regrettable with regard to the human right to water: it would have been exactly in this weighing – whether the underlying intentions of the state could justify the state's actions affecting the investor – where the right could have played a decisive role. Unfortunately, the tribunal did not ultimately have

---

[53] Ibid., at para 408.   [54] Ibid., at para 427.   [55] Ibid., at para 424.
[56] Ibid., at para 378.   [57] Ibid., at para 278.
[58] *Técnicas Medioambientales Tecmed, SA v Mexico*, ICSID Case No ARB(AF)/00/2, Award, 29 May 2003, (2004) 43 ILM 133, at paras 121–122.
[59] On the applicability of the proportionality principle in investor-state arbitration, see ch 18 in this volume.   [60] *James v United Kingdom*, ECtHR, App No 8793/79.
[61] *Azurix*, n 48 above, at para 311.   [62] Ibid., at para 322.

to carry out this weighing of values. At least it indicated its general pre-
paredness to consider the public interests underlying the state's action, of
which the right to water could certainly have been one. In future cases, however, the right to water could be used to justify a state's action as a legitimate
regulation.

Another interesting point with regard to the right to water in the arbitrators'
legal reasoning is the *reduced compensation* that was awarded to Azurix. The
tribunal determined that Azurix was only entitled to 'fair market value' compensation for the breaches of the BIT.[63] The tribunal even criticized Azurix for
the exaggerated amount it had laid out to obtain the concession as 'no well-
informed investor would have paid for the Concession at the price paid by
Azurix'.[64] Most essentially, the tribunal found that the canon payment could *not*
be considered as part of the recoverable asset base when it came to setting periodic tariff adjustments. In the arbitrators' eyes, no more than a fraction of the
canon payment could realistically have been recuperated under the existing
concession agreement.

Without naming it, the tribunal hereby applied one of the basic principles
and core elements of the right to water, as developed in General Comment No
15. Whereas a right to water does not mean a right to *free* water, it implies a
right to *affordable* water for all.[65] If water services were operated by third
parties, the states must prevent these parties from compromising affordable
access to water.[66] As a typical violation in respect of the right to water, the
General Comment explicitly names discriminatory or unaffordable increases in
the price of water.[67] In order to ensure that water prices remain affordable,
states must adopt necessary measures, which may include appropriate pricing
policies such as free or low-cost water;[68] prices must be based on the principle
of equity.[69]

In other words, water is not seen as a normal commodity open for profit-
making without limits in the General Comment. The prices for water must to a
certain extent remain connected to the actual costs of providing it. It was this
requirement that ultimately, but invisibly, caused the arbitrators to decide that
Azurix was not allowed fully to recover the canon payment through periodic
price increases. Implicitly the arbitrators thereby weighed the investors' economic freedom against the people's right to water, and the latter ultimately
outweighed the first.

It cannot be emphasized enough that the decisive element that tipped the
scales in Argentina's favour in the question of the compensation was, in essence,
nothing but an element of the human right to water.

---

[63] Ibid., at para 424.   [64] Ibid., at para 426.
[65] General Comment No 15, n 22 above, Art 12(c)(ii).   [66] Ibid., Art 24.
[67] Ibid., Art 44(a).   [68] Ibid., Art 27, s 1.   [69] Ibid., Art 27, s 2.

C. *Aguas del Tunari v Bolivia*[70]

Perhaps the most prominent investment dispute of all related to the privatization of a water supply system in the last few years is *Aguas del Tunari v Bolivia*, famously dubbed the 'water war' of Cochabamba.[71]

The World Bank had pressured Bolivia already by 1997 to privatize the water system of Cochabamba, Bolivia's third biggest city, by making additional aid for water development conditional upon this privatization. In September 1999, after a non-public process with one bidder, Bolivia granted a 40-year concession to take over the water system ('exclusive use' of water sources), previously held by the municipal company SEMAPA, to Aguas del Tunari, a subsidiary of the American engineering giant Bechtel. By 1997, SEMAPA had only provided water to 57 per cent of the 600,000 residents of Cochabamba, and the system was so inefficient that it lost around 50 per cent of its water during its transport.[72] Those without access to the system relied on private wells or purchased bottled water. Within a few weeks of the privatization, prices rose by an average of 35 per cent,[73] sparking a city-wide rebellion. The population also feared that plans to meter wells would cause charges for water that Aguas del Tunari had not supplied, and that alternative modes of access to water would be reduced.[74]

In November 1999, massive protests in Cochabamba had to be violently suppressed by the Bolivian Government. In April 2000, following a declaration of martial law by the Bolivian President, the army killed a Bolivian teenager and wounded more than 100 people.[75] As the citizens of Cochabamba continuously refused to back down, Bechtel gave up the project; Bolivia finally terminated the contract and replaced Aguas del Tunari with a public company again. However, the water supply in Cochabamba is still today considered insufficient.[76]

---

[70] For the facts and the procedural history, see *Aguas del Tunari, SA v Bolivia*, ICSID Case No ARB/02/3, Decision on Jurisdiction, 21 October 2005, 20 ICSID Review FILJ 450, pp 1–17.

[71] See in general on this case M McFarland Sanchez-Moreno and T Higgins, 'No Recourse: Transnational Corporations and the Protection of Economic, Social and Cultural Rights in Bolivia' (2004) 27 Fordham International Law Journal 1663; and R Glennon, 'Water Scarcity, Marketing and Privatization' (2005) 83 Texas Law Review 1873, 1894.

[72] See Sanchez-Moreno and Higgins, n 71 above, 1748.

[73] According to some consumers, water prices even increased by 200%; see Sanchez Moreno and Higgins, n 71 above, 1763; and J Naegele, 'What is wrong with Full-Fledged Water Privatization?' (2004) 6 Journal of Law and Social Challenges 99, 105, 125.

[74] At the time the unrest began, this had not been the case; however, under the contract, this would have been possible ('exclusive use' of water was granted to Aguas del Tunari); see on this issue PH Gleick, G Wolff, EL Chalecki, and R Reyes, 'The New Economy of Water: The Risks and Benefits of Globalization and Privatization of Freshwater', Pacific Institute for Studies in Development, Environment and Security (2002) 32; and Naegele, n 73 above, 125.

[75] The exact figures differ: see, for instance, Naegele, n 73 above, 125; and Glennon, n 71 above, 1890.   [76] Naegele, 126; and Glennon, 1891.

1. Procedure, Awards, and Agreements

Bechtel's claim against Bolivia under the Netherlands-Bolivia BIT was registered at the ICSID in July 2002. The company claimed US$50 million in damages and profits lost.

In August 2003, in a 'Petition of Non Governmental Organization to Intervene and for other forms of Involvement of Non Disputing Parties', the NGO 'Earthjustice', on behalf of civil society, requested permission to intervene in the arbitration. They applied for party status or status as *amicus curiae*.[77] Additionally, Earthjustice argued that the tribunal should publicly disclose all statements of both parties and open all hearings to the public. The petitioners claimed standing on the basis that each of them had a 'direct interest' in the matter and that their involvement would increase transparency.[78] Already in a letter before the decision the president of the tribunal advised the petitioners that only with the consent of both parties, and under the rules set out by the ICSID Convention and the BIT, could the tribunal allow a non-party or the general public to join the proceedings, or make the documents of proceedings public.[79] This consent being absent, the request for public participation was dismissed.[80]

In the beginning of 2006, the procedures were discontinued at the parties' request. Bechtel and Bolivia had signed an agreement in which they abandoned the ICSID case for a token payment of 2 bolivianos (approximately 30 cents). Both parties stated in their joint declaration that the concession was terminated only because of the civil unrest and the state of emergency in Cochabamba and not because of any act done or not done by the international shareholders. According to Bechtel officials,[81] the company wanted to clarify that Aguas del Tunari had acted entirely without fault, and that Bechtel had never been interested in monetary compensation from a country as poor as Bolivia. Observers of the case assume that it was not the expected outcome of an award, but the continued international pressure on Bechtel from civil society that led the company to consent to the agreement.[82] In 2007, Bolivia took the decision generally to withdraw itself from the jurisdiction of the ICSID arbitration.[83]

---

[77] *Aguas del Tunari, SA v Bolivia*, n 70 above, at 458.   [78] Ibid., at 458.
[79] Ibid., Decision on Respondent's Objections to Jurisdiction, Appendix III, at 575.
[80] Ibid., Decision, Appendix III, at 574–576.
[81] Statement by Jonathan Marshall, media relations manager for Bechtel, available at <http://www.bilaterals.org/article.php3?id_article=3612>.
[82] For instance, J Shultz, executive director of Democracy Centre, an advocacy group in Cochabamba, statement available at <http://www.bilaterals.org/article.php3?id_article=3612>.
[83] See, for instance, 'Bolivia notifies World Bank of withdrawal from ICSID, pursues BIT revision', Investment Treaty News, 9 May 2007, available at <http://www.iisd.org/pdf/2007/itn_may9_2007.pdf>.

2. Assessment of Award and Agreement in Light of the Right to Water

In considering the case in light of the right to water, first, one should acknowledge that one of the main problems in the *Aguas del Tunari* case was, as in the *Azurix* case, the missing guarantee of stable prices and the equity of pricing in the concession contract. This is in clear conflict with General Comment No 15, which clearly demands that 'services, whether publicly or privately provided, are affordable for all, including socially disadvantaged groups'.[84] Equity in this sense means that poorer households cannot be disproportionately affected by water expenses than richer households.[85] Given that the prices increased so dramatically after the privatization in Cochabamba and poorer households had to spend an enormous part of their budget on water expenses, the right to water was clearly violated in this sense.

A second crucial aspect of the *Aguas del Tunari* case is the jurisdiction of the ICSID arbitration. As we have seen in *Aquas de Aconquija*, the tribunal turned down the provisions in the concession contract that granted exclusive jurisdiction over the contract to Argentina's national courts. In the *Aguas del Tunari* case, the jurisdiction of the ICSID was based on a BIT which, at first glance, had nothing to do with the state or the origin of the company, namely on the Netherlands-Bolivia BIT. By building up an affiliate and settling it officially in the Netherlands, the US-based company Bechtel launched a clever manoeuvre to bridge the gap that a non-existent BIT of the United States with Bolivia had left open. In this way, it becomes rather easy for companies to create a legal basis for ICSID arbitration, namely by forming an affiliate in a state with whom the host state holds a BIT, and operating the water supply system through this subsidiary. Taking these two findings in *Aguas del Tunari* and *Aquas de Aconquija* together, ICSID arbitration may be unavoidable for states after a failed water privatization, regardless of the origin of the company or any jurisdiction-related clauses in the concession contract. In this scenario, the possibility of multinational corporations disrupting democratic processes and evading national laws lies potentially in the air. Article 24 of the Bolivian Constitution,[86] for instance, comparable to provisions in many other constitutions, states explicitly that all multinational corporations are subject to national law and jurisdiction. Placing the rulings of international tribunals such as the ICSID above Bolivian law and jurisdiction is thus likely to be considered unconstitutional by some. States with similar provisions in their constitutions as Bolivia would consequently have to consider dropping out from free trade

---

[84] General Comment No 15, n 22 above, Art 27.   [85] Ibid., Art 27.

[86] Art 24 of the Bolivian Constitution states: 'Las empresas y subditos extranjeros estan sometidos a las leyes bolivianas, sin que en ningun caso puedan invocar situacion excepcional ni apelar a reclamaciones diplomaticas'; text available at <http://www.constitution.org/cons/bolivi94.htm>.

agreements which include dispute settlement mechanisms such as the ICSID, or else be in breach of their own constitutions. This scenario becomes even more grotesque, if one recalls that many of the actions against which companies usually proceed – even if only in pursuit of their legitimate interests or their legal rights – are ultimately state actions to regulate or protect public interests.

Another interesting fact about the *Aguas del Tunari* case is that it also involved the cutting down of existing access to alternative water sources. This is another reason why the conflict in Cochabamba became so violent: the Bolivian state not only failed to further improve the water supply system of Cochabamba, but by granting 'exclusive' water rights to the private investor, existing access to alternative water sources was also impeded, at least according to the fears of many citizens. In doing so, Bolivia not only violated its duty of progressive realization, but also its immediate obligations not to interfere with existing access to water.

The fourth, and maybe most crucial, lesson to be learnt from the *Aguas del Tunari* case is one on public participation. From a formal point of view, no participation by interest groups or civil leaders is possible: only the state and the company in question are eligible as parties to the arbitration. However, substantive rights need to be procedurally reflected in order to be effective. It is likely that the right to water would have been brought forward in the arbitration process by interest groups or representatives of civil society. However, if the voice is not given the chance to speak, how is the message to be heard? Hence, detention of procedural rights often ultimately leads to a violation of substantial rights.[87] Bolivia should have made sure that its BITs allowed participation of third parties in the arbitration process, or should have tried to make an effort to convince the investor to allow third-party participation.

Finally, the right to water was also invoked as a substantial argument by the petitioners. They relied in their reasoning on a 'direct interest' in the matter, which should award them standing in the dispute. Even if in a blurred and elusive way, this is clearly another hint to the right to water. It is exactly the above-mentioned link between substantial law and procedural rights that the petitioners refer to. It would have been a stronger argument if the petitioners had clearly stated that the 'direct interest' was related to their right to water. However, given the ambiguous legal status of the right to water, it might also have been an invitation for the arbitrators to turn this reasoning down by simply replying that the right currently is not clearly accepted in international law. To hide behind the fuzzy term of 'direct interests' seemed to be more reliable for the petitioners in their attempt to get party status; yet it was, at the same time,

---

[87] See also Sanchez-Moreno and Higgins, n 71 above, 1777, who explicitly point out that the violation of procedural rights might have been the crucial aspect of the violation of the right to water in the *Aguas del Tunari* case.

another missed opportunity for the right to water to play a decisive role in the settlement of an international water dispute.

IV. Categories of Violations of the Right to Water and Some Legal and Political Answers

How can we now elevate the knowledge gained from the case studies to a more abstract or general level? The case studies have shown a variety of violations of the right to water associated with the privatization of water systems. In the following, the most common categories of these possible violations shall be identified, in order to better tackle the question of how these violations can be avoided in the future.[88]

A. Violation through the Concession Contract

Missing or insufficient provisions on the further development of tariffs in the concession contract are often chief causes for later arising conflicts, as seen in all of the three cases that have been discussed. The question, for instance, to what extent the price, possibly a highly exaggerated 'canon payment' paid for the concession contract, shall be recoverable by periodic tariff increases is often not specified sufficiently in the agreements between states and companies. Other typical violations of the right to water through the contract itself are insufficient provisions on quality control (as seen in the *Azurix* case after the algae outbreak) and the connected lack of sufficient obligatory investments through the investor or state. A third possible violation is that equal access to water for everyone is not sufficiently ensured in the agreements, thereby violating the equity requirement of the right to water as envisaged by the General Comment. Contingency plans in the case of a water crisis, such as water shortages or dramatic drops in water quality, are often also disregarded in the concession agreements. This leaves important questions open: who is in charge in cases of emergency? To what extent are states allowed to interfere in the operation of the private supplier? How serious must a situation be, so that states can give public warnings or make alternative water sources available?

The obvious answer to these raised problems is simply to require states to include stable and clear provisions on all of these issues in the concession contract. This is, of course, seeing things through rose-tinted glasses. States are often in a weaker situation, whereas the investors have the stronger hand. States are

---

[88] This is, of course, not an exclusive list, but just the attempt to capture and categorize the most common violations of the human right to water associated with the privatization of water supply systems.

often under high pressure, due to ailing public finances or to international agencies favouring privatization. The investor, on the contrary, will understandably only agree to the contract if it appears profitable. The imbalance is even bigger where, as in some of the cases above, there is only one bidder. However, states must be aware during the phase of the negotiation that they deal with a right that is their citizens', not their own. They should act as a trustee rather than as the holder of the right to water. States must therefore ensure that the development of prices – and their own possibilities for influence of this development – takes not a subordinate role to efficiency rules and economic principles in the concession contract. Exaggerated prices ('canon payments') that go beyond all economic reason are the responsibility of the investor and cannot be recovered through price increases. A purely economic calculation also cannot be applied to the question of increasing access to water. The operation of a water supply system is naturally more lucrative in urban than in rural areas. However, it is required under the principle of the right to water *for everyone* that a basic service must be provided also in remote areas. States will have to make sure in their agreements that investors do not only focus on optimizing service in lucrative areas, thereby neglecting their duties towards the rural population.

Furthermore, states should ensure in agreements that they themselves keep a 'safety net function' in cases of emergency. If water quality drops dramatically or if there is an overall water shortage, it is incompatible with the states' protective function for the right to water if clauses in the concession agreement ban the state from warning its citizens, or providing water from its own water reserves kept by states for emergency cases. Should concession contracts be in violation of any of these requirements, it will be in the hands of international judges and arbitrators to make the necessary corrections in interpreting the concession contracts.

A last question is over the period for which the privatization is envisaged. The fact that concessions are given to an investor for several decades is a problem, especially as the investor, once having signed the contract, has a powerful position of monopoly on water supply in the concession area. Competition, if any, on the water market is only possible as competition to get into the market rather than competition within the market itself. Of course, these long periods are envisaged for a good reason: investors need time to recoup some of the often costly investments they put into the infrastructure. However, states will have to address more critically the question in the future whether and under which conditions concession contracts granting exclusive water rights over several decades to one investor are compatible with the human right to water, especially given the fact that the states bear the main responsibility to respect, protect, and fulfil the right. The longer the envisaged time for a concession contract, the more states need to insist on the inclusion of a moderate right to cancel the contract. If such a right is not explicitly included in a concession contract, arbitrators will have to include an *implied* right of cancellation by means of 'contractual interpretation'.

B. Violation through Insufficient Monitoring and Control

After privatization, states have the duty to survey the operation of the water assets through the investor and, in cases of emergency, to intervene. Periodic documentation of price and quality development must be undertaken by states. If water prices go up, the water quality drops, or existing access to water sources is impeded, states have the duty to make immediate use of their possibilities for influence that they should have preserved in the concession agreement. Under no circumstances can states use the concession agreement as an excuse to end their responsibility. The states' responsibility changes after handing over the water supply systems to a private supplier. However, it does not end. To survey whether the operation of the water supplies complies with the concession agreement and the right to water is not an obligation that the states have towards themselves. It is a necessary step to *protect* the right of their people.

C. Violation through Denial of Procedural Rights

A third category of possible violations of the right to water is a procedural one. As procedural rights are necessary for the effective protection of substantive ESCR, it is possible to violate the right to water in its substance by denying the holders of the right a related *procedural* right.

The *Aguas del Tunari* case has shown a prime example for a lack of transparency and public participation: *during the time of the negotiation* only a few opportunities for public input were given and the Bolivian Government failed transparently to communicate the agreement to the public.[89] Furthermore, the subsequent water law, ratifying the deal between the government and Aguas del Tunari, was passed in a hurried manner, which undermined public participation.[90] More generally speaking, states that do not ensure public participation and transparency may violate the right to water itself: it is a logical part of any right to participate in procedures which may affect or dispose of it.

In the phase of the arbitrational dispute settlement, it is, oddly enough, typically the tribunal's procedural rules which can cause the procedural violation of the right to water. According to most BITs, participation is only possible if both parties – host state and investor – agree to the third-party participation. This is usually not the case: investors have an understandable interest in keeping the

[89] For a broader discussion, see Sánchez-Moreno and Higgins, n 71 above, 1663 (1747).
[90] Sánchez-Moreno and Higgins, 1663 (1747).

dispute settlement behind closed doors. In public discussions, they run the risk, rightly or wrongly, of being stigmatized as a profit-seeking 'Goliath' in a battle against a 'David-state' (the sued country often faces massive economic problems or national debts). Investors will understandably try to keep pressure from civil society initiatives out of the arbitrational rooms, and so the consent of both parties to allow third-party participation is often not given. It is due to the nature of the ICSID arbitration, which deals with the protection of investors' rights against states, that civil society and representatives of citizens are regarded as 'third parties'. However, this appears somewhat inappropriate, as the arbitrators often implicitly decide on the right to water, and therefore on a right of the people.

States must therefore allow public participation to the greatest extent possible at all times. This applies for the time of negotiating the concession agreement, where governments should make public input possible and inform the public about the negotiation and the final agreement. It also applies for the time after privatization, when governments should release regular reports about quality control and the development of prices. If it comes to a dispute settlement procedure, the states should try to influence the investor to allow third-party participation.

This endeavour, however, will often be difficult, if not impossible. Rather than relying on the consent of the investor on a case-by-case basis (when a conflict has already arisen), states should demand the general consent of home states, namely by including provisions on third-party participation in future BITs. Newer BITs, such as the BIT between Singapore and the United States, already generally allows for third-party participation, as the tribunal in the *Aguas del Tunari* case pointed out.[91] This is also in line with the new US Model BIT,[92] a prototype document for future BITs between the United States and other states. Article 28(3) of the US Model BIT explicitly states that tribunals shall have the authority to accept and consider *amicus curiae* submissions from a person or entity that is not a disputing party. However, one should note that Article 28(3) gives the tribunals only the *right* to consider and accept submissions of *amici curiae*. It does not oblige tribunals to do so. This is regrettable, but, as the correspondence in the *Aguas del Tunari* case between the arbitrators and the NGOs suggests, tribunals might have been willing to allow third-party participation in the past, but have not had the legal tools to do so. This, of course, would be different under a regime of BITs modelled after the US Model BIT.

---

[91] *Aguas del Tunari, SA v Bolivia*, Decision, Appendix III, n 79 above, at 575.
[92] 2004 Model BIT, Treaty between the government of the United States of America and the government of [country] concerning the encouragement and reciprocal protection of investment, available at <http://www.ustr.gov/assets/Trade_Sectors/Investment/Model_BIT/asset_upload_file847_6897.pdf>.

As long as these third-party provisions in BITs are the exception to the rule, the importance of civil protest outside the court rooms cannot be emphasized enough. It was not the expected outcome of the award in the *Aguas del Tunari* case that made Bechtel give in. It was the massive international protest in civil society that had started to damage the company's reputation. On this non-legal battlefield of public discussion and influencing economic behaviour, the right to water is an effective argument for NGOs and leaders of civil societies. There are, of course, no procedural rules that prevent the invocation of the right to water as a moral right in public discussion.

D. Violation through Lack of Judicial Review

ICSID arbitration has become one of the important institutions for the settlement of disputes after failed privatizations of water supply systems. However, given the ICSID's mandate, its main purpose is to protect foreign investment, not to investigate human rights violations. A counterpart for this ICSID arbitration, namely a jurisdiction for the protection of the economic rights of the people after failed water privatizations, does not yet exist. The recent adoption of the Optional Protocol to the International Covenant on Economic, Social, and Cultural Rights is just a first step along this road.[93] However, it will be a long time until the necessary number of ratifications is reached, and it remains to be seen how effective the procedure under the Optional Protocol will be.

ICSID arbitrators, in fact, have to decide on issues related to the right to water, but, oddly enough, must decide in the absence of the holders of the right (as individuals are not possible parties to ICSID arbitrations), without being able to apply the right directly (as the right is not part of the applicable law) and without facing any review of their awards, be it through an appellate review procedure[94] or through decisions of other courts or quasi-courts. The ICSID awards have therefore achieved a status of highest importance in areas that were not originally supposed to be within their jurisdiction.

However, it has been pointed out in the three case studies that arbitrators have tried hard to deal with this responsibly. In their struggle to find adequate solutions, they have applied different elements of the right to water, such as affordability or accessibility. However, they have done so only in implied and unspoken ways. A direct application has never been dared so far. This is regrettable, especially given the principle in customary international law to settle international treaty disputes and other international disputes in conformity with

---

[93] For an overview of the Adoption of the Optional Protocol to the International Covenant on Economic, Social, and Cultural rights, see, for instance, Reports and summaries of the 63rd General Assembly and the Third Committee in GA/SHC/3938 of 18 November 2008, available at <http://www.un.org/News/Press/docs/2008/gashc3938.doc.htm>.

[94] See in this respect the proposal by J Werner in ch 6 in this volume.

the 'principles of justice' and international law, including universal respect for human rights and fundamental freedoms.[95]

One of the main reasons for this reluctance to invoke human rights arguments[96] might be that it is often not considered to be part of the 'applicable law'. According to Article 42(1), section 1 of the ICSID Convention,[97] it is for the parties to choose the applicable substantive law that the arbitrators should apply to solve the dispute. In the absence of such an agreement, the tribunal will apply the host state's law and international law (Article 42(1), section 2). However, even if the parties do not include international law in their agreement on the applicable law, some tribunals have already stated – from the early 1990s – that they will ensure the application of international minimum standards. The most prominent example of this is the *Southern Pacific Properties v Egypt* case,[98] where the parties disagreed about whether the choice of national Egyptian law had been made clear, or whether international law was applicable in conformity with Article 42(1), section 2 of the ICSID Convention. The arbitrators, however, argued that this question was not decisive: they stated that, if municipal Egyptian law contained a lacuna or international law would be violated by the exclusive application of municipal law, the tribunal would still, in accordance with Article 42, directly apply the relevant principles and rules of international law instead.[99]

This award is often understood as being favourable for investors, in the sense that a tribunal would not uphold discriminatory or arbitrary actions by a host state just because they are in conformity with the applicable domestic law. However, one can consider the *Southern Pacific* award also in a broader way. This approach to the applicability of principles and rules of international law could also allow the invocation of human rights where appropriate. If the tribunals do not hold back in reading international minimum standards for the benefit of investors into the applicable law, the arbitrators might likewise also uphold minimum standards of human rights law, and thereby uphold the unity of international law,[100] not its fragmentation.

The question then, of course, is whether the human right to water belongs to this minimum canon of human rights that under no circumstances can be ignored. It is in this question that the fact that the human right to water is still contested in international law becomes tragic. Even if the arbitrators were to become more willing in the future to invoke human rights argument in their

---

[95] See an intensive discussion of these principles of justice in ch 8 in this volume.
[96] See on this more broadly chs 2 and 5 in this volume.
[97] Convention on the Settlement of Investment Disputes between States and Nationals of other States, available at <http://icsid.worldbank.org/ICSID/StaticFiles/basicdoc_en-archive/9.htm>.
[98] *Southern Pacific Properties v Egypt*, ICSID Case No ARB/84/3, Award, 20 May 1992, 3 ICSID Reports 189.   [99] Ibid., at para 85.
[100] See, for instance, PM Dupuy, 'L'unité de l'ordre juridique international, cours général de droit international public' (2005) Recueil des Cours de l'Academie de Droit 297.

awards, will they be willing to apply a right that is not recognized by the majority of states? This remains highly doubtful.

Therefore, states cannot rely on such interpretation of the applicable law favourable to human rights. They rather have to make sure in the conclusion of BITs and in the privatization agreements with investors that the applicable law includes the idea of the human right to water as laid down by the General Comment. In the absence of such provisions, the ball is in the field of the arbitrators to ensure that minimum human rights standards will always be upheld in the awards. It will be in their hands to decide whether they are willing to include the right to water in this canon of rights.

V. Conclusion and Outlook

The human right to water is still not accepted as a binding human right in international law. There might be strong tendencies in national constitutional law, in international conventions, and in national and international judgments and awards that point to the establishment of an increasingly recognized right. However, currently, the prevailing opinion in international human rights law still insists on the fact that the right has been mentioned and affirmed, but never accepted in a legally binding manner.

This absence of a clear legal status for the right to water is even more deplorable, as some important recent disputes in international investment law concern water privatization. In the settlement of these disputes, the arbitrators not only rule on rights of investors, but are at the same time confronted with essential human rights issues related to the right to water. However, as the three case studies *Aconquija*, *Azurix*, and *Aguas del Tunari* have shown, the right to water currently rarely results in an advantage for the states (or their people) in the arbitrational awards and, if so, only in subtle and indirect ways. States are therefore well advised to take special care for the protection and promotion of the right to water of their people *long before* disputes arise, namely during all phases of the privatization. During the negotiation of their BITs, states must negotiate carefully the applicable law and press for the allowance of third-party participation; during the negotiation of the concession contract, they must insist on the guarantee of stable water prices and quality and make public input in the negotiation possible; and in the aftermath of the privatization, states must closely monitor the investor's activity and ensure broad public information.

If this is not done or if these measures are still insufficient, then it is the arbitrators who will have to decide whether they nevertheless want to pay tribute to the right to water. The arbitrators have different options in how to do so. Tribunals can consider the right to water as part of the applicable law, as part of a minimum human right standard that cannot be neglected regardless of what the parties agreed upon as the applicable law, or they can invoke 'principles of justice' as a tool for treaty and contract interpretation and read elements of the right to water into these principles.

An overall clearer recognition of the human right to water as a legally binding human right would certainly be of great help, not only for the investment arbitrators, but also for all judges in courts and tribunals of national and international law. The 'double dilemma' of the right to water in international investment law would then have become a 'single' one: arbitrators and judges would only have to decide whether they regard human rights as part of the law they apply. They would no longer have to question whether the right to water is one of these fundamental human rights.

21

Human Rights Dimensions of Corporate Environmental Accountability

Elisa Morgera

I. Introduction

This study contributes to the previous analysis of the relation between human rights and international investment by exploring international practice outside the realm of international investment law and investor-state arbitration. It focuses on the impact of environmental human rights on foreign investors' *operations* and the role of intergovernmental organizations in ensuring that such operations respect in practice certain internationally agreed minimum standards. Instead of looking into issues of compensation for environmental damage, attention will be thus drawn to the *preventive* role of intergovernmental organizations vis-à-vis foreign investors' actual or potential negative impacts on environmental human rights in the country in which they are operating.

A growing international practice spearheaded by international organizations is based upon the interpretation and implementation of a combination of international soft and hard law instruments, with a view to 'translating'[1] inter-state obligations into normative benchmarks adapted to the reality of private operators, mainly foreign investors. Such practice may therefore be considered quasi-legal and quasi-judicial. It indeed seems to reflect an evolutionary trend in international (environmental) law that aims to fill a conceptual gap in the current legal system: the gap between inter-state obligations enshrined in treaty law and the growing expectation within the international community to apply international minimum standards based on treaty law to private companies, particularly foreign investors.[2]

---

[1] 'Because the main principles of international environmental law are written for public rather than private entities, they need to be 'translated' to the private sector: A Nollkaemper, 'Responsibility of Transnational Corporations in International Environmental Law: Three Perspectives' in G Winter (ed), *Multilevel Governance of Global Environmental Change: Perspectives from Science, Sociology and the Law* (2006) 179, 185.

[2] This is the main finding of the author's doctoral thesis: E Morgera, 'Corporate Accountability in International Environmental Law: Emerging Standards and the Contribution of Intergovernmental Organizations', D Phil thesis, European University Institute (2007).

International practice will be first related to the term *corporate environmental accountability*, and its ineffable legal significance, and then to its relevance for foreign investment. The initiative of different intergovernmental organizations will be then illustrated as it contributes to 'translating' inter-state obligations into minimum international standards targeting private companies and foreign investors. A few specific examples of environmental human rights standards that have been considered applicable to foreign investors will be illustrated. By way of example, the on-the-ground preventative action of intergovernmental organizations, through diplomatic pressure and conflict avoidance mechanisms, will also be explored. A brief assessment of such practice will point to the possible directions in which these standards may be incorporated in international investment law and dispute settlements.

II. What Is Corporate Environmental Accountability?

The term *corporate accountability* became a buzzword in early 2002, when the international community was gearing up to the World Summit on Sustainable Development (WSSD).[3] Even after the WSSD's endorsement, the significance and legal contours of corporate accountability in general, as well as in the specific context of international environmental law, remain a matter of contention.

The concept of *accountability* has developed in relation to the debate on global environmental governance.[4] The process of economic globalization has created increasing demands on transboundary environmental management: the interdependence of national economies, the increasing acceleration in international financial flows, and the privatization of services related to natural resources management allow the private sector, and particularly foreign investors, to make decisions on access to natural resources and environmental impacts in several countries, while increasing the likelihood of transboundary environmental damage.[5] In this context, multinational companies as 'global citizens' are expected to be included in the design of a more coherent and effective global framework for

[3] See para 49 of the WSSD Plan of Implementation (4 September 2002) UN Doc A/CONF.199/20, where the summit urges countries to:

> Actively promote corporate responsibility and accountability, based on the Rio principles including through the full development and effective implementation of intergovernmental agreements and measures, international initiatives and public-private partnerships and appropriate national regulations, and support continuous improvement in corporate practices in all countries.

[4] UN Development Programme (UNDP), *Human Development Report 1999* (1999) 100, where it was stated: 'Multinational corporations are already a dominant part of the global economy – yet many of their actions go unrecorded and unaccounted. They must however go far beyond reporting just to their shareholders. They need to be brought within the frame of global governance'.
[5] World Resources Institute, *World Resources 2002–2004: Decisions for the Earth: Balance, Voice, and Power* (2003).

environmentally relevant decision-making at all levels, in order to 'be *encouraged* to play an active role in bringing about sustainable development'.[6]

Accountability has been defined as a 'system of power control', as a means to furnish substantial reasons or a convincing explanation of one's actions, a system of 'quasi-juridical' answerability based on standards that are internationally defined and implemented.[7] Corporate environmental accountability, as opposed to responsibility, seems to make reference to the *means for*, rather than the result that should be achieved by, environmentally sound corporate conduct in light of public expectations. By focusing attention on means rather than results, corporate environmental accountability expresses the legitimate expectation that reasonable efforts, including a transparent and participatory framework for decision-making, will be put in place, according to international standards, by private companies and foreign investors for the protection of a certain global interest or the attainment of a certain internationally agreed environmental objective.[8]

In a nutshell, corporate environmental accountability refers to a pragmatic approach to ensure that private companies be more transparent, participatory, and proactive in their efforts to contribute to the protection of the environment, thus responding to the expectations of the international community in this direction. It represents an immediate response to a question for which traditional public international law and current international environmental law are inadequate to answer, and for which an international practice is developing.

III. Why Does Corporate Environmental Accountability Matter for International Investment?

International practice related to the definition and implementation of the novel concept of corporate environmental accountability is growing fast. On the one hand, the successive attempts of the United Nations[9] and the initiative of the Organization for Economic Development and Cooperation (OECD)[10] aimed

---

[6] N Yamamoto, 'Comment on the Paper by Nazli Choucri' in W Lang (ed), *Sustainable Development and International Law* (1995) 203–206 (emphasis added).

[7] N Rosemann, *The UN Norms on Corporate Human Rights Responsibilities: An Innovating Instrument to Strengthen Business' Human Rights Performance* (2005) 15.

[8] For a more in-depth discussion, see E Morgera, 'From Stockholm to Johannesburg: From Corporate Responsibility to Corporate Accountability for the Global Protection of the Environment?' (2004) 13 Review of European Community and International Environmental Law 214.

[9] For a more detailed discussion, see E Morgera, 'The UN and Corporate Environmental Responsibility: Between International Regulation and Partnerships' (2006) 15 Review of European Community and International Environmental Law 93.

[10] For more details, see E Morgera, 'An Environmental Outlook on the OECD Guidelines for Multinational Enterprises: Comparative Advantages, Legitimacy and Outstanding Questions in the Lead up to the 2006 Review' (2006) 18 Georgetown International Environmental Law Review 751.

to ensure the responsible conduct of multinational corporations, and of business in general. These initiatives include the draft Code of Conduct for Transnational Corporations,[11] the OECD Guidelines for Multinational Corporations,[12] the Global Compact,[13] and the Norms on the Responsibilities of Transnational Corporations and Other Business Enterprises with regard to Human Rights.[14] Regardless of the contested legal status of most of these initiatives, it should be stressed that they all build upon the same international standards for corporate environmental accountability.

In addition, international financial institutions have started to review proposed projects and determine the environmental conditions for their financing to the private sector (mostly foreign investors) against standards directly based on international environmental law. The most interesting example in this respect is the International Finance Corporation (IFC) of the World Bank Group, the largest multilateral source of financing for private sector projects in the developing world.[15] The IFC environmental guidelines and standards clearly identify the responsibility of the private sector on the basis of international environmental standards expressly based on international environmental agreements.[16]

Such fast-growing international practice, spearheaded by different international organizations, may, for example, fuel the possibility for foreign investors to be accused of breaching international environmental law before national and international courts, with at least a significant reputation damage for investors.[17] Indeed, victims and environmental activists are increasingly filing complaints before domestic courts and international fora against multinational corporations,[18] in order to hold them responsible for environmental damage. The private entities that have caused and benefited from such harm arguably have easier access to the relevant information and, above all, possess the financial

---

[11] UN Commission on Transnational Corporations (UNCTC), 'Proposed Text of the Draft Code of Conduct on Transnational Corporations' (12 June 1990) UN Doc E/1990/94 (UN Draft Code of Conduct).

[12] OECD, 'Guidelines on Multinational Corporations' (31 October 2001) DAFFE/IME/WPG (2000)15/FINAL (OECD Guidelines).

[13] The text of the principles of the Global Compact can be found at <http://www.unglobalcompact. org/AbouttheGC/TheTENPrinciples/index.html>.

[14] UN Commission on Human Rights (UNCHR) Sub-Commission, 'Norms on the Responsibilities of Transnational Corporations and Other Business Enterprises with regard to Human Rights' (26 August 2003) UN Doc E/CN.4/Sub.2/2003/12/Rev.2 (UN Norms).

[15] International Finance Corporation, IFC in Brief (2006) 3, available at <http://www.ifc.org/ifcext/about.nsf/Content/IFC_in_Brief>.

[16] For a more in-depth discussion, see E Morgera, 'Significant Trends in Corporate Environmental Accountability: The New Performance Standards of the International Finance Corporate' (2006) 18 Colorado Journal of International Environmental Law and Policy 147.

[17] See comments in IFC, *ILO Convention 169 and the Private Sector: Questions and Answers for IFC Clients* (March 2007) 1, available at <http://www.ifc.org/ifcext/sustainability.nsf/AttachmentsByTitle/p_ILO169/$FILE/ILO_169.pdf>.

[18] M Leighton, *From Concept to Design: Creating an International Environmental Ombudsperson. Legal and Normative References: Environmental Human Rights* (1998) 16–17.

resources to remedy it. This trend started already in the 1970s, but has much intensified in the last decade,[19] albeit with limited (if any) concrete results.

This contribution, however, will not focus on the case law on corporate environmental accountability, but rather on the use that intergovernmental organizations, and in particular international financial institutions, make of these standards. For instance, corporate environmental accountability standards could be included in the loan agreements between the IFC or other international financial institutions and foreign investors, thereby becoming contractually binding[20] and possibly sanctioned through the withdrawal of previously approved financing. In addition, commercial banks may adopt the same approach. The Equator Principles initiative is a framework for commercial banks to review, evaluate, mitigate, or avoid environmental impacts and risks associated with projects they finance, which is based upon the IFC environmental safeguard policies.[21]

Even when these standards are not formally included in loan agreements or other contractual instruments, they can still be used as benchmarks to assess the conduct of foreign investors who benefit from international financing, and discrepancies can motivate effective international action to influence private investors' behaviour towards a more environment- and human-rights-respecting conduct.

A *standard* involves an idea of reasonableness, of what is an acceptable conduct under the circumstances, thus functioning as a model against which to evaluate certain behaviours. The legal character of standards lies in their prescriptive purpose whose normative threshold can only be reached through the concrete application on a case-by-case basis.[22] In this chapter, legal standards describe the reasonable conduct expected from the private sector by the international community in light of the idea of good governance, due diligence, and other internationally recognized values within the international legal framework on environment protection. Standards may operate in different ways, and can evolve into other legal tools. They can, for instance, influence judicial practice, or form the basis upon which states may decide to hold corporations directly responsible by extraterritorial application of domestic law as the basis for establishing some form of international jurisdiction.[23] They can also influence the behaviour of

---

[19] P Muchlinski, 'The Accountability of Multinational Enterprises and the Right to Development: The Compensation of Industrial Accident Victims from Developing Countries' (1993) Third World Legal Studies 189, 190.

[20] IFC Compliance Advisor/Ombudsman, *A Review of IFC's Safeguard Policies* (January 2003) 20, available at <http://www.cao-ombudsman.org/html-english/documents/ReviewofIFCSPs finalreportenglish04-03-03.pdf> (hereinafter, IFC CAO 2003 Review).

[21] See <http://www.equator-principles.com>.

[22] R Dworkin, 'Is Law a System of Rules?' in R Dworkin (ed), *The Philosophy of Law* (1977) 38; R Pound, *Social Control through Law* (1942); and H Hart, *The Concept of Law* (1994).

[23] UNCHR, 'Interim Report of the Special Representative of the Secretary-General on the issue of Human Rights and Transnational Corporations and other Business Enterprises' (2006) UN Doc E/CN.4/2006/97, para 65.

private companies in their voluntary efforts, and back the claims of victims and international NGOs. They may also, in time, be developed into norms, either at the level of national legislation or at that of international law.

IV. What Are the Human Rights Dimensions of Corporate Environmental Accountability?

Certain corporate accountability standards based on international environmental law have a marked human rights dimension. Three of these standards have been consistently included in all major international initiatives: they are disclosure of environmental information, public consultation, and environmental impact assessment.

A. Disclosure of Environmental Information

Several cases of environmental damage led to aggravated consequences because of lack of timely disclosure of information to public authorities and affected communities.[24] For instance, a leak of lethal gas from a chemical storage facility of an American multinational company's subsidiary in Bhopal, India, in 1984, resulted in the death of between 7,000 and 10,000 people within three days; the chronic, debilitating illness of at least 12,000 people; and the pollution of groundwater and soil with toxins in concentrations exceeding six to 600 times the recommended limits.[25] In this case, the company did not immediately give the alarm when the gas leaked out, nor did it communicate information about its lethal nature to public authorities, thus exacerbating the consequences of the disaster.[26] The consequences of another egregious case of corporate environmental damage were significantly worsened by the late disclosure of information by the company:[27] in 1976, the operations of a subsidiary of the Swiss multinational Hoffman-LaRoche in Seveso, Italy, caused widespread pollution in an area of approximately 1,807 hectares due to a reactor burst that released a cloud of dioxin into the atmosphere.

Disclosure of environmental information is, therefore, the basis for the private sector's expected cooperation with local and other authorities, particularly for compliance with an international standard based on preventing

---

[24] RT Ako, 'Issues on Environmental Human Rights and Corporate Social Responsibility in the Niger Delta' (2005) 15(1) Lesotho Law Journal 1.

[25] Amnesty International, *Clouds of Injustice: Bhopal Twenty Years On* (2004).

[26] The International Council on Human Rights Policy, *Beyond Voluntarism: Human Rights and the Developing International Legal Obligations for Companies* (2002) 13.

[27] UNCTC, 'Environmental Aspects of the Activities of Transnational Corporations: A Survey' (1985) UN Doc ST/CTC/55, 93.

environmental harm.[28] In addition, disclosure of information is the precondition for meaningful public consultations, the standard discussed below.

Against this background, activists and scholars have advocated that information held by private companies should be disclosed when a key public interest such as the environment is at risk.[29] This is justified by practical reasons, namely it is argued that companies are well capable of providing timely response information, are likely to possess the most updated information on specific technologies, and are best placed to transmit such information across national borders.[30]

The fundamental character of the standard on disclosure of environmental information was already evident in the 1990 UN draft Code of Conduct.[31] The Global Compact considers disclosure of information as a necessary component of companies' multi-stakeholder dialogue.[32] The UN Norms, the OECD Guidelines, and the IFC Performance Standard link the need to integrate environmental concerns into management systems with disclosure of information. The OECD Guidelines point to disclosure of environmental information with potentially affected communities.[33] The UN Norms call for timely circulation of environmental impact assessment not only to interested governments and potentially affected groups, but also to international organizations and the public at large.[34] According to the IFC Standards, the private sector is expected to facilitate effective community engagement and consultation through disclosure of project-related information.[35] Thus, potentially affected communities should be able to rely on companies' timely, relevant, understandable (culturally appropriate), and accessible information.[36]

B. Public Consultations

An international standard for corporate environmental accountability, which is repeatedly referred to in international instruments, concerns the need for the private sector and foreign investors to facilitate the participation of affected

---

[28] The OECD Guidelines, for instance, call upon companies to put in place contingency plans for preventing, mitigating, and controlling serious environmental and health damage from their operations, including accidents and emergencies, as well as *mechanisms for immediate reporting to competent authorities* (OECD Guidelines, Ch V, para 5, emphasis added).
[29] The International Council on Human Rights Policy, n 26 above, 41.
[30] H Gleckman, 'Proposed Requirements for Transnational Corporations to Disclose Information on Product and Process Hazards' (1988) 6 Boston University International Law Journal 89–123, 90.   [31] UN Draft Code of Conduct, para 42.
[32] Office of the Global Compact, 'United Nations Guide to the Global Compact: A Practical Understanding of the Vision and the Nine Principles' (undated) 58, available at <http://www.cosco.com/en/pic/research/7573381391844063.pdf>.
[33] OECD Guidelines, Ch V, para 2(b).   [34] Commentary to the UN Norms, (b) and (c).
[35] IFC, 'Performance Standards on Social and Environmental Sustainability' (IFC Performance Standards), 30 April 2006, available at <http://www.ifc.org/sustainability>, IFC Performance Standard 1.   [36] Ibid., para 19.

communities, particularly indigenous ones. In light of the international civil
society's expectations, communities' involvement should be ensured by the
private sector and foreign investors, particularly in cases where expected or likely
environmental impacts may also hinder the enjoyment of local and indigenous
communities' rights to their traditional lifestyle, cultural practices, lands, and
natural resources. In addition, involvement of these communities in the environmental impact assessment and management of private sector's projects can
contribute to the quality of the assessments, the quality of information as the
basis for better decision-making, and the quality of solutions to mitigation and
contingency planning.

The Global Compact invites companies to hold multi-stakeholder dialogues,
without providing further information.[37] The OECD Guidelines recommend
'consultations with potentially affected communities'.[38] The IFC refers to
'community engagement' in relation to the environmental impact assessment;
'consultations with potentially affected communities' with regard to the environmental management system; specific consultations with protected areas
managers; and consultations with affected communities to identify heritage of
importance and integrate their views in the company's decision-making.[39]
Furthermore, the IFC expects foreign investors to set up a grievance system that
should be transparent, understandable, culturally appropriate, readily accessible,
and free of charge.[40] In addition, IFC clients are expected to foster good faith
negotiations and informed participation of indigenous peoples when projects are
to be located on traditional or customary lands used by indigenous peoples.[41]
Along these lines, IFC clients are expected to establish an 'ongoing' relationship
with affected communities of indigenous people 'from as early as possible in the
project planning and throughout the life of the project', with a process that is
'culturally appropriate and commensurate with the risks and potential impacts
to indigenous peoples'.[42]

C. Environmental Impact Assessment

Environmental impact assessments (EIAs) are now a well-established international and domestic legal technique for states to integrate environmental concerns into socio-economic development and decision-making.[43] Whether or not
the state in which a private company operates requires through national legislation foreign and national enterprises to undertake EIAs, an international
standard of corporate environmental accountability may entail that the private

[37] Guide to the Global Compact, 58.   [38] OECD Guidelines, Ch V, para 2.
[39] IFC Performance Standard 1, paras 19 and 23; and Performance Standard 6, para 11.
[40] Performance Standard 8, para 6.   [41] IFC Performance Standard 7, Objectives.
[42] Ibid., para 9.
[43] P Sands, *Principles of International Environmental Law* (2003) 800; and A Kiss and D Shelton,
International Environmental Law (2004) 236–244.

sector routinely assesses, prior to undertaking certain activities, the possible impacts on the environment, on the basis of scientific evidence and communication with likely affected communities. Companies are then expected to take such an assessment into account when deciding whether or not to carry out such activities, and if so with which cautions. The absence of prior environmental assessment and reporting requirements in the planning stages can increase the possible incidence and sources of environmental degradation in the area within the immediate vicinities of private developments or activities.[44]

A human-rights-based approach to the standard for environmental impact assessment can be found in the UN Norms on the Responsibility of Transnational Corporations, according to which business enterprises are to assess the environmental impacts of their activities on a periodic basis, in order to ensure that the burden of the negative environmental consequences does not fall on vulnerable racial, ethnic, and socio-economic groups.[45] The reports of such assessments are encouraged by the UN Norms to be circulated in a timely and accessible manner to the UN Environment Programme, International Labour Organization, and other international bodies, to the national governments of the host and home countries, and to other affected groups. In addition, the Norms suggest that these reports be accessible to the general public.[46] The OECD Guidelines also stress the need for a life-cycle assessment of impacts,[47] while the IFC expands the notion of EIAs also to cumulative impacts and possible global impacts through consideration of applicable multilateral environmental agreements, in particular the Convention on Biological Diversity.[48]

V. A Practical Example: the IFC Ombudsman's Role in Ensuring Corporate Environmental Accountability

The relevance of these standards not only relies on their translation of inter-state obligations into meaningful normative benchmarks for judging the conduct of foreign investors against international environmental law. There are some interesting instances in which follow-up or expert missions by international organizations or complaint mechanisms open to interested stakeholders have been based upon the international standards on corporate environmental accountability.

By way of example, let us focus on the specific case of the International Finance Corporation: complaints from those affected by IFC-financed projects can be filed before a Compliance Advisor/Ombudsman (CAO), an independent oversight

---

[44] D Ong, 'International Legal Developments in Environmental Protection: Implications for the Oil Industry' (1997) 4 Australian Journal of Natural Resources Law and Policy 55, 63.
[45] D Weissbrodt and M Kruger, 'Human Rights Responsibilities of Business as Non-State Actors' in P Alston (ed), *Non-State Actors and Human Rights* (2005) 315, 343.
[46] Commentary to the UN Norms, (b) and (c).   [47] OECD Guidelines, Ch V, para 3.
[48] IFC, Performance Standard 1, para 5; and IFC, Performance Standard 6, para 4.

authority that reports directly to the President of the World Bank Group.[49] The CAO has three functions: it is a complaint mechanism (ombudsman function); it can provide IFC with policy and process advice (advisory function); and it can conduct environmental and social audits and reviews as an aid to institution learning (review compliance function). In its ombudsman function, it 'attempts to resolve complaints through a flexible problem-solving approach and to enhance the environmental outcomes of the project'.[50] Any person, group or community affected, or likely to be affected, by a project is eligible, at any time in the project, to file complaints that may relate to any aspect of the planning, implementation, or impact of the project, without the need to allege necessarily violations of specific IFC procedures and standards.[51] When the complaint is accepted, the CAO decides the best course of action. Besides seeking to resolve issues for individuals who are directly or likely to be directly affected by IFC projects, the CAO is also mandated to provide IFC with policy and process advice on environmental and social performance, and conduct environmental and social audits and reviews as an aid to institution learning (review compliance function). The CAO can thus decide to resolve a complaint by undertaking a compliance audit or exercising advisory functions instead of its ombudsman functions. In the latter cases, the complainant no longer controls the process.[52]

The CAO may choose the means to resolve a complaint, thus being proactive in investigations.[53] In addition, complaints before the CAO do not need to refer to a particular policy or standard that has been allegedly violated.[54] If the CAO, in its ombudsman capacity, compiles its solution to the controversy, based on the parties' agreement, in a written form, one may argue that such written compromise may give rise to contractual obligations enforceable in local courts or arbitration.[55] NGOs have, however, noted with regret that when there are serious concerns of a credible threat of serious or irreversible harm to human health, the community, or the environment, there is no provision for the CAO to suspend project implementation.[56]

In all events, the possibility to file complaints before the CAO may well provide the only available forum to consider directly affected communities' claims regarding corporate environmentally irresponsible conduct.[57] It has also been suggested that in many cases the non-judicial procedures under IFC can

---

[49] IFC, 'Policy on Social and Environmental Sustainability' (30 April 2006), available at <http://www.ifc.org/sustainability>, paras 31–34.   [50] Ibid., para 33.

[51] CIEL, *A Handbook on the Office of the Compliance Advisor/Ombudsman of the International Finance Corporation and Multilateral Investment Guarantee Agency* (September 2000) 16, available at <http://www.ciel.org/Publications/CAOhandbook.pdf> (hereinafter, CIEL Handbook).

[52] Ibid., 8.

[53] H Hernández Uriz, 'Human Rights as the Business of Business: The Application of Human Rights Standards to the Oil Industry', D Phil thesis, European University Institute (2005) 207.   [54] Ibid., 208.

[55] Ibid., 209.   [56] CIEL, Letter to the IFC CAO, 2 March 2000.

[57] Hernández Uriz, n 53 above, 207.

potentially act as an incipient international administrative law system, which would establish uniform benchmarks of protection in the development of natural resources.[58]

The Ombudsman's *modus operandi* includes field visits to the site of contested projects and interviews with all parties involved: staff of the private company, local authorities, affected communities' representatives, other relevant local organizations, and IFC staff. Complaints, reports of field missions, and recommendations are all published on the CAO website, together with updates on ongoing investigations.[59] Among these, the most important document is the assessment report, which is intended both as a finding of facts by the CAO in relation to allegations contained in the complaint, and as an assessment of the 'ripeness' of any conflict or tension for resolution or management.[60]

Interestingly, after considering complaints, the CAO formulates recommendations not only to IFC itself on the basis of its Environmental Performance Policy, but also directly to the private company involved, albeit such recommendations will then need to be endorsed by the IFC President. The latter would then transmit them to the private company and/or request the IFC to take the appropriate action.[61] In some instances, the CAO also engages in follow-up monitoring and site visits.[62]

One of the most striking features of the CAO's recommendations is the paramount attention devoted to the perception of the environmental and social performance of IFC-funded projects by local communities. In some instances, the Ombudsman even concluded that in the absence of formal non-compliance with IFC standards, still companies should build a climate of trust and understanding with local communities with regard to the environmental impacts of the project. In the case of prospecting for diamond mining in Botswana, even if there were no ascertained impacts on the environment, the CAO suggested that the IFC and the private company disclose additional documents related to environmental scenarios and requirements, in order to build public trust in the project.[63] In the specific case of a gold and silver mine in Guatemala, the CAO concluded that no significant environmental risk from waterways contamination would result from the project and that the environmental impact assessment had adequately considered the risks and led to substantial improvements in the

---

[58] Ibid., citing B Kingsbury, 'Operational Policies of International Institutions as Part of the Law-Making Process: The World Bank and Indigenous Peoples' in GS Goodwin-Gill and S Talmon (eds), *The Reality of International Law: Essays in Honour of Ian Brownlie* (1999) 323.

[59] See the CAO website, <http://www.cao-ombudsman.org/html-english/ombudsman.htm>, where all of the CAO documents cited below can be found.

[60] CAO, Assessment Report on the complaint concerning COMSUR/Don Mario Mine, Bolivia (November 2003) (hereinafter, Bolivia Assessment Report). [61] Ibid., 4.

[62] CAO, Follow-up Assessment Report on Complaint regarding the Marlin Mining Project (May 2006).

[63] CAO, Assessment Report on the complaint regarding IFC's investment in Kalahari Diamonds Ltd, Botswana (June 2005).

project design. Nonetheless, given continuing public concerns, the Ombudsman suggested stepping up an already ongoing consultation process of the private company with affected communities through a participatory environmental monitoring and an analysis of Mayan customary perspectives and traditional decision-making in matters related to mining operations.[64]

In several instances, the Ombudsman considered whether the private company had undertaken an appropriate environmental impact assessment and whether IFC had appropriately reviewed such assessment. In a complaint concerning a copper mine in Zambia,[65] the Ombudsman found that certain aspects of the project appraisal timeline, in particular the environmental impact assessment, had been 'compressed' due to the complex nature of the project and its privatization. The assessment further indicated that IFC exited the project before making sure that environmental concerns, such as access to water and likely environmental impacts, were properly included in a resettlement action plan. Thus, the CAO suggested that IFC engage local and international NGOs with local presence to support project implementation after its exit.[66]

In other cases, the Ombudsman also highlighted that environmental impact assessments did not provide sufficient methodological rigour to provide appropriate information for decision-making, that the relevant information was not made available to the concerned communities, and that environmental commitments were not developed adequately to address the 'perceived social and cultural concerns of people affected'.[67]

The complaint regarding a hydropower project in India provided an opportunity for the Ombudsman to formulate recommendations directly to the private company.[68] The CAO recommended the company to provide for an independent study of environmental concerns, make it public, ensure public monitoring of resulting commitments, and generally engage more constructively local communities also through the intermediation of independent facilitators or observers. The CAO further called for developing a schedule for implementation of commitments resulting from the environmental impact assessment on the basis of each of the IFC performance standards.[69] In addition, the CAO provided for both the IFC and the private company to engage in quality monitoring. The IFC was requested to appoint an independent engineer to oversee the project and report on social and environmental matters, while the company was requested to report to IFC on a quarterly and annual basis on social, environmental, and health issues.[70]

Another extremely interesting intervention of the CAO regards a complaint for a project in Chile, which the Ombudsman accepted to consider notwithstanding

[64] CAO, Assessment Report of a complaint in relation to the Marlin Mining Project in Guatemala (September 2005).
[65] CAO, Assessment Report on the complaint regarding the Zambia Konkola Copper Mine Project (November 2003). [66] Ibid., 16.
[67] CAO, Assessment Report of the complaint regarding Allain Duhangan Hydropower Project, India (March 2005). [68] Ibid., 7.
[69] Ibid., 8–9. [70] Ibid., 14.

the corporation's exit from the project.[71] On this occasion, the CAO very openly criticized the 'degree of secrecy and the tentative approach to disclosure ... which hampered the ability of affected communities and internal constituencies of the IFC to understand the project'.[72] The CAO further argued that given the conditions of the loan agreement, the exit of the IFC should have taken place with an independent verification by IFC of the fulfilment of the loan conditions.[73] According to the IFC's interpretation that the agreement was still valid until all of its conditions were fulfilled, the CAO requested IFC to revisit its decision not to undertake any further external reviews of the project, to disclose the details of the agreement relating to environmental and social conditions, and to press the private company to disclose the results of monitoring and supervision in relation to downstream impacts.[74]

Where possible, the Ombudsman also engages directly in the resolution of complaints, facilitating an agreement between the private sector and the complainants. This was, for instance, the case of a pipeline project in Georgia.[75] During the site visit, the Ombudsman facilitated several agreements towards a resolution of the complaint, including mitigation of turbid water supply.

It can be concluded that through the conflict avoidance and resolution by the CAO, the IFC Standards have served as an instrument to ensure the respect of minimum environmental and human rights standards by companies. At the same time, the CAO provided individuals and communities with an avenue for expressing their complaints and receiving prompt consideration. Even without the intervention of national judges or international arbitrators, therefore, foreign investors can be effectively called upon to respect certain minimum international standards for the protection of the environment and the interests of local communities, through the standard-setting and follow-up actions of intergovernmental organizations.

VI. Conclusions

Already 15 years ago, the international community considered the need for subjecting multinational companies to public international law.[76] Since then, notwithstanding opposition, there has been growing discussion on this topic, with increasing work of different international organizations aimed at clarifying

---

[71] CAO, Assessment Report in relation to a complaint against IFC's investment in ENDESA Pangue SA (May 2003). [72] Ibid., 4.
[73] Ibid., 5. [74] Ibid., 6–7.
[75] CAO, Assessment Report in relation to a complaint regarding the Baku-Tbilisi-Ceyhan (BTC) Pipeline Project, Georgia (February 2006).
[76] P Sands, *International Environmental Law. Emerging Trends and Implications for Transnational Corporations* (1993) xv: 'the reasons for subjecting the activities of MNCs to some form of international regulation are widely recognized'; and UNCTC, n 27 above, 55(b): 'for MNCs to conform to provisions of international and regional environmental standards, guidelines and conventions to the extent they are applicable to corporate activities, *even though not mandatory under national law*'.

how and when the international law for the protection of the environment can be considered applicable to private companies and foreign investors, in addition to the primary responsibility for its implementation by states.[77] Meanwhile, international environmental principles and norms are increasingly impacting on corporate governance, through the preventive or remedial action of international organizations, their fact-finding missions or complaint mechanisms, regardless of whether specific legal obligations require companies to do so.[78]

Even if currently international environmental law does not impose legally binding obligations directly on private companies, the increasing practice of international organizations identifies minimum international standards for corporate environmental accountability that may be expected to be respected by private companies. And this expectation is independent from the absence of national laws to that effect, or from companies' pledges to comply with international standards on a voluntary basis. Disclosure of environmental information, environmental impact assessments, and public consultations are a case in point. These standards, as in the cases of the IFC and the Equator commercial banks, may become contractually binding on foreign investors. The inclusion of these standards in future investment treaties or their consideration by international investment arbitrators may also be another option for strengthening their legal nature. In the meantime, outside the systems of national and international dispute settlement, the pragmatic approach of international organizations may well serve the purpose of ensuring private investors' respect for certain minimum international standards and their human rights implications quite effectively.

---

[77] As stressed in Human Rights Council, 'Report of the Special Representative of the Secretary-General on the issue of Human Rights and Transnational Corporations and Other Business Enterprises: Protect, Respect and Remedy: A Framework for Business and Human Rights' (2008) UN Doc A/HRC/8/35.
[78] D Ong, 'The Impact of Environmental Law on Corporate Governance: International and Comparative Perspectives' (2001) 12 European Journal of International Law 685.

22

Environmental Rights, Sustainable Development, and Investor-State Case Law: A Critical Appraisal

Riccardo Pavoni

a Linda e Samuele

I. Introduction

We are witnessing a constant increase in international disputes where claims and considerations relating to environmental rights, sustainable development (SD), and foreign investment protections are inextricably intertwined. The *Pulp Mills* case,[1] currently pending on the merits before the International Court of Justice (ICJ), provides a quintessential example in that respect. The case concerns a major industrial project for the production of cellulose – described as the 'largest foreign investment in Uruguay's history'[2] – to be developed by two European (Finnish and Spanish) corporations on a section of the River Uruguay constituting the border between Uruguay and Argentina. The project is fiercely opposed by Argentina and the affected local population on account of its allegedly devastating environmental impact. Other than the ongoing ICJ proceedings, the dispute has already resulted in a decision by a Mercosur ad hoc arbitral tribunal,[3] finding that Argentina's tolerance of protesters' blockades of bridges and roads between the two states violated the basic freedoms of

---

[1] ICJ, *Case Concerning Pulp Mills on the River Uruguay (Argentina v Uruguay).* All documents relating to this case are available at <http://www.icj-cij.org>.

[2] Ibid., Order on Provisional Measures of 13 July 2006, at para 48. In addition, it is envisaged that the project 'would create many thousands of new jobs and that, once in service, the mills would have "an economic impact of more than $350 million per year", representing "an increase of fully 2 per cent in Uruguay's gross domestic product [GDP]"', ibid.

[3] *Omission of the Argentine State to Adopt Appropriate Measures to Prevent and/or Stop the Impediments to Free Circulation Arising from Blockage in Argentine Territory of the Access Roads to the International Bridges Gral. San Martin and Gral. Artigas, Which Connect the Argentine Republic with the Oriental Republic of Uruguay,* Arbitral Award, 6 September 2006, included as Annex 2 to Uruguay's request for the indication of provisional measures submitted on 30 November 2006.

commerce and transit as established by the Mercosur Treaty of Asunción.[4] In addition, a petition[5] against Uruguay has been lodged with the Inter-American Commission on Human Rights, alleging violation of a number of rights protected by the American Convention on Human Rights[6] (ACHR) and its San Salvador Protocol[7] as a result of the construction of the pulp mills, including the right to life and the right to a healthy environment. Should Uruguay abandon or downgrade the project as a consequence of adverse judicial decisions, it would run the risk of being sued by the two affected European corporations before an investment tribunal under the applicable bilateral investment treaty (BIT)[8] or contractual arbitral clause.

The *Pulp Mills* case is thus a powerful reminder of the risks inherent in jurisdictional competition among international dispute settlement bodies over investment, environment, and human rights claims, especially the risk of inconsistent judicial decisions on identical or similar matters. On a general level, this renders all the more urgent that investor-state tribunals, where many such disputes are bound to be heard and adjudicated, duly take into account the whole body of international law and avoid perceiving investment law as an essentially self-contained legal system.[9] At the same time, the impressive rise of investor-state arbitrations in recent years, and the realization that a good number of them have involved environmental, public health, and SD legal issues, warrant an appraisal of the relevant case law in order to determine how arbitrators have approached such issues and whether and to what extent they have taken environmental and SD principles and rules into consideration.

Throughout the chapter, I will try to highlight the relevance of the pertinent investor-state decisions for the protection and promotion of environmental human rights, especially in their procedural dimension. It is well known that such rights are broadly divided into two categories. On the one hand, the term 'substantive environmental rights' usually relates to the right to a healthy environment. Although this right in and of itself does not probably exist as a matter of customary international law, it nowadays finds recognition in a multitude of national

---

[4] Treaty Establishing a Common Market between the Argentine Republic, the Federal Republic of Brazil, the Republic of Paraguay, and the Eastern Republic of Uruguay, Asunción, 26 March 1991, (1991) 30 ILM 1041.

[5] *Jorge Pedro Busti and Pedro Guillermo Guastavino v Uruguay*, 19 September 2005 (on file with the author). Another complaint on behalf of several individuals has been brought before the International Finance Corporation's Compliance Advisory Ombudsman. The IFC is indeed deeply involved in the pulp mills project due to its substantial financial sponsorship.

[6] American Convention on Human Rights, San José, 22 November 1969, in force 18 July 1978, (1970) 9 ILM 673.

[7] Additional Protocol to the American Convention on Human Rights in the Area of Economic, Social, and Cultural Rights, San Salvador, 17 November 1988, (1989) 28 ILM 161.

[8] Namely, the 1992 Spain-Uruguay BIT and 2002 Finland-Uruguay BIT. All BITs cited throughout the chapter are available at <http://www.unctadxi.org/templates/DocSearch____779.aspx>.

[9] This emerges as a fundamental necessity since the booming of investor-state arbitration and the consequent advent of a legal system with marked public-law features. For compelling arguments in this sense, see G Van Harten, *Investment Treaty Arbitration and Public Law* (2007).

constitutions and is at least indirectly recognized by universal and regional human rights bodies and courts, first and foremost by the European Court of Human Rights' (ECtHR) jurisprudence on the rights to health and private life.

Accordingly, the ability and willingness of investor-state tribunals duly to take account of international environmental obligations of host states both vis-à-vis other states (via customary principles and treaty commitments) and individuals (via the positive obligation to protect the rights to environment and health) can thus be measured against the conclusions reached by such tribunals when those principles and obligations have been at stake. On the other hand, the term 'procedural environmental rights' (or 'participatory rights') refers to the individual rights of information, public participation, and access to justice in environmental matters, such as those protected under the 1998 Aarhus Convention[10] and Principle 10 of the 1992 Rio Declaration on Environment and Development.[11] These rights are not only increasingly recognized in environmental instruments and as an essential component of SD;[12] they are also rooted in classic human rights law (via the right to take part in the conduct of public affairs)[13] and their protection constitutes the most lively and significant aspect of the ECtHR environmental case law.

In section II of the chapter, I will focus on the status of international environmental principles and obligations in investor-state disputes and the relevance which various investor-state tribunals have attributed to them. I will treat general principles of environmental law separately from environmental treaty obligations as the latter have been at stake in a higher number of cases and stimulate broader reflections. In section III, I will examine a key issue, that relating to the 'like circumstances of investors test' for the purposes of non-discrimination obligations, in order to show how environmental principles and rights may effectively find their way into the arbitral process also by way of rules and concepts that are *internal* to investment law. Finally, in section IV, bearing in mind the framework emerging from the preceding sections, I will analyse the core issue of the relationship between investment law and the exercise of participatory rights. I will

---

[10] Convention on Access to Information, Public Participation in Decision-Making and Access to Justice in Environmental Matters, Aarhus, 25 June 1998, in force 30 October 2001, (1999) 38 ILM 517. As of 5 June 2008, there are 40 parties to the Convention, including the European Community.

[11] Rio Declaration on Environment and Development, 14 June 1992, (1992) 31 ILM 874.

[12] See most clearly, Principle 5 of the New Delhi Declaration of Principles of International Law Relating to Sustainable Development, adopted by the 70th Conference of the International Law Association, 6 April 2002, available at <http://www.ila-hq.org/en/committees/index.cfm/cid/25>.

[13] See International Covenant on Civil and Political Rights, 16 December 1966, in force 23 March 1976, (1967) 6 ILM 368, Art 25; ACHR, Art 23; and of the African Charter on Human and Peoples' Rights (ACHPR), Banjul, 27 June 1981, in force 21 October 1986, (1982) 21 ILM 59, Art 13. Cf Commission on Human Rights, 'Analytical Study of the High Commissioner for Human Rights on the Fundamental Principle of Participation and Its Application in the Context of Globalization', E/CN.4/2005/41, 23 December 2004; and J Ebbesson, 'Public Participation' in D Bodansky, J Brunnée, and E Hey (eds), *The Oxford Handbook of International Environmental Law* (2007) 681, 686, 687.

undertake a critical overview of the cases where the challenged environmental and public health measures were the result of significant participatory processes at the national level. The increasing recognition of *international* participatory rights for non-governmental organizations (NGOs) and other civil society actors in investor-state proceedings will constitute a background consideration throughout the chapter. Where pertinent, I will underscore the contribution made by NGO submissions to the tribunals' findings and accordingly develop my analysis.

II. Status and Relevance of International Environmental Law in Investor-State Disputes

As a branch of public international law, international environmental law is generally applicable in investor-state arbitrations.[14] However, applicability has not yet been translated into unequivocal and consistent reliance on environmental principles and rules by investment tribunals in the pertinent cases. Indeed, Moshe Hirsch has recently highlighted the reluctant, cautious, and sporadic approach of such tribunals to the application of non-investment human rights and environmental rules, and identified structural, both policy and legal, reasons for this state of affairs.[15] This is particularly true for general principles of environmental law or customary environmental rules, given that no investor-state tribunal has ever discussed or applied any such principles or rules.[16]

A different picture emerges with regard to environmental treaty obligations, as there are now several examples of investor-state arbitrations where specific multilateral environmental agreements (MEAs) have been examined and taken into account. However, this has not so far resulted in a uniform principled approach. The impact of environmental treaties on the adjudication of investor claims has indeed varied to a considerable degree.

A. General Principles of International Environmental Law, Including Sustainable Development

The absence of any reference to general environmental law principles in investor-state jurisprudence also pertains to SD, which is especially important in this context given its substantial human rights implications. As is well known,

---

[14] This is a very general remark which does not render justice to all of the persistent problems and distinctions (such as between treaty claims and contract claims) that are needed when dealing with applicable law in investment arbitrations. For an excellent and comprehensive account, see most recently, O Spiermann, 'Applicable Law' in P Muchlinski, F Ortino, and C Schreuer (eds), *The Oxford Handbook of International Investment Law* (2008) 89. Cf ICSID Convention, Art 42(1); NAFTA, Art 1131(1); and Energy Charter Treaty, Art 26(6).

[15] M Hirsch, 'Interactions between Investment and Non-Investment Obligations' in Muchlinski, Ortino, and Schreuer, ibid., 154; and M Hirsch, 'Conflicting Obligations in International Investment Law: Investment Tribunals' Perspective' in T Broude and Y Shany (eds), *The Shifting Allocation of Authority in International Law* (2008) 323.

[16] This is true also with regard to the *SD Myers* case (cf below nn 26–38 and accompanying text), which, however, evidences a much more progressive approach to the interpretation of investment law in line with general principles of international environmental law.

the status of SD is rather unclear in international law, as there is no consensus on whether it is a general principle of law producing substantive obligations, or a mere conceptual matrix, an objective, a process devoid of any law-creating character. A common denominator is, however, that SD plays an influential role in the interpretation and application of the law by courts and tribunals.[17]

In recent arbitrations squarely involving environmental and human rights issues and under the pressure of NGO submissions, investor-state tribunals have had the occasion to address the relevance of the concept of SD, but have failed to do so. In *Biwater Gauff*, a case concerning the privatization of the water and sewerage services of the city of Dar es Salaam (Tanzania), the ICSID tribunal refrained from discussing the possible significance of SD and human rights for adjudicating the claims at issue.[18] The tribunal merely reported the NGOs' opinion, according to which the question of the claimant's responsibility had to be addressed 'in the context of sustainable development and human rights',[19] since 'human rights and sustainable development issues are factors that condition the nature and extent of the investor's responsibilities, and the balance of rights and obligations as between the investor and the host State'.[20] Similarly, in the two awards rendered in the NAFTA/UNCITRAL *Methanex* case,[21] a case concerning a ban on the use of a chemical compound as a gasoline additive, no word is spent on the existence and scope of an obligation and/or right of states to regulate for the protection of the environment and the promotion of SD.[22] Nor did the tribunal mention,[23] at least for

---

[17] This is what Vaughan Lowe, in his seminal writings on SD, labels 'interstitial normativity': see V Lowe, 'Sustainable Development and Unsustainable Arguments' in A Boyle and D Freestone (eds), *International Law and Sustainable Development: Past Achievements and Future Challenges* (1999) 19, 31. According to this author (at 34), the concept of SD 'can be used by a tribunal to modify the application of other norms. It acquires a kind of normativity within the process of judicial decision-making … [T]he concept can plainly affect the outcome of cases … It will colour the understanding of the norms that it modifies.'
Cf WTO Appellate Body Report, *United States-Import Prohibition of Certain Shrimp and Shrimp Products*, WT/DS58/AB/R, 6 November 1998, (1999) 38 ILM 118: the reference to SD in the preamble of the WTO Agreement 'must add colour, texture and shading to our interpretation of the agreements annexed to the WTO Agreement', para 153.
[18] *Biwater Gauff (Tanzania) Ltd v United Republic of Tanzania*, ICSID Case No ARB/05/22, Award, 24 July 2008, available at <http://icsid.worldbank.org/ICSID/FrontServlet?requestType=CasesRH&actionVal=showDoc&docId=DC770_En&caseId=C67>. The jurisdiction of the ICSID tribunal was based on the 1994 UK-Tanzania BIT. [19] Ibid. at para 379.
[20] Ibid., at para 380. Cf *Amicus Curiae* Submission of Lawyers' Environmental Action Team, Legal and Human Rights Centre, Tanzania Gender Networking Programme, Center for International Environmental Law, and International Institute of Sustainable Development, 26 March 2007, available at <http://www.ciel.org/Publications/Biwater_Amicus_26March.pdf>, especially paras 10–11, 43–53, 98.
[21] *Methanex Corp v United States*, Partial Award on Jurisdiction and Admissibility, 7 August 2002, available at <http://www.state.gov/s/l/c5818.htm>, and Final Award on Jurisdiction and Merits, 3 August 2005, (2005) 44 ILM 1345.
[22] Cf *Methanex*, *Amicus Curiae* Submissions by the International Institute for Sustainable Development, 9 March 2004, especially at 16, 23, 27; and Submission of Non-Disputing Parties Bluewater Network, Communities for a Better Environment and Centre for International Environmental Law, 9 March 2004, especially at 3, 7, 10–11. These submissions are available at <http://www.state.gov/s/l/c5818.htm>. [23] Cf *Methanex*, Final Award, n 21 above, Pt II, Ch B.

interpretive purposes, the objective of SD as included in the preamble of NAFTA,[24] as well as the significant 'environmental context' of NAFTA itself, including the North American Agreement on Environmental Cooperation (NAAEC).[25]

A remarkably different approach was followed in the earlier NAFTA/ UNCITRAL *SD Myers* arbitration, a case relating to a Canadian ban on the export of polychlorinated biphenyl (PCB) wastes intended for disposal in the importing countries. This ban, which Canada alleged was enacted for reasons of environmental protection, was impugned by a US investor engaged in PCB waste treatment as a measure constituting, inter alia, an expropriation and a denial of national treatment and of fair and equitable treatment (FET). By referring to international law rules on treaty interpretation, the tribunal gave prominent weight to the preamble of NAFTA[26] and to its context, which included the pertinent international environmental agreements signed by the NAFTA parties,[27] the NAAEC,[28] and the principles affirmed by the NAAEC, including those of the Rio Declaration on Environment and Development.[29] According to the tribunal, the principles arising from such an environmentally coloured context were that NAFTA parties have the right to establish high levels of environmental protection, while not creating unnecessary distortions to trade, and that 'environmental protection and economic development can and should be mutually supportive'.[30]

Such a reference to a principle of mutual supportiveness between environmental protection and economic development is noteworthy. I have always held that mutual supportiveness must be considered as *the* key concept to describe the relationship of WTO and environmental law,[31] and I can find no overarching reason for not extending it to international economic law as a whole, including investment law. At the very least, this key concept must be seen as an acknowledgment of the importance of SD, in so

---

[24] Mexico, the United States, and Canada are resolved 'to promote sustainable development' and to undertake all the economic objectives of NAFTA 'in a manner consistent with environmental protection and conservation'. See preamble to the North American Free Trade Agreement, 17 December 1992, (1993) 32 ILM 289 and 605.
[25] North American Agreement on Environmental Cooperation, 14 September 1993, (1993) 32 ILM 1480.
[26] *SD Myers, Inc v Canada*, Partial Award, 13 November 2000, (2001) 40 ILM 1408, at para 196.
[27] Namely, the Convention on the Control of Transboundary Movement of Hazardous Wastes and Their Disposal, Basel, 22 March 1989, in force 5 May 1992, (1989) 28 ILM 657; and the Canada-US Agreement Concerning the Transboundary Movement of Hazardous Waste, Ottawa, 28 October 1986: ibid., at paras 103–108, 204–215, 255. See further section II.B.1. below. [28] Ibid., at paras 217–219, 247.
[29] Ibid., at para. 247. Cf the eighth paragraph of the preamble of NAAEC.
[30] Ibid., at paras 220 and 247. Cf NAAEC, Art 1(b).
[31] R Pavoni, 'Biodiversity and Biotechnology: Consolidation and Strains in the Emerging International Legal Regimes' in F Francioni and T Scovazzi (eds), *Biotechnology and International Law* (2006) 29, 50–56.

far as it shares the same rationale of integration of environmental, developmental, economic, and social values. Moreover, it can assist adjudicators at the interpretive level, as it invites a harmonious and consistent interpretation of apparently conflicting obligations. It seems indeed that the *SD Myers* tribunal espoused the concept in order to support its finding that there was no contradiction between the pertinent environmental principles and NAFTA Chapter 11 investment disciplines. By drawing on WTO law and practice, the tribunal held: 'where a state can achieve its chosen level of environmental protection through a variety of equally effective and reasonable means, it is obliged to adopt the alternative that is most consistent with open trade'.[32] Accordingly, rather than a sweeping trade ban, Canada might have adopted legitimate alternative measures, such as requirements conditioning exports, as well as subsidies to the domestic waste disposal industry.[33] In other words, the tribunal identified the criterion of the 'least-investment restrictive measure' as the line of equilibrium between investment and environmental rules. If only because it reads into NAFTA Chapter 11 a test not expressly provided for, this conclusion is very controversial and is reminiscent of the inherent flexibility that mutual supportiveness affords adjudicators. On the other hand, this does not diminish the significance of the *SD Myers* tribunal's approach to environmental principles and rules.[34] Indeed, the 'least-investment restrictive test' was devised in the context of a dispute involving a 'dual' measure, namely, a trade measure subject to challenge under both NAFTA Chapter 3 on trade in goods and Chapter 11 on investment. While no general environmental exception applies to Chapter 11, Article XX(b) and (g) of the WTO General Agreement on Tariffs and Trade (GATT)[35] are incorporated into Chapter III by virtue of NAFTA, Article 2101(1). The tribunal was aware both of the risk of circumvention of state-to-state dispute settlement procedures as envisaged by NAFTA for trade measures such as that at hand,[36] and of the unavailability of an environmental exception in the case of investor-state proceedings triggered by the same measures. Therefore, it conceded that the same GATT, Article XX exception might be read into Chapter 11.[37] As GATT, Article XX(b) (and/or Article XX, introductory paragraph) were at the time predominantly interpreted as including a

---

[32] *SD Myers*, n 26 above, at para 221. See also paras 195, 255, and 298.

[33] Ibid., at para 255.

[34] See further section III below, on the tribunal's interpretation of the test of 'like circumstances of investors'.

[35] Namely, measures 'necessary to protect human, animal or plant life or health' (Art XX(b)) and measures 'relating to the conservation of exhaustible natural resources' (Art XX(g)).

[36] *SD Myers*, n 26 above, at para 298.

[37] Ibid. In arriving at this conclusion, the tribunal seemed mindful also of NAFTA, Art 1112(1), according to which: 'In the event of any inconsistency between [Chapter 11] and another Chapter, the other Chapter shall prevail to the extent of the inconsistency'. Cf Canada's arguments on this point, ibid., at paras 158, 297.

'least-trade restrictive test', the tribunal held that the Canadian measures did not pass such test.[38]

The *SD Myers* case illustrates that, unlike arbitrations based on the over-whelming majority of existing BITs, NAFTA investor-state tribunals may be more naturally inclined to take due account of international environmental/SD general principles, even beyond the textual strictures of the NAFTA investment chapter.[39] This approach is in line with the significant environmental provisions included in NAFTA itself and with the far-reaching treaty and institutional framework of which NAFTA is a part. NAFTA cases and NAFTA parties' law-making processes are thus to be viewed as a catalyst for solutions in accordance with environmental rights and principles, which may serve as a model for BITs and ensuing litigation.[40]

B. Environmental Treaty Obligations

1. The SD Myers *Case and the Basel Convention*

Significant considerations arise from cases where environmental treaty obliga-tions have been at stake. First, even though there exists so far only a few such cases, investor-state tribunals – with one notable exception[41] – have duly asses-sed the possible relevance and effect of the pertinent obligations. This is important for environmental law, as treaty obligations constitute the most dynamic and entrenched source of this branch of international law. Second, although the relevant cases do not directly concern environmental human rights, there is no reason why the tribunals' open approach towards the applicability of environmental agreements should not extend to treaties such as the Aarhus

---

[38] Ibid., at para 298. A further corroborating contextual argument was drawn by the tribunal from NAFTA, Art 104, under which the primacy of selected multilateral and bilateral environmental treaties over NAFTA is qualified by a 'least-NAFTA restrictive test'. Cf ibid., at paras 214–215.

[39] On the other hand, the *Methanex* tribunal's different approach reminds of the absence of any reliable doctrine of precedent in investment arbitration. At the same time, some of *Methanex*'s substantive holdings may well be explained on the basis of a due, albeit concealed, consideration for the environmental and participatory aspects of the dispute. For an example, see section IV.A. below. Also, it must not be forgotten that the *Methanex* tribunal has been the first investor-state tribunal ever to accept the participation of NGOs in investor-state proceedings; see *Methanex*, Decision of the Tribunal on Petitions from Third Persons to Intervene as '*Amici Curiae*', 15 January 2001, available at <http://www.iisd.org/pdf/methanex_tribunal_first_amicus_decision.pdf>.

[40] See for instance the impact of NAFTA case law and NAFTA parties' practice about indirect expropriation on recent BITs and free trade agreements: L Cotula, 'Stabilization Clauses and the Evolution of Environmental Standards in Foreign Investment Contracts' (2006) 17 Yearbook of International Environmental Law 111, 116–119; OK Fauchald, 'International Investment Law and Environmental Protection' (2006) 17 YIEL 3, 22. See also the influence exerted by Canada and the United States on the new generation of BITs containing references to environmental protection and SD in their preambles and/or environmental provisions in their texts: Fauchald, ibid., 4–5, 36; and L Liberti, 'Investissements et droits de l'homme' in P Kahn and T Wälde (eds), *New Aspects of International Investment Law* (2007) 791, 814, 816.

[41] Namely, the *Santa Elena* tribunal, n 55 below, and nn 74–82 and accompanying text.

Convention,[42] or to those human rights treaties *stricto sensu* that explicitly or implicitly protect the right to a healthy environment, such as the ACHPR[43] and the European Convention on Human Rights[44] (ECHR), respectively.

As mentioned,[45] the *SD Myers* tribunal carried out a rather accurate analysis of the Basel Hazardous Wastes Convention in order to evaluate whether, as argued by the respondent,[46] the ban on the export of PCB wastes was a legitimate measure taken to comply with the Convention's basic principle of the 'environmentally sound management of hazardous wastes'. This principle requires, first and foremost, that states parties ensure that adequate disposal facilities are available within their territory[47] and that transboundary movements are reduced to the minimum.[48] If such were actually the case, the tribunal would have declared the primacy of the Basel Convention over the investment rules in NAFTA Chapter 11, and accordingly dismissed the claims. Such primacy is indeed expressly mandated by NAFTA, Article 104. However, the tribunal underscored that: (1) the measure at stake was not primarily motivated by environmental protection; it was a protectionist measure enacted to defend the domestic toxic waste disposal industry;[49] (2) the primacy clause in Article 104 was not applicable as the United States (namely, the state of nationality of the claimant) was not a party to the Basel Convention;[50] (3) allowing exports of PCBs between two border countries on the basis of a bilateral agreement was not at variance with the Convention;[51] and (4) in any event the respondent might have adopted measures less restrictive of investment flows and protection.[52]

On the one hand, like any NAFTA case, *SD Myers* must be distinguished, as the relevance accorded to the Basel Convention stems directly from Article 104; thus the tribunal's approach is just a matter of textual interpretation and application of NAFTA, with no need to resort to controversial interpretive criteria, such as evolutionary interpretation or systemic integration as per Article 31(3)(c) of the Vienna Convention on the Law of Treaties.[53] On the other hand, the Tribunal's

---

[42] See n 10 above. The hybrid *sui generis* nature of the Aarhus Convention is emblematically confirmed by its non-compliance procedure. See C Pitea, 'The Non-Compliance Procedure of the Aarhus Convention: Between Environmental and Human Rights Control Mechanisms' (2006) 16 Italian Yearbook of International Law 85.
[43] ACHPR, Art 24 provides: 'All peoples shall have the right to a general satisfactory environment favourable to their development'; see also Art 11 of the San Salvador Protocol to the ACHR, which reads: '1. Everyone shall have the right to live in a healthy environment and to have access to basic public services. 2. The States Parties shall promote the protection, preservation, and improvement of the environment'.
[44] European Convention for the Protection of Human Rights and Fundamental Freedoms, Rome, 4 November 1950, in force 3 September 1953, 213 UNTS 221.
[45] See section II.A. above.   [46] *SD Myers*, n 26 above, at paras 150, 153.
[47] Basel Convention, n 27 above, Art 4(2)(b).   [48] Ibid. , Art 4(2)(d). See also Art 4(9).
[49] *SD Myers*, n 26 above, at paras 162, 193–195.   [50] Ibid., at paras 214–215.
[51] Ibid., at para 213. Cf Basel Convention, n 27 above, Art 11(1). The bilateral agreement at stake was the 1986 Canada-US Agreement, n 27 above.
[52] *SD Myers*, n 26 above, at paras 215, 221, 255, 298.
[53] Convention on the Law of Treaties, Vienna, 23 May 1969, in force 27 January 1980, (1969) 8 ILM 679.

ad abundantiam multi-layered argumentation suggests a genuine attempt at giving due weight to all of the environmental legal and material aspects of the case.[54]

2. The World Heritage Convention As An Example: Revisiting the SPP and Santa Elena Cases

Outside the NAFTA framework, three distinct investor-state cases[55] have involved the UNESCO World Heritage Convention[56] (WHC). This cannot be a mere coincidence. The WHC is a rather unique treaty which adopts a holistic approach to the protection of cultural and natural properties of outstanding universal value.[57] It gains much legitimacy from its quasi-universal character[58] and from the recognition of the underlying interest of the international community as a whole in the conservation of such properties.[59] Given the basic obligation of protection of properties belonging to the cultural heritage[60] and the ever-expanding scope of the World Heritage List (WHL),[61] it is unsurprising that investment projects and activities may often collide with the WHC system – that is, whenever they are to be implemented within or close to protected sites, such as a city's historic centre, a nature conservation area, or an archaeological area.

The earliest of the mentioned arbitrations, *SPP v Egypt*,[62] is no doubt the one that has attached the most far-reaching consequences to the WHC. The case

[54] It must be borne in mind that Canada had a strong case under the Basel Convention, as the latter imposes a ban on trade in hazardous wastes between parties (such as Canada) and non-parties (such as the United States), with the exception of bilateral agreements that are in line with the Convention standards (cf Basel Convention, n 27 above, Arts 4(5) and 11(1)). The 1986 Canada-US Agreement may possibly be included among such agreements, but this point was contested by Canada.

[55] *Southern Pacific Properties (Middle East) Ltd v Egypt*, ICSID Case No ARB/84/3, Award on the Merits, 20 May 1992, 3 ICSID Reports 189; *Compañía del Desarrollo de Santa Elena, SA v Costa Rica*, ICSID Case No ARB/96/1, Final Award, 17 February 2000, 5 ICSID Reports 157; and *Parkerings-Compagniet AS v Lithuania*, ICSID Case No ARB/05/08, Award, 11 September 2007, available at <http://icsid.worldbank.org/ICSID/Index.jsp> (on this case see section III below). At the NAFTA level, the WHC, together with a number of instruments on cultural property protection and indigenous rights, is being invoked in the pending *Glamis Gold* arbitration, see nn 134–143 below and accompanying text.

[56] Convention Concerning the Protection of the World Cultural and Natural Heritage, Paris, 16 November 1972, in force 17 December 1975, 1037 UNTS 151.

[57] For an excellent appraisal of the WHC system, see F Francioni, 'Thirty Years On: Is the World Heritage Convention Ready for the 21st Century?' (2002) 12 Italian Yearbook of International Law 13.   [58] As of 6 October 2008, there are 185 states parties to the WHC.

[59] See especially WHC, Art 6 and the preamble's reference to the 'world heritage of mankind as a whole'. What the recognition of community interest actually entails here (eg with regard to *erga omnes* obligations) is a matter of debate: cf R O'Keefe, 'World Cultural Heritage: Obligations to the International Community as a Whole?' (2004) 53 ICLQ 189.

[60] According to WHC, Art 4, states parties are bound to do all they can, to the utmost of their resources, in order to protect such properties.

[61] Namely, the list administered by the World Heritage Committee (the Convention's most important body) which includes the properties nominated by states parties and accepted by the Committee (see WHC, Art 11). There are currently 878 properties included in the list, including 679 cultural, 174 natural, and 25 mixed properties located in 145 states parties, see <http://whc.unesco.org/en/list>.   [62] See n 55 above.

originated from the termination by Egyptian authorities of the 'Pyramids Oasis Project', which consisted in the development of large-scale touristic complexes and facilities within, or close to, an area that was eventually, in 1979, included in the WHL.[63] The investor submitted that Egypt's course of action amounted to a repudiation of the agreements for the execution of the project and demanded compensation for expropriation of contractual rights. Egypt contended that its actions were mandated, and thus justified, by the WHC, which it had ratified in 1974.

First of all, the ICSID Tribunal unhesitatingly declared the WHC relevant as applicable law.[64] This means that the tribunal was indeed going to *apply* the WHC to the investment dispute, rather than *interpreting* the latter in light of the former. Secondly, and most importantly, the tribunal seemed to accept the primacy of the WHC over investment rules, namely that a state's repudiation of contractual rights over an investment project which adversely affects the protection of cultural and natural properties *included in the UNESCO WHL* is lawful and non-compensable. This derives *a contrario* from the reasoning followed by the tribunal for rejecting Egypt's WHC arguments. The tribunal stated that '[i]t was only in 1979, after the Respondent nominated "the pyramid fields" and the World Heritage Committee accepted that nomination, that the relevant international obligations emanating from the Convention became binding on the Respondent'.[65] Thus, it was only from 1979 'that a hypothetical continuation of the Claimants' activities interfering with antiquities in the area could be considered as unlawful from the international law point of view'.[66] As the conclusion of the relevant contracts and their cancellation had taken place before 1979, the responsibility of the host state was engaged. In other words, the tribunal read the WHC basic obligation of protection of cultural and natural heritage as only applying to sites included in the WHL. It is important to note that this is one of the most debated interpretive issues raised by the WHC system. Leading commentators on the WHC have argued that its letter[67] and spirit make it clear that membership in the WHC 'obliges state parties to conserve and protect their own cultural properties even if these are *not* inscribed in the [WHL]',[68] while acknowledging that the core institutional and legal mechanisms of the WHC have little to

---

[63] The name of the UNESCO registered site is 'Memphis and its Necropolis-the Pyramids Fields from Giza to Dahshur'.
[64] *SPP v Egypt*, n 55 above, at para 78. On the significance of the tribunal's stance in this respect, see also Spiermann, n 14 above, 100.   [65] Ibid., at para 154.
[66] Ibid.
[67] Arts 4 and 12 jointly read. That the 'Pyramids Fields' site comes within the definition of cultural heritage of outstanding universal value as per WHC, Arts 1 and 2 is unquestionable.
[68] F Francioni and F Lenzerini, 'The Destruction of the Buddhas of Bamiyan and International Law' (2003) 14 European Journal of International Law 619, 631 (emphasis added).

offer to non-included sites.[69] Therefore, the tribunal's reading was not unreasonable[70] and, on the facts of the case, served as an exit strategy to the perceived primacy of the WHC over investment rules.

Moreover, the tribunal's willingness to attach far-reaching consequences to WHC obligations is evidenced by the part of the award dealing with the *quantum* of compensation. The tribunal refused to grant *lucrum cessans* as from the date of inclusion of the 'Pyramids Fields' in the WHL (1979), since:

[f]rom that date forward, the Claimants' activities on the Pyramids Plateau would have been in conflict with the [World Heritage] Convention and therefore in violation of international law, and any profits that might have resulted from such activities are consequently non-compensable.[71]

Even though the tribunal did not explicitly say so, its terminology ('conflict') and the overall structure of its reasoning must be taken to imply that state measures adopted to safeguard heritage sites *already* registered in the UNESCO WHL override investor protections and do not give rise to any compensable claim. Conversely, inclusion in the WHL occurring later than the challenged measures affects the amount of compensation[72] as heads of damage incurred from that date onwards are not recoverable. In addition, the tribunal did not give any weight to the doctrine of legitimate expectations of investors engaging in activities in heritage areas which the host state had, for the time being, refrained from nominating to the World Heritage Committee, nor to the fact that the host state's ratification of the WHC (and thus its knowledge of WHC obligations) predated the conclusion of the investment contracts.[73] According to the *SPP* award, then, investors should take notice of host states' WHC obligations and, with the help of international and national inventories, become aware of the possible cultural and natural sensitivity of the areas where they implement their activities; if they decide to go along with their projects in such areas, this is just a matter of typical business risk which is not recoverable by

---

[69] Francioni, n 57 above, 29–30.

[70] Especially if one considers that, at the time of the disputed facts, the WHC was taking its first steps and the 'Pyramids Fields' was indeed one of the first sites included in the WHL.

[71] *SPP v Egypt*, n 55 above, at para 191.

[72] Also the International Chamber of Commerce's court of arbitration, where the case was at first brought, substantially reduced the amount of compensation claimed by the investor on the ground, inter alia, that '[t]he project was a unique one in a very sensitive area from an environmental and political point of view', something which amplified the risk factor involved in the project, *SPP (Middle East) Ltd and Southern Pacific Properties Ltd v Egypt*, ICC Arbitration No YD/AS No 3493, Award, 16 February 1983, (1983) 22 ILM 752, at para 65.

[73] Contrary to what SPP contended, *SPP v Egypt*, n 55 above, at para 153. Along the same lines, see P Rambaud, 'L'affaire "des pyramides"' (1985) 30 Annuaire français de droit international 508, 519–520.

way of investor-state proceedings. Of course, the host state's measures must be genuinely taken to comply with WHC obligations.

The value of the *SPP* award as a precedent for investor-state disputes involving environmental treaty obligations is set at naught by the more recent *Santa Elena* award,[74] which displays a rather hostile and elusive approach to WHC and other environmental obligations. The case arose from a decree adopted in 1978 by Costa Rica and explicitly aimed at expropriating an area, known as Santa Elena, by reason of its exceptional importance for the conservation of biodiversity. The area was acquired in 1970 by a private company with US majority shareholding for tourism-development purposes. The parties were essentially agreed that an expropriation (a lawful one) had taken place and that the basic issue for determination by the tribunal was the *quantum* of compensation.[75]

The tribunal's elusive approach to international environmental obligations is evident in that the award does not even set out the arguments advanced in that respect by Costa Rica, nor – in stark contrast to the *SPP* award – does the tribunal mention the relevant treaties in its discussion about applicable law.[76] We indirectly know,[77] however, that Costa Rica invoked a number of environmental agreements to support its contention that the expropriation was a measure necessary to comply with them and that this should have led the tribunal to reduce substantially the amount of compensation.

It is also clear that the WHC was chief among such agreements. Costa Rica had ratified the WHC the year before (1977) the adoption of the expropriation decree. The Santa Elena property was in the very middle of a wider area of cardinal ecologic importance that Costa Rica duly wanted to nominate as a whole for inclusion in the WHL.[78] The expropriation was thus an essential means to protect the integrity of this area and pursue an integrated, SD-oriented approach to its conservation and management.

In a much-quoted passage, the tribunal declared:

While an expropriation ... for environmental reasons may be classified as a taking for a public purpose, and thus may be legitimate, the fact that the Property was taken for this reason does not affect either the nature *or the measure* of the compensation to be paid for the taking. That is, the purpose of protecting the environment ... does not alter the legal character of the taking for which adequate compensation must be paid.

---

[74] *Santa Elena*, n 55 above. The ICSID tribunal's jurisdiction was based on the ad hoc consent of Costa Rica, Ibid., at para 26.　　　　　　　　　　　　　　　　　[75] Ibid., at para 54.

[76] Cf Ibid., at paras 60–67.

[77] See P Sands, *Principles of International Environmental Law* (2003) 1070–1071, who mentions, as an example of MEAs invoked by Costa Rica, the Convention on Nature Protection and Wildlife Preservation in the Western Hemisphere, Washington, 12 October 1940, in force 1 May 1942, 161 UNTS 193. On this Convention, see ibid., 527–529.

[78] Costa Rica's intention and efforts in that respect were the object of witness statements before the tribunal: *Santa Elena*, n 55 above, at para 46.

The *international* source of the obligation to protect the environment makes no difference.[79]

In a footnote, the tribunal briskly explained that, accordingly, it had decided not to 'analyse the detailed evidence submitted regarding what Respondent refers to as its *international legal obligation* to preserve the unique ecological site that is the Santa Elena Property'.[80] Therefore, Costa Rica's environmental obligations, including those under the WHC, could have no bearing on the assessment of the *quantum* of compensation.

It is true that the circumstances of the *Santa Elena* and *SPP* cases were different: while in the former a classic taking of property on the basis of an expropriation decree had taken place, the latter was about a repudiation of contractual rights related to a development project. Moreover, from the perspective of the WHC and as mentioned below, in *Santa Elena* the relevant WHL inscription occurred much later in time than in *SPP* and did not at first encompass the expropriated property as such (which for some time remained in the investor's possession). Yet, while these specific considerations are absent in the *Santa Elena* award, the tribunal could have well accepted the overall rationale of the *SPP* award, and accordingly balanced environmental obligations against investor protections in the process of determination of the amount of compensation; all the more so given the eminently equitable nature of such a process.[81] To the contrary, it is striking that the tribunal essentially took into account elements of equity and fairness to attach compound interest (rather than the less controversial simple interest) to the basic sum awarded, so that its total amount rose from US$4,150,000 to US $16,000,000![82]

Santa Elena is an unwelcome decision for environmental law: such amounts of compensation are very significant for the budget of a developing country, such as Costa Rica. In addition, this country is renowned for its inestimable ecological heritage and extraordinary biodiversity, as well as for its long-standing commitment to environmental protection and conservation. Thus, the investor-state process may turn out to operate as a powerful disincentive for genuine efforts by host states to act for the protection of the environment in line with

---

[79] Ibid., at para 71, emphasis added. The tribunal further remarked:

> Expropriatory environmental measures – no matter how laudable and beneficial to society as a whole – are, in this respect, similar to any other expropriatory measures that a state may take in order to implement its policies: where property is expropriated, even for environmental purposes, whether domestic *or international*, the state's obligation to pay compensation remains.

Ibid., at para 72, emphasis added. This last passage is less significant as it refers to the persistence of the obligation to pay compensation as such, while the real bone of contention was the amount of compensation. [80] Ibid., fn 32, emphasis added.
[81] See F Francioni, 'Compensation for Nationalisation of Foreign Property: The Borderland Between Law and Equity' (1975) 24 ICLQ 255.
[82] *Santa Elena*, n 55 above, at paras 96–107.

international and national law.[83] The good faith of Costa Rica in this case is beyond dispute, as demonstrated by its actions before UNESCO/WHC bodies and by the latter's endorsement of Costa Rica's policies towards the Santa Elena property. As a matter of fact, the protracted dispute concerning the compensation owed to Santa Elena's investor prevented Costa Rica from immediately regaining possession of the whole area, with the result that in 1999 a 'mutilated site' was registered by the World Heritage Committee in the WHL.[84] On their part, the WHC bodies firmly backed[85] the incorporation of the investor's property into the wider area and it is thus unsurprising that the final settlement of the *Santa Elena* dispute was welcomed by them and paved the way to the extension of the existing site so as to include the Santa Elena sector. Indeed, in its 2004 decision approving this extension, the World Heritage Committee commended Costa Rica 'for its commitment and efforts in solving the legal process concerning the inclusion of this important sector'[86] in the existing site.

At the end of the day, it seems that the *Santa Elena* award advocated a sweeping, and in my view unacceptable, principle according to which the law on expropriation (and presumably investment protections in general) may not be affected by international environmental obligations. The ensuing picture was that of two areas of the law that operate in isolation and may not intersect and influence each other, contrary to the basic rationale of the concept of SD.

III. The 'Like Circumstances of Investors' Test as a Gateway to Environmental Principles and Rights: The *SD Myers, Methanex,* and *Parkerings* Cases

As seen above, investor-state tribunals may apply (and indeed have at times applied) international environmental law in and of itself, either as applicable law or through interpretive principles. In addition, environmental rights and principles may effectively find their way into the arbitral process by way of interpretation of *internal* rules and concepts of investment law. Case law illustrates that this alternative is primarily associated with the test of 'like circumstances' of investors and investments for the purposes of non-discrimination obligations – namely, national treatment (NT) and most-favoured-nation treatment (MFNT). Indeed, a breach of such obligations generally implies, inter alia, that the claiming foreign investor

[83] Another factor that the tribunal unduly failed to take into account in its considerations of fairness and equity was that Costa Rica consented to the *Santa Elena* arbitration under the threat of US financial sanctions, as provided by the so-called 1994 'Helms Amendment': ibid., at paras 24–26.   [84] The name of the site is 'Area de Conservación Guanacaste'.
[85] See World Heritage Nomination-IUCN Technical Evaluation, Area de Conservación Guanacaste (Costa Rica) – Extension to include the Santa Elena Sector, available at <http://whc.unesco.org/p_dynamic/sites/passfile.cfm?filename=928bis&filetype=pdf&category=nominations>.
[86] World Heritage Committee, 28th Session, Suzhou, China, 28 June – 7 July 2004, Decision 28COM 14B.18, available at <http://whc.unesco.org/en/decisions/101>.

was unlawfully discriminated against vis-à-vis domestic investors (NT) or other foreign investors (MFNT) 'in like circumstances'.

Recent jurisprudence is increasingly uniform in requiring that this test be fulfilled whether or *not* it is actually contemplated in the relevant treaty provisions.[87] Most importantly, uniformity is visible in the interpretation of the test, according to which investors are *not* in like circumstances whenever the discrepant treatment accorded to them stems from the pursuit by the host state of a *legitimate public policy objective*, such as first and foremost human rights and environmental protection. In other words, the circumstance that a given investment activity is environmentally hazardous and/or incompatible with the right to a healthy environment constitutes a valid criterion for subjecting it to prohibitions and constraints that are not applicable to domestic or (other) foreign non-hazardous investments, even though the latter pertain to the same (or to a similar) business sector and are thus potentially in competition with the former.

Although this principle encompasses a potentially endless variety of legitimate public policies, it is noteworthy that some of its most convincing applications may be found in investment-environment cases, thus acknowledging environmental concerns as public interest *par excellence*. In this context, the fact that the host state's regulatory measures are taken to comply with international environmental obligations is a major, albeit not indispensable, legitimizing factor.

Indeed, this principle was for the first time unambiguously upheld in the *SD Myers* arbitration,[88] where, as said, Canada tried to justify its ban on the export of PCB wastes with the need to observe the obligations arising from the Basel Hazardous Wastes Convention. In evaluating whether SD Myers was denied NT vis-à-vis the Canadian waste remediation industry under NAFTA, Article 1102, the tribunal said: 'The assessment of 'like circumstances' must also take into account circumstances that would justify governmental regulations that treat them differently in order to protect the public interest.'[89]

The tribunal duly recognized that compliance with the Basel Convention was indeed a matter of public interest which in theory would allow differentiations between foreign and domestic investors.[90] On the facts of the case, however, the tribunal had already determined that the impugned measure was in reality dictated by protectionist purposes and that Canada might have pursued its environmental objectives by way of least-investment restrictive means.[91] Nonetheless, this does not undermine the relevance and possible influence of the above statement of the *SD Myers* tribunal, according to which public environmental concerns may be a decisive factor for establishing that investments are in *unlike* circumstances. Perhaps, one would be tempted to confine such relevance to the NAFTA framework: the tribunal itself underlined that its interpretation of 'like

---

[87] See especially, below in this section, the *Parkerings* case, n 55 above. By contrast, NAFTA, Arts 1102 (NT) and 1103 (MFNT) are well-known examples of provisions textually setting out the 'like circumstances' test.   [88] *SD Myers*, n 26 above.
[89] Ibid., at para 250.   [90] Ibid., at para 255.   [91] Ibid., at paras 195 and 255.

circumstances' resulted from 'the legal context of the NAFTA, including ... its concern with the environment'.[92] Yet, once again the unpredictability of investment tribunals emerges from the subsequent *Methanex* award, which did not mention at all the principle at stake in its consideration of the NT claim under the same NAFTA, Article 1102. By contrast, the recent *Parkerings* award read into the MFNT clause of the relevant BIT a 'like circumstances' requirement sharing the rationale of, and operationalizing, the test coined by the *SD Myers* tribunal.

A closer look at the NT part of the *Methanex* award sheds light on the drawbacks arising from an approach not justified by reference to environmental public interests. The tribunal had to decide whether the California ban on the use of methyl tertiary butyl ether (MTBE) as a gasoline oxygenate resulted in a denial of NT to Methanex as a lead producer of a key MTBE ingredient, namely methanol. The tribunal was vigorously invited by the claimant to follow WTO case law relating to the test of 'like products' as set out in the MFNT and NT provisions (Articles I and III) of the GATT.[93] Since that case law had established that a finding of 'likeness' was fundamentally associated with a determination that two products were in competition, the *Methanex* tribunal should have selected the US ethanol industry as the proper comparator. This industry was indeed the chief competitor of Methanex in the US gasoline oxygenate market. The tribunal was unpersuaded by such arguments and first of all decided to look at Methanex's 'identical comparators'[94] – namely, US MTBE manufacturers[95] and/or US methanol producers – as a benchmark for the 'like circumstances' test under NAFTA, Article 1102. Accordingly, the NT claim was rejected as the treatment accorded to MTBE manufacturers and methanol producers was 'uniform',[96] namely, they were all equally affected by the MTBE ban. Second, the tribunal considered the comparison 'methanol-ethanol' and held that, even in this respect, no breach of NT could be found since methanol, *unlike ethanol*, was not a gasoline additive in its own right (that is, it could not be put directly into gasoline) and could only be used in the gasoline market as a feedstock for MTBE (namely, as an input product, not as an end-use product).[97] It is to be noted that the comparison

---

[92] Ibid., at para 250.
[93] *Methanex*, Final Award on Jurisdiction and Merits, n 21 above, Pt IV, Ch B, paras 4–7, 23.
[94] Ibid., at para 17.
[95] US MTBE manufacturers were neither an identical comparator nor an appropriate one vis-à-vis Methanex, as the latter's business was not the production of MTBE, but the production of an ingredient thereof. However, the tribunal's reference to MTBE producers was due to its conviction that the proper comparison on the facts of the case would precisely have been that between foreign and US MTBE manufacturers, as the challenged measure was a ban on MTBE and methanol was affected only in so far as used for manufacturing MTBE. Methanex's NT claim could have failed for this reason only. However, the tribunal went on to consider the comparisons methanol-methanol and methanol-ethanol. Indeed, in this part of the award, the tribunal had not yet finally determined that it had no jurisdiction to adjudicate the dispute, for the MTBE ban was not 'relating to' Methanex as per NAFTA, Art 1101 (see ibid., Pt IV, Ch E, paras 18–22).
[96] Ibid., Pt IV, Ch B, para 21.   [97] Ibid., para 28.

'methanol-ethanol' was undertaken by the tribunal in the light of the 'competition test' retained in the WTO/GATT context[98]: it was indeed a major criteria applicable as part of that test, namely, the product's end uses, which established the absence of likeness. No discussion of the possible relevance of environmental and health hazards linked to investments in methanol *as* an MTBE ingredient was offered.[99] Third, the tribunal completed its analysis by explaining that a textual interpretation of NAFTA disclosed that the expression 'like circumstances' in investment law had a different meaning vis-à-vis 'like products' in trade law, and that therefore 'trade provisions were not to be transported to investment provisions',[100] including of course the pertinent NAFTA and WTO case law.

This is a significant statement of principle, one which is firmly grounded on the much larger impact produced by foreign investment on the host state's territory and regulatory policies as compared to trade in goods: 'investment leaves a bigger footprint, both positive and negative, than trade',[101] and this may justify a broad array of restrictive measures aimed at protecting endangered public interests. Thus, in the assessment of 'like circumstances' of investments, an exclusive focus on competition, rather than on a 'regulatory context test',[102] would be fundamentally at variance with the above rationale. However, on the facts of the *Methanex* case, the same statement of principle proved rather useless, given that the tribunal had already determined that Methanex was unlike any relevant US comparator *on the basis of traditional economic considerations and criteria*. It is thus unsurprising that the above interpretive exercise carried out by the tribunal omitted any reference to the remarkable environmental and SD context of NAFTA.[103] What is most troubling is that, by sticking to this economic approach, the tribunal lent itself to criticism. With regard to the

[98] Ibid. ('the ethanol and methanol products cannot be said to be in competition, even assuming that this trade law criterion were to apply').

[99] This is duly acknowledged by N DiMascio and J Pauwelyn, 'Nondiscrimination in Trade and Investment Treaties: Worlds Apart or Two Sides of the Same Coin?' (2008) 102 AJIL 48, 84–85, even though they fail to recall that the tribunal had indeed discussed the comparison 'methanol-ethanol'.

[100] *Methanex*, Final Award on Jurisdiction and Merits, n 21 above, Pt IV, Ch B, para 37. This holding was perfectly in line with the arguments advanced by the NGOs, as the tribunal briskly acknowledged ('The International Institute for Sustainable Development (IISD), in its carefully reasoned Amicus submission, also disagrees with Methanex's contention that trade law approaches can simply be transferred to investment law', ibid., at para 27). See SE Gaines, 'Methanex Corp. v. United States' (2006) 100 AJIL 683, 687–688 (describing the tribunal's reference as 'an unusual nod to an amicus brief').

[101] DiMascio and Pauwelyn, n 99 above, 58 (ibid., 81). See also *Methanex*, *Amicus Curiae* Submissions by the International Institute for Sustainable Development, n 22 above, at para 39.

[102] The test of 'like circumstances' in the NT provisions of investment law is thus termed by DiMascio and Pauwelyn, ibid., 76 and *passim*.

[103] Cf *Methanex*, Final Award on Jurisdiction and Merits, n 21 above, Pt IV, Ch B, at paras 29–38. Cf the firm suggestion in the opposite direction by the *amici*: Submission of Non-Disputing Parties Bluewater Network, Communities for a Better Environment and Center for International Environmental Law, n 22 above, at paras 31–32.

comparison 'methanol-methanol', for instance, Sanford Gaines has submitted that the ban on MTBE probably triggered a de facto discrimination of Methanex vis-à-vis US methanol's producers not exposed to the methanol's *submarket* of gasoline additives.[104] Yet, the tribunal would have pre-empted this criticism had it simply pointed out that the methanol's MTBE submarket was discriminated against for legitimate reasons of environmental protection. Along the same lines and although it finally rejected the incorporation of WTO NT law into investment law, the tribunal might at least have mentioned the Appellate Body *Asbestos* decision for the proposition that health and environmental risks are 'pertinent in an examination of "likeness"'[105] under the GATT NT provision (Article III). However, the incontestable point is that there are solid grounds in investment law for excluding any breaches of non-discrimination obligations whenever investments and investors are treated differently on the basis of the different environmental adverse effects arising from their activities.[106]

The recent *Parkerings* award[107] is a key testimony to this. The case arose from a public tender launched by the Municipality of Vilnius (Lithuania) for the development and management of the city's parking system, including the construction of modern multi-storey car parks (MSCPs). The awarded bidder was a consortium comprising Parkerings, a Norwegian enterprise. In 1999, the consortium stipulated an agreement with the municipality spelling out the reciprocal obligations pertaining to the creation of the parking facilities. In the wake of substantial technical difficulties, legislative changes, and growing public opposition due to the cultural and environmental impact of the investor's project on the city's Old Town, such agreement was eventually terminated by the municipality. Vilnius historic centre, including its Old Town, had been included in the UNESCO WHL since 1994 and was therefore the object of special legal protections aimed at ensuring its preservation and integrity.

---

[104] Gaines, n 100 above, 688. The author recalls various methanol submarkets not exposed to the ban on MTBE (such as plastics and windshield washer fluid), ibid.

[105] WTO Appellate Body Report, *European Communities – Measures Affecting Asbestos and Asbestos-Containing Products*, WT/DS135/AB/R, 5 April 2001, at para 113. As is well known, the Appellate Body refused to consider health risk as a self-standing criterion of likeness, and rather retained its relevance as a factor for the examination of the well-established economic criteria of the physical properties of products and of consumers' tastes and habits (ibid., and at paras 114, 122, 128, 130, 135, 145). Cf *Methanex*, *Amicus Curiae* Submissions by the International Institute for Sustainable Development, n 22 above, at paras 47–55.

[106] It is also telling that, even in trade law, an analysis of NT obligations capable of accommodating 'legitimate regulatory concerns' is increasingly advocated. See most recently DiMascio and Pauwelyn, n 99 above, 83–84, who offer, as an example of legitimate measures, those discriminating as between prima facie 'like goods' in order to counter climate change. At the same time, it is quite inexplicable why, in reaching the latter conclusion, these authors ignore the WTO *Asbestos* decision (ibid.), which, however controversial, may be viewed as a significant inroad into the allegedly pure economic conception of 'like products' in GATT, Art III (see also the concurring statement of a member of the Appellate Body in *EC – Asbestos*, ibid., at paras 153–154).

[107] *Parkerings-Compagniet*, n 55 above. The jurisdiction of the ICSID tribunal was based on the 1992 Lithuania-Norway BIT.

One of Parkerings' claims before the ICSID tribunal was that Lithuania had breached the MFNT clause of the BIT as a result of an allegedly preferential treatment granted to a Dutch competitor, which, *unlike Parkerings*, had been authorized to build MSCPs and other facilities on a site close to the city's Old Town. The tribunal dismissed this claim as Parkerings and the Dutch company were *not* in like circumstances. Differential treatment was indeed justified because the impact of the claimant's project on the city's Old Town was larger than that of its Dutch competitor. Notably, the tribunal said: 'The historical and archaeological preservation and environmental protection could be and in this case were a justification for the refusal of the [claimant's] project'.[108] Therefore, 'despite similarities in objective and venue',[109] the tribunal concluded that:

[T]he differences in size of [the Dutch company] and [the claimant's] projects, as well as the significant extension of the latter into the Old Town near the Cathedral area, are important enough to determine that the two investors were not *in like circumstances*. Furthermore, the Municipality of Vilnius was faced with numerous and solid oppositions from various bodies that relied on archaeological and environmental concerns. In the record, nothing convincing would show that such concerns were not determinant or were built up to reject [the claimant's] project. Thus the City of Vilnius did have legitimate grounds to distinguish between the two projects.[110]

Parkerings is an important case for environmental law; contrary to the *Methanex* tribunal's reticence to address environmental protection issues raised by investor claims, the *Parkerings* tribunal showed genuine willingness to pay due attention to such issues as a powerful countervailing factor to investor protections. Compliance with the obligations flowing from the UNESCO WHC, albeit not specifically discussed, was certainly an underlying motive for the host state's actions and, probably, a significant consideration in the eyes of the tribunal.[111] In the case at hand and unlike the *SPP*[112] and *Santa Elena*[113] arbitrations, the requirements of the WHC were accommodated into an investor-state dispute through a concept internal to investment law, that of 'like circumstances of investors'. This concept is increasingly emerging as a crucial gateway to environmental principles and rights in investor-state case law. In this connection, it is also worth noting that the *Parkerings* tribunal unhesitatingly extended the 'like circumstances' test to the non-discrimination pillar of the FET standard.[114]

---

[108] Ibid., at para 392.   [109] Ibid., at para 396.   [110] Ibid. (emphasis in the original).

[111] See ibid., at para 385 ('Another feature does however call the Tribunal attention: the MSCP planned by [the claimant] extends significantly in the Old Town *as defined by UNESCO* and especially near the historical site of the Cathedral', emphasis added). See also ibid., at paras 381–382.   [112] See n 55 above.

[113] Ibid.

[114] *Parkerings-Compagniet*, n 55 above, at para 288 ('In order to determine if there is discrimination in violation of the standard of *the fair and equitable treatment*, one has to make a comparison with another investor in a similar position (*like circumstances*)', emphasis in the original).

It is to be hoped that the *Parkerings* award will be seen as a model to follow by other investor-state tribunals dealing with disputes involving the defence of public environmental interests.

IV. Participatory Rights at the National Level and Investor-State Case Law

Whereas the increasing involvement of civil society and NGOs in international arbitral proceedings has already been massively commented upon,[115] much less attention has been paid to the relationship between investment law and the exercise of environmental participatory rights at the *national* level. Still, in several instances, investor-state tribunals have been called upon to decide over the lawfulness under investment disciplines of environmental measures which were taken following extensive national processes of public participation, consultation, and opposition. A careful review of such cases is certainly warranted. First, public participation is closely linked to other general principles, concepts, and requirements of vital importance, not only for environmental law, but also as a matter of international public policy, such as democracy, legitimacy, accountability, non-discrimination, and subsidiarity. Second, the principle of public participation and procedural environmental rights are growingly upheld in international human rights law. As Alan Boyle put it, the environmental jurisprudence of human rights courts:

suggests that what existing international law has most to offer with regard to environ-mental protection is the empowerment of individuals and groups most affected by environmental problems, and for whom the opportunity to participate in decisions is the most useful and direct means of influencing the balance of environmental, social and economic interests.[116]

When settling investment-environment disputes, investor-state tribunals should thus be mindful and duly take account of the general principles and human rights obligations underlying public participation in environmental matters.

A. Environmental Impact Assessment and Management: From *Maffezini* to *Glamis Gold*

Environmental impact assessment (EIA) is the term of art used to describe the fundamentally scientific process through which the potential ecological risks associated with a particular project, substance, or activity are evaluated prior to their

---

[115] See also for further references E Savarese, '*Amicus curiae* Participation in Investor-State Arbitral Proceedings' (2007) 17 Italian Yearbook of International Law 99; J Delaney and D Barstow Magraw, 'Procedural Transparency' in Muchlinski, Ortino and Schreuer, n 14 above, 721; and C Tams and C-S Zoellner, 'Amici Curiae im internationalen Investitionsschutzrecht' (2007) 45 Archiv des Völkerrechts 217.

[116] A Boyle, 'Human Rights or Environmental Rights? A Reassessment' (2007) 18 Fordham Environmental Law Review 471, 498.

authorization, then communicated to the public, and finally submitted to the government authorities as an essential basis of their regulatory policies and decisions (the so-called 'impact/risk management' phase of political decision-making). In environmental law, EIA is usually associated with, and viewed as, a technique for implementing the principle of preventive action. Although the status and scope of EIA in customary international law are not entirely clear, there is no doubt that this is a key environmental principle, as demonstrated by its growing recognition in treaties, regional instruments, domestic legislation, and judicial practice.

Two reasons make it particularly convenient to deal with EIA in this context. First, a critical feature of any legitimate EIA is the significant participatory rights to which the concerned public is entitled throughout the process. EIA may thus be viewed as the process where substantive environmental obligations meet (and merge with) individual rights of information, participation, and access to justice. There now exists a well-established jurisprudence of the ECtHR, according to which any national authorization of projects with potentially harmful environmental consequences must be preceded by an EIA. Indeed, the main reason for this requirement is that modern EIA legislation usually establishes that the concerned public be adequately informed of the nature of the proposed project, given the opportunity to submit its comments and views during the procedure, as well as to access justice when it considers that such views and comments have not been duly taken into account in the decision-making process.[117] Lack of EIA, or existence of an EIA/risk management process flawed by a denial of (or an insufficient regard for) participatory rights, may entail a violation of the right to private life[118] and, in the most serious situations, of the right to life[119] (Articles 8 and 2 of the ECHR).

Second, as it is obvious, EIA may be a far-reaching form of interference with investment activities. More specifically, EIA may undermine the expectations an investor had at the time the investment was first made. For instance, an EIA may conclude that the available scientific evidence indicates that: (1) a given project or business is not environmentally safe; (2) the project or business should be

---

[117] Most explicitly in this sense, see ECtHR, *Giacomelli v Italy*, App No 59909/00, judgment, 2 November 2006, at paras 83–94. See also *Hatton and ors v United Kingdom*, App No 36022/97, judgment, 8 July 2003, at para 128; and *Taşkin and ors v Turkey*, App No 46117/99, judgment, 10 November 2004, at paras 119–125. As rightly noted, this case law of the ECtHR brings about a de facto incorporation of the participatory rights established by the Aarhus Convention into the ECHR: see Boyle, n 116 above, 499, 503, 510.

[118] *Giacomelli*, ibid., at paras 86, 93–94, 96–97 (lack of EIA for a plant for the treatment of toxic industrial waste); *Taşkin*, ibid., at paras 120–126 (lack of appropriate EIA and flawed EIA/risk management process for the authorization of a gold mine because of non-enforcement of judicial decisions revoking permit to operate the mine); *Öçkan and ors v Turkey*, App No 46771/99, judgment, 28 March 2006, at paras 44–50 (same); *Lemke v Turkey*, App No 17381/02, judgment, 5 June 2007, at paras 43–46 (same); and *Fadeyeva v Russia*, App No 55723/00, judgment, 9 June 2005, at paras 129–134 (flawed EIA/risk management process relating to a highly polluting steel plant because of insufficient disclosure of information and non-enforcement of national legislation).

[119] *Öneryildiz v Turkey*, App No 48939/99, judgment, 30 November 2004, at para 90.

authorized, or continue to be carried out, only if additional information and studies are provided, or technical precautions implemented, at the investor's expense; or, finally and more problematically, (3) an initially favourable EIA opinion must be reversed following an EIA monitoring study or other review and/or novel more demanding legislation.[120] Do such interferences with foreign investment amount to a violation of investor protections, such as the prohibition of expropriation without compensation and/or the minimum standard of treatment, including FET?

It seems appropriate to distinguish the three situations above, as investor-state disputes offer examples of each of them. The situation of an EIA resulting in (allegedly unforeseen) additional economic and technical burden for the investor (point (2) of list above) was at stake in the *Maffezini* case,[121] concerning inter alia a claim for denial of FET brought by the owner of a failed investment in a plant for the production of toxic chemicals. The ICSID tribunal resolutely dismissed the investor's contention that the failure of its business was partly due to the additional costs ensuing from the EIA process.[122] Notably, the tribunal explained that the reason for its special attention to this aspect of the case was that 'the Environmental Impact Assessment procedure is *basic for the adequate protection of the environment and the application of appropriate preventive measures*',[123] further underlining how this was true 'not only under Spanish and [European Economic Community] law, but also increasingly so under international law'.[124] This is a rare statement from an investor-state tribunal, one that shows due consideration, not only for the protection of the environment in general, but also for specific MEAs[125] and certain authoritative literature existing in this area.[126] At the same time, this approach cannot be overstated, as the tribunal's main conclusion on this part of the claim was that the host state did no more than complying with national and European legislation;[127] nor can this approach be generalized, as the situation at hand is that of an EIA resulting in a delayed and more onerous authorization, not of an EIA which prompts denial of an authorization or far-reaching amendments to an existing one. Moreover, by initiating to develop its investment project before completion of the EIA, the investor assumed the foreseeable risk of eventual unfavourable EIA findings: in

---

[120] In all of these hypotheses, I assume that the political authorities would act upon the EIA conclusions in the risk management phase and, accordingly, either formally deny the requisite authorizations, withdraw them, grant conditional authorizations, or amend existing authorizations.

[121] *Maffezini v Spain*, ICSID Case No ARB/97/7, Award, 13 November 2000, 5 ICSID Reports 419. The jurisdiction of the ICSID tribunal was based on the 1991 Argentine-Spain BIT.

[122] Ibid., at paras 65–71.   [123] Ibid., at para 67, emphasis added.   [124] Ibid.

[125] The tribunal quotes the Convention on Environmental Impact Assessment in a Trans-boundary Context, Espoo, 19 February 1991, (1991) 30 ILM 800. Ibid., fn 17.

[126] The tribunal quotes P Sands, *Principles of International Environmental Law* (Vol 1, 1995), ch 15. Ibid.

[127] In accordance with the BIT clause of 'conformity of investments with national legislation' (*Maffezini*, n 121 above, at para 71); the tribunal thus places itself on the more comfortable realm of investment disciplines.

short, the underestimation of EIA requirements was one of the investor's 'bad business judgments'[128] and entailed that legitimate expectations could not be invoked.

The *Methanex* case is an apt illustration of an EIA process which determines that a given use of a product, that is, the use of MTBE as a gasoline oxygenate, is not environmentally safe and should accordingly be discontinued (point (1) of list above).[129] The EIA findings were duly acted upon by Californian authorities which set up a schedule for the phasing out of MTBE. The arguments that Methanex advanced before the NAFTA tribunal in relation to EIA requirements were necessarily different from those of the claimant in the *Maffezini* case. On the one hand, Methanex contested the validity of the scientific conclusions at the basis of the trade ban, and on the other, it raised serious doubts about the impartiality and legitimacy of the entire regulatory process (allegedly tainted by corruption and bias, and hence depicted as a political sham), including the EIA. The tribunal was favourably impressed by the structure, timing, and orderly unfolding of the EIA process, which consisted in a thorough scientific report by the University of California (UC) accompanied by extensive peer review and public participation,[130] and concluded that the UC Report reflected 'a serious, objective and scientific approach to a complex problem'.[131] Scientific disagreement was not able to affect this finding, particularly because the report 'was subjected at the time to public hearings, testimony and peer-review; and its emergence as a serious scientific work *from such an open and informed debate* is the best evidence that it was not the product of a political sham'.[132] Although not justified by reference to international human rights or environmental principles, the tribunal's conclusion is noteworthy for its deference to national regulatory processes and EIA schemes which display democratic, transparent, and scientific features such as the one at hand here.[133] Ultimately, this approach acknowledges, albeit indirectly, the underlying environmental participatory

---

[128] Indeed, the 2000 *Maffezini* Award is most famous and quoted for the tribunal's statement that 'Bilateral Investment Treaties are not insurance policies against bad business judgments' (ibid., at para 64).

[129] The *Methanex* situation may also suit the third hypothesis outlined above (ie that of a reversal of an initially favourable EIA), as California originally encouraged use of oxygenates such as MTBE in gasoline (as they help reduce air pollution). However, the EIA process recalled in the text appears as a rather self-standing and fresh exercise carried out by the Californian authorities to respond to reports and public disquiet about significant groundwater contamination due to dispersal of MTBE.

[130] cf *Methanex*, Final Award on Jurisdiction and Merits, n 21 above, Pt II, Ch D, at paras 7–22, and Pt III, Ch A, at paras 1–36.   [131] Ibid., Pt III, Ch A, at para 101.

[132] Ibid., emphasis added. The treatment of the issue of scientific controversies in this passage of the award may also be taken as an implicit acceptance (as a matter of principle) of the legality of precautionary measures vis-à-vis investment disciplines. See A Newcombe, 'Sustainable Development and Investment Treaty Law' (2007) 8 JWIT 357, 381.

[133] For further convincing comments on this aspect of the *Methanex* Award, cf MA Orellana, 'The Role of Science in Investment Arbitrations Concerning Public Health and the Environment' (2006) 17 YIEL 48, 70–72.

rights and the associated host states' responsibility for safeguarding them, in line with the jurisprudence of human rights courts and bodies.

California's stringent environmental policies and legislation are again at stake in a pending NAFTA/UNCITRAL arbitration, the *Glamis Gold* case. The available factual record[134] exhibits typical features of a situation consisting of successive complex, multilevel, manifold, and contradictory EIA findings, coupled with policy and regulatory changes (point (3) of list above). The claimant asserts that the EIA process resulting in the final rejection of its proposed plan of operation of a major open-pit gold mine located in the California Desert Conservation Area, as well as newly introduced legislation on open-pit mining, have the effect of depriving of all value its investment (that is, previously acquired mining rights) and therefore constitute an expropriation and a denial of FET. Like in *Maffezini*, the claimant undertook the risk of injecting capital in its investment project before completion of the EIA/risk management process. At the same time, the situation appears far more complicated than in *Maffezini*: scientific and political assessments of the necessity of the measures at stake were complex and divergent, and the outcome of the process was denial of the requisite authorization, not its postponement. On the other hand, a powerful countervailing factor is again represented by the far-reaching transparent and participatory arrangements implemented throughout the decision-making procedure by the Californian authorities. In particular, these arrangements included the extensive involvement of the indigenous communities[135] affected by the gold mine project, which is located in close proximity to Native American sacred sites. It is worth recalling that the principle of public participation receives enhanced protection in international law when applied in the context of indigenous rights,[136] as the jurisprudence of human rights bodies illustrates.[137] Moreover, it will be extremely interesting to see whether the tribunal will take a look at the ECtHR *Taşkin* and related mining cases,[138] which display striking similarities with the facts underlying the *Glamis Gold* dispute. In the *Taşkin* case, the ECtHR emphasized the paramount importance of respect for participatory

---

[134] cf *Glamis Gold Ltd v United States*, Notice of Arbitration, 9 December 2003, and Non-Party Submission, Submission of the Quechan Indian Nation, 19 August 2005, 1–6. All documents of the case are available at <http://www.state.gov/s/l/c10986.htm>.
[135] See *Glamis Gold*, Application for Leave to File a Non-Party Submission, Submission of the Quechan Indian Nation, 19 August 2005, at fn 1.
[136] See, for instance, ILO Convention (No 169) Concerning Indigenous and Tribal Peoples in Independent Countries, Geneva, 27 June 1989, (1989) 28 ILM 1382, Art 15(2).
[137] Among the most recent and significant decisions, see African Commission on Human and Peoples' Rights, *Social and Economic Rights Action Center/Center for Economic and Social Rights v Nigeria*, Comm No 155/96, Decision, 13–27 October 2001, at para 53 and *dispositif* (see the commentary by D Shelton (2002) 96 AJIL 937); Inter-American Commission on Human Rights, *Maya Indigenous Community of the Toledo District v Belize*, Case 12.053, Report No 40/04, 12 October 2004, at paras 194, 197; and Human Rights Committee, *Mahuika and ors v New Zealand*, Comm No 547/1993, Views, 15 November 2000, at paras 9.5–9.8.
[138] *Taşkin*, n 117 above; *Öçkan*, n 118 above; and *Lemke*, n 118 above.

rights 'where a State must determine complex issues of environmental and economic policy',[139] and concluded that Turkey had violated the applicants' right to private life by nullifying the procedural safeguards formally available to them during the authorization process for the gold mine at stake.[140]

It is submitted that the *Glamis Gold* tribunal may have two valuable reasons for clarifying that the EIA process undertaken by the US authorities does not violate any investment discipline. First, it may establish that the adherence of the process to the principles of sound science, transparency, and public participation is dictated by human rights law. Secondly, if the tribunal wants to remain within the bounds of familiar investment rules, it may find that the doctrine of legitimate expectations has no role to play where such an open, informed, and inclusive EIA decision-making process has been carried out as part of a good faith effort duly to take into account all interests of the affected stakeholders. Most frequently, legitimate expectations are relied on in the context of the FET standard. Violation of this standard is usually associated with host states' conduct seriously tainted by, inter alia, arbitrariness, unfairness, denial of procedural due process, or lack of transparency in the decision-making process.[141] Given that participatory rights in EIA/risk management processes aim at fulfilling these very same values (albeit for different reasons), their consistent observance by a host state should be able to neutralize allegations of denial of FET.[142]

The *Glamis Gold* case also calls into question regulatory changes in the field of human rights and environmental law. In the context of EIA, these may relate to novel legal or technical requirements, such as the need for additional preventive measures or participatory procedures, which may result in updated EIA reports that overturn previous findings and trigger the withdrawal or withholding of authorizations. Is this course of action inconsistent with host states' obligations owed to foreign investors? Here, I entirely share the opinion[143] according to which host states are bound not to abdicate their human rights and environmental responsibilities in the name of stability of the regulatory framework affecting investments, be it by way of contractual/treaty arrangements or representations offered to prospective investors. The obligations to protect human rights and the environment do not have a fixed content that is valid once and for all; on the contrary, they are bound to acquire new dimensions to cope with

---

[139] *Taşkin*, ibid., at para 119.
[140] Ibid., at paras 124–126. In most cases, the same conclusion results from a violation of the principle of proportionality, ie from the defendant state's failure to strike a fair balance between the competing interests of the individual and the community as a whole and/or other private actors, cf *Fadeyeva*, n 118 above, at para 134.
[141] cf the celebrated definition of the FET standard given by the NAFTA tribunal in *Waste Management, Inc v Mexico*, Case No ARB(AF)/00/3, Award, 30 April 2004, (2004) 43 ILM 967, at para 98.   [142] cf Orellana, n 133 above, 55–57, 63–66.
[143] Most recently see, along these lines, Cotula, n 40 above, 129–131. See also *Suez, Sociedad General de Aguas de Barcelona, SA and Vivendi Universal, SA v Argentina*, ICSID Case No ARB/03/19, *Amicus Curiae* Submission, 4 April 2007, at 19–21, available at <http://www.ciel.org/Publications/SUEZ_Amicus_English_4Apr07.pdf>.

emerging threats and challenges and changing societal values and perceptions. In this context, science represents a compelling legitimizing factor for national measures. Accordingly, stabilization should never, as a matter of principle, apply to environmental and human rights legislation based on plausible scientific evidence. This would be fundamentally at variance with the dynamic and evolutionary nature of environmental and human rights obligations, as well as with the intertemporal dimension of the concept of SD.

B. Downplaying Participatory Rights and Subsidiarity: The *Metalclad* and *Tecmed* Cases

Whereas the *Methanex* tribunal's deference for and due consideration of national participatory processes is to be praised, other investor-state jurisprudence has substantially downplayed participatory rights and related concepts. The *Metalclad*[144] and *Tecmed*[145] cases must be singled out in this connection. Many elements were common to these cases: (1) they both related to failed investments in the very sensitive area of hazardous waste treatment and management; (2) the defendant was the same, namely, Mexico, as were therefore most national authorities involved in the challenged regulatory actions; (3) in both cases, such actions targeted investments in hazardous waste landfills, inter alia by denying a municipal construction permit in *Metalclad* and by refusing to renew an existing federal operating licence in *Tecmed*; (4) in both cases, these regulatory measures were taken for alleged reasons of environmental protection; and finally and most importantly, (5) such measures were strongly supported by various NGOs, as well as by groups of citizens living in the vicinity of the landfills and thus most affected by their operation. By contrast, applicable law was different in the two cases: *Metalclad* was a NAFTA case, while *Tecmed* was a BIT case.[146] This might have spurred a more environmentally oriented outcome in the *Metalclad* case.[147] To the contrary, the unpredictability of investor-state tribunals comes again to the fore, since, as shown below, the *Tecmed* tribunal at least demonstrated willingness to get to grips with the environmental and participatory issues raised by the dispute.

The *Metalclad* tribunal held that the decision-making processes and structures culminating in the denial of a municipal construction permit for a disputed landfill amounted to a violation of the FET standard.[148] Moreover, this denial

---

[144] *Metalclad v Mexico*, ICSID Case No ARB(AF)/97/1, Award, 30 August 2000, 5 ICSID Reports 212.
[145] *Técnicas Medioambientales Tecmed SA v Mexico*, ICSID Case No ARB(AF)/00/2, Award, 29 May 2003, (2004) 43 ILM 133.
[146] The jurisdiction of the ICSID tribunal was based on the 1995 Spain-Mexico BIT.
[147] This illusion fades away soon after reading the section of the *Metalclad* Award devoted to applicable law, *Metalclad*, n 144 above, at paras 70–71. No mention is made therein of the considerable environmental context and objectives of NAFTA.   [148] Ibid., at paras 97, 100–101.

552 Case Studies on Protection Standards and Specific Human Rights

and associated actions taken by Mexican authorities constituted a measure tantamount to expropriation.[149] 'Although not strictly necessary for its conclusion',[150] the tribunal also held that a further ground for its finding of expropriation was a state (sub-federal) Ecological Decree proclaiming a nature conservation area encompassing the landfill, as this decree 'had the effect of barring forever the operation of the landfill'.[151]

Both findings of the tribunal were to a large extent motivated by the absence of a clear legal basis for the denial of the construction permit by the *municipal* authorities.[152] These authorities had denied the permit in the light of the *opposition of the local population* and *ecological concerns* regarding the impact of the landfill on the surrounding environment and *communities*.[153] In the tribunal's view, the only lawful ground available to the municipal authorities for refusing the permit were construction considerations (for example, physical defects in the landfill). Therefore, the municipality 'acted outside its authority'[154] and its denial of the permit 'by reference to environmental impact considerations',[155] or 'for *any* reason other than those related to the physical construction',[156] was improper. Thus, environmental protection could not be seen as a valid justification for the disputed measures as the *federal* authorities, by granting the requisite *federal* permits, had thereby excluded the existence of environmental risks.[157]

The tribunal's findings are very controversial from the perspective of environmental law. First, they completely ignore that the municipal and state (sub-federal) authorities' actions were not capricious or discriminatory; on the contrary, they were responsive to civil society's legitimate concerns and opposition to the landfill.[158] Second, the environmental genuineness of such actions was eventually evidenced by the establishment of an ecological preserve. It is certainly no coincidence that the tribunal expressly refrained from inquiring into the motivations behind the Ecological Decree and retained instead a 'sole effects test' in concluding that the decree amounted to indirect expropriation.[159]

Moreover, and most importantly, the tribunal's findings are fundamentally at variance with the principle of subsidiarity in environmental matters.[160] Indeed, in order to arrive at its conclusion that the municipality could not invoke environmental concerns, the tribunal got entangled in settling a controversial Mexican constitutional issue relating to the allocation of powers between different levels of government in matters of hazardous waste.[161] It said that the municipality had authority only with respect to *non*-hazardous waste, while the

---

[149] Ibid., at paras 104, 107.   [150] Ibid., at para 109.   [151] Ibid.
[152] Ibid., at paras 97 ('procedural and substantive deficiencies of the denial') and 107 ('absence of a timely, orderly or substantive basis for the denial').   [153] Ibid., at para 92.
[154] Ibid., at para 106.   [155] Ibid., at para 86.   [156] Ibid., emphasis added.
[157] Ibid., at para 98.
[158] Some facts relating to public participation and opposition to the landfill are recalled in the award; see ibid., at paras 46 and 48.   [159] Ibid., at para 111.
[160] As noted, eg by Sands, n 77 above, 1072–1073.
[161] *Metalclad*, n 144 above, at paras 79–86.

disputed landfill was '*basically* a hazardous waste disposal landfill'.[162] My point is that, by doing so, investor-state tribunals, like any other international adjudicatory body, misinterpret their role in disputes involving environmental (and similar public policy) issues. This role should be confined to ascertaining whether allegedly environmental measures taken by host states are incompatible with investor protections. It should not be that of an arbiter of complex domestic controversies about the distribution of environmental powers between the various levels of government. In this context, the appropriate standard of review should be a very deferential one, especially when, like in *Metalclad*, the challenged measures are authored by the lowest levels of government, namely, by the authorities most representative of (and proximate to) citizens' needs and concerns, and are indeed aimed at responding to such concerns.

Subsidiarity is a structural principle of human rights and environmental law. The ECtHR environmental jurisprudence is telling in this respect and provides further evidence of the unsoundness of the *Metalclad* tribunal's reasoning. While the essentially subsidiary function of the ECtHR is generally linked to the consideration that 'national authorities have direct democratic legitimation and are ... in principle better placed than an international court to evaluate local needs and conditions',[163] in that jurisprudence this has translated into affording a *wide* margin of appreciation to domestic authorities in environmental issues.[164] However controversial, this means self-restraint on the part of the Court when assessing whether national measures violate environmental rights. In the *Fadeyeva* case,[165] the Court went even further. It offered another reason for its subsidiary nature, namely, 'the complexity of the issues involved with regard to environmental protection'.[166] Accordingly, it said that its role ought to be essentially confined to examining 'whether the decision-making process was fair and such as to afford due respect to the interests [of] the individual ... and only in *exceptional* circumstances may it go beyond this line and revise the material conclusions of the domestic authorities'.[167]

In other words, the ECtHR fundamental role in environmental cases is that of assessing whether *procedural* or *participatory* rights have been safeguarded.[168] It is evident that the outcome of the *Metalclad* case points to the opposite direction: the tribunal substituted its own judgment to that of the domestic authorities with regard to the *substantive* merits of their environmental decisions, while ignoring the participatory and subsidiarity issues underlying those

---

[162] Ibid., at para 86, emphasis added.   [163] *Hatton*, n 117 above, at para 97.
[164] Ibid., at para 100; *Taşkin*, n 117 above, at para 116; and *Fadeyeva*, n 118 above, at para 134.
[165] Ibid.   [166] Ibid., at para 105.   [167] Ibid., emphasis added.
[168] As rightly noted, this case law brings about the absorption of the substantive dimension of environmental rights by their procedural dimension. See E Lambert Abdelgawab, 'Convention européenne des droits de l'homme, droit à l'environnement et proportionnalité', paper presented at a workshop on 'émergence et circulation de concepts juridiques en droit international de l'environnement: entre mondialisation et fragmentation', Paris I Sorbonne, 18 April 2008 (on file with the author).

decisions, that is, precisely the issues which are increasingly covered by human rights obligations and doctrines.

The ultimate findings of the *Tecmed* tribunal were identical to those of the *Metalclad* tribunal: the refusal by a federal agency of the Mexican Ministry of the Environment to renew a licence for the operation of a hazardous industrial waste landfill, and the concomitant request to draw up a plan for its closure, amounted to a de facto expropriation and a violation of the FET standard.[169] Nonetheless, there is an essential difference between the *Tecmed* and *Metalclad* tribunals' approaches: the former did not neglect the participatory issues underlying the facts of the case. Indeed, the tribunal accepted to balance the 'widespread and aggressive'[170] public opposition to the landfill against the deprivation of investor rights within the proportionality test which it devised in order to assess whether the host state's actions were expropriatory.[171] At least prima facie, public participation was thus duly considered as a matter of public interest, since that test, as usual, aimed at establishing whether there was a reasonable relationship of proportionality between a measure interfering with individual (investor) rights and a legitimate public policy objective.

In my view, however, the tribunal's application of the proportionality test ended up in downplaying participatory rights. The tribunal held, first, that there was no genuine environmental problem behind the host state's measures. The indisputable breaches by the claimant of Mexican environmental regulations were minor and not such as to 'seriously or imminently affect[...] public health, ecological balance or the environment'.[172] Second, the tribunal, seemingly unaware of the human rights implications of public participation, labelled 'community pressure' as mere 'socio-political circumstances' or 'political problems'[173] *tout court*. The concerned public's *political* goals – namely, the relocation and closure of the landfill – were unsupported by severe environmental adverse effects.[174] Third, the tribunal nonetheless carried out its balancing exercise and determined that investor rights overrode public participation, since the latter did not in this case give rise to 'a serious urgent situation, crisis, need or social emergency'.[175] It said:

the Respondent has not presented any evidence that community opposition to the Landfill – however intense, aggressive and sustained – was in any way massive or went any further than the positions assumed by some individuals or the members of some groups that were opposed to the Landfill. Even after having gained substantial momentum, community opposition, although it had been sustained by its advocates through an insistent, active and continuous public campaign in the mass media, could gather on two occasions a crowd of only two hundred people the first time and of four

---

[169] Under Arts 4 and 5 of the Spain-Mexico BIT.   [170] *Tecmed*, n 145 above, at para 108.
[171] The *Tecmed* Award is indeed well known especially for this proportionality test retained by the tribunal within its expropriation analysis. The test is set out in ibid., at para 122.
[172] Ibid., at para 130. See also, eg para 124.   [173] Ibid., at paras 129–130.
[174] Ibid., at para 131.   [175] Ibid., at para 139. See also paras 133 and 137.

hundred people, the second time out of a community with a population of almost one million inhabitants ... Additionally, the 'blockage' of the Landfill was carried out by small groups of no more than forty people.[176]

It is not clear whether the tribunal, in referring to a 'social emergency or crisis' as a yardstick for public participation to trump investor protections, had in mind a state of necessity as a circumstance precluding wrongfulness or, rather, more pragmatic considerations relating to good governance, legitimacy, and representativeness of civil society claims. Either way, it should explicitly have stated so. At any rate, public participation cannot simply be reduced to its numerical dimensions or to an effective lobbying campaign, especially in the case of developing countries, where meaningful participatory structures and opportunities may at best be minimal. The *Tecmed* tribunal embarked upon highly discretionary assessments, instead of acknowledging that the situation was that of a legitimate regulatory process led by a ministry of a federal state responsive to subsidiarity concerns[177] and to those of the affected public.

Even though the tribunal's analysis starting point was 'due deference'[178] to a state's choices related to 'its public policy or the interests of society as a whole',[179] it then overstepped the proper role of an international adjudicatory body in disputes involving environmental and participatory issues. In supporting a high threshold of magnitude for public participation, it unreasonably second-guessed the legitimate choices made by domestic authorities. This is all the more so, since the tribunal's reasoning on the environmental problems associated with the landfill cannot be shared. How can the relocation of a hazardous waste landfill, situated in the proximity of a densely populated urban centre in breach of the applicable host state's regulations,[180] be regarded as a mere 'political problem'?[181] And how can the repeated infringements of environmental standards by the investor, including unauthorized transfer and storage of hazardous wastes, be understated? At the very least, the regulatory decision at stake ought to be viewed as a measure consistent with the principles of preventive and/or precautionary action. Yet, there is no room in the tribunal's reasoning for such principles, since 'it would be excessively formalistic ... to understand that the [regulatory measure] is proportional to [the investor's

---

[176] Ibid., at para 144. See also para 147.
[177] Although not prominently as in the *Metalclad* case, subsidiarity was at issue also in the *Tecmed* case, given the emphasis of the tribunal on the exclusive environmental authority of the federal government, which in its view rendered consultation with the subfederal levels of government legally unnecessary, ibid., at para 129.   [178] Ibid., at para 122.
[179] Ibid.
[180] That is, at a distance of 8 km from the city's centre, instead of 25 km (see ibid., at para 106). This is a supervening host state's environmental standard, ie one that entered into force after the investment was made. The tribunal gave prominent weight to this factor as generating legitimate expectations on the part of the investor (see, eg ibid., at para 141). I have already criticized this approach (n 143 above and accompanying text). Here, the reference to the host state's applicable laws is only made to show that an actual environmental problem was indeed at stake.
[181] Ibid., at para 129.

infringements] when such infringements do not pose a *present or imminent risk* to the ecological balance or to people's health'.[182]

Ironically, the *Tecmed* tribunal is often recalled with approval for its extensive quotes from the ECtHR case law about property rights and proportionality.[183] It will now be apparent that those quotes did not involve some critical tenets upheld in that case law, such as subsidiarity and the wide national margin of appreciation in environmental matters, or the essential importance of environmental procedural rights in assessing whether there has been a violation of the ECHR.[184]

V. Conclusion

Investor-state cases involving environmental issues are paradigmatic examples of SD disputes. Their adjudication should therefore invite a systematic balancing and integration of ecologic, economic, social, human rights, and developmental factors. The existing investor-state jurisprudence reviewed throughout this chapter reveals some modest steps in that direction. First, certain awards, such as *SD Myers* and *Parkerings*, may be seen as reasonable attempts at weighing up all of the circumstances relevant to a meaningful SD balancing exercise. By contrast, other decisions, such as *Metalclad* and *Santa Elena*, show resistance on the part of the tribunals to broaden their perspective. It is evident how these tribunals unduly interpreted their mission as essentially limited to applying investment rules and doctrines. Second, some investor-state tribunals, prominently the *Methanex* tribunal, but to some extent also the *Maffezini* tribunal, rendered decisions which are in line with the protection of environmental procedural human rights. These tribunals actually endorsed host states' regulatory processes characterized by legal techniques and instruments, such as EIA, public hearings, and peer scientific review, which are essential to the realization of participatory rights.

In the light of its growing recognition in theory, jurisprudence, and practice, the principle of public participation will most likely represent the critical benchmark for future tribunals dealing with disputes at the intersection of environmental law, human rights, and investment protections.

---

[182] Ibid., at para 149, emphasis added. The alleged absence of genuine environmental concerns was also a chief reason for the tribunal's finding of violation of the FET standard; see, eg ibid., at para 164.   [183] Ibid., at para 122.

[184] Admittedly, the *Tecmed* Award was rendered at a time when the ECtHR jurisprudence on environmental procedural rights was embryonic (the *Hatton* and *Taşkin* judgments, n 117 above, were made on the same year as, and a year later than, the award, respectively); but see the 1998 *Guerra* judgment, where the Court famously held that failure to provide the affected individuals with information on environmental risks and emergency procedures relating to hazardous industrial activities violated their right to private and family life: *Guerra and ors v Italy*, judgment, 19 February 1998, at para 60.

23

The Relevance of Non-Investment Treaty Obligations in Assessing Compensation

*Lahra Liberti**

I. Introduction

The role of non-investment treaty obligations in the assessment of compensation has not been fully explored so far. The approach to this challenging issue cannot be but problematic, especially in an area in which clear-cut solutions are not easily at hand, because of the complex relationship between international obligations arising in different normative subject matters. The question is whether and to what extent a measure adopted by the state *in the furtherance* of international obligations other than those provided for in the investment treaty bears any consequences not only in the appreciation of state liability,[1] but also in the determination of the quantum of compensation and in the choice of the method of valuation. This chapter reviews existing jurisprudence and aims to identify key issues for consideration.

II. Non-Investment Treaty Obligations in Investment Disputes Case Law: Are They Relevant in the Assessment of Compensation?

It could be pointed out at the very outset that the question of the relevance of international obligations other than those provided for in investment treaties for

---

* This chapter is based on the text of the presentation delivered at the Eighth Investment Treaty Forum Public Conference on 'Remedies under International Investment Law', London, 11 May 2007 (published online in Transnational Dispute Management, 2007, vol 4, issue 6) and at the European University Institute Workshop on 'Is there a role for human rights in international investment law and dispute settlement', Fiesole, 12–13 June 2007. The views expressed in this chapter are exclusively those of the author and do not represent those of the OECD or its member governments. This chapter cannot be construed as prejudging ongoing or future negotiations or disputes pertaining to international investment agreements.

[1] The important question of whether the existence of international obligations has a bearing on the determination of whether or not a taking or any other violation of the standards of treatment set forth under investment treaties has occurred is beyond the scope of this chapter. This issue will be only partially addressed while illustrating the *SPP v Egypt* case below.

the settlement of a given dispute might deserve little or no consideration after the ICSID tribunal in *Compañia del Desarrollo de Santa Elena SA v Costa Rica* plainly dismissed the argument, stating that it would not analyse the detailed evidence submitted by what the respondent referred to as its international obligation to preserve a unique ecological site. The arbitral tribunal ruled as follows:

While an expropriation or taking for environmental reasons may be classified as a taking for a public purpose, and thus may be legitimate, the fact that the property was taken for this reason does not affect either the *nature* or the *measure* of the compensation to be paid for the taking. That is, the purpose of protecting the environment for which the Property was taken does not alter the legal character of the taking for which adequate compensation must be paid. *The international source of the obligation to protect the environment makes no difference.*

Expropriatory environmental measures – no matter how laudable and beneficial to society as a whole – are, in this respect, similar to any other expropriatory measures that a state may take in order to implement its policies: where property is expropriated, even for environmental purposes, *whether domestic or international, the state's obligation to pay compensation remains.*[2]

By relying on the 'sole effect doctrine', the arbitral tribunal left no room for an argument that the existence of international obligations to protect the environment has a bearing on the nature and measure of compensation.

It might be tempting to dismiss international obligations other than those provided for under international investment treaties as simply irrelevant, both with regard to the application of the standard of compensation and methodologies of valuation. However, a closer look at the awards rendered in the *Siemens v Argentina* and *SPP v Egypt* cases would suffice to question this conclusion as belonging 'to the things of which we may doubt' – *dubium sapientiae initium.*

In the award rendered in the *Siemens v Argentina* case,[3] the arbitral tribunal did not refuse to consider the defence of the respondent based on international human rights law. The respondent first argued that the protection of property rights of the investor, if upheld, would have constituted a breach of international human rights law. The tribunal held that the argument, without the benefit of further elaboration and substantiation, did not bear prima facie any relationship to the merit of the case.

Then, with specific regard to the assessment of compensation, Argentina further contended that: 'the fair market value of an expropriated property as the measure of compensation for an expropriated investment is not always applicable when an expropriation becomes necessary for social policy reasons'.[4]

---

[2] *Compañia del Desarrollo de Santa Elena SA v Costa Rica*, ICSID Case No ARB/96/1, Final Award, 17 February 2000, 39 ILM 1317, at paras 71–72 (emphasis added).
[3] *Siemens AG v Argentina*, ICSID Case No ARB/02/08, Award, 6 February 2007, available at <http://ita.law.uvic.ca/alphabetical_list_content.htm#su>.   [4] Ibid., at para 346.

Argentina questioned the way in which Siemens drew the line to delimit the state's legitimate actions from actions entitling an investor to compensation, relying on the proportionality test advanced by *Tecmed*.[5] Argentina also referred to the jurisprudence of the European Court of Human Rights, which in *James v UK* held that Article 1 of the First Protocol to the European Convention on Human Rights does not 'guarantee a right to full compensation in all circumstances. Legitimate objectives of "public interest" such as pursued in measures of economic reform or measures designed to achieve greater social justice, may call for less than reimbursement of full market value'. Argentina deemed these considerations to be applicable in the case before the ICSID tribunal, concluding that 'even if there was an expropriation, the Claimant would not be entitled to more than the direct losses and not to the *lucrum cessans*'.[6]

The arbitral tribunal rejected this argument on the following three grounds. First, Argentina did not develop the argument according to which, when a state expropriates for social or economic reasons, fair market value does not apply because otherwise this would limit the sovereignty of a country to introduce reforms. Second, the tribunal found that Argentina erroneously relied on *Tecmed*, since the considerations on the purpose and proportionality of the measures taken related to the determination of whether an expropriation had occurred and not to the assessment of compensation. Third, Article 1 of the First Protocol to the European Convention on Human Rights permits a margin of appreciation not found in customary international law or the bilateral investment treaty between Germany and Argentina.[7]

The arbitral tribunal did not endorse Argentina's argument that less than 'fair market value' should be the measure of the compensation more on the basis of the shortcomings in the argument put forward by the respondent rather than on the theoretical impossibility to make a successful argument. Thus, the tribunal, while taking into account the argument *in abstracto*, ultimately ruled against it *in concreto*. It also found that without the benefit of further elaboration and substantiation, the reference made by Argentina to international human rights law

---

[5] *Técnicas Medioambientales Tecmed, SA v Mexico*, ICSID Case No ARB(AF)/00/2, Award, 29 May 2003, 19 ICSID Review FILJ (2004) 158.   [6] Ibid., at paras 346–347.
[7] Ibid., at para 354:

Argentina has pleaded that, when a State expropriates for social or economic reasons, fair market value does not apply because otherwise this would limit the sovereignty of a country to introduce reforms in particular of poor countries. Argentina has not developed this argument, nor justified on what basis Argentina would be considered a poor country, nor specified the reforms it sought to carry out at the time. Argentina in its allegations has relied on *Tecmed* as an example to follow in terms of considering the purpose and proportionality of the measures taken. The Tribunal observes that these considerations were part of that tribunal's determination of whether an expropriation had occurred and not of its determination of compensation. The Tribunal further observes that Article I of the First Protocol to the European Convention on Human Rights permits a margin of appreciation not found in customary international law or the Treaty.

did not prima facie bear any relationship to the merits of the case. This means that had Argentina further developed it, the conclusion might have been different.

Therefore, as it was pointed out in the *Amicus Curiae* submission filed in the *Biwater v Tanzania* case, the crucial issue for consideration 'is not whether this is theoretically possible, but how might it be specifically relevant' under the specific circumstances of each case.[8]

III. The Specific Relevance of the Obligations of the UNESCO Convention in the *SPP v Egypt* Case

The issue of the relevance of non-investment treaty obligations in the assessment of compensation has been raised and dealt with in depth by the ICSID arbitral tribunal in the *SPP v Egypt* award.[9] In this case, the tribunal had no doubt as to the relevance of the international obligations deriving from the Convention concerning the protection of the World Cultural and Natural Heritage (hereinafter, the UNESCO Convention) – the divergencies on the interpretation of Article 42 of the ICSID Convention on the applicable law did not matter.

Moreover, the relevance of the UNESCO Convention was not disputed between the parties. Egypt considered the UNESCO Convention applicable as a treaty ratified and incorporated under Egyptian law. The tribunal also reported that:

the Claimants themselves acknowledged during the proceedings before the French Cour d'Appel that the Convention obligated the Respondent to abstain from acts or contracts contrary to the Convention, stating: 'que les Etats etaient susceptibles d'engager leur responsabilité internationale envers les autres Etats signataires en persistant dans des actes ou contrats devenus contraires aux règles de la Convention'.[10]

The crucial issue was how the UNESCO Convention could be deemed to be specifically relevant under the specific circumstances of the case.

A. The Relevance of the UNESCO Convention in the Appreciation of the Legal Nature of the Measures Taken by Egypt

Egypt maintained that the entry into force of the UNESCO Convention on 17 December 1975 made it obligatory to cancel the Pyramids Oasis Project. The

---

[8] *Biwater Gauff (Tanzania) Ltd v Tanzania*, ICSID Case No ARB/05/22. The *Amicus Curiae* submission is available at <http://www.ciel.org/Publications/Biwater_Amicus_26March.pdf>, at para 43.

[9] *Southern Pacific Properties (Middle East) Ltd v Egypt*, ICSID Case No ARB/84/3, Award, 20 May 1992, 32 ILM 933 (1993), at para 78.   [10] Ibid., at para 78.

respondent relied on Articles 4 and 5 of the UNESCO Convention. Article 4 provides that:

Each State Party to this Convention recognizes that the duty of ensuring the identification, protection, conservation, presentation and transmission to future generations of the cultural and natural heritage referred to in Articles 1 and 2 and situated on its territory, belongs primarily to that State. It will do all it can to this end, to the utmost of its own resources and, where appropriate, with any international assistance and co-operation, in particular, financial, artistic, scientific and technical, which it may be able to obtain.

Article 5(d) further provides:

To ensure that effective and active measures are taken for the protection, conservation and presentation of the cultural and natural heritage situated on its territory, each State Party to this Convention shall endeavour, in so far as possible, and as appropriate for each country: ... to take the appropriate legal, scientific, technical, administrative and financial measures necessary for the identification, protection, conservation, presentation and rehabilitation of this heritage ...

The claimants contended that the expropriatory measures had not been taken pursuant to the UNESCO Convention, since the Convention was ratified by Egypt on 7 February 1974 and the Pyramids Oasis Project was approved more than a year later in 1976. As a matter of consequence, in the claimants' view, the expropriatory acts were not based on the UNESCO Convention, since Egypt did not rely on it when it cancelled the project, but only invoked it as a 'post hoc rationalization for an act of expropriation which in fact had nothing to do with the Convention'.[11] In addition, the claimants further argued that the UNESCO Convention did not require the cancellation of the project and that other measures short of cancellation could have been taken in conformity with the Convention to protect the antiquities on the plateau.

The tribunal rejected the respondent's argument that it cancelled the construction project pursuant to the UNESCO Convention, since the Convention entered into force for Egypt in December 1975, while the construction project was approved in 1976; the decision to cancel the project was taken in 1978 after the approval of the Decree No 90 which declared lands on the project site to be public property, while the Pyramids Fields was included in the inventory of property to be protected only in 1979. In the tribunal's view, the obligations to protect and preserve the antiquities became binding only from the date on which the respondent's nomination of the Pyramid Fields was accepted for inclusion in the inventory of property to be protected under the UNESCO Convention in 1979. That is the reason why under the specific circumstances of the case the tribunal held that the UNESCO Convention by itself did not

---

[11] Ibid., at para 153.

justify the measures taken by Egypt. The cancellation of the project was characterized as a lawful taking of contractual rights, for which compensation should be paid.

At the same time, the tribunal recognized that after the World Heritage Committee accepted Egypt's nomination of the Pyramid Fields for inclusion in the inventory of protected property, Egypt was entitled under the UNESCO Convention to consider that the 'Pyramids Oasis Project was not compatible with its obligations under the Convention to protect and conserve antiquities in the areas registered with the World Heritage Committee'[12] and that 'a hypothetical continuation of the Claimants' activities interfering with antiquities in the area could be considered as unlawful from the international point of view'.[13]

Because of belated registration of the Pyramids Fields under the UNESCO Convention, the tribunal could not go any further in considering whether the international obligations to protect and conserve the antiquities might alter the very legal nature of the measures taken as amounting to a compensable expropriation (the lawful character of which was never disputed).

However, it could be argued that the conclusions of the tribunal might have been different, had the cancellation of the project occurred after the registration in 1979, since after that date any activities interfering with the antiquities would have become internationally unlawful. The tribunal expressly recognized that Egypt was entitled under the Convention to determine 'that the Pyramids Oasis Project was not compatible with its obligations under the Convention to protect and conserve antiquities in the areas registered with the World Heritage Committee'. Moreover, as reported by the tribunal, the claimants themselves acknowledged during the proceedings before the French *Cour d'Appel* that the Convention obligated the respondent to abstain from acts or contracts contrary to the Convention.

B. The Relevance of the UNESCO Convention in the Determination of the Quantum of Compensation and Method of Valuation

Although the tribunal held that the UNESCO Convention did not alter the legal nature of the measures taken as a lawful compensable taking, the determination that the claimants' activities on the Pyramids Plateau would have become internationally unlawful in 1979 had 'significant consequences' in terms of determining the quantum of compensation, with special regard to the methodology for valuing the tourist project. As pointed out by the tribunal: 'The cardinal point to be borne in mind, then, in determining the appropriate compensation is that, ... the contracts could no longer be performed'.[14] The tribunal rejected the discounted cash flow (DCF) method invoked by the

---

[12] Ibid., at para 156.   [13] Ibid., at para 154.   [14] Ibid., at para 183.

claimants as not appropriate for determining the fair compensation not only with regard to the short life span of the project, which was not sufficient to generate the data necessary for a meaningful calculation, but more importantly because:

> ... the Claimants' DCF approach would in effect award lucrum cessans through the year 1995 on the assumption that lot sales would have continued through that year. Yet lot sales in the areas registered with the World Heritage Committee under the UNESCO Convention would have been illegal under both international law and Egyptian law after 1979, when the registration was made. Obviously, the allowance of lucrum cessans may only involve those profits which are legitimate. As A. de Laubadere has stated: 'le lucrum cessans correspond au "benefice legitime" que le co-contractant pouvait normalement escompter' ...

Thus, even if the Tribunal were disposed to accept the validity of the Claimants' DCF calculations, it could only award lucrum cessans until 1979, when the obligations resulting from the UNESCO Convention with respect to the Pyramids Plateau became binding on the Respondent. From that date forward, the Claimants' activities on the Pyramids Plateau would have been in conflict with the Convention and therefore in violation of international law, and any profits that might have resulted from such activities are consequently non-compensable.[15]

Alternatively, the claimants claimed for their out-of-pocket expenses and 'an additional amount ... to compensate for loss of the chance or opportunity of making a commercial success of the project'[16] intended to recover the value of the investment.

Taking into account the portion of the sales revenues actually made during the short life of the project in the period between February 1977 and May 1978, the tribunal found that the investment had a value that exceeded the claimants' out-of-pocket expenses, amounting to the difference between the expenditures incurred by the claimants to generate the revenues imputed to the lot sales and the portion of imputed revenues corresponding to the claimants' shareholding in the joint venture.

As a result, the overall sum awarded to the claimants amounted to US$27,661,000, instead of $41,000,000 initially claimed by the claimants on the basis of the DCF method.

The tribunal expressly acknowledged that it did factor into the determination of the quantum of compensation the fact that the reclassification of the land on the Pyramids Plateau was a lawful act as well as the fact that the claimant should have known the risk that antiquities would be discovered in the tourist project area, by not awarding compensation based on profits that might have accrued to the claimants after the date on which areas on the plateau were registered with the World Heritage Committee under the UNESCO Convention.

---

[15] Ibid., at para 190–191.   [16] Ibid., at para 180.

IV. Concluding Remarks

The *SPP v Egypt* award clearly shows how, under the specific circumstances of the case, international obligations arising from different subject-matter areas of international law can be relevant while adjudicating investment disputes. It seems that the belated registration of the Pyramids Fields with the UNESCO Convention which occurred after the cancellation of the project lies at the heart of the tribunal's finding of a compensable expropriation. Nevertheless, the *SPP* case also shows that it is possible to demonstrate that a state is in violation of a particular treaty (or customary obligation) because of a particular investment: since 1979, the tourist project of the Pyramids Plateau would have been in conflict with the UNESCO Convention and therefore Egypt would have been in violation of international law. The existence of the international legal obligations deriving from the UNESCO Convention to preserve and protect the Pyramids Fields did have significant consequences in the assessment of compensation, bearing in mind that the activities in the Pyramids Fields would have become unlawful after the registration of the area with the UNESCO Convention.

Although not a BIT case, the rationale of the *SPP v Egypt* award might serve as a useful precedent for future tribunals. It might reasonably be expected that arbitral tribunals will be increasingly confronted with the defence argument that the taking measure or any other measure deemed to be in violation of any other substantive standard of investment protection was adopted by the state *in furtherance* of an international obligation. In particular, in the water privatization disputes and in the context of the implementation of South Africa's reforms to redress past racial discrimination, it is conceivable that respondent states might argue that the measures adopted have been taken to comply with existing international obligations arising from human rights conventions.[17] The arbitral tribunals will be thus called to appreciate the consequences of measures genuinely taken in furtherance of an international obligation in terms of liability of the state as well as in the assessment of compensation.

---

[17] See the pending ICSID case *Piero Foresti, Laura de Carli and ors v South Africa*, ICSID Case No ARB(AF)/07/1.

24

EC Free Trade Agreements: An Alternative Model for Addressing Human Rights in Foreign Investment Regulation and Dispute Settlement?

Angelos Dimopoulos

I. Introduction

The rising interest in foreign investment is born mainly out of the widespread conviction that foreign investment contributes to growth and development.[1] In recognition of the positive effects of foreign investment flows, most countries have made moves towards developing a legal and economic environment favourable to foreign investment and greater capital mobility, which has led to a patchwork of more than 2500 bilateral agreements dealing with foreign investment.[2] Dealing mainly with concerns about the protection of foreign investors against host state interventions, bilateral investment treaties (BITs) have become the backbone of international investment law, including the most common norms regulating foreign investment. The most important innovation that they have introduced is the establishment of a rigorous and efficient dispute settlement mechanism, which has allowed private investors to challenge any measures adopted by the host state that contravene the provisions of the BIT, by initiating institutionalized or ad hoc arbitration.

---

[1] According to many economic studies, foreign investment contributes to home and host country development in many ways, adding to their economic wealth and social welfare. For an indicative bibliography, see UNCTAD, *Economic Development in Africa, Rethinking the Role of Foreign Direct Investment* (2006); T Moran, *Does Foreign Investment promote development?* (2005); H Kehal, *Foreign Investment in Developing Countries* (2004); and J Dunning and S Lundan, *Multinational Enterprises and the Global Economy* (2008).
[2] UNCTAD, *World Investment Report* (2006) XVII, 26.

However, BITs and investment arbitration conducted under their auspices have generated fierce criticism. In many cases foreign investors, in their attempt to protect their property against alleged unlawful actions of the host state, have challenged national measures implementing public policies seeking to promote or protect human rights interests. A series of controversial disputes centred upon environmental and public health measures of the host state have been arbitrated so far,[3] having given in fact little space for human rights considerations to be taken into account. Furthermore, BITs do not address how investment activity might affect the enjoyment of various human rights in the host country (for example, labour rights, freedom of expression, freedom of assembly), thus minimizing the possibility of successfully raising human rights arguments in future BIT arbitrations. Hence, since BITs do not introduce their own human rights obligations, and investment tribunals have a limited jurisdiction to arbitrate investment disputes as defined under BITs, there appears to be little scope for human rights issues to play a determinative role in investment treaty disputes.[4]

In addition, BITs are considered to have failed in their primary purpose to increase capital flows and attract foreign investment.[5] They have focused mainly on protection against expropriation and have been unsuccessful in addressing the main location determinants of foreign investment, namely market access and profitability.[6] On the contrary, the broad protection offered against expropriation, including 'regulatory expropriation', has led many developing countries to adopt protectionist measures, deterred them from opening their markets to foreign investors, or forced them to pay enormous sums to foreign

---

[3] See, eg *Metalclad Corp v Mexico*, Award, 30 August 2000, ICSID Case No ARB(AF)/97/1, (2001) 6 ICSID Review – FILJ 168; *Aguas del Tunari SA v Bolivia*, Decision on Jurisdiction, 21 October 2005, ICSID Case No ARB/02/3, (2005) 20 ICSID Review – FILJ 450; and *Azurix Corp v Argentina*, Award, 14 July 2006, ICSID Case No ARB/01/12.

[4] L Peterson and K Gray, *International Human Rights in Bilateral Investment Treaties and in Investment Treaty Arbitration* (2005) 6.

[5] Recent studies revealed that although investment flows have increased considerably in the last few years, most of it is directed to other developed countries and economies in transition, while developing countries receive only a small percentage of it. Even though the failure of the investment policy followed to attract foreign investment may be explained by economic reasons, such as lack of natural resources or small markets, the chosen legal regime of foreign investment is also responsible for low investment flows and unsustainable practices in developing countries. UNCTAD, n 2 above, 2–4, 44–45. T Moran, 'What policies should developing country governments adopt toward outward FDI? Lessons from the experience of developed countries' in KP Sauvant, K Mendoza, and I Ince (eds), *The Rise of TNCs from Emerging Markets: Threat or Opportunity?* (2008) ch 13; and L Sachs and K Sauvant (eds), *The Impact of Bilateral Investment and Double Taxation Treaties on Foreign Direct Investment Flows* (2008).

[6] S Griffith-Jones, *Global Capital Flows* (1998) 158–160, 171–175; and UNCTAD, *World Investment Report* (2003) 99–145.

investors in order to promote their environmental, public health, and development policies.[7]

This situation has been severely criticized within the current legal framework on foreign investment,[8] and the international community has been put under pressure to reassess the relationship between foreign investment and human rights. As a result, the European Community (EC)[9] has tried to incorporate foreign investment in a broader framework and link foreign investment regulation with human rights concerns and development principles. Within its limited mandate, the EC has attempted to reflect its policy orientation in its external economic relations and in particular in the bilateral free trade agreements (FTAs) that it has concluded with third (non-EU) countries, promoting an alternative regulatory framework of foreign investment, which takes into account economic and social policy considerations.

This chapter aims to present the relation between foreign investment and human rights, as established in EC FTAs and in particular in their dispute settlement mechanisms. The first part offers a brief analysis of the substantive provisions of EC FTAs dealing with foreign investment, focusing on their innovative character in relation to traditional BITs and addressing their human rights implications. The second part presents the dispute settlement mechanisms that are established in EC FTAs and assesses their suitability for investment disputes, while the third part discusses the role of human rights in EC FTAs and their relation with investment provisions. The fourth part highlights the practical implications of the described EU model and, finally, the fifth part outlines the future perspectives of EC FTAs in terms of readdressing the relation between foreign investment and human rights.

II. The Substantive Scope of EC FTA Provisions on Foreign Investment

The EC was not initially a key player of the international community in the field of foreign investment regulation. Unlike trade, where the EC's exclusive competence has long been well established, its competence on foreign investment

---

[7] A Cosbey et al, *Investment and Sustainable Development: A guide to the Use and Potential of International Investment Agreements* (2004) 9–14; and A Guzman, 'Why LDCs Sign Treaties That Hurt Them: Explaining the Popularity of Bilateral Investment Treaties' (1975) 38 Virginia Journal of International Law 640, 680–684.

[8] For a discussion on the adverse effects of foreign investment law on human rights interests, see U Kriebaum, 'Privatizing Human Rights. The Interface between International Investment Protection and Human Rights' in A Reinisch and U Kriebaum (eds), *The Law of International Relations – Liber Amicorum H. Neuhold* (2007) 165.

[9] In this chapter the term European Community (EC) will be used for identifying the legal person concluding the FTAs and the term European Union (EU) will be used for referring to the Member States and their nationals.

was limited[10] and still remains vague.[11] However, the gradual expansion of foreign investment regulation as well as the continuous process of European integration has rendered the EC an important actor in the field of foreign investment regulation. It has been a pioneer in the introduction of investment-related norms in sectoral agreements, such as GATS in the WTO and the Energy Charter Treaty, and simultaneously it has promoted the inclusion of investment provisions in its bilateral and regional trade agreements.[12] Despite Member States' objections that the EC would encroach on their competence and substitute favourable provisions of their BITs, the EC promotes its own, complementary investment policy, establishing not only free trade areas, but also a framework for broad economic, political, and social cooperation and underlining the strong connection between trade, investment, and development.

A. EC FTAs Including Provisions on Foreign Investment

Investment-related provisions are included in the vast majority of the FTAs that the EC has concluded with third countries. First, the Stabilization and Association Agreements (SAAs) with Balkan countries,[13] the Association Agreement with Turkey,[14] and the European Economic Area Agreement (EEAA),[15] which all aim at the future accession of the respective countries to the EU or to the creation of an internal market, adopt the same rules which currently apply to investments between EU Member States or provide for their gradual approximation. However, due to their proximity with EC law and their integration objectives, these agreements are not representative of EC FTAs, thus, they will not be analytically addressed in this chapter. A second category of EC FTAs, aiming at the future creation of a free trade area, are those concluded with EU neighboring countries, namely the Euro-Mediterranean Agreements[16] and the

---

[10] W Shan, 'Towards a Common European Community Policy on Investment Issues' (2001) 2 JWIT 603; L Mola, 'Which Role for the EU in the Development of International Investment Law?', Society of International Economic Law, Working Paper 26/08 (2008); and C Söderlund, 'Intra-EU BIT Investment Protection and the EC Treaty' (2007) 24 Journal of International Arbitration 455–468.

[11] For an analysis of EC competence over foreign investment under the Constitutional Treaty, see J Ceyssens, 'Towards a Common Foreign Investment Policy? – Foreign Investment in the European Constitution' (2005) 32 Legal Issues of Economic Integration 259; and J Karl, 'The Competence for Foreign Direct Investment' (2003) 4 JWIT 414.

[12] B Hoekman and R Newfarmer, 'Preferential Trade Agreements, Investment Disciplines and Investment Flows' (2005) 5 Journal of World Trade 949, 961–966.

[13] The EU has concluded Stability and Association agreements with Croatia [2001] OJ L-26/3, the Former Yugoslav Republic of Macedonia [2004] OJ L-84/13, Albania [2006] OJ L239, Montenegro [2007] OJ L-345, Bosnia and Herzegovina [2008] OJ L169/1, and Serbia [2008] OJ L-119.

[14] [1973] OJ C113/1.   [15] [1994] OJ L1/3.

[16] The EU has concluded Euro-Mediterranean Association Agreements with Algeria [2005] OJ L.265, Egypt [2004] OJ L-345/115, Israel [2000] OJ L147/3, Jordan [2002] OJ L129/3, Palestine [1997] OJ L187/3, Morocco [2000] OJ L70/2, and Tunisia [1998] OJ L97/2, and has concluded the negotiations with Syria.

Partnership and Cooperation Agreements (PCAs).[17] Even though the majority of these FTAs limit their investment regulation only to capital movements, the most recent agreements, like those with Algeria and Jordan, also contain far-reaching provisions on foreign investment. Third, the association agreements, which the EC has concluded with South Africa, Mexico, and Chile,[18] as well as the Economic and Partnership Agreement (EPA) with CARIFORUM States,[19] constitute the purest form of EC FTAs, as they are based essentially on economic reasoning, and include the most extensive provisions concerning foreign investment. Finally, it is noteworthy that the negotiations of EPAs with the other groups of African, Caribbean, and Pacific (ACP) countries and the FTAs with the Gulf Council Cooperation (GCC) countries and MERCOSUR are expected to offer more comprehensive provisions on foreign investment, thus setting the model for future Community agreements.

B. Regulation of Foreign Investment in EC FTAs

EC FTAs approach foreign investment from a different perspective than BITs in their effort to complement their content and address the criticism raised against the latter. Recognizing the ever-growing importance attributed by foreign investors to market access as the major regulatory determinant of the investment location, EC FTAs deal explicitly with the admission of foreign investment, namely the degree of liberalization of capital movements and the conditions for the establishment of foreign investors – issues that are not dealt with in any European BIT. In addition to listing the freedoms enjoyed by and the restrictions placed on foreign investors wishing to establish themselves in the host country, certain agreements go a step further by offering specific standards of treatment of foreign investors, both before and after their establishment in the

[17] The EU has concluded Partnership and Cooperation Agreements with Armenia [1999] OJ L239/1, Azerbaijan [1999] OJ L246/46, Georgia [1999] OJ L205/1, Kazakhstan [1999] OJ L-196/1, Kyrgyzstan [1999] OJ L196/46, Moldova [1998] OJ L181, Russia [1997] OJ L327, Ukraine [1998] OJ L49, and Uzbekistan [1999] OJ L229/1.

[18] (a) Agreement on Trade, Development and Cooperation between the European Community and its Member States, of the one Part, and the Republic of South of Africa, of the other part ([2000] OJ L311); (b) Decision No 2/2001 of the EU-Mexico Joint Council of 27 February 2001 implementing Articles 6, 9, 12(2)(b), and 50 of the Economic Partnership, Political Coordination, and Cooperation Agreement ([2001] OJ L276/45); (c) Agreement establishing an association between the European Community and its Member States, of the one Part, and the Republic of Chile, of the other part ([2002] OJ L352).

[19] Economic Partnership Agreement between the CARIFORUM States, of the one part, and the European Community and its Member States, of the other Part, concluded on 21 December 2007, available at <http://ec.europa.eu/trade/issues/bilateral/regions/acp/pr220208_en.htm>.

The CARIFORUM States are a regional grouping of 15 Caribbean countries, namely Antigua and Barbuda, the Bahamas, Barbados, Belize, Dominica, the Dominican Republic, Grenada, Gyana, Haiti, Jamaica, Saint Kitts and Nevis, Saint Lucia, Saint Vincent and the Grenadines, Surinam, and Trinidad and Tobago.

host country. However, they stop short of including provisions on expropriation and property protection. For example, Mexico and Chile proposed that an investment chapter be included in their association agreements in line with that existing in regional trade agreements concluded by the United States, but most EU Member States objected to this, fearing that it would substitute favourable provisions of their BITs.[20]

More specifically, almost all EC FTAs provide for the liberalization of capital movements related to foreign investment, reflecting the belief that the free movement of capital is a prerequisite for an increase of foreign investment flows and, consequently, economic growth. Nevertheless, such liberalization is subject to specific limitations, different from one agreement to the other, which serves economic, monetary, and other public interest goals, thus proving the EC's respect for third countries' priorities and needs.[21]

Second, certain EC FTAs, namely those with Algeria, Mexico, Jordan, Chile, and CARIFORUM States, regulate the establishment of foreign investors,[22] granting MFN and National Treatment to foreign investors with regard to specific sectors of the economy and subject to specific limitations. In particular, the agreements with Algeria, Mexico, and Chile[23] adopt a GATS approach, thus regulating the conditions for entry of foreign investment in services sectors.[24] The agreement with Chile[25] also includes a specific chapter on establishment, which provides for the national treatment of foreign investors, subject to specific limitations, in all other sectors besides services, while the PCAs and the

---

[20] J Reiter, 'The EU-Mexico Free Trade Agreement: Assessing the EU Approach Regulatory Issues' in GP Sampson and S Woolcock (eds), *Regionalism, Multilateralism and Economic Integration* (2003) 88–95.

[21] The most common restrictions that are provided in EC FTAs are those relating to outward investment and the preservation of current restrictions, which aim primarily at enhancing the economies of third countries and at preparing them for complete liberalization, when their level of economic development is advanced. S Fares, 'Current Payments and Capital Movements in the EU-Mediterranean Association Agreements' (2003) 30 Legal Issues of Economic Integration 15, 23–28.

[22] Establishment concerns the setting up and management of a primary or dependent under-taking in the host state. Regulation of establishment, which aims at the identification and gradual abolition of the domestic regulatory restrictions that impede market access to foreign investors, such as foreign equity ownership limitations and quantitative restrictions, ranges from transparency provisions, which allow investors to be aware of the relevant national laws, to provisions offering Most Favoured Nation and National Treatment to foreign investors, which bring about their assimilation to domestic or investors from other countries. UNCTAD, *Admission and Establishment* (1999) 1–4; and J Salacuse, 'Towards a Global Treaty on Foreign Investment: the Search for a Grand Bargain' in N Horn (ed), *Arbitrating Foreign Investment Disputes* (2004) 73.

[23] Arts 32 and 34, Decision 02/2001 and Arts 95–135 respectively of the agreements.

[24] The GATS in essence regulates the conditions for entry of foreign investment in services sectors, as it recognizes commercial presence as a mode of supply of trade in services. It adopts a 'bottom-up' approach on liberalization, obliging WTO members to make specific commitments so as to provide market access and national treatment to foreign investors, indicating any possible limitations in specific sectors. See M Koulen, 'Foreign Investment in the WTO' in E Nieuwenhuys and M Brus (eds), *Multilateral Regulation on Investment* (2001) 288.

[25] Arts 130–134 of the agreement.

agreements with Jordan[26] and CARIFORUM States[27] regulate the establishment of foreign investors jointly for services sectors and all other economic sectors.[28] Furthermore, it is noteworthy that the remaining FTAs with Mediterranean countries and the Trade, Development and Cooperation Agreement reaffirm the parties' GATS commitments and provide for future negotiations on establishment.[29] Last but not least, establishment constitutes the main subject of the ongoing negotiations on investment that the EC is currently conducting with ACP, GCC, and MERCOSUR countries.

The EC FTAs that regulate establishment also include provisions on post-admission treatment of foreign investors. Following the model adopted worldwide of offering general, abstract standards of treatment of foreign investment, the agreements with Algeria, Chile, Jordan, Mexico, and CARIFORUM States provide for qualified Most-Favoured Nation and National Treatment of foreign investors in the regulated sector at the post-establishment phase.[30] In addition, they include specific provisions allowing the employment of foreign key personnel, thus regulating an important aspect of post-admission operation of foreign investment. Nevertheless, EC FTAs do not regulate issues of protection of foreign investors in cases of expropriation of their assets, as they respect and safeguard the BITs concluded by EU Member States, thus avoiding any potential conflict with them.[31]

C. The Impact of EC FTAs' Foreign Investment Provisions on Human Rights Protection

Regulating primarily market access and admission of foreign investment, EC FTAs do not seem at first glance to raise the same human rights concerns as BITs, which are essentially focused on protection of investors' properties. Domestic public policies do not appear to 'threaten' investors' property, nor does their entrance into the market of the host state immediately affect the enjoyment of human rights by the local population. Nevertheless, the regulation of admission of foreign investment can have a considerable impact on human rights interests.

[26] Arts 30–36 of the agreement.   [27] Arts 67–70 of the agreement.
[28] M Roy, J Marchetti, and H Lim, 'Services Liberalization in the New Generation Preferential Trade Agreements (PTAs): How much further than the GATS?', WTO Working Paper ERSD-2006-07 (2006) 13–31; and S Szepesi, *Comparing EU Free Trade Agreements: Investment*, InBrief 6D of European Centre for Development Policy Management (2004) 3–7.
[29] B Gavin, 'Trade and Investment in Wider Europe: EU Neighborhood Policy for Enhanced Regional Integration' (2003) 4 Journal of World Trade 893, 898–903.
[30] The inclusion in future EC FTAs of an additional provision offering fair and equitable treatment to foreign investors at the post-admission stage is under discussion.
[31] eg the most recent agreement with CARIFORUM States provides in Art 71 that: 'Nothing in this Title shall be taken to limit the rights of investors of the Parties to benefit from any more favourable treatment provided for in any existing or future international agreement relating to investment to which a Member State of the European Community and a Signatory CARIFORUM State are Parties'.

First, by creating a rigid and inflexible regime, market access commitments may impede future policy orientation of the host state, aiming at protecting and/or preserving human rights. For example, the liberalization of investment rules in economic sectors which provide essential goods and services to the population, such as water, electricity, transport, education, and health services, may contravene the obligations of the host state to protect and promote basic economic, social, and cultural rights. If market access commitments are not followed by positive measures ensuring that foreign investors' activities will have a positive impact on the realization of specific policies promoting human rights concerns, it is arguable that liberalization of investment rules in these sectors might lead to a deterioration of the human rights standards enjoyed by the local population.

Secondly, the degree of the liberalization of capital movements, which allows foreign investors to enter and leave a country without any restrictions, has considerable influence on the standards of living of the local population and can have a severe impact on their enjoyment of human rights. The most illustrative example would be the impact on the employment of local population. The unrestricted exit of a foreign investor can lead to the unemployment not only of those who were employed in its undertaking, but also of all of those who were economically dependent on its presence. Hence, regulation of foreign investment in EC FTAs raises important human rights concerns which require specific consideration.

III. Dispute Settlement in EC FTAs

All EC FTAs provide for the settlement of disputes arising out of the application of the agreements. Despite the recognition of the importance of judicial or quasi-judicial dispute settlement mechanisms for the resolution of trade and investment disputes, the vast majority of EC FTAs adopt the traditional 'diplomatic' model of settlement for all disputes arising out of the application of their provisions. Nevertheless, newer agreements present a shift of EU preferences, by establishing more judicialized mechanisms suitable for the settlement of investment disputes, thus following the trend of increased judicialization of international economic relations[32] and recognizing the prominent role of dispute settlement in foreign investment regulation.

A. Political Settlement of Disputes

An institutionalized political framework for the political settlement of disputes arising out of the application of foreign investment provisions is established in the Euro-Mediterranean agreements and the PCAs. Following the tradition

---

[32] See EU Petersmann, 'Justice as Conflict Resolution: Proliferation, Fragmentation and Decentralization of Dispute Settlement in International Trade' (2006) 37 University of Pennsylvania Journal of International Economic Law 280.

established by the Association Agreements concluded in the 1970s, when there was limited experience, even in the international context of the GATT, with legal adjudication as an instrument for solving trade disputes, these FTAs have opted for diplomatic means of dispute settlement, thus expressing the existing considerations at the time that recourse to legal adjudication could be potentially disruptive of important bilateral relationships.[33] Furthermore, given that most association agreements were concluded with third countries aiming at accession to the EU, for example, the Europe Agreements, and that these agreements made frequent references to the *acquis communautaire* and provided for its application in bilateral relationships with third countries, the EC's hesitancy to adopt legal adjudication methods for resolving trade and economic disputes can also be explained by the fact that the EC wanted to avoid the application of Community law by arbitration panels, which thus could undermine the autonomy of Community law role and the importance of the European Court of Justice.[34] Hence, the historical setting of EC FTAs has resulted in the establishment of a loose mechanism for dispute settlement, usually described very broadly in only one provision.

More specifically, dispute settlement relies essentially on consultations and negotiations. It is provided that disputes should be resolved by a joint political organ established by the agreement, usually named the Association Council or Committee, and in case of disagreement by arbitration or conciliation. However, arbitration presents an alternative only in so far as there is consensus, as each party can block the establishment of an arbitration panel. The minimal importance attributed to arbitration is also confirmed by the fact that these agreements do not provide detailed legal rules determining arbitration procedures, and lack any reference to compliance, thus relying only on the 'best efforts' of the parties. For these reasons, these EC FTAs include a self-help provision, allowing the parties to adopt 'any appropriate measures', if they consider that the other party has failed to fulfil its obligations under the relevant agreement, without, however, conditioning unilateral measures to prior recourse to dispute settlement and without defining the limits on the measures that can be adopted.[35]

B. Interstate Dispute Settlement

Dissatisfaction with the effectiveness of the diplomatic model of dispute settlement as well as the increasing use of legal adjudication of trade disputes in other international fora, and most notably in the WTO, has initiated a shift in EC

---

[33] IG Bercero, 'Dispute Settlement in European Union Free Trade Agreements: Lesson Learned?' in L Bartels and F Ortino (eds), *Regional Trade Agreements and the WTO System* (2006) 389–390.   [34] Ibid., 390.
[35] ER Robles, 'Political & Quasi-Adjudicative Dispute Settlement Models in European Union Free Trade Agreements', WTO Economic and Research Statistics Division, Staff Working Paper ERSD-2006-09 (2006) 11–21.

FTAs. The TDCA with South Africa and the Cotonou agreements presented the first timid steps towards more judicialized dispute settlement systems. Ensuring the establishment of an arbitration panel even in cases where there is no consensus, providing detailed rules on arbitration procedure, and binding the parties to implement arbitral decisions, these EC FTAs have introduced important adjudicative elements in their dispute settlement mechanisms.[36] Nevertheless, it was the agreements with Mexico and Chile that introduced for the first time adjudicative or quasi-adjudicative models for settlement of investment disputes. This trend has been affirmed by the EPA with CARIFORUM States, which provides for an even more rigorous dispute settlement mechanism.

In line with the spirit of the WTO dispute settlement, the trade agreements with Mexico, Chile, and the CARIFORUM States have marked a shift in bilateral agreements concluded by the EC in the sense that they include more judicialized systems of dispute settlement.[37] Following the WTO model, the agreements provide for compulsory recourse to arbitration,[38] detailed procedures, and enforcement mechanisms; however, they introduce important differentiations from WTO rules. On the one hand, they are more complete than WTO rules, as they ameliorate procedural efficiency and compliance by providing for shorter time frames and for rules on sequencing of compliance procedures and enhance transparency by allowing public hearings and guaranteeing the admissibility of *amicus curiae*. On the other hand, they present drawbacks, as they lack a system of checks and balances similar to the Appellate Body, while in the FTA with Chile the adoption of panel reports can be blocked if there is no consensus between the parties.

Contrary to NAFTA, which provides for different dispute settlement mechanisms for trade and investment, the agreements with Mexico, Chile, and CARIFORUM States do not contain rules specifically pertaining to the settlement of investment disputes.[39] In sharp contrast to international investment agreements that grant direct rights to foreign investors and allow their participation in the settlement procedure, these EC FTAs establish only one dispute settlement mechanism applying to all trade and trade-related matters, including foreign investment, thus applying all elements of interstate dispute settlement to

---

[36] Bercero, n 33 above, 391.

[37] S Szepesi, *Comparing EU Free Trade Agreements: Dispute Settlement*, InBrief 6G of the European Centre for Development Policy Management (2004) 5–6; and Robles, n 35 above, 28.

[38] The agreements attempt to delimitate the jurisdiction of arbitration panels established under them from WTO jurisdiction, by excluding concurrent proceedings and, in the EU-Chile Agreement, by including a rule on forum exclusivity. Nevertheless, these rules appear to be incomplete and unsatisfactory, as they do not fully address the complex relationship between WTO law and FTA law, which is drafted and dependent to a great extent upon WTO law, threatening the justiciability and effectiveness of the WTO plus provisions of the FTAs and questioning the status of WTO panels and the Appellate Body as the sole competent organs to interpret and apply WTO law. See Bercero, n 33 above, 401–404.

[39] Hoekman and Newfarmer, n 12 above, 954–957.

investment disputes. More specifically, private individuals are prevented from initiating or participating in a dispute, being given only the possibility of submitting *amicus curiae* briefs,[40] thus needing to convince their home states to espouse their claim and initiate interstate settlement proceedings. Even though European companies and individuals can use the mechanism established under the Trade Barriers Regulation (TBR),[41] which was devised so as to facilitate complaints by private persons regarding trade obstacles they encountered in third countries, the TBR does not allow for effective indirect participation of private persons in interstate arbitration, as it grants a wide margin of appreciation to the European Commission and to the Council on whether a complaint should be initiated, which is only partially scrutinized under legal review by the ECJ.[42] Hence, the FTAs with Mexico and Chile draw away from the model of investor-state arbitration, which has been successfully adopted by most international investment treaties, as it allows private investors to pursue their interests independently from their home country, thus promoting depoliticization of investment disputes.[43] Furthermore, private investors cannot benefit directly from the remedies provided by the agreement, which consist of the withdrawal of inconsistent commitments, compensation, and retaliation in situations similar to those described in the WTO DSU. Private investors' damages are not taken into account nor does compensation present a possible remedy, thus diminishing the effectiveness of investment dispute settlement.

Despite the strengthening of adjudicative elements, no disputes concerning foreign investment have yet been launched under any EC FTAs. The advocates[44] of the choices adopted in EC FTAs argue that the innovative character of the provisions and the fact that the agreements are still in their infancy period can explain why the dispute settlement provisions have not yet been used. However, the (un)suitability of the dispute settlement system for resolving investment disputes provides a more credible explanation. The limited extent of foreign investment provisions and the adoption of the diplomatic model for dispute settlement in most FTAs fail to address the demands of foreign investors, who prefer rigorous and effective systems of legal adjudication. Furthermore, the adoption of interstate dispute settlement mechanisms in the FTAs with Mexico, Chile, and CARIFORUM States has mitigated their effectiveness, as they do not provide the

[40] It is noteworthy that Art 217 of the EPA with CARIFORUM States explicitly secures the right for private individuals to submit *amicus curiae*.
[41] Council Regulation 2641/84 of 17 September 1984 on the strengthening of the common commercial policy with regard in particular to protection against illicit commercial practices, [1984] OJ L252.
[42] Case C-69/89 *Nakajima* [1991] ECR I-2069; Case C-70/87 *Fediol IV* [1989] ECR 1781; and R McLean, *EU Trade Barrier Regulation: Tackling Unfair Foreign Trade Practices* (2000) ch 9.
[43] R Echandi, 'A New Generation of International Investment Agreements in the Americas: Impact of Investor State Dispute Settlement over Investment Rulemaking', Fourth Annual Conference of the Euro-Latin Study Network on Integration and Trade (2006) 5–7.
[44] Szepesi, n 37 above, 8–9; and Robles, n 35 above, 30.

necessary incentives either for private investors to put pressure on their home countries to initiate a dispute or for states to undertake legal adjudication with another country, risking their bilateral relations. Parties still give their preference to existing and well-tested mechanisms of dispute settlement, like the WTO and especially ICSID arbitration, which are viewed as more legitimate and effective systems, thus contributing to the lack of use and consequently 'failure' of EC FTAs dispute settlement provisions.

IV. Human Rights Considerations in EC FTAs

EC FTAs do not only create a framework for trade and investment regulation; they also promote political and social cooperation, establishing a multi-levelled association between the EC and third countries. Following the long-standing tradition of EC Association Agreements, the EC has, in its external relations, been promoting the model of a broad association addressing political, social, and economic considerations under a single agreement, thus contributing to the coherence and effectiveness of EC bilateral relationships with third countries.[45] Recognizing the significance of economic cooperation for the achievement of the general objectives set in EU external relations, trade and investment liberalization has gradually acquired an important role in EC Association Agreements, becoming in many cases the dominant characteristic of the agreements. However, political and social cooperation remains a vital aspect of the agreements, inserting objectives, principles, and characteristics that go beyond traditional FTAs.

Within this context, human rights occupy a prominent role in EC FTAs, being inextricably linked to trade and investment regulation. The formation of an EC policy 'on Human Rights, Democracy and Development',[46] which was a result of the ever-growing importance attributed to human rights and development in EC external relations, has gradually led to the inclusion of direct and indirect references to human rights in all association agreements concluded by the EC. More specifically, the majority of EC FTAs contain a human rights clause, commonly referred to as the essential elements clause, which, in combination with a non-execution clause, constitutes the main instrument for incorporation of human rights concerns in EC Association Agreements and FTAs. Furthermore, all EC FTAs contain direct or indirect references to human

---

[45] S Peers, 'EC Frameworks of International Relations: Co-operation, Partnership and Association' in A Dashwood and C Hillion (eds), *The General Law of EC External Relations* (2000) 175–176.

[46] Commission Communication on Human Rights, Democracy, and Development Cooperation Policy, SEC (91) 61, 6; Resolution of the Council and of the Member States Meeting in the Council on Human Rights, Democracy and Development, 28 November 1991, Bull EC 11-1991, 122.

rights in their preamble, in their objectives, or as a separate field of cooperation between the parties. Last, and more importantly, the EPA with CARIFORUM States addresses for the first time directly the link between human rights concerns and foreign investment regulation, as it provides for specific standards of investors' behaviour, safeguards the maintenance of environmental, health, and labour standards and provides for a general exception from the application of investment norms, thus setting the framework for a clear and coherent reading of foreign investment and human rights norms.

Due to their diverse nature and normative scope and consequently their different impact on foreign investment regulation, human rights references in EC FTAs will be addressed separately. First, respect for human rights as an objective of EC FTAs will be examined; second, an analysis of the scope and impact of essential elements clauses on foreign investment provisions; third, the normative content of the innovative provisions on investors' behaviour, maintenance of standards, and the general exception. Looking at these features of EC FTAs, I will underline the attempt to reconcile investment liberalization with human rights concerns. Finally, bringing together all of the above, I will examine the role of human rights norms as applicable law in foreign investment dispute settlement with regard to both EC FTAs dispute settlement and BIT arbitration.

A. Respect and Protection of Human Rights as an Objective of EC FTAs

The recognition of respect and protection of human rights as objectives of EC FTAs has important implications for their investment regime. According to public international law, the objectives of international treaties like EC FTAs establish a relevant context for the interpretation of the other provisions of the treaty,[47] hence investment provisions as well. Furthermore, parties may undertake the obligation not to frustrate or to achieve the objectives of a treaty, thus rendering treaty objectives into an overarching obligation influencing the application and implementation of all other treaty obligations.[48] Such an obligation to achieve the treaty objectives has been inserted into all EC FTAs, which provide in the first paragraph of their non-execution clause that 'the parties shall see to it that the objectives of this Agreement are attained'. For these reasons, it is important to identify first whether and which references to human rights constitute objectives of EC FTAs and what is their normative scope and second what is their effect on foreign investment provisions.

---

[47] Art 31(1) of the Vienna Convention on the Law of Treaties (VCLT) states that '[a] treaty shall be interpreted in good faith in accordance with the ordinary meaning to be given to the terms of the treaty in their context and in the light of its object and purpose'.
[48] L Bartels, *Human Rights Conditionality in the EU's International Agreements* (2005) 81–82.

1. The General Objectives of EC FTAs

References to human rights interests and values in the preamble of EC FTAs have become commonplace. Emphasizing the 'paramount importance of respect for human rights' and the 'firm commitment' of the parties to respecting human rights,[49] all EC FTAs have introduced in their preamble human rights concerns. However, these preambular references to human rights do not usually carry normative weight, as they are only assumptions upon which EC FTAs are predicated. Given that international courts have ruled on numerous occasions that mere assumptions stated in a treaty, usually in its preamble, should be distinguished from the treaty's actual objectives,[50] especially in cases where there are express statements of the objectives of a treaty, it is widely accepted that references in the preamble of EC FTAs represent a statement of shared values rather than their actual objectives.[51] Confirming this position and in sharp contrast with their preambular statements, none of the EC FTAs recognizes explicitly respect, protection, and promotion of human rights as their objective. Their objectives clauses focus on institutional and economic aims, with no mention of human rights or democratic principles.

Nevertheless, the majority of EC FTAs recognize respect for human rights as a special objective in the field of political and/or social cooperation. The PCAs, the TDCA with South Africa, and the FTAs with Mexico and Chile include a specific chapter on political cooperation or on cooperation on human rights and democracy, providing that respect and promotion of human rights is the main objective of cooperation in this field.[52] Even though respect for human rights appears at first sight to be limited only with regard to political and social cooperation, the inclusion of trade and investment provisions alongside human rights under a single agreement connotes that human rights considerations shall be indirectly considered also in the field of economic cooperation. A coherent and consistent application of all provisions of an international treaty requires

---

[49] The first wording is mainly used in the PCAs, while the commitment of the parties to respecting human rights is underlined in the Euro-Med Agreements, the TDCA with South Africa, the FTAs with Mexico and Chile, and the EPA with CARIFORUM States.

[50] *Case Concerning Rights of Nationals of the United States of America in Morocco (France v USA)*, ICJ Reports (1952) 176. For an analysis of numerous cases, see I Buffard and K Zemanek, 'The "Object and Purpose" of a Treaty: An Enigma?' (1998) 3 Austrian Review of International and European Law 330, 331–332.

[51] As the EC Council has acknowledged, 'the human rights clause does not transform the basic nature of the agreements, which are otherwise concerned with matters not directly related to the promotion of human rights'. EU Annual Report on Human Rights, adopted by the Council in October 1999 (2000) 21. B Brandtner and A Rosas, 'Human Rights and the External Relations of the European Community: An Analysis of Doctrine and Practice' (1998) 9 European Journal of International Law 468, 472.

[52] eg Arts 6, 4, 39, and 12 of the Association Agreements with Russia, South Africa, Mexico, and Chile respectively establish a cooperation framework focusing on the promotion and protection of human rights.

that the specific objectives under one part of the treaty cannot be frustrated by the application of the provisions of a different part of the same treaty. Hence, human rights objectives shall be taken into account in the field of economic cooperation, at least to the extent that action taken within the scope of the latter field does not impede the accomplishment of these human rights objectives.

2. The Objective of Sustainable Development

Apart from being specific objectives of the political cooperation framework established in EC FTAs, respect and promotion of at least some human rights are basic objectives of many EC FTAs due to their direct link to the notion of sustainable development. Contribution to the sustainable economic, social, and environmental development of EC counterparties is a main objective of many EC FTAs[53] as well as of the Cotonou Agreement, which provides the general framework under which future EPAs with ACP countries will function. It is noteworthy that the EPA with CARIFORUM States, implementing the general objectives of the Cotonou Agreement, stresses the role of sustainable development as an objective 'to be applied and integrated at every level of their economic partnership'.[54]

Furthermore, sustainable economic and social development is considered in the majority of EC agreements as the main objective of economic cooperation, thus rendering sustainable development a main objective of their foreign investment provisions. Hence, sustainable development is the basic principle which runs through the entire content of these agreements, and as all policies and strategies aim at serving sustainable development goals, it has a considerable impact on the application and interpretation of foreign investment provisions.[55]

The reference to sustainable development relates directly to human rights norms, elevating them to objectives of EC FTAs. The EPA with CARIFORUM States, by reference to the Cotonou Agreement, and the TDCA provide an explicit link between sustainable development and human rights, stating that 'respect for all human rights ... are an integral part of sustainable development'.[56] However, despite the lack of an explicit link between sustainable development and human rights, it is widely argued[57] that sustainable development connotes

[53] All Euro-Mediterranean Agreements, as well as the TDCA with South Africa, the FTA with Chile, and the EPA with CARIFORUM States explicitly acknowledge that support of the economic and social development of the parties is a main objective of the agreement.
[54] Art 3 of the agreement.
[55] J Nwobike, 'The Emerging Trade Regime under the Cotonou Agreement: Its Human Rights Implications' (2006) 40 Journal of World Trade 291, 300–301.
[56] Art 9 of the Cotonou Agreement and Art 65 of the TDCA with South Africa.
[57] For an analysis of the interlinkages between human rights and development, see P Alston, 'What's in a Name: Does it Really Matter if Development Policies Refer to Goals, Ideals or Human Rights?' 95–106 and C Dais, 'Mainstreaming Human Rights in Development Assistance. Moving from Projects to Strategies' 72–94, both in H Helmich et al, *Human Rights in Development Cooperation* (1998).

respect of at least certain human rights. Linking sustainable development with the 'continuous improvement of the quality of life and well-being on Earth for present and future generations'[58] which is promoted via 'a dynamic economy with full employment and a high level of education, health protection, social and territorial cohesion and environmental protection',[59] it is obvious that promotion and protection of fundamental human rights are at the heart of the notion of sustainable development.

As a result, respect and protection of human rights is a basic objective of all EC FTAs, influencing the application and interpretation of their foreign investment norms. Liberalization of foreign investment must not result in severe violations of human rights in the host state, nor may it affect the enjoyment of fundamental human rights. On the contrary, it must contribute to the promotion of human rights, at least of those that are directly linked with sustainable development, namely, concerning the eradication of poverty. Given that the human rights implications of foreign investment liberalization cannot be judged *in abstracto* and *a priori*, excluding foreign investors from the beneficial scope of foreign investment provisions, human rights considerations in fact gain a decisive role in the field of dispute settlement, where the actual human rights implications of foreign investment activity based on provisions of EC FTAs can be assessed and play an important role for the outcome of the dispute, as will be discussed below.

B. Essential Elements Clauses

The main instrument used for addressing human rights concerns in EC FTAs is the inclusion of essential elements clauses. Following the adoption of various human rights clauses in EC Association Agreements in the early 1990s,[60] a standardized clause has gradually developed, which the EC has successfully integrated in all of its international agreements, including all of its FTAs with third countries. In particular, in one of their first articles under the heading of 'principles', all EC FTAs provide that 'respect for democratic principles and fundamental human rights . . . inspires the domestic and external policies of the [parties] and constitutes an essential element of this Agreement'. The essential elements clause is complemented in most FTAs by a non-execution clause, completing its effectiveness by offering the possibility to the parties to take appropriate unilateral measures, if the other party fails to fulfil an obligation under the agreement. Considering that violation of the essential elements clause

---

[58] Brussels Presidency Conclusions, Review of EU Sustainable Development Strategy, 15–16 June 2006, available at <http://register.consilium.europa.eu/pdf/en/06/st10/st10117.en06.pdf>.
[59] Ibid.
[60] For the history, development, and typology of human rights clauses in EC FTAs, see E Fierro, *The EU's Approach to Human Rights Conditionality in Practice* (2003) 213–243.

is a 'material breach' of the agreement or a case of 'special urgency',[61] the non-execution clause allows for immediate action to be taken bypassing the dispute settlement mechanism established in the agreement.[62]

The recognition of respect for human rights as an essential element of EC FTAs followed by a non-execution clause significantly affects the investment regime established therein in multiple ways. First, the inclusion of essential elements clauses in EC FTAs has important implications for their normative content and the obligations of the parties under the agreement. It is widely argued that the essential elements clause introduces an autonomous and binding obligation of the parties to respect and promote human rights.[63] Since non-execution clauses allow for self-help measures only in cases of violations of parties' obligations under the agreements and the violation of the essential elements clause is considered as a material breach (violation) of the agreement giving rise to self-help measures, the conclusion can be drawn that essential elements clauses oblige the parties to respect human rights.[64]

The obligation to respect and promote human rights, as it is established in essential elements clauses, has a specific normative content, which is usually stricter than under customary international law. The vast majority of EC FTAs contain in their essential elements clause a reference to international human rights instruments, namely to the Universal Declaration on Human Rights and/or the Helsinki Final Act and the Charter of Paris,[65] thus revealing the EU's approach to international human rights based on the principles of universality, indivisibility,

---

[61] Non-execution clauses can be found in all EC FTAs. Nevertheless, a declaration that violation of the essential elements clause is a case of special urgency or a material breach, usually called a Czech/Slovak declaration, is missing from Euro-Mediterranean Agreements (except for the agreement with Egypt).

[62] For an analysis of the suspension mechanism under human rights clauses, see A Rosas, 'Human Rights in the External Trade Policy of the European Union' in *World Trade and the Protection of Human Rights. Human Rights in Face of Global Economic Challenges*, Publications de l'Institut International des Droits de l'Homme (2001) 193; and M Cremona, 'Human Rights and Democracy Clauses in the EC's Trade Agreements' in N Emiliou and D O'Keefe (eds), *The European Union and World Trade Law* (1996) 62.

[63] Bartels, n 48 above, 93–97; and Fierro, n 60 above, 239–240.

[64] Despite the lack of a Czech/Slovak declaration, it has been argued by La Pergola AG in Case C-268/94 *Portugal v Council* [1996] ECR I-6177 that essential elements clauses include per se an obligation to respect human rights. Even though the ECJ did not affirm this position, it chose a careful wording which allows for a similar interpretation to be adopted. In any case, even if it is accepted that essential elements clauses do not impose an autonomous obligation to respect human rights, their violation may have similar consequences to a non-execution clause, according to public international law rules concerning repudiation of a Treaty. See Bartels, n 48 above, 99–106.

[65] Except for the agreements with Israel and Tunisia, the other Euro-Mediterranean Agreements, the TDCA, the EPA with CARIFORUM States by reference to the Cotonou Agreement, and the FTAs with Mexico and Chile link their reference to human rights to the Universal Declaration on Human Rights, while the PCAs link the reference to the Helsinki Final Act and the Charter of Paris.

and interdependence.[66] Providing that respect for human rights 'as defined in' or 'as set out in' these international human rights instruments is an essential element of the agreement, EC FTAs incorporate these human rights instruments in their content,[67] thus setting high standards for respect of human rights, which exceed the human rights obligations of the parties under customary international law.

The establishment of a strict obligation to respect human rights, as they are defined in international legal instruments, has a major impact on foreign investment regulation in EC FTAs. As already mentioned, the parties can resort to unilateral measures, if they observe a violation of human rights, and can suspend the application of FTA provisions. The parties can take measures varying from the suspension of technical and financial cooperation provisions, which are vital for economic development, thus coercing their counterpart to respect human rights, to suspension of trade and investment commitments, thus blocking the function of the FTA.[68] Hence, human rights violations which are linked directly with foreign investment activity can be addressed by sanctioning the host state for not protecting human rights in its territory efficiently.

Furthermore, the threat of suspension of favourable provisions can also act preventively. The possibility that the violation of human rights will be punished with sanctions may act as a deterrent for host states from lowering or waiving their human rights obligations standards in order to encourage the establishment, acquisition, or retention of an investment in their territory. In addition, it may prevent European investors from 'violating' human rights in the course of their activities in the host country, as the suspension of trade and investment provisions would mean the loss of the preferential treatment upon which their establishment was based, and of preferential trade commitments, upon which the profitability of their business may depend.

Finally, the obligation to respect human rights may play a decisive role in the settlement of investment disputes. A harmonious interpretation of the essential elements clause and the provisions on foreign investment is required, since both include binding obligations of the parties and therefore must be consistently interpreted, without the one frustrating the fulfilment of the other.[69] As a result, the essential elements clause allows for specific human rights norms, as they are

---

[66] For a critical analysis of the legal principles defining EU's human rights policy, see P Leino, 'European Universalism? The EU and Human Rights Conditionality' (2005) 24 Yearbook of European Law 329; and cf DC Horng, 'The Human Rights Clause in the European Union's External Trade and Development Agreements' (2003) 9 European Law Journal 677.

[67] The use of the term 'in particular' in the PCAs breaks the equation of the norms in the essential elements clause and the norms as they are established in the Helsinki Final Act and the Charter of Paris, thus reaffirming only the parties' human rights obligations under those instruments.

[68] On the nature of the measures that can be taken and their limitations, see Bartels, n 48 above, 110–120.

[69] VCLT, Art 31(1), n 47 above. See also I Sinclair, *The Vienna Convention on the Law of the Treaties* (1984) 130 ff.

described in the above-mentioned international human rights instruments, to be raised in foreign investment disputes, in order to determine the scope of the provisions on foreign investment and to define the limits of foreign investment liberalization.

C. Behaviour of Investors, Maintenance of Standards, and General Exceptions from the Application of Investment Rules

The EPA with CARIFORUM States, providing for a complex and elaborated chapter on foreign investment, grants for the first time a more prominent role to human rights considerations in the field of foreign investment regulation. Besides the references to respect for human rights and sustainable development, which are strengthened by their recognition as objectives of the agreements and their tie to international human rights norms, it introduces human rights concerns in the chapter dealing with foreign investment. Articles 72 and 73 of the agreement on investors' behaviour and maintenance of standards as well as Article 224 on general exceptions from the application of the investment rules create an innovative framework for balancing human rights concerns and foreign investment regulation.

1. Behaviour of Investors

More specifically, Article 72 sets out the basic obligations of foreign investors, which are inherently linked with the protection of certain fundamental human rights. It provides that the parties 'shall take . . . measures as may be necessary to ensure' that bribery of officials by foreign investors is forbidden, that core labour standards as required by the ILO Declaration on Fundamental Principles and Rights of Work 1998 are respected, and that international environmental or labour obligations arising from agreements signed by the parties are not breached by investors' activities.

A primary conclusion that can be drawn from a careful reading of this innovative provision is that the EPA clearly sets minimum labour and environmental standards that are inextricably linked with the protection of certain core human rights, which are the most vulnerable under foreign investors' activities. The use of the wording 'shall' not only recognizes the right of the parties to pursue policies that ensure respect for the above-mentioned core human rights, but it imposes an obligation on the parties to take the appropriate and necessary measures.

It is also noteworthy that the provision explicitly links minimum labour and environmental standards to international law instruments. This approach, which follows the established EU practice to adhere to internationally accepted standards and avoids imposing its own standards in its relations with third countries,[70]

---

[70] Leino, n 66 above, 379–382.

creates a bridge between foreign investment law and other areas of international law. It proves that foreign investment law is not standing in 'splendid isolation' from international environmental or labour law; on the contrary, it creates a solid and clear legal provision which leaves no doubt that environmental and labour law considerations must be taken into account in determining foreign investors' rights and obligations.

Another important characteristic of this provision is that it incorporates in an international legally binding agreement principles of corporate social responsibility. Taking inspiration for the UN Code of Conduct for Transnational Corporations[71] and the OECD Guidelines for Multinational Corporations,[72] this provision, which is titled behaviour of investors, illustrates that foreign investors' activity is subject to rules of good conduct, at least in the fields of labour and environmental law.[73] Without imposing direct obligations on private individuals, which would be controversial under public international law principles,[74] the text is carefully drafted so that it incorporates fundamental limits on foreign investment activity.

It could be argued that, due to its limited scope, the EPA with CARIFORUM States is of trivial practical importance. The agreement relates only to international environmental and labour instruments that have been signed and ratified by the parties, without including a general obligation to respect human rights or even national policies with regard to labour conditions or the environment that go beyond the minimum levels recognized by the above-mentioned international treaties. However, many of these deficiencies are covered by the provisions on maintenance of standards and general exceptions, and it is undeniable that this EPA constitutes the first international investment agreement that recognizes minimum standards of environmental and labour protection and explicitly recognizes the interrelation between foreign investment law and other areas of international law.

2. Maintenance of Standards

The establishment of minimum standards of protection of environmental and labour-related human rights in Article 72 is complemented by the succeeding provision, which concerns the maintenance of standards. Article 73 of the EPA with CARIFORUM States provides that the parties 'shall ensure that foreign

[71] UN Centre on Transnational Corporations (UNCTC), *UN Code of Conduct for Transnational Corporations* (1986).

[72] OECD, *OECD Guidelines for Multinational Corporations* (1972 as amended in 2001).

[73] For a discussion of voluntary codes of corporate social responsibility, see F McLeay, 'Corporate Codes of Conduct and the Human Rights Accountability of Transnational Corporations: a Small Piece of a Larger Puzzle' in O De Schutter (ed), *Transnational Corporations and Human Rights* (2006) 219–241.

[74] O De Schutter, 'The Challenge of Imposing Human Rights Norms on Corporate Actors' in O De Schutter (ed), *Transnational Corporations and Human Rights* (2006) 1–43.

direct investment is not encouraged by lowering domestic environmental, labour or occupational health and safety legislation and standards or by relaxing core labour standards or laws aimed at protecting and promoting cultural diversity'. Similar provisions are found in Articles 188 and 193 of the EPA, which reiterate the obligation of the parties not to lower the standards of their domestic environmental, health, social, and labour legislation in order to encourage foreign investment.

A first comment on these provisions is that they include a legally binding obligation of the parties to retain their existing national legislation on environmental, social, labour, health, and safety standards and on promotion of cultural diversity in so far as encouragement of foreign investment is concerned. Even though this article was modelled on Article 1114 of the NAFTA Agreement, it goes beyond the latter's scope, as it includes a much clearer and stronger wording (in the EPA the term 'shall ensure' is used, while NAFTA, Article 1114 uses words such as 'it is inappropriate' and 'should not') and it incorporates social, labour, and cultural concerns. Hence, the EPA does not only include an appeal to the parties' 'best efforts', but obliges them to avoid lowering their national standards for the purpose of attracting foreign investment.

In that regard, it is indisputable that this provision safeguards the respect of core human rights in the specific fields. Given that national legislations may usually include higher standards of labour, environmental, health, and cultural diversity human rights than those incorporated in the international instruments mentioned in Article 72, it becomes apparent that this provision enhances the direct link between human rights and foreign investment regulation and limits investors' rights within the national framework of protection of the above human rights.

3. General Exceptions

Apart from environmental, labour, social, health, and cultural human rights, the EPA with CARIFORUM States also provides for another indirect means for linking human rights concerns with foreign investment regulation. Article 224 provides for a general exception from the provisions of the agreement, allowing the parties to adopt any measures that are proportionate and non-discriminatory in so far as they: (1) are *necessary to protect* public morals, the public order, human, animal or plant life, or health and national cultural treasures and *to secure* compliance with legislation on data protection, fraud, and security; or (2) *relate to* the conservation of exhaustible natural resources, the products of prison labour, and the importation or exportation of gold or silver.

A first reading of this provision makes it clear that the EPA includes a general exception provision drafted on similar terms to the GATT, Article XX and GATS, Article XIV exceptions. Nevertheless, it is the first international agreement that extends the scope of the exception to investment provisions, thus allowing the parties to invoke its application for derogating from the rules on foreign investment. Linking this provision with human rights concerns, it is arguable that due to the similarity of its wording with the WTO provisions, it is expected that human rights considerations are to be taken into account in a similar way to that applying under GATT, Article XX.[75] Hence, human rights considerations and national policies aiming at protection and promotion of human rights can be justified, even if they violate investment rules, as long as they fulfil the conditions set in the general exception clause.

The EPA with CARIFORUM States initiated a new era for the relation between foreign investment and human rights. Going beyond mere references to respect for human rights, it includes specific provisions that safeguard minimum levels of protection of certain human rights and enable states to promote their human rights policies without fearing that they will be in violation of their investment obligations. Of course, this agreement does not explicitly incorporate human rights in investment regulation. Instead of adopting a 'constitutional' approach to human rights,[76] it vests the parties to the agreement with the power to set their priorities and promote their own human rights policy. In that respect, the EPA adopts a more traditional approach regarding the relation between foreign investment and human rights and considers the parties as guardians of human rights interests.

D. Human Rights as Applicable Law in Foreign Investment Dispute Settlement

In practical terms, the added value of the above-described direct and indirect references to human rights interests is revealed by the fact that they allow for human rights considerations to be taken into account in foreign investment dispute settlement as part of the applicable law. The obligation to respect and protect human rights as it is formulated in the essential elements clause as well as the references to human rights in the objectives of EC FTAs can significantly influence the application and interpretation of foreign investment provisions in dispute settlement proceedings. By extending the scope of the applicable law to all provisions of the relevant agreement, EC FTAs provide the opportunity for human rights considerations to be heard and taken into account in foreign investment arbitrations. Even though arbitration under both the diplomatic and adjudicative models is limited to the subject matter of the dispute, namely foreign investment regulation, arbitral tribunals are not prohibited from examining

---

[75] For a general discussion on human rights and GATT, Art XX, see J Harrison, 'The Impact of the World Trade Organisation on the Protection and Promotion of Human Rights', EUI Thesis (2005) chs 6 and 11.

[76] On the 'constitutional approach' to international law, see EU Petersmann, 'Constitutional Primacy and Indivisibility of Human Rights in International Law' in S Griller (ed), *International Economic Governance and Non-Economic Concerns* (2003) 211–266.

provisions other than those relating directly to foreign investment; on the contrary, they are obliged to do so.

Furthermore, the EPA with CARIFORUM States provides a more solid basis for raising human rights arguments in foreign investment arbitration. An arbitral tribunal would take into consideration human rights arguments raised by the parties or by third persons submitting *amici curiae*, in so far as the compatibility of a national measure aiming at the protection and respect of human rights with Articles 72, 73, and 224 would be under scrutiny.

As mentioned, EC FTAs that adopt a diplomatic model for dispute settlement do not contain any rules on arbitration procedures and applicable law. The jurisdiction of the arbitral panel as well as the rules on procedure will be defined by the parties, as in other cases of ad hoc interstate arbitration. In determining the consistency of national measures with foreign investment provisions, arbitral tribunals are bound by the general principles of treaty interpretation, as they have been established in Articles 31 and 32 of the VCLT, to consider the context of a treaty provision when interpreting its content. Hence, the objectives of the treaty as well as the fundamental obligations set in them, like the essential elements clause, constitute the broader context within which the normative content of the provisions on foreign investment shall be defined.

This approach is also adopted in the FTAs with Chile and Mexico and the EPA with CARIFORUM States, which establish a quasi-judicial dispute settlement system, as they make explicit references to applicable law and methods of interpretation. They provide that the arbitration panel shall consider the consistency of challenged measures with the provisions of the agreement, while customary rules of interpretation of public international law also apply in order to clarify the provisions of the agreements.[77] Hence, human rights norms can affect the interpretation of foreign investment provisions, as they constitute an integral part of the agreement and thus of the applicable law, ensuring consistency among the provisions of these FTAs. Even in the FTA with Chile, where dispute settlement is reserved only for trade and trade-related matters, and arbitral tribunals do not have jurisdiction over disputes concerning the application of other provisions of the agreement, this does not affect the above-described relevance of human rights norms: although arbitral tribunals cannot decide whether there has been a violation of the parties' human rights obligations, they can still, and in fact they must, consider these provisions as the context when defining the scope and interpreting foreign investment provisions.

Last but not least, it could be argued that human rights considerations under EC FTAs can also be raised in arbitration proceedings conducted under a BIT concluded between an EU Member State and a third country which is party to an

---

[77] Art 187 and rule 9 of Annex XV of the FTA with Chile, rr 5 and 34 of Annex III of Decision 2/2001 of the EU-Mexico Joint Council (EC-Mexico FTA), Art 219 of the EPA with CARIFORUM States.

EC FTA. Given that EC FTAs are mixed agreements, which are concluded individually by the Member States as well, and given that they do not contain a clear delimitation of competence between the EC and the Member States, they are binding on the Member States as a matter of international law[78] and affect their international responsibility.[79] Thus, in accordance with the *lex posterior* principle of public international law, it is arguable that EC FTAs substitute the parts of the BITs with which they overlap and as a result allow for human rights considerations to be taken into account. However, given the partial overlap of EC FTAs and Member States BITs, which concerns mainly capital movements and national treatment standards, there is limited scope for EC FTA law and consequently human rights arguments to be raised in BITs arbitration, in particular in cases concerning expropriation. Furthermore, the vast majority of EC FTAs provide that they do not limit investors' rights and do not affect BITs between an EU Member State and the third country which is party to the FTA.[80] As a result, EC FTAs leave intact the scope of EU Member States BITs, aiming, for the time being, at supplementing their content rather than at substituting them.

V. Practical Implications of EC FTAs Human Rights Considerations

A. Effectiveness and Suitability of EC FTAs for Addressing the Human Rights Implications of Foreign Investment Regulation

Despite the introduction of human rights considerations in EC FTAs, it is not yet clear how effective and suitable they are for addressing the human rights implications of foreign investment regulation. Neither the suspension mechanism under the essential elements clause, nor the indirect use of human rights as objectives limiting the scope of foreign investment provisions seem to address all of the human rights concerns that foreign investment regulation presents. Furthermore, the inclusion of a general exception clause and of provisions on maintenance of standards and investors' behaviour provides only a limited framework for addressing human rights concerns in foreign investment regulation.

First, human rights conditionality, as expressed through the essential elements and the non-execution clause, is a political mechanism used by the EU to

---

[78] EC FTAs may also have an effect on prior BITs concluded individually by EU Member States under Community law and in particular Art 307 of the EC Treaty. However, an analysis of the Community law obligations of the Member States goes beyond the scope of the present chapter.

[79] For an overview of Member States' international responsibility under mixed agreements, see M Cremona, 'External Relations of the EU and the Member States: Competence, Mixed Agreements, International Responsibility, and Effects of International Law', EUI Working Paper (2006) 20–25.   [80] See above n 31.

'sanction' third countries for severe violations of human rights and not a legal instrument allowing for an automatic response to specific human rights violations arising from a particular action. Serving as 'a restrictive measure to uphold respect for human rights, democracy, the rule of law and good governance',[81] the suspension mechanism has actually been invoked only in cases of manifest and gross violations of human rights.[82] Hence, it is questionable whether economic sanctions through the use of the non-execution clause would actually be imposed in cases of specific violations of human rights resulting from a specific investment activity in the host country.

The unsuitability of the suspension mechanism for addressing the negative impact of investment activity on human rights is better illustrated by the fact that such human rights violations would result from the application of the FTAs. Given that the investment activity that could lead to human rights violations is based on the provisions of the FTAs, the inclusion of which the EU has strongly supported and insisted on, the EU would appear paradoxical by questioning the positive impact that foreign investment provisions purportedly have, as it would recognize that they can give rise to severe human rights violations. The willingness of the EU to make use of the suspension mechanism would become even less likely in cases where human rights violations did not result from the laxity of host states' laws and standards, but from the activity and behaviour of European investors established in the host country. In such cases, the imposition of sanctions would condemn the host state for other actors' actions and instead of contributing to the amelioration of human rights conditions in the host state, it would turn a blind eye to the latter's political and legal inability to protect human rights effectively.

Second, the use of respect for human rights as an objective of EC FTAs limiting the scope of foreign investment provisions presents practical deficiencies. Even though it constitutes an influential tool for addressing human rights considerations in investment disputes, the contested nature of the references to human rights in EC FTAs as well as their vagueness may discourage future arbitrators from using them. Given that no disputes have yet been launched under EC FTAs and that there are other competitive fora offering an alternative option for foreign investors, it is possible that, in order to enhance the attractiveness of the dispute settlement mechanism established under EC FTAs, arbitral tribunals will follow the path of other investment arbitrations and restrain from using obscure human rights references in an investment dispute.

---

[81] Notification of the Council of the European Union on Basic Principles on the use of restrictive measures (sanctions), Brussels, 7 June 2004.
[82] eg human rights clauses have been invoked with regard to bilateral relations with Belarus and Myanmar. For an overview of the practical application of human rights clauses, see Bartels, n 48 above, 35–40.

Third, the new provisions of the EPA with CARIFORUM States allow for only partial interaction between human rights and foreign investment. Similar to the criticism of the relation between human rights and trade in the framework of the WTO,[83] it is obvious that these provisions of the EPA do not provide for a complete integration of human rights law in FTA law, nor do they include the proper mechanisms for ensuring that the affected parties can effectively raise their human rights concerns. A manifest example of the incomplete system of the EPA is that if the provisions of the agreement on minimum standards and maintenance of standards are breached, the persons whose human rights are directly affected are not provided with any means for demanding the enforcement of these provisions, as such violations may be economically beneficial for both the host state and the home state and its investors.

Nevertheless, it is arguable that these provisions will provide a specific legal basis for safeguarding and undertaking national measures aiming at the promotion and protection of human rights. Even if national measures have an adverse effect on foreign investors' rights and the home state initiates dispute settlement proceedings, it is expected that arbitrators will take into account the specific limitations of foreign investment liberalization, as the latter are expressed in the provisions of the EPA.

B. Hypothetical Application: the *UPS v Canada* and *Tecmed* Cases

In order to illustrate the potential influence of the above analysed human rights considerations in real investment arbitration, we will examine whether and how human rights interests could be taken into account if two of the most famous investment disputes were initiated under the auspices of EC FTAs. The *UPS v Canada*[84] and *Tecmed*[85] cases serve as perfect examples for illustrating how human rights considerations that were underlying the challenged national measures could be successfully raised in the arbitration proceedings.

The *UPS v Canada* case initiated the trend to challenge public services aiming at the promotion and protection of fundamental human rights in the NAFTA framework. The claim raised in this case belongs to the broader category of cases, where public services that are offered on a competitive basis are challenged on the grounds that the principles of MFN and National Treatment are breached by the host countries, which provide subsidies and other forms of preferential treatment to their national public services providers. In the specific case,

[83] See EU Petersmann, 'Human Rights and International Trade Law – Defining and Connecting the Two Fields' in T Cottier and L Bürgi (eds), *Human Rights and International Trade* (2005); and Harrison, n 75 above, ch 12.
[84] *United Parcel Service of America v Canada*, Award, 24 May 2007, (2007) 46 ILM 922.
[85] *Técnicas Medioambientales Tecmed, SA v Mexico*, Award, 29 May 2003, ICSID Case No ARB (AF)/00/2, 19 ICSID Review – FILJ (2004) 158.

the tribunal rejected UPS' claim on the grounds that its services were not in 'like circumstances' to those offered by Canada Post and that the subsidies received by Canada Post with regard to the Publication Assistance Programme fell under the cultural exception from NAFTA rules (Article 2106).[86]

Even though UPS' claim was rejected, the case reveals that an investor can successfully challenge a public service which aims at the promotion and protection of human rights, in particular in fields where competition conditions are fully liberalized. Despite the lack of 'likeness' between courier and postal services, it would be difficult for states to support the different character of the services supplied in other fields, such as electricity or water supply. Furthermore, most subsidies granted to state-owned service providers are necessary for ensuring their public purpose and would be only rarely linked to specific exceptions from the scope of investment rules, such as the cultural exception in NAFTA.

Were a similar challenge of public services to be raised under the EPA with CARIFORUM States, it is most probable that it would fail. The host state would be most likely to protect its public services from any attack by another state endorsing its investor's claim by invoking the general exception. In that respect, it could retain the preferential treatment of its national services provider, provided that it was not disproportionate and served one of the public policy goals mentioned in the general exception. Given the broad degree of deference in WTO jurisprudence, which focuses more on the proportionality test than on the public purpose,[87] it is expected that an arbitral tribunal applying the EPA would reject challenges of measures granting preferential treatment to state services providers, as long as they are proportionate and are based on a specific and sufficient public purpose.

The *Tecmed* case provides another example of how national measures aiming at promoting human rights, in this case human rights linked with environmental protection, can be considered a violation of foreign investment rules. More specifically, the tribunal found that a refusal to renew an operating permit for a landfill constituted a violation of the Spain-Mexico BIT provision on expropriation. Adopting a combination of the effects and purpose doctrines and balancing them via a proportionality test,[88] the tribunal examined the public

---

[86] For a detailed analysis of the case in relation to cultural rights, see V Vadi, 'Cultural Heritage and International Investment Law: A Stormy Relationship?' (2008) 15 International Journal of Cultural Property 19.

[87] It is not argued that the general exception clause can be interpreted as accommodating general economic or social considerations; however, if a specific measure provides a sufficient public policy justification which falls under one of the categories listed, then the panels avoid examining the underlying rationale of the policy pursued. S Balman, 'International Free Trade Agreements and Human Rights: Reinterpreting Article XX GATT' (2001) 10 Minnesota Journal of Global Trade 62.

[88] For an analysis of the *Tecmed* case, see J Coe and N Rubins, 'Regulatory Expropriation and the Tecmed case: Context and Contributions' in T Weiler (ed), *International Investment Law and Arbitration* (2005) 597.

purpose of the contested measure; however, it ruled that it was not proportionate to the weight imposed on the foreign investor.

As the case concerned indirect expropriation, it could never have arisen under the scope of the EC-Mexico FTA. However, given that expropriation provisions are most likely to be included in the EC-Mexico FTA in the future in the light of the current negotiations under the review clause of the agreement,[89] it is worth examining whether human rights considerations could be raised by Mexico, if the case was brought under a revised version of the EC-Mexico FTA. As Ryan Suda argues,[90] Mexico could support the non-expropriatiory character of its measure based on human rights arguments by reference to the International Covenant on Economic, Social, and Cultural Rights (ICESCR) and the International Covenant on Civil and Political Rights (ICCPR). Given that both parties have concluded the above human rights instruments, a balanced approach between their human rights and BIT obligations would require a reading of the investment provisions consistent with the ICESCR and the ICCPR. However, the lack of explicit reference to the ICESCR and the ICCPR in current investment agreements means that they can only be invoked by virtue of the general principles of treaty interpretation. At this point the added value of the EC-Mexico FTA is apparent: instead of entering the highly controversial debate over whether principles of treaty interpretation can be used for invoking human rights in investment arbitration, the integration of human rights obligations in the EC FTAs would, as argued above, allow, and in fact oblige, arbitral tribunals to undertake a balancing of human rights and foreign investment rules.

VI. Future Developments

There is no doubt that EC FTAs present a first significant effort to integrate foreign investment regulation with human rights considerations. By focusing on the admission of foreign investment and promoting liberalization, EC FTAs present a new generation of international investment agreements, addressing increasingly important aspects of investment regulation and many of foreign investors' regulatory concerns, without, however, providing a complete framework of foreign investment regulation. Due to the exclusion from their scope of protection against expropriation, the system that EC FTAs adopt for the settlement of investment disputes goes a step back, as they opt for diplomatic settlement or interstate arbitration. Nevertheless, recent agreements follow the

---

[89] See below the part on Future Developments.
[90] R Suda, 'The Effect of Bilateral Investment Treaties on Human Rights Enforcement and Realization' in O De Schutter (ed), *Transnational Corporations and Human Rights* (2006) 140–143.

trend for adjudication of investment disputes bringing significant improvements in comparison to the rules governing interstate dispute settlement in the WTO and other international fora. However, the most important innovation introduced by EC FTAs is a framework for considering human rights and broader policy concerns when examining the limits of foreign investment liberalization. EC FTAs increasingly adopt sustainable development goals as their overarching principles and recognize respect for human rights as an objective, an essential element, and a specific obligation of the parties, hence displaying the interactions between different legal fields. The EPA goes a step further by incorporating specific provisions that safeguard minimum standards and allow for exceptions from investment rules when they serve specific public policy goals. This constantly evolving character of EC FTAs indicates the dynamic relationship between international foreign investment regulation and human rights, which can be better illustrated by the future challenges and perspectives of EC FTAs with regard to foreign investment and human rights.

First, the EU is eager to expand the scope of foreign investment provisions in its future FTAs. It is expected that future EPAs as well as the FTAs with MERCOSUR and GCC, which are bound to be concluded soon, will include a regulatory framework on foreign investment, with more far-reaching commitments than the existing FTAs. Furthermore, the EU has recently launched negotiations for FTAs with India, Korea, and ASEAN, emphasizing the need to establish a regulatory framework for foreign investment.[91] Given that under the Lisbon Treaty,[92] the new constitutional charter of the EU, foreign direct investment becomes part of the EU Common Commercial Policy and thus falls under exclusive EU competence, it is widely anticipated that the EU will engage more actively in foreign investment negotiations, expanding its regulation to all aspects of foreign investment, including protection against expropriation.[93] Hence, the EU is expected to assume an even greater role in the international field of foreign investment regulation, freed from internal competence delimitations that undermine its negotiating position.

Within this context it is very likely to expect a strengthening of the dispute settlement mechanisms established in future EU FTAs, adopting an adjudicative

---

[91] On the EU's approach to bilateral FTAs, see Commission Communication, Global Europe: Competing in the World, COM(2006) 567, Brussels, 4 October 2006.

[92] Treaty of Lisbon amending the Treaty on European Union and the Treaty establishing the European Community, [2007] OJ C306 of 17 December 2007.

[93] Art 207 of the Treaty on the Functioning of the European Union provides that: 'The common commercial policy shall be based on uniform principles, particularly with regard to changes in tariff rates, the conclusion of tariff and trade agreements relating to ... foreign direct investment', while Art 3 provides that 'the Union shall have exclusive competence in the following areas: ... (e) common commercial policy'. On the author's approach to EU competence on investment after the Lisbon Treaty, see A Dimopoulos, 'The Common Commercial Policy after Lisbon: Establishing parallelism between internal and external economic policy?' (2008) 4 Croatian Yearbook of European Law and Policy 101.

model for the settlement of investment disputes. However, the possibility of allowing for investor-state arbitration remains unlikely in the near future, at least until provisions on expropriation are included in future FTAs. Nevertheless, this perspective does not imply that the current system of interstate arbitration will remain inactive. On the contrary, the recent challenges of public services, like the *UPS v Canada* case, illustrate that such disputes can be brought to arbitration under EC FTAs, which present considerable human rights implications, in so far as the challenged public service serves to implement the obligation of host states to take positive action to fulfil human rights.

Finally, future EC FTAs may give a more prominent role to human rights considerations in the field of foreign investment regulation. The EPA with CARIFORUM States initiated a new era in international investment law, where basic aspects of investors' social responsibility and minimum labour, health, and environmental standards become binding obligations. Furthermore, the introduction of a general exception clause indicates that public policy considerations are an important aspect of foreign investment regulation. Within this broader framework of respect for public policy concerns, it is expected than the introduction of expropriation clauses in EC FTAs will entail further elaboration of public policy and human rights concerns.

EC FTAs present a new source of international investment law, adding to the existing complicated network of international investment agreements. They introduce important innovations, aiming at redefining the purposes and objectives of investment regulation. In view of their evolving character, much is expected from future EC FTAs; however, whether they will be able to supersede BITs and offer an alternative framework for addressing human rights in foreign investment regulation and dispute settlement remains to be seen.

Index

Printed in Great Britain
by Amazon.co.uk, Ltd.,
Marston Gate.